Management of Construction Projects

A Constructor's Perspective

JOHN E. SCHAUFELBERGER

and

LEN HOLM

University of Washington

Prentice Hall

Upper Saddle River, New Jersey
Columbus, Ohio

Library of Congress Cataloging-in-Publication Data

Schaufelberger, John
Management of construction projects: a constructor's perspective / John E. Schaufelberger, Len Holm.
p. cm
Includes index.
ISBN 0-13-084678-3
1. Building—Superintendence. I. Holm, Len. II. Title.

TH438 .S395 2002
692—dc21

2001021509

Editor in Chief: Stephen Helba
Editor: Ed Francis
Production Editor: Christine M. Buckendahl
Production Coordinator: Lithokraft II
Design Coordinator: Robin G. Chukes
Cover Designer: Rod Harris
Cover photo: FPG
Production Manager: Matt Ottenweller
Marketing Manager: Jamie Van Voorhis

This book was set in Times Roman by Lithokraft II and was printed and bound by Courier Kendallville, Inc. The cover was printed by The Lehigh Press, Inc.

Prentice-Hall International (UK) Limited, *London*
Prentice-Hall of Australia Pty. Limited, *Sydney*
Prentice-Hall Canada, Inc., *Toronto*
Prentice-Hall Hispanoamericana, S.A., *Mexico*
Prentice-Hall of India Private Limited, *New Delhi*
Prentice-Hall of Japan, Inc., *Tokyo*
Prentice-Hall Singapore Pte. Ltd.
Editora Prentice-Hall do Brasil, Ltda., *Rio de Janeiro*

Prentice Hall

10 9 8 7 6 5 4 3 2 1
ISBN 0-13-084678-3

Preface

Successful construction projects are delivered by skilled project managers. This book examines the skills, knowledge, tools, and techniques needed to be a successful project manager from the perspective of the construction contractor's project manager. The construction industry has become increasingly competitive in the last decade, placing greater emphasis on effective construction project management, and many books have been written from the perspective of the owner's project manager. Few, however, have approached the subject from the contractor's perspective.

This book was developed for use as a text for undergraduate courses in construction project management and as a reference for construction contractors. It assumes that readers have a basic understanding of the construction process, the construction methods used in the industry, cost estimating, and project planning and scheduling. Topics are addressed just as a project manager would in managing a construction project. The focus is on the individual management processes and techniques needed to manage a project, and tools are provided to assist in the performance of these processes. While the context for the discussion is management of commercial projects, the principles and techniques presented also are applicable to residential, industrial, and heavy construction projects.

Each chapter has a similar organization. Topics are first discussed in general terms, then individual issues are discussed in detail and illustrated. A single construction project is used throughout the book, providing a context for concept illustration and student exercises. Although the construction company used in this text is fictitious, the project was actually constructed in Juneau, Alaska. Construction progress photographs are shown in Chapters 10 through 22. Forms illustrated in the text that normally would be handwritten are shown as handwritten. Forms that could be handwritten, typewritten, or computer-generated are shown with project-specific information entered in italics. The chapters conclude with a set of review questions that emphasize the major points covered in the chapter, and an instructor's manual containing answers to the review questions is available. Exercises allow students to apply the principles learned. Most chapters have a list of other publications for those interested in additional information on the topics covered in the chapter.

A listing of all abbreviations used in the text is in Appendix A, and a glossary of construction terms is in Appendix B. Terms defined in the glossary are highlighted in bold italics the first time the term is used in the text. An index of forms used in the text has been included at the end of the book to help readers locate particular forms quickly.

Acknowledgments

This book could not have been written without the help of many people. We wish to acknowledge the following: Mike Matter for his input and use of a draft of the text in the classroom; Deborah Gardner for her assistance with the review questions; the Huna Totem Corporation of Juneau, Alaska, for allowing us to use their building and photographs of what turned out to be an excellent example of a team-built project; the Jensen Yorba Lott Architectural Partnership of Juneau, Alaska, for allowing us to use their drawings; the American Institute of Architects and the Associated General Contractors of America for granting us permission to reproduce their contract forms; several construction firms in the Northwest who have adopted drafts of this text as project management guides for their firms; and most of all, the many University of Washington students who have used various drafts of the material presented in the text and provided significant input regarding its content. We also want to thank the following reviewers of the manuscript for their helpful comments: David Bilbo, Texas A & M University; Charles R. Cole, Southern Polytechnic State University; O. C. Duffy, Jr., University of Arkansas; Chris Ray, Purdue University; and Darlene Septelka, Washington State University.

John Schaufelberger
Len Holm

This book is dedicated to construction project managers—the team leaders of our industry.

Contents

1 Introduction 1

2 Construction Contracts 13

6 Contract Development 73

7 Partnering and Team Building 79

8 Subcontracting 91

9 Material Management 115

10 Project Start-Up 127

11 Document and Record Keeping 141

12 Communications 151

13 Field Questions 163

14 Submittals 173

15 Progress Payments 183

16 Cost and Time Control 197

17 Quality Management 211

18 Safety Management 223

19 Contract Change Orders 237

23 Advanced Topics in Project Management 279

Appendices 293

Index of Forms 425

Index 427

1

Introduction

1.1 PROJECT MANAGEMENT CONCEPT

Project management is the application of knowledge, skills, tools, and techniques to the many activities required to complete a project successfully. In construction, project success generally is defined in terms of safety, quality, cost, and schedule. These project attributes are depicted in Figure 1–1. The project manager's challenge is to balance quality, cost, and schedule within the context of a safe project environment. While cost and schedule may be compromised to produce a quality project, there can be no compromise regarding safety.

In this book, we will examine project management from the perspective of the construction contractor. Other project managers typically are involved in a project representing the owner and the designer, but our focus is on the knowledge, skills, tools, and techniques needed to be successful as a project manager for a construction contractor. Our context will be that of a project manager for a commercial general contractor. The principles and techniques discussed, however, are equally applicable to residential, industrial, and infrastructure or heavy construction projects.

The ***project manager*** is the leader of the contractor's project team and is responsible for identifying project requirements and ensuring that all are accomplished safely and within the desired budget and time frame. To accomplish this challenging task, the project manager must organize his or her ***project team***, establish a project management system that monitors project execution, and resolve issues that arise during project execution. In successive chapters, we will discuss the many tools that a project manager should use in managing a project. They all may not apply to every project, but the project manager must select those that are applicable for each project.

The major phases of a construction project are:

- Project planning
- Project start-up

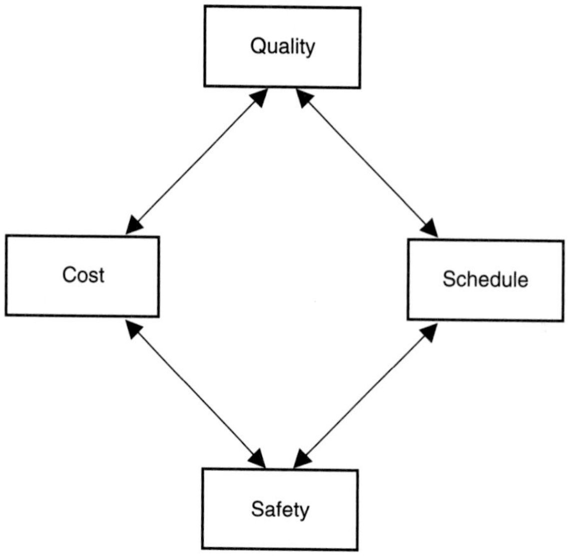

FIGURE 1–1 Critical Project Attributes

- Project control
- Project close-out
- Post-project analysis

The sequence of the chapters in this text generally follows these phases.

During ***project planning***, the project manager evaluates the risks that are associated with the project, particularly those related to safety, cost, quality, and schedule. Risk analysis and risk management are critical skills essential to successful project management. The project manager develops the organizational structure needed to manage the project and the communications strategy to be used within the ***project management organization*** and with other project stakeholders. The project manager also develops material procurement and subcontracting strategies during the planning phase. Topics relating to project planning are discussed in Chapters 3 through 9.

Project start-up involves mobilizing the project management team, educating them regarding the project and associated risks, and conducting team-building activities. The project management office is established, and project documentation management systems are created. Initial project ***submittals*** are provided to the owner or the owner's representative. Vendor accounts are established, and materials and subcontract procurement initiated. Project cost, schedule, and quality control systems are established to manage project execution. Topics relating to project start-up are addressed in Chapters 10 and 11.

Project control involves controlling the project, interfacing with external members of the project team, anticipating risk by taking measures to mitigate its potential impacts, and adjusting the project schedule to accommodate changing conditions. The project manager monitors the document management system, the quality management system, cost control system, and schedule control system and makes adjustments where appropriate. He or she reviews performance reports to look for variances from expected performance and takes action to minimize their impacts. Topics relating to project control are addressed in Chapters 12 through 20.

Project close-out involves completing the physical construction of the project, submitting all required documentation to the owner, and financially closing out the project. The project manager must pay close attention to detail and motivate the project team to close out the project expeditiously to minimize overhead costs. Project close-out is discussed in Chapter 21.

Post-project analysis involves reviewing all aspects of the project to determine lessons that can be applied to future projects. Such issues as anticipated cost versus actual cost, anticipated schedule versus actual schedule, ***quality control***, subcontractor performance, material supplier and construction equipment performance, effectiveness of communications systems, and work force productivity should be analyzed. Many contractors skip this phase and simply go to the next project. Those who conduct post-project analyses learn from their experiences and continually improve their procedures and techniques. This is the primary focus of ***total quality management***, as you will see in Chapter 7.

1.2 PROJECT DELIVERY METHODS

The principal participants in any construction project are the owner or client, the designer (architect or engineer), and the ***general contractor***. The relationships among these participants are defined by the delivery method used for the project. The choice of delivery method is the owner's, but it has an impact on the scope of responsibility of the contractor's project manager. Owners typically select project delivery methods based on the amount of risk they are willing to assume and the size and experience of their own contract management staffs. In this section, we will examine the five most common delivery methods used in the United States.

Traditional Delivery Method

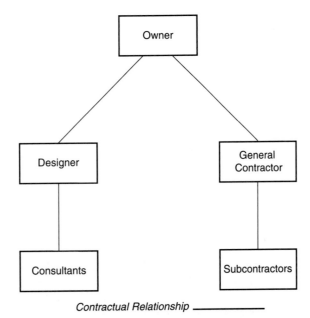

The ***traditional delivery method*** is illustrated in Figure 1–2. The owner has separate contracts with both the designer and the general contractor. There is no contractual relationship between the designer and the general contractor. In this delivery method, the design is typically completed before the contractor is hired. The contractor's project manager is responsible for obtaining the project plans and specifications, developing a cost estimate and project schedule for construction, establishing a project management system to manage the construction activities, and managing the construction.

FIGURE 1–2
Traditional Delivery Method

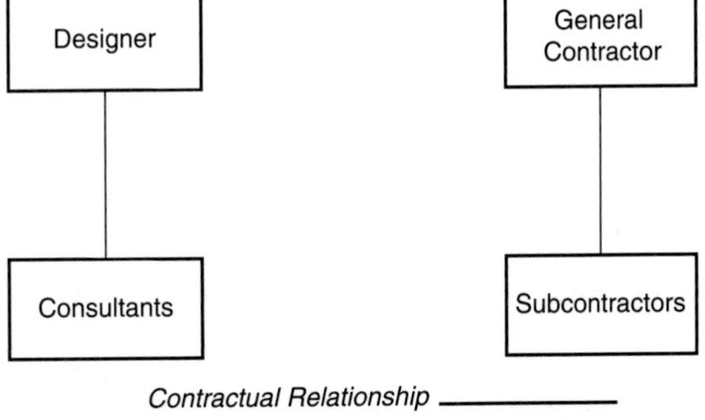

Agency Construction Management Delivery Method

In the ***agency construction management delivery method***, the owner has three separate contracts: one with the designer, one with the general contractor, and one with the construction manager. These are illustrated in Figure 1–3. The construction manager acts as the owner's agent and coordinates design and construction issues with the designer and the general contractor. The construction manager usually is the first contract awarded, and he or she is involved in hiring both the designer and the general contractor. The general contractor usually is not hired until the design is completed. In this delivery method, the general contractor's project manager has similar responsibilities to those listed for the traditional delivery method. The primary difference is that the project manager interfaces with the construction manager instead of the owner, as in the traditional method.

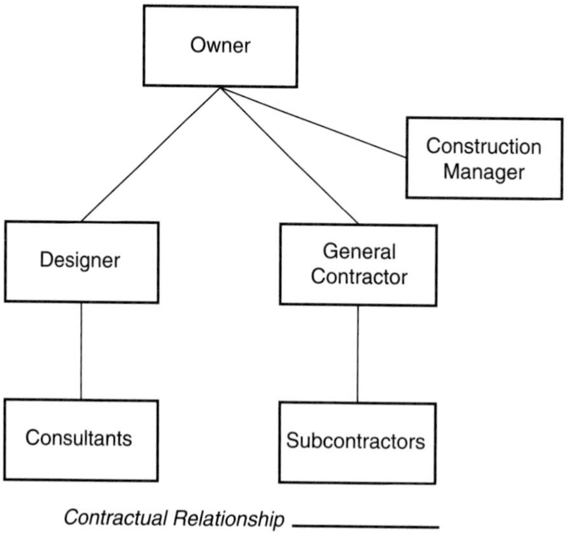

FIGURE 1–3 Agency Construction Management Delivery Method

Construction-Manager-at-Risk Delivery Method

In the ***construction-manager-at-risk delivery method***, the owner has two contracts, one with the designer and one with the construction manager/general contractor, as illustrated in Figure 1–4. This delivery method is also known as the ***construction manager/general contractor delivery method***. In this method, the designer usually is hired first. The construction manager/general contractor typically is hired early in the design development to perform a variety of ***preconstruction services***, such as cost estimating, ***constructability analysis***, and ***value engineering*** studies. Once the design is completed, the construction manager/general contractor constructs the project. In some cases, project construction may be initiated before the entire design is completed. This is known as ***fast-track*** (or ***phased***) ***construction***. The contractor's project manager interfaces with the designer and manages the execution of preconstruction tasks. Once construction starts, the project manager's responsibilities are similar to those in the traditional method.

Design-Build Delivery Method

In the ***design-build delivery method***, the owner has a single contract with the design-build contractor for both the design and construction of the project as illustrated in Figure 1–5. The design-build contractor may have a design capability within its own organization, may choose to enter into a ***joint venture*** with a design firm, or may hire

FIGURE 1–4
Construction-Manager-at-Risk Delivery Method

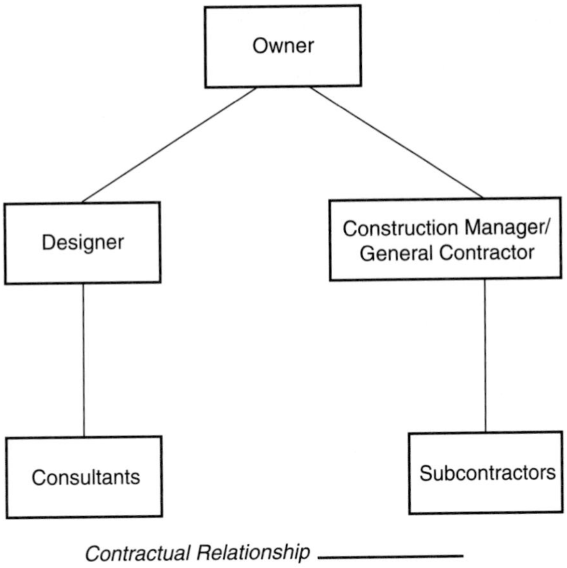

a design firm to develop the design. On some projects, a design firm may sign the contract and hire the construction firm. Construction may be initiated early in the design process using fast-track procedures or may wait until the design is completed. In this delivery method, the contractor's project manager is responsible for interfacing with the owner and managing both the design and the construction of the project. Variations to this method are ***design-build-operate*** and ***build-operate-transfer***. In the design-build-operate delivery method, the contractor charges an annual fee to operate the facility after construction for a specified period. This delivery method often is used for utilities projects such as water treatment or sewage treatment plants. In the build-operate-transfer delivery method, the contractor finances the design and construction of the project and is paid an annual fee to operate the completed facility for a specified period of time. At the end of the operating period, the project is transferred to the owner. This delivery method often is used for large infrastructure projects such as toll roads and electric power plants.

FIGURE 1–5 Design-Build Delivery Method

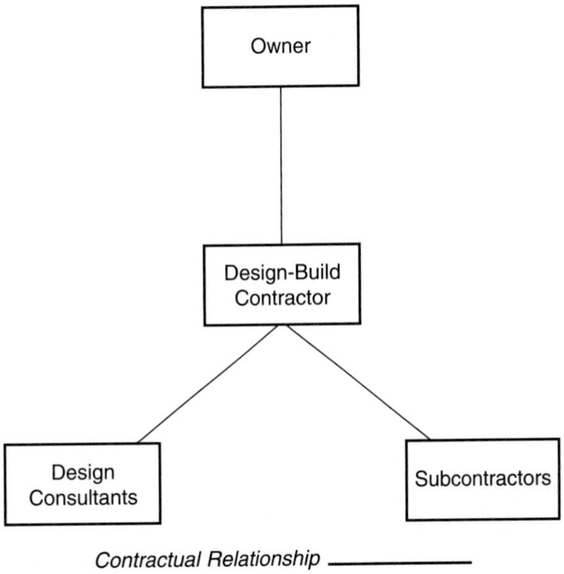

Bridging Delivery Method

The ***bridging delivery method*** is a hybrid of the traditional and the design-build delivery methods. The owner contracts with a design firm for the preparation of partial design documents. These documents typically define functional layout and appearance requirements. A design-build contractor is then selected by the owner to complete the design and construct the project.

1.3 PROJECT MANAGEMENT ORGANIZATION

The size and structure of the project management organization depends on the size of the project, its complexity, and its location with respect to other projects or the contractor's home office. The cost of the project management organization is considered job overhead and must be kept economical to ensure that the cost of the contractor's construction operation is competitive with other contractors. The goal in developing a project management organization is to create the minimum organization needed to manage the project effectively. If the project is unusually complex, it may require more technical people than would be required for a simpler project. If the project is located near other projects or the contractor's home office, technical personnel can be shared among projects, or backup support can be provided from the home office. If the project is located far from other contractor activities, it must be self sufficient.

General contractors typically organize their project management teams using one of three models. In one type of project management concept, estimating and scheduling are performed in the contractor's home office, as illustrated in Figure 1–6. The ***officer-in-charge*** is the project manager's supervisor. He or she may have various titles as described in Section 1.5. In an alternative organizational structure, shown in Figure 1–7, estimating and scheduling are the project manager's responsibilities. Both the project manager and the superintendent may report to the officer-in-charge as illustrated in Figure 1–7, or the superintendent may report to the project manager, as illustrated in Figure 1–8 on page 8. The choice of project management organizational structures depends on the contractor's approach to managing projects.

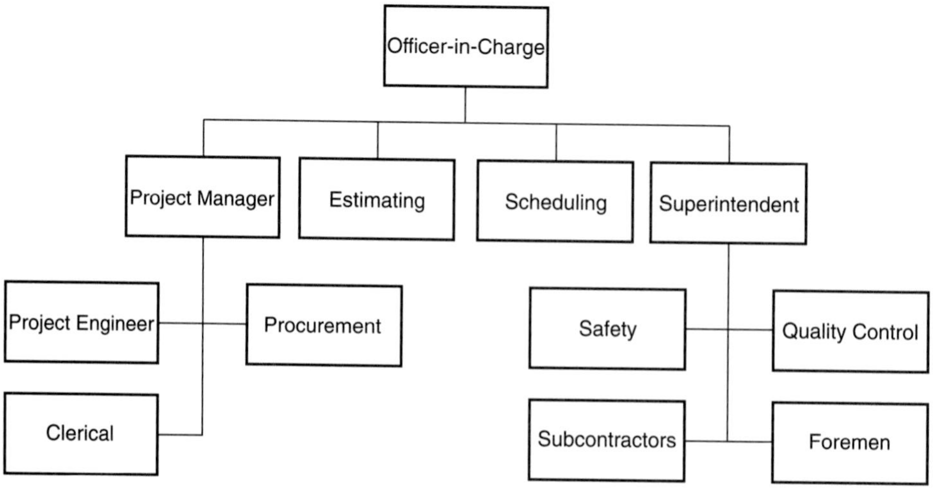

FIGURE 1–6 Contractor's Project Management Organization with Estimating and Scheduling at Home Office

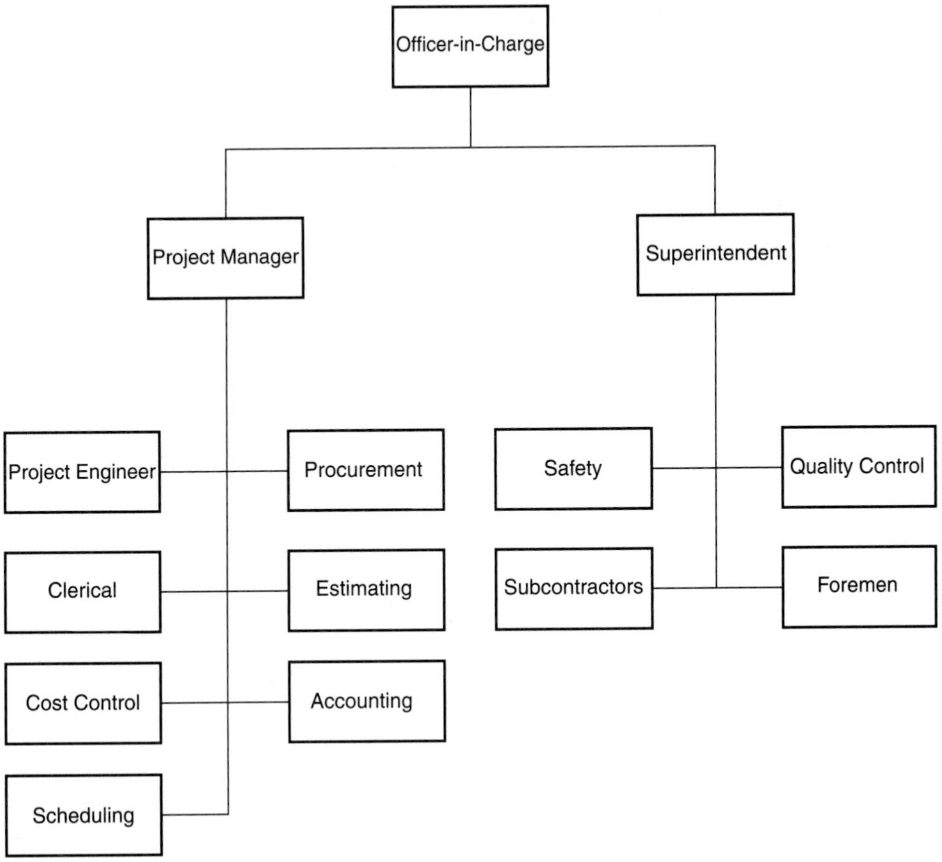

FIGURE 1–7 Contractor's Project Management Organization with Estimating and Scheduling Under Project Manager

1.4 PROJECT TEAM DEVELOPMENT

Once the project management organization is selected for a project, the project manager identifies the individuals to be assigned to each position. Most people will come from within the contractor's organization, but some may be hired externally. Selection of project team members from inside the construction firm may be made by the project manager or by senior company managers. If new people are hired, the project manager must write a job description for each position, prepare a list of skills needed to perform the job, recruit and select new employees, and train them on the contractor's methods of doing business. These human resource management responsibilities are explained in more detail in Chapter 23. Once all the team members have been selected, the project manager must forge them into a cohesive team. This requires team building, which may be a significant challenge for the project manager. Team building is discussed in Chapter 7.

1.5 PROJECT TEAM MEMBER RESPONSIBILITIES

Individual team member responsibilities may vary from project to project, but in general they are as described below. The superintendent is the only position that is specified in most construction contracts. Article 3.9 of the general conditions shown in Appendix E is an example of such contract language.

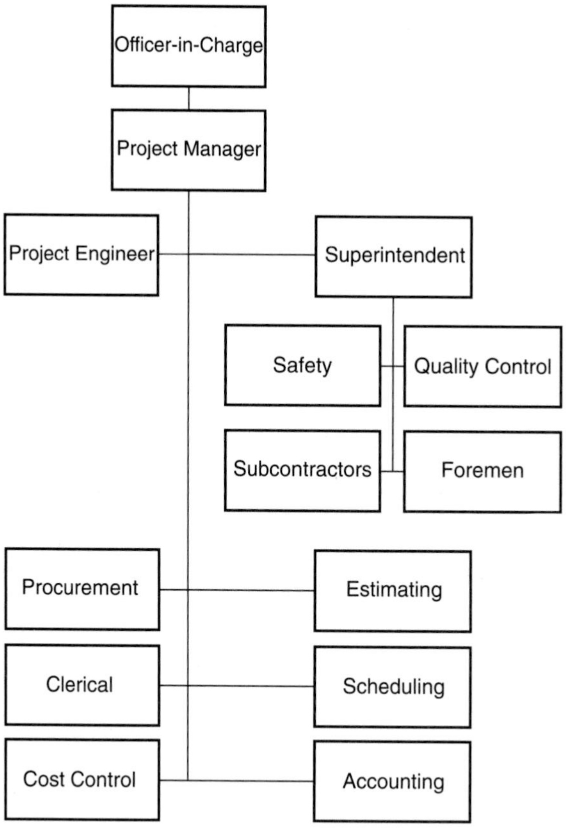

FIGURE 1–8 Contractor's Project Management Organization with Superintendent Reporting to Project Manager

Officer-in-Charge

The officer-in-charge is the principal official within the construction company who is responsible for construction operations. He or she generally signs the construction contract and is the individual to whom the owner turns in the event of any problems with the project manager. This individual often carries the title of vice president for operations, operations manager, district manager, senior project manager, or may be the owner or chief executive officer.

Project Manager

The project manager has overall responsibility for completing the project in compliance with all contract requirements, within budget, and on time. He or she organizes and manages the contractor's project team. Specific responsibilities of the position include:

- Coordinating and participating in the development of the project budget and schedule.
- Developing a strategy for executing the project in terms of what work to subcontract.
- Communicating frequently with the owner and the designer.
- Soliciting, issuing contract packages, evaluating, and awarding ***subcontracts*** and material ***purchase orders***.
- Negotiating and finalizing contract change orders with the owner and subcontractors.

- Implementing project cost and schedule control procedures.
- Scheduling and managing project team meetings.
- Supervising project office staff.
- Submitting monthly ***progress payment requests*** to the owner.
- Managing project close-out activities.

Superintendent

The ***superintendent*** is responsible for the direct daily supervision of construction activities on the project, whether the work is performed by the contractor's workers or those employed by subcontractors. Specific responsibilities include:

- Planning, scheduling, and coordinating the daily activities of all ***craftspeople*** working on the site.
- Determining the construction building methods and work strategies for work performed by the contractor's own work force.
- Preparing a three-week look-ahead schedule and coordinating equipment requirements and material deliveries.
- Preparing daily reports of project activities.
- Submitting daily time cards for self-performed work.
- Ensuring all work performed conforms to contract requirements.
- Ensuring all construction activities are conducted safely.

Project Engineer

The ***project engineer*** is responsible for resolving any technical issues relating to completion of the project. On small projects, the project engineer's responsibilities may be performed by the project manager. Specific responsibilities include:

- Maintaining submittal and ***field question logs***.
- Reviewing submittals and transmitting them to the owner or designer.
- Preparing and submitting ***field questions***.
- Preparing contract documents and correspondence and maintaining the contract file.
- Reviewing subcontractor invoices and requests for payment.

Foreman

The foreman is responsible for the direct supervision of the project workers. The construction firm will assign foremen to oversee work that is performed by the company's own construction workers. Foremen for all subcontracted work will be assigned by each subcontractor. Specific responsibilities include:

- Coordinating the layout and execution of individual trade work on the project site.
- Verifying that all required tools, equipment, and materials are available on site.
- Ensuring all craft work conforms to contract requirements.
- Preparing daily time sheets for all supervised personnel.

1.6 SUMMARY

The contractor's project manager is the leader of the contractor's project management team. He or she is responsible for managing all the activities required to complete the job on time, within budget, and in conformance with quality requirements specified in the contract. The major phases of a construction project are: project planning, project start-up, project control, project close-out, and post-project analysis.

There are five major project delivery methods used in the United States. The primary differences among them are the relationships between the project participants. In the traditional delivery method, there is no contractual relationship between the designer and the general contractor; the owner has separate contracts with each one. In the agency construction management delivery method, the owner has separate contracts with the construction manager, designer, and the general contractor. The construction manager acts as the owner's representative on the project but has no contractual relationship with either the designer or the general contractor. In the construction-manager-at-risk delivery method, the owner has two separate contracts, one with the designer and one with the general contractor, who also acts as the construction manager. In the design-build delivery method, the owner has a single contract with the design-build contractor, who is responsible for both designing and constructing the project. Variations to this method include design-build-operate and build-operate-transfer. The bridging delivery method is a hybrid method in which the owner first contracts with a designer for a partial design and then contracts with a design-build firm to complete the design and construct the project.

Contractors establish project management organizations to manage construction activities. The project team typically consists of a project manager, superintendent, project engineer, foremen for self-performed work, and administrative support personnel depending upon project size and complexity.

1.7 REVIEW QUESTIONS

1. What are four critical project attributes that the project manager must integrate?
2. What are the major phases of a construction project, and what occurs during each phase?
3. What is the difference between the traditional and the construction management delivery methods?
4. What is the difference between the construction-manager-at-risk and the design-build delivery methods?
5. How do the responsibilities of the project manager differ from those of the project superintendent?
6. What are the major duties of the project engineer?

1.8 EXERCISES

1. Develop an organization chart for a project management organization to manage the construction of a $20 million office complex that is to be completed within one year.
2. Describe the advantages and disadvantages of the project management organization shown in Figure 1–8, as compared with the organization shown in Figure 1–7.

3. Redraw Figure 1–3, depicting the lines of communication among the project participants.

1.9 SOURCES OF ADDITIONAL INFORMATION

Barrie, Donald S., and Boyd C. Paulson. *Professional Construction Management.* 3d ed. New York: McGraw-Hill, Inc., 1992.

Clough, Richard H., and Glenn A. Sears. *Construction Contracting.* 6th ed. New York: John Wiley and Sons, Inc., 1994.

Collier, Keith. *Construction Contracts.* 3d ed. Upper Saddle River, N.J.: Prentice-Hall, Inc., 2001.

Dorsey, Robert W. *Project Delivery Systems for Building Construction.* Washington, D.C.: Associated General Contractors of America, 1997.

Haltenhoff, C. Edwin. *The CM Contracting System: Fundamentals and Practices.* Upper Saddle River, N.J.: Prentice-Hall, Inc., 1999.

Hinze, Jimmie. *Construction Contracts.* New York: McGraw-Hill, Inc., 1993.

2

Construction Contracts

2.1 INTRODUCTION

A ***contract*** is a legal document that describes the rights and responsibilities of the parties involved, for example, the owner and the general contractor. The terms and conditions of their relationship are defined solely within the contract documents. These documents should be read and completely understood by the contractor before deciding to pursue a project. They also are the basis for determining a project budget and schedule. To manage a project successfully, the project manager must understand the organization of the contract documents, as well as the contractual requirements for the project. This knowledge is essential if the project manager expects to satisfy all contractual requirements.

The contract documents describe the completed project and the terms and conditions of the contractual relationship between the owner and the contractor. Usually there is no description of the sequence of work or the means and methods to be used by the contractor in completing the project. The contractor is expected to have the professional expertise required to understand the contract documents and select appropriate subcontractors and qualified tradespeople, materials, and equipment to complete the project safely, as well as achieve the quality requirements specified. For example, the contract documents specify the dimensions and workmanship requirements for cast concrete structural elements, but will not provide the design for required formwork.

2.2 ORGANIZATION OF CONTRACT DOCUMENTS

A typical construction contract consists of the five documents shown in Figure 2–1. A special conditions section is not always used, unless there are some specific requirements or restrictions placed on the contractor for the project. The ***invitation to bid*** and ***request for proposals*** generally are not considered contract documents. Any of the

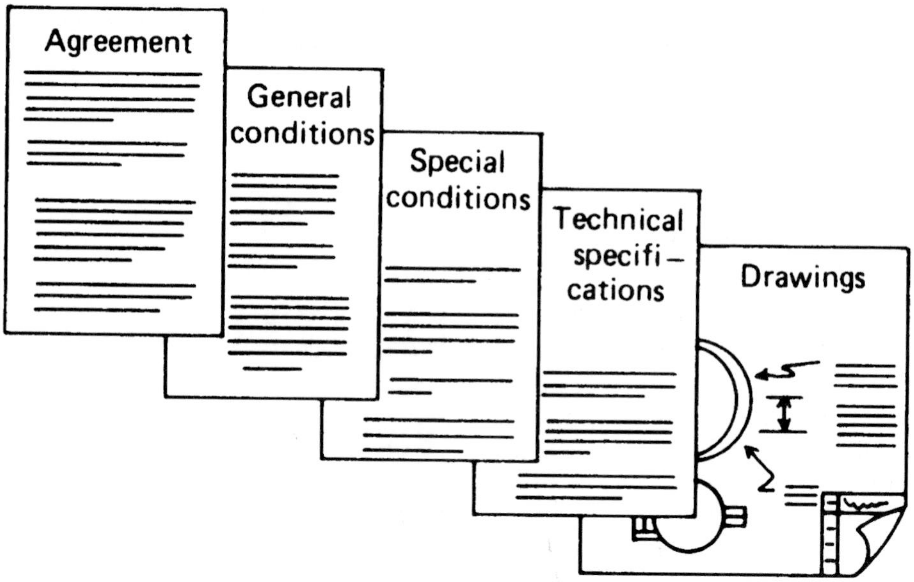

FIGURE 2–1 Contract Documents

contract documents can be modified by ***amendments*** or ***addenda*** or by ***change orders***. Amendments or addenda are issued by the owner prior to award of the contract, whereas change orders are executed between the owner and the contractor after the contract award. Any amendments, addenda, or change orders used also are considered to be contract documents.

The ***agreement*** describes the project to be constructed, the pricing method to be used (the cost, if lump-sum, or the fee structure, if cost-plus), the time allowed for construction, any ***liquidated damages***, and the name of the owner and the contractor. Supporting documents may be incorporated into the agreement by reference or as exhibits. These documents then become part of the contract documents. Examples of supporting documents might be a geotechnical evaluation of the project site or a project manual produced by the designer.

The ***general conditions*** provide a set of operating procedures that the owner typically uses on all projects. They describe the relationship between the owner and the contractor, the authorities of the owner's representatives or agents, and the terms of the contract. Some owners use standard general conditions published by professional organizations such as those discussed in Section 2.5. Topics typically addressed in the general conditions are:

- Rights and responsibilities of the owner
- Authorities of the designer or construction manager
- Rights and responsibilities of the contractor
- Bonds and insurance
- Changes in contract scope of work
- Changes in contract price or fee
- Changes in contract time
- Inspections
- Uncovering defects and correction of work
- Protection of personnel and property
- Progress payments
- Subcontracting
- Contract close-out procedures
- Warranty of work
- Resolution of disputes
- Early termination of the contract

The ***special*** or ***supplementary conditions*** contain any unique requirements for the specific project. Examples of special conditions requirements are:

- Site access restrictions
- Site security requirements
- Permission requirements for night work
- Location of parking for contractor's workers
- Listing of equipment furnished by owner
- Required insurance coverage limits
- Mandatory wage rates (usually only for public projects)

Owners who use standard general conditions also may use the special conditions to modify selected general conditions requirements for a specific project.

The ***technical specifications*** provide the qualitative requirements for construction materials, equipment to be installed, and workmanship. They typically are organized using the ***MasterFormat*** shown in Figure 2–2 that was developed by the ***Construction Specifications Institute (CSI)***. Each division of the specifications is further subdivided using a standard five-digit code developed by CSI. Figure 2–3 shows an example for site work. There are four types of technical specifications used in construction contracts:

- Descriptive specifications that detail the required properties and quality of a material, assembly of materials, or products.
- Performance specifications that establish functional criteria for acceptable materials or products.
- Proprietary specifications that identify acceptable products by brand name, model number, or trade name.
- Reference standard specifications that reference well-known standards such as the American Society for Testing and Materials (ASTM).

The types of specifications are not mutually exclusive. A single specification may contain descriptive and reference requirements.

FIGURE 2–2 MasterFormat for Technical Specifications

Division 01.	General Requirements
Division 02.	Site Work
Division 03.	Concrete
Division 04.	Masonry
Division 05.	Metals
Division 06.	Wood and Plastics
Division 07.	Weather Protection
Division 08.	Doors, Windows, and Glass
Division 09.	Finishes
Division 10.	Specialties
Division 11.	Equipment
Division 12.	Furnishings
Division 13.	Special Systems
Division 14.	Hoisting Systems
Division 15.	Mechanical
Division 16.	Electrical

Division 02. Site Work

02010	Subsurface Investigation
02050	Demolition
02100	Site Preparation
02150	Underpinning
02200	Earthwork
02300	Tunneling
02350	Piles, Caissons, and Cofferdams
02400	Drainage
02440	Site Improvements
02480	Landscaping
02500	Paving and Surfacing
02590	Ponds and Reservoirs
02600	Piped Utility Materials and Methods
02700	Piped Utilities
02800	Power and Communications Utilities
02850	Railroad Work
02880	Marine Work

FIGURE 2–3 MasterFormat for Site Work Specifications

The drawings show the quantitative requirements for the project and how the various components go together to form the completed project. The drawings may be done on paper or produced electronically using computer-aided design (CAD) equipment. The initial set of drawings issued to the contractor are updated as required throughout the duration of the project to reflect modifications made by change orders. These updated construction drawings become the basis for the set of ***as-built*** (or record) ***drawings*** that the contractor provides to the owner at project close-out. The drawings for a typical construction contract are organized as shown below. Not all of these types of drawings will be used on all projects.

- Architectural drawings
- Controls drawings
- Electrical drawings
- Equipment drawings
- Fire protection drawings
- Landscaping drawings
- Low-voltage data systems drawings
- Mechanical drawings
- Plumbing drawings
- Shoring drawings
- Site or civil drawings
- Structural drawings

2.3 CONTRACT PRICING METHODS

There are several methods for pricing contracts used in the construction industry. The owner chooses a method for a particular project based on the risk associated with the project, deciding how much risk to assume and how much to impose on the contractor. Contractors want compensation for risk they assume.

Lump-Sum Contracts

Lump-sum (sometimes called stipulated-sum or fixed-price) contracts are used when the scope of work can be defined. The owner provides a set of drawings and specifications and the contractor agrees to complete the project for a lump sum. Lump-sum contracts also are used for design-build projects where the owner specifies design criteria and the contractor agrees to design and construct the project for a single price. While the exact scope of work is not defined in a design-build project, the contractor controls the design process and produces a design that can be built for the contract price. In a lump-sum contract, the contractor is responsible for determining all the material, labor, equipment, and subcontract costs to establish the project cost. The initial contract price accepted by the owner at contract award may be modified during the life of the project by contract change orders, as we will see in Chapter 19.

Unit-Price Contracts

Unit-price contracts are used when the exact quantities of work are not known at the time the contract is executed. The designer provides an estimate of the quantity of each material required, and the contractor determines a unit price for each material. An example of a unit-price bid schedule for a utility project is shown in Figure 2–4. The cost data shown in italics would be entered on the form by the contractor and submitted to the owner as the bid for the project. The actual contract value for each item is not determined until the completion of the project. The actual quantities of work are measured throughout the completion of the project, and the cost is determined by multiplying the actual quantity by the unit price established by the contractor. Unit-price contracts are used extensively on highway jobs or environmental clean-up jobs where exact quantities of work are difficult to define. Unit-price and lump-sum methods can both be used in the same contract. Sometimes the foundation portion of a building may be unit price, while the remainder of the building is lump sum.

Work Items	Unit	Estimated Quantity	Unit Price	Bid Amount
Soil excavation	cubic yards	12,000	*$6.00*	*$72,000*
12" concrete pipe	linear feet	1,000	*$18.00*	*$18,000*
Crushed rock fill	cubic yards	3,000	*$24.00*	*$72,000*
Compacted fill	cubic yards	9,000	*$15.00*	*$135,000*
TOTAL				*$297,000*

FIGURE 2–4 Sample Unit-Price Bid Form

Cost-Plus Contracts

Cost-plus contracts are used when the scope of work cannot be defined. They are sometimes referred to as ***cost-reimbursable contracts***. All specified contractor's project-related costs are reimbursed by the owner, and a ***fee*** is added to cover ***profit*** and company ***overhead***. Only those costs identified in the contract are reimbursable.[1] The fee may be a fixed amount, a percentage of project costs, or may have an incentive component. The fee in a ***cost-plus-fixed-fee contract*** is a fixed amount irrespective of the actual construction cost. The fee in a ***cost-plus-percentage-fee contract*** is a percentage of the actual project cost. The fee in a ***cost-plus-incentive-fee*** or ***cost-plus-award-fee contract*** is variable, based on the contractor's performance. The owner establishes a set of criteria that are used to determine the actual fee.

Cost-plus contracts typically are awarded based on an agreed fee structure, since project costs are not known until the project has been completed. Cost-plus contracts generally are used when the construction contract is awarded prior to the completion

[1]Article 7 of the contract agreement shown in Appendix D is an example listing of reimbursable contractor costs.

of the design. They also frequently are used in emergency conditions such as reconstruction after a major natural disaster, including hurricanes, earthquakes, or floods.

A special type of a cost-plus contract is known as a ***time-and-materials contract***. In this type of contract, the owner and the contractor agree to a labor rate that includes the contractor's profit and overhead. The contractor's reimbursements are based on actual costs for materials and the agreed labor rate multiplied by the number of hours worked. Time-and-materials contracts generally are used only for small projects, maintenance and repair, or material testing.

Cost-Plus Contracts with Guaranteed Maximum Price

A cost-plus contract with ***guaranteed-maximum-price (GMP)***, or simply a guaranteed-maximum-price contract, is a type of cost-plus contract in which the contractor agrees to construct the project at or below a specified cost. Any cost exceeding the GMP would be borne by the contractor. Some of these contracts have a saving-sharing formula if the actual cost is less than the guaranteed maximum value. This is to provide an incentive to the contractor to control costs. For example, 30% of the savings might go to the contractor and 70% to the owner. In other GMP contracts, all the savings accrue to the owner.

2.4 PROCUREMENT METHODS

Owners who procure contracts use either a bid or a negotiated procedure. Public owners, such as government agencies, use public solicitation or procurement methods. These owners may require potential contractors to submit documentation of their qualifications for review before being allowed to submit a bid or proposal, or the owners may open the solicitations to all qualified contractors. The first method is known as ***prequalification of contractors***, and only the most qualified contractors are invited to submit a bid or proposal. Private owners can use any method they like to select a contractor, but most use contractors they have had good experience with in the past and may ask a select few or even only one contractor to submit a proposal.

Bid Method

Bid contracts generally are awarded solely on price. The owner defines the scope of the project, and the contractors submit lump-sum bids, unit-price bids, or a combination of both. The owner awards the contract to the contractor submitting the lowest total price for the project. Since actual quantities of work are not known for unit-priced items, the contractor's unit prices are multiplied by the estimated quantities provided on the bid form and summed. The contractor submitting the lowest sum is selected for award. The steps in awarding a contract using a bid procedure are shown in Figure 2–5. The ***pre-bid conference*** usually is held in the designer's office or at the project site to resolve any questions contractors may have relating to the project or the contract.

Negotiated Method

Negotiated contracts are awarded based on any criteria the owner selects. They are more prevalent in the private sector than they are in the public sector. Typical criteria include: cost (or fee in the case of a cost-plus contract), project duration, expertise of the project management team, plan for managing the project, contractor's safety record, contractor's existing work load, and contractor's experience with similar projects. Most

FIGURE 2–5 Procedure for Awarding a Contract on a Bid Basis

- Advertisement (Invitation to Bid)
- Pre-Bid Conference
- Site Visit
- Bid Opening
- Verification of Responsiveness of Low Bid
- Verification of Low Bidder's Qualifications
- Proof of Bonding Ability
- Contract Award

negotiated contracts involve a two-step procedure. First, prospective contractors are prequalified after review of their prior work experiences and safety records. Then the most qualified contractors (generally four to six) are invited to submit proposals containing project specific information required by the owner. As a part of the evaluation procedure, owners may require the proposed project management teams to brief their plans for managing the project. This may include preparation of a project schedule and budget. The owner then selects the contractor submitting the best proposal and negotiates a contract price, and maybe a project duration. The steps in awarding a contract using a negotiated procedure are shown in Figure 2–6. The ***pre-proposal conference*** is similar to the pre-bid conference used in a bid procedure. The major difference in a negotiated procedure is the opportunity for the owner to discuss the contractors' proposals, modify contract requirements, and clarify any issues before requesting best and final offers. The owner then selects the contractor submitting the best final proposal.

Some owners use a more informal negotiating procedure, particularly if they have long-term relationships with their contractors. Such an owner may simply ask one or a few contractors to submit proposals. After reviewing the proposals, the owner negotiates contract terms with the selected contractor.

FIGURE 2–6 Procedure for Awarding a Contract on a Negotiated Basis

- Advertisement (Request for Proposal)
- Pre-Proposal Conference
- Receipt of Proposals
- Evaluation of Proposals
- Discussion/Clarification/Interview
- Request for Best and Final Offer
- Negotiations
- Proof of Bonding Ability (if used)
- Contract Award

2.5 STANDARD CONTRACT FORMS

Contracts are either standard or specially prepared agreements. Most government agencies use standard formats for developing construction contract documents. Federal and state agencies typically have standardized general conditions and agreement language. Many local government agencies and private owners use contract formats developed by the ***American Institute of Architects*** (***AIA***). Standard contract formats also have been developed by the following professional organizations:

- ***Associated General Contractors of America*** (***AGC***)
- National Association of Home Builders (NAHB)
- Engineers Joint Council Document Committee (EJCDC)
- Design Build Institute of America (DBIA)

Contracts should not be signed until they have been subjected to a thorough legal review. This is to ensure that the documents are legally enforceable in the event of a disagreement and that there is a clear, legal description of each party's responsibilities. The advantage of using standard contract forms is that they have been developed by individuals skilled at contract law and have been tested in and out of courts. Care should be exercised when modifying any of these standard forms. Most are available in electronic format and are easy to tailor for specific projects. Sample contract documents are shown in Appendices D and E. We will illustrate the use of selected AIA and AGC contract forms throughout this text.

2.6 BONDS AND INSURANCE

Bonds and insurance are used to protect the owner and the contractor from some of the risks associated with construction. A bond is provided by a third party (called the ***surety***), which guarantees to the owner that the contractor will perform, as illustrated in Figure 2–7. When the contractor completes its obligations under the terms of the contract, the bond expires. Most public owners require bonds on projects exceeding a certain value, such as $100,000 or maybe $250,000. Similar bonds also may be required by general contractors to guarantee the performance of subcontractors. This is discussed in Chapter 8.

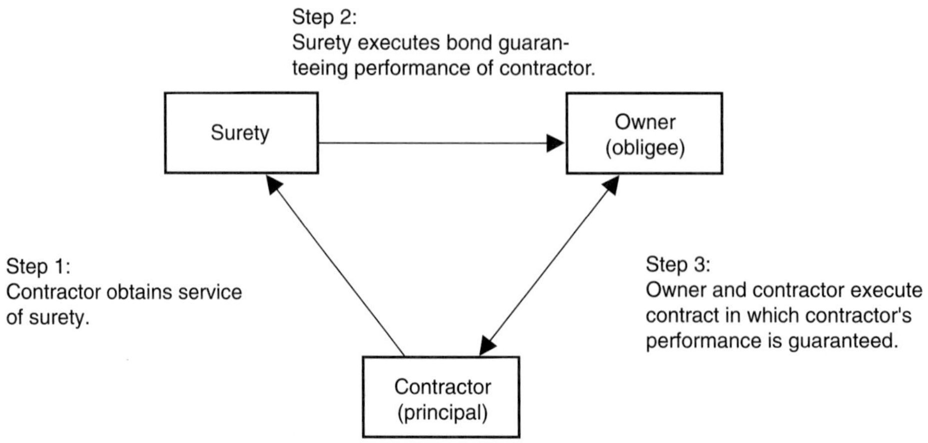

FIGURE 2–7 Relationship Between Owner, Surety, and Contractor

There are three primary types of bonds used in construction:

- **bid bond**

  guarantees that the low bidder will submit performance and payment bonds and execute a contract to complete the project at the price bid. If the contractor does not, the bid bond becomes payable to the owner as compensation for damages sustained, which are the additional costs incurred by awarding the contract to the next lowest bidder.

- **performance bond**

  guarantees that the contractor will complete the project in accordance with the contract plans and specifications. If the contractor defaults or fails to perform, the bonding company either must complete the project in accordance with contract requirements or compensate the owner for additional costs incurred by hiring another contractor to complete the project.

- **labor-and-material payment bond**

  guarantees that the contractor will pay all suppliers and subcontractors and that no ***liens*** will be placed on the completed project. If the contractor is unable or refuses to pay for work performed or materials used on the project, the surety will pay the claimants.

Private owners may or may not require bonds on their projects. However, lending institutions often require bonds before financing private projects. Contractors purchase the bonds from a surety (also known as a bonding company) typically through a broker. Surety underwriters determine the amount of bonding that they will provide to an individual contractor after evaluating the character, capacity, and capital resources of the contractor. *Capital* refers to the financial strength of the contractor, *capacity* refers to the number and sizes of projects the contractor can handle, and *character* refers to the contractor's reputation for completing projects on time and satisfying owners. A sample bond rate schedule for a medium-size general contractor with a good reputation and good financial condition is shown in Figure 2–8. Rates will vary among contractors based on the underwriter's assessment and market conditions. Rates shown are for performance bonds as well as labor-and-material payment bonds.

Contract Price	Premium Cost per $1,000 of Contract Price for the First 12 Months of a Project (Additional Time Would Add Additional Cost)
$1 to $100,000	$30
Next $400,000	$20
Next $1,000,000	$15
Next $2,000,000	$10
Next $2,000,000	$7
Next $2,000,000	$6
Over $7,500,000	$5

FIGURE 2–8 Bond Rate Schedule

Bid bonds usually are one-page documents that must be submitted with the bid documents. Some owners allow a certified cashiers check to be submitted in lieu of a bond as ***bid security***. Performance and payment bonds are not submitted until the owner indicates its intention to award the contract to a specific contractor. Bond coverage requirements specified by owners typically is 5 to 20% of the contract price for bid bonds and 50 to 100% for performance and payment bonds. Bonds impose no obligation on either the surety or the contractor beyond that contained in the construction contract. The AIA standard formats for bid, performance, and labor-and-material payment bonds are illustrated in Appendix H.

Insurance is purchased by the contractor to cover some of the risks associated with the project. An insurance policy is a contract under which the insurer promises, for a consideration (fee or premium), to assume the financial responsibility for a specified loss or liability. Coverage requirements generally are specified in the contract documents, and deductibles may be used to reduce insurance premiums if the contractor is willing to assume a portion of the risk. The following seven types of insurance policies typically are purchased by the contractor:

- **builder's risk insurance**

  protects the contractor in the event the project is damaged or destroyed while under construction. Builder's risk insurance may be all-risk or limited to named perils such as fire, wind, hail, and explosion. All-risk insurance covers all damage unless there is a risk exclusion such as earthquake. Builder's risk insurance generally includes coverage of materials stored on site and may include coverage of materials in transit and stored off site. Builder's risk policies typically include a standard exclusion for loss or damage resulting from faulty or defective workmanship or material.

- **general liability insurance**

  protects the contractor against claims from a third party for bodily injury or property damage.

- **property damage insurance**

  protects the contractor against financial loss due to damage to the contractor's property.

- **equipment floater insurance**

  protects the contractor against financial loss due to physical damage to equipment from named perils or all risks and theft. Coverage is for owned, leased, and rented equipment not operated on streets and highways.

- **automobile insurance**

  protects the contractor against claims from another party for bodily injury or property damage caused by contractor-owned, leased, or rented automobiles and equipment operated over the highway. Coverage may include damages to the automobiles and equipment.

- **umbrella liability insurance**

  provides coverage against liability claims exceeding that covered by standard general liability or automobile insurance. For example, a contractor may have a general liability insurance policy covering up to $2 million per occurrence and an umbrella policy covering up to $50 million per occurrence.

- **workers' compensation insurance**

  protects the contractor from a claim due to injury or death of an employee on the project site.

Some owners purchase the builder's risk insurance, while others require the contractor to purchase it. Coverage expires upon acceptance of the completed project by the owner. Workers' compensation insurance is either purchased from a commercial insurance company or a state fund. Some state governments require employers to purchase worker's compensation insurance from a monopolistic state fund, unless they choose to be self-insuring. To be self-insuring, the contractor typically must meet certain size and financial requirements. Contractors executing design-build projects also may purchase ***errors and omissions insurance*** to provide coverage against claims resulting from incomplete or defective design documents.

2.7 IMPACT ON PROJECT MANAGEMENT

The contract documents have a significant impact on the responsibilities of the project manager. Specific requirements are contained in the general conditions and special conditions of the contract. Unit-price and cost-plus contracts have more owner involvement than do lump-sum contracts. The actual quantities of work are jointly determined by the owner and the project manager in a unit-price contract. Project expenditures often require owner approval in cost-plus contracts, and invoices must be collected on the project site and submitted to the owner for reimbursement. A comparison of lump-sum and cost-plus contracts from a contractor's perspective is shown in Figure 2–9.

Lump-Sum Contract	Cost-Plus Contract
Riskiest to contractor	Least risk for contractor
Sometimes adversarial	Team atmosphere
Little owner input to project management	May be significant owner involvement in project management
Owner controls funding on disputed work	All direct project cost reimbursed
Savings resulting from innovation go to contractor	Savings resulting from innovation may be shared between owner and contractor

FIGURE 2–9 Comparison of Lump-Sum and Cost-Plus Contracts

2.8 SUMMARY

The construction contract describes the responsibilities of the owner and the contractor and the terms and conditions of their relationship. A thorough understanding of all contractual requirements is essential if a project manager expects to complete the project successfully.

There are five basic documents that comprise most construction contracts. They are the agreement, the general conditions, the special conditions, the technical specifications, and the contract drawings. The agreement describes the project to be constructed, the pricing method to be used, the time allowed for construction, any liquidated damages, and the names of the parties to the contract, the owner and the contractor. The general conditions of the contract provide a set of operating procedures that a specific owner typically uses on all projects. The special conditions of the contract contain any unique requirements for the project. Some construction contracts do not contain any special conditions. The technical specifications provide the qualitative requirements for construction materials, equipment to be installed, and workmanship. The contract drawings show the quantitative requirements for the project and how the various components go together to form the completed project.

There are several pricing methods that typically are used on construction contracts. Lump-sum contracts are awarded on the basis of a single lump-sum estimate for a specified scope of work. Unit-price contracts are used when the exact quantities of work cannot be defined. The designer estimates the quantities of work, and the contractor submits unit prices for each work item. The actual quantities required are multiplied by the unit prices to determine the contract price. Cost-plus contracts are used when the scope of work cannot be defined. All the contractor's project-related costs are reimbursed by the owner, and a fee is paid to cover profit and contractor general overhead. A guaranteed-maximum-price contract is a cost-plus contract in which the contractor agrees not to exceed a specified cost.

Owners select contractors by one of two methods. In a bid procedure, the contractor is selected solely on the cost data submitted on the owner's bid form. In a negotiated procedure, the contractor is selected based on any criteria the owner wishes to establish.

Contracts are either standard or specifically prepared documents. Standard contracts generally are preferred because they have been legally tested in and out of courts. Such documents have been developed by AIA, AGC, and other professional organizations.

Construction is a very risky activity, and bonds and insurance are used by owners and contractors to cover some of the risks. Owners often require bid bonds to guarantee that the low bidder will accept the contract, performance bonds to guarantee that the contractor will complete the project, and labor and materials payment bonds to guarantee that there will be no liens placed on the project. Contractors purchase insurance contracts to protect against financial loss due to damage to the uncompleted project (builder's risk), claims from third parties (general liability), damage to their property (property damage), damage to or loss of equipment (equipment floater), and claims resulting from injury or death of an employee on the project (workers' compensation).

2.9 REVIEW QUESTIONS

1. Why is it essential that a project manager fully understand the requirements and procedures specified in the contract documents?
2. What types of information would you find in each of the following contract documents?
   a. Agreement
   b. General conditions
   c. Special conditions
   d. Technical specifications
   e. Contract drawings
3. What is the difference between contract addenda and a contract change order?
4. Why might an owner decide to include a special conditions section in a construction contract?
5. Name and describe the four types of technical specifications.
6. What type of construction materials are covered in division 8 of the technical specifications of a construction contract?

7. What type of construction materials are covered in division 9 of the technical specifications of a construction contract?
8. What is the difference between a lump-sum and a unit-price contract?
9. Under what conditions might an owner decide to use a unit-price contract?
10. What is the difference between a lump-sum and a cost-plus construction contract?
11. What is the difference between the bid and the negotiated methods of contract procurement?
12. On what basis is the successful contractor selected in a bid method of contract procurement?
13. On what basis is the successful contractor selected in a negotiated method of contract procurement?
14. What does contractor prequalification mean in the context of a construction contract procurement strategy?
15. What are the three types of bonds used in construction? Why do owners require them?
16. What is the difference between builder's risk and general liability insurance?
17. What is the difference between named-peril and all-risk builder's risk insurance?
18. What contractor's risk is covered by workers' compensation insurance?

2.10 EXERCISES

1. What requirements might be included in the special conditions of a contract for the construction of a major addition to an existing hospital in a major metropolitan area? What impacts would these requirements have on the scheduled completion and cost of the project?
2. An owner wants to identify the best-qualified contractors for negotiating a design-build contract for the construction of a major manufacturing plant. What information might the owner require contractors to submit for review during the prequalification process?
3. What criteria might an owner use when negotiating a lump-sum contract for the construction of a shopping complex that she desires be completed prior to the start of the Christmas shopping season?
4. Calculate a contractor's cost for performance and labor and material payment bonds using the rate schedule shown in Figure 2–8 for each of the following:
   a. A construction project with an estimated cost of $750,000.
   b. A construction project with an estimated cost of $25 million.

   What is the calculated bond fee (bond cost as a percentage of the construction cost) for each project? How does the bond fee vary as the project cost is increased?

2.11 SOURCES OF ADDITIONAL INFORMATION

Barrie, Donald S., and Boyd C. Paulson. *Professional Construction Management.* 3d ed. New York: McGraw-Hill, Inc., 1992.

Bartholomew, Stuart H. *Construction Contracting: Business and Legal Principles.* Upper Saddle River, N.J.: Prentice-Hall, Inc., 1998.

Clough, Richard H., and Glenn A. Sears. *Construction Contracting*. 6th ed. New York: John Wiley and Sons, Inc., 1994.

Collier, Keith. *Construction Contracts*. 3d ed. Upper Saddle River, N.J.: Prentice-Hall, Inc., 2001.

Dorsey, Robert W. *Project Delivery Systems for Building Construction*. Washington, D.C.: Associated General Contractors of America, 1997.

Hinze, Jimmie. *Construction Contracts*. New York: McGraw-Hill, Inc., 1993.

3

Selecting a Project

3.1 INTRODUCTION

Now that we have discussed basic project management concepts and organizations as well as construction contracts, we will examine selection and acquisition of a project to manage. In this chapter, we will discuss risk analysis, marketing techniques, and bidding or negotiating strategies. In many construction firms, the selection of projects to pursue is made by senior executives, not individual project managers. In other firms, the project managers recommend projects for senior executive approval. At the end of the chapter, you will be introduced to an example project that we will use throughout the remainder of the book to illustrate specific concepts and procedures. The project is large enough to illustrate project management procedures and tools, yet small enough to demonstrate concepts without getting lost in the detail sometimes involved in the management of larger, more complex projects.

3.2 RISK ANALYSIS

Construction is a risky business, as evidenced by the high number of construction firm failures each year. About 1.2% of the construction firms in the United States go out of business each year, according to Dun & Bradstreet's annual *Business Failure Record.*[1] To minimize the possibility for financial difficulty, a contractor should analyze each potential project to determine the risks involved and whether or not the projected rewards justify acceptance of the risk exposure.

---

[1] *The Business Failure Record.* (Wilton, Conn.: The Dunn & Bradstreet Corporation, 1996), p. 6.

The basic steps in performing a risk analysis are:

- Identify the sources of risk.
- Identify the range of possible risk events.
- Assess the potential impacts of risk events on the project.
- Identify alternative responses to mitigate the hypothetical impacts of risk events.
- Identify the consequences of the alternative responses.
- Select risk management strategies including the allocation of risk.

The sources of risk on a project may involve such things as unusually adverse weather, material cost inflation, owner's inability to finance the project, limited availability of skilled craftspeople or subcontractors, bankruptcy of subcontractors, incomplete design documents, project size, project location, and project constructability and complexity. The contractor needs to forecast the likelihood of such risks, the range of possibilities, and the impact of each on the contractor's ability to complete the project profitably. This is particularly true of constructability risks identified during analysis of the ***geotechnical*** or ***soils report*** for the project site.

The primary risk responses are:

- Avoiding the risk by walking away from the project.
- Mitigating the risk by sharing it with a joint-venture partner or hiring a subcontractor.
- Transferring the risk by purchasing insurance.
- Accepting the risk.

Selection of risk management strategies involves choosing the appropriate response to each of the identified risks. Insurance coverage generally is limited to protection against financial loss due to damage to the project under construction (builder's risk), injury of workers on the project site (workers' compensation), injury or property loss to a third party (liability), and damage to equipment (equipment floater).

Internal risks must be identified also and appropriate management strategies selected. The three most common internal risks are unrealistic cost estimates, unrealistic construction schedules, and ineffective project management, including cost and schedule control, material management, and subcontractor coordination. Contractors must adopt strategies to minimize occurrence of these problems. Often the basic issue to be addressed is the selection of qualified people to manage the project, particularly the project manager.

The output of a risk analysis is a decision whether or not to pursue a project, the amount of contingency to include in the bid or cost proposal, whether or not to joint-venture with another firm, the portions of work to subcontract, and the type and amount of insurance to purchase.

3.3 MARKETING

Marketing is acquiring and retaining customers. This is an essential project management skill, because the most effective marketing resource is a satisfied customer. In most projects, the customer is the owner, and customer satisfaction is measured in terms of cost of construction, time to complete, and the resulting quality of the completed project. These project characteristics are the responsibility of the project manager, as discussed in Chapter 1.

The initial marketing task is to determine which segment of the overall market the contractor wants for its customers. Some contractors may want to bid for public projects such as schools, government office buildings, or highways. Others may be interested only in privately-funded projects such as shopping centers, private office buildings, hotels, or condominiums. Once the market segment has been selected, the contractor needs to target its marketing activities toward those prospective customers. Then, the contractor organizes its services to cater to the specific market segment selected. This requires an understanding of how the targeted owners select contractors for their projects and what project characteristics they value. For example, some private owners are more interested in high-quality, short-duration projects than they are in low cost. The contractor should emphasize the characteristics that are important to the targeted group in its marketing initiatives. For example, a contractor wanting to enter the hotel construction market will want to ensure that his or her project managers understand the prospective customers' requirements (typically reasonable cost, high quality, and early completion) and are skilled at preparing proposals and making presentations for that specific market and owner.

While the contractor's business development staff may identify potential clients, it usually is up to the project manager to obtain the project. This may be done by bidding on the project or by preparing a quality proposal and making a winning presentation to the potential customer. Good marketing and presentation skills are just as important as good technical skills to be a successful project manager. Once a project has been acquired, it is the responsibility of the project manager to complete the project to the owner's requirements. This is to ensure the construction firm is considered for future projects built by the owner.

Everything that occurs on a project should be a part of the contractor's marketing strategy. The project sign, the organization and cleanliness of the project site, the treatment of subcontractors and suppliers, the condition of its equipment, and the accident rate all shape the public and prospective owners' opinions regarding the contractor. Public relations also is a part of marketing. Participation in professional organizations and public service projects establishes a network of contacts for the project manager and significantly aids in marketing. Networking also results in new insights on marketing strategies and lessons learned.

3.4 BIDDING

Most contracts awarded on a bid basis are either lump-sum or unit-price contracts, or a combination of both. A lump-sum contract may require a single price for the entire scope of work, or separate prices for individual portions. Some contracts may have additive or deductive items that must be priced during the bidding process. The owner selects which combination of ***additive*** and/or ***deductive alternates*** to award once the bids have been opened. Figure 3–1 illustrates a bid form containing additive and deductive alternates. Some contracts may contain a combination of lump-sum and unit-price items as shown in Figure 3–2 on page 31.

Sometimes cost-plus contracts are awarded on a bid basis. Since the construction costs are not known, the basis for award is the size of the fee and possibly the cost of preconstruction services. The owner provides an estimated cost of construction, and the contractor bids a fee based on the owner's estimate. Cost-plus contracts generally are awarded on a negotiated basis but on occasion are awarded on a bid basis.

Bidding may be open to any qualified contractor or may be restricted to those firms prequalified by the owner. If prequalification is used, the project manager must ensure that the documentation submitted in response to the ***request for qualifications*** presents a strong basis for prequalifying the firm. A project manager cannot win the project if he or she does not first make the list of best-qualified contractors who are invited

BASE BID

Pursuant to and in compliance with the Advertisement for Bids and Instructions to Bidders, the undersigned hereby certifies having carefully examined the Contract Documents entitled

South Central High School,
prepared by Stellar Architects

and conditions affecting the work, and is familiar with the site; and having made the necessary examinations, hereby proposes to furnish all labor, materials, equipment, and services necessary to complete the work in strict accordance with the above named documents for the sum of

____ Dollars ($ _______________)

which sum is hereby designated as the Base Bid.

ALTERNATES

The undersigned proposes to perform work called for in the following alternates, as described in Section 01030 and the drawings of the Contract Documents, for the following resulting additions to or deductions from the Base Bid.

Alternate #1: Delete Selected Landscaping

____ Dollars ($ _______________)

Alternate #2: Delete Paved Parking Lot

____ Dollars ($ _______________)

Alternate #3: Add First Floor Upgrade

____ Dollars ($ _______________)

Alternate #4: Add Second Floor Upgrade

____ Dollars ($ _______________)

Legal Name of Bidder: ____

By: ____
Signature/Title

Date: ____________________

FIGURE 3–1 Contract Bid Form Containing Alternates

BID

Pursuant to and in compliance with the Advertisement for Bids and Instructions to Bidders, the undersigned hereby certifies having carefully examined the Contract Documents entitled

Olympic Office Tower,
prepared by Cascade Designers, Inc.

and conditions affecting the work, and is familiar with the site; and having made the necessary examinations, hereby proposes to furnish all labor, materials, equipment, and services necessary to complete the work, less the drilled pier foundations, in strict accordance with the above named documents for the sum of

______________________________ Dollars ($ ______________)

The undersigned proposes to furnish all labor, materials, equipment, and services necessary to construct the drilled pier foundation for the following schedule of prices. Exact quantities will be determined upon completion of the work.

Item	Est. Quantity	Unit	Unit Price	Amount
24-inch diameter drilled piers	600	linear feet		
36-inch diameter drilled piers	800	linear feet		
48-inch diameter drilled piers	900	linear feet		

Total for Unit Priced Items:

______________________________ Dollars ($ ______________)

Total Bid Price:

______________________________ Dollars ($ ______________)

Legal Name of Bidder: ______________________________

By: ______________________________
Signature/Title

Date: ____________________

FIGURE 3–2 Contract Bid Form Containing Lump-Sum and Unit-Price Bid Items

to submit bids. Good marketing and presentation skills are essential in preparing the prequalification documentation describing the contractor's and the project team's qualifications for the project.

Pricing the specific items on the bid form requires an understanding of the construction costs, risks involved, desired profit, and the bidding climate. Bidding climate refers to the number of anticipated competitors bidding and the availability of construction work in the local market. When there are many contractors pursing a few projects, profit margins tend to be small. When there is considerable construction activity, profit margins tend to be larger.

3.5 NEGOTIATING

Negotiated contracts may be lump-sum, unit-price, or cost-plus. Most are awarded using a two-step process. First, the prospective contractors are invited to submit statement of their firms' qualifications and those of the designated project management team members. Sometimes owners also request statements of qualifications for the major subcontractors. Once these qualifications have been evaluated, the best-qualified project teams are invited to make presentations to the owner and sometimes the designer. Those teams presenting the best management approaches are then asked to submit cost, and sometimes schedule, proposals. Negotiations then take place between the owner and the highest-ranked construction firm to reach an agreement regarding contract parameters such as estimated cost, fee, and schedule. These negotiations also may involve adjustments to contract language.

In negotiating a lump-sum contract, the project manager generally is required to provide a detailed breakdown of the cost estimate and a complete project schedule. Initial discussions usually involve reaching agreement on the ***direct construction costs***. Once agreement is reached, ***indirect construction costs*** and ***mark-up*** are discussed. In cost-plus contracts, negotiations focus on the guaranteed maximum price (if one is used in the contract), the fee, the schedule, and the cost control system to be used.

Good marketing and presentation skills are essential for a project manager to be successful in the negotiated construction market. Some private owners may not use the prequalification procedure; rather, they simply invite one or two construction firms who have worked with them previously to submit proposals. This is where previous project success is critical, whether it be for the prospective client or someone known by the prospective client.

3.6 EXAMPLE PROJECT

Project Description

The project selected as the example project for this text is a two-story, wood-frame office building of approximately 13,000 square feet with two mechanical penthouses of approximately 600 square feet with a thirty-two-space asphalt parking lot in front. The project is called the Huna Office Building project, and it was constructed in Alaska. An artist's rendering of the completed project is shown in Figure 3–3, and a site plan is shown in Appendix C.

The wood frame building was constructed on concrete footings and covered with stained cedar siding. Wood trusses were placed above the wood frame, and a standing-seam metal roof was installed. Typical building sections are shown in Figures 3–4 and 3–5. Representative construction drawings are shown in Appendix C. Construction photographs are shown in Chapters 10 though 22 to illustrate activities performed on the Huna Office Building project.

FIGURE 3–3 Artist's Rendering of Completed Project
(Huna Totem Corporation and Jensen Yorba Lott, Inc.)

Contracting Method

The construction contract for this project was a cost-plus-fixed-fee contract awarded on a negotiated basis. The contract contained a guaranteed maximum price and a provision for sharing any savings, 30% to the contractor and 70% to the owner. Three selected contractors were invited to make proposals for its construction. The contract documents are shown in Appendices D and E.

Project Participants

The owner of the project was the Huna Totem Corporation and the architect was Jensen Yorba Lott, Inc., both located in Juneau, Alaska. The fictitious contractor used in this text is the Northwest Construction Company. An organization chart for the project is shown in Figure 3–6.

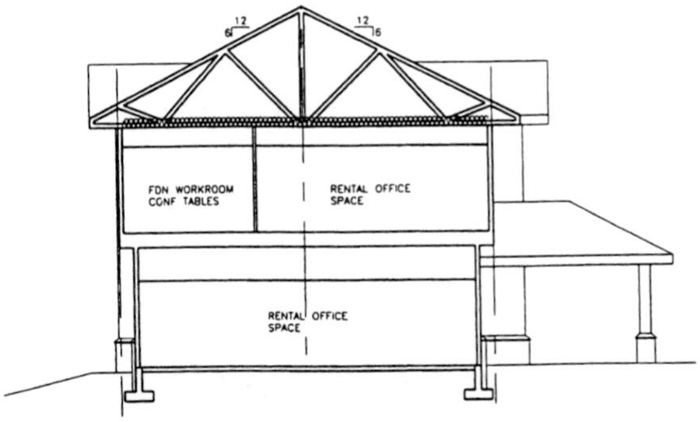

FIGURE 3–4 Building Section
(Jensen Yorba Lott, Inc.)

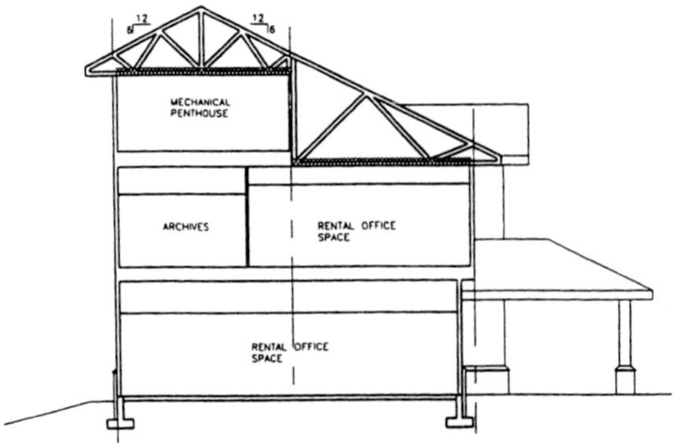

FIGURE 3–5 Building Section through Mechanical Penthouse (Jensen Yorba Lott, Inc.)

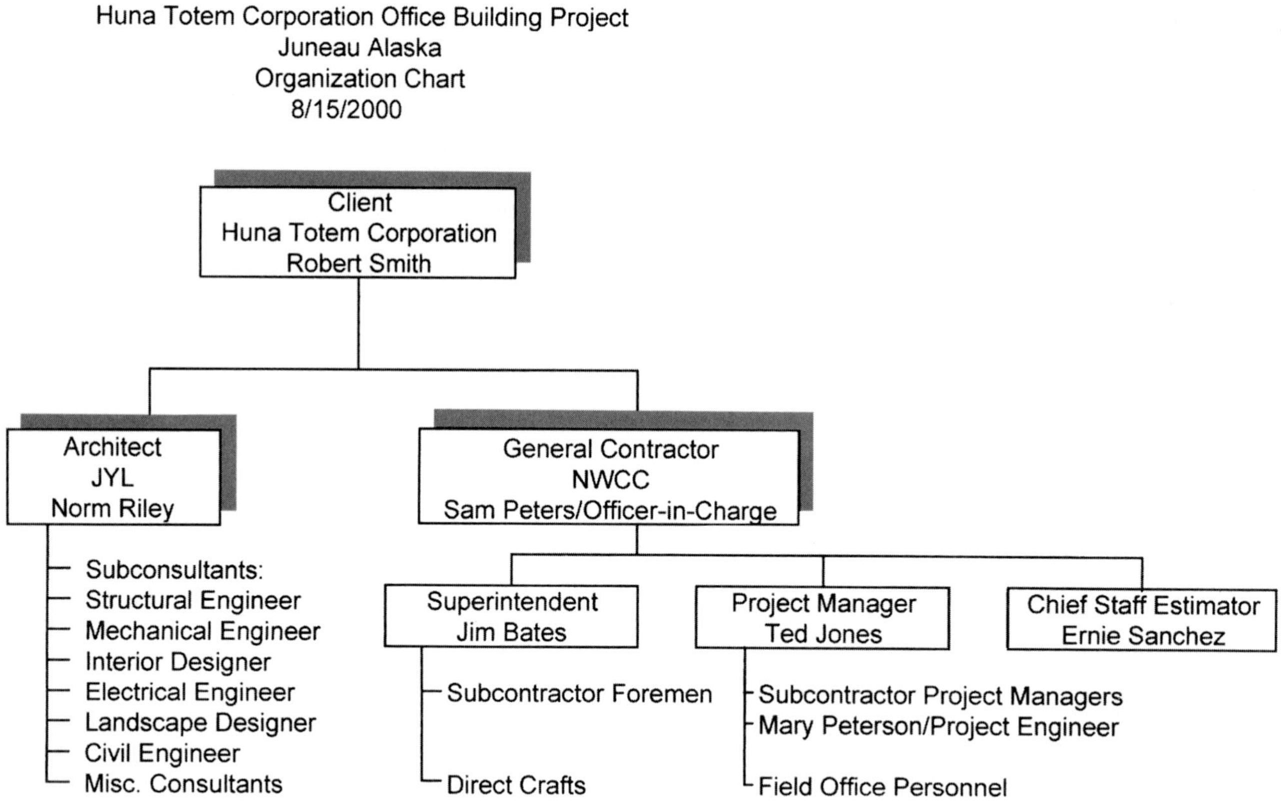

FIGURE 3–6 Project Organization Chart

3.7 SUMMARY

Construction is a risky business, and project managers must assess carefully the risks associated with a prospective project. Once the risks have been identified, strategies are selected to manage them. In some cases, the risks are too great and the project should not be pursued. In other cases, the risk can be mitigated by obtaining a joint-venture partner or hiring subcontractors.

Marketing is a critical project manager skill, necessary for attracting and retaining customers. Successful marketing is based on understanding existing and prospective customers' needs and criteria for selecting contractors. Good communication and presentation skills are essential to effective marketing.

Projects may be awarded on either a bid or a negotiation basis. Bidding may be open to any contractor or may be restricted to a short list of contractors developed during prequalification. Generally, only prequalified or preselected contractors are invited to submit proposals for negotiated contracts. The project manager must ensure that bid forms or proposal documents fully comply with owner requirements.

3.8 REVIEW QUESTIONS

1. What are five potential risks that a contractor might face on a construction project?
2. What are four alternative risk response strategies that a contractor might consider in developing a risk management plan?

3. What are three common internal risks a project manager faces on a construction project?
4. What are three risks a contractor might face in the construction of a public school project that is to be awarded on a bid basis?
5. Why is marketing an essential project manager skill?
6. What does *segmenting the market* mean in the development of a marketing plan?
7. What is the value gained by membership in professional organizations?
8. What is the difference between a bid and a negotiation procedure for awarding a construction contract?
9. In some cases, only prequalified contractors are invited to submit a bid for a project. How does a contractor become prequalified?
10. Why are good presentation skills critical to a project manager pursuing a project that is to be awarded on a negotiated basis?

3.9 EXERCISES

1. What risks does a contractor face in a lump-sum contract for the construction of an office building for a private real estate developer?
2. What risks does a contractor face when bidding on a construction project located in a city in which she has never had a previous project?
3. What criteria should a contractor use in deciding which projects to submit bids on?

3.10 SOURCES OF ADDITIONAL INFORMATION

Kubal, Michael T., Kevin T. Miller, and Ronald D. Worth. *Building Profits in the Construction Industry*. New York: McGraw-Hill, Inc., 2000.

Management of Project Risks and Uncertainties. Publication 6–8, Austin, Tex.: Construction Industry Institute, October 1989.

4

Cost Estimating

4.1 INTRODUCTION

As discussed in Chapter 1, cost is one of the critical attributes that must be controlled by the project manager. Project costs are estimated to develop a budget within which the project manager must work. All project costs are estimated in preparing bids for lump-sum or unit-price contracts and negotiating the guaranteed maximum price on cost-plus contracts. Non-reimbursable costs are estimated in developing fee proposals for cost-plus contracts.

Cost estimating is the process of collecting, analyzing, and summarizing data in order to prepare an educated projection of the anticipated cost of a project. Cost estimates may be prepared either by the project manager or by the estimating department of the construction firm. Even if the estimate is prepared by the estimating department, the project manager must understand how it was prepared, because he or she must build the project within the budget developed from the estimate. This project budget becomes the basis for the cost control system discussed in Chapter 16.

Our goal in this chapter is not to reproduce all of the information that is available in other publications, but to highlight some of the major issues in developing cost estimates. There are many good texts and references available on estimating. Some are listed at the end of this chapter. We will discuss estimating from a manual perspective to illustrate some basic issues. Many contractors use software to develop their estimates. There are several on the market such as Timberline Precision, MC^2, WinEstimator, BID2WIN, and HCSS.

Good cost-estimating skills are essential if one is to be an effective project manager. The quantity take-off procedure for a few major building systems will be briefly discussed in this chapter. For discussion of other building systems, readers should refer to the texts listed at the end of the chapter. If a project manager can calculate the quantity of concrete in a spot footing, or count the quantity of hollow core doors, then he or she has the skills needed to measure almost any material quantity. The rules of measuring, counting, and extending apply to most systems.

It is assumed that the reader has experience in construction means and methods. An understanding of the differences between basic building systems, such as concrete foundations from wood framing, is essential. It is also assumed that document reading is a tool that the reader has already acquired and is familiar with terms and abbreviations such as SF (square foot) and CY (cubic yard).

There is no correct estimate for any project. There are many good estimates, although some are better than others. Adjustments in pricing, subcontractor and labor strategy, overhead structures, and fee calculations are individual contractor decisions that will determine "the estimate" for those conditions at that time. The process of developing an estimate is illustrated in Figure 4–1. The first step, gathering information, is the foundation for the process. As the estimator proceeds through the process, information continues to be analyzed and summarized, until eventually there is only one figure left, the final estimate or bid.

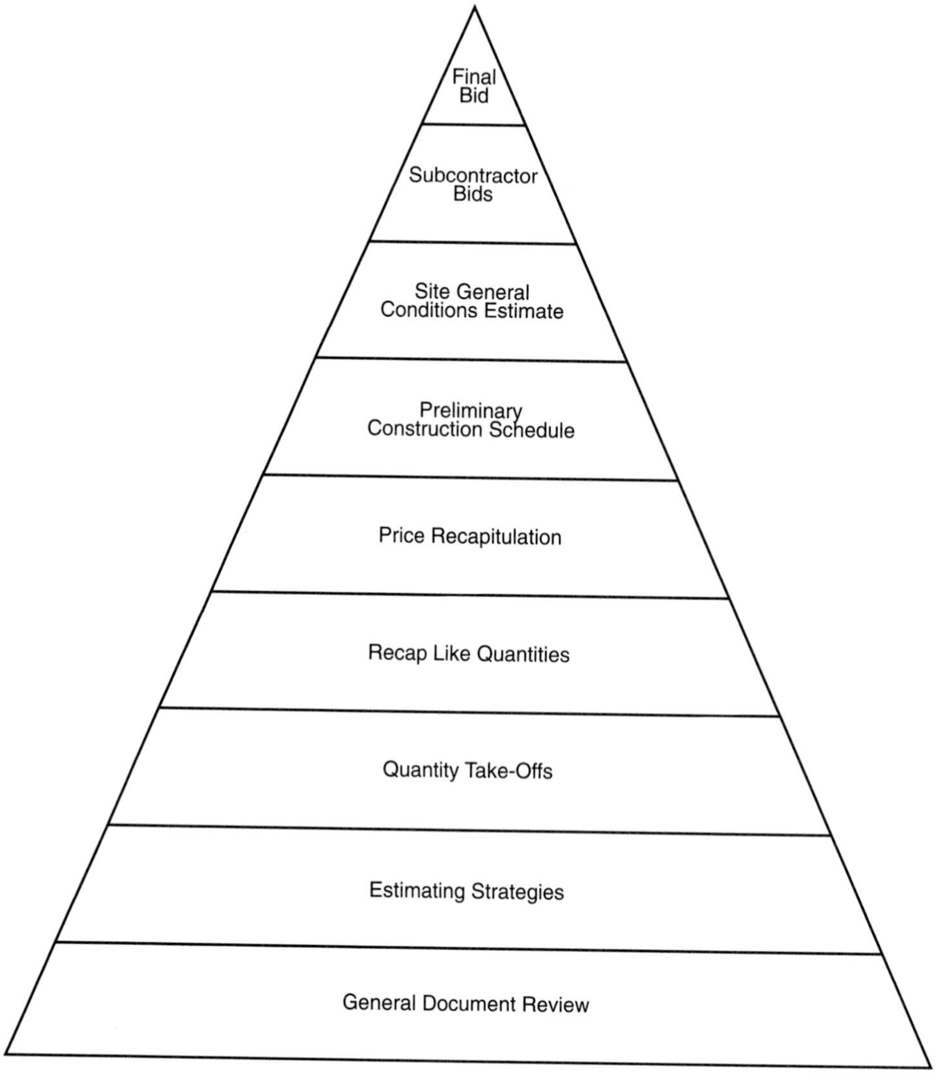

FIGURE 4–1 The Estimating Process

4.2 TYPES OF COST ESTIMATES

There are several different types of cost estimates. ***Conceptual cost estimates*** are developed using incomplete project documentation, while ***detailed cost estimates*** are prepared using complete drawings and specifications. The typical accuracy for each type of estimate is shown in Figure 4–2. A type of conceptual cost estimate called a ***rough order-of-magnitude (ROM) estimate*** is developed from the first document overview to establish a preliminary project budget and determine if the contractor intends to pursue the project.

4.3 RISK ANALYSIS

The greatest risk in developing a cost estimate is predicting the productivity of the craftworkers. Other risks involve counting some element of work twice or not at all. To minimize the potential for making errors when developing an estimate, the project manager should

- Rely on good estimating practices and procedures.
- Choose good in-house project management and supervision teams not only to manage the project but also to assist with the estimating.
- Choose qualified subcontractors and suppliers.
- Plan to build the project in less time than specified in the contract to save overhead expenses.
- Be selective on which projects are chosen to bid. Familiarity with the owner, designer, and building location and type are important. Selection of projects may be made by senior managers in the construction firm. Sometimes they may ask for the project manager's recommendations.

4.4 ESTIMATING STRATEGIES

When possible, the project manager and superintendent should be responsible for developing the estimate, or at a minimum, work as integral members of the estimating team. Their individual inputs regarding constructability and their personal commitments to the estimating product are essential to assure not only the success of the estimate, but also the ultimate success of the project. One of the first assignments for

Type of Estimate	Document Development	Accuracy
Budget or Rough Order of Magnitude	Schematics, Design Development, 30% Construction Documents	10–20%
Guaranteed Maximum Price for Cost-Plus Project	60–90% Construction Documents	5%
Lump-Sum Bid	100% Plans and Specifications	2%

FIGURE 4–2 Accuracy of Different Cost Estimates

the project manager and the estimating team is to develop a responsibility list and to schedule the estimate. Each team member relies on the others to do their jobs efficiently and accurately. If one member falls behind, the team and the estimate will suffer. A list of the team responsibilities for the Huna Office Building project is shown in Figure 4–3.

The estimating process should be scheduled for each project. The start date is known, most probably a pre-bid conference is scheduled, and the date the bid is due is also scheduled. With these milestones established, a short ***bar chart schedule*** should be developed which shows each step and assigns due dates to each estimating task. Familiarity with the steps or building blocks shown in Figure 4–1 is essential in developing the schedule. Similar to a construction schedule, if one of the individuals falls behind on any one activity, the completion date may be in jeopardy, or more commonly, the quality of the finished estimate will be affected unless other resources are applied. An ***estimate schedule*** for the Huna Office Building project is shown in Figure 4–4 on page 42.

Many factors will affect the estimating strategy for each project. These include:

- Project location
- Complexity of the project
- Type of contract
- Familiarity with architect
- Workload of the construction company
- Season of the year
- Familiarity with owner
- Adequacy of contract documents
- Availability of estimating resources

4.5 WORK BREAKDOWN

The ***work breakdown structure (WBS)*** for the project is an early compilation of the significant work items that will have associated cost or schedule considerations. This includes areas of work such as foundations, utilities, drywall, floor covering, plumbing and so on. Before any detailed estimating is performed, the estimator should have a general idea of the work that will be included on the WBS. The first step is to perform a document overview, slowly leafing through the drawings and specifications to develop a good understanding of the type of project and the systems that are included. The estimator should not start measuring or pricing any work items until this overview is complete.

One of the tools utilized in this process is the project item list. Figure 4–5 on page 43 shows a partial example for the Huna Office Building project. This list is a good reference to use throughout the estimating process as well as a final checklist to review again prior to finalizing the bid. This item list is not to be considered a complete work breakdown structure, just a good first step.

At this stage, the estimator needs to know which categories of work will be estimated in detail and subsequently self-performed by the contractor's own forces and which will be supplied and installed by subcontractors. The project item list has boxes to check for this purpose. The types of work general contractors most often perform include:

- Hand excavation and backfill
- Concrete formwork
- Concrete reinforcement placement
- Concrete placement
- Concrete slab finishing
- Structural steel erection
- Rough carpentry
- Finish carpentry, including doors, specialties, and accessories
- Siding
- Window placement

NORTHWEST CONSTRUCTION COMPANY

1242 First Avenue, Cascade, Washington 98202
(206) 239-1422

HUNA PROJECT ESTIMATE
TEAM RESPONSIBILITY LIST

Mary Peterson, Project Engineer:

- Call subcontractors to verify interest in bidding.
- Perform quantity take-offs for CSI divisions 2, 3, 6, 8, and 10.
- Prepare computer schedule for proposal based upon Jim's schedule input.
- Receive subcontractor fax and phone quotes on bid day with the assistance of other office personnel.

Jim Bates, Project Superintendent:

- Work with Mary for sequencing of work, slab joints, etc.
- Work with Ted for jobsite equipment requirements.
- Review general conditions estimate with Ted.
- Prepare preliminary construction schedule.
- Review pricing sheets developed by Ted and Ernie.

Ernie Sanchez, Chief Staff Estimator:

- Work with Mary to perform balance of quantity take-offs.
- Input quantities into computer. Apply company productivity rates and material pricing as appropriate.
- Prepare estimates for subcontractor scopes of work.
- Review Ted's general conditions estimate.
- Work in bid room on bid day.

Ted Jones, Project Manager:

- Act as bid captain.
- Develop general conditions estimate.
- Review spec section 1 and contract.
- Send contract to legal, insurance, and bonding companies for review.
- Review pricing sheets developed by Ernie.
- Price CSI divisions 3 and 6.
- Review schedule developed by Mary and Jim.
- Prepare sub-bid tab sheets for bid day postings.
- Fill in bid form and attach all requested data.
- Work in bid room on bid day.

Sam Peters, Officer-in-Charge:

- Develop fee markups.
- Review contract.
- Sign the bid form.
- Review completed "plug" estimate day prior to bid.

FIGURE 4–3 Team Responsibility List

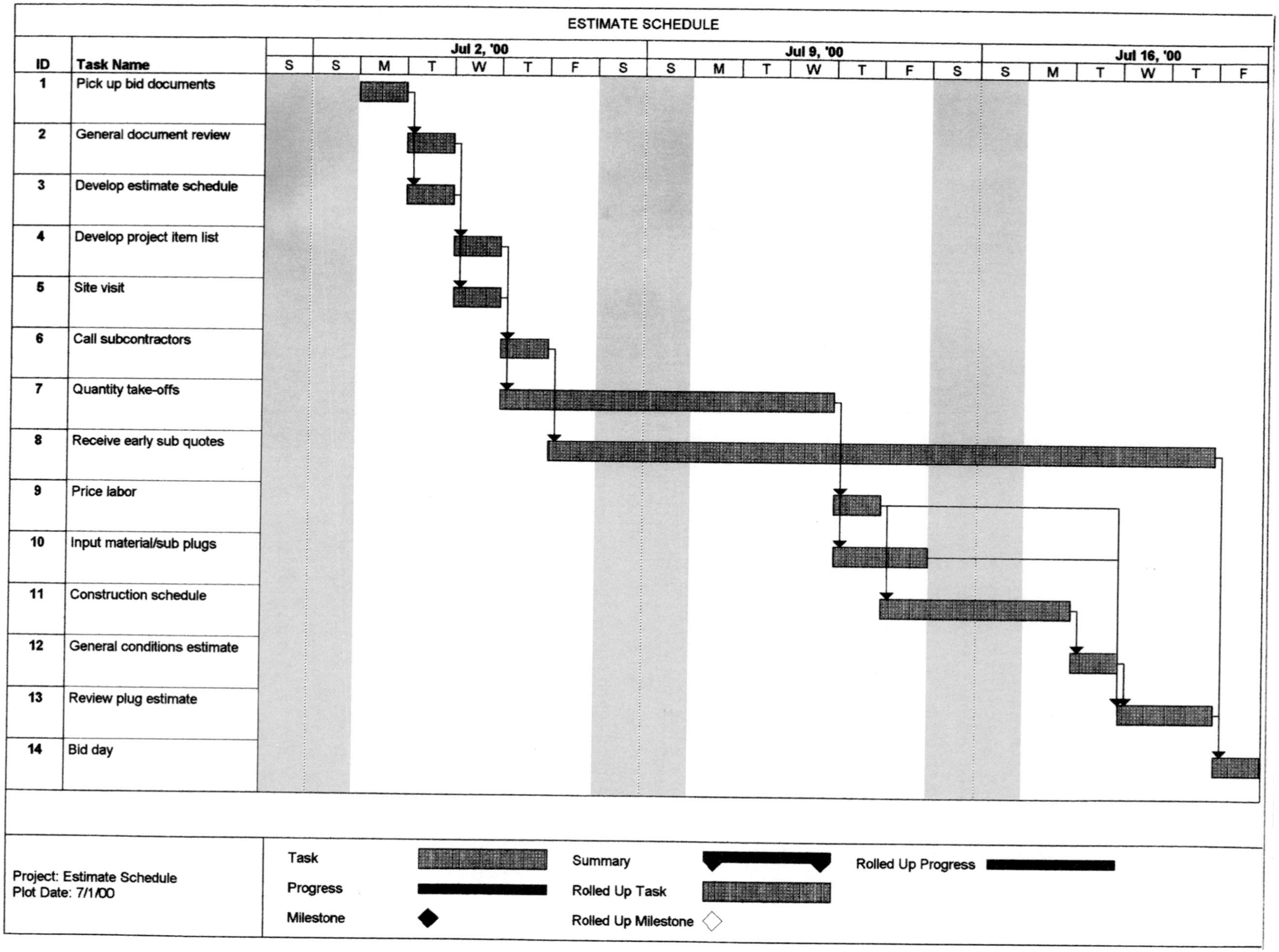

FIGURE 4–4 Estimate Schedule

NORTHWEST CONSTRUCTION COMPANY

1242 First Avenue, Cascade, Washington 98202
(206) 239-1422

PROJECT ITEM LIST

Project: HUNA OFFICE BUILDING		Date:	JULY 7, 2000
Estimator: TED JONES		Page	1 of 5

Drawing Detail	CSI	Description	Provider: General Contractor Labor	Provider: General Contractor Material	Provider: Subcontractor Labor	Provider: Subcontractor Material
		FOUNDATIONS:				
	2	STRUCTURAL EXCAVATION			X	X
		AND BACKFILL				
	3	FORMWORK	X	X		
	3	REINFORCING STEEL	?	X	?	
	3	PUMP CONCRETE ?			X	
	3	PLACE CONCRETE	X	P.O.		
		SLAB ON GRADE:				
	7	VISQUEEN	X	X		
	2	SAND	X	X		
	15	PLUMBING			X	X
	3	PUMP CONCRETE			X	
	3	FINISH			X	
	3	PLACE SLAB	X			
	3	EMBEDS	X	X		
	3/7	SAW CUT JOINTS	?		?	
	3/7	CAULK JOINTS	?		?	
	3	PRE-CAST WAINSCOT WALLS				
		(EVALUATE OFF-SITE VS. ON-SITE VS. PURCHASE				
		FROM SUPPLIER)				
		PERF SYSTEM:				
	2	PIPE	X	X		
	2	GRAVEL	?	X	?	
	2	FABRIC ? ASK FQ OF ARCHITECT				

FIGURE 4–5 Project Item List

Decisions regarding which scopes of work to self-perform and which to subcontract are based on several criteria:

- Labor. Subcontractors must be used if the trades needed are not employed by the general contractor.
- Specialization. If a subcontractor specializes in finishing concrete, he or she may have the most efficient and least expensive way to perform the work.
- Quality. If this is an area the subcontractor specializes in, he or she often can perform it better. Also, if there are problems with quality, a subcontractor is required to repair the work without increase in cost to the general contractor. However, if the general contractor is required to repair self-performed work, the general contractor's cost will increase and the profit margin will correspondingly decrease.
- Price. If a subcontractor can perform the work on a fixed price contract for less than what the general contractor has estimated with no guarantee of price, then the work may be awarded to the subcontractor.
- Work load. If the general contractor's labor forces are tied up on other work, some normally self-performed items may be awarded to subcontractors. Conversely, if the general contractor is low on work and wants to keep his or her labor force together, he or she may choose to self-perform more work items.
- Schedule. Many general contractors will argue that they can control and assure project schedule and quality better with their own forces.

After the decisions have been made regarding which scopes of work to subcontract, subcontractors should be notified about the project. It is a good idea to have the subcontractors working to assist with the estimate in parallel with the general contractor developing its own estimates for ***self-performed work***. A ***subcontractor call sheet*** similar to the one illustrated in Figure 4–6 can be used to both call subcontractors and verify interest in estimating the project, as well as to assist with developing individual subcontractors' scopes of work. When subcontractors are called, they will ask the estimator questions regarding specifications, quantities, and materials. The general contractor should be somewhat informed at that time about specific subcontractor scope but should be cautious about providing too much detail to the subcontractor. Estimators do not want to place themselves in the position that subcontractors have based their prices on information the estimators have given them. Each subcontractor should develop a completely independent estimate. Incorporating the cost of subcontracted portions of the work into the project estimate is discussed more fully in Section 4.8.

Information obtained through review of all of the above processes and documents will assist the estimator with preparation of the initial WBS. This WBS development will continue to evolve throughout the estimating, scheduling, and buyout processes which are all discussed later in this text. A work breakdown structure for the Huna Office Building project is shown in Figure 4–7 on page 46.

4.6 QUANTITY TAKE-OFF

The estimator takes material quantities directly off the drawings. The goal is to measure and count each item of work that has previously been selected to be self-performed. After each item has been taken off and recorded on ***quantity take-off (QTO)*** sheets, the drawings can be momentarily set aside. The take-off process is one of the most time-consuming building blocks in the estimating triangle shown in

NORTHWEST CONSTRUCTION COMPANY
1242 First Avenue, Cascade, Washington 98202
(206) 239-1422

SUBCONTRACTOR CALL SHEET

Job: HUNA OFFICE BUILDING   Date: 7/8/00

Subcontract/Supply Item: FLOOR COVERING
Specification Section: 09

Firm	Contact	Telephone	Will bid? Yes or No
OMAR'S FLOORING	OMAR SMITH	214-1992	YES
COYOTE COVERING	CLANCY TORRENCE		NO
STEIN'S	RANDY REDFISH	214-1444	YES
UNITED TILE	TERRY JONES	214-9829	TILE ONLY
SOFT TOUCH	SHERRI BRADFORD	214-0372	CARPET ONLY

General Scope of Work: ALL FLOOR COVERING SYSTEMS

Specific Inclusions: CARPET, SHEET VINYL, RUBBER BASE, EXIT STAIR TREADS (REQUIRED? — ASK ARCHITECT)

Related Drawings or Details: FLOOR PLANS: A201 AND A202
FINISH SCHEDULE: A200
SPECIFICATIONS
TOILET ROOM DETAILS: A401

Specific Exclusions: FLOOR PREPARATION BY NORTHWEST CONSTRUCTION COMPANY

Other Notes: ALSO: WAINSCOT? PLAM COUNTER TOPS?

FIGURE 4–6 Subcontractor Call Sheet

NORTHWEST CONSTRUCTION COMPANY
1242 First Avenue, Cascade, Washington 98202
(206) 239-1422

Work Breakdown Structure
Huna Office Building
7/15/2000

CSI Division	Description	
1	Job Site General Conditions	
2	Sitework:	
		Earthwork & Utilities
		Paving
		Walks & Miscellaneous Sitework
3	Concrete:	
		Purchase Reinforcement Steel
		Foundations
		Walls & Slabs
4	Masonry	
5	Structural & Miscellaneous Metals	
6	Wood & Plastic:	
		Rough Carpentry
		Finish Carpentry/Wood Floors
7	Thermal & Moisture Protection	
		Insulation
		Roof & Accessories
		Gutters & Downspouts
8	Doors, Windows, Glass	
		Doors
		Windows & Storefront
		Door Hardware
9	Finishes:	
		Drywall
		Painting
		Acoustical Ceilings
		Floor Covering: Carpet
		Floor Covering: Ceramic, Vinyl, Base
10	Specialties	
11, 12, 13	Equipment, Furnishings, Special Construction	
14	Conveying Systems (Elevator)	
15	Mechanical Systems:	
		Plumbing
		Fire Protection
		HVAC
		Controls
16		Electrical Systems

FIGURE 4–7 Work Breakdown Structure

Figure 4–1 and is an important step towards preparing the final figure. Order-of-magnitude estimates are initially developed for subcontracted work to be replaced later with cost estimates provided by the subcontractors.

Is it necessary to count every nail? No. Is it necessary to count every window? Yes. Eighty percent of the costs are included with twenty percent of the work items (***eighty–twenty rule***). Focus on the majority of the cost exposure and the minor items will get covered.

The quantity take-off process starts with the work items that will be constructed first, the foundations. This will accomplish several tasks. First, it will force the estimator to think like the constructor; the floor system is built before the walls. Organization of the estimate in this fashion will later assist with the schedule development and will aid with the development of the project cost control systems discussed in Chapter 16. All the work items are taken off prior to pricing. Material quantities are recorded and later extended out and summarized on quantity take-off sheets similar to the one shown in Figure 4–8. Suggested procedures for taking off the footing illustrated in Figure 4–8 are shown in Figure 4–9 on page 49.

Good estimating habits are worth noting:

- A clear paper trail is important. The estimate will be used later for schedule development and cost control systems that are discussed in Chapter 16.
- The estimate should appear neat and professional. Others will want to review the estimator's work for completeness and accuracy. The neater the document, the more confidence it will exude.
- The drawings should be marked up with colored pencils and highlighters, indicating what items of work have been taken off. This will help minimize errors.
- Sketches and assumptions should be developed and noted on either the drawings or in the estimate file.
- Quantities should be measured, extended, and summarized as they will be purchased. For example concrete is initially measured in cubic feet but it is purchased in cubic yards (CY). It does not do any good to summarize concrete in cubic feet on the pricing sheets if it will be purchased in CY. Similarly, cedar shake roofing is measured in square feet but is purchased by the square (100 SF or CSF).
- Waste factors for all quantities should be included on the quantity take-off sheets. Figure 4–10 on page 50 provides some commonly used waste factors.

After all of the materials have been taken off of the drawings, the estimator recaps or groups like sizes and material products together in preparation for transfer onto the pricing pages. All areas of concrete are grouped and added together. This way only total yardage is brought to the pricing pages in only one location. Purchase of other major materials which may be recapped include reinforcement steel and framing lumber. Some contractors may add together all of the millwork, regardless of size; or all of the exterior rough-sawn cedar trim, regardless of size. This may be done because the labor to install such materials will be the same per linear foot. Other materials that should be grouped together include items such as doors and windows.

The amount of waste to apply will vary with the installer, project, and estimator. Allowing between 5 and 10% is common. Purchase of enough, but not too much, material is important to maintain labor productivity. Items such as nails, glue, and framing hardware can be estimated or allowed for, but determining exact quantities is difficult. The amount of time and cost the estimator expends exceeds the value of the materials. Allowances are usually sufficient at this stage.

QUANTITY SHEET

COMPANY: NORTHWEST CONSTRUCTION COMPANY — ESTIMATOR: TJ
PROJECT: HUNA OFFICE — ESTIMATE NO.: 1
LOCATION: JUNEAU — SHEET NO.: 1 OF
DESIGNER: JYL — DATE: 7-7-00
SYSTEMS CLASSIFICATION: CONTINUOUS FOOTINGS

DESCRIPTION	QTY	DIMENSIONS L	W/T	D/H	LF EDGEFORM	CF CONCRETE	SF FINEGRADE	LF REBAR	CF EXCAVATION	
DETAIL 1/S5		52	1.67	.83				3 #5	(W+4.67) 2.67	
1'-8"x10"		37						CONT.	= (1.67+4.67) 2.67	
		26							= 17 SF/LF FTG	
		34								
		4								
		155								
		4								
		34								
		4								
		350	1.67	.83	700	485	585	1050	5950	
2'-0"x10"		12	2.0	.83					= 18 SF/LF FTG	
		6								
		12								
		6								
		36	2.0	.83	72	60	72	108	648	
					772 LF	545 CF	657 SF	1158 LF	6598 CF	
WASTE AND LAP CONVERSIONS:						x 1.05		x 1.1	X1.33 TCF/BCF	
						= 572		=1274	= 8775 TCF	
						÷ 27 CF/CY		x1.043	÷ 27 CF/CY	
						= 21 CY		=1329	= 325 TCY	
								÷2000		
								= 0.7 TONS		

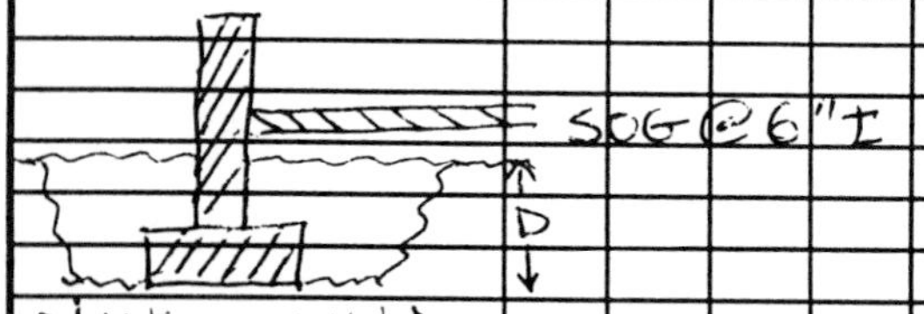

D*1'* W*1'*D

SF EXCAVATION/LF FOOTING = [W+1'+1'+(D+D)/2] x D

STRUCTURAL EXCAVATION − FOOTING CY − WALL CY = STRUCTURAL BACKFILL

= 325 TCY
− 21 CY
− 40 CY
264 TCY

NOTE: THICKENED SLAB @ SHEAR WALLS INCL W/SOG TAKE-OFF ✓

X

FIGURE 4–8 Quantity Take-Off Sheet

- The structural excavator may be an individual subcontractor who owns one backhoe. This subcontractor will dig the footings to prepare the formwork. The same firm also backfills the foundations after the walls are placed. The usual means of contracting will be hourly, but for the general contractor to estimate the costs involved, the cubic yards of excavation and backfill are calculated by measuring the cubic feet of cut, including slope, and allowing for expansion and compaction.
- Fine-grade or hand excavation is calculated by measuring the square footage of the bottom of the footing. Although it is expected that the structural excavation will be accurate to plus or minus 2 inches, the footings need to be placed within 1/4 inch. Some hand shovel work will be required. An alternative to fine grade is to include an allowance of between 1% and 10% of structural excavation yardage, which will be estimated to be performed by hand.
- Spot footings are also referred to as spread or pad footings. They generally are designed to receive point loading from columns. The quantity of formwork is calculated by measuring the length of each of the sides (usually four sides). The formwork is determined in linear feet (LF) and will be constructed with dimensional lumber. For example, if a footing is 8 inches deep, a 2 x 8 will be used for the form. If the footing is greater than 12 inches deep, the formwork will be constructed from a plywood system and is measured in square feet of contact area (SFCA).
- Reinforcing steel is measured by counting similar bars and measuring and extending out in linear feet (LF). It will later be converted to tons. An allowance of 10% should be used to account for bends and laps on small projects.
- Concrete finishing is generally not included for foundations; they will eventually be buried, so appearance is not a factor. The time to finish with a wood trowel or screed is assumed to be included in the placement costs.
- Continuous footings are measured similar to spot footings except that four equal sides are replaced with two long sides. Footings with like widths and like depths are measured and added together, and all quantities are recapped. It is not important exactly where the footing is measured with respect to an intersecting footing, just that it is calculated once and only once.

FIGURE 4–9 Procedures for Taking Off Footing

4.7 PRICING SELF-PERFORMED WORK

Pricing recap sheets are developed for each system or CSI division that is utilized. An example of a pricing sheet is shown in Figure 4–11 on page 51. All of the recapped material quantities are brought forward and entered onto the pricing sheets. The estimator should not start pricing until all of the materials have been taken off the quantity sheets and entered on the pricing sheets, similar to the process of taking the materials off of the drawings. Each quantity is marked or highlighted indicating it has been brought forward. After every quantity has been taken off a quantity sheet, the sheet is marked, indicating that it has been completed. After all of the quantity sheets have been marked, the estimator begins labor pricing.

Labor productivity is the most difficult item for a contractor to estimate and is therefore the most risky. Often a general contractor will review the amount of labor in an estimate and use this figure as a basis for determining overall project risk and therefore the appropriate fee to apply. Labor productivity is estimated as man-hours per unit of

Common Waste Factors for Cost Estimating

Concrete:	5% for most work; 3% for large placements
Wire mesh:	10% for lapping of mesh
Building paper:	10% for lapping of paper
Vapor barrier:	10% for lapping of material
Gravel:	20% for volume decrease due to compaction
Earth fill:	30–50% for volume decrease due to compaction
Framing lumber:	10%

FIGURE 4–10 Common Waste Factors

work, such as 1 man-hour per window. This is referred to as *unit man-hours* or *UMH*. This system allows for fluctuation of labor rates, union versus open shop, geographic variations, and time. If it takes 0.8 man-hours per yard to pour a strip footing in Atlanta, it probably takes the same in Alaska. Appropriate wage rates can be applied for the specific project. The best source of labor productivity rates is from the estimator's desk drawer. Each estimator should develop a database from previous estimates and previously developed labor factors. Other sources of UMH would include published databases or reference guides, such as Means' *Building Construction Cost Data.*

It is important to round off man-hours. Fractional extended man-hours should not be retained on the pricing recap sheet. Partial man-hours are difficult to schedule and monitor against for cost control, let alone difficult to explain to a superintendent who questions why he has only 1.7 man-hours to place gravel for a perforated drain system and not two hours. Estimating is not an exact science. The man-hours are totaled at the bottom of each pricing page. This figure will be valuable information for scheduling and cost control.

The wage rates used are determined by the company, location, and type of work to be performed. Sources of wage rates may include ***Davis-Bacon rates***, which are established by the Department of Labor; prevailing wage rates; union rates; or in-house rates. An example wage schedule for Juneau area unions is shown in Figure 4–12 on page 52. A measured material quantity of 6500 SF of slab-on-grade requiring finishing is multiplied by the historical UMH of .01 MH/SF to yield 65 MH. The cement finisher's wage rate of $25 per hour is applied yielding a total of $1,625 to finish the slab.

Labor burdens or labor taxes will add between 30 and 60%, depending upon craft. Labor burdens are in addition to the labor estimate for expenses to the general contractor for items such as workers' compensation, union benefits, unemployment, FICA (social security), and medical insurance. These percentages fluctuate with time and location. The estimator should check with his or her company's current accounting data before applying a figure.

The best sources of material unit prices are suppliers. Suppliers are requested to provide prices for each item that will be purchased by the general contractor. Price

NORTHWEST CONSTRUCTION COMPANY

1242 First Avenue, Cascade, Washington 98202

(206) 239-1422

Huna Office Building | Owner: Huna Totem | Estimator: Ted Jones | EST # 1

GMP Estimate | Architect: JYL | Date: 07/15/00 | SHEET: 1

Description	Quantity	Unit	Labor UMH	Labor MH	Labor Rate	Labor Cost	Material UP	Material Cost
SYSTEM:	**CONCRETE FOUNDATIONS**							
Layout	1	DAY	24.00	24	25.00	600	500.00	500
Excavate and export foundations	485	TCY	0.10	49	25.00	1,213	15.00	7,275
Import and place backfill	196	TCY	0.10	20	25.00	490	22.00	4,312
Perforated drain system: Pipe	350	LF	0.10	35	25.00	875	2.50	875
Gravel	17	TCY	0.10	2	25.00	43	25.00	425
Fabric	700	SF	0.02	14	25.00	350	0.50	350
Fine grade under foundations	985	SF	0.05	49	25.00	1,231	0.25	246
Form continuous footings	772	LF	0.08	62	25.00	1,544	0.80	618
Form spot footings	280	SF	0.10	28	25.00	700	1.00	280
Form pilasters	180	SF	0.20	36	25.00	900	1.20	216
Form elevator pit	130	SF	0.20	26	25.00	650	1.20	156
Rebar: See separate recap	0		0.00	0	25.00	0	0.00	0
Pour continuos footings	21	CY	0.80	17	25.00	420	10.00	210
Pour spot footings	11	CY	1.00	11	25.00	275	10.00	110
Pour pilasters	6	CY	2.00	12	25.00	300	10.00	60
Pour elevator pit	2	CY	2.00	4	25.00	100	11.00	22
Buy concrete	40	CY	0.00	0	25.00	0	75.00	3,000
Pump concrete	40	CY	0.00	0	25.00	0	15.25	610
Thickened slab @ shear walls	0		0.00	0	25.00	0	0.00	0
Quantities with SOG recap	0		0.00	0	25.00	0	0.00	0
Embeds for pre-cast walls	90	EA	1.00	90	25.00	2,250	15.00	1,350
Concrete equipment	40	CY	0.00	0	25.00	0	50.00	2,000
Concrete accessories	40	CY	0.00	0	25.00	0	15.00	600
Tubesteel column embeds	14	EA	1.00	14	25.00	350	25.00	350
SUB TOTAL				492		12,290		23,565
LABOR TAX				@50% of labor:		6145		
LABOR						18,435		18,435
TOTAL SYSTEM:								42,000
Total CY:								40
System cost $/CY:								$1,050

(System cost is high but many non-foundation items are included here, project is in Alaska, and quantities are small, therefore, acceptable.)

FIGURE 4–11 Pricing Sheet

quotations should be received in writing on the supplier's letterhead. If telephone quotations are received, forms such as the one illustrated in Figure 4–13 on page 53 should be used for recording material pricing, although pricing on the vendor's letterhead is always preferred. Other sources of material prices include historical costs or previous estimates. This is old data, however, and is therefore not as reliable data, but

Juneau Area Union Hourly Wage Rates

Effective: June 1, 2000 through May 31, 2001

Carpenters:		**Concrete Finishers:**	
Foreman	$26.50	Journeyman	$25.00
Journeyman	$25.00		
1st Apprentice	$15.00	Pipefitters:	
2nd Apprentice	$17.50	Foreman (heavy industrial)	$28.50
3rd Apprentice	$20.00	Journeyman (heavy industrial)	$26.75
4th Apprentice	$22.50	Foreman (light industrial)	$26.50
		Journeyman (light industrial)	$24.75
Laborers:			
Foreman ($1 above highest classification)		**Plumbers:**	
Power Tools	$23.10	Residential	$24.00
General Construction	$22.50	Commercial	$24.75
Janitorial	$19.00	Industrial	$26.75
		Irrigation	$19.50
Iron Workers:			
General Foreman	$25.75	**Operating Engineers:**	
Foreman	$24.75	Foreman	$28.25
Journeyman	$23.75	Journeyman	$26.25
Fabrication	$23.75		
		Millwrights:	
Electricians:		Journeyman	$26.00
Foreman	$27.00		
Journeyman	$26.00		
Low Voltage	$22.50		

FIGURE 4–12 Sample Wage Rates

it is better than leaving an item blank if the information is not available. The third choice for material prices is data bases or reference guides. These sources are useful for unusual items for which local quotes cannot be obtained.

The material prices are extended by multiplying the quantity of 40 cubic yards of concrete times the concrete supplier's quote of $75 per CY to yield a material price of $3,000. Extended prices should be rounded to the nearest dollar. Fractional man-hours and cents are applicable in the unit price or UMH columns of the pricing recap page only, not the extended columns. After all of the unit prices have been applied to the quantities, totals are brought down in preparation to be brought forward to the estimate summary page.

A good reality check of the estimate for a given system, foundations, for example, can be made at this time on the pricing recap page. Add together the labor cost, material cost, and calculated portion of labor taxes to come up with a quick total cost for that system. Then divide that figure by the total predominant material quantity, such as 40 cubic yards of concrete, to arrive at a total unit price for that system or assembly. There are many available references that are used for conceptual estimating and budgeting against which this number can be checked. There is also the more relevant personal list of figures the estimator has on hand, such as $1,000 per cubic yard for concrete foundations. If the calculation is in the range, the estimator is comfortable. If it is way off, for example, one half or twice as much, then maybe an error occurred, and a double check should be made.

NORTHWEST CONSTRUCTION COMPANY
1242 First Avenue, Cascade, Washington 98202
(206) 239-1422

BID PROPOSAL

Firm: *Juneau Redi-Mix Supply, Inc.*
Telephone: *242-1922*
City: *Juneau*
Quoted By: *Rose*
Price Valid Until: *30 days*

Date: *July 18, 2000*
Time: *3:00 p.m.*
Project: *Huna Office Building*
Union: *Trucks*
Merit Shop: *NA*

Spec. Sect.	Bid Item/Inclusions	Amount
03300	*Supply 4,000 PSI Concrete*	*$75.00 per CY*

BASIC BID *$75.00 per CY*

Addenda Nos. *NA* through *NA*
Per Plans and Specs: *yes*
Furnish Only: *yes*
Delivery Time: *NA*
Installed: *no*
FOB Job Site: *yes*
Erected Only: *no*
Trucks: *NA*

Exclusions and Clarifications	Alternates or Unit Prices	Amount
Installation		
Admixtures		
Hot Water		
Pumping		

Received By: *Ted Jones*

FIGURE 4–13 Supplier or Subcontractor Telephone Quote Sheet

4.8 PRICING SUBCONTRACTED WORK

The best source of subcontractor pricing is from subcontractors. They are the ones who will ultimately be required to sign a contract and guarantee performance of an established amount of work for a fixed amount of compensation. General contractors should estimate subcontractor work to develop pre-bid day budgets and to check the reasonableness of subcontractor bids. If one low bid of $1,000 for floor covering comes in and one higher bid of $7,000 is available, the general contractor can feel comfortable throwing the low bid out if his or her own estimate was $7,500. The low bidder obviously does not have the right scope. The reverse may be true if the general contractor's estimate was nearer the lower bid.

Once a reliable subcontractor price is received, the estimator's figures should be replaced with the subcontractor's price. The estimator should not assume that the firms who specialize in areas of floor covering are all in error and that his or her figure is the most correct one. A spreadsheet should be developed which aids in the analysis of subcontractor and supplier pricing. A sample bid analysis for the floor covering for the Huna Office Building project is shown in Figure 4–14.

4.9 PRICING JOB SITE GENERAL CONDITIONS

Even if the general contractor is not required to turn in a construction schedule, it is still necessary to develop a rough schedule prior to preparing a general conditions estimate. Utilizing past experience coupled with the estimated man-hours and superintendent's input, it is fairly simple to prepare a ten- to twenty-line item schedule. It is not necessary to determine if it will take exactly 165 days to build the building, but it is important to know that this structure will take approximately eight months (not six or ten) to construct given the site conditions, project complexity, long-lead material deliveries, anticipated weather, and available manpower.

There are many different uses of the term *general conditions*. ***Job site general conditions costs***, or direct general conditions, are project specific and are measurable. It was discussed earlier in Section 4.7 that estimating direct labor costs is one of the most difficult and riskiest tasks of the construction estimating team. Estimating job site general conditions is also difficult and risky, but it is easier to quantify than estimating home office indirect costs, which may be applicable to a project. Site general conditions could also be referred to as job site administration costs. These job site expenses will be based upon the specific project's duration, needs, and risks.

A list of typical job site general conditions is shown in Figure 4–15 on page 56. There is not an exact rule of thumb for what these costs should be. They could range anywhere from less than 5% to greater than 10% for that specific project. Many of the individual general conditions line items are project and site specific, and others are time dependent.

Before the job site general conditions estimate can be developed, the anticipated labor hours must be obtained from the direct work portion of the estimate. The superintendent and project manager then rough out a schedule based upon these hours, the project's complexity, and even subcontractor and supplier input on durations and deliveries. This schedule is used to develop overall durations for estimating site administration and equipment rental type durations for the job site general conditions estimate.

The general conditions costs are not estimated until after the schedule is developed. A reasonable approximation of construction time is one of the most crucial elements to estimating general conditions. If the project lasts eight months, then certain support individuals, equipment, and material will need to be on site for that duration.

NORTHWEST CONSTRUCTION COMPANY

1242 First Avenue, Cascade, Washington 98202

(206) 239-1422

SUBCONTRACT AND SUPPLIER BID ANALYSIS

Project: HUNA OFFICE BUILDING Owner: HUNA TOTEM

Location: JUNEAU, AK Project Manager: TED JONES

Date: JULY 22, 2000

Work Classification: FLOOR COVERING

Description / Contractors:	NWCC Budget	OMAR	COYOTE	STEIN	UNITED	SOFT TOUCH
Bid per spec?		ALT PRODUCT		YES	YES	YES
Union labor?		NO		YES	YES	YES
Delivery time?		2 MO		60 DAY	IN-STOCK	?
Exclusions:	TREADS NOT SHOWN	PREP PLAM STAIR TREADS			CARPET AND BASE	VINYL TILE STAIR TREADS
Include tax?	NO	NO		NO	NO	NO
Alternate pricing **Quantities:** **Unit prices**		CARPET $30/SY TILE $10/SF	NO BID		TILE $1,000/LF	BASE $1,500/LF
Other questions – FLOOR PREP?	WITH CONCRETE					
Acknowledge addenda	ϕ	ϕ		ϕ	ϕ	ϕ
Base bid price:		$48,000		$35,000	$17,100	
CARPET	$30,000	INCL		INCL	EXCL	$20,000
BASE - RUBBER	5,000	INCL		EXCL	EXCL	2,950
SHEET VINYL	5,000	INCL		INCL	INCL	EXCL
CERAMIC TILE	10,000	INCL		EXCL	INCL	EXCL
Subtotal:	$50,000	$48,000		$35,000	$17,100	$22,950
Necessary adjustments:	ϕ	ϕ		BASE - $3,000 TILE - $10,000	ϕ	ϕ
Adjusted bid:	$50,000	$48,000		$48,000	$17,100	$22,950

UNITED + SOFT TOUCH = $40,050

FIGURE 4–14 Subcontractor Bid Analysis

NORTHWEST CONSTRUCTION COMPANY

Huna Office Building | Owner: Huna Totem | Estimator: Ted Jones | Estimate #: 1
GMP Estimate | Architect: JYL | Date: 07/18/00 | Sheet: 1

Description	Quantity	Unit	Labor UMH	Labor Rate	Labor Cost	Material UP	Material Cost
SYSTEM:	**JOB SITE GENERAL CONDITIONS**						
Project Manager	5	wks	0.00	1,200.00	6,000	0.00	0
Superintendent	43	wks	0.00	1,150.00	49,450	0.00	0
Project Engineer	10	wks	0.00	800.00	8,000	0.00	0
Field Survey	6	wks	0.00	200.00	1,200	200.00	1,200
Schedules	1	LS	0.00	0.00	0.00	250.00	250
Blueprinting	1	LS	0.00	0.00	0.00	250.00	250
Safety supplies	10	mo	0.00	0.00	0.00	100.00	1,000
Job phone and fax	10	mo	0.00	0.00	0.00	500.00	5,000
Set up phones	1	LS	0.00	0.00	0.00	500.00	500
Office supplies	1	LS	0.00	0.00	0.00	350.00	350
Outside equipment rental	1	LS	0.00	0.00	0.00	10,000.00	10,000
Owned equipment rental	1	LS	0.00	0.00	0.00	12,000.00	12,000
Pickup truck	10	mo	0.00	0.00	0.00	450.00	4,500
Forklift rental	5	mo	0.00	0.00	0.00	3,000.00	15,000
Small Tools	302,335	DL$	0.00	0.00	0.00	0.04	12,093
Equipment fuel & maint.	41,500	EQ$	0.00	0.00	0.00	0.15	6,225
Job office/trailer	10	mo	0.00	0.00	0.00	400.00	4,000
Tool shed	10	mo	0.00	0.00	0.00	250.00	2,500
Trailer transportation	2	trip	0.00	0.00	0.00	250.00	500
Camp set up/tear down	2	ea	0.00	275.00	550	500.00	1,000
Water system	10	mo	0.00	0.00	0.00	250.00	2,500
Temp power hookup	1	LS	0.00	0.00	0.00	1,500.00	1,500
Temp lighting operation	4	mo	0.00	200.00	800	250.00	1,000
Temp heat setup	1	LS	0.00	0.00	0	350.00	350
Operate temp heat	3	mo	0.00	200.00	600	1,000.00	3,000
Job radio system	10	mo	0.00	0.00	0	250.00	2,500
Temporary handrails	1	LS	0.00	500.00	500	1,500.00	1,500
Liability insurance	1,700,000	est $	0.00	0.00	0.00	0.01	17,000
Power bills	10	mo	0.00	0.00	0.00	750.00	7,500
Drinking water	10	mo	0.00	0.00	0.00	250.00	2,500
Chemical toilets	20	mo	0.00	0.00	0.00	150.00	3,000
Job photographs	10	mo	0.00	0.00	0.00	150.00	1,500
Rubbish removal	10	mo	0.00	0.00	0.00	600.00	6,000
Periodic cleanup	10	mo	0.00	300.00	3,000	0.00	0
Final cleanup	1	LS	0.00	0.00	0.00	5,182.00	5,182
Glass cleaning	1	LS	0.00	0.00	0.00	3,500.00	3,500
SUB TOTAL					70,100		$134,900
TOTAL SYSTEM:							$205,000
Cost per month	10						$20,500
Percentage of direct cost	$1,472,000						13.93%

Percentage is high, but job is small, and duration is long (compared to job size), therefore acceptable.

FIGURE 4–15 Site General Conditions Estimate

4.10 PRICING COMPANY OVERHEAD INDIRECT COSTS

Company overhead indirect costs include items such as accounting, marketing, and officer salaries. These costs usually are a relatively fixed figure based upon staffing per annum. An average-size general contractor may need to generate 2 to 5% of their annual volume to cover these costs. This mark up is applied to the total estimated direct project cost and sometimes is called the ***overhead burden***. In addition to covering the indirect costs, the contractor desires to earn a profit on each project. The desired profit plus the overhead indirect cost is called the fee. Fees can range anywhere from 3 to 10% for commercial work. Smaller commercial projects require higher fees due to smaller annual volumes of the firms involved. If the general contractor performs much of the work itself, it assumes a proportionally increased risk and fee. On cost-plus contracts, conceptual cost estimates may be used to establish the guaranteed maximum price, but company overhead costs still need to be estimated to develop the fee proposal.

4.11 ESTIMATE SUMMARY WRAP-UP

In addition to choosing the fee, there are several other final steps in putting the estimate together. A sample summary page is shown in Figure 4–16. This form should be filled out completely the night prior to bid day. Subcontractor pricing that has not been received yet should be priced with in-house estimates. These in-house estimates often are referred to as ***plugs***. This is just a refinement of the first rough order-of-magnitude estimate that was developed the day the documents came in. As the estimator completes the estimate, he or she should use the most current and relevant information. All of the pricing recap pages are brought forward by posting the values on the summary sheet. If a certain project has specific needs that the estimate summary page does not account for, a project specific summary must be prepared.

Some of the other percentage markups or add-ons that are shown but have not been previously discussed include:

- Material tax. Varies between states. Sometimes these values are already included in the pricing. Sometimes they apply only to materials that are not incorporated into the project, for example concrete forms.
- Contingency. If the project is competitively bid with relatively complete documents, the amount of contingency applied is usually zero. Most general contractors account for the contingency, if there is any, with their choice of fee on competitive projects. Stated contingencies will show up on negotiated projects which have incomplete documents.
- Insurance. Liability insurance is volume related. The insurance rate will range significantly between contractors depending upon their safety records. The range generally is .5% for large commercial contractors to 2% for smaller contractors.
- Business tax or excise tax. This is also volume related and is dependent upon the state, city, and county.
- Bond. Performance and payment bond rates are also annual volume related, but the project bond costs are project specific. They generally do not appear on negotiated projects. On larger lump-sum commercial projects, they may be required, especially for public work, and the cost will vary depending upon the size of the project and the past performance of the contractor. A sample bond rate schedule was shown in Chapter 2 (Figure 2–8).

NORTHWEST CONSTRUCTION COMPANY
1242 First Avenue, Cascade, Washington 98202
(206) 239-1422

ESTIMATE SUMMARY FOR HUNA OFFICE BUILDING
8/15/00

Line Item	Description	Labor Hours	Labor	Material	Subcontract	Value
1.0	General Conditions	1,869	70,100	134,900	0	205,000
2.1	Earthwork and utilities	0	0	0	124,000	124,000
2.2	Paving	0	0	0	24,000	24,000
2.3	Miscellaneous sitework	93	3,500	4,500	40,000	48,000
	Subtotal Sitework:	93	3,500	4,500	188,000	196,000
3.1	Reinforcement	123	4,600	8,400		13,000
3.2	Foundations	492	18,435	23,565		42,000
3.3	Walls and slabs	760	28,500	53,500		82,000
	Subtotal Concrete:	1,374	51,535	85,465		137,000
4.0	Masonry	0	0	0	0	0
5.0	Steel	40	1,500	4,500	0	6,000
6.1	Rough carpentry and siding	4,907	184,000	200,000		384,000
6.2	Finish carpentry	1,133	42,500	42,500		85,000
	Subtotal Carpentry:	6,040	226,500	242,500		469,000
7.1	Insulation				19,000	19,000
7.2	Roofing				59,000	59,000
7.3	Gutters				3,000	3,000
	Subtotal Division 7:				81,000	81,000
8.1	Doors and frames	124	4,650	24,350	0	29,000
8.2	Glazing	253	9,500	8,000	1,500	19,000
8.3	Door hardware	67	2,500	12,500	0	15,000
	Subtotal Division 8:	444	16,650	44,850	1,500	63,000
9.1	Drywall				25,000	25,000
9.2	Painting				28,000	28,000
9.3	Acoustical ceilings				8,000	8,000
9.4	Carpet				23,000	23,000
9.5	Balance of floorcovering				17,000	17,000
	Subtotal Finishes:				101,000	101,000
10.0	Specialties	71	2,650	8,350	0	11,000
11, 12, 13	Equipment	0	0	0	0	0
14.0	Elevator				30,000	30,000
15.1	Plumbing				49,000	49,000
15.2	Fire protection				29,000	29,000
15.3	HVAC				145,000	145,000
15.4	Controls				35,000	35,000
	Subtotal Mechanical				258,000	258,000
16.0	Electrical				120,000	120,000
	Subtotal Job Costs:	9,932	372,435	525,065	779,500	1,677,000
	Fee @ 5%					83,000
	Total					$1,760,000

Notes: Labor taxes of 50% included with wage rate for total loaded wage rate of $37.50/hour.
Insurance and excise taxes included with site general conditions estimate.
Home office overhead included with Fee.

FIGURE 4–16 Estimate Summary

As much of the estimate summary as possible should be filled out prior to bid day. The estimator should have someone else check the math, since many gross errors occur at this stage. An estimate summary form, similar to other estimating forms, should be developed and used consistently. It may require slight modification for individual projects, but its consistency is important to provide the project manager a quick and comfortable overview prior to and during bid day. A hard copy should be printed out and saved.

The final bid value is determined on bid day. Subcontractor quotations will be received, and the bid revised. The final bid generally is approved by an executive of the construction firm. The bid must be submitted to the owner on the form specified in the instructions before the indicated time.

4.12 SUMMARY

Estimating is a series of steps, the first being project overview to determine if the project is going to be pursued. The quantity take-off step is a compilation of counting items and measuring volumes. Pricing is divided between material pricing, labor pricing, and subcontract pricing. Labor is computed using productivity rates and labor rates. Material and subcontract prices are developed most accurately using supplier and subcontractor quotations. Job site general conditions cost is a schedule-dependent job cost. Home office indirect costs are often combined with fee. The fee calculation depends on several conditions, including company volume, market conditions, labor risk, and resource allocations. There are three major lessons to be learned in estimating. The first is to be organized. If proper organization and procedures are utilized, good estimates will result. The second is to estimate and estimate a lot. Practice and good organization will eventually develop thorough and reasonable estimates. The third is to maintain and use historical databases of cost and productivity data from previous projects.

4.13 REVIEW QUESTIONS

1. What is the difference between a conceptual cost estimate and a detailed cost estimate?
2. What is the greatest risk the contractor faces when developing a cost estimate?
3. How does an estimator develop the work breakdown structure for a project?
4. When is a construction schedule developed in the estimating process and why?
5. What is the difference between job site general conditions and home office indirect costs?
6. What are two sources for labor productivity rates?
7. List five of the general contractor's personnel who should participate in developing an estimate for the project and what their specific roles would be.
8. Why is it important that the first conceptual estimate developed by a contractor be somewhat accurate?
9. What is wrong with using unit prices from published references for material and subcontract items of work?
10. What is the difference between a construction schedule and an estimate schedule?
11. What is the eighty–twenty rule, and how does it apply to estimating concrete formwork?

12. If a general contractor is certain of receiving at least one or two subcontract bids on bid day, why should he bother with estimating that area of work himself?
13. What is an acceptable job site general conditions percentage? Should straight percentage calculations be used in developing an estimate?
14. Where do most estimate errors occur?

4.14 EXERCISES

1. Complete the project list shown in Figure 4–5 for the Huna Office Building project. Items that require decision regarding self-performed or subcontractor work should be noted.
2. Using Figures 4–3 and 4–4, determine a required completion date for each of the assigned tasks listed in Figure 4–3 for each member of the estimating team.

4.15 SOURCES OF ADDITIONAL INFORMATION

Building Construction Cost Data. Kingston, Mass.: R. S. Means Co., Inc., 2001.

Dagostino, Frank R., and Leslie Feigenbaum. *Estimating in Building Construction*. 5th ed. Upper Saddle River, N.J.: Prentice-Hall, Inc., 1999.

Goldman, Jeffrey, ed. *Means Estimating Handbook*. Kingston, Mass.: R. S. Means Co., Inc., 1990.

Siddens, Scott, ed. *The Building Estimator's Reference Book*. 26th ed. Lisle, Ill.: Frank R. Walker Co., 1999.

5

Planning and Scheduling

5.1 INTRODUCTION

Like estimating, scheduling has been covered extensively in other books, several of which are listed in Section 5.11 at the end of the chapter. Our purpose in this chapter is to briefly discuss schedule development and then focus on using the schedule as a project management tool. As discussed in Chapter 1, time management is just as important to project success as is cost management. The key to effective time management is to carefully plan the work to be performed, develop a realistic construction schedule, and then manage the performance of the work. Schedules are working documents that need updating as conditions change on the project. For example, contract change orders generally modify some aspect of the scope of work, requiring an adjustment to part of the schedule. In addition to aiding management of the project, updated schedules also can be used to justify additional contract time on change orders and claims. Some texts use the terms scheduling and project management identically. The two are, however, not identical. Project management, as can be seen within the context of this book, involves many other aspects of construction management than just scheduling.

5.2 PROJECT PLANNING

Project planning is the process of selecting the construction methods and the sequence of work to be used on a project. Planning must be completed before a schedule can be developed. It starts with the assembly of all the information necessary to produce a schedule. Other steps in planning the project include:

- Developing the work breakdown structure (WBS) which is a listing of all the activities that must be performed to complete the project (A WBS for the Huna Office Building project was shown in Chapter 4).

- Acquiring input from the key members of the project team including:
    1. Company specialists
    2. Field supervisors
    3. Subcontractors
    4. Suppliers
- Making decisions with field supervisors regarding:
    1. Site layout
    2. Sequence in which work will be performed
    3. Direction of work flow: bottom up, left to right, or east to west
    4. Means and methods of construction
    5. Type of concrete forming system to be used
    6. Type of equipment to be used
    7. Safety requirements
- Making decisions regarding performing work with the general contractor's own work crews or with subcontractors.
- Identifying all restraining factors such as:
    1. Skilled labor: crew makeup and sizes
    2. Material and equipment delivery date estimations
    3. Weather
    4. Permits
    5. Financing
- Preparing the estimate. The schedule is not prepared until the estimate has been completed, at least up to and including work that is to be performed by the contractor's work force. The estimated craft hours from the estimate are needed to determine ***activity durations*** for the schedule.

The project plan may be an outline, notes, minutes of meetings with responsible parties, or a roughed-out schedule. This information is then provided to the scheduler, who in some instances may be the same individual as the planner. On some projects, the project manager may do the planning and develop the schedule.

5.3 TYPES OF SCHEDULES

There are two primary types of schedules: bar charts and ***network diagrams***. Bar charts relate activities to a calendar, but generally show no relationship among the activities. Network diagrams show the relationship among the activities and may be time-scaled on a calendar. Two techniques are used in developing network schedules. The first is known as the ***arrow-diagramming method,*** in which arrows depict the individual activities. The other is known as the ***precedence-diagramming method,*** in which the activities are represented by nodes. The arrow-diagramming method often is used on schedules prepared manually, while the precedence-diagramming method is used on computer-generated schedules. Network diagram schedules are sometimes referred to as *critical path* schedules because the ***critical path*** is the longest path through the schedule and determines the overall project duration. A delay in any activity on the critical path results in a delay in the completion of the project. Both types of schedules are good and may be appropriate in different applications.

Schedules can be prepared in different formats depending upon the anticipated use.

- Formal schedules may be developed and provided to the owner as required by contract or prepared and submitted with a proposal for a negotiated contract.
- ***Summary schedules***, like the one illustrated in Figure 5–1, often are used for presentations or management reporting.
- Detailed schedules, like the one illustrated in Figure 5–2, are posted on the walls of meeting rooms. They are marked up with comments and progress. Figure 5–2 is set as a fold-out at the back of the book.
- Short-interval "look ahead" schedules are developed by each foreman and each subcontractor on a weekly basis. They are often hand-drafted in bar chart form. The form or system does not matter. What is important is that they are produced by the people who are doing the work and that they are communicated and distributed to all involved. In this way, they are tools of the construction trade. These schedules can be in two-, three-, or four-week increments, depending upon the job and level of activity. Figure 5–3 on page 65 shows an example of a three-week schedule during the footing operations for the Huna Office Building project.
- Minischedules, also called area or system schedules, allow additional detail for certain portions of the work that can not be adequately represented in the project schedule and have longer duration than the short-interval schedule.
- Other specialized schedules include submittal schedule, buyout schedule, material delivery schedule, equipment start-up schedule, and close-out schedule.

5.4 SCHEDULE DEVELOPMENT

Once the project plan has been completed, it is time to develop a construction schedule. Individual tasks or activities to be accomplished were identified during the development of the WBS. The next task is to determine the sequence in which the activities are to be completed. This involves answering the following questions for each activity:

- What activities must be completed before this activity can start?
- What activities can be started once this activity has been completed?
- What activities can be performed concurrently with this activity?

Based on the answers to these questions, the schedule structure can be developed using the interdependencies among the activities. The duration for each activity is determined by using the crew productivity factors used in developing the cost estimate. Now the start and finish dates for each activity can be determined, and the overall scheduled project completion date is compared with the contractual completion date. If the schedule shows completion later than the contract requires, some of the activities on the critical path must be accelerated to produce a schedule that meets contractual requirements.

Computers can assist in developing the schedule. The identification of the activities, the duration for each, and the sequence in which they are to be completed must be input into the computer for it to develop the schedule. The computer will plot the schedule and calculate the start and finish time for each activity. Computer-generated schedules allow the scheduler and project manager to determine quickly the effects of changes in schedule logic, delays in delivery of critical materials, or adjustments to resource requirements.

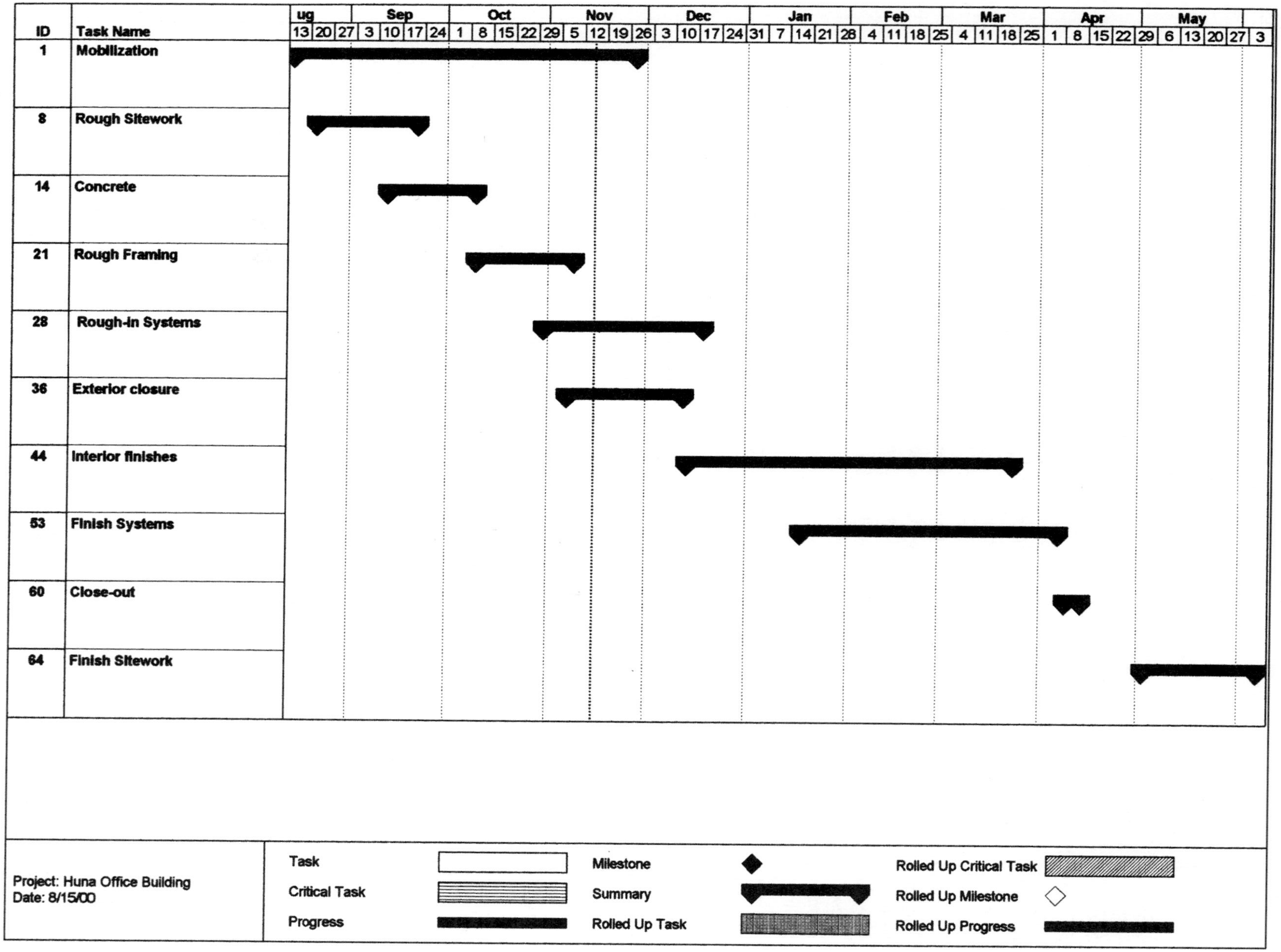

FIGURE 5–1 Huna Project Summary Schedule

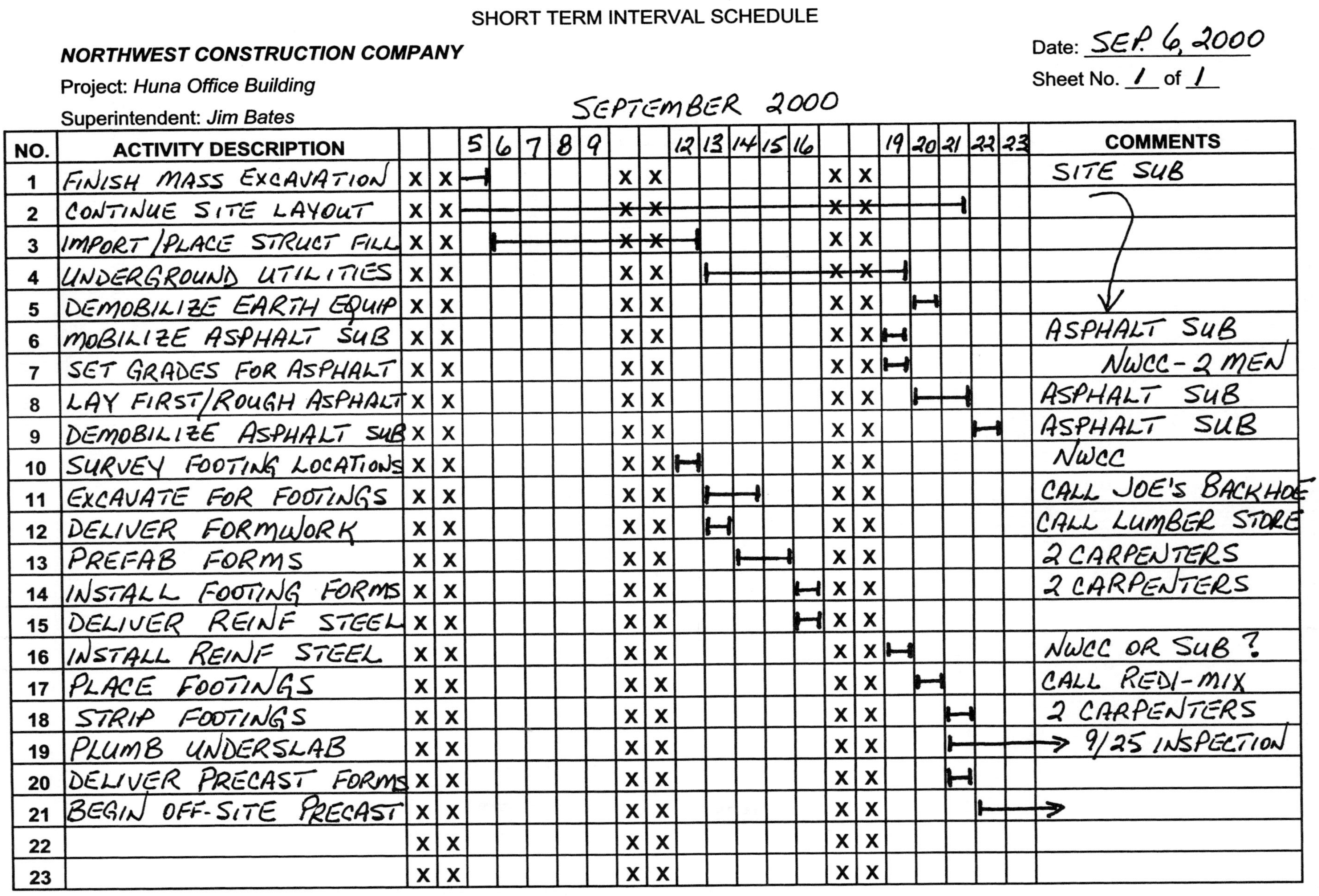
SHORT TERM INTERVAL SCHEDULE
NORTHWEST CONSTRUCTION COMPANY
Project: Huna Office Building
Superintendent: Jim Bates
Date: SEP. 6, 2000
Sheet No. 1 of 1
SEPTEMBER 2000
NO.
ACTIVITY DESCRIPTION
5 6 7 8 9 12 13 14 15 16 19 20 21 22 23
COMMENTS
1 FINISH MASS EXCAVATION
2 CONTINUE SITE LAYOUT
3 IMPORT/PLACE STRUCT FILL
4 UNDERGROUND UTILITIES
5 DEMOBILIZE EARTH EQUIP
6 MOBILIZE ASPHALT SUB
7 SET GRADES FOR ASPHALT
8 LAY FIRST/ROUGH ASPHALT
9 DEMOBILIZE ASPHALT SUB
10 SURVEY FOOTING LOCATIONS
11 EXCAVATE FOR FOOTINGS
12 DELIVER FORMWORK
13 PREFAB FORMS
14 INSTALL FOOTING FORMS
15 DELIVER REINF STEEL
16 INSTALL REINF STEEL
17 PLACE FOOTINGS
18 STRIP FOOTINGS
19 PLUMB UNDERSLAB
20 DELIVER PRECAST FORMS
21 BEGIN OFF-SITE PRECAST
22
23
SITE SUB
ASPHALT SUB
NWCC - 2 MEN
ASPHALT SUB
ASPHALT SUB
NWCC
CALL JOE'S BACKHOE
CALL LUMBER STORE
2 CARPENTERS
2 CARPENTERS
NWCC OR SUB ?
CALL REDI-MIX
2 CARPENTERS
9/25 INSPECTION

FIGURE 5–3 Huna Three-Week Schedule

The project manager and superintendent should be actively involved in developing the construction schedule; they are responsible for completing the project on time. This provides buy-in by the project leadership. If they agree with the schedule, they will do everything they can to make it happen.

5.5 SCHEDULE UPDATES

A schedule must be used to be an effective management tool; ***schedule updates*** should be added weekly to monitor progress. The superintendent or project manager should report progress at the weekly owner/designer/contractor meetings. Highlighters can be used to visually emphasize activities that are ahead or behind. Scheduling software programs also can depict schedule progress. The overall schedule status and any important issues should be documented in the weekly meeting notes, which are discussed in Chapter 12.

Should the project manager update or revise a schedule? If so, when and how? This depends on the contract requirements as well as project progress. If the project is proceeding more or less as planned, the schedule need not be updated. If the project is significantly behind schedule or there have been many change orders, an update is necessary. Current computer scheduling software allows revisions to the schedule to be saved, which enables the user to compare the current schedule with the original schedule. The project manager can, therefore, document schedule impacts when negotiating change orders.

The original schedule should remain intact if at all possible. If a revised schedule is developed, it must be submitted to all subcontractors to be evaluated for impact. Upon acceptance, the new schedule must be incorporated into every contracting and supplying firm's respective contracts. Similar to incorporating new drawings into contracts, this is a change order opportunity for subcontractors.

Schedules, like estimates, provide a map of where the project manager wants to go and how he or she is going to get there. The objective is not to complete each activity exactly within its scheduled duration, but to complete the project within the scheduled time. Many activities will be completed early, and others late. The project manager just wants to keep from finishing the entire project late. The objective is for the variances to average out.

Sometimes it is necessary to revise the schedule, either because of a contract requirement or because of a substantial change in scope or progress. It is recommended that some system be used to retain the original commitments of all of the parties. If it appears that construction progress is significantly behind, it may be necessary to develop a new schedule. This may have been caused by a variety of reasons including:

- Late material deliveries
- Owner-induced delays
- Architect-induced delays
- Weather
- Additional scope
- Labor shortages or inefficiencies
- Equipment availability
- Inadequate estimate or schedule
- Incorrect schedule logic.

Just as the project manager should not work off an incorrect cost estimate, he or she should not use an incorrect construction schedule. The construction team must first understand what the problems are and then endeavor to correct them. This may be done through a variety of methods including:

- Paying extra for expedited material deliveries, such as airfreight
- Increasing manpower

- Working double shifts
- Working overtime
- Changing general contractor workers
- Removing and replacing a subcontractor or supplier

All of these are not without increased costs and other impacts, including production inefficiencies. The project manager must carefully assess the impacts of each method selected and their importance to the project. Schedule make up can occur only by accelerating activities on the critical path.

5.6 CASH FLOW CURVES

A ***cash flow curve*** is a projection of the total value of the work to be completed each month during project construction. It is created by adding the estimated cost to each activity on the schedule and plotting the estimated monthly project costs. Often, it is one of the first things the owner will ask of the project manager and may be specifically required by the construction contract. One reason this is required is to provide information to the bank for anticipated monthly payments. Some project managers hestitate to do a cash flow curve on the basis that it might be wrong and that they may be penalized for it. However, if the owner requires a cash flow curve, the project manager must provide one.

The cash flow curve is easy to prepare. The estimated costs are applied across the schedule activities. If an activity will take five months and its value is $100,000, then $20,000 is spread over each of the five months. Costs such as administration, taxes, and fees should be distributed proportionately over the entire project. The cost data are totaled at the bottom of the schedule for each month to develop anticipated monthly expenses. The likelihood of the general contractor being billed by each material supplier and subcontractor according to any anticipated schedule is somewhat remote. It would be the exception to the rule, but the project manager may be limited on monthly payment requests by these cash flow projections. The contract requirements should be reviewed to determine if there are any restrictions. Figure 5–4 shows a ***cash-loaded schedule*** for Huna Office Building project.

Now a cash flow curve can be plotted. This can be displayed in either bell shape or *S* shape. The bell-shaped curve represents a plot of the estimated value of work to be completed each month. The *S*-shaped curve represents a plot of the cumulative value of work completed each month. Some project managers will adjust the monthly figures to reflect somewhat a standard bell curve. Within reason, this is acceptable for presentation purposes but is not a requirement. Many cash flow curves actually depict more of a double-hump camel than a bell. This occurs when there are significant project costs early on the project, such as prepayment for long-lead equipment, and late in the project, such as expensive finishes. The actual cash flow can later be tracked against the schedule. Figure 5–5 on page 69 shows the cash flow curve for the cash-loaded schedule in Figure 5–4.

One interesting twist to the cash flow analysis is that there are actually several different means of measurement:

- Committed costs. Once the purchase orders have been issued and the subcontracts have been awarded, the project manager and the owner have committed to spend the money, but it may not yet be paid.
- On-site materials. The reinforcement steel was received, but the project manager has not received an invoice for it, and therefore, has not made payment.
- Costs in place. The reinforcement steel that was delivered last month is installed this month. Costs for materials are not counted until the materials are actually installed on the project.

NORTHWEST CONSTRUCTION COMPANY
1242 First Avenue, Cascade, Washington 98202
HUNA OFFICE BUILDING CASH-LOADED SCHEDULE

CSI Division	Description	GMP Value Inc below	Week of: 8/20	8/27	9/3	9/10	9/17	9/24	10/1	10/8	10/15	10/22	10/29	11/5	11/12	11/19	11/26	12/3	12/10	12/17	12/24	12/31	1/7	1/14	1/21	1/28	2/4	2/11	2/18	2/25	3/4	3/11	3/18	3/25	4/1	4/8	4/15	$x1000 Total
1	Job Site General Conditions																																					
2	Sitework:																																					
	Earthwork & Utilities	124,000		25	25	25	25	24																														124
	Paving	24,000						12																					12									24
	Misc. Site	48,000																									24	24										48
	Sitework Subtotal:	196,000																																				
3	Concrete:																																					
	Reinforcement	13,000																																				
	Foundations	42,000																																				
	Walls & Slabs	82,000																																				
	Concrete Subtotal:	137,000					34	34	34	35																												137
4	Masonry	0																																				
5	Structural & Misc. Metals	6,000									2	1	1	1	1																							6
6	Wood & Plastic:																																					
	Rough Carpentry	384,000									68	69	69	69	82	14	13																					384
	Finish Carpentry	85,000																													29	28	28					85
	Carpentry Subtotal:	469,000																																				
7	Thermal & Moisture Protection																																					
	Insulation	19,000																			19																	19
	Roof & Accessories	59,000													59																							59
	Gutters	3,000																3																				3
	Division 7 Subtotal:	81,000																																				
8	Doors, Windows, Glass																																					
	Doors	29,000																										29										29
	Glazing	19,000												19																								19
	Door Hardware	15,000																										15										15
	Division 8 Subtotal:	63,000																																				
9	Finishes:																																					
	Drywall	25,000																			5	5	5	5	5													25
	Painting	28,000																	14							5	5	4										28
	Acoustical Ceilings	8,000																											8									8
	Carpet	23,000																											8	8	7							23
	Floor Covering	17,000																											6	6	5							17
	Finishes Subtotal:	101,000																																				
10	Specialties	11,000																															11					11
11,12,13	Equipment	0																																				0
14	Conveying Systems (Elevator)	30,000																							7	8	8	7										30
15	Mechanical Systems:																																					
	Plumbing	49,000												10	10	9																		20				49
	Fire Protection	29,000														5	5	5	4									10										29
	HVAC	145,000														22	22	23	23	10								45										145
	Controls	35,000																										35										35
	Mechanical Subtotal:	258,000																																				
16	Electrical Systems	120,000														20	20	20									20	20	20									120
	Subtotal w/o GC's and Fee:	1,472,000	0	25	25	25	25	59	70	34	35	70	70	70	99	152	70	60	51	41	10	24	5	5	5	12	13	57	189	54	14	41	28	39	20	0	0	1,472
	General Conditions	205,000	6	6	6	6	6	6	6	6	6	6	6	6	6	6	6	6	6	6	6	6	6	6	6	6	6	6	6	6	6	6	5	5	5	5	5	205
	Fee	83,000	2	2	2	2	2	2	2	3	3	3	3	3	3	3	3	3	3	2	2	2	2	2	2	2	3	3	3	2	2	2	2	2	2	2	2	83
	Subtotal GC's & Fee	**288,000**	8	8	8	8	8	8	8	9	9	9	9	9	9	9	9	9	9	8	8	8	8	8	8	8	9	9	9	8	8	8	7	7	7	7	7	288
	TOTAL GMP:	**1,760,000**	8	33	33	33	67	78	42	44	79	79	79	108	161	79	69	60	50	18	32	13	13	13	20	21	66	198	63	22	49	36	46	27	7	7	7	1,760
				41					253				281				417					173				67				349					165		14	1,760

FIGURE 5–4 Cash-Loaded Schedule

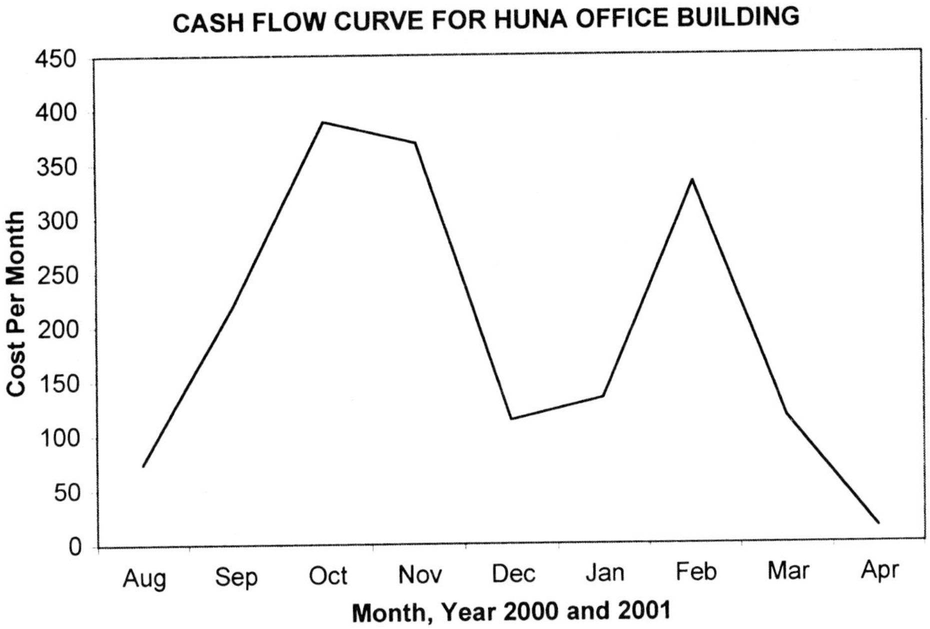

FIGURE 5–5 Cash Flow Curve

- Costs billed to the general contractor. This reflects invoices received from suppliers and subcontractors. It usually lags behind the costs committed and in place.
- Monthly pay request to the owner. This follows receipt of invoices from suppliers and subcontractors. Payment can be up to thirty days after some of the labor was paid and materials have been received.
- Payment received. This reflects when payment was received by the contractor from the owner. It will lag behind the formal monthly payment request by ten to thirty days.
- Payment distributed. This curve reflects payments distributed to subcontractors and suppliers. It will generally lag behind payment received from the owner by an additional ten to thirty days.

So which measure of cash flow should the curve represent? In most instances, the project manager will develop the curve based on the schedule of construction that reflects the anticipated costs in place. This was the method used developing the curve shown in Figure 5–5. The formal invoice will be one to four weeks behind this curve, and the receipt of cash and subsequent disbursement up to a total of two months behind the time when the work was accomplished. In this way, the actual cash flow falls behind the projection. This is beneficial to the owner and the lender. The owner's and/or the bank's actual outflow of cash will be slower than had been scheduled. The only time a problem can occur is when the outflow of cash by the contractor is faster than had been scheduled and the money is not yet available from the owner or bank.

5.7 PROJECT MANAGEMENT ISSUES

The schedule should be referenced in the contract as an exhibit. It should be referred to in each subcontract and purchase order by title and date. The project manager may insert language into all subcontracts placing the subcontractors on notice that they are required to achieve the project schedule, and that if the general contractor determines they are falling behind, the subcontractors will work overtime and/or increase crew sizes at their expense to catch up.

Day one for the project schedule for the general contractor should hinge upon four things from the owner:

- Verification of adequate construction financing
- Receipt of all building permits
- Receipt of a signed contract
- Receipt of a notice to proceed

Most owners and general contractors will avoid using a specific date in either the commencement or completion articles of the construction contract. This will be discussed more extensively in Chapter 6. Completion is usually defined in calendar days or work days, for example 165, after issuance of the notice to proceed.

Performing construction on a fast-track basis was a buzzword of the 1980s. Many construction projects are fast track now. Basically this means that activities are overlapping and occurring in parallel in lieu of in series. Few schedules are completely linear in that the preceding activity is 100% complete before the subsequent activity starts.

Activity ***float*** represents the flexibility available to schedule activities not on the critical path without delaying the overall completion of the project. The float is owned by the first party who uses it. The owner may claim the float and use it to introduce new scope. The architect may use some of the float when responding to field questions and submittals. Subcontractors and suppliers may use some of the float and either start their work late or deliver materials late. There have been numerous debates over float ownership, including many resolved by the courts.

Similar to cost control, the schedule should be developed with sufficient detail that it can be adequately measured, monitored, and corrected if necessary. An excessively detailed schedule will take on a life of its own and become too burdensome to monitor. The eighty–twenty rule should be applied to schedules the same way it is applied to estimates, filing, and cost control work packages. Eighty percent of the work is included in 20% of the activities. The project team should focus on that critical 20%.

Does the general contractor schedule the subcontractors or do the subcontractors schedule themselves? The same principle of commitment applies to the subcontractor-developed schedules as it does to superintendent-developed estimates and schedules. If the subcontractor develops the schedule, and if it fits within the overall plan, he or she has made a commitment to achieve the schedule. Whereas, if the general contractor dictates to the subcontractors when and how long they will be on the job, the subcontractors may accomplish the task, but if they don't finish on time, they will always have the excuse that they did not get the opportunity to provide input.

Schedules should be maintained in a manner similar to the way drawings and estimates are maintained. They should be marked up and commented on to reflect when activities started, when they were completed, material delivery dates, rain days, crew sizes, and whatever else the project manager feels is appropriate. The ***as-built schedule***, similar to the ***daily job diary***, becomes a legal tool in the case of a dispute. The recording of actual durations can also be used to more accurately develop future schedules and estimates.

Unfortunately, many schedules today are used largely for claim preparation. On a recent project, a sizable subcontractor refused to provide any schedules of any value during the entire two years they were on the project. Remarkably, two months after completion, the subcontractor submitted a claim for extra costs incurred due to schedule delays. An exhibit to that claim was an incredibly detailed, computer-generated schedule, in color, with floats, deliveries, and manpower restraints indicated that had not been shared while the job was in progress. The reason this happened was because the document did not exist until after the fact. This schedule was not a construction tool. If it had been available early in the project, maybe the subcontractor would have managed his work properly and communicated with the general contractor, and a claim would not have been submitted.

5.8 SUMMARY

Schedules are important tools of all members for the owner, design, and construction team. Proper planning of the project and the schedule, with input from the relevant personnel such as the superintendent and the subcontractors, are keys to developing a useful management tool. Schedule development begins with proper planning, which considers many variables such as deliveries, manpower, and equipment availabilities. There are many different types of schedules, each of which has a use on a construction project. Updating or revising the schedule can be an expensive task and does not need to be a monthly occurrence, if the project remains on track. Using the schedule to monitor progress is the superintendent's responsibility and occurs during the weekly owner/designer/contractor coordination meeting. Development of a cash flow curve is a simple task and one that the project manager should do to analyze financing requirements.

5.9 REVIEW QUESTIONS

1. What is the difference between scheduling and planning?
2. Which members of the construction team provide input to the project plan?
3. How many items should be included in the work breakdown structure?
4. What is the difference between a bar chart schedule and a network diagram schedule?
5. Who should develop a three-week schedule?
6. What is the difference between updating the schedule and using it to monitor progress?
7. Who indicates progress on the schedule? When should it be done?
8. Why should contractors avoid updating the schedule?
9. Are schedules contract documents?
10. Why do project managers resist developing cash flow curves?
11. Should a cash flow curve always be a perfect bell-shaped curve?
12. When does day one of the contract schedule occur?
13. How many activities should be on the project schedule?
14. How does the eighty–twenty rule apply to developing schedules?
15. When is it appropriate to revise the schedule?
16. How is an as-built schedule developed, and when should it be developed?

5.10 EXERCISES

1. Develop a short interval schedule for the construction of the site work for the Huna Office Building project. Identify the activities and logic, but not the durations for the activities.

5.11 SOURCES OF ADDITIONAL INFORMATION

Antill, James M., and Ronald W. Woodhead. *Critical Path Methods in Construction Practice.* 4th ed. New York: John Wiley and Sons, Inc., 1990.

Callahan, Michael T., Daniel G. Quackenbush, and James E. Rowings. *Construction Project Scheduling.* New York: McGraw-Hill, Inc., 1992.

Hinze, Jimmie W. *Construction Planning and Scheduling.* Upper Saddle River, N.J.: Prentice-Hall, Inc., 1998.

Pierce, David R. *Project Scheduling and Management for Construction.* 2d ed. Kingston, Mass.: R. S. Means Company, Inc., 1998.

6

Contract Development

6.1 INTRODUCTION

As stated in Chapter 2, the construction contract describes the rights and responsibilities of the owner and the general contractor, as well as the terms and conditions of their relationship. There are five basic documents that comprise most construction contracts: the agreement, the general conditions, the special conditions, the technical specifications, and the construction drawings. The agreement identifies the parties to the contract, the pricing method to be used, the time allowed for construction, any ***retention***, and any liquidated damages. The general and special conditions describe management procedures for the project. The technical specifications and the construction drawings describe the project that is to be constructed.

Since the contractor's responsibilities are defined by the contract documents, the project manager must read and understand each document to identify contract requirements and any associated risks. This knowledge is essential if the project manager is to supervise the project effectively. On a negotiated project, the project manager may be able to arrange contract language to reduce the contractor's risks. This generally is not possible on bid projects, particularly those awarded by public agencies.

In this chapter, we will examine the specific contract that was used for the Huna Office Building project, and how the project manager was able to influence some of the language in the contract agreement. The agreement portion of the contract (AIA Form A111–1997) is in Appendix D, and the general conditions (AIA Form A201–1997) are in Appendix E.

6.2 CONTRACT LANGUAGE

There are several different sources for contract documents. Some construction firms have prepared their own contract forms or have had their attorneys customize documents for their firms, while others use standard formats. It is not recommended that a project manager prepare his or her own contract documents. Such documents, for the most part, are unproven; they are easily challenged and may end up in court. It is best to use a proven, copyrighted document, such as those prepared by the organizations listed in Section 2.5 in Chapter 2. The advantage of using contract documents that have been developed and updated by professional associations is that they have been drafted by attorneys and have been in existence for some time. These documents, in contrast to forms prepared by a construction firm, have been challenged and tested in courts, and they are understood and accepted within the construction industry. Which family of contract documents are used on a project generally is decided by the owner, but the project manager may have an opportunity to provide input.

The AIA family of contract documents was chosen for the Huna Office Building project. The parties involved in this project had not worked together before, and the use of a widely accepted copyrighted document seemed to be the fairest for all involved. The AIA family of documents is used extensively by many private owners, and therefore, would be familiar to most contractors. A cost-plus contract with a guaranteed maximum price was chosen by the owner. The market in Juneau was not conducive to lump-sum bidding because of the limited availability of contracting and supplier firms. The owner and the architect both wanted to negotiate with a general contractor early in design development. The design team wanted to have the contractor on the team early to assist with reviewing the design as it was being developed. The owner and designer also wanted to bring the contractor on board as a team member and not an adversary.

The solicitation was sent to five general contractors. Three indicated they were interested in submitting a proposal. A detailed request for proposal (RFP) was issued to the three contractors, allowing them two weeks to respond. Attached to the RFP were rough schematic documents from which the contractors were to prepare a preliminary budget and an AIA A111 contract for a guaranteed maximum price (GMP). Three competitive proposals were received, and one firm, Northwest Construction Company, was chosen because of the experience of its project management team and its cost proposal.

On a negotiated project, the construction contract can be executed early. Either a budget or an ***allowance*** may be used as a GMP, or the contractor may receive a ***letter of intent*** or a ***preconstruction agreement***, in which case the contract document is executed after the design is complete and the GMP finalized. This second method was the one chosen for the Huna Office Building project.

Even though a proven copyrighted contract is used, many contractors, architects, and owners have standard revisions they make to the original wording. Beyond these changes, much of the contract language and execution is a process of filling in the blanks. The contract agreement for the project is in Appendix D. The following are additional specific drafting guidelines for the contract agreement.

General Issues

- Names and addresses should be shown on page one.
- Any previously issued letters of intent, letters of authorization, or preconstruction agreements may also be referred to and attached as ***exhibits***.
- The contract defines the agreement. It is the most important document on the project and is to be all encompassing. All relevant information and documents must be tied into the contract by reference and attached as exhibits. All exhibits are to be numbered or lettered, dated, and attached.
- Any article that does not apply to the specific project should either be crossed out or annotated with an *NA*. This indicates that a blank article was not overlooked.

Specific Article Issues

Article 4.1: Work should commence upon receipt of four items:

(a) Permits

(b) Verification of financing

(c) Notice to proceed

(d) Signed and executed contract

Specific dates that are out of the contractor's control should not be used.

Article 4.3: Completion is established as calendar or work days (165 work days for the Huna Office Building contract) after commencement. The project manager should also avoid using a specific date that may be out of his or her control. The summary schedule should be referred to and attached as an exhibit. This is for backup only and is dependent upon Article 4.1. Exhibit A for the Huna Office Building contract (Appendix D) is also shown in Figure 5.1 in Chapter 5.

Article 5.1.2: The fee should either be a specific amount or a percentage of the actual cost. If there is an incentive component, the criteria for determining the fee should be explained. All parties should be clear about the fee amount.

Article 5.2.1: The guaranteed maximum price, if used, should be written into the contract in both alpha and numeric methods, similar to writing a check. A ***schedule of values*** is commonly included as an exhibit on negotiated projects. Exhibit B for the Huna Office Building contract (Appendix D) is the summary estimate that was introduced in Chapter 4. A savings split, with a possible ceiling on the contractor's portion of the savings, would also be identified here.

Article 7.2.2: The general contractor may want to insert the project manager as a designated ***reimbursable cost*** here, particularly if the project manager is dedicated only to this project.

Article 7.5.1: General contractors often negotiate an allowance for hand tools to avoid the necessity to track tool costs. If an allowance is to be used, its value should be stated here.

Article 12.1.3: The exact timing of the payment request cycle should be indicated. This is more thoroughly discussed in Chapter 15.

Articles 12.1.7 and 12.1.8: The retention rate is indicated in the appropriate blanks. Retention is discussed in Chapters 15 and 21.

Article 12.2.2: If special attention should be brought to any close-out documents, such as ***lien releases***, this is the place to emphasize them.

Article 14.2: The interest rates for late payment should be indicated. Because interest is a variable and can be subject to change on long projects, it is best to tie it to a percentage (2% in the Huna Office Building project) above the prime rate as established by the lending institution involved in the project.

Article 15: A detailed list of documents is included in each section. The author of the documents should also be listed. For example: "Drawing A001, dated August 18, 1997, revision 1, prepared by JYL Architects" would be listed in detail in Article 15.1.5, along with all other drawings on the project. An alternative to listing each document in the different subsections is to attach and refer to an exhibit that lists all of the documents. Exhibit C for the Huna Office Building contract in Appendix D was prepared in this manner. There are several advantages to the separate document. First, it is easy to modify and update. Second, once created, it can be re-used for subcontracts and subsequent contract change orders. The inclusion, exclusion, or clarification list that may have been developed with the bid or proposal could be referred to and also attached as an exhibit. It is important with documents such as this not to have conflicts with other contract documents.

6.3 ATTACHMENTS

The contract agreement is the most important construction document. All other documents on the project should be linked to it. The agreement should be self-sustaining and stand on its own. It should make reference to all relevant supporting documents, and they should be attached as exhibits. Some of the documents that could be linked to the contract agreement are:

- Construction schedule (Exhibit A in the Huna Office Building contract)
- Specifications
- ***Project manual***
- Drawings
- Document exhibit which lists all of the relevant documents (Exhibit C in the Huna Office Building contract)
- Geotechnical report
- Bid addenda including pre-bid meeting notes
- Approved submittals (Submittals are discussed in Chapter 14.)
- The request for proposal
- Letter of intent to award a contract from the owner to the contractor
- Preconstruction agreement between the owner and the contractor
- The contractor's prescribed bid form
- Pre-bid site inspection certification form
- Either a summary of the contractor's estimate (Exhibit B in the Huna Office Building contract) or the entire detailed estimate.

If these documents are to be considered contract documents, they must be referenced in the contract agreement by title and date. In some contracts, each party will sign or initial each exhibit, similar to the execution of the contract itself.

6.4 EXECUTION

When allowed by the owner, the project manager should participate in developing the construction contract agreement. This section discusses several basic principles that should be followed when preparing owner/contractor contracts, regardless of contract format.

In many cases the contract itself is included or referred to in the RFP. This is a good practice from the owner's position. The party issuing the RFP may even go so far as to have the bidders acknowledge the contract format to be used and agree to accept its terms and conditions without any revisions. Wording similar to the following often is used in RFPs:

> Submittal of a proposal by a general contractor shall serve as evidence and acceptance of the contract format to be used and enclosed herein without any modifications, except as proposed by the contractor, for acceptance by the owner, and noted and attached to the contractor's proposal.

In these cases, the project manager has no choice regarding the contract and must make a decision whether or not to bid the project.

When drafting or executing a contract, project managers should:

- Request two blank copies of the contract, if the format is specified by the owner.
- If no format is specified, select the standard contract document developed by the association that best represents his or her firm's business and the specific project.
- Avoid the use of double-sided documents. Sometimes the back side of pages does not get copied and without proper initialing of each page, as discussed below, cases have been made that the reverse side was not read.
- Request two original copies of the contract from the association.
- Make a photocopy of one of the originals and begin drafting the contract.
- Route drafts through the office for input from superiors and peers.
- Revise language based on company input and submit to the owner for review.
- Revise language, if required, based on the owner's input and prepare two original documents. All exhibits that are referred to in the body of the contract must be attached.
- Initial each page of both originals. Pass the contract on to the officer-in-charge and ask for his or her initials on all pages, as well as a signature on each of the originals in the appropriate blank.
- Initials and signatures should be original and not stamped, and they should be done with blue ink. Original black ink is sometimes difficult to discern from copies due to the high quality copy machines that are available. Pencil should not be used because it can be erased easily.
- Deliver both originals to the owner or architect, whichever is called out as the recipient and reviewer. Request that the owner also initial every page and return one executed contract back for the project manager's files. This way both the owner and the project manager will have an original copy.
- If the owner wishes to make a minor revision, he or she can simply indicate that text should be added or deleted and initial the change on both originals. Then all originals will need to be returned to the project manager for the counterinitial on the change. This allows the contract to be executed and avoids redrafting due to minor changes. If a major change is necessary, redrafting may be the only choice.

Many of these same principles apply to development of subcontract agreements and purchase orders as well. Development of these documents will be discussed in Chapters 8 and 9.

6.5 SUMMARY

Contract language should be reviewed carefully. The contract defines the agreement between and responsibilities of the owner and the contractor. The project manager should volunteer to draft the contract, if allowed by the owner, since he or she will ultimately end up administering it. Other people in the construction firm should be involved in selecting the choice of formats and in reviewing drafts. If the construction firm is going to use an owner's in-house contract, or if substantial changes to a copyrighted contract's text have been proposed, an attorney should review the language. All relevant documents should be referred to and attached as exhibits.

6.6 REVIEW QUESTIONS

1. How many firms are involved in the execution of a contract?
2. Why should the project manager volunteer to draft the contract?
3. Why are black ink and pencil not suggested in contract execution?
4. How many attachments and exhibits should a contract have?
5. Why is the contract not tied into a specific start or end date?
6. When does day one of the construction schedule start?
7. Why was a negotiated contract format chosen for the Huna Office Building?
8. How many exhibits did the Huna Office Building contract have? What were they?
9. What are two advantages in using a document exhibit versus listing every design document on the contract itself?

6.7 EXERCISES

1. Prepare a list of exhibits for a construction contract for the construction of an elementary school that is to be awarded as a publicly bid lump-sum contract.
2. Prepare a guaranteed-maximum-price contract using AIA A111–1997 for the construction of a medical clinic.

6.8 SOURCES OF ADDITIONAL INFORMATION

Bartholomew, Stuart H. *Construction Contracting: Business and Legal Principles.* Upper Saddle River, N.J.: Prentice-Hall, Inc., 1998.

7

Partnering and Team Building

7.1 INTRODUCTION

Executing a construction project involves the participation of many people representing numerous organizations. The ability of the project manager to produce a successful project depends on close working relationships among project participants. These contractual relationships generally are defined by contract language that many have viewed as creating adversarial situations. The result of this lack of teamwork often is seen in a significant number of contract disputes and resulting ***litigation.*** Owners, designers, contractors, and subcontractors are beginning to recognize that there is a better way to deliver projects. By working together in a cooperative spirit, strained relationships can be avoided, and participants can walk away from a completed project feeling that they have been successful.

In this chapter, we will discuss three concepts that can be used to foster better working relationships among project participants. These concepts have been adopted by many in the construction industry to avoid the claims and disputes that are discussed in Chapter 20. First we will discuss ***partnering***, a concept originated in 1988 by the U.S. Army Corps of Engineers during the construction of a lock and dam project in Alabama. Then we will discuss team-building techniques that can be used to forge groups of individuals with different objectives into cohesive, effective teams. Lastly, we will discuss total quality management (TQM), which is a continuous process-improvement philosophy initially implemented in Japan as it recovered at the end of World War II. Introduced in the United States in the 1980s, TQM has been adopted by many manufacturing and service companies.

7.2 PARTNERING CONCEPT

Partnering is a cooperative approach to project management that recognizes the importance of all members of the project team, establishes harmonious working relationships among them, and resolves issues in a timely manner, minimizing impact on project execution. The team focuses on common goals and benefits to be achieved collectively during project execution and develops processes to keep the team working toward these goals. Partnering does not eliminate conflict, but assumes all participants are committed to quality and will act in good faith toward issue resolution. Successful partnering requires not only a process such as that described in the next section, but also an attitude shift among project participants. They must view the project in terms of making it a collective success, rather than from their narrow parochial perspectives. Mutual trust and commitment are the trademarks of a successful partnering relationship.

Partnering has been used successfully to build cooperative relationships between the owner, the designer, and the contractor on projects. Project results, however, often were unsatisfactory because major subcontractors were not included in the partnering structure. Subcontractors often perform the majority of the work on a construction project and have a great impact on project cost, duration, and quality. Major subcontractors must be included in the partnering structure if a cohesive project delivery team is to be forged.

The basic components of a partnering relationship are:

- A collectively developed mission statement
- A collectively developed charter that contains specific goals and objectives
- An effective communication system
- An effective monitoring and evaluation system
- An effective conflict resolution system

Partnering will work only when there is total commitment from all participants to open, frequent communications and mutual trust. This commitment must originate at the leadership of all organizations represented on the project team. Unless there is commitment and support from the top, mutual trust will not permeate each organization represented on the project. This requires clear articulation regarding partnering intentions and a willingness to participate in initial partnering activities and succeeding periodic evaluations.

The primary objectives of partnering are to break down barriers that otherwise hinder good working relations among project participants and to prevent destructive and expensive conflict. Its key elements are:

- Respect
- Trust
- Commitment
- Open communication
- Shared goals
- Continuous education
- Timely responsiveness

Mutual respect, trust, and commitment to partnering are essential if the relationship is to work. If this is lacking, the relationship will soon break down into the adversarial relationships found on many projects. Continuous, open communications are essential to resolving project-related issues. A shared set of goals developed at the initial partnering workshop provides the underpinning for the relationship. All must participate in the development of these goals that become the partnering charter used to evaluate project success. Project participants must understand what partnering is and what it is not. This comes only from continuous education and reinforcement. Each participant must understand the needs of the others and help team members find timely solutions to questions and issues. The overall objective of partnering is to make the project a winning endeavor for all participants.

Successful partnering relationships result in profitable jobs for participants, less time and cost growth, higher quality, and safer projects. Evaluation of successful partnering relationships has identified the following steps for success:

- Assume the other parties are honest and intend to do a good job.
- Understand and believe that the best way to have an effective team is to create win-win relationships that begin with respect.
- Start the process before the project starts.
- Involve management: this is necessary to set the tone and reinforce and support the process.
- Select project objectives for cost, schedule, safety, etc., that are specific and mutually agreed upon.
- Develop an issue escalation process that any party can invoke.
- Evaluate progress towards accomplishment of project and partnering goals jointly.
- Encourage and develop partnering skills throughout the project.

The decision to partner on a project usually rests with the owner. Contract provisions similar to that shown in Figure 7–1 are used by an owner desiring to create a partnering relationship for a project. Such provisions would appear in the special conditions of the contract. Even though the owner has the lead, the contractor must be involved in the initial planning to ensure that all critical team members, including major subcontractors, are included. Sometimes critical suppliers and building inspectors also are included. Project success depends on the inclusion and commitment of all key members of the project team.

7.3 PARTNERING TECHNIQUES

The partnering process begins when top management from each participating organization commits to the strategy. Once the commitment has been made, a workshop is conducted by an external facilitator who is not involved in the project. Workshop attendees should include senior managers from all organizations represented as well as all personnel involved in managing activities on the project site. Senior personnel are needed to emphasize the dedication of each organization to the partnering relationship and ultimately to making the project a success for all participants.

An effective workshop requires careful planning. Both the owner's and the contractor's project managers should be involved. Specific issues to be addressed during workshop planning are:

- What are the results desired from the partnership?
- How is top management support to be obtained?
- What is the budget for the workshop and who pays the cost?
- Who should attend?
- Who is to be the facilitator?
- Does the facilitator understand the project and major concerns regarding its completion?

PARTNERING

1. Owner proposes to utilize a partnering process for his or her project. Partnering emphasizes a cooperative approach to problem solving involving all key parties to the project: owner, designer, contractor, principal subcontractors, principal suppliers, and primary building inspectors.

2. Participation in partnering will be voluntary. Upon contract award, contractor will be given the option to participate in partnering.

3. If contractor decides to participate, one- to two-day workshops to define partnering relationships will be scheduled. The purpose of the workshops will be:

   a. To establish mutual understanding of partnering concepts,

   b. To develop the mission statement and project goals, and

   c. To develop a process for quick resolution of critical issues.

4. Owner will be responsible for obtaining the facilities for the workshop, as well as the facilitator and any workshop materials. Contractor is requested to pay half of the cost for the facilitator and facilities in an amount not to exceed $5,000. Contractor, designer, and major subcontractors are expected to provide project personnel for the workshop at no cost to the owner.

5. At the conclusion of the workshop, it is anticipated that a definitive on-going working arrangement for partnering will be agreed upon and committed to in writing by participants. Parties may withdraw from the partnering arrangement upon written notice to the others. Should the partnering arrangement be terminated, claims or disputes settled or changes approved during the existence of the partnering arrangement will not be affected.

FIGURE 7–1 Sample Partnering Contract Provision

- Do attendees understand how partnering works and their responsibilities for making it successful?
- Where will the workshop be conducted?
- What will the workshop agenda be?
- Will the facilitator be involved in follow-up evaluation sessions?

The objectives of the workshop are:

- For project participants to get to know each other
- For participants to understand the project success criteria of each other
- To identify potential problems and mitigation measures
- To begin team building
- To develop a ***partnering charter*** containing a mission statement and collective goals and objectives for the project
- To establish effective lines of communication
- To develop a system for timely resolution of issues
- To establish an evaluation system

A sample workshop agenda is shown in Figure 7–2. To be effective, the partnering workshop should be limited to about twenty-five people. If more participants are needed, a small group of key team leaders may be used to conduct a preworkshop meeting to craft tentative partnering documents (charter, communication guidelines, issue resolution system, and evaluation system). During the workshop, these preliminary documents are used by the facilitator to expedite development of final documents.

A team-developed charter is fundamental to a successful partnering relationship. It defines the project team's mission and identifies collective goals they established to define project success. The project goals should be specific, measurable, action-oriented, and realistic. Once the partnering charter has been crafted, it is signed by all workshop attendees, as illustrated in the partnering charter for the Huna Office Building project shown in Figure 7–3 on page 84.

The communication systems to be used on the project must be responsive to the needs of all project participants. A meeting schedule needs to be developed and participants identified. Specific media should be selected for keeping all parties informed of project issues and their resolutions. Meetings, telephone conference calls, and electronic mail generally are more responsive than formal correspondence. Time frames for responding to inquiries should be established.

An issue resolution system must be developed for timely escalation of open issues to minimize the impact on project execution. This system should delegate the initial attempt at issue resolution to the lowest levels in participating organizations. Issues that cannot be resolved within a specified time frame are then elevated to the next level for resolution. Each level is provided specific timelines until the open issue is elevated to the principal officers of the effected organizations. An example issue resolution system is shown in Figure 7–4 on page 85. The following rules are suggested for using the system:

- Start at the lowest level to resolve problems.
- Escalate unresolved problems upward in a timely manner.
- Do not jump levels of authority.
- Do not ignore the problem or fail to make a decision.
- Make only those decisions you feel comfortable with; escalate unresolved issues upward.

FIGURE 7–2 Sample Partnering Workshop Agenda

Workshop Agenda

1. Participant introductions
2. Project description
3. Description of partnering
4. Success factors for participants
5. Identification of probable obstacles
6. Team building
7. Development of partnering charter
8. Development of communication system
9. Development of issue resolution system
10. Establishment of evaluation/follow-up system

Partnering Charter

Mission Statement

We the partners of the Huna Office Building Project commit to combine our strengths and expertise as a team to construct a quality project safely in an atmosphere of mutual trust and respect achieving the following goals:

Performance Goals

- Excellent safety performance by completing the project with no fatalities, lost-time accidents, or public liability claims over $400.
- Completing a quality project that is built right the first time in conformance with the design intent. Built like it was ours.
- Completing the project on time through timely resolution of issues and joint management of the schedule.
- Maximizing cooperation to limit cost growth to 2%, minimize contractor and subcontractor costs, and minimize paperwork.
- Submittals reviewed and approved or approved with comments within 14 days.
- No unresolved claims.

Communications Goals

- Positive working relationship; be courteous, cordial, honest and listen.
- Open communications between all levels.
- Issue resolution at lowest level.
- Focus on issues and not personalities.
- Have productive meetings.
- Act responsibly.
- Develop a sense of pride, enthusiasm, integrity, and enjoyment on the project. Have fun.

Robert Smith	Mary Peterson
Norm Riley	Jerry Brown
Sam Peters	Jack Alexander
Ted Jones	Alice Jackson
Linda White	Ernie Sanchez
Jim Bates	Barry Smith

FIGURE 7–3 Partnering Charter for Huna Office Building

Designer	**Owner**	**Contractor**	**Time**
Managing Partner	Chief Executive	Chief Executive	2 days
Project Sponsor	Vice President	Vice President	1 day
Project Manager	Project Manager	Project Manager	4 hours
Design Coordinator	Project Engineer	Superintendent	4 hours
Designer	Inspector	Foreman	2 hours

FIGURE 7–4 Example Issue Resolution System

Periodic evaluation of project performance is essential to monitor the success of the partnering relationship. Monthly performance reviews may be attended by project management personnel, with principals attending quarterly reviews. Progress toward accomplishment of the charter goals and the effectiveness of the communications and issue resolution systems should also be reviewed. Project executives should publicly state their commitment to making the relationship work and support their project personnel. Partnering successes should be recognized at these evaluation meetings to reinforce the value of maintaining the relationship. A sample agenda for an evaluation meeting is shown in Figure 7–5. Project participants, not just managers attending formal evaluation meetings, should be asked to evaluate the relationship periodically. Forms similar to the sample shown in Figure 7–6 can be used to collect individual opinions regarding the relationship.

Just as a company's goals and objectives are defined in its business plan and its methods of operation are defined in its operating procedures, the partnering documents shown in Figure 7–7 on page 87 define the goals and objectives and operating procedures for the entire project team. These documents, however, may not lead to project success. It requires an attitude shift and total commitment to trust and open, honest communications from all members of the project team.

7.4 TEAM BUILDING

For partnering to succeed, project participants must agree to work together as a team to share responsibility for completing the project successfully. Since many of the participants may have never worked together previously, the first task is to get them to

FIGURE 7–5 Sample Evaluation Meeting Agenda

EVALUATION MEETING AGENDA

1. Reaffirm charter objectives and commitment.
2. Review evaluation data to identify weak and strong areas.
3. Evaluate strong areas.
4. Develop action plans for weak areas.
5. Discuss new issues and concerns.
6. Celebrate successes.

PARTNERING EVALUATION FORM

Name: ______________________________

Date: ______________________________

Organization: ______________________________

Please complete the following table based on your personal experiences and observations. Please provide comments in the remarks section for any evaluation rating given of 3 or below.

	Poor 1	Marginal 2	Good 3	Very Good 4	Excellent 5
Commitment to partnering					
Conflict resolution					
Job satisfaction					
Teamwork					
Timely issue resolution					

Remarks: ______________________________

____

____

____

____

FIGURE 7–6 Partnering Evaluation Form

know one another to develop mutual trust. It will not happen in one meeting; developing trusting relationships takes time. Team members must learn to support one another and to collaborate freely and frequently. This generally is a greater problem on bid projects than it is on negotiated projects where team members may have worked together previously.

Many construction projects are not managed in this manner. Unfortunately information may be withheld for later use, and project participants may posture for their own advantage. Team members must establish guidelines that they will use in their team meetings. They must recognize that there may be conflicts among team participants, but that they must not take any issue personally. All team members should be encouraged to state their views, and issues should be addressed objectively. Effective communication—listening, presenting, and discussing—is at the heart of teamwork. The team needs to discuss issues collaboratively, seek responsive solutions, and adopt a shared sense of accountability for achieving their collective goals and objectives. Effective teams are characterized by open communication, mutual trust, concern, support, and respect. This results from working together to solve mutual problems in a nonthreatening, supportive environment.

Team building is the process of bringing together a diverse group of individuals and seeking to resolve differences, remove impediments, and proactively develop the group into a focused, motivated team that strives to accomplish a common mission. A typical team-building process is illustrated in Figure 7–8 on page 88. A facilitator often is used

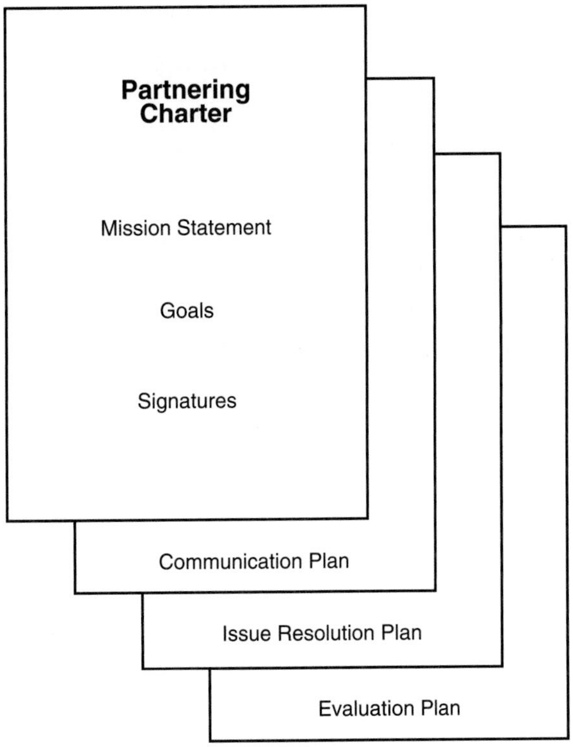

FIGURE 7–7 Partnering Documents

for the initial two steps in the process to minimize the time needed to complete them. Note the similarity between the team-building process shown in Figure 7–8 and the partnering process discussed in Section 7.3.

7.5 TOTAL QUALITY MANAGEMENT

Total quality management is a management philosophy that focuses on continuous process improvement and customer satisfaction. The customer is defined as the recipient of the service provided by or the product produced by a management process, such as processing field questions or requests for information. Customers may be internal or external to the contractor's organization or even to the project team. The objective is to achieve customer satisfaction, regardless of whether they are internal or external. Small teams known as ***process action*** or ***quality improvement teams*** are organized to study a specific process and identify means for improving it. Once process improvements have been identified and implemented, the revised process is evaluated by the team. This continuous improvement cycle repeats itself until the service meets customer expectations.

The steps the process action team takes in identifying improvements are:

- Document and define the process.
- Determine the customer's expectations.
- Measure process performance against the customer's expectations.
- Identify inefficient, wasteful, or redundant steps in the process.
- Select process changes that improve the process's capability to meet customer's expectations.

Team-Building Process

1. Collectively develop team charter that defines the team's mission, goals, and operating procedures.
2. Collectively identify specific team tasks and frequency of team meetings.
3. Work together.
4. Evaluate team performance.

FIGURE 7–8 Team-Building Process

The key to making total quality management work is empowering the people closest to each process with the authority to make changes. This capitalizes on the knowledge and experience of those individuals in the best position to identify and effect improvements. A process action team should include individuals who work with and provide input to the process and customers of the process. This ensures that all aspects of the process are understood by the team and that all perspectives are considered during team deliberations.

Individual team members must be trained regarding the total management philosophy and the need to find collective or team suggestions regarding process improvements. Since team members on a project may come from many different organizations, the first step in team development is ensuring each member understands the collective goals and objectives for the project and how the process in question impacts accomplishment of those goals. These project goals and objectives are contained in the partnering charter developed at the initial partnering workshop. Team building exercises may be required if team members have not worked with each other previously.

Implementing total quality management on a construction project requires establishment of an oversight group and individual process action teams. The senior project managers from each participating organization should be used to form the oversight group. This will allow total quality management activities to be reviewed as an agenda item at their coordination meetings. Process action team recommendations should be discussed, and team members should be recognized for their contributions. Just as with partnering, total quality management will succeed only if there is commitment from upper management of all participating organizations. The objectives are to prevent mistakes, not correct them, and to improve management procedures. This requires both teamwork and commitment.

Management of quality in the construction project is discussed in Chapter 17. This is different than total quality management, which looks at management processes such as submittal review, material procurement, subcontractor selection, processing progress payment requests or field questions, and inspection and acceptance of subcontractor work. While some of these processes directly impact the quality of the completed project, others do not.

7.6 SUMMARY

Construction projects are built by teams of people representing many organizations. Historically, the relationships between some of these organizations have been adversarial, resulting in costly disputes and litigation. Partnering was developed as a cooperative team approach to project management. The objective is to get project participants to recognize the importance of all team members and to strive for collective success for all.

Partnering begins with an initial workshop to create a cohesive team perspective on project management, develop a partnering charter that contains the team mission statement and project goals and objectives, and establish systems for frequent communication, effective issue resolution, and periodic evaluation. Successful partnering relationships depend on total commitment to trust and open, honest communication from all members of the project team.

For partnering to succeed, project participants must agree to work together as a team and share responsibility for project success. Since team members may be new to each other, a period of team building may be needed to create effective bonds of trust, concern, support, and respect.

To improve the quality of project management processes, a total quality management structure can be implemented. Process action teams are organized to evaluate critical management processes and identify methods for improvement. Total quality management is a tool for enhancing the effectiveness of the project management team.

7.7 REVIEW QUESTIONS

1. Why was the concept of partnering developed?
2. What is a partnering charter, and how is it developed?
3. Whom do you recommend to participate in the initial partnering workshop?
4. Why is the partnering charter a critical document in developing and maintaining a partnering relationship?
5. What is an issue resolution system, and why is it a critical component of partnering?
6. What information relating to the Huna Office Building project should be reviewed during partnering evaluation meetings?
7. What is meant by total quality management?
8. What are process action teams, and how do they function?

7.8 EXERCISES

1. You have been asked to organize a partnering workshop for a major hospital renovation project. Whom would you invite to the workshop? What specific issues should be addressed in the development of the partnering charter?
2. Who should participate in the partnering workshop for the Huna Office Building project?
3. Develop a communication plan for the Huna Office Building project. Identify media for daily communication, a schedule of periodic meetings, a list of attendees for each type meeting, and the individual responsible for conducting each type meeting.
4. You have been asked to organize a process action team to evaluate the process used for submission and approval of contractor's progress payments. What five people would you assign to the team?
5. How would you organize the total quality management oversight group for the Huna Office Building project?

7.9 SOURCES OF ADDITIONAL INFORMATION

Chase, Gerald W. *Implementing TQM in a Construction Company*. Washington, D.C.: Associated General Contractors of America, 1993.

Clark, Neil. *Team Building: A Practical Guide for Trainers*. New York: McGraw-Hill, Inc., 1994.

Fisher, Kimball. *Leading Self-Directed Teams*. New York: McGraw-Hill, Inc., 1993.

Godfrey, Kneeland A. *Partnering in Design and Construction*. New York: McGraw-Hill, Inc., 1996.

Harrington-Macklin, Deborah. *The Team-Building Tool Kit: Tips, Tactics, and Rules for Effective Workplace Teams*. New York: American Management Association, 1994.

Hensey, Mel. *Collective Excellence: Building Effective Teams*. New York: American Society of Civil Engineers, 1992.

Implementing TQM in Engineering and Construction. Special Publication 31–1, Austin: Construction Industry Institute, 1994.

Lewis, James P. *How to Build and Manage a Winning Project Team*. New York: American Management Association, 1991.

Ronoco, William C., and Jean S. Ronoco. *Partnering Manual for Design and Construction*. New York: McGraw-Hill, Inc. 1996.

Schultzel, Henry J., and V. Paul Unruh. *Successful Partnering: Fundamentals for Project Owners and Contractors*. New York: John Wiley and Sons, Inc., 1996.

Stephenson, Ralph J. *Project Partnering for the Design and Construction Industry*. New York: John Wiley and Sons, Inc., 1996.

Team Building: Improving Project Performance. Publication 37–1, Austin: Construction Industry Institute, July 1993.

Tenner, Arthur R., and Irving J. DeToro. *Total Quality Management: Three Steps to Continuous Improvement*. Reading, Mass.: Addison-Wesley Publishing Company, 1992.

Thompson, Paul, Travis Crane, and Steve Sanders. *The Partnering Process—Its Benefits, Implementation, and Measurement*. Research Report 102–11, Austin: Construction Industry Institute, 1996.

Warne, Thomas R. *Partnering for Success*. New York: ASCE Press, 1994.

8

Subcontracting

8.1 INTRODUCTION

General contractors typically use ***subcontractors*** to execute most of the construction tasks involved in a project. Indeed, a typical general contractor subcontracts 75 to 85% of the project scope of work. Subcontractors, often referred to as ***specialty contractors***, therefore, are important members of the general contractor's project delivery team and have a significant impact on the project manager's success or failure. The relationship of the subcontractors to the other members of the project delivery team is illustrated in Section 1.2 of Chapter 1. Since subcontractors have such a great impact on the overall quality, cost, and schedule for a project, they must be selected carefully and managed efficiently. There must be mutual trust and respect between the project manager and the subcontractors, because each can achieve success only by working cooperatively with the other. Consequently, general contractors and their project managers find it advantageous to develop and nurture positive, enduring relationships with reliable subcontractors. Project managers must treat subcontractors fairly to ensure the subcontractors remain financially viable as business enterprises. This will ensure that the subcontractors will be available for future projects.

General contractors use subcontractors to reduce risk and provide access to specialized skilled craftworkers and equipment. One of the major risks in contracting is accurately forecasting the amount and cost of labor required to complete a project. By subcontracting significant segments of work, the project manager can transfer much of the risk to subcontractors. When the project manager asks a subcontractor for a price to perform a specific scope of work, the subcontractor bears the risk of properly estimating the labor, material, and equipment costs. Craftspeople experienced in the many specialized trades required for major construction projects are expensive to hire and generally used on a project site only for limited periods of time. Unless general contractors have continuous need for such specialized labor, it is not cost effective to employ them as a part of the contractor's own work force.

Subcontracting is not without risk. The project manager gives up some control when working with subcontractors. The scope and terms of the subcontract define the responsibilities of each subcontractor. If some aspect of the work is inadvertently omitted, the project manager is still responsible for ensuring that the general contract requirements are achieved. Specialty contractors are required to perform only those tasks that are specifically stated in the subcontract documents. Consistent quality control, particularly the quality of workmanship, may be more difficult with subcontractors. Owners expect to receive a quality project and will hold the project manager accountable for the quality of all work whether performed by the general contractor's crews or by subcontractors.

Subcontractor bankruptcy is another risky aspect of subcontracting, which can be minimized by good prequalification procedures and timely payment for subcontract work. Scheduling subcontractor work often is more difficult than scheduling the general contractor's crews because the subcontractor's workers may be committed to other projects. Safety procedures and practices among subcontractors may not be as effective as those used by the general contractor presenting an additional challenge to the superintendent.

The major subcontracting challenges to be faced are:

- Defining well-understood, specific scopes of work.
- Selecting qualified subcontractors.
- Negotiating fair prices for the subcontracted scopes of work.
- Scheduling and coordinating subcontractor work to ensure timely completion of the project.
- Causing precedent subcontractors to perform their work on time and in accordance with contract requirements.
- Resolving technical issues involving subcontractors' work.
- Ensuring the quality of subcontractors' work.
- Paying subcontractors on time for properly completed work.
- Developing enduring relationships with reliable subcontractors.

In this chapter, we will discuss subcontractor selection, acquisition, and management. Selection and acquisition of subcontractors are part of project start-up activities, as we will discuss in Chapter 10. Selecting quality subcontractors is essential if the project manager is to produce a quality project on time and within budget. Project managers must remember that poor subcontractor performance will reflect negatively on their professional reputations and their ability to secure future projects. Once the subcontractors have been selected, contract documents are executed, defining the scopes of work and the terms and conditions of the agreement. Subcontractor management is an integral part of project management. While the project superintendent manages the field performance of the subcontractors, the project manager oversees all subcontract documentation and communication and is responsible for ensuring that the subcontractors are treated fairly.

8.2 SUBCONTRACT SCOPES OF WORK

During the initial work breakdown, the project manager identifies the work items that are to be self-performed by the general contractor and those that are to be subcontracted. He or she develops a subcontract plan identifying which work items to include in each subcontract. This plan becomes the basis for creating the specific scope of work for each subcontract.

A well-defined scope of work is essential to ensuring that prospective specialty contractors understand what is expected of them. Poorly defined scopes of work lead to conflicts and often result in cost escalation, time delays, and litigation. The subcontract must state clearly the exact scope of work to be performed and either include or make reference to all relevant drawings and specifications, ensuring a clear understanding of the subcontractor's responsibilities.

The subcontract scope of work should contain:

- A description of the work to be performed
- A list of specific scope items to be included
- A list of items that are to be excluded (if applicable)

The scope may include construction services only, or it may include both design and construction services. Construction services may include labor and equipment only or labor, materials, and equipment. Action words should be used in writing scopes of work to minimize misunderstandings. Words such as *provide* and *install* should be used to define clearly the subcontractor's responsibilities.

The following is an example of a scope of work involving labor and equipment only:

> Subcontractor agrees to provide all labor, supervision, equipment, supplies, and other items necessary or required to install the roofing and perform all such work in accordance with the contract drawings, specifications, and any addenda contained in the general contract documents for the construction of the Central Office Building. Exclusion: Roofing material will be provided by general contractor.

The following is an example of a scope of work involving labor, materials, and equipment:

> Subcontractor agrees to provide all materials, labor, supervision, equipment, supplies, and other items necessary or required to perform all electrical work in accordance with the contract drawings, specifications, and any addenda contained in the general contract documents for the construction of the Central Office Building. The intent is to provide and install a complete electrical system that meets local code requirements. Includes conduit required for installation of telephone cabling by others.

The following is an example of a scope of work involving design and construction:

> Subcontractor agrees to design the automatic fire protection sprinkler system for the Huna Office Building and provide all materials, labor, supervision, tools, equipment, supplies, and other items necessary or required to install the sprinkler system in accordance with the approved design.

Project managers must ensure that all work items to be subcontracted are included in a subcontract scope of work. Omitted items eventually become change orders to the subcontract, resulting in unanticipated expenses for the project manager. Project managers must also ensure that individual work items do not appear in multiple subcontracts to avoid paying for them more than once. An audit of subcontract scopes of work is completed before specialty contractors are asked to submit cost proposals. This audit involves reviewing all work items identified in the work breakdown and ensuring that each work item selected for subcontractor performance is included in one, and only one, subcontract scope of work.

Now that we have concluded our discussion of the scope of work, let's examine subcontract documents.

8.3 SUBCONTRACT DOCUMENTS

The subcontract is a record of the agreement between the general contractor and each specialty contractor used on the project. It usually is based on the requirements and specifications contained in the general contract with the project owner. Once the scope of work has been established, the specific terms and conditions are defined for each subcontract. These terms and conditions establish the operating procedures the project manager intends to use to manage each subcontract. Topics that should be addressed are:

- Subcontract price
- List of subcontract documents
- Commencement and progress of work
- Availability of temporary utilities
- Job site clean-up requirements
- Availability of lifting support and scaffolding
- Insurance
- Indemnification
- Bonds (if required)
- Safety
- Disposal of hazardous waste
- Inspection and acceptance of completed work
- Change order procedures
- Claims procedures
- Payment procedures
- Warranty
- Dispute resolution
- Termination or suspension

Standard subcontract documents have been developed by the American Institute of Architects, the American Subcontractors Association, and the Associated General Contractors of America. The latter document is illustrated in Appendix G. Project managers should select one of these documents because they are used widely in the industry and are understood by specialty contractors. The advantage of using copyrighted documents is that they have been tested in court and found legally sufficient. Project managers who choose not to use one of these standard subcontracts should consult with legal counsel when crafting subcontract language. Creating original subcontracts is very risky and not recommended.

8.4 SUBCONTRACTOR PREQUALIFICATION

To ensure quality work, project managers should prequalify specialty contractors before asking them to submit a price for the work. Historically too much emphasis has been placed on price and not enough on quality and experience. Project managers should select subcontractors based on their ability to provide the greatest overall value to the project. Proven performers should be selected based on their professional approach to producing quality work.

Potential subcontractors should be evaluated using a standard set of criteria, such as:

- Experience and technical skills required
- Technical and supervisory competency of management and field supervisors
- Stability and financial strength
- Adequacy of specialized equipment and labor
- Past safety performance
- Reputation for working cooperatively, proven history of responding to warranty calls, and past project performance

One technique for gathering much of this information is to require prospective subcontractors to respond to a detailed questionnaire, such as the example illustrated in Figure 8–1. Additional information should be acquired from other project managers, and personal interviews may be required before selecting the set of prequalified subcontractors invited to submit proposals. Owners and designers should be invited to participate in reviewing the prospective subcontractors' qualifications. Project managers should use only quality subcontractors as members of their project delivery teams. Specialty contractors reviewed during prequalification should be evaluated against a set of criteria similar to that listed in the preceding paragraph. Each firm should be ranked based on the project manager's assessment of its capability to provide quality service as a member of the project delivery team.

8.5 SUBCONTRACTOR SELECTION

Selecting quality specialty contractors for each subcontract is essential for project success. The ideal specialty contractor has a good safety record, experienced craftspeople, good equipment, and is able to complete the project to the desired standards without experiencing financial problems. Some project managers select subcontractors simply on price, which often leads to problems on the project with quality control or timely execution. On some projects, the owner reserves the right to approve subcontractors. Article 10 of the contract agreement for the Huna Office Building project shown in Appendix D addresses subcontracting. Additional subcontracting requirements are contained in Article 5 of the contract general conditions in Appendix E. While qualification-based selection of subcontractors is highly recommended, some owners, particularly public agencies on cost-plus contracts, may require that an open bidding system be used for subcontractors. Subcontracts are then awarded to the lowest responsive bidder.

The recommended strategy is to select the top five or six specialty contractors identified during prequalification and invite them either to submit a proposal or a quotation (bid) for the scope of work. Requests for proposal typically are used for design-build or cost-plus scopes of work. ***Requests for quotation*** are used for lump-sum or unit-price scopes of work. A sample request for quotation or invitation to bid is shown in Figure 8–2 on page 98, and a sample request for proposal is shown in Figure 8–3 on page 99. Some project managers solicit quotations by telephone, but a better practice is to use written solicitations to ensure each prospective subcontractor understands the project requirements.

Subcontractor quotations typically are received by the project manager by telephone or facsimile. Quotations received from one subcontractor should not be disclosed to another. This practice is known as ***bid shopping*** and is considered unethical. Subcontractors expect project managers to treat their quotations as confidential information until the subcontracts are awarded. Project managers who practice bid shopping may find subcontractors unwilling to bid on their projects.

Once the proposals or quotations have been received, they are evaluated to select a specific specialty contractor for each subcontract. A subcontractor analysis form similar to the one shown in Chapter 4 (Figure 4–14) can be used to assist in subcontractor selection. To ensure each subcontractor's cost proposal is realistic, the project manager should have previously developed an order-of-magnitude cost estimate for each subcontract. Unrealistically low or high quotations generally indicate that the subcontractor

- Was uncertain regarding the exact scope of work,
- Found ambiguities regarding some of the conditions of work,
- Erred when preparing the quotation, or
- Omitted items.

NORTHWEST CONSTRUCTION COMPANY
1242 First Avenue, Cascade, Washington 98202
(206) 239-1422

SUBCONTRACTOR QUESTIONNAIRE

1. **General Company Information**:

Name: *Arctic Mechanical*

Address: *1736 Main Street*

City: *Juneau* State: *AK* Zip: *99801*

Telephone: *907-292-1412* FAX: *907-292-1413*

Type of firm. (check appropriate box)

☒ Sole owner. Name: *Joe Johnson*

☐ Partnership. List names of partners.

____
____
____

☐ Corporation.

President:____________________

Vice President:____________________

Number of years in business under present name: *12 years*

Trade(s) normally performed by company: *HVAC, ductwork, plumbing, fire protection, and sometimes controls.*

Number of trade and office personnel currently employed:

Trade employees: *15* Office employees: *3*

2. **Financial Information**:

What is the maximum dollar value of work the company is capable of handling at one time?

$650,000

Attach last 2 years audited financial statements at end of questionnaire.

FIGURE 8–1 Subcontractor Questionnaire

3. **Insurance Information**:

What is the company's workers' compensation experience modification rate for the 3 most recent years?

1997: 1.2 *1998: 0.8* *1999: 0.6*

How much insurance coverage does the company currently carry?

	Yes	No	Amount
General Liability	*X*		*$2,000,000*
Automobile Liability	*X*		*$2,000,000*
Workers' Compensation	*X*		

4. **Safety Information**:

Does the company have a written safety program? *Yes*

Use your OSHA Form 200 to complete the following table.

	1997	**1998**	**1999**
Total Number of Workers' Compensation Claims	*7*	*5*	*5*
Number of Lost Time Workers' Comp. Claims	*7*	*4*	*2*
Number of Accident Liability Claims	*1*	*0*	*0*
Number of Fatalities	*0*	*0*	*0*

5. **Project Information**:

List current, ongoing projects with approximate dollar value and estimated completion date.

Project	Amount	Completion Date
Rest Home	*$250,000*	*June 15, 2001*
2 residences	*$40,000*	*October 1, 2000*
Texaco	*$75,000*	*April 1, 2001*
Airplane hangar tenant improvement	*$10,000*	*August 15, 2000*

Has the company failed to complete any work assigned to it during the past 5 years? *No*
If Yes, explain:

Attach a list of projects completed in the last 3 years and a list of contractor references whom we may contact.

6. **Equipment Information**:

Attach a list of owned construction equipment with capacity, age, type, and attachments.

This questionnaire was completed by:

Name: *Joe Johnson* Title: *Owner*

Signature: Joe Johnson Date: *June 1, 2000*

FIGURE 8–1 Subcontractor Questionnaire *(Continued)*

INVITATION TO BID/SUBBID PROPOSAL

SUBCONTRACTOR ACME Roofing
Address 1437 First Avenue
Juneau, AK 99801
CONTRACTOR Northwest Construction Co.
Address 1242 First Avenue
Cascade, WA 98202

OWNER HUNA Totem
Project Office Building
Location Juneau, AK
A/E JYL
Subbid Date & Time July 21, 2000 10 AM
Bid Date & Time July 21, 2000 1 PM

Type of work (including specification sections) Supply and install all roofing materials, including flashing and paper

(List the category(ies) this proposal will cover, such as plumbing, heating, air conditioning and ventilation, electrical and elevators.)

This proposal includes furnishing all materials and performing all work in the category(ies) listed above, as required by the plans, specifications, general and special conditions and addenda,
NA
(List addenda by number.)

which are available at NA
Identify work to be **excluded** by specification paragraph otherwise the Subcontractor will be responsible for all work in the above category(ies) required by the specifications and plans. Metal Gutters and Snow Brakes

Subbid must be given to the Contractor by subbbid date and time set forth above in time for tabulation and evaluation before the general bid date and time.

If this proposal, including prices, is accepted, the Subcontractor agrees to enter into a subcontract and, if required, furnish performance and payment bonds from AAA Insurance Inc.
(Name of surety company or agency)
guaranteeing full performance of the work and payment of all costs incident thereto. The cost of the bond is not included in this proposal, but will be added to the subcontract price at a cost of 1.2 % of the base and and alternates.

This proposal will remain in effect and will not be withdrawn by the Subcontractor for a period of 30 days or for the same period of time required by the contract documents for the Contractor in regard to the prime bid, plus 15 days, whichever period is longer.

BASE BID $59,000.00

ALTERNATES

Identification	Add	Deduct	No Change
Gutters	$3.00/LF	$	
Downspouts	$2.50/LF	$	
Snow Brakes	$75.00/EA	$	
	$	$	
	$	$	
	$	$	
	$	$	

If gutters are required, then snow brakes are needed, or no warranty. J.T.

Northwest Construction Company
Contractor
By Ted Jones — Project Manager (Title)
July 7, 2000
Date

ACME Roofing
Subcontractor
By Jamick Truson — Estimator (Title)
July 21, 2000
Date

AGC Document 605 • INVITATION TO BID/SUBBID PROPOSAL • 1992

FIGURE 8–2 Subcontract Request for Quotation or Bid
Associated General Contractors of America

NORTHWEST CONSTRUCTION COMPANY
1242 First Avenue, Cascade, Washington 98202
(206) 239-1422

REQUEST FOR PROPOSAL

To: Arctic Mechanical
Attention: Joe Johnson
1736 Main Street
Juneau, Alaska 99801

Date: July 7, 2000

Project: Huna Office Building

Project Address: 9301 Glacier Highway
Juneau, Alaska 99801

Northwest Construction Company is soliciting Design-Build proposals for the mechanical systems in the above named project. Subcontract is to be awarded on a cost-reimbursable plus fee basis. Proposals are due in three copies no later than July 20, 2000. Selection will be dependent upon the overall subcontractor responsiveness with particular emphasis on the creative and detailed response to the "Proposed Systems", "Proposed Team", and "Proposed Budget" portions of this RFP.

Proposal Requirements:

1. Subcontractor's Fee for the Work:
   State proposed fee as a percentage of the estimated cost of the work.
2. Subcontractor Labor Cost:
   Provide a list of your proposed hourly labor costs for all direct and indirect reimbursable labor.
3. Proposed Subcontractor Team and Management Plan:
   Provide a list of proposed project personnel including project manager, design engineer(s), and project superintendent. Provide a comprehensive and concise project management plan detailing how you plan to complete the subcontract scope of work. Describe how this team differentiates itself and what measures will be taken to provide competitive budgets, cost control, and innovation.
4. Proposed System Narratives:
   Provide mechanical system design narrative including description of major components selected.
5. Proposed System Detailed Budget:
   Provide a detailed mechanical systems budget for project.

Sincerely,

Ted Jones

Ted Jones

FIGURE 8–3 Subcontract Request for Proposal

A high quotation also may indicate that the subcontractor is fully committed on other projects and not interested in the work. Any ambiguities regarding the scope of work should be resolved, and all subcontractors invited to submit new quotations.

Subcontractor performance and payment bonds often are not required when subcontractors are selected based on their technical competence, reputation, and financial condition. However, bonds generally are required by contractors if the contract with the owner requires subcontracts to be awarded using a public bid procedure. If bonds are required by the project manager as a part of the project risk management strategy, forms similar to those illustrated in Figure 8–4 and Figure 8–5 on pages 101–04 should be used. Any bond requirements would be shown in Section 3.27 of the subcontract in Appendix G. Bonds are not free. If required, premiums will be included in each subcontractor's price quotation. Bonds protect the project manager against subcontractor default, bankruptcy, and liens, but do not guarantee successful subcontractor performance. Subcontractor bonds are similar to the general contractor bonds discussed in Section 2.6 of Chapter 2. The major difference is that the surety guarantees the subcontractor's performance to the general contractor rather than the general contractor's performance to the owner.

Once each specialty contractor is selected, the price is entered on the subcontract, and the project manager and the specialty contractor sign the agreement. The procedures used are similar to those for executing the contract between the owner and the general contractor, discussed in Chapters 2 and 6.

8.6 SUBCONTRACTOR MANAGEMENT

Once the subcontracts are awarded and construction begins, the project manager and the superintendent work together to schedule and coordinate the subcontractors' work to ensure the project is completed on time, within budget, and in conformance with contract requirements. Since most of the construction work is performed by subcontractors, efficient management of their work is critical to the project manager's ability to control costs and complete the project on time. Before allowing subcontractors to start work on the project, they should be required to provide a certificate of insurance, and the coverage requirements should be stated in the subcontract. Section 9.2 of the subcontract in Appendix G contains insurance coverage requirements. An example of a subcontractor insurance certificate is shown in Figure 10–6 in Chapter 10.

The first challenge is to mold the subcontractors into a cohesive, successful project delivery team, which requires an understanding of their concerns and proper work sequencing. It is essential that the superintendent establish a cooperative relationship with the subcontractors and their foremen by conducting regular coordination meetings to discuss their concerns. Frequent, open communications coupled with mutual goals will help foster subcontractor relationships that are built on trust. The superintendent should require each subcontractor to submit a daily report of activities. This provides a daily record of each subcontractor's progress and any obstacles encountered in performing the work.

The success of any project is dependent on a viable schedule. The superintendent is responsible for coordinating start and completion dates with each subcontractor. They need adequate time to arrange their jobs, obtain equipment and materials, and schedule their crews. This means the superintendent must provide adequate notice to each subcontractor regarding the planned start date for his or her phase of the work. In addition to being timely, the notice should also indicate the scheduled completion date to preclude interfering with the work of following subcontractors. If different subcontractors work concurrently on the project site, the superintendent must ensure that they are compatible and that each receives notice. All subcontractors must be aware of their safety responsibilities including those toward other subcontractors working on the

THE ASSOCIATED GENERAL CONTRACTORS OF AMERICA

SUBCONTRACT PERFORMANCE BOND

Any singular reference to Principal, Surety, Obligee or other party shall be considered plural where applicable.

PRINCIPAL (SUBCONTRACTOR)
(Name and Address):
Arctic Mechanical, 1736 Main Street
Juneau, AK 99801

SURETY (Name and Address of Surety Company Office):
Southeast Surety
1221 Third Avenue
Juneau, AK 99801

OBLIGEE (CONTRACTOR)
(Name and Address):
Northwest Construction Co., 1242 First Avenue
Cascade, WA 98202

SUBCONTRACT
Date: September 1, 2000
Amount: $145,000.00
Description of Project (Name and Location): Huna Office Building
9301 Glacier Highway
Juneau, AK 99801

BOND
Date (Not earlier than Subcontract Date): September 1, 2000
Penal Amount: $ 145,000.00

SUBCONTRACTOR AS PRINCIPAL
Company: (Corporate Seal)
Arctic Mechanical
Signature: Jason Sams
Name and Title: Jason Sams, Treasurer

SURETY
Company: (Corporate Seal)
Southeast Surety
Signature: Francis Tenure
Name and Title: Francis Tenure, Vice President
Attach Power of Attorney

Witness: Mary Jones

Witness: Jerry Hill

(Any additional signatures appear on page attached)

FOR INFORMATION ONLY
AGENT or BROKER:
(Name, Address and Telephone)
AAA Insurance LLC
12247 Hilltop #403
Anchorage, AK 99772

AGC DOCUMENT NO. 606 • SUBCONTRACT PERFORMANCE BOND • 1988

FIGURE 8–4 Subcontract Performance Bond
Associated General Contractors of America

Articles

1. **SCOPE OF BOND.** The Principal and the Surety, jointly and severally, bind themselves, their heirs, executors, administrators, successors and assigns to the Obligee for the performance of the Subcontract, which is incorporated in this bond by reference. In no event shall the Surety's total obligation exceed the penal amount of this bond.
2. **EFFECT OF OBLIGATION.** If the Principal performs the Subcontract, then this bond shall be null and void; otherwise it shall remain in full force and effect.
3. **ALTERATION NOTICE WAIVER.** The Surety hereby waives notice of any alteration or extension of the Subcontract, including but not limited to the Subcontract price and/or time, made by the Obligee. This waiver shall not apply to the time for suit provided by paragraph 5 hereunder.
4. **PRINCIPAL DEFAULT.** Whenever the Principal shall be, and is declared by the Obligee to be in default under the Subcontract, with the Obligee having performed its obligations in the Subcontract, the Surety may promptly remedy the default, or shall promptly:

   4.1 **COMPLETE SUBCONTRACT.** Complete the Subcontract in accordance with its terms and conditions; or

   4.2 **OBTAIN NEW CONTRACTORS.** Obtain a bid or bids formally, informally or negotiated for completing the Subcontract in accordance with its terms and conditions, and upon determination by the Surety of the lowest responsible bidder, or negotiated proposal, or, if the Obligee elects, upon determination by the Obligee and the Surety jointly of the lowest responsible bidder, or negotiated proposal, arrange for a contract between such party and the Obligee. The Surety will make available as work progresses sufficient funds to pay the cost of completion less the balance of the contract price. The cost of completion includes responsibilities of the Principal for correction of defective work and completion of the Subcontract; the Obligee's legal and design professional costs resulting directly from the Principal's default, and; liquidated damages or actual damages if no liquidated damages are specified in the Subcontract. The term "balance of the contract price," as used in this paragraph, shall mean the total amount payable by the Obligee to the Principal under the Subcontract and any amendments to it, less the amount properly paid by the Obligee to the principal; or

   4.3 **PAY OBLIGEE.** Determine the amount for which it is liable to the Obligee and pay the Obligee that amount as soon as practicable; or

   4.4 **DENY LIABILITY.** Deny its liability in whole or in part and notify and explain to the Obligee the reasons why the Surety believes it does not have responsibility for this liability.
5. **TIME FOR SUIT.** Any suit under this bond must be instituted before the expiration of two (2) years from the date of substantial completion as established by the contract documents.
6. **RIGHT OF ACTION.** No right of action shall accrue on this bond to or for the use of any person or entity other than the Obligee named herein, its heirs, executors, administrators or successors.

AGC DOCUMENT NO. 606 • SUBCONTRACT PERFORMANCE BOND • 1988

FIGURE 8–4 Subcontract Performance Bond (*Continued*)
Associated General Contractors of America

THE ASSOCIATED GENERAL CONTRACTORS OF AMERICA

SUBCONTRACT PAYMENT BOND

Any singular reference to Principal, Surety, Obligee or other party shall be considered plural where applicable.

PRINCIPAL (SUBCONTRACTOR)
(Name and Address):
Arctic Mechanical, 1736 Main Street
Juneau, AK 99801

SURETY (Name and Address of Surety Company Office):
Southeast Surety
1221 Third Avenue
Juneau, AK 99801

OBLIGEE (CONTRACTOR)
(Name and Address):
Northwest Construction Co., 1242 First Avenue
Cascade, WA 98202

SUBCONTRACT
Date: September 1, 2000
Amount: $ 145,000.00
Description of Project (Name and Location): Huna Office Building
9301 Glacier Highway
Juneau, AK 99801

BOND
Date (Not earlier than Subcontract Date): September 1, 2000
Penal Amount: $ 145,000.00

SUBCONTRACTOR AS PRINCIPAL
Company: (Corporate Seal)
Arctic Mechanical

Signature: Jason Sams
Name and Title: Jason Sams, Treasurer

Witness: Mary Jones

SURETY
Company: (Corporate Seal)
Southeast Surety

Signature: Francis Tenure
Name and Title: Francis Tenure, Vice President
Attach Power of Attorney

Witness: Jerry Hill

(Any additional signatures appear on page attached)

FOR INFORMATION ONLY
AGENT or BROKER:
(Name, Address and Telephone)
AAA Insurance LLC
12247 Hilltop #403
Anchorage, AK 99772

AGC DOCUMENT NO. 607 • SUBCONTRACT PAYMENT BOND • 1988

FIGURE 8–5 Subcontract Payment Bond
Associated General Contractors of America

Articles

1. **SCOPE OF BOND.** The Principal and the Surety, jointly and severally, bind themselves, their heirs, executor, administrators, successors and assigns to the Obligee to pay for labor, materials and equipment furnishea for use in the performance of the Subcontract, which is incorporated in this bond by reference and pursuant to which this bond is issued. In no event shall the Surety's total obligation exceed the penal amount of this bond.

2. **EFFECT OF OBLIGATION.** If the Principal shall promptly make payment directly or indirectly to all Claimants as defined in this bond, for all labor, material and equipment used in the performance of the Subcontract, then this bond shall be null and void; otherwise it shall remain in full force and effect, subject, however, to the following conditions:

   2.1 **TIME FOR CLAIM.** The Principal and Surety hereby jointly and severally agree with the Obligee that every Claimant, who has not been paid in full before the expiration of a period of ninety (90) days after the date on which the last of such Claimant's work or labor was done or performed, or materials were furnished by such Claimant, for which claim is made, may have a right of action on this bond. The Obligee shall not be liable for the payment of any costs or expenses including attorneys' fees which the Obligee may incur in connection with its defense of any such right of action.

   2.2 **RIGHT OF ACTION.** No suit or action shall be commenced on this bond by any Claimant:

   2.2.1 Unless Claimant, other than one having a direct contract with the Principal, shall have given written notice to any two of the following: Principal, Obligee, or the Surety above named, within ninety (90) days after such Claimant did or performed the last of the work or labor, or furnished the last of the materials for which said claim is made, stating with substantial accuracy the amount claimed and the name of the party to whom the materials were furnished, or for whom the work or labor was done or performed. Such notice shall be served by mailing the same by registered mail or certified mail, postage prepaid, in an envelope addressed to the Principal, Obligee or Surety, at any place within the United States where an office is regularly maintaine for the transaction of business, or served in any manner in which legal process may be serve in the state in which the aforesaid Project is located, however, such service need not be made by a public officer.

   2.2.2 After the expiration of one (1) year from the date (1) on which the Claimant gave the notice required by Subparagraph 2.2.1, or (2) on which the last labor or service was performed by anyone or the last materials or equipment were furnished by anyone on the Project, whichever first occurs. Any limitation embodied in this bond, which is prohibited by any law controlling the Project, shall be deemed to be amended so as to be equal to the minimum period of limitation permitted by such law.

   2.2.3 Other than in a state court of competent jurisdiction in and for the county or other political subdivision of the state in which the Project, or any part thereof, is situated, or in the United States District Court for the district in which the Project, or any part thereof, is situated, and not elsewhere.

3. **CLAIMANT.** A Claimant is defined as an individual or entity having a direct contract with the Principal to furnish labor, materials or equipment for use in the performance of the Subcontract or any individual or entity having valid lien rights which may be asserted in the jurisdiction where the Project is located. The intent of this bond shall be to include without limitation in the terms "labor, materials or equipment" that part of water, gas, power, light, heat, oil, gasoline, telephone service or rental equipment used in the Subcontract, architectural and engineering services required for performance of the work of the Principal, and all other items for which a mechanic's lien may be asserted in the jurisdiction where the labor, materials or equipment were furnished.

4. **AMOUNT OF BOND.** The amount of this bond shall be reduced by and to the extent of any payment or payments made in good faith by the Surety.

5. **ALTERATION NOTICE WAIVER.** The Surety waives notice of any alteration or extension of the Subcontrac including but not limited to the Subcontract price and/or time, made by the Obligee. This waiver shall not apply to the time for suit provided by Paragraph 2.2 hereunder.

AGC DOCUMENT NO. 607 • SUBCONTRACT PAYMENT BOND • 1988

FIGURE 8–5 Subcontract Payment Bond (*Continued*)
Associated General Contractors of America

site. The superintendent must ensure that the job site is ready for a subcontractor before scheduling him or her to start work. Requiring subcontractors to arrive on a site that is not ready causes a hardship on them and can result in lost time and increased project cost. The superintendent also is responsible for resolving any conflicts between subcontractors. Even though the work is being performed by a subcontractor, the general contractor is still responsible.

The superintendent must ensure that subcontractor work conforms to quality requirements specified in the contract. Subcontractors must understand workmanship requirements before being allowed to proceed with the work. The project manager should conduct preconstruction meetings with subcontractors before allowing them to start work on the project. A sample agenda for these meetings is shown in Figure 8–6. The owner and designer should be invited to participate in all ***subcontractor preconstruction meetings***. Often ***mock-ups***, which are stand-alone samples of completed work, are required for exterior and interior finishes. This allows the superintendent and the designer to evaluate the work and establish a standard of workmanship. Project site cleaning policies also should be discussed at the preconstruction conference. Generally, all subcontractors should be required to clean their work areas when they have completed their scopes of work.

Subcontractors must not be allowed to build over work that has been improperly done by a previous subcontractor. The superintendent should walk the project when each subcontractor finishes its portion to identify any needed rework. An inspection report similar to the one illustrated in Figure 8–7 should be used to document the results of each inspection. This is better than waiting until the end of the construction and trying to get several subcontractors to return and do rework. Early identification and correction of deficiencies is a key part of an ***active quality management program***, as will be discussed in Chapter 17.

FIGURE 8–6
Subcontractor Preconstruction Meeting Agenda

Subcontractor Preconstruction Meeting Agenda

1. Scope review
2. Work status
   - Submittal status
   - Permit status
   - Material status
3. Schedule review
4. Coordination and safety
5. Quality control
6. Field administration
   - Daily foreman's report
   - Job site maintenance and clean up
   - Job site meetings
   - Back-charge notification
   - Field questions
7. Contract administration
   - Pay requests—lien releases
   - Notification of changed conditions
   - Change-order procedures
   - Close-out requirements

NORTHWEST CONSTRUCTION COMPANY

1242 First Avenue, Cascade, Washington 98202
(206) 239-1422

PROJECT INSPECTION REPORT

Project: HUNA OFFICE BUILDING Date: NOV. 15, 2000

Subcontractor: ACME ROOFING

Area of Work: METAL ROOF PANELS

Inspection Participants:

JEREMY - TTI TESTING — ACME FOREMAN

RILEY - JYL — OWNER - PART TIME

BATES - NWCC

Scope of Inspection:

SCAFFOLD NEEDS TO COME DOWN, SO NEED ROOF BUYOFF — REVIEWED ALL PANELS, FLASHING, RIDGE, AND PLUMBING VENTS.

Items Requiring Correction	Date Corrected	Date Reinspected
1) GABLE FLASHING ON NW CORNER NOT FASTENED	11/16	11/16 - BATES
2) NEED ADDITIONAL SILICONE CAULK ON EXEC BATH VENT	11/16	11/16 - BATES
3) ONE SLIGHTLY DENTED PANEL - NOT VISIBLE FROM GROUND - OK WITH ARCHITECT IF OK WITH MANUFACTURER - ACME TO CHECK AND RESPOND IN WRITING		

FIGURE 8–7 Project Inspection Report

Subcontractors may have questions regarding some aspects of their scopes of work. A field question procedure should be established to document subcontractor questions and the responses. Many questions can be answered by the project superintendent or project engineer, but others may require information from the project designer. Simple forms, such as the example illustrated in Chapter 13 (Figure 13–1), should be used to expedite the processing of subcontractor field questions. To ensure that all subcontractor questions have been answered, a log similar to the one shown in Figure 13–2 in Chapter 13 is maintained. The project manager should review the subcontractor field question logs periodically to ensure timely responses are provided to subcontractors.

Situations may arise when the scope of work needs to be modified. All such modifications should be documented as subcontract change orders to identify clearly the changes in scope and the impact on the subcontract price. Some changes affect multiple subcontractors, in which case all affected subcontracts must be altered appropriately. Prior to negotiating the cost of a change order, the project manager sends a change order request to the affected subcontractors. An example for the Huna Office Building project is shown in Figure 8–8 on page 108. All change orders should be issued in written form, as illustrated in Figure 8–9 on page 109. A change order register such as the one shown in Figure 8–10 on page 110 should be maintained for each subcontract to document all changes.

Subcontractors submit requests for payment as their work progresses, at the end of each phase of their work, or according to the payment schedule provided in the subcontracts. A sample subcontract payment request is shown in Figure 8–11 on page 111. Once the project engineer approves a payment request, payment should be made to the subcontractor within the timeline established in the subcontract. Most subcontracts contain a provision that the subcontractor will be compensated for the work performed once the owner reimburses the general contractor. Article 8 of the subcontract in Appendix G contains this provision; it states that the subcontractor relies on the credit of the owner, not the general contractor, for payment. Such contracts place significant financial burdens on subcontractors when owners fail to make timely progress payments to general contractors. There are other standard subcontracts that contain a provision that the general contractor will pay the subcontractor for work completed within a reasonable time, whether or not the owner has paid the general contractor for the work. These contracts place the total risk of owner nonpayment on the general contractor. Since the subcontractor has performed its responsibilities under the terms of the subcontract, many people in the construction industry believe payment should be made whether or not the owner has paid the general contractor. Subcontractors should be paid on time to avoid causing them cash flow problems and to ensure their financial health. Before making final payment, the subcontractor should submit a ***final lien release***, similar to the sample shown in Figure 8–12 on page 112.

8.7 SUMMARY

Subcontractors are essential members of the project manager's team; typically, they perform most of the work on a construction project. During the initial work breakdown for a project, the project manager determines which work items are to be subcontracted and which will be included in each subcontract. Based on this subcontract plan, the project manager crafts a specific scope of work for each subcontract. Once the scope of work has been developed, the project manager prepares the terms and conditions of the subcontract or selects a standard subcontract format.

NORTHWEST CONSTRUCTION COMPANY
1242 First Avenue, Cascade, Washington 98202
(206) 239-1422

SUBCONTRACTOR CHANGE ORDER REQUEST

Date: *October 12, 2000*

SCOR No.: *003*

Distribution: *Arctic Mechanical*
Richardson Electric

Attached are the following documents: *Field Question #5, Sketch #6, and Construction Change Directive #2*

Description of Change: *First and second floor systems which pass through both lobbies are to be routed in a chase (to be constructed by Northwest Construction Company) above first floor lobby ceiling.*

Please prepare an estimate and schedule impact for the enclosed. Your response is required to be submitted to the above address, in detail, with all supporting estimating backup, no later than:

Date Due: *October 26, 2000*
Time Due: *Noon*

If a response is not received by the above date and time we will assume that the enclosed has no impact to your scheduled or estimated cost of work and will issue a change modification to your subcontract/purchase order incorporating these documents indicating no impact.

Submitted by: Mary Peterson

File code: *9821/COP #003*

FIGURE 8–8 Subcontractor Change Order Request

NORTHWEST CONSTRUCTION COMPANY
1242 First Avenue, Cascade, Washington 98202
(206) 239-1422

SUBCONTRACT CHANGE ORDER

Change Order Number *001*

Project: *Huna Office Building*

Subcontract: *Richardson Electric*

We agree to make the following change(s) in the subcontract scope of work:

Route conduits from second floor lobby through new first floor lobby pipe chase per Field Question #5 and Construction Change Directive #2.

Change(s) will affect the following plans and/or specifications:

Drawing E 2.1

Subject to the following adjustment to the subcontract value:

Cost of this Change: *$1,150.00*

Previous Subcontract Amount: *$120,000.00*

Revised Subcontract Amount: *$121,150.00*

Revised Completion Date: *No change*

Contractor: NORTHWEST CONSTRUCTION COMPANY

By: ➢ Ted Jones Date *November 7, 2000*
Authorized Signature/Title

Subcontractor: *Richardson Electric*

By: ➢ Rick Richardson Date *November 7, 2000*
Authorized Signature/Title

FIGURE 8–9 Subcontract Change Order

Because subcontractors are so critical to project success, project managers should prequalify them before asking for price quotations. Subcontractors should be selected based on their ability to provide the greatest overall value as members of the project delivery team. Once the subcontractor has been selected, the price is entered on the subcontract, and the agreement is signed both by the project manager and the subcontractor.

NORTHWEST CONSTRUCTION COMPANY
1242 First Avenue, Cascade, Washington 98202
(206) 239-1422

SUBCONTRACT CHANGE ORDER REGISTER

Project: *Huna Office Building*

Subcontractor: *Richardson Electric*

Date Awarded: *September 15, 2000*

Change Order Number	Date of Change Order	Scope of Change Order	Change Order Value	Subcontract Value
			Original Subcontract Value	*$120,000.00*
1	*11/7/00*	*Lobby pipe chase*	*$1,150.00*	*$121,150.00*
2	*2/15/01*	*Exterior lighting*	*$4,200.00*	*$125,350.00*
3	*2/17/01*	*Value engineering*	*<$900.00>*	*$124,450.00*
—	———	*Changes reconciliation*	———	———

FIGURE 8–10 Subcontract Change Order Register

Once the subcontracts are awarded and construction begins, the project manager and the superintendent work together to coordinate the subcontractors' work to ensure the project is completed on time, within budget, and in conformance with contract requirements. The success of the project is dependent on a viable schedule that provides adequate notice to all subcontractors regarding the scheduled start times for their phases of work. Subcontract management includes ensuring quality performance of work, responding to field questions, issuing change orders when needed, and promptly paying subcontractors for accepted work.

SUBCONTRACTOR'S APPLICATION FOR PAYMENT

TO: Northwest Construction Company
FROM: Hi-Gloss Painting

PROJECT: Huna Office Building, 9301 Glacier Highway, Juneau, AK 99801
PAYMENT REQUEST: #1
PERIOD December 1, , 2000, to December 31, , 2000

STATEMENT OF CONTRACT ACCOUNT:

1.	Original Contract Amount	$ 28,000	
2.	Approved Changer Order Nos. NA	$ 0	
3.	Adjusted Contract Amount		$ 28,000
4.	Value of Work Complete to Date: (As per attached breakdown)	$ 14,000	
5.	Value of Approved Change Orders Completed: (As per attached breakdown)	$ 0	
6.	Material Stored on Site: (As per attached breakdown)	$ 0	
7.	Value of Completed Work and Stored Materials		$ 14,000
8.	Net Total to Date		$ 14,000
9.	Less Amount Retained (5%)	($ 700)	
10.	Total Less Retainage		$ 13,300
11.	Total Previously Certified (Deduct)	$ 0	
12.	Amount Due This Request		$ 13,300

CERTIFICATION OF THE SUBCONTRACTOR:

I hereby certify that the work performed and the materials supplied to date, as shown on the above represent the actual value of accomplishment under the terms of the Contract (and all authorized changes thereto) between the undersigned and Northwest Construction Co. relating to the above referenced project.

I also certify that the payments, less applicable retention, have been marked through the period covered by previous payments received from the contractor, to (1) all my subcontractors (sub-contractors) and (2) for all material and labor used in or in connection with the performance of this Contract. I further certify I have complied with Federal, State and local tax laws, including Social Security laws, Unemployment Compensation laws and Worker's Çompensation laws insofar as applicable to the performance of this Contract.

Furthermore, in consideration of the payments received, and upon receipt of the amount of this request, the undersigned does hereby waive, release and relinquish all claim or right of which the undersigned may now have upon the premised above described except for claims or right of lein for contract and/or change order work performed to the extent that payment is being retained or will subsequently become due.

Date December 28, 2000

Hi-Gloss Painting Company
Subcontractor

Subscribed and sworn before me this ________ Day of ________, 19________

By: Mark Jackson
Authorized Signature

Notary Public: ________
My Commission Expires: ________

Title: Owner

Subcontractor's Federal Tax ID No.: 522-32-1101

Subcontractor's State of local license number, if applicable: ________

AGC Document No. 610 - SUBCONTRACTOR'S APPLICATION FOR PAYMENT - 1992

FIGURE 8–11 Subcontract Payment Request
Associated General Contractors of America

FINAL LIEN RELEASE
UPON RECEIPT OF FINAL PAYMENT

Upon receipt by the undersigned of a check from *Northwest Construction Company* in the sum of *$1,200.00* payable to *ATB Asphalt* and when the check has been properly endorsed and paid by the bank upon which it is drawn, this document shall become effective to release any mechanic's lien rights the undersigned has on the project of

Asphalt paving work for Huna Office Building

located at *Juneau, Alaska.*
The undersigned has been paid in full for all labor, services, material and equipment furnished to *Northwest Construction Company.*

Dated: *June 30, 2000*

By: *Randy Jones, President*

FIGURE 8–12 Final Lien Release

8.8 REVIEW QUESTIONS

1. Why do general contractors use subcontractors rather than performing all the work on a project?
2. What risks do general contractors incur by using subcontractors?
3. Why might a project manager require performance and payment bonds from a subcontractor?
4. Why is a termination or suspension provision included in most subcontracts?
5. Why is subcontractor bid shopping considered unethical behavior?
6. Why do subcontractors need reasonable notice regarding the scheduled start times for their phases of work? Why does the superintendent not determine the exact start times for each subcontractor at the beginning of the project?
7. What are mock-ups, and how are they used for project quality control?
8. How are subcontractors' requests for payment processed on a typical project?
9. Why is a subcontractor's ability to finance his or her cash flow requirements on a project of concern to the project manager?
10. What is the difference between a request for quotation and a request for proposal? What type of subcontract is awarded using a request for quotation? What type is awarded using a request for proposal?

8.9 EXERCISES

1. Write a clear scope of work for a subcontract for the site work subcontract for the Huna Office Building project.
2. What are five criteria that you suggest be used to prequalify site work contractors for the Huna Office Building project?
3. What basis do you suggest the project manager use to select the electrical subcontractors for the Huna Office Building project?

8.10 SOURCES OF ADDITIONAL INFORMATION

Barfield, Thomas J. *Mastering Subcontracts: A Reference Guide*. Alexandria, Va.: Subcontractors Education Trust, 1998.

Bartholomew, Stuart H. *Construction Contracting: Business and Legal Principles*. Upper Saddle River, N.J.: Prentice-Hall, Inc., 1998.

Hinze, Jimmie. *Construction Contracts*. New York: McGraw-Hill, Inc., 1993.

Liebing, Ralph W. *Construction Contract Administration*. Upper Saddle River, N.J.: Prentice-Hall, Inc., 1998.

9

Material Management

9.1 INTRODUCTION

Building materials are necessary to complete the project. As discussed in Chapter 8, some materials are furnished by the subcontractors, while others are procured by the general contractor. All materials required for self-performed work must be obtained by the general contractor. The general contractor also may purchase materials requiring special manufacturing or long-lead time for installation by subcontractors. This gives the contractor control of the cost of these items and the ability to influence their delivery times. But the general contractor assumes responsibility for any subcontractor impacts caused by late delivery of contractor-procured materials. Materials should be ordered early in the construction process to minimize the risk of price inflation and to ensure that construction activities are not delayed because of a lack of materials.

Material deliveries should be phased so they arrive on the project site near the time they are needed to support construction activities. Most project sites are not large enough to store all supplies on site at the same time, and ***just-in-time delivery of materials*** prevents congesting the construction site with storage of materials. In addition, stored materials need to be protected against theft, damage, and weather. Damaged supplies do not meet contract specifications and must be replaced at the contractor's expense. Limiting the length of on-site storage minimizes the cost of providing adequate protection.

In fixed-price contracts, owners may choose not to pay contractors for materials stored on the project site but wait until the materials are incorporated into the project. Early delivery of materials on such projects may adversely impact the contractor's cash flow because ***material suppliers*** may request payment before the owner pays the contractor for the materials. On cost-plus contracts, like the one in Appendix D, the cost of materials stored on site is reimbursable.

Major materials are those which require approvals and have a significant lead or delivery time. These include structural steel, reinforcing steel, specialized mechanical or electrical equipment, and some interior finish items. Such materials typically require designer approval before being ordered. The normal procedure is to select the supplier; issue a purchase order; receive ***shop drawings, product data sheets*** and/or product samples; obtain approval of the shop drawings, product data sheets and/or product samples; receive the materials; and store the materials on site until installed. Shop drawings are drawings or diagrams prepared by suppliers to illustrate their products. Product data sheets are used to illustrate performance characteristics of materials described in shop drawings or are submitted as verification that the materials meet contract specifications. Shop drawings, product data, and product samples are known as *submittals*. The submittal process is discussed in Chapter 14. A member of the design team verifies that the supplied shop drawings and product data sheets correctly interpret contract requirements. Material dimensions are the responsibility of the general contractor. Structural steel typically is fabricated by a supplier and erected by a subcontractor. First the fabrication shop drawings are approved, then the supplier cuts the steel elements to the correct dimensions and drills the holes for bolted connections. The steel erection subcontractor submits shop drawings showing the erection sequence. Once these have been approved, the subcontractor can begin erecting the steel. The typical material procurement process is illustrated in Figure 9–1.

Materials are ordered using supply contracts called *purchase orders*. Suppliers provide invoices with the materials at time of delivery, and contractors make payment to suppliers using the invoices as reference documents. Some suppliers offer material discounts if the invoices are paid within a specified time after material delivery. Project managers should analyze their cash flow capabilities and take advantage of these discounts to increase their profit margins. This may mean paying suppliers before being paid by the owner. Small quantities of common hardware and hand tools may be purchased from local vendors using a credit card. A unique credit account generally is established for each project, and expenditure limits are established by company policy.

9.2 SUPPLIER SELECTION

Just as the selection of quality subcontractors is critical to the project manager's ability to delivery a quality project, so is the selection of reliable, quality suppliers. Material requirements for a project are determined from the contract plans and specifications. The plans provide the quantitative requirements, while the specifications provide the qualitative requirements. Some suppliers might only sell materials, while others may manufacture and sell the materials. An example of the former is a lumberyard that sells lumber, masonry materials, and hardware. An example of the latter is the concrete supplier who mixes the concrete and delivers it to the site ready for placement. Suppliers typically are asked for price quotations before purchase orders are executed. They should be selected based on the quality of their products, the quoted prices, and their ability to deliver the materials to meet construction schedule requirements.

9.3 PURCHASE ORDERS

Purchase orders are short form contracts for the manufacture and/or sale of materials and equipment. There are two different types used on construction projects. The first is a ***long-form purchase order***, illustrated in Figure 9–2 on pages 118–21, that is used for major material purchases, typically by the project manager or the construction firm's purchasing department. The second is a ***short-form purchase order***, illustrated in Figure 9–3 on page 122, typically used in the field by superintendents to order materials from local suppliers. When preparing a purchase order, the project manager needs to provide a complete description, the quantity required, the unit price, and total

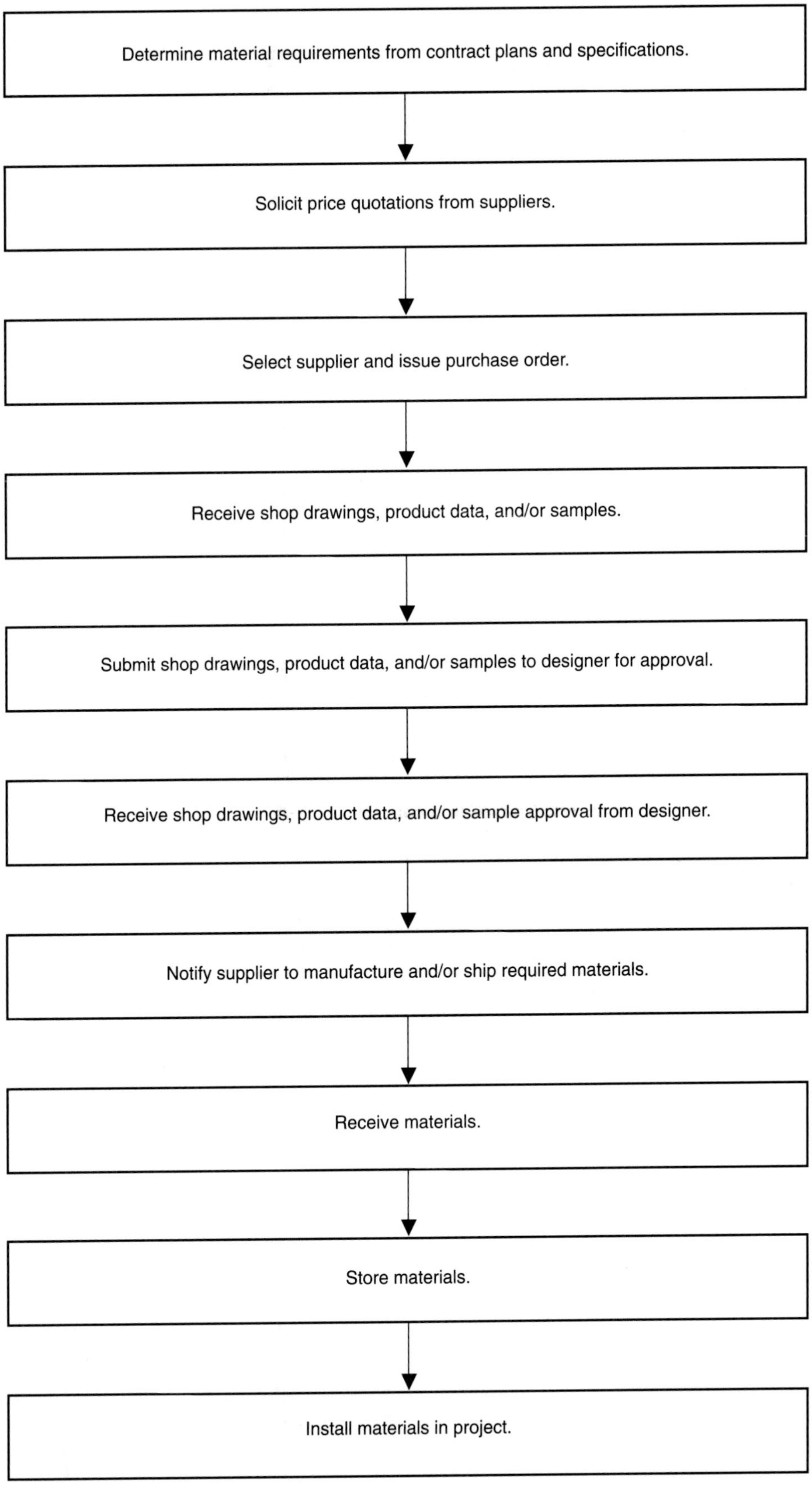

FIGURE 9–1 Material Procurement Process

MATERIAL PURCHASE ORDER CONTRACT

Northwest Construction Company
1242 First Avenue
Cascade, Washington 98202
(206) 239-1422

CONTRACT NO. *9821/08.70*

FOR: *Huna Office Building*

TO *Glacier Glazing, Inc.*
Post Office Box 113
Juneau, Alaska 99801

ORDER NO. *08.70*

QUOTATION

TERMS *30 days*

DATE *September 1, 2000*

SHIP TO: *Job Site:*
9309 Glacier Highway
Juneau, Alaska 99801

VIA *Your trucks*

MARKED FOR

REQUIRED DELIVERY DATE *10/31/00*

Item No.	Quantity	Description	Code or Equip. No.	Unit Price	Amount
		Supply all windows for installation by			
		Northwest Construction Company			
		Excludes all screens		*lump sum*	*$8,000.00*

This contract is not assignable by Seller.
This Purchase Order Contract is subject to the terms and provisions printed on the reverse hereof.

SELLER:

By *Arnie Atkinson*

Title *Project Manager*

BUYER:

Northwest Construction Company

By *Ted Jones*

FIGURE 9–2 Long-Form Purchase Order

PURCHASE ORDER CONTRACT TERMS AND PROVISIONS

I. Where materials (including manufactured articles) are furnished, *not subject* to provisions of applicable plans and/or specifications pertaining to a general construction contract, Seller agrees and warrants as follows:

a. To furnish the materials described in this Purchase Order Contract within the time or times specified therefor and at the price indicated, and to deliver same where required free and clear of any lien, lien right, royalties, or extra charges whatever nature, including taxes of any description not shown on the face hereof.

b. Full or partial payment shall not be construed as acceptance of defective workmanship or improper materials.

II. Where materials (including manufactured articles) are furnished subject to the provisions of applicable plans and/or specifications pertaining to a general condition contract, Seller agrees to comply with all provisions of Section I above and in addition agrees and warrants as follows:

a. That materials furnished comply with all provisions of applicable plans and specifications, that no materials are furnished which may involve a patent infringement action or claim, and that all materials shall be subject to the guarantee provisions of the specifications.

b. That any changes, modification, increase or decrease in the work or quantities as covered in this Purchase Order Contract or in the plans and specifications in connection therewith shall be in writing and approved by Buyer before the same shall be binding on said company.

c. Unless specifically provided otherwise on the face of this Purchase Order Contract, payment for the materials furnished shall be made to Seller when Buyer has received payment from the Owner for same, less 10% of the amount due to be retained by Buyer until the materials are approved in accordance with the requirements of the plans and specifications and final payment has been received from the Owner; provided that Buyer may also withhold payment per paragraph d, following.

d. On request by Buyer, Seller shall provide releases of lien, claims against bonds, claims against retention, or other claims, either by Seller or its suppliers, employees, or other persons who may have claims against the project Owner, the Buyer or sureties on the project. Failing such releases in form and substance reasonably satisfactory to Buyer, the latter may withhold all or part payment hereunder until such liens or claims are released or satisfied.

e. Buyer's receipt of the goods covered by this Purchase Order Contract shall not constitute waiver of any claims for damages due to delay in delivery, defective goods, or goods not in conformity with this Purchase Order Contract. Buyer shall have the right to reject the goods delivered within a reasonable time after delivery and inspection, which shall not be less than ten (10) days.

f. Buyer reserves the right to postpone delivery of goods covered by this Purchase Order Contract for a reasonable time.

g. Deliveries must be made within the time(s) stated on this Purchase Order Contract. Late delivery can cause Buyer to incur substantial extra costs (including liquidated damages for late project completion, added costs of project performance, and other forms of incidental and consequential damages). Because time is of the essence under this Purchase Order Contract, the Seller expressly

ab/17

FIGURE 9–2 Long-Form Purchase Order (*Continued*)

agrees to reimburse Buyer for all additional penalties, damages, and other expenses that may arise from failure to deliver in accordance with the deadline(s) or schedule established in this Purchase Order Contract.

h. If Seller fails to maintain progress consistent with the delivery deadline(s) or schedule established under this Purchase Order Contract, Buyer may, without prejudice to any other legal right, elect (after three days' written notice) to terminate all or part of this Purchase Order Contract. In that event, Buyer may, in addition to any other remedies backcharge or otherwise obtain reimbursement from Seller for the cost of procuring the items ordered in this Purchase Order Contract.

i. Upon termination of the project or contract for which Buyer placed this Purchase Order Contract, Buyer may (upon written notice) terminate this Purchase Order Contract, with Seller's compensation to be equitably adjusted as a change under paragraph o herein.

j. All deliveries to Buyer's jobsite must be accompanied by delivery slips. Signed delivery slips must accompany all invoices as a prerequisite for payment under this Purchase Order Contract.

k. All costs of delivery shall be prepaid by Seller. Seller agrees to protect and hold Buyer harmless against all costs or claims for transportation, freight, express, and other charges incidental to delivery of goods under this Purchase Order Contract.

l. If shop drawings are required, they shall be prepared and submitted timely, as required by Buyer.

m. This Purchase Order Contract is subject to all warranties, express or implied, provided in the Uniform Commercial Code, none of which is waived by Buyer or disclaimed by Seller.

n. Seller agrees to defend and hold harmless from all liens, claims, or assessments arising from purchase, manufacture, or delivery pursuant to this Purchase Order Contract. This applies (without limitation) to all labor costs, material and taxes, provided, however, that Buyer shall be responsible for all sales taxes imposed on this purchase transaction.

o. Buyer reserves the right to make changes, deviations, additions, or deletions to the work herein contracted, and in that event the price shall be equitably adjusted. If such changes have been initiated by the project Owner or other party for whom Buyer entered this Purchase Order Contract, then the change in Seller's price shall be controlled by the change in Buyer's compensation from the third party.

p. With regard to goods delivered under this Purchase Order Contract, Seller agrees to defend and save harmless the Buyer and any other transferee of the goods on the project referenced herein from all liability for patent or trademark infringement, or for injuries to any person, employees and/or property, and from damages by any fire, in any way caused by Seller, its agents, employees, subcontractors or their employees or agents or persons, firms or corporations to whom Seller sublets work, caused by, or incidental to, the execution of work under this Purchase Order Contract, and from all damages, judgments, charges and other related expenses arising or to arise, though any act or omission of any of the said persons. Seller also expressly assumes with respect to the goods to be furnished hereunder, all of the liability imposed on Buyer by the construction contract between Buyer and its project owner or prime contractor. If there are any claims for injuries to persons or property unsettled upon completion of this Purchase Order contract, final settlement between Buyer and Seller may be deferred at Buyer's option until such claims are adjusted or until Seller furnishes indemnity acceptable to Buyer.

FIGURE 9–2 Long-Form Purchase Order (*Continued*)

q. In the event that Seller totally or partially breaches this contract, resulting in litigation or arbitration, Seller agrees to pay Buyer's reasonable attorney's fees.

r. Seller agrees not to assign any portion of the work covered by this Purchase Order Contract without the Buyer's written consent.

s. Any controversy or claim arising out of or relating to this Purchase Order Contract or breach thereof shall be settled by arbitration in accordance with the Construction Industry Arbitration Rules of the American Arbitration Association, and judgment upon award rendered by the arbitrator(s) may be entered in any court having jurisdiction hereof.

FIGURE 9–2 Long-Form Purchase Order (*Continued*)

cost for each item. Extracts from the specifications may be attached to clarify material or performance requirements. An example of a material specification for rough carpentry is shown in Appendix F.

When preparing purchase orders, the project manager or project engineer must decide where the contractor desires to assume ownership of the materials. The alternatives are either the shipping point or the job site. Most materials will be ordered ***free on board*** (***FOB***) job site, which means the price quoted by the supplier includes the transportation to the job site. In this case, the supplier selects the transporting carrier. In some instances, it might be advantageous to order materials FOB shipping point, which means the price quoted by the supplier does not include transportation costs. In this case, the contractor selects the transporting carrier and pays the transportation cost.

Project managers should maintain a purchase order log similar to the one shown in Figure 9–4 on page 123 to manage their procurement activities. Some materials, such as ready-mix concrete, may be purchased on an ***open purchase order***, which sometimes is called a ***blanket purchase order***. The project superintendent simply contacts the supplier providing the mix number, quantity, and required time of delivery. An open purchase order is similar to a unit-price contract. The contractor and supplier agree to a unit price, but the exact quantity to be used is not stated. The cost invoiced to the contractor is the quantity delivered multiplied by the unit price. A superintendent may request deliveries on different dates using the same purchase order. Open purchase orders often contain a not-to-exceed quantity or cost and have an expiration date.

9.4 SCHEDULING MATERIAL DELIVERIES

Project managers should initiate material procurement early in the construction process to ensure that materials are available on site when needed by the construction workers. Special manufactured items and items that must be shipped long distances must be ordered early. The project manager must order materials early to lock in prices and avoid inflation. Adequate time must be allowed for the submittal and review of shop drawings, product data, and product samples. The project manager or project

PURCHASE ORDER

Northwest Construction Company
1242 First Avenue
Cascade, Washington 98202
(206) 239-1422

Purchase Order No.
149

To: JUNEAU LUMBER

Date: SEPT. 2, 2000

Job Name: HUNA OFFICE BUILDING

Attention: JEFF

Job Address: 9309 GLACIER HIGHWAY

Phone No. 907-477-2992

When Required: SEPT. 8, 2000			Ship Via:		
No.	**Quantity**	**Unit**	**Description**	**Unit Price**	**Amount**
1	500	LF	(1 ROLL) SILT FENCE	$250/ROLL	$250.00
2					
3					
4					
5					
6					
7					
				TOTAL	$250.00

Purchase Order Instructions

1. Accept orders only from duly authorized Buyer and obtain a purchase order number at time of purchase.
2. All packages or pieces must show this purchase order number.
3. Do not back order or substitute without prior approval.

1. Render separate invoices for each shipment.
2. Invoices received without purchase order number will be considered incorrect.

Requested By:	Approved By:	Purchased By:
Jim Bates	Jim Bates	Mary Peterson

FIGURE 9–3 Short-Form Purchase Order

NORTHWEST CONSTRUCTION COMPANY
1242 First Avenue, Cascade, Washington 98202
(206) 239-1422

PURCHASE ORDER LOG

Project No.: *9821* Project Name: *Huna Office Building* Project Manager: *Ted Jones*

P.O. No.	Supplier	Materials Delivered	Date Sent	Date Materials Due	Date Materials Received	Date Supplier Paid
145	Juneau Lumber	Surveying and flagging stakes	8/15/00	8/17/00	8/17/00	9/1/00
146	Juneau Lumber	2x4s and plywood	8/20/00	8/20/00	8/21/00	9/1/00
147	Arctic Mechanical	Temporary drain pipe	8/20/00	8/25/00	8/24/00	9/1/00
148	Acme Roofing	Miscellaneous flashing and reflectors	8/27/00	8/27/00	8/27/00	9/1/00
149	Juneau Lumber	Silt fence	9/2/00	9/9/00		
150	Alaska Redi-Mix	1 load quarry spalls				

FIGURE 9–4 Purchase Order Log

engineer may prepare the purchase orders for major materials, or they may be prepared by the construction firm's purchasing department. In either case, the project manager or project engineer must establish the qualitative requirements, quantities, and required delivery dates. Supplier submittals must be reviewed by the project manager or project engineer to ascertain that materials are adequately described in the submitted documents and that they conform to contract requirements. Poor submittals often are rejected by the designer and must be resubmitted, which may result in delayed deliveries and late project completion. Required delivery dates are established based on material need dates derived from the project schedule. Deliveries should be scheduled so that the supplies arrive on site at the time they are needed for installation on the project. This just-in-time approach to material delivery minimizes the need for material storage on the project site. Materials must be ordered early enough to allow normal transportation modes to be used. Expedited transportation, such as air freight, is costly and may not have been considered when developing a bid or proposing a guaranteed maximum price.

Project managers or project engineers should ***expedite*** or actively monitor major purchases to ensure compliance with purchase order requirements. An expediting log similar to the one shown in Figure 14–3 in Chapter 14 may be used for this purpose.

9.5 MATERIAL MANAGEMENT AT PROJECT SITE

Construction productivity is greatly influenced by the organization of the project site and the flow of equipment, labor, and materials through the site. Site planning is discussed in the next chapter, but here we will examine some issues related to material management on the project site. Material storage sites should be selected where they have the least impact on the efficient construction of the project. This means they typically are not adjacent to the project. In determining the size and location of storage areas, the project manager and the superintendent must anticipate the material requirements of the entire project, including those provided by the subcontractors. Supplies should be stored as near as possible to the location of installation without adversely impacting the productivity of the workforce. Storage areas should be organized so materials are only moved once on the project site—from the storage location to the place of installation. Materials should be stored so they are accessible when needed. Delivery routes should be selected to avoid impacting construction operations, and materials procured by the general contractor should be inspected upon delivery to ensure that the correct items and quantities were delivered. This is an important part of an active quality management program that is discussed in Chapter 17. Also, materials should be properly protected from the weather until installed. Pallets or dunnage typically are placed under stored materials to keep them off the ground. Items damaged in storage may not be accepted by the owner and must be replaced at the contractor's cost.

9.6 SUMMARY

Effective material management is essential to the timely completion of the construction project. Construction materials must be procured in time to meet project schedule requirements. Most of them may be provided by subcontractors, but some typically are obtained by the general contractor. The project manager decides which materials the contractor will procure and initiates the procurement process. Suppliers are selected based on their ability to provide quality materials at a reasonable price and in the time frames needed to meet schedule requirements. Long-form purchase orders are used by the project manager to purchase major materials, whereas short-form purchase orders are used in the field to request materials from local suppliers. Required delivery dates must meet project schedule requirements. Effective material management on the project site is essential for efficient construction operations. Supplies should be handled only once on the project site and stored near the point of installation in an area that does not adversely impact productivity on the project.

9.7 REVIEW QUESTIONS

1. Why is effective material management an essential project management function?
2. What type of construction materials would a general contractor typically purchase on a long-form purchase order on a project involving the construction of a four-story structural steel office building?
3. Why are submittals (i.e. shop drawings, product data, or product samples) required from suppliers? Who reviews these submittals?
4. Why are submittal approvals obtained before the supplier ships the required materials?
5. How would you determine the required delivery date for the lumber needed to construct the exterior walls for the Huna Office Building project?
6. What criteria should a project manager use when selecting a material supplier for a project?
7. How does the organization of a job site affect material management efficiency on a construction project?
8. What is a purchase order? What are its main components? Why should a project manager keep a purchase order log?
9. Why might a project manager choose to pay suppliers for materials received before being paid by the project owner?
10. What criteria should the project manager use in selecting material storage areas on a construction work site?

9.8 EXERCISES

1. Prepare a long-form purchase order for the procurement of 600 pounds of #8 reinforcing steel.
2. Prepare a short-form purchase order for the procurement of 60 pounds of 16d nails and 100 board feet of 2 × 8 lumber.

9.9 SOURCES OF ADDITIONAL INFORMATION

Barrie, Donald S., and Boyd S. Paulson. *Professional Construction Management*. 3d ed. New York: McGraw-Hill, Inc., 1992.

Civitello, Andrew M., Jr. *Construction Operations Manual of Policies and Procedures*. 3d ed. New York: McGraw-Hill, Inc., 2000.

Halpin, Daniel W., and Ronald W. Woodhead. *Construction Management.* 2d ed. New York: John Wiley and Sons, Inc., 1998.

Levy, Sidney M. *Project Management in Construction.* 3d ed. New York: McGraw-Hill, Inc., 2000.

Mincks, William R., and Hal Johnston. *Construction Jobsite Management.* Albany, N.Y.: Delmar Publishers, 1998.

Stukhart, George. *Construction Materials Management.* New York: Marcel Dekker, Inc., 1995.

10

Project Start-Up

10.1 INTRODUCTION

Once the project manager has been notified that the project has been won, he or she must plan project start-up activities. Efficient project start-up activities are dependent on a good start-up plan. Start-up activities involve establishment and organization of the project office and staff, construction site layout, and mobilization of the job site. The project manager selects the project management team and involves them in start-up planning. Contract files, project office administrative procedures, and correspondence management systems are established. These will be discussed in Chapter 11. Award of subcontracts, procurement of materials, and actual mobilization must wait until the ***notice to proceed*** is received, but the planning should be completed prior to its receipt so that implementation can begin immediately upon receipt of the notice. The actual mobilization of the job site is the responsibility of the project superintendent.

Both the project manager and the superintendent participate in the ***preconstruction conference***. This meeting is conducted either by the owner or the designer to introduce project participants and to discuss project issues and management procedures. Section 01200 of the specifications in Appendix F discusses the preconstruction conference for the Huna Office Building project. The notice to proceed authorizes the contractor to start work on the project and often is issued at the end of the preconstruction conference. An example notice to proceed is shown in Figure 10–1.

Once the notice to proceed has been received, the project manager should ***buy out*** the project by awarding subcontracts and ordering needed materials and equipment. The notice to proceed often is provided at the preconstruction conference along with verification of owner financing and needed permits. Project-specific quality control (see Chapter 17) and safety plans (see Chapter 18) need to be finalized, and if required by contract, submitted to the owner or owner's representative. A schedule of values (see Chapter 15) and a ***schedule of submittals*** (see Chapter 14) also are prepared and submitted to the owner or the owner's representative for approval.

NOTICE TO PROCEED

To: *Northwest Construction Company* **Date:** *August 16, 2000*
1242 First Avenue
Cascade, Washington 98202

Project Name: *Huna Office Building*

You are hereby notified to commence WORK in accordance with subject contract dated *August 15, 2000* on *August 17,2000* and you are to complete the WORK within *165* consecutive work days thereafter. The date for completion of all WORK is therefore *April 9, 2001*.

By *Robert Smith*
Title: *Chairman*
Company: *Huna Totem Corporation*

ACCEPTANCE OF NOTICE

Receipt of the above NOTICE TO PROCEED is hereby acknowledged by *Northwest Construction Company* this the *seventeenth* day of *August, 2000*.

By *Sam Peters*
Title: *Vice President*
Company: *Northwest Construction Company*

FIGURE 10–1 Notice to Proceed

10.2 JOB SITE PLANNING

Efficient job site organization is essential for a productive construction project. The job site layout affects the cost of material handling, labor, and the use of major equipment by the general contractor and the subcontractors. A well-organized site has a positive effect on the productivity and safety of the entire project workforce. The job site layout plan should identify locations for temporary facilities, as well as material movement, storage, and handling equipment. Although developed by the superintendent, it should consider the needs and requirements of all subcontractors working on site. The site plan should:

- Show existing conditions, such as adjacent buildings, utility lines, and streets.
- Indicate the planned locations for all temporary facilities such as fences and gates, trailers, temporary utilities, sanitary facilities, erosion control, and drainage.

- Indicate areas for material handling, material storage, equipment storage, worker and visitor parking, and material handling equipment.

In developing the site plan, the superintendent should consider site constraints, equipment constraints, job site productivity, material handling, and safety. A good site plan should:

- Eliminate any bottlenecks to equipment movement on site.
- Locate material storage areas near where the materials are to be used.
- Locate staging areas where they are accessible to material handling equipment, such as cranes.
- Place project office near the main entrance for visitor control.
- Provide turnaround areas for haul vehicles.
- Minimize traffic impact on adjacent streets.

A site plan[1] for the Huna Office Building project is shown in Figure 10–2.

Separate project gates should be provided for union and non-union workers; these gates will be used by both the contractor's and subcontractors' workforces, as well as by suppliers making material deliveries. In the event of a labor dispute, only the union gate may be picketed. This practice minimizes the potential for costly job stoppages caused by labor disputes and is allowed under the National Labor Relations Act. To avoid confusion, each gate must be labeled conspicuously with a sign similar to the one illustrated in Figure 10–3 on page 131, and each subcontractor and supplier must be notified in writing which gate to use.

10.3 MOBILIZATION

The actual mobilization and move onto the job site is the superintendent's responsibility. The project office is established and temporary utilities (i.e. electricity, water, sewer, and telephone) are installed. Site access is secured with adequate fencing, and gates are installed to provide needed site access for workers and material delivery. Erosion control measures are installed to keep soil-laden water from leaving the project site and entering streams or wetlands. A project sign is installed at a visible location on the project site. Mobilization occurs soon after receipt of the notice to proceed to demonstrate the project manager's commitment to starting the project.

Mobilization for the project manager involves organizing the project team and setting up the project files, control systems, and project logs. A ***start-up checklist*** similar to the one shown in Figure 10–4 on page 132 will help the project manager ensure that all needed tasks are completed. The schedule of values is discussed in Chapter 15, the ***change order proposal log*** in Chapter 19, the ***field question log*** in Chapter 12, and the submittal and expediting logs in Chapter 14. The filing system and project files are important tools of the project manager, so they must be organized in a logical sequence and clearly identified. The test of a good filing system is the ease with which needed records can be retrieved. Project files will be discussed in Chapter 11. The project manager also ensures that all contractually required initial documentation is submitted to the owner. At a minimum, this will include a schedule of values and a project schedule. It also may include a subcontracting plan, a quality control plan, and a safety plan.

[1] This is a great proposal/interview/marketing tool. It shows the owner that the contractor has thought through the project—a personal touch. It may make a difference on a close award decision.

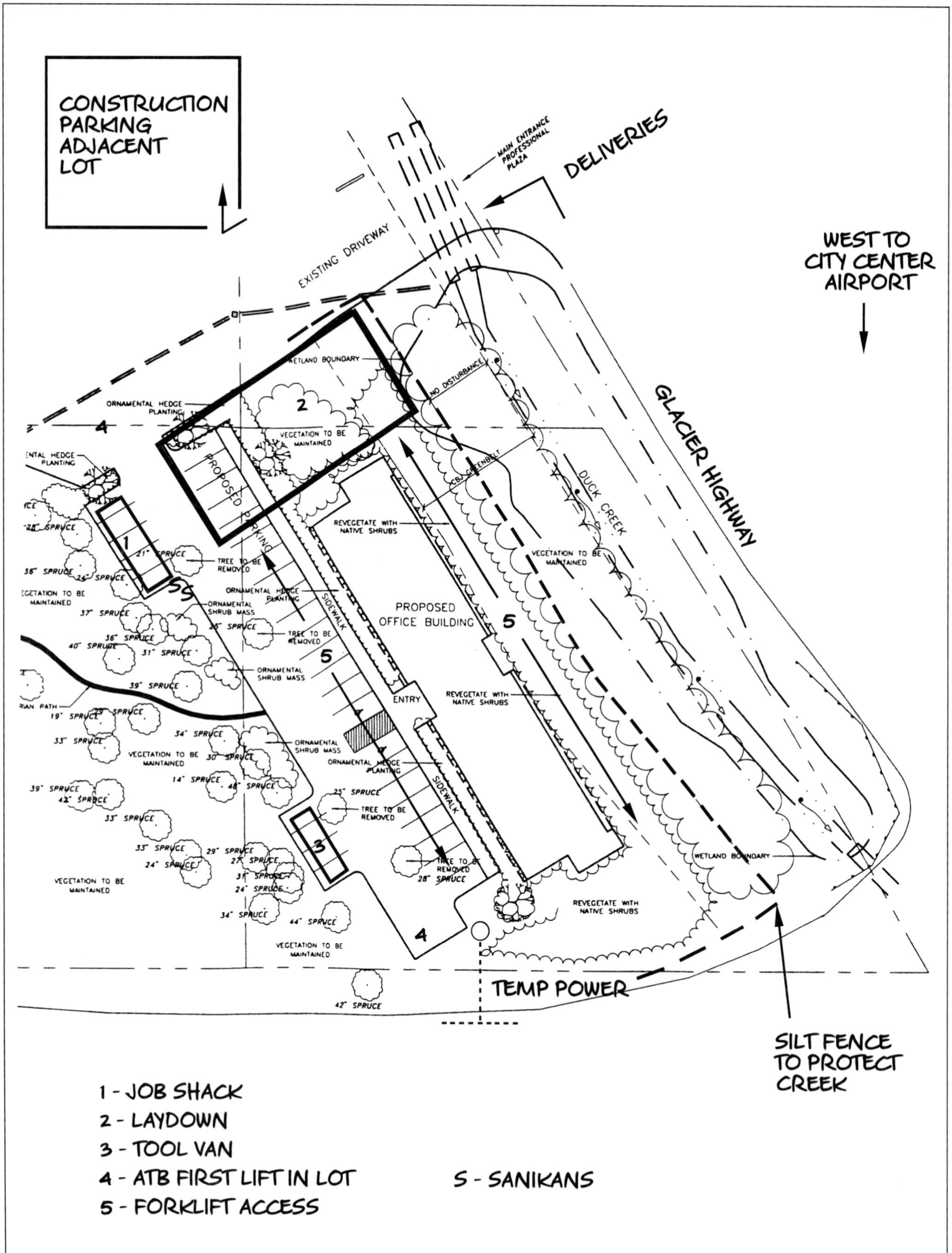

FIGURE 10–2 Project Site Plan

FIGURE 10–3
Project Gate Sign

THIS GATE RESERVED EXCLUSIVELY FOR THE EMPLOYEES, AGENTS, SUBCONTRACTORS, AND SUPPLIERS OF:

Richardson Electric, Inc.

Acme Roofing Company

Smith Fencing Company

Hi Gloss Painting Contractors

All other persons <u>must</u> use the gate located on 15th Avenue on the east side of the project.

A ***start-up log*** such as the one shown in Figure 10–5 on page 133 is a useful tool for managing start-up activities relating to subcontractors and suppliers. The project manager should require a ***certificate of insurance*** from each subcontractor before allowing her or him to start work and provide one to the owner, thus ensuring that all parties working on the project have required coverage. A typical certificate of insurance is shown in Figure 10–6 on page 134.

The general contractor typically is required to demonstrate proof of liability insurance and name the owner as an additional insured. This protects both the owner and the general contractor from financial loss due to damage to third-party property or injury to third parties. Builder's risk insurance protects the project under construction by covering the cost of damage due to fire or severe storms. This insurance is purchased either by the owner or by the general contractor. Whoever purchases the insurance needs to ascertain that the policy regards the other party as an additional named insured. Workers' compensation insurance is no-fault insurance that covers the cost due to injury or death of an employee on the project site. Such insurance is required by law and may be obtained from an insurance company, or if the state has a monopoly it must be purchased from the appropriate state fund. Workers' compensation insurance is discussed in more detail in Chapter 18. Insurance requirements are contained in Article 11 of the AIA General Conditions in Appendix E.

10.4 INITIAL SUBMITTALS

The technical specifications of the construction contract may require that specific shop drawings, product data sheets, or samples be submitted to the designers for review and approval. These are called *submittals* and are used by design professionals to ensure correct materials are used on the project. They were discussed as part of the material purchasing process in Chapter 9, and Article 3.12 of the AIA General Conditions in Appendix E also addresses submittal requirements.

Shop drawings are produced by the general contractor, subcontractors, or suppliers to show construction details not shown on the contract drawings. They typically are required for reinforcing steel, precast concrete, structural steel, duct work, electrical equipment, fire protection systems, millwork, casework, metal doors, curtain walls, and manufactured roofs. Product data sheet submittals generally are manufacturers' product information describing model or type, performance characteristics, and physical characteristics. Samples are physical parts of specified products. A detailed

NORTHWEST CONSTRUCTION COMPANY
1242 First Avenue, Cascade, Washington 98202
(206) 239-1422

PROJECT START-UP CHECKLIST

Project No.: *9821* Project Name: *Huna Office Building*

Project Manager: *Ted Jones*

	Scheduled Completion	Date Completed
Cost codes set up	*9/1*	*9/1*
Work packages set up	*9/1*	*9/15*
Buyout complete	*9/1*	
Draft contract complete	*8/15*	*8/15*
Certificate of insurance submitted to owner	*8/15*	*8/15*
Subcontracting plan submitted to owner	*9/1*	*9/1*
Safety plan submitted to owner	*8/15*	*8/17*
Quality control plan submitted to owner	*8/15*	*9/1*
Subcontracts drafted	*9/15*	
Subcontracts awarded	*9/30*	
Subcontractor insurance certificates received	*9/30*	
Subcontractor safety manuals received	*9/30*	
Subcontractor preconstruction meeting conducted	*9/30*	
Building permit in hand	*8/15*	*8/15*
Construction schedule submitted to owner	*8/15*	*8/15*
Schedule of values submitted to owner	*8/15*	*8/15*
Telephone list completed	*9/15*	*9/7*
Change order proposal log established	*9/15*	
Purchase order log established	*9/15*	*9/10*
Field question log established	*9/15*	*9/1*
Expediting log established	*9/15*	*9/1*

FIGURE 10–4 Project Start-Up Checklist

NORTHWEST CONSTRUCTION COMPANY
1242 First Avenue, Cascade, Washington 98202
(206) 239-1422

PROJECT START-UP LOG

Project No.: *9821* Project Name: *Huna Office Building* Project Manager: *Ted Jones*

Code	Category	Subcontractor/Supplier	Letter of Intent	Rough Sub/P.O.	Final Sub/P.O. Sent	Final Sub/P.O. Rec.	Insur. Cert. Rec.	Insur. Expir. Date	Safety Plan Rec.
	Temp Fence	*Smith Fencing*	—	—	*8/17/00*	—	*NA*	*NA*	*NA*
02200	*Struct/Mass Excavation*	*Earth Enterprises*	—	*8/17/00*	*8/18/00*	*8/21/00*	*8/18/00*	*12/31/00*	*8/18/00*
02600	*Asphalt*	*ATB Asphalt*	*8/21/00*	*8/28/00*	*8/29/00*				
03200	*Rebar Supply*	*Steel Fabrication*	*8/21/00*	*8/28/00*	*8/29/00*		*NA*	*NA*	*NA*
03300	*Concrete*	*Juneau Redi Mix*	—	*8/28/00*	*8/29/00*	*8/30/00*	*NA*	*NA*	*NA*
15000	*Plumbing*	*Arctic Mechanical*	*8/21/00*	*8/25/00*			*8/30/00*	*12/31/00*	
16000	*Electrical*	*Richardson Electric*	*8/21/00*	*8/25/00*					

FIGURE 10–5 Project Start-Up Log

CERTIFICATE OF INSURANCE

Producer (Insurance Broker) *ACME Insurance Agency*	THIS CERTIFICATE IS ISSUED AS A MATTER OF INFORMATION ONLY AND CONFERS NO RIGHTS UPON THE CERTIFICATE HOLDER. THIS CERTIFICATE DOES NOT AMMEND, EXTEND OR ALTER THE COVERAGE AFFORDED BY THE POLICIES BELOW.

Insured

Glacier Glazing

COMPANIES AFFORDING COVERAGE

	INSURANCE COMPANY	BEST RATING
Company Letter A	*National Insurance*	*AAA*
Company Letter B	*National Insurance*	*AAA*
Company Letter C	*National Insurance*	*AAA*
Company Letter D		

COVERAGES

THIS IS TO CERTIFY THAT THE INSURANCE POLICIES LISTED BELOW HAVE BEEN ISSUED TO THE INSURED NAMED ABOVE FOR THE POLICY PERIOD INDICATED. NOTHWITHSTANDING ANY REQUIREMENT, TERM, OR CONDITION OF ANY CONTRACT OR OTHER DOCUMENT WITH RESPECT TO WHICH THIS CERTIFICATE MAY BE ISSUED OR MAY PERTAIN, THE INSURANCE AFFORDED BY THE POLICIES DESCRIBED BELOW IS SUBJECT TO ALL THE TERMS, EXCLUSIONS, AND CONDITIONS OF SUCH POLICIES. LIMITS MAY HAVE BEEN REDUCED BY PAID CLAIMS.

Co. Ltr.	Type of Insurance	Policy Number	Policy Effective Date (M/D/Y)	Policy Expiration Date (M/D/Y)	Limits
A	**General Liability** X Commercial General Liability _ _	*27ABC649*	*10/1/00*	*9/30/01*	General Aggregate *$1,000,000* Products/Comp Ops Agg *$1,000,000* Pers. & Adv. Injury *$1,000,000* Each Occurrence *$1,000,000* Fire Damage (any one fire) *$50,000* Med. Expenses (any one person) *$10,000*
B	**Automobile Liability** X Any Automobile _	*27ABC659*	*10/1/00*	*9/30/01*	Combined Single Limit *$1,000,000* Bodily Injury (per person) *$500,000* Bodily Injury (per accident) *$1,000,000* Property Damage *$500,000*
C	**Excess Liability** X Umbrella Form _	*27ABC789*	*10/1/00*	*9/30/01*	Each Occurrence *$5,000,000* Aggregate *$7,500,000*
D	**Workers' Compensation**				Each Accident $ Disease Policy Limit $ Disease (each employee) $

PROJECT NAME OR ALL OPERATIONS:

Northwest Construction Company is an additional insured per attached endorsement. The liability insurance referred to in this certificate is primary and non-contributory to any insurance carried by *Glacier Glazing* per attached endorsement.

CERTIFICATE HOLDER	**CANCELLATION**
Northwest Construction Company	SHOULD ANY OF THE ABOVE DESCRIBED POLICIES BE CANCELED BEFORE THE EXPIRATION DATE LISTED, THE ISSUING COMPANY WILL PROVIDE 7 DAYS WRITTEN NOTICE TO CERTIFICATE HOLDER NAMED TO LEFT. **AUTHORIZED REPRESENTATIVE** *Bill Brown*

FIGURE 10–6 Subcontractor Certificate of Insurance

discussion of submittals and the submittal process is contained in Chapter 14. Section 01300 of the specifications in Appendix F contain the procedures used on the Huna Office Building project.

The following is an example specification requirement for manufactured roof panels for the Huna Office Building project:

> Submittals: In addition to product data, submit shop drawings, installation instructions, color samples, and general recommendations, as applicable to materials and finishes for each component and for total panel assemblies.

To manage the submittal review and approval process, the project manager often is required by contract to prepare a schedule of all submittals required by the contract specifications. Submittals need to be turned in and approved before the products are installed on the project. If products are needed for early phases of the project, the submittals should be considered part of project start-up. This provides time for the designers to approve them and for the materials to be delivered to the project site without delaying scheduled activities. Proper management of the submittal process is critical to the quality and schedule of the project. Late submittals often lead to late delivery of materials and late completion of scheduled elements of work.

10.5 PROJECT BUYOUT

Project buyout is awarding the subcontracts and procuring materials being furnished by the general contractor and comparing the actual costs to the budgeted costs. This helps determine the status of the project with respect to the contractor's budget. A ***buyout log*** such as the one illustrated in Figure 10–7 can be used to buy out the project. The major unknown variable is the labor cost for self-performed work. This must be monitored weekly to track actual expenditures versus budgeted costs, as will be discussed in Chapter 16. Some project managers may choose to use an electronic spreadsheet, such as Microsoft Excel, to compare buyout costs with budgeted costs.

As was discussed in Chapter 8, subcontractors should be selected based on the value they contribute to the project team. Selection solely on price often leads to problems with quality and timely execution. Prior to being invited to submit proposals, the specialty contractors should be prequalified as recommended in Chapter 8. A subcontractor bid analysis form, similar to the one illustrated in Chapter 4 (see Figure 4–14), can be used to assist in subcontractor selection. The project manager wants to ensure that the intended scope of work is included in the price quotation and uses an analysis form to compare all proposals for each scope of work. Prior to selecting the specialty contractor for each subcontract, the project manager should conduct pre-award meetings with the best-value firms. The best-value firms are those who propose reasonable prices, have experienced craftspeople, are in sound financial condition, have excellent safety records, and have reputations for high quality work. The project manager meets with one specialty contractor at a time to:

- Review the drawings and specifications to ensure the correct scope of work was considered in preparing the proposal.
- Review any exclusions listed on the specialty contractor's proposal.
- Discuss any questions submitted with the proposal.
- Discuss the size of the contractor's proposed workforce and schedule.

Based on the results of the pre-award meetings and annotated subcontractor proposal analysis forms, subcontractors are selected for all scopes of work that will not be performed by the general contractor's workforce. Each subcontract value is then entered in the project buyout log shown in Figure 10–7.

NORTHWEST CONSTRUCTION COMPANY

1242 First Avenue, Cascade, Washington 98202
(206) 239-1422

PROJECT BUYOUT LOG

Project No.: *9821* Project Name: *Huna Office Building* Project Manager: *Ted Jones*

Spec/Code	Description	Budget	Buyout	Variance	Date	Subcontractor/ Supplier	Comment
02200	*Mass Excavation*	*127,200*	*124,000*	*3,200*	*8/15/00*	*Earth Enterprises*	
03200	*Reinforcement Steel*	*22,000*	*23,565*	*<1,565>*	*8/16/00*	*Steel Fabrication*	*Quantity increase*
07411	*Metal Roof*	*75,000*	*59,000*	*16,000*	*8/16/00*	*Acme*	
09680	*Carpet*		*22,950*		*8/20/00*	*Soft Touch*	*Split package between*
09652	*Vinyl Tile*		*17,100*		*8/20/00*	*United*	*two subcontractors*
	Total	*50,000*	*40,050*	*9,950*			
15000	*Mechanical*	*145,000*				*Arctic Mechanical*	*Combine packages*
15400	*Plumbing*	*75,000*				*Arctic Mechanical*	*and award to one*
15900	*Controls*	*22,000*				*Arctic Mechanical*	*subcontractor*
	Total	*242,000*	*258,000*	*<16,000>*	*8/17/00*		

FIGURE 10–7 Project Buyout Log

Site Clearing and Grading for the Huna Office Building

10.6 THREE-WEEK SCHEDULES

While project schedules, such as those discussed in Chapter 5, are developed for overall project control, ***short-interval schedules*** generally are used by the superintendent to manage the day-to-day activities on the project. These are developed each week throughout the duration of the project. Three-week schedules typically provide sufficient information for managing the project. The initial three-week schedule must be prepared during project start-up to schedule the contractor's and subcontractors' workforces to minimize interference and smoothly plan the flow of work. The initial three-week schedule for the Huna Office Building project is shown in Figure 10–8.

10.7 SUMMARY

The project manager and the superintendent are responsible for planning project start-up and mobilizing the job site. This involves planning the job site, organizing the project office, and physically mobilizing on site. The organization of the job site has a significant impact on the productivity of the entire workforce. The site layout plan should identify locations for temporary facilities, material movement, material storage, and material handling equipment. The project manager mobilizes by organizing the project team and establishing the project files, control systems, and project logs. Initial submittals must be prepared and submitted for review so construction will not be delayed by lack of materials. The project manager buys out the project by awarding subcontracts and purchase orders. An initial short-interval schedule is prepared to schedule the trades needed to initiate construction.

SHORT TERM INTERVAL SCHEDULE

NORTHWEST CONSTRUCTION COMPANY

Project: *Huna Office Building*

Superintendent: *Jim Bates*

Date: AUG. 15, 2000

Sheet No. 1 of 1

AUGUST 2000

NO.	ACTIVITY DESCRIPTION			14	15	16	17	18			21	22	23	24	25			28	29	30	31	9/1	COMMENTS
1	NOTICE TO PROCEED	X	X				⊢⊣		X	X						X	X						
2	MOVE TRAILER TO LOT	X	X				⊢⊣		X	X						X	X						
3	INSTALL SILT FENCE	X	X					⊢	X	X	—	⊣				X	X						
4	SURVEY CORNERS	X	X					⊢⊣	X	X						X	X						
5	LOCATE UTILITIES	X	X						X	X	⊢⊣					X	X						
6	BRING-IN TEMP PHONES	X	X						X	X				⊢	⊣	X	X						
7	BRING-IN TEMP POWER	X	X						X	X				⊢	⊣	X	X						
8	CLEAR AND GRUB SITE	X	X						X	X	⊢⊣					X	X						
9	MASS EXCAVATION	X	X						X	X		⊢	—	—	—	X	X	—	—	—	—	→	→ 9/5
10	INSPECTOR APPROVE IMPORT	X	X						X	X	⊢	—	—	—	—	X	X	⊣					
11		X	X						X	X						X	X						
12		X	X						X	X						X	X						
13		X	X						X	X						X	X						
14		X	X						X	X						X	X						
15		X	X						X	X						X	X						
16		X	X						X	X						X	X						
17		X	X						X	X						X	X						
18		X	X						X	X						X	X						
19		X	X						X	X						X	X						
20		X	X						X	X						X	X						
21		X	X						X	X						X	X						
22		X	X						X	X						X	X						
23		X	X						X	X						X	X						

FIGURE 10–8 Initial Three-Week Schedule for Huna Office Building Project

10.8 REVIEW QUESTIONS

1. Why does the project manager not initiate project start-up activities prior to receipt of the notice to proceed?
2. What are three factors that should be considered when planning the organization of a job site?
3. What type of information should be shown on a job site layout plan?
4. Why are two entrance gates sometimes required?
5. What are the superintendent's responsibilities during job site mobilization?
6. What are the project manager's responsibilities during job site mobilization?
7. What are certificates of insurance, and why are they used?
8. What is workers' compensation insurance?
9. What are submittals, and how do they impact the construction schedule?
10. What is meant by project buyout?

10.9 EXERCISES

1. Draw a site plan for a construction site involving the construction of a three-story motel.
2. Prepare a start-up checklist for the project superintendent on the Huna Office Building project.
3. Prepare a mobilization schedule for the superintendent on the Huna Office Building project.

10.10 SOURCES OF ADDITIONAL INFORMATION

Civitello, Andrew M., Jr. *Construction Operations Manual of Policies & Procedures.* 3d ed. New York: McGraw-Hill, 2000.

Levy, Sidney M. *Project Management in Construction.* 3d ed. New York: McGraw-Hill, Inc., 1999.

Mincks, William R., and Hal Johnston. *Construction Jobsite Management.* Albany, N.Y.: Delmar Publishing, 1998.

11

Document and Record Keeping

11.1 INTRODUCTION

The physical move onto the job site and beginning construction work are the responsibility of the superintendent. The project manager mobilizes in a different fashion. Although on larger projects, he or she also will move into the job office or trailer. The project manager's mobilization responsibilities are focused primarily on starting the paper flow. This includes setting up the document systems and logs, employing subcontractors, and staffing the site management team. While previous chapters have discussed the project manager's contractual start-up responsibilities, this chapter contains a description of his or her document- and record-keeping responsibilities. In this chapter, we will discuss manual documents and record keeping. Use of project management software for these functions is discussed in Chapter 23. Safety documentation and record keeping are discussed in Chapter 18.

11.2 PROJECT FILES

The project ***filing system*** and the files are important tools for the project manager. Files, properly prepared, are indispensable for managing the project; they are not just storage locations. The key to a good filing system that allows easy retrieval is first that it has a logical organization and second that documents are filed properly. All the information on a particular subject or involving a specific subcontractor should be placed in the appropriate file. This includes documents such as submittals, letters, change orders, and telephone conversations. The file should be kept in chronological order with the most current information on top. One filing method that has been used successfully by project managers is illustrated in Figure 11–1. All contractual

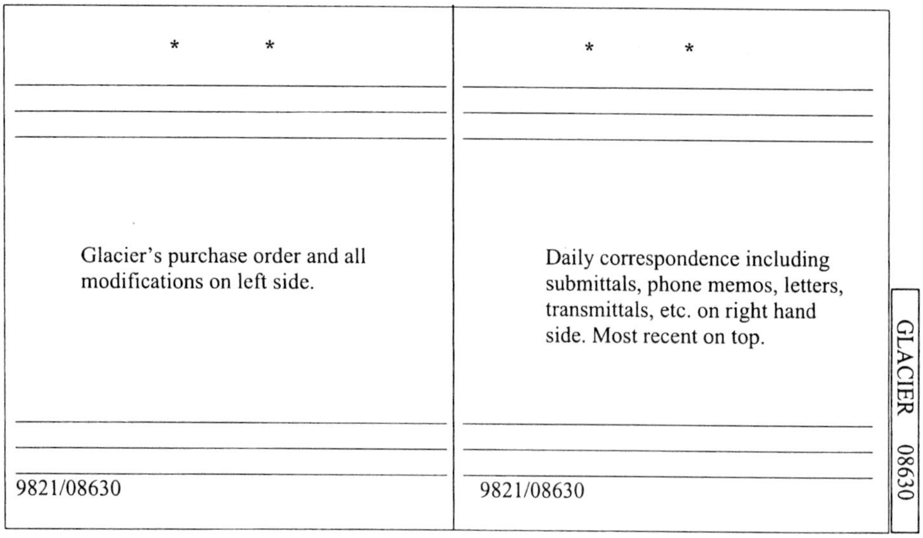

FIGURE 11–1 File Folder for Glacier Glazing

information for a particular supplier or subcontractor is placed on the left side of a file folder with the most recent document on top; all other correspondence is placed on the right side, once again with the most recent on top.

The filing system and the file codes to be used should be set up early in the job. It is not necessary to set up job files during the bidding process. However, as soon as the project manager is notified of a successful bid, the file system should be established. The files may be set up by the project manager or a designee, such as the project engineer. The project clerk may be the one to maintain and file project information during the course of the job, but the project manager or the project engineer should develop the filing system.

The file coding system should be either alpha or numeric. Often subcontractors' codes correlate with their CSI sections of the contract specifications. The important lessons here are that a coding system must be established and that this system should be used consistently throughout the construction firm. It is recommended that the codes assigned to estimate line items match those in the filing system, on the contracts, and on the invoices. An example of a portion of a file log for the Huna Office Building project is shown in Figure 11–2.

Because files are used as a resource, they need to be located where the project manager can have ready access. If the project management team is working on a medium to large project, say greater than $10 million dollars, it is likely that the team is physically located at the site, and the files should be at the site also. One exception to this is the original contract documents. These should be located in fireproof files and safely secured in the construction firm's corporate office.

The file cabinets can become filled with numerous duplicate copies. To avoid creating unnecessary duplicate copies of correspondence, a ***routing stamp*** or ***reading file*** should be used. A routing stamp, such as the one shown in Figure 11–3, is an inexpensive way to ensure and verify that all individuals who need to see a document do so. After all parties have seen and initialed it, the document can be filed. One of the problems with this system is that the document may take a long time to be routed completely around the office and may not be filed for some time. An alternate system is to file the original document and make one copy for inclusion in a reading file. The reading file includes all incoming and outgoing correspondence over a given time period, say one week. The routing stamp can also be utilized to verify that all relevant parties have reviewed the week's documents by stamping the outside cover of the reading file.

NORTHWEST CONSTRUCTION COMPANY
1242 First Avenue, Cascade, Washington 98202
(206) 239-1422

HUNA PROJECT FILE LOG
JOB NO. 9821

CODE	DESCRIPTION	COMPANY
AC	Architect correspondence	JYL
DAY	Daily diaries	NWCC
GC	General correspondence	
PMT	Permits and city correspondence	Juneau
02200	Mass excavation and import subcontractor	Earth Enterprises
02600	Asphalt paving subcontractor	ATB Asphalt
03200	Reinforcing steel supply	Steel Fabrication
03300	Concrete supply	Juneau Redi Mix
06100	Rough carpentry supply	Juneau Lumber
07411	Roofing subcontractor	Acme
08630	Glazing supplier	Glacier
09652	Tile and vinyl subcontractor	United
09680	Carpet subcontractor	Soft Touch
09900	Painting subcontractor	Hi-Gloss Painting
15000	Mechanical subcontractor	Arctic Mechanical
15500	Fire protection subcontractor	Alaskan Fire Protection
16000	Electrical subcontractor	Richardson Electric

FIGURE 11–2 Huna Project File Log

FIGURE 11–3 Routing Stamp

NWCC
ROUTING STAMP
HUNA PROJECT

☐ CEO ____________________

☐ PM ____________________

☐ SUPT ____________________

☐ PE ____________________

☐ CLERK ____________________

After complete routing, the archive in its entirety can be filed chronologically. This provides a backup to the standard file system.

The job files not only serve as an active tool during construction, they provide a permanent written record of the project. If the project is unfortunate enough to end up in a legal dispute, this is one of the first places the attorneys will begin their review. After the project's completion, the files should be kept safe for an established period of time. Sometimes this duration is dictated by local statute, other times by the contract terms, and still others by the construction firm's corporate philosophy. A common period is three years after the project is completed and all claims resolved.

11.3 DAILY JOB DIARY

The daily job diary is an important project management document. Some construction professionals refer to the diary as a daily journal or a daily report. The name is not as important as the fact that the document is used properly. The job diary is one of the most important project management tools and job site records. It is viewed as a contemporary record of each day's events. Its uses include:

- Legal record of daily job site activity
- Change-order backup documentation
- ***Back charge*** and claim documentation
- Historical record of schedule progress

An example of a job diary for the Huna Office Building project is shown in Figure 11–4. There are a variety of forms which are utilized throughout the industry. Each construction firm should select a standard format to use on all projects. The important items to be included with any diary include:

- Superintendent's name
- Job name and reference number
- Date and day the diary is filled out
- Weather
- Manpower for both the general contractor and subcontractors
- Routing or distribution of copies
- Hindrance to normal progress
- Deliveries received
- Visitors to the site
- Equipment on site
- Accidents
- Inspections

The project superintendent should fill out the diary. Often this is delegated to the assistant superintendent, foreman, or field engineer. However, because of the historical importance of the diary, it should be prepared by the project superintendent, who is responsible for all field activities. The diary should be completed at the end of every day. Postponing completing the diary until the next morning, or doing five of them at the end of the week, dilutes their accuracy. The diary should be copied and distributed to those who have a need for the information, such as the project manager and the officer in charge of the project. On negotiated projects, the owner also may request copies. Some superintendents have been known to write one diary on Monday and make four photocopies, just changing the date for the remaining four days of the week. This completely eliminates the purpose of the form.

The diary should be written out by hand in ink. This helps support authenticity and originality. Some superintendents are now preparing their diaries on their desktop computers. To some extent, this also negates the originality of the document. There are two schools of thought regarding loose sheet or bound diaries. Looseleaf can be copied, distributed, and filed easily. But loose sheets may also get lost. If they are bound and consecutively numbered, there is less chance of a diary getting rewritten to reflect a desired viewpoint or recollection. Conversely, bound diaries are more difficult to use as a tool on the job site with regard to distribution.

NORTHWEST CONSTRUCTION COMPANY
1242 First Avenue, Cascade, Washington 98202
(206) 239-1422

DAILY JOB DIARY

Project: HUNA TOTEM Superintendent: JIM BATES
Date: 10/04/00 Day: WEDS Job No.: 9821
Today's Weather: RAIN - STEADY, TEMP : 42° ±

Activities Completed:
'COMPLETED PRE-CAST OPERATION OFFSITE, CLEANED UP SHOP FROM PRE-CAST, 'CONTINUED ERECTION OF P-C ON EAST AND WEST ENDS, WILL FINISH NO. SIDE MONDAY 'CONTINUED FINEGRADE AND REBAR ON NO. SIDE 'CONTINUED REBAR FOR CLOSURE POURS 'JOE AND EDDY CLEANED MUD OFF SOG AND ATB.

Problems Encountered:
FORKLIFT BOGGED DOWN IN MUD ERECTING PRECAST. RAIN IS SLOWING US DOWN.

Visitors: NORM RILEY / JYL, FRED - CITY INSPECTOR - APPROVED REBAR IN CLOSURES SO FAR.

Materials and Equipment Received Today:
'SANIKANS CLEANED OUT, '4TH DELIVERY OF PRE-CAST, ONE MORE TO GO, 'LAST DELIVERY OF DOWELS FROM STEEL FAB, WILL POUR CLOSURES NEXT WEEK.

Rental Equipment Returned Today: **Returned to:**
N/A

On-Site Labor/Crafts/Subs/Hours worked:

Carpenters:	4 @ 8H/E		
Laborers:	2 @ 8H/E		
Ironworkers:	1 @ 8H, 1 NO-SHOW (CALLED IN SICK)		
CM Finishers:			
Masons:			
Electricians:			
Drywallers:			
Plumbers:	ARCTIC: 1 PLUMBER @ 4H/UNDERSLAB ROUGH-IN.		
HVAC:			
Painters:			
Other:			
Other:			

cc:

FIGURE 11–4 Daily Job Diary

Placing Concrete Foundation for Huna Office Building

As discussed in Chapter 8, it is a good practice to require on-site subcontractors also to complete daily reports and provide a copy to the project manager. This way the general contractor has evidence of their manpower and their view of daily progress, recorded in the subcontractor's original written hand. If there is a problem or restraint noted on a subcontractor's diary, the project manager should deal with it immediately. Some owners also may require copies of the subcontractors' daily reports as well as the general contractor's diaries.

11.4 CONTROL LOGS

Some of the types of logs which are used on a construction project include:

- Purchase order
- Field question
- Submittal
- Contract change directive
- Sketch
- Drawing
- Change order proposal
- Transmittal
- Letter
- Telephone conversation
- Subcontract modification
- Close-out

Examples of many of these logs are shown in other chapters. To many beginning project engineers, the development and maintenance of the job site logs will be a major focus. All logs are important tools of the project management process. They provide summary reports of much of the communication processes on the job site and with the owner, design team, subcontractors, and suppliers. Although the production of the logs may be a project engineer's responsibility, it is still the ultimate responsibility of the project manager to ensure that they are correct, similar to files and meeting notes. Many of the logs are used for reference or as a summary, but most importantly, logs are used as the focus of discussion during coordination meetings. Many of the logs reviewed during a meeting should then be attached to the meeting notes.

11.5 RECORD DRAWINGS

There can be several different types of record drawings. The set of drawings used and referenced in the original contract is kept as a set of record drawings. The current set of contract drawings, as incorporated into the contract through change orders is a record set of drawings. The permit set of drawings as stamped by the municipality is a record set of drawings and must be available in the contractor's project office for review by the inspector. Approved submittal drawings are also to be maintained as record drawings.

An example of a portion of a drawing log for the Huna Office Building project is shown in Figure 11–5. This log may be maintained by the design team, the construction team, or both. It should be periodically distributed to make sure that all contracting parties have the current set of drawings and that these drawings have been incorporated into all contracts, subcontracts, and purchase orders. The requirements for posting and storage of different types of record drawings are usually defined in the specifications or in the special conditions to the contract. The record drawing requirements for the Huna Office Building project are contained in Section 01700 of the specifications in Appendix F.

Another type of record drawing is the set of as-built drawings, which are discussed in Chapter 21. As-built drawings are developed by marking up exact construction conditions on a copy of the construction drawings. These will be used by the owner as a reference of the manner in which the project was actually constructed. Some contracts require that the as-built drawings either be submitted or reviewed each month to assure that they are being kept up to date as a part of the pay request process. The superintendent is responsible for maintaining the as-built drawings to ensure they reflect any changes made during the construction of the project.

11.6 SUMMARY

Documents and document control are important tools for the construction team. The project manager is responsible for setting these systems up properly at the beginning of the project. The project manager may delegate the maintenance of these systems to an engineer or assistant, but it is still his or her responsibility to make sure that they are operating properly.

The files for a construction project should be developed consistent with other projects of the construction company. The files should be kept current and located where they can be readily accessed by the construction team. The daily job diary and the project files are valuable historical tools in case of a dispute. The diary should be maintained by the project superintendent. There are numerous logs that are used on a construction project. They provide a summary of the construction documentation and are often reviewed during construction meetings and attached to meeting notes as exhibits.

There are also various types of record drawings. The requirements for maintenance and storage generally are defined in the specifications. As a historical reference, the contractor will want to store different sets of contract or reference drawings for extended periods after the project is completed.

11.7 REVIEW QUESTIONS

1. Which member of the construction team is responsible for physically mobilizing onto the job site?

NORTHWEST CONSTRUCTION COMPANY
1242 First Avenue, Cascade, Washington 98202
(206) 239-1422

Huna Office Building
DRAWING LOG
10/10/00
Page 1 of 2

Document Number	Description	Date	Current Revisions: Rev. 1	Rev. 2	Rev. 3
	ARCHITECTURAL DRAWINGS:				
A001	Cover and Administrative Information	8/18/97	8/24/97		
A102	Site Section	8/18/97	8/24/97		
A200	Door & Finish Schedules	8/18/97	8/24/97	9/15/97	
A201	First Floor Plan	8/18/97	8/24/97		
A202	Second Floor Plan	8/18/97	8/24/97	9/15/97	
A203	Mechanical Penthouse Plan	8/18/97	8/24/97		
A204	Roof Plan	8/18/97	8/24/97		
A301	Exterior Elevations	8/18/97			
A302	Exterior Elevations	8/18/97	8/27/97	9/15/97	10/10/97
A303	Building Sections	8/18/97			
A304	Building Sections	8/18/97			
A305	Building Sections	8/18/97			
A306	Wall Sections	8/18/97			
A307	Wall Sections	8/18/97	8/24/97		
A401	Toilet Rooms	8/18/97	8/24/97		
A501	Interior Elevations	8/18/97			
A502	Interior Elevations	8/18/97			
A601	First Floor Reflected Ceiling Plan	8/18/97	8/27/97	9/15/97	10/10/97
A602	Second Floor Reflected Ceiling Plan	8/18/97	8/27/97	9/15/97	10/10/97
A701	Elevator Section	8/18/97			
A801	Exterior Details	8/18/97			
A901	Interior Details	8/18/97			

FIGURE 11–5 Drawing Log

2. Which member of the construction team is responsible for mobilizing the paper flow?
3. The file code system on a job site should be similar to what other code systems?
4. Where should the project files be located?
5. What is the difference between a reading file and a routing stamp?

6. How many copies of a particular piece of communication should be made?
7. How long are files kept in storage?
8. What is a journal or daily report?
9. List at least five important types of information that is recorded on a daily job diary.
10. Who should originate a diary?
11. List three misuses of a diary.
12. Why would it be important for a log to be up to date?
13. How would it be possible for different members of the team to be working from different revisions of construction drawings?
14. How are as-built drawings created?
15. List three types of record drawings.

11.8 EXERCISES

1. On the Huna Office Building project, what is the date of and the revision number for Drawing A601 that the drywall subcontractor should use as a reference in her daily diary?
2. Create a typical job diary for the Huna Office Building project for the following dates. Use the project schedule folded inside the back cover for reference.
   a. September 21, 2000 (a clear day)
   b. December 21, 2000 (a snowy day)

Weather Protection of Concrete Foundation for Huna Office Building

11.9 SOURCES OF ADDITIONAL INFORMATION

Bartholomew, Stuart H. *Construction Contracting: Business and Legal Principles.* Upper Saddle River, N.J.: Prentice-Hall, Inc., 1998.

Civitello, Andrew, Jr. *Construction Operations Manual of Policies & Procedures.* 3d ed. New York: McGraw-Hill, Inc., 2000.

Grimes, J. Edward. *Construction Paperwork: An Efficient Management System.* Kingston, Mass.: R. S. Means Company, Inc., 1989.

Levy, Sidney M. *Project Management in Construction.* 3d ed. New York: McGraw-Hill, Inc., 1999.

Liebing, Ralph W. *Construction Contract Administration.* Upper Saddle River, N.J.: Prentice-Hall, Inc., 1998.

Mincks, William R., and Hal Johnston. *Construction Jobsite Management.* Albany, N.Y.: Delmar Publishers, 1998.

12

Communications

12.1 INTRODUCTION

Communication means acquiring and transmitting information. It is the most critical project management tool. A good technical project manager who knows how to estimate, plan, schedule, and execute most likely will fail unless he or she also has good communication skills. Unless the project manager can communicate his or her needs, wants, and expectations, they probably will be unfulfilled. Construction communications involve exchanging information regarding a project. Several formats and techniques have been developed to expedite the flow of information among members of the project team. Many communication tools such as contracts, schedules, logs, and start-up documents have been introduced in previous chapters. This chapter describes the use of several additional communication tools that are essential to the project manager.

12.2 COMMUNICATION SKILLS

To be a skilled communicator, the project manager must clearly understand what message he or she is trying to send, how the message will be interpreted by the recipient, and what action will be initiated as a consequence of receiving the message. Communication must be clear and concise to avoid confusion. Simple language is more effective than cryptic jargon. Acquiring good writing and speaking skills requires patience and practice, but is essential if one is to become an effective project manager.

12.3 WRITTEN COMMUNICATIONS

Effective written communications are essential. Most people have short memories and often hear what they want to hear. People may hear and interpret the same communications differently. The project manager does not want to stifle verbal communications, teamwork, and camaraderie for the sake of the written word, but it is necessary to make a written record of discussions affecting a project. Written forms are used to document verbal communications, such as meetings and telephone conversations. They form a clear record of what happened and what was intended or directed to happen. Unfortunately some people see written forms of communications only as documentation to support claims or disputes. This does not have to be the case. If project communications are properly handled, there should be no need for disputes. Written communications should be seen as tools to help build the project, not solely as support for future litigation.

Transmittals are one of the most common construction communication tools. An example is shown in Figure 12–1. This document works as the cover sheet for other types of documents. For example, a transmittal may be used to send a request for payment to the owner or to send a revised schedule to a subcontractor. They are widely used with the fax machine unless the documents being sent are bulky. A transmittal should clearly tell recipients what they are being given, what they are expected to do with the attached documents, and when they are to do it. It is important to use simple, direct language to avoid confusion. Multipart paper works well for transmittals. The original top copy is sent to the recipient with the documents being transmitted. A second copy is placed in the project file to serve as a record of when and what was sent. A third copy could be sent to either the project superintendent or the officer-in-charge so that he or she also is aware of what documents are changing hands.

Some other common types of written construction communication documents include:

- Change orders (see Chapter 19)
- Contracts (see Chapters 2 and 6)
- ***Electronic mail***
- Estimates (see Chapter 4)
- Field questions (see Chapter 13)
- Job diaries (see Chapter 11)
- Letters
- ***Meeting notes***
- ***Project team lists*** (companies, individuals, telephones, and addresses)
- Schedules (see Chapter 5)
- Submittals (see Chapter 14)
- ***Warranties*** (see Chapter 22)

The major issue is that they be prepared in simple, direct language to eliminate the potential for misinterpretation.

12.4 ORAL COMMUNICATIONS

Oral communications are important and are often essential. Typical oral communications include making presentations and informally discussing issues with other project team members, either individually or collectively in meetings. Written documentation

NORTHWEST CONSTRUCTION COMPANY
1242 First Avenue, Cascade, Washington 98202
(206) 239-1422

TRANSMITTAL

Date: *August 16, 2000*

To: *Huna Totem Corporation*
9922 Glacier Highway
Juneau, Alaska 99801

Attn: *Mr. Robert Smith*

Re: *Contracts*

Enclosed: *X* Fax: ____ Mailed: ____ Prior, w/o transmittal: ____
Hand Delivered: *X* Fax Number: ________________

Item(s) Transmitted: *2 each original AIA contracts #A111, dated August 15, 2000, with attachments*

Remarks: *We have completed the contracts as agreed and have executed both original copies. Please initial each page, including attached exhibits, and return one completely executed original for our files. If you have any questions regarding the enclosed, please call.*

Transmitted by: ________________ *Ted Jones, Project Manager*

Job/File code: *9821*

cc: *Mr. Sam Peters, NWCC*
Mr. Norm Riley, JYL Architects

FIGURE 12–1 Transmittal

should also be used to document oral communications. Two methods are discussed in this chapter: meeting notes, which are discussed in the next section, and ***telephone memorandums***. The telephone memorandum, illustrated in Figure 12–2, is a standard tool extensively used in the construction industry. A copy should always be routed to those on the other end of the conversation, as well as to any others involved in the

NORTHWEST CONSTRUCTION COMPANY
1242 First Avenue, Cascade, Washington 98202
(206) 239-1422

TO/WITH: ROBERT SMITH	DATE: 8/20/00
	TIME: 11:15 AM
COMPANY: HUNA TOTEM	JOB NO.: 9821
	PAGE: 1 of 1

MEMORANDUM: ☐ Conference ☒ Telephone ☐ File ☐ Information ☐ Fax

PHONE NO.: (907) 929-4923 FAX NO.: (907) 929-4922

PROJECT: HUNA OFFICE BUILDING

LOCATION: JUNEAU, AK

SUBJECT: CONTRACT DOCUMENT EXHIBIT

DISCUSSION:
ROBERT CALLED AND ASKED WHEN WE WOULD REVISE THE DOCUMENT EXHIBIT INCLUDED WITH THE CONTRACT DELIVERED EARLIER THIS WEEK. I INDICATED THAT, ALTHOUGH THE DESIGN TEAM IS CURRENTLY REVISING THE DRAWINGS AND SPECIFICATIONS TO REFLECT CITY PERMIT COMMENTS, I DID NOT ANTICIPATE ANY MAJOR COST IMPACTS. WE WILL REVISE THE EXHIBIT UPON RECEIPT OF THOSE DOCUMENTS AND THEN MODIFY THE CONTRACT WITH A CHANGE ORDER.

FILE CODE: 9821 BY: Ted Jones

COPIES: NORM RILEY, JYL

FIGURE 12–2 Telephone Memorandum

subject. This is sometimes viewed negatively, but if the practice is started early in the job, it will soon be accepted by all as sound business practice. A copy of each telephone memorandum should be included in the routed reading file discussed in Chapter 11 and the original placed in the project file.

12.5 ELECTRONIC COMMUNICATIONS

Electronic mail (e-mail) has completely changed construction communications. E-mail is an excellent substitute for telephonic communication and provides a written record of each communication, substituting for the telephone memorandum shown in Figure 12–2. Electronic mail is being used to coordinate field questions with designers and subcontractors, coordinate material deliveries with suppliers, and coordinate project issues with owners. Electronic mail does not, however, eliminate the need for periodic coordination meetings and formal letters.

12.6 PROJECT MEETINGS

The primary purpose of a meeting is to provide a forum for direct communication and timely and efficient information exchange. This allows the parties involved to take appropriate action and make the decisions necessary to maintain the scheduled flow of work. The meeting is a tool that is to be used to assist in constructing a project.

Types and Frequency of Meetings

Informal meetings are held every day. If two people pass in the hall and stop and exchange information, a meeting has occurred. Our discussion will be focused on the more formal scheduled meetings. The project manager will be involved with various

Pumping Concrete for Huna Office Building

types of meetings, each with its purpose, attendees, format, and notes arranged according to the subject of that particular meeting. The project manager's role also varies with regard to the subject of the meeting. Some of the types of meetings that occur on a typical project are shown in Figure 12–3. Owners may include meeting requirements in their contract specifications. Section 01200 of the specifications in Appendix F contains the meeting requirements for the Huna Office Building project.

Meetings should be announced in sufficient time so that all responsible parties can arrange to attend. A ***meeting notice***, similar to the one shown in Figure 12–4, works well for this purpose. Meetings should be held in the office of the firm conducting the meeting. The project manager should chair all meetings that are appropriate. Only those parties with pertinent information should attend; too large a group causes simultaneous third-party conversations. A short memorandum to remind the required attendees of their expected attendance is sometimes helpful. The meeting notes, discussed below, will provide the appropriate notice for the next meeting. Meeting attendance should be taken and a list of attendees attached to the meeting notes. This reminds attendees of the importance of their presence and serves as a permanent record of their attendance.

Meeting Agenda

If a particular meeting is not a continuation of a previous meeting, a ***meeting agenda*** is required. The agenda is a sequential listing of the topics to be addressed at the meeting. This document forces the meeting to proceed in a formal manner, which allows the project manager the opportunity to accomplish his or her goals and limits digression. The project manager first establishes himself or herself as the meeting leader or chair by sending out the agenda and meeting notice. It is a good procedure to distribute this agenda at least one day prior to the meeting allowing all parties to prepare properly. If this is not possible, a typed agenda distributed at the beginning of the meeting is still beneficial.

TITLE	OCCURRENCE	CHAIR
Owner/Architect Meeting	Weekly	Project Manager
Safety	Weekly	Assistant Superintendent or General Foreman
Scheduling	As Needed	Project Manager or Superintendent
Preconstruction meetings:		
• with Owner and Architect	Once	Owner or Architect
• with Subcontractors	Once per Subcontractor	Project Manager
• with Unions (jurisdictions)	Once	General Superintendent
• with City (permits, utilities)	Once	Project Manager or Superintendent
• coordination meetings	As Needed	Project Manager or Architect
• design coordination	Weekly	Architect
Labor Relations	As Needed	General Superintendent
Foremen's meetings	Weekly	Superintendent or Assistant Superintendent
Change order status/review	Weekly	Project Manager or Architect
Pay request review	Monthly	Project Manager or Architect
Punch list meeting (end of job)	Weekly	Project Manager, Superintendent, or Architect
Subcontractor coordination	Weekly	Project Manager
Field question/submittal coordination	Weekly	Project Manager or Project Engineer

FIGURE 12–3 Types of Meetings

NORTHWEST CONSTRUCTION COMPANY
1242 First Avenue, Cascade, Washington 98202
(206) 239-1422

MEETING NOTICE

Date: *March 10, 2001*

To: Required Attendees
Optional Attendees

Subject: *The city has asked to meet with the owner and construction teams and environmental agencies about protection of Duck Creek before the spring thaw.*

Date of meeting:	*March 17, 2001*
Meeting start time:	*9:00 a.m.*
Anticipated completion:	*10:30 a.m.*
Location of meeting:	*General contractor's project site trailer*
Required attendees:	Representing:
Ted Jones and Jim Bates	*Northwest Construction Company*
Norm Riley	*JLY Architects*
Robert Smith	*Huna Totem*
Mary Jackson	*City of Juneau*
Jerry Hopkins	*Environmental Protection Agency*
Optional attendees:	Representing:
Frank Waters	*Civil Engineer consultant*
Neighbors	*Notice posted and distributed in neighborhood*
Attendance comfirmation required?	Yes: _X_ Please call: (206) 239-1422. No: __
Transmitted by:	*Mary Peterson, Project Engineer*

Job/File code: *9821/MN*

FIGURE 12–4 Meeting Notice

Meeting Notes

The multifaceted nature of meeting notes allows them to:

- Provide a written record of meeting discussions and decisions
- Provide a formal list of meeting attendees
- Remind attendees of action required prior to the next meeting
- Create responsibility through action items with due dates
- Provide an agenda for next meeting

- Solicit corrections to the project manager's understanding of meeting results
- Announce the next meeting

It is the project manager's responsibility to chair the weekly project coordination meeting and publish meeting notes. A meeting may be too large for the project manager to both chair and record meeting notes. In such instances, a project engineer or assistant project manager may assist with taking the notes. The project manager should always take and publish his or her own set of notes, even when the meeting has been called by, chaired by, or hosted by another party. The note publisher will, if only subconsciously, tend to slant the notes towards his or her desired outcome. Notes should be prepared and distributed the same day the meeting is conducted. This minimizes the possibility of memory loss and provides a timely notification to attendees of their commitments and actions due. The project manager may telephone attendees a couple of days later and verify that they received their notes, remind them of the next meeting, and question them regarding accuracy and the status of open action items. Project managers should not assume that the notes were received and read just because they were mailed (or faxed or e-mailed).

Meeting notes serve as a formal and sometimes legal record; they are important documents that should be regarded seriously. Meeting notes often serve as supportive data for letters, change orders, and field questions. They should be filed and stored as part of the project files. The format for meeting notes should follow the basic format shown in Figure 12–5 on pages 159–60. Meeting notes may occasionally vary according to specific projects, topics, and attendees. Individual meeting notes used within a construction firm should follow the same format. At a minimum, the notes should contain the following:

- Heading: project name, construction firm's letterhead, date and time of meeting, meeting number, location of meeting.
- Typed attendance list and the firm each attendee represents.
- Paragraph notifying attendees that they are expected to be qualified to make decisions that accurately represent their firms.
- Paragraph notifying participants and note recipients that they have up to seven days to notify the note taker of any errors or omissions. After that time, the notes will be considered statements of fact and entered into the project's records.
- Item numbers: Each new business note item shall be numbered with that meeting number as its prefix. This will eliminate duplicate numbers and allows the next week's notes to tie in. Additionally, open, unresolved items can be carried forward as old business; the meeting number prefix indicates the age of open issues.
- Discussion, action items, and decisions.
- Company or individual responsible for taking action.
- Date the action is to be due and the individual responsible for making it happen.
- Full sentences wherever possible.
- Use of **bold**, or *italics*, or underline are beneficial to bring attention to topics.
- Handouts, regardless of source and references to them. This way the project manager can avoid one party indicating it did not receive a copy of an item distributed during the meeting.
- Note taker's name.
- Distribution to all attendees, absentees, and others whom the notes affect.
- Logs distributed and discussed such as: field question log, submittal log, sketch log, and change order proposal log.

NORTHWEST CONSTRUCTION COMPANY
1242 First Avenue, Cascade, Washington 98202
(206) 239-1422

Construction Coordination Meeting Number 6
September 20, 2000 @ Job site
Job number 9821
Page 1 of 5

Attendance:	Representing:
Robert Smith	Huna Totem
Norm Riley	JYL
Ted Jones	NWCC
Jim Bates	NWCC
Mary Peterson	NWCC

Representatives attending this meeting shall be qualified and authorized to act on behalf of the entity that each represents.

To the best of our knowledge this is an accurate summary of the discussions, decisions, etc. which occurred during this meeting. Notification of exceptions to this summary are to be made within 7 days of receipt.

Please bring your copy of these notes to the next meeting as they shall serve as the preliminary agenda.

Item	Discussion	Responsible	Date Due
Permits:			
1.02	The building permit has been picked up and is posted at the job site. The design team is in the process of incorporating city comments and will issue revisions to the contract set for pricing.	Riley	9/22/00
Schedule:			
6.01	Project superintendent Jim Bates reports that the project is currently plus or minus one to two days from the original contract schedule. There do not appear to be any current problems. The attached three week look ahead schedule was distributed and discussed in detail.	Bates	Ongoing
Safety:			
6.02	Jim reported that there have been no safety incidents to date resulting in lost work days. Each subcontractor will be required to submit a site specific safety plan to NWCC before mobilizing onto the job site.	Bates	Ongoing

FIGURE 12–5 Sample Meeting Notes

- Numbered pages, for example, *page 2 of 4.*
- *End of Meeting* added underneath the last discussion held in the meeting
- Every document on a construction job should be filed and given a file code number that includes the job number. This code goes on the bottom of the last page of the meeting notes.

NORTHWEST CONSTRUCTION COMPANY
1242 First Avenue, Cascade, Washington 98202
(206) 239-1422

Construction Coordination Meeting Number 6
September 20, 2000 @ Job site
Job number 9821
Page 2 of 5

Item	Discussion	Responsible	Date Due
Old Business:			
1.02	There are still five value engineering items open which require resolution by the project team. The attached log was reviewed. Robert indicated he will discuss in-house and provide the client's decisions by no later than next week's meeting.	Smith	9/27/00
3.09	Temporary power still has not been established on the job site. NWCC is currently pulling power cords from adjacent buildings. Jim will keep in touch with the utility company. It was agreed that the service will be established in Huna's name and they will pay for the utility bills direct. NWCC to develop a credit change order proposal for the amount of funds estimated for temporary power hookup fees and monthly bills.	Bates Jones	Ongoing 9/27/00
New Business:			
6.03	JYL is revising the owner-furnished equipment list with current cut sheet information. Several items previously anticipated to be provided by Huna will not be requested to be provided by NWCC. A CCD will be issued with this revised list, and NWCC will prepare a corresponding COP.	Riley Jones	10/1/00 10/14/00
6.04	NWCC requested that if a tenant is identified for the second floor shell space that formal design be issued as soon as possible for pricing and incorporation into the work. If this tenant improvement work can not be done concurrent with other TI work, there will be additional job site overhead expenses. All parties understood, but to date there has not been a tenant identified. It was agreed that this item be tracked on a weekly basis.	JYL/Huna	Ongoing
6.05	The attached field question and submittal logs were reviewed in detail. There are currently not any items which have been open for longer than one week.	Peterson Riley	Ongoing

FIGURE 12–5 Sample Meeting Notes *(Continued)*

Conducting the Meeting

The weekly owner/architect meeting, also called the project coordination meeting, is the project manager's primary means of communication with the entire project team at one time and in one place. It is either held in the general contractor's main office or in the field office depending upon project progress and size. This meeting ideally takes place at the job site trailer, which helps instill the importance of timely decisions on the team members. It is imperative that both the architect and the owner attend this meeting.

The meeting chair should make every endeavor to follow an agenda. All items requiring discussion and resolution should be addressed. If a meeting wanders from the agenda or contains multiple simultaneous conversations, it will be excessively long, causing issues to be tabled, postponing action items, and possibly even delaying the project. It is preferable to hold individual conversations until after the meeting has ended. Workshops and task forces are utilized effectively for this purpose. The smaller group can then report back to the larger group at the next coordination meeting. The project manager must avoid being too rigid by not allowing discussion of new items, which may also be important. If attendees are not getting what they want out of the meeting, their attention and attendance may diminish. The project manager is also the peacekeeper, head communicator, and principal compromiser and must lead by example in all cases. He or she must have the ability to bring discussion to a close and identify specific actions to be taken regarding open issues.

Choice of seating is important. The important decision makers should not be standing against the wall or sitting in the second row. There are two seats of choice for the project manager.

- The head of the table establishes a position of power and leadership. If the project manager has a message to deliver, this may be the best chair. If the project manager has not established himself or herself as the leader of the group, this also may be the best chair.
- The middle of a long side of the table offers the project manager the best opportunity to communicate with many people. If the goal of the meeting is to achieve a compromise, the project manager may choose this softer or friendlier position.

As indicated previously, the coordination meeting should follow an agenda. Use of the previous meeting's notes provides an easy and natural path to follow. The following general outline works in most situations:

- Status of the project schedule (superintendent's responsibility)
- Safety issues (superintendent's responsibility)
- Review of various document logs (often presented by project engineer)
- Review of open items from previous meeting
- New business items for discussion (All participants are given an opportunity to introduce new items.)
- Summary of decisions made
- Announcement of next meeting date and time

Some project managers summarize many of the important issues decided upon during the meeting or actions due prior to the next meeting. This is done verbally to all in attendance at the end of each meeting. This process is similar to reading the first draft of the meeting notes. This is a good reminder and offers all the opportunity to disagree if their understanding is not the same as the project manager's.

12.7 SUMMARY

Construction communications involve exchanging information regarding a project. They may be written, oral, or electronic. Good communications are concise and focused to avoid misinterpretation. Transmittals are used to transmit documents and provide a written record. Other common written documents include daily job diaries, field questions, change orders, telephone memorandums, and meeting notes. Telephone memorandums are used to record the major points discussed in telephone conversations. Meeting notes are used to record the issues discussed and decisions reached at project meetings. They also list open action items and individuals tasked with resolving them. Meetings, especially owner/architect/contractor coordination meetings, are important communication tools for the project manager. Each meeting needs an agenda to provide focus and a note taker to prepare the meeting notes. The exact format for the meeting notes is not as important as the fact that the notes were prepared and distributed to all attendees.

12.8 REVIEW QUESTIONS

1. List five types of written communications.
2. How often should records of telephone conversations be made?
3. What is the most common form of written communication documents?
4. Who should chair the weekly job site safety meeting?
5. Who on the project management team is often responsible for preparation of meeting notes?
6. Who on the project management team is responsible for the accuracy of the owner/contractor/architect coordination meeting notes?
7. List five uses of meeting notes.
8. Where should the project manager sit at a meeting?
9. What documents should be attached to the meeting notes and why?
10. When should the meeting notes be distributed and why?

12.9 EXERCISES

1. Prepare a transmittal for Northwest Construction Company to submit its monthly request for payment to the owner of the Huna Office Building project.
2. Prepare a telephone memorandum of a conversation between the project manager and the electrical subcontractor on the Huna Office Building project regarding the scheduled delivery of electrical switch gear.
3. Prepare a set of meeting notes for the classroom discussion as if it were a construction meeting.

12.10 SOURCES OF ADDITIONAL INFORMATION

Civitello, Andrew M., Jr. *Construction Operations Manual of Policies and Procedures.* 3d ed. New York: McGraw-Hill, Inc., 2000.

Grimes, J. Edward. *Construction Paperwork: An Efficient Management System.* Kingston, Mass: R. S. Means Company, Inc., 1989.

Mincks, William R., and Hal Johnston. *Construction Jobsite Management.* Albany, N.Y.: Delmar Publishers, 1998.

13

Field Questions

13.1 INTRODUCTION

Field questions are asked when a subcontractor or the general contractor discovers a discrepancy in the construction documents or with existing site conditions and needs assistance or confirmation from the designer or owner for resolution. The field question is a specific type of written communication, transmitted on paper or electronically, that is used to document the inquiry and record the response. There are many terms used for field questions in construction. The most common are:

- Design change verification request
- Field information memorandum
- Request for clarification
- Request for information

While the format of each may be slightly different, the basic concept is the same. Field questions generally are managed by the project engineer, who maintains a log indicating the status of each question. Questions generated by subcontractors or suppliers are submitted to the project engineer for review prior to their submission to the owner or designer.

13.2 PREPARATION

Field questions can be originated by several of the construction participants. They may be written either by subcontractors, suppliers, or the general contractor. Regardless of who discovers the conflict or needs assistance, there are a few rules that should be followed when preparing a field question.

- The questions always should be asked in writing. Sometimes the project engineer contacts the structural engineer verbally with a critical question. These verbal questions should always be followed up requesting written confirmation of the discussion held.
- Subcontractors and suppliers should always route questions through the general contractor. Many subcontractors use their own forms. The project manager may allow subcontractors to prepare field questions on their own forms, and then use the general contractor's form as a cover with his or her own numerical identifier. Some project managers require subcontractors to use the general contractor's form. The exact form used is not as important as the information it should contain. Some contract specifications may dictate the form to be used on a specific project.
- The number of questions asked on a single form should be limited to one. If more questions are asked, the designer will wait to respond until he or she has answers to all questions. This will delay the response.
- Each question must be clear, complete, concise, and accurate. It must refer to specific contract sections or be supported with appropriate documentation. Such documentation may include sketches and material data.
- Each form should have a unique number for identification.

An example field question for the Huna Office Building project is shown in Figure 13–1 on pages 165–66.

All field questions should be tracked on a log, such as the one in Figure 13–2 on page 167. This log generally is maintained by the project engineer. It is important to note who generated the question as well as who is expected to respond. Open items on the log should be reviewed during the owner/architect/contractor coordination meeting. This log should be an attachment to the meeting notes, as discussed in Chapter 12.

Verbal responses to field questions should not be accepted. If the reviewer refuses to write a response, the project manager should write the designer's verbal direction regarding the question in the answer portion, document the source and time, and route the form back through, similar to copying the other party with a telephone memorandum.

All responded questions should be routed to the appropriate office and field staff as well as the originating subcontractor. They also should be sent to any other subcontractors and suppliers who may possibly be involved or impacted. All responded questions need to be reviewed for project impact. They may change project scope or impact the schedule. Impact analysis will be discussed in Section 13.4.

13.3 MANAGEMENT

Like the submittals that are discussed in Chapter 14, field questions are part of the final stages of the design process. Many conflicts could not have been anticipated until the duct and pipe are actually installed on the job site. Many unforeseen conditions are exposed when the backhoe excavates for the foundations. If the field question process is used properly, it can be a real tool for the construction team. However, many architects and owners dislike the field question process; it costs time and money to respond, and they feel many questions are superfluous or that the contractor is just digging for change orders. Unfortunately, some contractors use field questions for just that purpose. If the issue is identified or anticipated early enough, the designers do not feel like they are always being asked for an immediate response. Many designers who realize that the construction and design processes are not independent disciplines also acknowledge that field questions from the contractors, installers, craftspeople, and fabricators are really a process of assistance rather than annoyance.

NORTHWEST CONSTRUCTION COMPANY
1242 First Avenue, Cascade, Washington 98202
(206) 239-1422

FIELD QUESTION

Project: *Huna Office Building*
Area/System: *lobby piping*
To: *JYL Architects*
Address: *522 West 10th Street*
Juneau, Alaska 99801
Attention: *Norm Riley*
Required Response Date: *October 14, 2000*

Date: *October 7, 2000*
Field Question No. *5*
Related Field Questions: *NA*

Subcontractor/Supplier providing FQ: *NA*

Originator's Number: *NA*

Subject: *Pipe chase in lobby*

Detailed Description/Request: *The plumbing, HVAC piping, electrical, and fire protection are required to traverse from south to north through the first and second story lobbies, Rooms 100 and 200. The piping drawings indicate "adjacent to beam, concealed from view." There are no drop or false ceilings in this area. Please advise if these pipes are to be run exposed.*

Attached/Referenced/Supporting Documentation: *Drawings M1.1 and M2.1*

Please reply to: *Mary Peterson, Project Engineer*

Space below for Architect/Engineer:

Reply: *Attached is sketch #6 and CCD #2. Please provide a change order proposal to fur below the joist and drop the first floor ceiling to cover the pipes. Route all first and second story piping through this space.*

Signed: Norm Riley

Date: *October 12, 2000*

Contractor's Job No./File Code: *9821*

FIGURE 13–1 Field Question

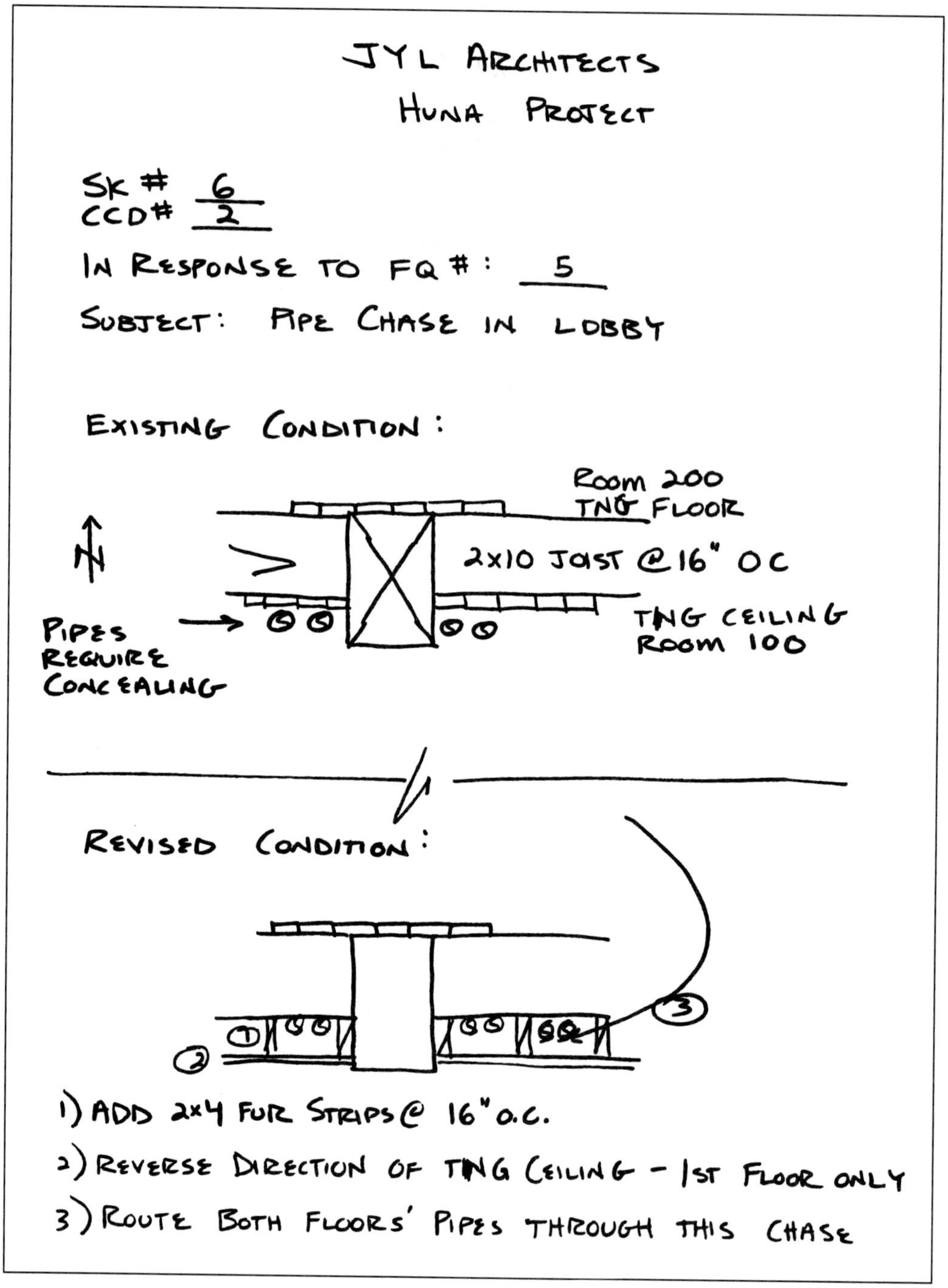

FIGURE 13–1 Field Question *(Continued)*

Some construction participants advocate conducting a meeting to discuss several questions at the same time. This often is unavoidable and can be helpful. Sometimes the only way to visualize the conflict is for everyone to meet on the project site. Meetings such as these also can have a positive impact on team relationships. The resolutions should still be documented, either during or after the meeting.

Designer-originated question forms often have spaces for the contractor to indicate if the issue will result in cost or schedule impacts to the project. This is a difficult situation for the project manager. The issue, conflict, or question should be resolved first,

NORTHWEST CONSTRUCTION COMPANY
1242 First Avenue, Cascade, Washington 98202
(206) 239-1422

FIELD QUESTION LOG

Project No.: *9821* Project Name: *Huna Office Building* Project Manager: *Ted Jones*

FQ No.	Originator	Subcontractor FQ No.	Supporting Documents	Description	Date Submitted	Requested Return Date	Date Returned	COP Issued
1	*Northwest Construction*	*NA*	*S1*	*Need dimensions clarified*	*8/17/00*	*8/24/00*	*8/23/00*	*no*
2	*Northwest Construction*	*NA*	*S1 & A201*	*SOG elevation?*	*8/17/00*	*8/24/00*	*8/24/00*	*no*
3	*Arctic Mechanical*	*1*	*M & S Dwgs*	*Duct and beam conflict*	*9/15/00*	*10/1/00*	*11/1/00*	*no*
4	*Richardson Electric*	*1*	*NA*	*Underslab conduit*	*10/1/00*	*10/8/00*	*10/15/00*	*no*
5	*Richardson Electric*	*2*	*M1.1 & M2.1*	*Pipe chase at lobbies*	*10/7/00*	*10/14/00*	*10/12/00*	*yes, #3*

FIGURE 13–2 Field Question Log

best, and expediently, rather than forcing the designer into a position in which he or she may taint the answer because of a potential change order and possible retaliation from the owner. If the issue is always cost first and constructability later, the field question's use as a tool is diminished.

Field questions are part of the active quality control process. If there is a problem, it should be addressed, not covered over. Project managers cannot assume that they know how the owner or designer will answer a question, and, therefore, not ask it. How many questions can a job have? It depends on the parties involved, the type of contract, the complexity of the job, and the value of the contract. It also depends upon the quality of the design documents. The better and more complete and coordinated the design, the fewer questions that will arise in the field. Project teams that have worked together previously tend to have fewer questions. It is important to follow correct project management procedures to ensure a successful outcome, especially on projects that require many field clarifications.

The project engineer and subcontractors must be as clear as possible when asking field questions. The specific problem must be clearly stated in simple language. Photocopied portions of drawings or specifications should be attached if needed to clarify the issue. Photographs of exact field conditions also are often attached. Test reports, letters, submittals, or other documentation may be required as well. Even if the reviewing party already has some of this information, the question must be drafted so that it is completely self-explanatory. The drafter should do all that is possible to assist the designer in answering the question, and all pertinent information must be included. If the project engineer knows of a good and logical solution, he or she should recommend it. However, the contractor cannot assume the architect's or engineer's design responsibilities.

Most importantly, the project engineer should research the problem and always be right. Designers are busy, and at this stage of the project, they have moved on to another design. Their construction administration budget may be nearly expended. The construction team should not waste the designer's time and money, challenge their patience, and jeopardize the team relationship that has been built by asking irrelevant or superfluous questions. The project manager needs to ensure that the project engineer and the subcontractors have attempted to resolve the issue internally before submitting it to the designer.

All sketches issued by the design team to accompany a field question response should be numbered, dated, and refer to a construction drawing. Most designers are using 8½-by-11-inch sheets for minor drawing revisions. It is easier and quicker to produce sketches on this size of paper rather than reissue a new drawing. Sometimes the change is complex enough that a new drawing is necessary. Any sketches produced by different members of the design team should all be routed through the architect for sequential numbering. This is the same as subcontractors routing their field questions and submittals through the project manager. If the designer does not produce a log of all sketches, the project manager should. This log should be periodically distributed at both subcontractor and owner/architect meetings to test its completeness.

Also, along with field questions and submittals, these sketches are of great value in beginning the as-built drawing process discussed in Chapter 11. They can be taped to the back of the previous drawing, with a red circle annotating the impacted area and a reference made to the sketch number. For example, if a new wall layout is necessary in room number 210 which is shown on drawing A202, the sketch showing the change, say sketch number SK-49, is attached to the back of drawing A201, the previous drawing. Drawing A202 then has a red circle around room 210 with the note, "See sketch #49 on previous page."

Revised drawings should also be logged on a drawing log. The contract document exhibit should be revised, reissued, and reincorporated into all contracts. This can be quite an administrative task, but if an impacted party does not receive a revised room

Erecting Prefabricated Wall Panels on Precast Foundation Walls on Huna Office Building

layout, the quality control program has just failed. All sketches and revised drawings should be issued through the project architect and should be accompanied by a numbered document that provides clear and concise direction as to what the construction team is expected to do. This direction may come in the form of one of the following documents:

- Construction change directive
- Design change notice
- Design change proposal
- Design change verification
- Engineering or architectural change notice
- Field change notice
- Field order

13.4 IMPACT ANALYSIS

The response to each field question should be reviewed carefully by the project manager to determine if it results in any of the following:

- Change in the scope of the project
- Additional construction costs
- Adverse impact on the construction schedule

If so, the project manager should request a contract change order from the owner. The document used for this purpose is known as a ***change order proposal*** (***COP***). In some instances, the designer will recognize that the response will result in a change order, and the owner will issue a ***construction change directive*** (***CCD***). The use of COP and CCD will be discussed in Chapter 19. Both documents should be numbered sequentially, logged, and discussed at the owner/architect and subcontractor meetings. All involved should be informed. The CCD should provide clear direction to the construction team delineating required actions. Common direction choices include:

- Proceed with the work; estimate to be provided later.
- Proceed with preparation of an estimate. Do not begin work until the estimate is approved.
- Proceed with the work on a time and material basis. Track actual costs.

All sketches, revised drawings, and CCDs are contract documents, and should be treated as such. They should be evaluated by the construction team and incorporated into the prime contract and all appropriate subcontract agreements by change orders.

13.5 SUMMARY

Field questions are used to quickly obtain answers to issues relating to construction of the project. They may be prepared by the general contractor, subcontractors, or suppliers. The field question is one of the last steps in the design process and is an important quality control measure. Sometimes the field question is the first step in the change order process. Although the change order possibility is undesirable for some, it is often unavoidable. The project manager is responsible for informing all parties of field questions, which are an important tool for improving communication and achieving a successful project. Field question forms, similar to other documentation, should be consistent on each project and within the construction firm. All questions and responses should be documented in writing. The field question log is reviewed at the owner/contractor/architect coordination meeting. The construction team should thoroughly review an issue before writing a question and should include as much backup as necessary to fully explain the problem to the design reviewer.

13.6 REVIEW QUESTIONS

1. Why are field questions used on construction projects?
2. Why do some designers resist field questions?
3. Why do some designers welcome field questions?
4. When is the field question log reviewed?
5. Who should prepare a field question?
6. Are verbal responses to field questions sometimes acceptable? If so, how should they be ultimately documented?
7. Do all field questions result in change orders?

13.7 EXERCISES

1. As the roofing subcontractor on the Huna Office Building project, prepare a field question asking for direction regarding the gutters and snow brakes. Include the time when you need a response.

2. You found a conflict in the drawings for the Huna Office Building project. The finish schedule on Drawing A200 shows the walls of the conference room to be tan, but the interior elevation shown in Drawing A501 shows the walls to be light green. Prepare a field question to resolve the discrepancy.

13.8 SOURCES OF ADDITIONAL INFORMATION

Civitello, Andrew M., Jr. *Construction Operations Manual of Policies and Procedures*. 3d ed. New York: McGraw-Hill, Inc., 2000.

Grimes, J. Edward. *Construction Paperwork: An Efficient Management System*. Kingston, Mass: R. S. Means Company, Inc., 1989.

14

Submittals

14.1 INTRODUCTION

The project manager's primary responsibility is to complete the project on time, within budget, and to the specified quality requirements. In this chapter, we will discuss submittals and the submittal process. The submittal process is a key part of the overall quality management program for the project. Our discussion of quality management will wait until Chapter 17.

A submittal is a document or product turned in by the construction team to verify that what they plan to purchase, deliver, and ultimately install is in fact what the design team intended by their drawings and specifications. It serves as one last check. Submittals were introduced in Chapter 9 in our discussion of material purchasing. Submittal requirements for a project are contained in the specifications of the contract. Project managers should look at submittals as a first step in quality control, and, therefore, as a tool to complete a successful project. Article 3.12 of the AIA General Conditions in Appendix E describes submittals.

14.2 TYPES OF SUBMITTALS

A submittal can be any of the following:

- Color charts
- Coordination drawings
- Cut sheets of product data
- Fabrication drawings
- Samples
- Mock-ups
- Shop drawings

Regardless of the type, submittals are one of the final design steps and also one of the first quality control steps. The construction drawings prepared by the designer, although adequate for cost estimating and general construction, do not show sufficient detail to be suitable for fabrication and production of many required construction products. Manufacture of required materials often requires that the contract drawings be amplified by detailed shop drawings that supplement, enlarge, or clarify the project design. These descriptive shop drawings are prepared by the manufacturers or fabricators and provided to the purchasing organization, either the general contractor or a subcontractor. These shop drawings are reviewed by the project engineer to ensure conformance with contract drawings and specifications before being forwarded to the designer. Cover sheets, similar to the transmittals discussed in Chapter 12, are used to transmit shop drawings to the designer.

Other submittals are used to demonstrate that materials selected for the project conform to contract requirements. These may be performance requirements, descriptive requirements, such as color of carpeting or wall covering, or proprietary requirements. Again, cover sheets are used to transmit manufacturer's technical data and product samples to the designer.

14.3 REVIEW AND APPROVAL

The procedures for processing submittals are generally in Division 1 of the contract specifications. Section 01300 of the specifications in Appendix F contains submittal procedures for the Huna Office Building project. Note that it contains specific instructions regarding submittal preparation, copies to be provided, and the review process.

There have been recent changes in the approval that is received back from the designer. It is difficult today to find a submittal stamp or any other correspondence from a designer with the word *approved* on it. Figure 14–1 illustrates some of the wording commonly used on submittal approval stamps. The word *approved* has been replaced with *reviewed*. This also occurs on the designers' field reports where *inspected* has been replaced with noncommittal words such as *visited*, *witnessed*, *reviewed*, or *observed*. The wording used on approval stamps has been selected so that the reviewer does not assume any of the legal responsibility of the party seeking approval.

Some designers will require the contractor to stamp a submittal *approved* before the designer stamps it *reviewed*. Most contractors also have noncommittal stamps that are similar to those of many designers. Some general contractors use a stamp that indicates that the submittal has been received and forwarded. Many general contractors are now asking the subcontractor and supplier to stamp a submittal *approved* prior to submitting it, therefore passing some of the responsibility to them. To some extent, this is a good practice. It requires the submittal originator and the general contractor to at least read the submittal and not just pass it through. Some designers return submittals without any stamp, signature, or comment. Regardless of what the stamp says, it is recommended that project managers submit, submit early, submit everything, and submit often. A good argument can be made that if the reinforcing steel shop drawings were turned in and returned without any marks or comments, they have been accepted. After all, they were not rejected. Unfortunately many owners get caught in the middle with neither party taking responsibility.

The construction team must submit everything that the specifications require as a minimum. If the specifications do not specifically require that the fire extinguishers be submitted, yet the specifications clearly indicate the color of the extinguishers as purple, the project manager has reason to believe that this is an error. If an error is assumed and red extinguishers ordered, the project manager may be surprised. Conversely, if a custom color is ordered and the owner and designer are surprised during the final

Date Rec'd	Date Ret'd	Reviewed by

☐ No exception taken
☐ Make Corrections noted
☐ Revise & Resubmit
☐ Rejected

This review is for general conformance with contract documents only and does not release the contractor of his responsibility for compliance with applicable drawings and specifications.

This submittal review shall not be construed as a complete check and indicates only that information presented conforms generally with contract documents. In no case is subcontractor or supplier relieved of full responsibility for adherence to the contract documents and satisfactory construction of all work.
Returned to contractor for final approval.

Name ____________ Date ____________

☐ Conforms to design concept
☐ Conforms to design concept with revisions as shown
☐ Non-conformance. Revise and resubmit

This document has been reviewed for general conformance with design concept only and does not relieve the subcontractor, fabricator, or supplier of responsibility for conformance with design drawings and specifications all of which have priority over this document.

By: ____________ Date: ____________

Ref. Submittal No. ________
Date Received ________
To Architect ________
From Architect ________

This submittal has been reviewed by the general contractor in accordance with the requirements of the contract documents.
This submittal is forwarded to the Architect and/or engineer for review and final approval.

Name ____________ Date ____________

No exceptions taken ☐
Make corrections noted ☐
Revise & resubmit ☐

FIGURE 14–1 Sample Approval Stamps

inspection, turnover may be affected. The project manager should be proactive. Even though a fire extinguisher submittal was not required, the project manager should still forward one. In the long run, the designers will appreciate this sort of early notification and validity check. Many subcontractors and suppliers fight the submittal process, but it is in their best interest to participate fully. The more documents that are received back from an owner or architect with their approval signature and stamps on them, the better off the subcontractors and suppliers are.

14.4 SUBMITTAL MANAGEMENT

Submittals allow the project manager to identify some of the hidden errors and exceptions the subcontractors and suppliers have taken in their bids. Although they bid it "per plans and specifications," and although the subcontract clearly reinforced this, the project manager does not want to be surprised three months later when the door frames which the chosen supplier has delivered are really cherry veneer and not solid cherry. Although the project manager may be contractually correct, this does not help get the building turned over, the owner moved in, and retention released.

Internal Bracing of First Floor Wall Panels on Huna Office Building

Sometimes project managers do not want the designer to complete the design. Sometimes it is in the construction team's best interest to have some of the choices of field routing, material selections, and construction applications left up to the contractor. This is referred to as "means and methods," an area some owners and architects do not want to step in to, and those who do, shouldn't have. Examples would include the choice of concrete forming systems, or a structural steel joint which if bolted, in lieu of welded, would assist with the installation.

The submittal process also is one of the early checks of the validity of the construction schedule. If the toilet accessory cut sheets are late being submitted by the supplier, a good case could be made that the delivery will also be late. The timing of submittals, as well as deliveries and construction installation, should be noted on all of the purchase orders and subcontracts.

Owners and architects cannot always make up their minds on all possible product choices prior to awarding the contract. An example would be plastic laminate counter top colors. If a product brand is specified with the note, "color to be selected later by the owner," this is adequate to get competitive pricing and issue contracts.

Submittal planning involves the development of a schedule of submittals that is given to the architect for review and an ***expediting log*** to manage the submittal process with subcontractors and suppliers. A flow chart of the planning process is shown in Figure 14–2. Article 3.10.2 of the AIA General Conditions in Appendix E contains the requirement for the contractor to prepare a schedule of submittals. Shortly after receiving award of the contract, the project manager should review each specification section for submittal requirements. Language should be included in each subcontract and purchase order regarding quantity and timing of submittals. The construction schedule is then reviewed with the superintendent and submittals scheduled. A preliminary submittal list or expediting log with all potential submittals is prepared, with the understanding that some items may be grouped or dropped at a later date. An example is shown in Figure 14–3 on page 178. A letter is sent to each subcontractor and supplier with the expediting log attached, asking for their acceptance of or

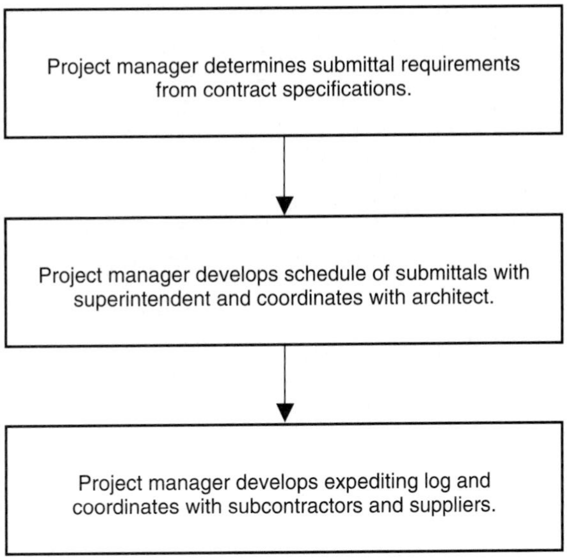
Project manager determines submittal requirements from contract specifications.
Project manager develops schedule of submittals with superintendent and coordinates with architect.
Project manager develops expediting log and coordinates with subcontractors and suppliers.

FIGURE 14–2
Submittal Planning

disagreement with the items that will be submitted, as well as the dates materials are required. A required response date should be set and recipients notified that nonresponses will be considered as approvals.

The process for managing submittals is illustrated in Figure 14–4 on page 179. After a submittal is received, it should be reviewed with respect to the specifications and the drawings. The project manager does not want to be in a position of explaining why the floor covering contractor submitted vinyl tile when slate was clearly required. Vendors have been known to attempt to substitute a cheaper, nonspecified product. The shop drawings should be reviewed for requested dimensions, and the submittal should be stamped with the company's stamp. Each submittal is assigned a number and entered on a ***submittal register***, also known as a submittal log. This log is updated and discussed at the owner/architect/contractor coordination meeting as well as at subcontractor coordination meetings. This is different than the expediting log. Expediting issues and problems with subcontractors should be kept out of meetings with the owner. Discussion should be limited to materials and documents that the designers have. Some project managers will assign a submittal number for every item prior to processing any submittals. These can be tied into the specification section numbers. For example, reinforcing steel may be simply submittal 5 for the entire project, or may be number 03200–1 for the first submittal in reinforcing steel specification 03200. Regardless of the numbering system utilized, the important point to remember is to number each submittal individually. This allows for efficient tracking and future reference. A submittal log is illustrated in Figure 14–5 on page 180.

A submittal cover sheet is similar to a transmittal, except it is used exclusively for submittals. Each construction firm will have its own format. The architect, for example, may have a required form and may have even included it in the specifications. A submittal cover sheet is illustrated in Figure 14–6 on page 181. The approval stamps discussed in Section 14.3 are applied to the actual submittal documents, not the cover sheet.

Submittals may be processed by the architect, the owner, the city, consultants, or subconsultant designers. They may be reviewed by several people, either concurrently or sequentially. The project manager or project engineer should set up the submittal log so that it can document the entire review process. After receipt of the submittal from the reviewing party, the project manager needs to review it for disposition and log it accordingly. If changes have been made to the products, the project manager needs to note them for potential change orders. Submittals should be reviewed both by the project engineer and by the superintendent when they are first received from the subcontractor or supplier and again after review by the design team.

NORTHWEST CONSTRUCTION COMPANY
1242 First Avenue, Cascade, Washington 98202
(206) 239-1422

EXPEDITING LOG

Project No.: *9821* Project Name: *Huna Office Building* Project Manager: *Ted Jones*

No.	Description	Supplier	Committed Shop Dwg Submittal	Actual Shop Dwg Submittal	Fabricate/ Delivery Duration	Scheduled Delivery Date	Actual Delivery Date	Responsible Person
1	Import sample	Earth Enterprises	8/20/00	8/20/00	NA	9/6/00	9/6/00	Peterson
2	Pea gravel	Earth Enterprises	8/20/00	8/20/00	NA	9/14/00	9/13/00	Peterson
3	Silt fence	Juneau Lumber	8/20/00	8/21/00	NA	9/17/00	9/16/00	Peterson
4	Perforated pipe	Juneau Lumber	8/20/00	8/28/00	2 days	9/20/00	9/1600	Peterson
5	Footing rebar	Steel Fabrication	9/1/00	10/7/00	2 weeks	9/16/00	9/19/00	Peterson
6	Embed steel	Steel Fabrication	9/6/00	10/7/00	2 weeks	9/22/00	9/19/00	Peterson
7	Concrete mix	Juneau Redi-Mix	9/6/00	9/15/00	NA	9/20/00	9/20/00	Peterson
8	SOG wire mesh	Steel Fabrication	9/1/00		1 week	9/24/00	9/24/00	Peterson
9	Asphalt specification	ATB Asphalt			NA	9/19/00	9/19/00	Peterson
10	Column rebar	Steel Fabrication	9/1/00		2 weeks	9/25/00		Peterson

FIGURE 14–3 Expediting Log

FIGURE 14–4
Submittal Management Process

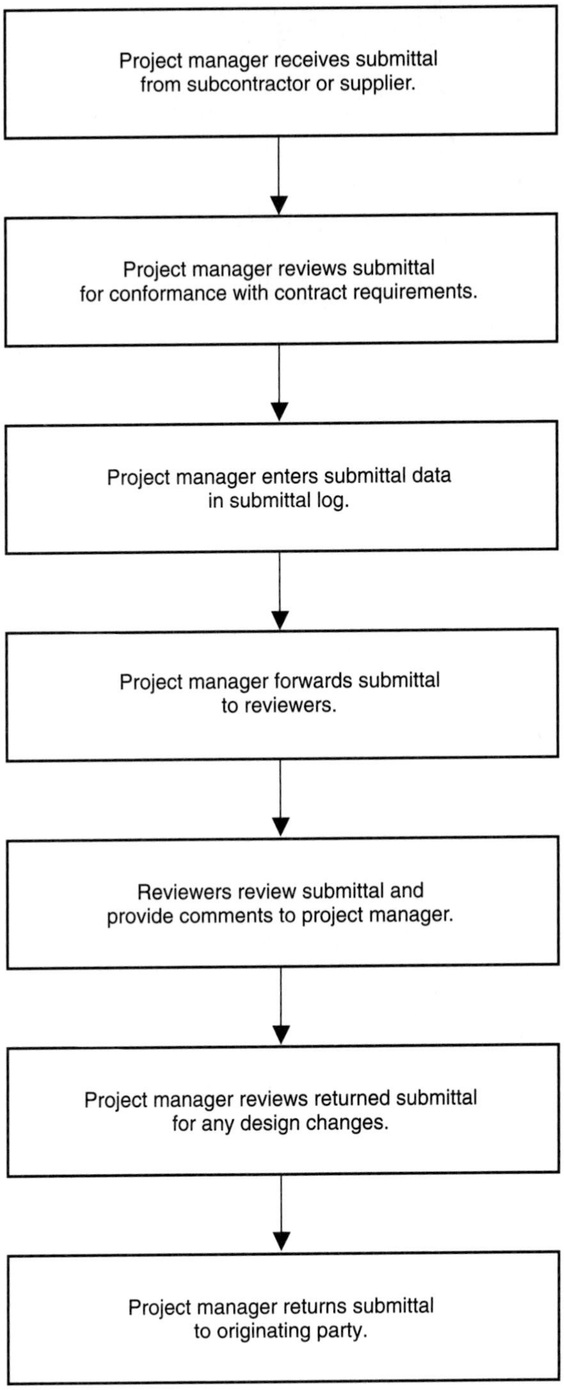
Project manager receives submittal from subcontractor or supplier.
Project manager reviews submittal for conformance with contract requirements.
Project manager enters submittal data in submittal log.
Project manager forwards submittal to reviewers.
Reviewers review submittal and provide comments to project manager.
Project manager reviews returned submittal for any design changes.
Project manager returns submittal to originating party.

The submittal should be sent back to the originating party who will then take action. Other contractors and suppliers may need to review the final submittals. For example, a steel erector will need to see the steel fabricator's drawings. It is the subcontractor's responsibility to notify the project manager if any change of scope has arisen due to comments received. The designer and owner may not only use the submittal process as a vehicle to finish the design, they may also use it to change the design. If a change of scope is included, for example changing all of the #4 reinforcement steel to #5, a formal change document should have accompanied the submittal return. The change order process is discussed in Chapter 19.

NORTHWEST CONSTRUCTION COMPANY
1242 First Avenue, Cascade, Washington 98202
(206) 239-1422

SUBMITTAL LOG

Project No.: *9821* Project Name: *Huna Office Building* Project Manager: *Ted Jones*

No.	Originator	Sub's No.	Specification Section	Description	Date Submitted	Date Return Requested	Date Returned	Disposition*
1	*Earth Enterprises*	*1*	*Civil drawings*	*Import sample*	*8/20/00*	*8/27/00*	*8/26/00*	*A*
2	*Earth Enterprises*	*2*	*Civil drawings*	*Pea gravel pipe bedding*	*8/20/00*	*8/27/00*	*8/26/00*	*A*
3	*Northwest Construction*	*NA*	*Civil drawings*	*Silt fence data sheet*	*8/21/00*	*8/22/00*	*8/23/00*	*A*
4	*Northwest Construction*	*NA*	*Civil drawings*	*Perforated pipe sample*	*8/28/00*	*9/15/00*	*9/10/00*	*AN*
5	*Steel Fabrication*	*1*	*03200*	*Footing rebar shop drawings*	*10/7/00*	*10/14/00*	*10/15/00*	*AN*
6	*Steel Fabrication*	*2*	*Structural drawings*	*Steel embed shop drawings*	*10/7/00*	*10/14/00*		

*A — approved, AN — approved as noted, RR — revise and resubmit, and R — rejected

FIGURE 14–5 Submittal Log

NORTHWEST CONSTRUCTION COMPANY

1242 First Avenue, Cascade, Washington 98202
(206) 239-1422

SUBMITTAL

Project: *Huna Office Building*
Area/System: *Footing rebar*
To: *JYL Architects*
Address: *522 West 10th Street*
Juneau, Alaska 99801
Attention: *Norm Riley*
Required Response Date: *October 14, 2000*

Date: *October 7, 2000*
Submittal Number *5*
First Submittal? *Y*
Re-Submittal? *NA*
Previous Number(s) *NA*

Subcontractor/Supplier providing submittal: *Steel Fabrication* Originator's Number: *1*

Specification Section	Description	Drawing No.	Action Taken
03200	*Two sheets of shop drawings*	*S1 & S2 sepias*	*Checked*

Remarks by Contractor: *Please review and approve. Keep one set of blue line drawings for record. Return sepias for copying and distribution.*

Submitted by: *Mary Peterson, Project Engineer*

Space below for Architect/Engineer:

Reply: *Approved as noted.*

Signed: Norm Riley

Date: *October 16, 2000*

Contractor's Job No./File Code: *9821/03200*

FIGURE 14–6 Submittal Cover Sheet

14.5 SUMMARY

Submittals are documents or products that are submitted to the designer for review. They represent the final phase of the design process and are key components of the project manager's quality management program. Submittals include shop drawings, manufacturer's technical data, and product samples. They may be prepared by subcontractors, suppliers, or the project manager's technical staff. Because of their potential impact on the construction schedule, all submittal requirements should be identified at the beginning of the project and tracked using a submittal log. The submittal log is used for managing the submittal process with the design team, and an expediting log is used for managing the submittal process with subcontractors and suppliers. An effectively managed submittal program is a necessary tool to achieve a successful construction project.

14.6 REVIEW QUESTIONS

1. Who are responsible for preparing submittals?
2. Who is responsible for approving submittals?
3. What is the difference between a contract drawing and a shop drawing?
4. List five items that would require a submittal on a construction project.
5. Why would a contractor not want the design team to completely design an item of work?
6. How is a submittal considered part of the quality control process?
7. How is a submittal considered part of the design process?
8. List two different methods of numbering a submittal.
9. When is the submittal log reviewed?

14.7 EXERCISES

1. Prepare a submittal coversheet for manufactured roof panels for the Huna Office Building project. The submittal requirements are shown in Chapter 10. Use the project schedule folded inside the back cover to assist in identifying approximate dates and lead times.
2. Prepare a submittal coversheet for an item on the Huna Office Building project that may not normally require a submittal. Select an item that may involve some uncertainty. Explain why you selected the item.

14.8 SOURCES OF ADDITIONAL INFORMATION

Civitello, Andrew M., Jr. *Construction Operations Manual of Policies and Procedures.* 3d ed. New York: McGraw-Hill, Inc., 2000.

Grimes, J. Edward. *Construction Paperwork: An Efficient Management System.* Kingston, Mass.: R. S. Means Company, Inc., 1989.

Mincks, William R., and Hal Johnston. *Construction Jobsite Management.* Albany, N.Y.: Delmar Publishers, 1998.

15

Progress Payments

15.1 INTRODUCTION

One of the most important project management functions is to receive payment for the work performed. A project manager may have all of the tools necessary to earn a profit on a job, but if the owner does not pay for the work, the project manager will not be able to realize a profit. Some project managers do not acknowledge the importance of preparing prompt payment requests; this is true with subcontractors, as well. If a payment request is not submitted on time, the project manager will not likely get paid on time. Cash management is essential, or the project manager may find that he or she may be unable to pay suppliers, workers, or subcontractors. Good cash management skills, just like good communications skills, are essential if one is to be an effective project manager.

15.2 CONTRACT TYPES

On most construction projects, requests for payment are submitted monthly, and ***progress payments*** are made during the following month. The formats and times are specified in the general conditions of the contract. Payment procedures used on the Huna Office Building project are contained in Article 12 of the contract agreement in Appendix D and in Article 9 of the AIA General Conditions in Appendix E. Regardless of the type of contract, many of the procedures are similar. In this section, we will discuss some of the pay request differences that result from different types of contracts.

Cost-plus contracts, including those with a GMP, have the following characteristics:

- Project managers request payment based on actual expenses; therefore, they have to have already received the invoices from subcontractors and suppliers.

- The project manager generally is required to submit invoices and general contractor payrolls to the owner with the payment request.
- It is almost impossible to overbill.
- Fees and any lump sum items, such as general conditions expenses, are billed using a schedule of values and percentage completion.
- The project manager may be subjected to periodic owner audits of actual costs incurred.

Payment on a lump-sum contract is based on a schedule of values and percentage completion. ***Front loading*** and ***overbilling*** can occur on this type contract, as will be discussed in the next section. Project manager records are rarely audited in a lump-sum contract.

A unit-price contract allows for payment based upon quantities actually installed. If the contractor is to be paid $2,000 per ton for structural steel installed and installs fifty tons, then he or she will be paid $100,000, less any agreed-upon ***retention***. This process is quite objective and can be facilitated by an outside quantity measurement individual, firm, or team.

Payment on a time-and-materials contract is based on actual labor hours times a contract labor rate plus reimbursement for materials based on supplier invoices.

15.3 SCHEDULE OF VALUES

The first step in developing the pay request is establishing a schedule of values or an agreed-upon breakdown of the contract cost. Often the contract will require that a schedule of values be submitted for approval within a certain time after executing the contract, for example two weeks. This schedule of values should be established and agreed upon early in the job, well before the first request for payment is submitted, but after all subcontracts have been awarded.

Developing the schedule of values starts with the summary estimate that has been corrected for actual buyout values. This is shown as the first two cost columns in the center of Figure 15–1. This would be the schedule of values used on a cost-plus contract because the general conditions and fee are listed separately. On a lump-sum contract, the general conditions and fee would be distributed proportionately across all payment items as shown on the right side of Figure 15–1. The schedule of values that the project manager would submit for a lump-sum contract is the far right column of the figure which is entitled adjusted totals.

Some contractors try to combine items into single line items. In this way, they believe they can possibly overbill or hide the true subcontract values from the owner. The schedule of values should be as detailed as is reasonable. The project manager should do all that is possible to assist the owner in paying completely and promptly. Nothing should be hidden. At a minimum, the sixteen CSI divisions should be used as line items. Major subcontractors should be listed where possible. Separate building components, building wings or distinct site areas, separate buildings, phases, or systems should be listed individually in a detailed schedule of values.

Even if the contract does not require early submission of the schedule of values for approval, it is good practice to do so. The project manager does not want any future arguments with an owner or architect over a payment request. The schedule of values should be submitted for approval. Most owners will appreciate the openness, and this may help with facilitating prompt payment, as well as establishing a high level of respect and trust.

The fee on cost-plus contracts can be invoiced based on the percentage of the project that is complete. If the project is 60% complete, then 60% of the fee has been

NORTHWEST CONSTRUCTION COMPANY
1242 First Avenue, Cascade, Washington 98202
(206) 239-1422
Huna Office Building
8/15/00

CSI Division	Description		GMP Value	% of Subtotal	GC & Fee Prorated	Adjusted Totals
1	Jobsite General Conditions		0			
2	Sitework:					
	Earthwork & Utilities	124,000		8.42%	24,261	148,261
	Paving	24,000		1.63%	4,696	28,696
	Misc. Site	48,000		3.26%	9,391	57,391
	Sitework Subtotal:		196,000	13.32%	38,348	234,348
3	Concrete:					
	Reinforcement	13,000		0.88%	2,543	15,543
	Foundations	42,000		2.85%	8,217	50,217
	Walls & Slabs	82,000		5.57%	16,043	98,043
	Concrete Subtotal:		137,000	9.31%	26,804	163,804
4	Masonry		0			
5	Structural & Misc. Metals		6,000	0.41%	1,174	7,174
6	Wood & Plastic:					
	Rough Carpentry	384,000		26.09%	75,130	459,130
	Finish Carpentry	85,000		5.77%	16,630	101,630
	Carpentry Subtotal:		469,000	31.86%	91,761	560,761
7	Thermal & Moisture Protection					
	Insulation	19,000		1.29%	3,717	22,717
	Roof & Accessories	59,000		4.01%	11,543	70,543
	Gutters	3,000		0.20%	587	3,587
	Division 7 Subtotal:		81,000	5.50%	15,848	96,848
8	Doors, Windows, Glass					
	Doors	29,000		1.97%	5,674	34,674
	Glazing	19,000		1.29%	3,717	22,717
	Door Hardware	15,000		1.02%	2,935	17,935
	Division 8 Subtotal:		63,000	4.28%	12,326	75,326
9	Finishes:					
	Drywall	25,000		1.70%	4,891	29,891
	Painting	28,000		1.90%	5,478	33,478
	Acoustical Ceilings	8,000		0.54%	1,565	9,565
	Carpet	23,000		1.56%	4,500	27,500
	Floor Covering	17,000		1.15%	3,326	20,326
	Finishes Subtotal:		101,000	6.86%	19,761	120,761
10	Specialties		11,000	0.75%	2,152	13,152
11,12,13	Equipment		0			
14	Conveying Systems (Elevator)		30,000	2.04%	5,870	35,870
15	Mechanical Systems:					
	Plumbing	49,000		3.33%	9,587	58,587
	Fire Protection	29,000		1.97%	5,674	34,674
	HVAC	145,000		9.85%	28,370	173,370
	Controls	35,000		2.38%	6,848	41,848
	Mechanical Subtotal:		258,000	17.53%	50,478	308,478
16	Electrical Systems		120,000	8.15%	23,478	143,478
	Subtotal w/o GC's and Fee:		1,472,000	100.00%	**288,000**	**1,760,000**
	General Conditions		205,000			
	Fee		83,000			
	Subtotal GC's & Fee		**288,000**			
	TOTAL GMP:		**1,760,000**			

FIGURE 15–1 Schedule of Values

earned. Most owners will not take issue with this approach. General conditions on cost-plus contracts can be invoiced three different ways:

- Actual costs incurred
- Percentage complete based on work constructed
- Straight line with equal payments for each month

Approved change orders can either be spread across the schedule of values as they are received or added to the bottom as separate line items. This second method generally is the easiest to administer. Reformatting the schedule of values each month is similar to re-drafting the construction schedule. The original schedule of values record is lost, and it may create an issue with the owner or the architect.

Some project managers advocate hiding the fee and general conditions, or front loading them. This is more prevalent on a bid contract than with negotiated work. It is recommended that the fee and general conditions be listed just as they would in the project cost accounting system. The schedule of values should look like the final estimate. Trying to explain during an audit or a claim situation why the cost of the foundations was stated as $70,000 in the pay estimate but was only $42,000 in the original estimate will be difficult. Spreading, but still hiding, the fee and general conditions as a weighted average over the schedule of values may be fair, but it will be difficult for the owner to track lien releases, as will be discussed in Section 15.7.

15.4 PAYMENT REQUEST PROCESS

The most common billing practice is to request payment at the end of each month. The project manager must gather all of the costs and prepare the monthly request that is submitted to the architect or owner for approval. This process should start on the twentieth of the month, and subcontractors and major suppliers should be required to have their monthly invoices to the project manager by that date. If subcontractors are having problems managing their cash flow, the project manager needs to push them to submit their monthly billings. Some project managers think that if the subcontractors do not get their bills in on time, that is the subcontractors' problem and they will not get paid this month. While this may be contractually correct, it is counterproductive. The project manager must do all that is reasonable to give the subcontractors enough capital to keep them from going broke, at least while they are on the project.

On the twentieth of the month, all of the subcontractors should estimate what percentage of work they believe will be complete and in place through the end of the month, and the suppliers estimate what they believe will be delivered to the site through the end of the month. The project manager also forecasts what direct work he or she believes will be in place through the end of the month.

Subcontractors and suppliers will want to be paid for materials purchased for the job that they are storing in their own warehouses. Perhaps fabrication is necessary, as is the case with ductwork or structural steel, or maybe the supplier is ahead of schedule or the general contractor is behind. Payment for materials stored off the project site should be avoided. Sometimes payment for such stored materials is unavoidable due to scheduling reasons. Occasionally it may be financially beneficial for all parties, for example, if the mechanical subcontractor was able to purchase the stainless material at discount because it was purchased with materials needed for another larger project. In these cases, the project manager needs to be sure that his or her interests are protected. The material must be stored in an insured and bonded warehouse.

The project manager collects all of the forecasts, estimates, and requests and assembles a draft pay request to submit for approval. This involves estimating the percentage complete for each item on the schedule of values at the end of the month. These percentages are multiplied by the value of each line item to produce the schedule of values shown in Figure 15–2.[1] About the twenty-fifth of the month, the project manager should hold a short informal meeting with the architect, the owner, and maybe the bank at the job site to review the month's anticipated pay request. The request is submitted as a draft for discussion and approval. If any of the approving parties has a problem with a particular line item or percentage, the project manger still has time to request an explanation from the submitting party or develop additional detail. A job walk during this meeting is extremely helpful to visualize how much work is complete or will be in place by the end of the month. Only percentage completions are usually reviewed, not dollars. If necessary, subcontractor invoices can be attached to this draft for backup. This draft pay estimate and the meeting promote teamwork among the owner, the architect, and the general contractor's project manager.

Some contracts may require that the monthly pay request review and approval coincides with review of the ongoing as-built drawing process. As will be discussed later, general contractors generally do not do a good job of developing as-built drawings. They often put it off until the end of the job and have them prepared by individuals who were not involved or who have forgotten what occurred. Some contracts will require that a monthly submittal of as-built drawings accompany the pay request. This may be overkill and is excessively expensive. Monthly review of as-built drawings on the contractor's and subcontractor's job site plan tables should suffice.

The project manager submits the formal pay request, as revised (if necessary), for formal approval and payment to the owner no later than the end of the month. This can be submitted earlier if possible. Some contracts and lenders may also request that the architect sign off in the approval process. The project manager should carry the payment request through the approval process to ensure that there are not issues with its content.

AIA Form G702, which is illustrated in Figure 15–3 on page 189, is an example of a pay request summary and approval page that accompanies the detailed schedule of values shown in Figure 15–2. All blanks should be filled in. If any are not applicable, *NA* should be entered. The form should be either typed or prepared in ink.

The contract will dictate payment terms. It is customary for the general contractor to be paid by the tenth of the following month if the payment request is submitted by the end of the current month. The specific timeframes used on the Huna Office Building project are contained in Article 12.1.3 of the contract agreement in Appendix D. After the project manager has received the monthly payment from the owner, he or she disburses funds to the suppliers and subcontractors. This usually is done within one week to ten days after receipt. A project manager should not delay paying the suppliers and subcontractors.

Some ***third-tier subcontractors*** and suppliers may want to enter into ***joint check agreements*** with the project manager to ensure that they are paid direct by the contractor. Although some project managers see this as unnecessary effort, it ultimately benefits and protects the project manager and the owner from the possibility that some subcontractors may not make payment, resulting in third-tier firms placing liens on the project.

15.5 CASH AS A TOOL

Cash is one of the most useful tools the project manager has. If a construction firm has a reputation of paying their subcontractors and suppliers fast and fairly, they may

[1]This is a customized form for the Huna Office Building project. Many project managers use similar spreadsheets for their monthly schedule of values submissions. AIA Form G703 may be specified in the contract as the required schedule of values worksheet.

NORTHWEST CONSTRUCTION COMPANY

1242 First Avenue, Cascade, Washington 98202

(206) 239-1422

Billing Period:
From: 12/01/00
To: 12/31/00

Huna Office Building

PAY REQUEST CONTINUATION SHEET

Request # 5
Invoice # 1234

A	B	C	D	E	G	G.1	H
					(D+E)	(G/C)	(C-G)
Line Item	**Description**	**Contract Value**	**Previous Complete**	**Complete This Mo.**	**Complete To date**	**% Complete**	**To Go**
1.0	General Conditions	205,000	96,000	24,000	120,000	59%	85,000
2.1	Earthwork & Utilities	124,000	124,000	0	124,000	100%	0
2.2	Paving	24,000	12,000	0	12,000	50%	12,000
2.3	Misc. Site	48,000	0	0	0	0%	48,000
3.1	Reinforcement	13,000	13,000	0	13,000	100%	0
3.2	Foundations	42,000	42,000	0	42,000	100%	0
3.3	Walls & Slabs	82,000	82,000	0	82,000	100%	0
5.0	Steel	6,000	6,000	0	6,000	100%	0
6.1	Rough Carpentry & Siding	344,000	344,000	0	344,000	100%	0
6.11	Siding	40,000	40,000	0	40,000	100%	0
6.2	Finish Carpentry	85,000	0	0	0	0%	85,000
7.1	Insulation	19,000	0	19,000	19,000	100%	0
7.2	Roofing	59,000	59,000	0	59,000	100%	0
7.3	Gutters	3,000	3,000	0	3,000	100%	0
8.1	Doors & Frames	29,000	0	0	0	0%	29,000
8.2	Glazing	19,000	19,000	0	19,000	100%	0
8.3	Door Hardware	15,000	0	0	0	0%	15,000
9.1	Drywall	25,000	0	10,000	10,000	40%	15,000
9.2	Painting	28,000	0	14,000	14,000	50%	14,000
9.3	Acoustical Ceilings	8,000	0	0	0	0%	8,000
9.4	Carpet	23,000	0	0	0	0%	23,000
9.5	Balance of floorcovering	17,000	0	0	0	0%	17,000
10.0	Specialties	11,000	0	0	0	0%	11,000
14.0	Elevator	30,000	0	0	0	0%	30,000
15.1	Plumbing: underslab	9,000	9,000	0	9,000	100%	0
15.11	rough-in	20,000	20,000	0	20,000	100%	0
15.12	fixtures & trim	20,000	0	0	0	0%	20,000
15.2	Fire Protection: rough-in	19,000	15,000	4,000	19,000	100%	0
15.21	Fire Protection: trim	10,000	0	0	0	0%	10,000
15.3	HVAC: rough-in	50,000	43,000	7,000	50,000	100%	0
15.31	equipment	50,000	24,000	23,000	47,000	94%	3,000
15.32	trim	45,000	0	3,000	3,000	7%	42,000
15.4	Controls	35,000	0	0	0	0%	35,000
16.0	Electrical: rough-in	60,000	60,000	0	60,000	100%	0
16.1	trim	60,000	0	0	0	0%	60,000
90.0	Fee	83,000	41,000	9,000	50,000	60%	33,000
	Original Total	1,760,000	1,052,000	113,000	1,165,000	66%	595,000
99.1	Change Order No. 1	4,623	3,000	1,623	4,623	100%	0
99.2	Change Order No. 2	0	0	0	0	0%	0
	Current Total	**1,764,623**	**1,055,000**	**114,623**	**1,169,623**	66%	**595,000**

FIGURE 15–2 Pay Request Continuation Sheet

APPLICATION AND CERTIFICATE FOR PAYMENT AIA DOCUMENT G702 (Instructions on reverse side) PAGE ONE OF PAGES

TO OWNER: *Huna Totem Corporation*

PROJECT: *Huna Office Building*

APPLICATION NO.: 5
PERIOD TO: Dec 31, 2000
PROJECT NOS.: 9821

Distribution to:
☒ OWNER
☒ ARCHITECT
☒ CONTRACTOR
☐
☐

FROM CONTRACTOR: *Northwest Construction Co.*

VIA ARCHITECT: *Jensen Yorba Lott, Inc.*

CONTRACT DATE: August 15, 2000

CONTRACT FOR: *New Office Building*

CONTRACTOR'S APPLICATION FOR PAYMENT

Application is made for payment, as shown below, in connection with the Contract. Continuation Sheet, AIA Document G703, is attached.

1. **ORIGINAL CONTRACT SUM** $1,760,000.00
2. **Net change by Change Orders** .... $ 4,623.00
3. **CONTRACT SUM TO DATE** (Line 1 ± 2) $1,764,623.00
4. **TOTAL COMPLETED & STORED TO DATE** $1,169,623.00
   (Column G on G703)
5. **RETAINAGE:**
   a. 5 % of Completed Work $ 58,481.00
   (Columns D + E on G703)
   b. 5 % of Stored Material $ NA
   (Column F on G703)
   Total Retainage (Line 5a + 5b or Total in Column I of G703) .... $ 58,481.00
6. **TOTAL EARNED LESS RETAINAGE** $1,111,142.00
   (Line 4 less Line 5 Total)
7. **LESS PREVIOUS CERTIFICATES FOR PAYMENT**
   (Line 6 from prior Certificate) $1,002,250.00
8. **CURRENT PAYMENT DUE** .... $ 108,892.00
9. **BALANCE TO FINISH, INCLUDING RETAINAGE** $ 653,481.00
   (Line 3 less Line 6)

CHANGE ORDER SUMMARY	ADDITIONS	DEDUCTIONS
Total changes approved in previous months by Owner	$4,623.00	NA
Total approved this Month	NA	NA
TOTALS	$4,623.00	NA
NET CHANGES by Change Order	$4,623.00	

The undersigned Contractor certifies that to the best of the Contractor's knowledge, information and belief the Work covered by this Application for Payment has been completed in accordance with the Contract Documents, that all amounts have been paid by the Contractor for Work for which previous Certificates for Payment were issued and payments received from the Owner, and that current payment shown herein is now due.

CONTRACTOR:

By: Ted Jones Date: Dec. 29, 2000

State of:
County of:
Subscribed and sworn to before me this day of

Notary Public:
My Commission expires:

ARCHITECT'S CERTIFICATE FOR PAYMENT

In accordance with the Contract Documents, based on on-site observations and the data comprising this application, the Architect certifies to the Owner that to the best of the Architect's knowledge, information and belief the Work has progressed as indicated, the quality of the Work is in accordance with the Contract Documents, and the Contractor is entitled to payment of the AMOUNT CERTIFIED.

AMOUNT CERTIFIED .... $ 108,892.00

(Attach explanation if amount certified differs from the amount applied for. Initial all figures on this Application and on the Continuation Sheet that are changed to conform to the amount certified.)

ARCHITECT:

By: Norm Riley Date: Dec. 30, 2000

This Certificate is not negotiable. The AMOUNT CERTIFIED is payable only to the Contractor named herein. Issuance, payment and acceptance of payment are without prejudice to any rights of the Owner or Contractor under this Contract.

FIGURE 15–3 Pay Request Summary Page

Installing Prefabricated Second Floor Structure on Huna Office Building

receive more favorable prices on bid day. This will result in the contractor getting more work.

General contractors, as well as subcontractors, are not banks. The general contractor's role on the construction project is to build the building, not provide construction financing. The project manager begins incurring labor and material expenses on the first of the month. Bills for these expenses are submitted at the end of the month, and payment is not received until the tenth of the next month. This means the general contractor has provided funding for these expenses for a minimum of forty and maybe up to sixty days. These time periods may be up to thirty days longer for subcontractors. This is the reason some project managers attempt to overbill the owner.

If the project manager overbills too much, the owner and bank may become suspicious, and trust and faith in the project manager are lost. The owner may allow a little overbilling so as not to place the contractor in a situation with an excessively large negative cash flow. The project manager should compromise by not overbilling too much, as it might impede the monthly payment request process.

The way some project managers overbill on lump-sum contracts is to front load the schedule of values. Ways of accomplishing this are to place all of the fee and general conditions (if not separately listed) on the early scheduled construction activities, such as foundations or concrete slabs. Another way is to artificially inflate these early activities or to falsify the amounts requested by subcontractors. These methods are also counter productive to building with a team attitude and will most often ultimately be discovered through interim lien releases or during an audit.

Another example of cash as a tool is the use of discounts. Discounts may be offered by material suppliers for early payment. If a project manager pays within a certain time period, say ten days, he or she can receive a discount off the invoice price. For this reason, a project manager may elect to pay suppliers early, even though the owner has not made a payment. In effect, the general contractor is acting as a bank. Many owners will want to benefit from these discounts also. If the owner has not paid the general contractor and the contractor is utilizing his or her own cash to realize the discount, the discount should belong to the contractor. If the owner is willing to pay up front and the general contractor is using the owner's cash to achieve the discount, then the discounts should apply to the owner.

15.6 RETENTION

A portion of the monthly pay request is commonly held back by the owner and subsequently by the general contractor with respect to subcontractors. This is referred to as retention, or retainage, and is another cash tool. The purpose of retention is to assure that the contractor's attention is focused on completion of the project, including close-out of all paperwork activities. Discussion of close-out activities and the process required to release the retention is contained in Chapter 21.

The amount of retention will be dictated by the contract and may be a subject for negotiation, or during the course of the project, renegotiation. In the past, 10% was standard, but as the size of contracts has increased along with the value of money, 10% may be excessive in today's market. The most common percentages today are either 5% through the course of the job or alternatively 10% until the project is 50% complete and no further retention thereafter, which also equals 5% upon completion. Article 21.1.7 of the contract agreement for the Huna Office Building project in Appendix D indicates a retention rate of 5%.

A subcontractor's contract is tied into the prime contract. In this way, the subcontractor is also tied into whatever retention terms the general contractor has with the owner. This is usually in the subcontractor's best interest and prohibits the general contractor from overwithholding.

One twist to retention is the length of time a particular subcontractor's money is held. If the owner retains 5% of the entire job until thirty days after substantial completion (the standard time frame), does this mean that the site work subcontractor has to wait to receive final payment until all of the floor covering punchlist items are complete? This is not fair to the early subcontractors and can result in undesirable financial burdens that can ultimately impact both the general contractor and the owner. It is a good idea to include text in the contract that allows for release of that portion of the overall retention to facilitate paying off these early subcontractors. The utility contractor can go broke on another project, and the project manager may receive a lien on the project because of the retention. This is not as applicable on short duration projects but is extremely important on jobs that last a year or longer. Early subcontractors should be paid and their final and unconditional lien releases received soon after their work is completed.

Sometimes on cost-plus contracts, the project manager can negotiate that retention is limited to a percentage held on the fee, for example 25% of the fee. Retention serves two purposes. First, it establishes an account to finish the work of those parties who refuse or cannot do so, and it also serves as an incentive for the project manager to finish the project expeditiously. A project manager often may be able to convince the owner that he or she does not need to hold much retention if the project manager and the owner have worked together previously.

15.7 LIEN MANAGEMENT

A lien is a legal right to secure payment for work performed and materials provided in the improvement of land. This right attaches to the land in a manner similar to a mortgage. If a contractor is owed money and the owner refuses payment, the contractor can attach a lien to the owner's property. If the lien is not removed by payment, the lien claimant can demand legal foreclosure of the property and have the obligation satisfied out of the proceeds of the sale of the property. Liens should be avoided at all costs. They are expensive to deal with, they cause bad feelings, and any party involved receives bad press from them.

The project manager should work to protect the owner from liens from subcontractors and suppliers and from their subcontractors and suppliers. The most common liens are filed from third- or even fourth-tiered parties. These may be from a supplier to a supplier to a subcontractor to a subcontractor. The farther removed, the more difficult it is to prevent and ultimately resolve.

The supplier's rights are protected by law to assure payment for goods received by the end user and the ultimate beneficiary. In most jurisdictions, suppliers are required to file what is known as a ***materialman's notice***, similar to the one illustrated in Figure 15–4. This notice is sent to the property owner notifying him or her that the supplier will be delivering material to their project. The notice is technically required in order to preserve the supplier's lien rights. Some notices are also sent to the general contractor. The project manager should file all material notices received with each subcontract. At the end of the project, it is appropriate to request an ***unconditional lien release*** from each party who filed such a notice. If they went to the trouble of preserving their lien rights, they have the responsibility to release them when paid.

Conditional lien releases should accompany each request for payment from suppliers and subcontractors. An example was shown in Chapter 8 (Figure 8–12). The contract may require submission of interim (or conditional) lien releases from suppliers and subcontractors with each payment request to the owner. A project manager should require suppliers and subcontractors to submit conditional lien releases with their pay requests, regardless of the owner's requirements. Interim lien releases should be collected and filed just in case a problem occurs. If the owner requests copies of them, the project manager should not resist, but comply.

A conditional lien release is just that; the release of lien rights is conditional upon receipt of payment. An unconditional lien release means that all payments have been received, and all lien rights are unconditionally released. Some payment request procedures will require conditional releases to accompany each request for payment along with an unconditional release for the previous month's payment. Some owners will go so far as to physically trade checks for lien releases.

There are several different release forms. Many states produce forms which comply with local law. Some owners will try to get project managers to release lien rights that are not required to be released by law. Releasing rights to claim for extra work are also sometimes hidden within the lien release or payment request forms. An example lien release form is shown in Figure 15–5 on page 194. Lien releases are an area where legal counsel should be sought. The conditional release covers the month for which payment is requested, and the unconditional release is for the month that was covered by the payment that was received. A ***final lien release*** will be submitted for the entire contract at close-out to receive retention release. This is discussed in Chapter 21.

So what happens if a supplier does not get paid? The time limits involved vary with jurisdiction. Usually a pre-lien notice is filed which is not a lien, but is just a warning that if the supplier does not get paid by a certain date, it will file a lien. Common timing is that if the supplier has not filed its lien within ninety days after delivery, the supplier has waived its lien rights. After the lien is filed, it has an additional ninety days to foreclose. Sometimes a lien is filed too quickly by a supplier. Liens are very difficult to have removed, and every precaution should be made to assure they are not filed erroneously.

The project manager needs to follow all of the appropriate rules and take all of the necessary precautions but should not count on rules regarding timing of filing documentation for protection. Despite several court cases, if a supplier has delivered material for which the property owner is benefiting and for which the supplier has not been paid, some courts may find that the supplier is due payment, regardless of the technicalities with respect to filing.

ATB Asphalt

518 Third Avenue
Juneau, Alaska 99801

September 21, 2000

Huna Totem Corporation
9309 Glacier Highway
Juneau, Alaska 99801

Re: Materialman's/Suppliers Notice to Owner

Dear Sir:

We are pleased to communicate that on September 20, 2000, our firm commenced to furnish materials for use on your construction project known as Huna Office Building which is located at the premises commonly described as 9301 Glacier Highway, Juneau, Alaska 99801. Delivery was commenced at the request and upon the order of Northwest Construction Company, a contractor whose business address is 1242 First Avenue, Cascade, Washington 98202. Even though we do not have the opportunity of dealing with you directly, be assured that we are pleased to be able to make a contribution to your project.

In order to preserve our lien rights, the laws of this state require that we advise you that we are furnishing materials for use upon your property, and that we may claim a lien for the value of those materials. We certainly have no reason to anticipate the necessity of making such a claim of lien, and trust that you will not construe this notification as any reflection upon either you or Northwest Construction Company.

Our experience has been that everyone in the construction industry recognizes that it is simply good business practice to protect one's lien rights. We sincerely hope that you will be pleased with the materials we are furnishing, and trust that we may be of further service to you in the future.

Sincerely,

Randy Jones

Randy Jones
President

FIGURE 15–4 Materialman's Notice

INTERIM LIEN/CLAIM WAIVER

From: *Northwest Construction Company*
1242 First Avenue
Cascade, Washington 98202

Contact Person: *Ted Jones*
Contact Telephone: *206-239-1422*

Project: *Huna Office Building*
9301 Glacier Highway
Juneau, Alaska 99801

Project Manager: *Ted Jones*
Project Telephone: *907-586-1113*

CONDITIONAL RELEASE

The undersigned does hereby acknowledge that upon receipt by the undersigned of a check from *Huna Totem Corporation* in the sum of *$108,892.00* and when the check has been properly endorsed and has been paid by the bank upon which it was drawn, this document shall become effective to release any and all claims and rights of lien which the undersigned has on the above referenced project for labor, services, equipment, materials furnished and/or any claims through *December 31, 2000,* except it does not cover any retention or items furnished thereafter. Before any recipient of this documents relies on it, said party should verify evidence of payment to the undersigned.

I CERTIFY UNDER PENALTY OF PERJURY UNDER THE LAWS OF THE STATE OF ALASKA THAT THE ABOVE IS A TRUE AND CORRECT STATEMENT.

Signature: Sam Peters
(Authorized Corporate Officer)
Vice President

Dated: *December 29, 2000*

UNCONDITIONAL RELEASE

The undersigned does hereby acknowledge that the undersigned has been paid and has received progress payments in the sum of *$1,002,250.00* for labor, services, equipment or materials furnished to the above referenced project and does hereby release any and all claims and rights of lien which the undersigned has on the above referenced project. This release covers all payment for labor, services, equipment, materials furnished and/or claims to the above referenced project through *November 30, 2000* only and does not cover any retention or items furnished after that date.

I CERTIFY UNDER PENALTY OF PERJURY UNDER THE LAWS OF THE STATE OF ALASKA THAT THE ABOVE IS A TRUE AND CORRECT STATEMENT.

Signature: Sam Peters
(Authorized Corporate Officer)
Vice President

Dated: *December 29, 2000*

FIGURE 15–5 Lien Release

Since liens are filed against the owner's property, why should the project manager worry about them? Liens are a problem. They reflect poorly on all of the parties involved. It is the owner who has received a lien from the contractor's supplier. The project manager is expected to protect the owner from these unfortunate occurrences. On the other hand, the contractor's right to lien and the lien itself are sometimes necessary tools which the project manager must understand and use.

15.8 SUMMARY

Receipt of timely payment is one of the most important responsibilities of the project manager. The exact format for submitting payment requests will vary depending on the type of contract. A schedule of values is used to support payment applications on lump-sum contracts and fee payments on cost-plus contracts. The project manager is responsible to develop the payment request, make sure payment is received, and subsequently see that the subcontractors and suppliers are paid. If payment has not been received on time, the project manager should contact the owner to determine the cause. The owner and the project are the project manager's responsibility. The same scenario holds true with respect to subcontractors and suppliers. The project manager ensures that they are paid promptly. Owners may withhold a portion of each payment to ensure timely completion of the project. This is known as retention. The retention rate is specified in the contract. Liens can be placed on a project if workers or suppliers are not paid for their labor or materials. To preclude liens, owners require lien releases with payment applications.

15.9 REVIEW QUESTIONS

1. How does the type of contract influence the format of the payment request?
2. What is a schedule of values? Why is it required by project owners?
3. What type of data is submitted to support a payment request on a lump-sum contract?
4. What is retention? What is it used for?
5. What is a lien?
6. What is the relationship between a payment bond (Chapter 2) and a lien?
7. What are interim lien releases used for?
8. Why are final lien releases requested by owners as part of the final payment process?
9. How can slow payment from the owner affect the financial stability of a contractor?

15.10 EXERCISES

1. Prepare a schedule of values similar to the one shown in Figure 15–2 using the adjusted totals shown on the right side of Figure 15–1.
2. Prepare a pay request for the month ending January 2001 for the Huna Office Building project, including all supporting documentation and lien releases.

15.11 SOURCES OF ADDITIONAL INFORMATION

Civitello, Andrew M., Jr. *Construction Operations Manual of Policies and Procedures*. 3d ed. New York: McGraw-Hill, Inc., 2000.

Clough, Richard H., and Glenn A. Sears. *Construction Contracting*. 6th ed. New York: John Wiley and Sons, Inc., 1994.

Mincks, William R., and Hal Johnston. *Construction Jobsite Management*. Albany, N.Y.: Delmar Publishers, 1998.

16

Cost and Time Control

16.1 INTRODUCTION

The project manager is responsible for ensuring that a project is completed within the time allowed by the contract and the project budget. To accomplish this challenging task, cost and time controls are established to monitor progress throughout the duration of the project. The project manager wants to ensure that all contractual requirements are completed as early as possible while earning a profit on the project. Early completion of a project results in reduced project overhead costs enhancing anticipated profits. In this chapter, we will examine several techniques for cost and time control.

16.2 COST CONTROL

Cost control begins with assigning ***cost codes*** to the elements of work identified during the work breakdown phase (see Chapters 4 and 5) of developing the cost estimate. These cost codes allow the project manager to monitor project costs and compare them to the estimated costs. The objective is not to keep the cost of each element of work under its estimated value, but to ensure that the total cost of the completed project is under the estimated cost.

Some uses of actual cost data are:

- To monitor project costs, identify any problem areas, and select mitigation measures.
- To identify additional costs incurred as a result of changes in the project scope of work.

- To identify costs for completing work that was the responsibility of a subcontractor. These are called back charges.
- To develop a database of historical cost data that can be used in estimating the cost of future projects.
- To evaluate the effectiveness of the project management team.
- To provide the project owner with a cost report, which may be a contract requirement.

The cost control process involves the following steps:

- Cost codes are assigned to each element of work in the cost estimate.
- The cost estimate is corrected based on buyout costs (see Chapter 10).
- Actual costs are tracked for each work item using the assigned cost codes.
- The construction process is adjusted, if necessary, to reduce cost overruns.
- Actual quantities, costs, and productivity rates are recorded and an ***as-built estimate*** is prepared.

While all costs should be monitored, the items that generally involve the greatest risk are:

- Direct labor
- Equipment usage or rental
- Job site overhead or project administration

It is possible to lose money on material purchases, but with good estimating skills, it is not probable, and the risk is not as great as it is on labor. The same holds true with subcontractors. They have quoted prices for specific scopes of work and therefore bear the risk associated with labor and equipment.

It is difficult to control costs if the project manager does not start with a detailed estimate. For example, let's suppose there was a $4,000 cost overrun on 4,000 square feet of concrete slab-on-grade (SOG). The aggregate cost analysis shown in Figure 16–1 does not provide sufficient detail to identify the cause. Project managers should use a more detailed cost breakdown, as shown in Figure 16–2, to determine the cause of the cost overrun.

Now it is easy see that the problem is not with the carpenters forming the slab, nor the laborers placing the slab, but the majority of the overrun is with reinforcing steel and concrete finishing. There are multiple reasons why this could have happened: rain, more steel was needed than was estimated, personnel changes, or the estimate was too low. There could be a variety of reasons. The point is the project manager and the superintendent can now focus on evaluating these specific issues.

	Quantity	Estimated Unit Price	Estimated Cost	Actual Unit Price	Actual Cost	Variance
SOG	4,000 SF	$2/SF	$8,000	$3/SF	$12,000	+$4,000

FIGURE 16–1 Aggregate Cost Analysis

	Quantity	Estimated Unit Price	Estimated Cost	Actual Unit Price	Actual Cost	Variance
Formwork	440 LF	$2.05/LF	$900	$2.15/LF	$950	+$50
Reinf. Steel	2 ton	$750/ton	$1,500	$1,500/ton	$3,000	+$1,500
Concrete	50 CY	$60/CY	$3,000	$70/CY	$3,500	+$500
Placement	50 CY	$12/CY	$600	$11/CY	$550	−$50
Finish	4,000 SF	$0.50/SF	$2,000	$1/SF	$4,000	+$2,000
Total system:			$8,000	$3/SF	$12,000	+$4,000

FIGURE 16–2 Detailed Cost Analysis

Cost Codes

To be able to control costs, they must be tracked accurately and compared against the ***corrected estimate***. The first step is to record the actual costs incurred and input the information into a cost control database. Cost codes are used to allow comparison of actual cost data with the estimated values. There are several types of cost codes used in the industry. The best system to use on most projects is the coding system selected for the project files. Such systems were discussed in Chapter 11. Many construction firms have adopted the CSI MasterFormat system described in Chapter 2. An example of this type of coding system is:

__________ . __________ . __________

(project number) (CSI work package) (element of cost)

Here the project number is assigned by the construction firm, the CSI work package code is from the MasterFormat, and the element of expense is the type of cost. An example element of cost coding is:

.1 labor
.2 equipment
.3 material
.4 subcontract

Using this system, the cost code for rough carpentry direct labor on the Huna Office Building project would be:

9821.06100.1

and for material would be:

9821.06100.3

Depending on the size of the construction firm, the type of work, and the type of owner and contract agreement, the project manager may perform job-cost accounting in the home office or in the field. Generally, the smaller the firm and the smaller the contract value, the more likely all accounting functions will be performed in the home office. On larger projects, the project team may have a job site accountant. The type of contract and how it addresses reimbursable costs may also have some affect on where the construction firm performs the accounting function. Suppose the project is a $20 million pharmaceutical facility that has a negotiated guaranteed maximum price contract allowing for all on-site accounting to be reimbursed. It may be more cost effective to perform accounting out of the home office with the assistance of an accounting department, but according to the terms of the contract, the owner will not pay for activities conducted off the project site.

Regardless of where the cost data is collected and where the checks are prepared, most of the accounting functions on a project are the same. The process begins with a corrected estimate. Then actual costs are incurred, either in the form of direct labor, material purchase or subcontract invoice. Cost codes (those matching the estimate) are recorded on the time sheets and invoices. Often this process begins with the project engineer. The coded time sheets and invoices are then passed to the superintendent and the project manager for approval. Sometimes the officer-in-charge or maybe the owner (on cost-plus projects) may also want to initial approval on each invoice. After the time sheets and invoices are coded and approved, the cost data is input into the cost control system.

One important aspect of this phase of cost recording is the accurate coding of actual costs. If costs are intentionally or accidentally coded incorrectly, the project team will not really know how they are doing on that specific item of work. Some superintendents and project mangers may intentionally code costs against codes where there is money remaining, not necessarily against the correct work activity, thereby hiding overruns. Others have been known to intentionally exceed the estimate on a specific line item of work to prove a point that the estimator is not covering the item correctly. Regardless of the reason, the project manager will not be able to monitor and collect accurate cost data if coding errors occur. All costs should be coded correctly to provide the project manager an accurate accounting of all expenditures.

Work Packages

Control of direct craft labor and equipment rental costs is the responsibility of the superintendent. The key to getting the field supervisors involved in cost control is to get their personal commitment to the process. One successful way for the project manager to do

Erecting Prefabricated Second Floor Wall Panels on Huna Office Building

this is to have the superintendent actively involved in developing the original estimate. If the superintendent said it will take four people working two weeks to form a particular wall, he or she will often see to it that the task is completed within that time.

Work packages are a method of breaking down the estimate into distinct packages or systems that match measurable work activities. These were previously discussed as part of the work breakdown in Chapters 4 and 5. For example footings, including forming, reinforcing steel, and placement could be a work package. The work is planned according to the amount of hours in the estimate and monitored for feedback. When the footings are complete, the project manager will have immediate cost-control feedback. Work packages apply best to those who estimate and track costs by system rather than the pure CSI approach. When a system is complete, such as footings or slab-on-grade, the project manger and the superintendent immediately know how they are doing with respect to the overall estimate.

Some project managers believe the field supervisors should not be told the budgeted value of each work package. This is a poor practice, because the field supervisors are key members of the project team and have critical roles in making the project a success. They should be provided the actual budgeted cost, both in materials and man hours for each work package.

A good technique for monitoring project cost is to develop a ***project labor curve*** similar to the one shown in Figure 16–3 for the Huna Office Building project. It is important to have the superintendent or foreman record the actual hours incurred weekly and chart them against the estimate. If the actual labor used is under the curve, the field supervisors are either beating the estimate or behind schedule. The opposite is true if the hours are above the curve. This simple method of recording the man hours provides immediate and positive feedback to field supervisors. It is better to use hours and not dollars when monitoring direct labor. The advantages of estimating using unit man hours (UMH) over unit prices for labor were previously discussed in Chapter 4. Field supervisors think in terms of crew size and duration. They do not think in terms of $3.50 per square foot.

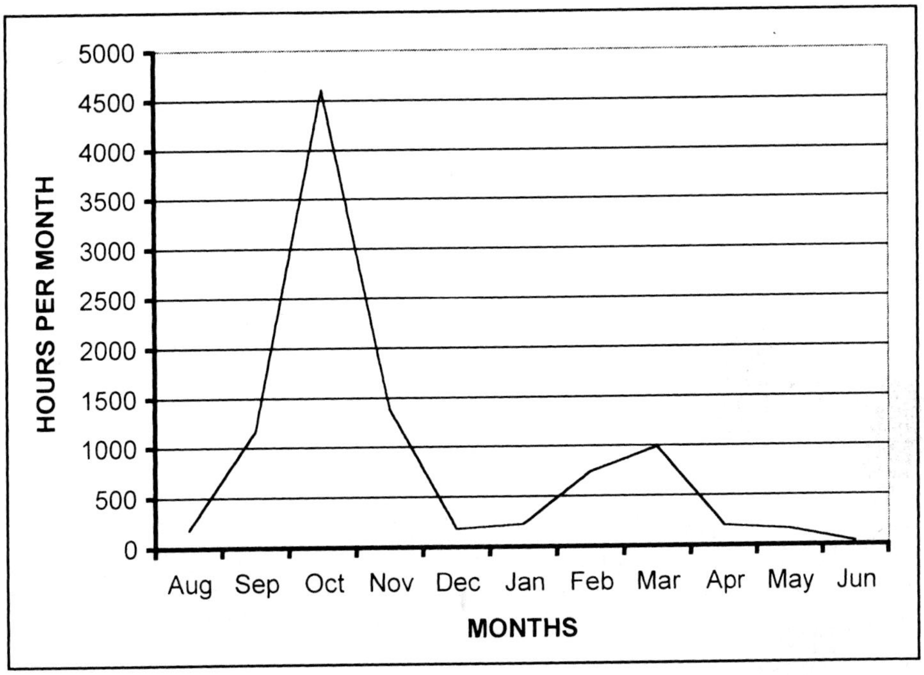

FIGURE 16–3 Project Labor Curve

When the question arises of which items the project team should track, the eighty–twenty rule can apply. The project manager should evaluate the risks. The estimate should be reviewed to identify those items that have the most labor hours, or in the case of equipment rental, the most cost. Work packages should be prepared for those items the project manager and superintendent believe are worthy of tracking and monitoring. Each work package should be developed by the foreman who is responsible for accomplishing the work. Figure 16–4 shows an example work package cost-control worksheet for the Huna Office Building project.

Management Reports

The project manager should develop a monthly forecast for the project that is shared with the superintendent and the officer-in-charge. The owner may also be included in the case of a cost-plus contract. This forecast includes line items for all areas of the estimate, cost to date, and estimated cost to complete. All major categories of the estimate should receive a separate forecast page, with one summary page for the entire project. The major categories of the estimate include:

- Direct labor
- Direct material
- Major purchase order items
- Subcontractors
- Job site administration
- Equipment rental
- Taxes, permits, and insurance
- Fee

Field Foreman's Work Package Cost Control Worksheet

Project: HUNA OFFICE BUILDING   Foreman: BLAIR

System/Area: FOUNDATIONS   Date: 10-10-00   Page: 1 OF 1

Date:	12 (SEPT)	13	14	15	16	19	20	21	22	23	26	27	28	29	30	3 (OCT)	4	5	6	7	10			Totals
Estimated Crew Size	3	8	→				8	½	0	0	0	2	1½	½	0	→		2	2	1	1½			
Estimated daily hours	24	64	→					3	0	0	0	16	10	4	0	0	0	16	16	9	10			
Est'd Accumulated hrs	24	88	152	216	280	344	408	411	→			427	437	441	→			457	473	482	492			492
Actual Crew Size	0	4	6	8	10	10	10	10	1	½	½	0	0	0	0	0	2	2	0	0	0			
Actual daily hours	0	32	48	64	80	80	80	80	8	4	4	0	0	0	0	0	16	16	0	0	0			
Actual Accum'd hours	0	32	80	144	224	304	384	464	472	476	480	480	480	480	480	480	496	512	512	→				512

← FOOTINGS →   → ELEV PIT ←   → PERF PIPE ←

Manpower curve:

Hours:

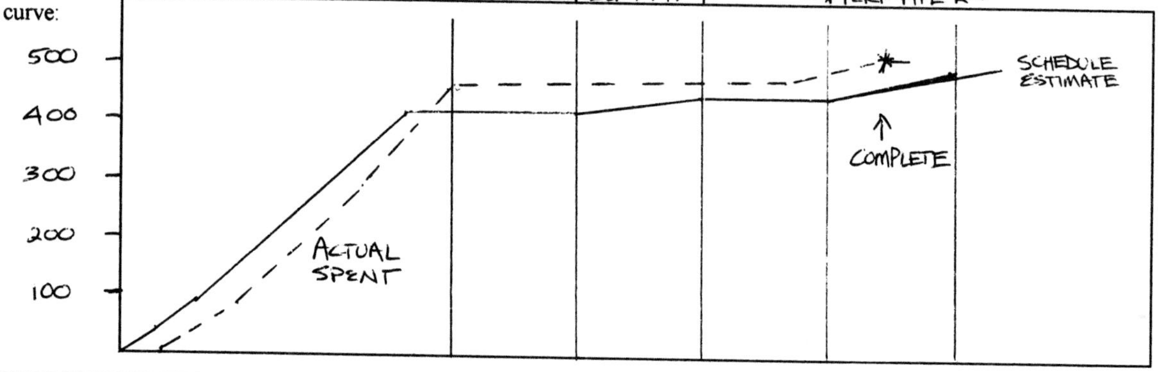

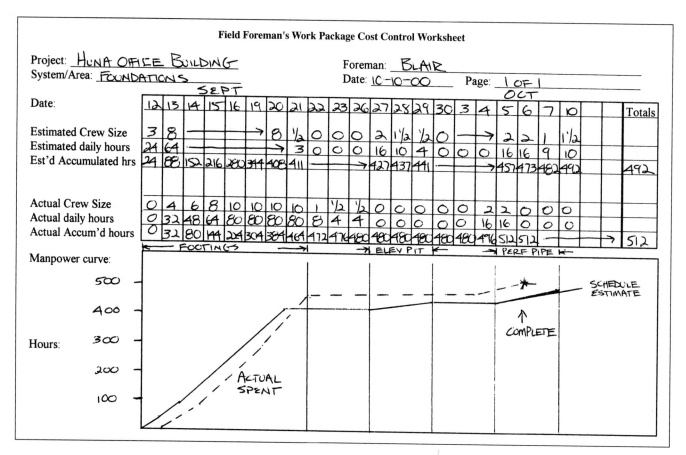

FIGURE 16–4 Foreman's Work Package Cost-Control Worksheet

Figure 16–5 illustrates the project manager's forecast for the Huna Office Building. It is a good practice to include a narrative with the monthly forecast explaining the significant differences from the previous month's forecast, as well as a work plan for continuing or improving performance throughout the remainder of the project. The project manager cannot afford to wait until the project is over to measure and report the overall project cost. It is not only too late to take any corrective actions, it is also too late to accurately determine why the team deviated from the plan.

There can be several other management reports either generated by the project manager or the accounting department according to the construction firm's practices and the requirements of any specific client or project. Most of the reports are computer generated and are accurate to the degree that the information regarding actual costs was accurately input. They can occur weekly or monthly, but either way, home office-generated cost-control reports are likely to be too late for implementing any corrective action in the field.

As-Built Estimate

Project managers usually are too busy and excited about starting the next project to develop as-built estimates for a completed project. As-built estimates, like as-built drawings and as-built schedules, are important historical reporting tools. Revising the estimate with actual cost data assists in developing better future estimates. This is particularly true if actual unit price data, which requires input of actual quantities as well as actual cost, is determined. This data can help with developing the firm's database as well as providing project managers with their own accurate cost factors for future use. There are many different types of databases, which can be used for a variety of different purposes. There are several software systems available which allow a project manager to prepare a customized database.

16.3 SCHEDULE CONTROL

Schedule control involves monitoring the progress of each activity in the construction schedule and determining the impact of any delayed activities on the overall completion of the project. Schedule control is just as important as cost control, because the project manager wants to ensure substantial completion is achieved prior to the contractual completion date. If this does not occur, liquidated damages may be owed to the owner to compensate for the project not being completed on time.

Schedule development and updates were discussed in Chapter 5. The superintendent should report construction progress at the weekly project coordination meetings. The project manager should review the progress with the project team and identify the causes of any delays. He or she should select appropriate mitigation measures with the superintendent. Such measures may include expediting material delivery, increasing the size of the workforce, or working extended hours. Short-interval schedules would be developed to intensively manage all accelerated work.

Just as an as-built estimate is important for estimating future work, an as-built schedule is helpful in scheduling future projects. The greatest risk in scheduling is the determination of workforce productivity, and the project manager should develop a personal set of productivity factors based on actual experience. These factors will help the project manager and superintendent establish realistic activity durations when scheduling future projects.

NORTHWEST CONSTRUCTION COMPANY

PROJECT:	Huna Totem Office Building		Page 1 of 5
		DATE:	10-Jan-01
PROJECT NUMBER:	9,821	JOB COST SUMMARY DATE:	31-Dec-00
PROJECT MANAGER:	Jones	LABOR REPORT DATE:	31-Dec-00
PROJECT SUPT.:	Bates	PROJECT MANAGER:	Jones
FILE CODE:	9821/fore	PROJECT SUPT.:	Bates

JOB FORECAST

December 2000

	SYSTEM	ORIGINAL ESTIMATE	C.O. TO ESTIMATE Through # 1	ADJ. TO ESTIMATE AAA	CURRENT ESTIMATE	COST TO DATE	COST TO COMPLETE	CONTRACT FEE	TOTAL COST INCL FEE	(OVER) UNDER
00	FEE	83,000	221	0	83,221	0	0	83,221	83,221	0
01	SUBCONTRACTS	779,500	0	0	779,500	485,000	294,500		779,500	0
02	PURCHASE ORDERS	305,065	0	0	305,065	195,275	109,790		305,065	0
03	INDIRECT LABOR	70,100	0	0	70,100	55,250	25,000		80,250	(10,150)
04	INDIRECT MATERIAL/Taxes/Insur	134,900	0	0	134,900	74,442	56,000		130,442	4,458
05	DIRECT MATERIAL	85,100	0	0	85,100	0	85,100		85,100	0
06	BACKCHARGES	0	0	0	0	0	0		0	0
07	WORK ORDERS	0	0	0	0	0	0		0	0
10-49	DIRECT LABOR	302,335	0	0	302,335	220,000	60,000		280,000	22,335
	Change Orders Approved	0	4,402	0	4,402	4,219	0		4,219	183
		1,760,000	4,623	0	1,764,623	1,034,186	630,390	83,221	1,747,797	16,826

FORECAST SAVINGS/LOSS			16,826
FORECAST SAVINGS			16,826
	NWCC %	30.00%	5,048
	HUNA%	70.00%	11,778

FEE DATA

ORIGINAL FEE	83,000
ADJUSTED BY C.O.'S #1	220
TOTAL CONTRACT FEE	83,220
PENDING C.O. FEE	0
SAVINGS (LOSS)	5,048
FORECAST FEE	88,268
% OF CONTRACT AMOUNT	5.05%
% OF CONTRACT COST	5.30%

CONTRACT DATA

ORIGINAL CONTRACT		1,760,000
APPROVED CHANGE ORDERS	1	4,623
SUBTOTAL		1,764,623
PENDING CHANGE ORDERS ESTIMATE		0
SAVINGS ADJUSTMENT		11,778
CURRENT CONTRACT AMOUNT		1,764,623
CONTRACT COMPLETION DATE:		03-Jun-01
PROJECTED COMPLETION DATE:		03-Jun-01

BILLING DATA

TO DATE:	1,169,632
OVER:	142,221
UNDER:	0
% COMPLETE	58.61
% BILLED	66.28
INCLUDES RETENTION	

FIGURE 16–5 Project Manager's Job Forecast

Constructing Third Floor Mechanical Rooms on Huna Office Building

16.4 EARNED VALUE

Earned value is a technique for determining the estimated or budgeted value of the work completed to date (or earned value) and comparing it with the actual cost of work completed. The most effective use of earned value to a general contractor's project manager is to track direct labor, which represents the project manager's greatest project risk. As discussed earlier in this chapter, man hours generally are used for monitoring direct labor.

The work-package curve shown in Figure 16–4 shows the man hours planned by the foreman and the actual man hours used for the footing installation. If the actual man-hour curve is below the estimated curve, does this necessarily represent that the foreman is under budget? Could he be behind schedule? He could actually be ahead or behind schedule and over or under budget and just about any combination in between.

Introduction of a third, or earned-value curve, shows the estimated hours the foreman has earned based upon the estimated quantities which were actually installed. This curve is determined by plotting the total number of man hours estimated for the work package multiplied by the cumulative percent completed. With this third curve, an actual measure of productivity can be made. This method of monitoring will provide more accurate feedback to the project team for appropriate correction.

The schedule status is determined by subtracting the actual time used to perform the work from the time scheduled for the work that has been performed. This is the same as measuring the horizontal distance between the earned-value and the estimated curves shown in Figure 16–6. The actual time used to complete the budgeted or estimated 90 man hours of work was 6 days, while the time scheduled for that amount of work was 9 days. Therefore, the foreman is 9 minus 6 or 3 days ahead of schedule.

The cost status is determined by subtracting the actual cost of work performed from the earned value of the work performed. This is the same as measuring the vertical distance between the actual and earned-value curves. Looking again at Figure 16–6, we see that the actual value of work performed was 48 man hours while the earned value was 90 man hours. Therefore, the foreman is 90 minus 48 or 42 man hours under budget.

Figure 16–7 shows a different situation. The foreman is 54 minus 72 or 18 man hours over budget and 5.5 minus 6 or 0.5 days behind schedule.

16.5 SUMMARY

Project cost control and time control are essential project manager functions. The project manager wants to ensure that the project is completed within budget and within the time allowed by the contract. Cost codes are used to track project costs and compare them with the budgeted or estimated value for each element of work. Work-package

Time	1	2	3	4	5	6	7	8	9	10	11	12	Total
Estimated - per day	10	10	10	10	10	10	10	10	10	10	10	10	
Estimated - cumulative	**10**	**20**	**30**	**40**	**50**	**60**	**70**	**80**	**90**	**100**	**110**	**120**	**120**
Estimated % spent/complete	8%	17%	25%	33%	42%	50%	58%	67%	75%	83%	92%	100%	
Actual - per day	8	8	8	8	8	8							
Actual - cumulative	**8**	**16**	**24**	**32**	**40**	**48**							
Actual % spent	7%	13%	20%	27%	33%	40%							
Earned - per day	15	15	15	15	15	15							
Earned - cumulative	**15**	**30**	**45**	**60**	**75**	**90**							
Actual % earned	13%	25%	38%	50%	63%	75%							

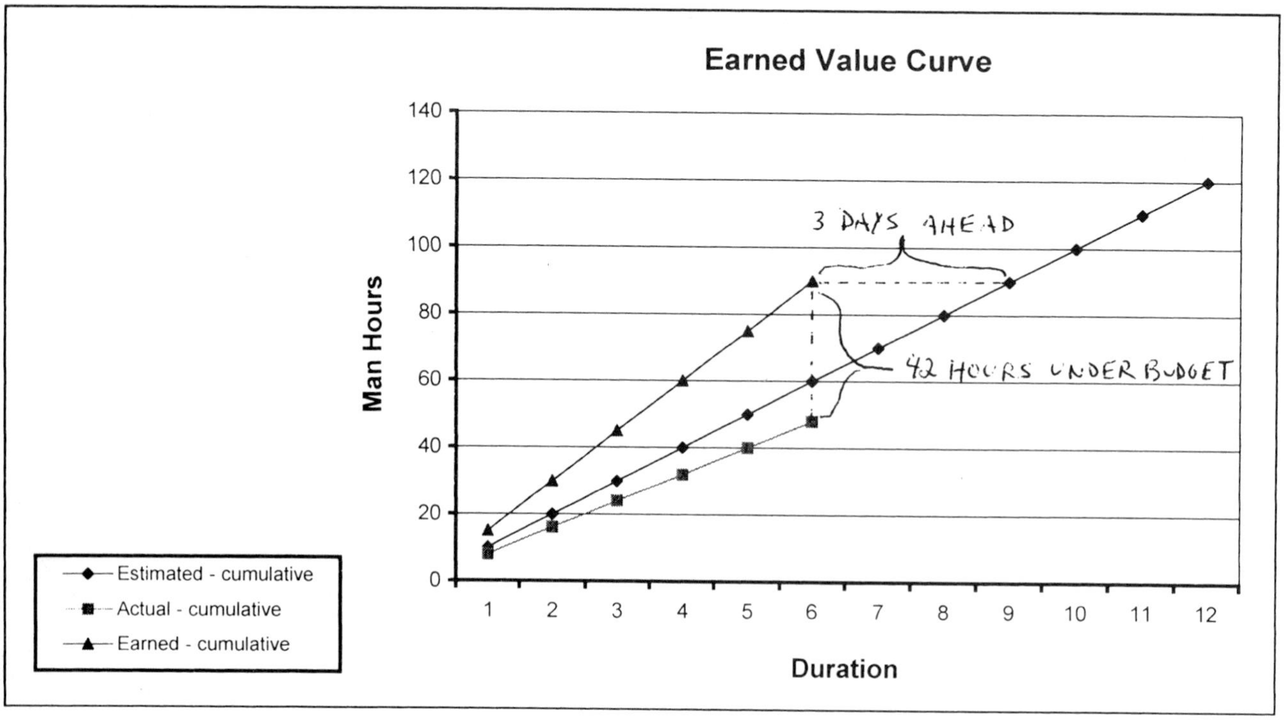

FIGURE 16–6 Earned-Value Curve Ahead of Schedule

analysis provides the project manager and the superintendent a method for tracking direct labor cost, which represents the greatest risk on the project. As-built estimates are developed to create unit-price data that can be used on future estimates. Schedule control involves monitoring the progress of each scheduled activity and selecting appropriate mitigation measures to overcome the effects of any schedule delays. As-built schedules are prepared to allow project managers to develop historical productivity factors for use on future projects. Another technique for cost and time control is earned value analysis, which compares the budgeted value of work completed with the actual cost incurred.

16.6 REVIEW QUESTIONS

1. What are four uses of actual project cost data?
2. Why is the original cost estimate corrected based on buyout data?

Time	1	2	3	4	5	6	7	8	9	10	11	12	Total
Estimated - per day	10	10	10	10	10	10	10	10	10	10	10	10	
Estimated - cumulative	**10**	**20**	**30**	**40**	**50**	**60**	**70**	**80**	**90**	**100**	**110**	**120**	**120**
Estimated % spent/complete	8%	17%	25%	33%	42%	50%	58%	67%	75%	83%	92%	100%	
Actual - per day	12	12	12	12	12	12							
Actual - cumulative	**12**	**24**	**36**	**48**	**60**	**72**							
Actual % spent	10%	20%	30%	40%	50%	60%							
Earned - per day	8	8	8	10	10	10							
Earned - cumulative	**8**	**16**	**24**	**34**	**44**	**54**							
Actual % earned	7%	13%	20%	28%	37%	45%							

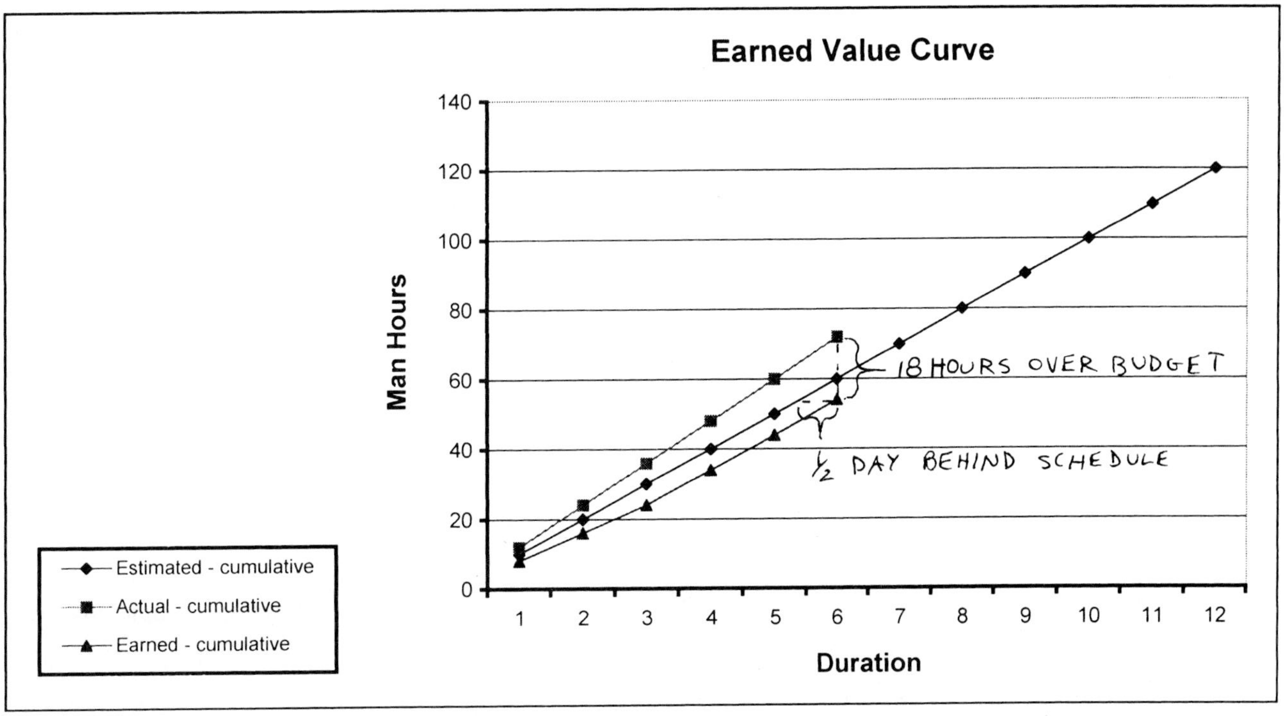

FIGURE 16–7 Earned-Value Curve Behind Schedule

3. What three types of project costs present the greatest risk to the project manager?
4. Why are cost codes used for monitoring actual project costs?
5. What are project labor curves used for?
6. What is a foreman's work package cost-control worksheet used for?
7. How frequently should a project manager develop a forecast of the estimated cost to complete a project?
8. What are as-built estimates used for?
9. What are as-built schedules used for?
10. What is an earned value analysis used for?
11. What would the CSI MasterFormat cost codes be on the Huna Office Building project for:
    a. Carpet?
    b. Concrete placement?
    c. Reinforcing steel purchase?

16.7 EXERCISES

1. Prepare a work package for direct labor for a system of work such as concrete foundations, cast-in-place concrete walls, tilt-up concrete walls, or slab-on-grade. Attach the original portion of the estimate that refers to this work package. Assume the following percentages complete and spent:

	Portion of Work Complete	Portion of Estimate Spent
Excavation:	100%	80%
Form work:	90%	100%
Reinforcement steel or mesh:	85%	110%
Concrete placement:	50%	40%
Slab finish (if appropriate):	40%	75%
Tilt-up panel erection (if appropriate):	10%	7%

2. Prepare a cost forecast for the above work activities. Based upon the work packages developed, forecast the remaining hours needed and calculate the total over- or under-run this system will achieve. Convert the hours to dollars using current wage rates. List the possible reasons the over- or under-runs could be occurring and what corrective actions could be taken. If the project proceeds at the same rate it has been, calculate what the historical as-built unit man hours will be.
3. Prepare additional earned-value curves for the footing example discussed earlier in the chapter. Draw a curve where the foreman is over budget and behind schedule and another where he is on budget and ahead of schedule. Prepare a narrative explaining why these situations might be occurring.

16.8 SOURCES OF ADDITIONAL INFORMATION

Barrie, Donald S., and Boyd C. Paulson. *Professional Construction Management.* 3d ed. New York: McGraw-Hill, Inc., 1992.

Civitello, Andrew M., Jr. *Construction Operations Manual of Policies and Procedures.* 3d ed. New York: McGraw-Hill, Inc., 2000.

Clough, Richard H., and Glenn A. Sears. *Construction Contracting.* 6th ed. New York: McGraw-Hill, Inc., 1994.

Halpin, Daniel W., and Ronald W. Woodhead. *Construction Management.* 2d ed. New York: John Wiley and Sons, Inc., 1998.

Hinze, Jimmie. *Construction Planning and Scheduling.* Upper Saddle River, N.J.: Prentice-Hall, Inc., 1998.

Levy, Sidney M. *Project Management in Construction.* 3d ed. New York: McGraw-Hill, Inc., 1999.

Mincks, William R., and Hal Johnston. *Construction Jobsite Management.* Albany, N.Y.: Delmar Publishers, 1998.

17

Quality Management

17.1 INTRODUCTION

Quality management is an important project management function. As stated in Chapter 1, it is one of the critical attributes of project success, with the others being cost, time, and safety. It has short-term implications affecting material and labor costs on a project and long-term implications affecting the overall reputation of the construction firm. The firm's greatest marketing assets are satisfied owners, and delivering quality projects is critical to achieving customer satisfaction. The project manager and superintendent must work together to ensure that all materials used and all work performed on a project conform to the requirements of the contract plans and specifications. Nonconforming materials and work must be replaced at the contractor's cost, both in terms of time and money. This means that the contractor must bear the financial cost of tearing out and replacing unsatisfactory work and that additional contract time is not granted for the impact the rework has on the overall construction schedule. Quality management is essential to ensure all contract requirements are achieved with a minimum of rework. This requires a proactive quality focus from all members of the project team.

Quality control plans are developed prior to initiating actual construction to document the quality control organization and procedures to be used on the project. Some owners on negotiated contracts require project quality control plans to be submitted with cost and schedule proposals and project-specific safety plans during contract negotiation. Other owners may require that quality control plans be submitted at preconstruction meetings that were discussed in Chapter 10.

Full-time quality control inspectors often are specified in the contracts for large, complex projects. Some contractors attempt to substitute a foreman or assistant superintendent who already has other responsibilities. If a full-time inspector is specified, the project manager must provide one and include the cost in the general conditions part of the estimate. On smaller projects, the quality control and safety inspection functions may be combined and performed by the same person.

Quality management involves the following processes:

- Setting quality standards
- Scheduling inspections
- Managing any required rework
- Documenting corrections

The exact procedures to be used and the organization of the quality control team are identified in the project-specific quality control plan.

17.2 QUALITY CONTROL PLANNING

To achieve quality in the completed project, the project manager must see that systems are in place to assure that quality materials are procured and received, quality craftworkers and subcontractors are selected, and all workmanship meets or exceeds contract requirements. This proactive approach to selecting effective procedures and processes to deliver quality projects is the focus of total quality management, which was discussed in Chapter 7. This involves careful planning and an effective inspection process to ensure quality results. Variations from standards are measured, and appropriate actions are taken to correct all variations or deficiencies. Effective quality control planning starts with detailed study of the contract documents to determine all unique quality and testing requirements. A project-specific quality control plan is developed that identifies quality control systems for each major work package. Qualified inspectors are selected and trained, if necessary, to ensure that all self-performed and subcontractor work meets contract specifications. These inspectors also should participate in the submittal process discussed in Chapter 14 to ensure that quality materials are being submitted and that only approved materials are installed. Mock-ups, which are stand-alone samples of completed work, should be planned to establish workmanship standards for critical architectural features. Systems testing, balancing, and ***commissioning*** are scheduled to ensure all systems meet contractual performance criteria.

Checklists often are developed and included in the quality-control plan to ensure inspectors do not overlook critical items. An example checklist for concrete formwork is shown in Figure 17–1. Formal quality control reports should be required and acted upon. These reports list any deficiencies that have been identified as a part of the inspection process. All deficiencies identified should be listed in a deficiency log such as the one shown in Figure 17–2 on page 214. The superintendent should discuss the status of uncorrected deficiencies during the weekly coordination meeting, which was described in Chapter 12.

Proper materials must be procured to ensure conformance with contract requirements. Shop drawings and certificates of compliance with reference standards submitted by the suppliers or subcontractors must be carefully reviewed to ensure all materials used on the project meet contract requirements. As mentioned previously, the quality control inspectors should actively participate in the submittal process discussed in Chapter 14 so they can become familiar with the materials being proposed and have an opportunity to compare material characteristics with contractual requirements.

17.3 SUBCONTRACTED WORK

As discussed in Chapter 8, subcontractors perform most of the work on a construction project. The general contractor's reputation for quality work, therefore, is greatly affected by the quality of each subcontractor's work. Quality subcontractors are not necessarily the least-cost subcontractors, but in the long term they provide a superior project.

NORTHWEST CONSTRUCTION COMPANY

1242 First Avenue, Cascade, Washington 98202

(206) 239-1422

INSPECTION CHECKLIST

03100 – CONCRETE FORMWORK

Date: SEPT. 16, 2000

Project: HUNA OFFICE BUILDING

		YES	NO
1.	Location, dimensions, and grades are as required.	X	
2.	Formwork materials as specified.	X	
3.	Reused formwork is properly conditioned and treated for reuse.	X	
4.	Completed formwork provides structural sections required.	X	
5.	Temporary spreaders are arranged for easy removal.	X	
6.	Forms are secured against movement during concrete placement.	X	
7.	Forms are in alignment.	X	
8.	Forms are properly cleaned and surface-treated as required.	NEED ADDITIONAL WASH DOWN	
9.	Shoring is checked for location and bearing. (NA)		
10.	Free movement of expansion and contraction joints can occur. No reinforcement through the joints.	X	
11.	Filler is installed and securely fastened in expansion joints.	X	
12.	Ties are of proper type and spacing. (NA)		

NOTES: INSPECTOR NOTED: (1) DIRT ON REBAR (2) REBAR ON GROUND (3) SCRAP WOOD IN FORM — ALL THESE CONDITIONS WERE CORRECTED SAME DAY.

INSPECTOR: Jim Bates, SUPERINTENDENT

FIGURE 17–1 Inspection Checklist for Concrete Formwork

NORTHWEST CONSTRUCTION COMPANY
1242 First Avenue, Cascade, Washington 98202
(206) 239-1422

PROJECT DEFICIENCY LOG

Project No.: *9821* Project Name: *Huna Office Building* Project Manager: *Ted Jones*

No.	Description	Location	Responsible Party	Date Identified	Date Corrected	Date Inspected
1	*Silt fence does not protect creek*	*South end Duck Creek*	*Northwest Construction*	*9/10/00*	*9/10/00*	*9/11/00*
2	*Mud on reinforcing steel*	*Strip footing*	*Northwest Construction*	*9/19/00*	*9/19/00*	*9/19/00*
3	*Reinforcing steel stored on ground*	*Strip footing*	*Northwest Construction*	*9/19/00*	*9/19/00*	*9/19/00*
4	*Wood debris in forms*	*Strip footing*	*Northwest Construction*	*9/19/00*	*9/19/00*	*9/19/00*
5	*Concrete break @2250 PSI*	*Foundation wall*	*Northwest Construction/ Juneau*	*9/26/00*		*Hold 28 days for break*
6	*EMT conduit in SOG in lieu of PVC*	*East end SOG*	*Richardson*	*9/27/00*	*9/30/00*	*9/30/00*

FIGURE 17–2 Deficiency Log

Installing Roof Trusses on Huna Office Building

The project superintendent must ensure the job site is ready for a subcontractor before scheduling him or her to start work. Quality requirements should be emphasized at subcontractor preconstruction meetings that were discussed in Chapter 8. Subcontractors may be required to prepare mock-ups for exterior or interior finishes to establish the required level of workmanship. They must fully understand their quality requirements before being allowed to start work on the project. Subcontractors should not be allowed to build over work that has been improperly done by a previous subcontractor.

The superintendent should walk the project when each subcontractor finishes its portion of the work to identify any needed rework. Any deficiencies noted should be listed in the log shown in Figure 17–2. All rework should be completed before follow-on subcontractors are allowed to start work. Deficiencies should be corrected as the work progresses to minimize the size of the ***punch list***, which is a list of items to be completed or corrected that were identified at the ***pre-final inspection***.

17.4 TESTING AND INSPECTION

Quality control starts with the submittal process described in Chapter 14. Approved materials and equipment are then procured using the methods described in Chapter 9. All materials and equipment should be inspected as they are being delivered to the project site. They should be examined and compared to the appropriate purchase orders and submittal documentation. If the materials and/or equipment are not as specified, they should not even be unloaded from the truck; they should be rejected. Materials stored on site also need to be inspected periodically to ensure they are properly protected against weather damage.

Mock-ups required either by contract or the quality control plan are constructed prior to initiating work to establish workmanship standards. An example of a mock-up is a construction of 6-foot-by-6-foot section of a brick wall to establish the brick pattern and mortar workmanship. Mock-ups are examined as a part of the ***preparatory inspection*** for each phase of the work. These inspections should ensure that all preliminary work has been completed on the project site either by the general contractor's or appropriate subcontractor's work force. All materials and equipment are inspected to ensure they are appropriate for the tasks to be performed.

Once the work starts, the inspector conducts an ***initial inspection*** to ensure workmanship meets quality standards and dimensional requirements are met. Daily follow-up inspections are conducted to ensure continuing compliance with contract requirements. Quality control inspectors prepare daily reports, similar to the one illustrated in Figure 17–3, to document their inspection activities and any deficiencies identified. These daily inspection reports should be reviewed both by the superintendent and by the project manager. Outstanding deficiencies should be entered in the deficiency log and tracked until they have been corrected. Building inspectors and design team members should be scheduled to visit the site throughout the completion of the project to ensure that all work is inspected prior to being covered. This avoids the need to uncover work for inspection.

Article 12.1 of the AIA General Conditions in Appendix E addresses uncovering work for inspection. Work covered contrary to the architect's request or to contract requirements is to be uncovered at the contractor's expense. The architect may request that additional work be uncovered for inspection. If the uncovered work is found to conform to contract requirements, a change order will be issued to cover the impact costs. If the work is found not to conform with contract requirements, the inspection and correction costs are the contractor's responsibility.

The specifications identify which items are to be tested and how they are to be tested. Other testing directed by the architect or owner requires a change order to compensate the contractor for the additional work. Professional testing and inspection agencies are used to perform required testing. Contracts often require independent monitoring and testing of:

- Concrete
- Fireproofing
- Glazing and window walls
- Post-tension cables
- Precast concrete
- Reinforcing steel
- Roofing
- Shoring systems
- Soil compaction
- Structural steel fabrication, erection welds, and field bolt torque
- Underground utilities

Reports provided by testing agencies are reviewed by the quality control inspectors and filed with their daily inspection reports. The contract may require that copies of the reports be submitted to the owner. Materials not meeting test standards must be replaced.

When the project is nearing completion, the project manager schedules the prefinal inspection. Generally, this inspection is conducted by the superintendent, an owner's representative, and a representative of the design firm. All deficiencies noted are recorded on a punch list. If an active quality management system has been used on the project, the size of the punch list should be minimal. When all deficiencies listed on the punch list have been corrected, the project manager schedules the ***final inspection***

NORTHWEST CONSTRUCTION COMPANY
1242 First Avenue, Cascade, Washington 98202
(206) 239-1422

DAILY INSPECTION REPORT

Date: SEPT. 19, 2000

Project: HUNA OFFICE BUILDING

Weather Conditions: RAIN AND GRAY

WORK INSPECTED: REBAR FOR FOOTINGS

WORK FOUND TO BE IN ACCORDANCE WITH APPROVED PLANS AND SPECIFICATIONS WITH EXCEPTIONS AS NOTED BELOW. TALKED TO BATES (SUPERINTENDENT) AND THESE ITEMS WILL BE CORRECTED PRIOR TO CONCRETE PLACEMENT SCHEDULED FOR TOMORROW.

DEFICIENCIES NOTED: (1) SOME MUD ON REBAR. (2) SOME REBAR LAYING ON GROUND – NOT YET HUNG. (3) MINOR WOOD AND DEBRIS LAYING IN FORMS.

INSPECTOR: JEREMY SHAKER – TTI TESTING, INC.

FIGURE 17–3 Daily Inspection Report

to verify that all required work has been completed in conformance with contract requirements. The final inspection is conducted by the superintendent, an owner's representative, and a representative of the design firm. Other aspects of project close-out are discussed in Chapter 21.

17.5 ISO 9000

In 1987, the International Organization for Standardization, a federation of the national standards organizations of over 90 countries, published ***ISO 9000 international standards*** for quality management and quality assurance. These standards, which have been adopted by many countries throughout the world, provide quality management guidance and identify generic quality system elements necessary for quality assurance. They provide direction regarding what needs to be done but do not prescribe how it is to be accomplished. The basic structure of the standards is illustrated in Figure 17–4. ISO 9000–1 and ISO 9004–1 are considered guidance standards, while ISO 9001, ISO 9002, and ISO 9003 are conformance standards. These standards are continuously reviewed and periodically updated.

ISO 9000–1, *Quality Management and Quality Assurance Standards—Guidelines for Selection and Use*, introduces the series, explains how to use ISO 9004–1 for internal quality management, and provides guidance for selecting, using, and tailoring ISO 9001, ISO 9002, and ISO 9003 for external quality assurance programs. Some of the key topics discussed in ISO 9000–1 are:

- Quality objectives of an organization
- Work as a process
- Management review of quality systems
- Role of documentation
- Tailoring the standard to a contract

ISO 9004–1, *Quality Management and Quality System Elements—Guidelines*, expounds on internal quality management. Some of the key topics discussed in the standard are:

- Organizational quality goals
- Management responsibility
- Quality system elements
- Quality in marketing
- Quality in specification and design
- Quality in purchasing
- Quality of processes
- Control of processes
- Product verification
- Control of inspection, measuring and test equipment
- Control of nonconforming products
- Corrective action
- Quality records
- Personnel
- Safety

ISO 9001, *Quality Systems—Model for Quality Assurance in Design/Development, Production, Installation, and Servicing*, is used when there is a design effort involved in service delivery. It addresses quality planning, measurement, and documentation throughout all stages of the service life cycle, from design development to warranty. The following quality system requirements are contained in this standard.

- Management responsibility
  - Quality policy
  - Quality management organization
  - Quality system management review

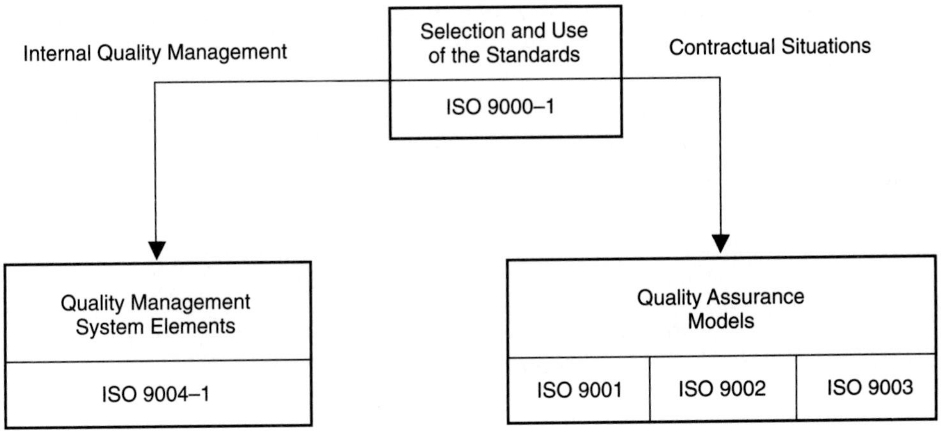

FIGURE 17–4 Structure of ISO 9000 Standards

- Quality management system
    - Quality system procedures
    - Quality planning
- Contract review
- Design control
- Document and data control
- Purchasing control
- Control of customer-supplied products
- Product identification and traceability
- Process control
- Inspection and testing
- Control of inspection, testing, and measuring equipment
- Inspection and test status
- Control of nonconforming product
- Corrective and preventive action
- Handling, storage, packaging, preservation, and delivery
- Control of quality records
- Internal quality audits
- Training
- Servicing
- Statistical measurement

ISO 9002, *Quality Systems—Model for Quality Assurance in Production, Installation, and Servicing*, is used when there is no design effort involved in service delivery. Quality system requirements contained in this standard are the same as those contained in ISO 9001, except there is no design control requirement.

ISO 9003, *Model for Quality Assurance in Final Inspection and Test*, addresses requirements for detection and control of problems during final inspection and testing. Quality system requirements contained in this standard are the same as those contained in ISO 9001, except there are no requirements for design control, purchasing control, process control, or servicing.

ISO 9004–2, *Quality Management and Quality System Elements—Part 2: Guidelines for Services*, builds on the quality management principles contained in

Installing Roof Sheeting on Huna Office Building

ISO 9000–1, ISO 9001, and ISO 9002 and provides guidance regarding establishment and implementation of quality systems for service industries, such as construction. Topics covered in the standard include:

- Management of customer relations
- Measurement of customer satisfaction
- Emphasis on the critical need for process management
- Dependence of service quality on employee knowledge, skills, and motivation
- Employee involvement and teamwork
- Quality planning and life-cycle management of services
- Prevention-oriented quality management systems
- Importance of continuous improvement based on quantitative measurement

Within the United States, most contractors who are ISO 9000 certified have selected certification under ISO 9001. A few have opted for certification under ISO 9002. To become certified, a contractor must be audited by a third-party registrar to ensure the construction firm complies with all of the requirements listed within the standard. Once certified, the registrar conducts follow-up surveillance audits every six months. The construction industry in the United States has been slow to adopt ISO 9000 standards and certification. Many international contractors have adopted these standards because ISO 9000 certification often is a requirement to receiving a construction contract in many European and Middle Eastern countries.

17.6 SUMMARY

An effective quality management program is essential to project success, both in terms of a satisfied owner and a profitable project for the general contractor. Poor quality work costs the contractor both time and money and can cause the loss of future projects from the owner. The project manager must ensure that all materials and work conform to contract requirements. The objective of a quality management program is to achieve required quality standards with a minimum of rework. Quality materials must be procured and qualified craftworkers selected to install them. Workmanship must meet or exceed contractual requirements.

Quality control inspectors should be used to inspect all work, whether performed by the contractor's workforce or a subcontractor's. Materials are inspected for conformance with contract specifications upon arrival on the job site. Mock-ups may be required to establish workmanship standards. Each phase of work is inspected as it progresses, and a prefinal inspection is conducted when most of the work has been completed. All deficiencies identified during the prefinal inspection are recorded on the punch list. When all outstanding deficiencies have been corrected, the final inspection is conducted.

International ISO 9000 quality management and quality assurance standards have been published to guide the development of comprehensive quality management programs. While not used extensively in the United States domestic construction market, they are widely used in the international construction market.

17.7 REVIEW QUESTIONS

1. What is the primary objective of quality management programs?
2. What four processes are used in managing quality on a construction project?
3. Why are project-specific quality control plans needed? Why are generic quality control plans not acceptable?
4. What are mock-ups, and why are they used?
5. Why should quality control inspectors be involved in the submittal process?
6. Why should subcontractors not be allowed to build over work that was improperly done by a previous subcontractor?
7. Why are materials that are stored on site periodically inspected?
8. What is the purpose of a prepatory inspection?
9. What is the purpose of an initial inspection?
10. What is a prefinal inspection, and when is it conducted?
11. What are ISO 9000 standards?
12. What is the difference between ISO 9001 and ISO 9002 standards?
13. How does a contractor become ISO 9000 certified?
14. Why might a contractor be interested in becoming ISO 9000 certified?

17.8 EXERCISES

1. What quality control organization do you recommend the contractor use on the Huna Office Building project?
2. What are two mock-ups the general contractor should require subcontractors to construct for the Huna Office Building project?

3. Develop a quality control checklist for rough carpentry for the Huna Office Building project. The technical specification is in Appendix F.
4. Develop a quality control checklist for gypsum board assemblies for the Huna Office Building project. The technical specification is in Appendix F.

17.9 SOURCES OF ADDITIONAL INFORMATION

Davies, James S. *ISO 9000 Management Systems Manual*. New York: McGraw-Hill Companies, Inc., 1997.

Mahoney, William D., and Edward B. Wetherill, ed. *Construction Inspection Manual*. 6th ed. Los Angeles: BNI Publications, Inc. 1994.

Nee, Paul A. *ISO 9000 in Construction*. New York: John Wiley and Sons, Inc., 1996.

Peach, Robert W., ed. *The ISO 9000 Handbook*. 2d ed. Fairfax, Vir.: CEEM Information Services, 1994.

18

Safety Management

18.1 INTRODUCTION

Construction is one of the most dangerous occupations in the United States, accounting for about 10% of the disability injuries and 20% of the fatalities that occur in the industrial work force. Primary causes of job site injuries are falling from an elevation, being struck by something, being caught between two objects, and electrical shock. Within the United States, the ***Occupational Safety and Health Administration*** (***OSHA***) has the primary responsibility for establishing safety standards and enforcing them through inspection of construction work sites. The Occupational Safety and Health Act which established OSHA contains a provision that allows states who desire to administer their own industrial safety programs to do so as long as their requirements are at least as stringent as those imposed by OSHA. About half of the states have opted to administer their own programs. In this text, we discuss only the OSHA requirements, but they are similar to those imposed by state-mandated programs.

Most successful construction companies have recognized the importance of safety management and have developed effective company safety programs that include new employee orientation, safety training, and job site safety surveillance. The effectiveness of these programs, however, is directly related to management's commitment to safety. Project managers and superintendents are responsible for the safety of the workers, equipment, and materials on their project sites. They must set the standard regarding safety on their projects and enforce safety standards at all times. A continual safety awareness campaign that is focused on reducing accidents is necessary. Frequent (at least weekly) job site safety inspections should be conducted to identify hazards and ensure compliance with job-specific safety rules. Every project meeting should address safety in some manner. Many construction firms require their foremen to conduct weekly safety meetings with workers to maintain a continuous emphasis on hazard removal and safe work practices.

Job site safety is a significant project management issue. A safe working environment results in increased worker productivity and reduces the risk of injury. Accidents are costly, leading to disruption of the construction schedule and demanding significant management time for investigation and reporting. The indirect costs that can result from an accident are shown in Figure 18–1. They can be significant and generally are not covered by insurance, and thus adversely impact the profitability of a project. OSHA compliance inspectors can issue citations for safety violations and shut down operations considered to be life threatening. Stiff fines may be levied for violations. Project labor cost is greatly influenced by a construction firm's safety record. The workers' compensation premium rates for a company are directly related to the firm's safety record, as we will see in Section 18.9.

Article 10 of the AIA General Conditions in Appendix E prescribes the contractor's responsibility for job site safety. OSHA or state requirements are incorporated into the contract by reference in Article 10.2.2. Therefore, compliance is a contractual requirement. Similar provisions should be included in all subcontracts. Project managers often itemize specific job site safety requirements and attach them as an exhibit to the subcontract agreement.

18.2 ACCIDENT PREVENTION

Most job site accidents occur either as a result of unsafe conditions or unsafe acts. They generally can be prevented by eliminating unsafe conditions and by training workers to perform construction tasks safely. Job site accident prevention starts with an analysis of all the hazards that are associated with each task that is to be performed on the project. This ***job hazard analysis*** is performed during the project planning process that was discussed in Chapter 5. It involves the following three elements:

- A description of the construction operation
- A listing of the hazards associated with the operation
- A plan for eliminating, reducing, or responding to the hazardous situations

This job hazard analysis becomes the primary focus of the project-specific phased safety plan that is discussed in Section 18.6. A form such as the one illustrated in Figure 18–2 can be used for the analysis.

- First aid expenses
- Damage or destruction of materials
- Clean-up and repair costs
- Idle equipment time
- Unproductive labor time
- Schedule delays
- Loss of skilled workers
- Work slowdown
- Administrative and legal expenses
- Lowered employee morale
- Third-party lawsuits

FIGURE 18–1
Indirect Accident Costs

NORTHWEST CONSTRUCTION COMPANY
1242 First Avenue, Cascade, Washington 98202
(206) 239-1422

JOB HAZARD ANALYSIS

Project: *Huna Office Building Project*

Phase: *Clear and grade; Mass excavation*

Sequence of Construction Tasks	Potential Hazards	Hazard Mitigation Measures
Survey site	*Automobile traffic*	*1) Wear orange vests* *2) Put one man on automobile watch*
Erosion control	*Driving stakes*	*1) Protective eyewear* *2) Steel toe boots*
Logging	*Tree falling* *Saw kickback*	*1) Orange vests 2) Secure site* *3) Traffic watch 4) Saw guards*
*Tree/brush removal**	*Automobile traffic* *Debris falling from trucks*	*1) Orange vests 2) Automobile watch* *3) Clean truck tires* *4) Don't over-fill trucks*
*Mass excavation**	*Automobile traffic* *Operators not seeing workers on ground*	*1) Orange vests 2) Full-time flagger* *3) Clean tires*
	**Contaminate spill into creek*	*Check hoses daily to protect against spills into creek; have sand ready for absorption*
Equipment to be Used	**Inspection Requirements**	**Training Requirements**
Chain saws *Sledge hammers* *Track excavator* *Dump truck* *Dozer*	*Sharp chains* *New handles* *[Hydraulics, mirrors, and clean windshield]*	*Sharpen every hour* *Daily inspection* *[Inspect every vehicle entering and leaving site]*

Prepared by: Jim Bates Date: *August 15, 2000*

CC: subcontractors, employees, architect, owner, project manager, and project engineer

FIGURE 18–2 Job Hazard Analysis Form

Safe construction procedures and techniques should be identified for each phase of the work to minimize the potential for accidents. Some of the ways to reduce the risk created by a hazard are:

- Modify construction techniques to eliminate or minimize the hazard.
- Guard the hazard, for example, by fencing in the site.
- Provide a warning, such as back-up alarms on mobile equipment or warning signs.
- Provide special training.
- Equip workers with personal protective equipment, such as hard hats and hearing protection.

The hazards associated with each phase of work and selected mitigation strategies should be discussed with both contractor and subcontractor work crews prior to allowing them to start work. Many superintendents require daily safety meetings prior to allowing the workers to start work. These meetings address risks and mitigation strategies for the work to be performed that day.

18.3 SUBSTANCE ABUSE

As was mentioned at the beginning of this chapter, construction is one of the most dangerous occupations in the United States. Workers under the influence of drugs or alcohol on the job site pose serious safety and health risks, not only to themselves, but also to all those who work in the proximity of the users.

To combat the problem of substance abuse, many contractors have established specific policies prohibiting substance use on project sites and people from working on site who are under the influence. A key element of this program is a requirement for periodic drug and/or alcohol testing. Testing requirements usually apply to all individuals working on the project site, whether they are employed by the contractor or by a subcontractor. Subcontractors generally are required to administer their own substance-testing programs, or they are not allowed to work on the project site. Individuals refusing testing or failing to pass a test are removed from the job site. Many contractors require testing during the hiring process, after an accident, and when a supervisor believes the individual's behavior warrants testing. Others also require random testing.

Contractors use third parties to administer their testing programs to ensure fairness in implementation and compliance with legal requirements. Selected administrators should be members of the Substance Abuse Program Administrators Association to keep updated on rules and court cases at state and national levels.

18.4 PERSONAL PROTECTIVE EQUIPMENT

One of the methods for reducing the risk of job site injuries is to provide personal protective equipment, including:

- Body protection (protective clothing)
- Eye protection (safety glasses and goggles)
- Foot protection (safety shoes)
- Hand protection (gloves)
- Head protection (hard hats)

- Hearing protection (earplugs and earmuffs)
- Protection from falls (lifelines and safety harnesses)
- Respiratory protection (respirators)

Project managers and superintendents identify personal protective equipment requirements as part of the job hazard analysis discussed in Section 18.2 and require that all contractor and subcontractor workers use the proper equipment on the construction site. These requirements are specified in the project-specific phased safety plan discussed in Section 18.6. The wearing of hard hats, safety glasses, and safety shoes generally is required of all personnel at all times when working on or visiting the job site.

18.5 HAZARDOUS MATERIALS COMMUNICATIONS

OSHA regulations require that all personnel working on a construction site be informed of all chemicals being used on the site and of any harmful effect they may cause. The transmittal of this information is to be accomplished by means of a hazardous materials communication program that includes:

- Warning labels on all containers indicating the specific hazard posed
- Posting of ***material safety data sheets*** (***MSDS***)
- Specialized training regarding the safe handling, transporting, storage, and use of the chemicals

MSDS must be obtained from the manufacturer of each chemical used on site. The format for these sheets is shown in Figure 18–3. They basically are short technical reports that identify all known hazards associated with particular materials and provide procedures for using, handling, and storing the materials safely. Information contained on these sheets includes:

- Material identification and use
- Chemical data and hazardous composition
- Physical data
- Fire and explosion hazard data
- Health hazard data including emergency and first aid procedures
- Reactivity data
- Spill or leak procedures
- Protective equipment and ventilation requirements
- Special precautions for handling and storing

A copy of the MSDS for each hazardous chemical must be made available to all potentially exposed workers before the chemical is used on the project site. Copies of all sheets for materials used on site should be maintained in an accessible location in the project office.

18.6 PROJECT-SPECIFIC PHASED SAFETY PLAN

A ***project-specific phased safety plan*** is a detailed accident prevention plan that is focused directly on the hazards that will exist on a specific project and the specific measures to be taken to reduce the likelihood of accidents. Many owners require

Material Safety Data Sheet
May be used to comply with OSHA's Hazard Communication Standard, 29 CFR 1910 1200. Standard must be consulted for specific requirements.

U.S. Department of Labor
Occupational Safety and Health Administration
(Non-Mandatory Form)
Form Approved
OMB No. 1218-0072

IDENTITY *(as Used on Label and List)*	*Note: Blank spaces are not permitted. If any item is not applicable or no information is available, the space must be marked to indicate that.*

Section I

Manufacturer's name	Emergency Telephone Number
Address *(Number, Street, City, State and ZIP Code)*	Telephone Number for Information
	Date Prepared
	Signature of Preparer *(optional)*

Section II—Hazardous Ingredients/Identity Information

Hazardous Components (Specific Chemical Identity, Common Name(s))	OSHA PEL	ACGIH TLV	Other Limits Recommended	% (optional)

Section III—Physical/Chemical Characteristics

Boiling Point		Specific Gravity (H_2O = 1)	
Vapor Pressure (mm Hg)		Melting Point	
Vapor Density (AIR = 1)		Evaporation Rate (Butyl Acetate = 1)	
Solubility in Water			
Appearance and Odor			

Section IV—Fire and Explosion Hazard Data

Flash Point (Method Used)	Flammable Limits	LEL	UEL
Extinguishing Media			
Special Fire Fighting Procedures			
Unusual Fire and Explosion Hazards			

(Reproduce locally) OSHA 174 Sept. 1985

FIGURE 18–3 Material Safety Data Sheet

Section V—Reactivity Data

Stability	Unstable		Conditions to Avoid
	Stable		

Incompatibility *(Materials to Avoid)*

Hazardous Decomposition or Byproducts

Hazardous Polymerization	May Occur		Conditions to Avoid
	Will Not Occur		

Section VI—Health Hazard Data

Route(s) of Entry	Inhalation?	Skin?	Ingestion?

Health Hazards *(Acute and Chronic)*

Carcinogenicity	NTP?	IARC Monographs?	OSHA Regulated?

Signs and Symptoms of Exposure

Medical Conditions
Generally Aggravated by Exposure

Emergency and First Aid Procedures

Section VII—Precautions for Safe Handling and Use

Steps to Be Taken in Case Material Is Released or Spilled

Waste Disposal Method

Precautions to Be Taken in Handling and Storing

Other Precautions

Section VII—Control Measures

Respiratory Protection *(Specify Type)*

Ventilation	Local Exhaust	Special
	Mechanical *(General)*	Other

Protective Gloves	Eye Protection

Other Protective Clothing or Equipment

Work/Hygienic Practices

FIGURE 18–3 Material Safety Data Sheet *(Continued)*

project managers to submit such plans at preconstruction conferences. Other owners may require that these plans be submitted with the proposal package on negotiated contracts. A project-specific phased safety plan serves several purposes:

- Defines individual hazard prevention responsibilities of each member of the project management team.
- Identifies potential hazards that may occur on the job site during each phase of construction and identifies specific avoidance or mitigation measures to be taken.
- Lists equipment to be used on the project, the hazards associated with each, and specific safeguards to be taken.
- Lists construction methods to be employed during each phase of construction and safety procedures that are to be incorporated with each method.
- Describes the specific safety awareness training program to be used on the site.

The table of contents for the phased safety plan for the Huna Office Building project is shown in Figure 18–4. The analysis contained in Section 14 of the plan involves dividing the total scope of work into different phases, such as site preparation, excavation, concrete formwork, concrete placement, framing, roofing, exterior, interior, mechanical system, and electrical system. A job hazard analysis, such as illustrated in Figure 18–2, is prepared for each phase and included in the plan.

TABLE OF CONTENTS

1. Company Safety Policy
2. Safety Responsibilities of Project Management Team Members
3. Substance Abuse Program
4. Hazardous Materials Communication Program
5. Personal Protective Equipment
6. Emergency Procedures and First Aid
7. Fire Protection
8. Job Site Sanitation
9. Severe Weather Contingency Plans
10. Safety Training
11. Safety Meetings
12. Safety Inspections
13. Accident and Illness Recording and Reporting
14. Hazard Analysis of Each Phase of Construction
    a. Hazard Prevention Responsibilities
    b. Potential Hazards and Mitigation Measures
    c. Protective Equipment Required
    d. Specific Safety Procedures to be Used
    e. Safety Awareness Training

FIGURE 18–4
Phased Safety Plan for Huna Office Building

Placing Concrete on Huna Office Building

18.7 ACCIDENT INVESTIGATION

All accidents and near-miss incidents should be investigated promptly, whether or not injuries and/or damage occurred. An inspection team may be needed for serious accidents, such as collapse of some portion of a project. A single investigator should be adequate for less complex accidents. Supervisors or safety professionals should be used to conduct accident investigations to avoid biased findings. The objective of the investigation is to:

- Determine what happened.
- Determine why the accident or incident happened.
- Determine procedures or policies that should be adopted to minimize the potential for future occurrence of similar accidents or incidents.

The results of the investigation should be recorded by the superintendent and retained in the project files. A form similar to the one illustrated in Figure 18–5 may be used to record the investigator's findings and recommendations. Photographs should be included with the report to document conditions at the accident site. Some owners will require a copy of each accident report. If injuries occur as a consequence of the accident, a report must be submitted to OSHA and a copy kept on file at the construction firm for five years.

18.8 REPORTING REQUIREMENTS

All construction firms employing more than ten individuals are required to maintain detailed records for OSHA. They are required to maintain a log of all job site injuries

NORTHWEST CONSTRUCTION COMPANY
1242 First Avenue, Cascade, Washington 98202
(206) 239-1422

ACCIDENT INVESTIGATION REPORT

Project: ______________________________

Date of Accident: ______________ Time of Accident: ______________

Location of Accident: ______________________________

Description of Accident: ______________________________

____

____

____

Cause of Accident: ______________________________

____

____

____

Injured Personnel and Medical Treatment Required: ______________________________

____

____

____

Safety Equipment in Use at Time of Accident: ______________________________

____

____

Recommended Actions to Prevent Reoccurrence: ______________________________

____

____

____

Prepared by: ______________ Date: ______________

FIGURE 18–5 Accident Investigation Report

and illnesses and submit an annual report to OSHA no later than February 1 of the following year. The log must contain the following information for each recorded illness or injury:

- The date of the illness or injury
- The name of the affected employee
- The occupation of the employee
- A description of the illness or injury
- The amount of time lost due to the illness or injury.

In addition to the log, contractors are required to submit a separate one-page description of each illness or injury. This supplementary record of occupational illness or injury includes a description of how the illness exposure or injury occurred, the place of the exposure or accident, the employee's activity at time of exposure or injury, and the exact nature of the illness or injury, including affected body parts.

18.9 RELATIONSHIP TO LABOR COST

All states have workers' compensation laws mandating coverage for all workers on a job site. Workers' compensation is a no-fault insurance program that protects a contractor from being sued by his or her employees as a consequence of injuries sustained on the job site and provides compensation to workers who are injured or contract an illness on the job. Worker benefits include:

- Coverage of medical expenses
- Compensation for lost wages
- Vocational rehabilitation
- Disability pensions

Some states are monopolistic and provide workers' compensation insurance through state-administered funds, while others rely on private insurance companies.

Premiums are calculated by multiplying an established base rate for a particular trade, such as carpentry, by a predetermined factor based on the contractor's safety record. This factor is the ***experience-modification rating***, or ***EMR*** as it is known in the industry. It is based on the volume of claims made by a contractor's employees and goes back four years but excludes the previous year. For example, the EMR for 2001 would include data from 1999, 1998, and 1997. Typical company EMRs range from 0.5 to 2.0. The actual premium paid, therefore, is the product of the insurance base rate and the EMR. For example, suppose the base rate for carpenters is $2.50 per hour and the construction firm's EMR is 0.9. The premium rate to be paid is

$$(0.9)(\$2.50 \text{ per hour}) = \$2.25 \text{ per hour}$$

This means the contractor must pay $2.25 per hour for each carpenter working on the job site. The base rate for trades with higher accident rates, such as roofing, might be as much as $5.00 per hour.

Since a contractor must pay workers' compensation premiums for each hour a worker is on the job site, they significantly add to the labor cost. Firms that have poor safety records have high EMRs, making their labor costs higher than those with good safety records, which result in low EMRs. Project managers, therefore, must emphasize safety on their projects so their employers earn low EMRs and have competitive labor rates.

18.10 SUMMARY

Construction projects are dangerous work environments that pose many hazards to people working on them. To minimize the potential for worker injury, OSHA has established national safety standards that are enforced through a job site inspection program. Because of the importance of safety management, most construction firms have developed safety programs and hired safety professionals. Since project managers are responsible for safety on their project sites, they must establish safety awareness programs and enforce good safety practices.

The key to a good safety program is accident prevention. This is accomplished by identifying all the hazards that are associated with each work activity and developing plans for eliminating, reducing, or responding to these hazards. This is known as job hazard analysis. Substance abuse also can result in accidents, so an effective substance abuse program is needed to remove individuals from the job site who are under the influence. Personal protective equipment is provided and its use required to reduce the risk of job site injuries. Workers need to be informed of all hazardous chemicals that will be used on the project, their potential effects, and emergency and first aid procedures. Phased safety plans are developed for each project to identify hazards likely to occur during each phase of the work and specific measures to be taken to reduce the likelihood of accidents.

All accidents or near-miss incidents should be thoroughly investigated for lessons learned. The objective is to determine why the accident or incident occurred and identify procedures or policies to minimize the potential for future occurrence of similar accidents or incidents. A construction firm's safety record has significant impact on its labor cost. Workers' compensation premium rates are adjusted based on the history of claims submitted by the firm's employees.

18.11 REVIEW QUESTIONS

1. What are the four prime causes of injuries on construction projects?
2. What is OSHA's role in safety management on construction sites?
3. Why is job site safety a significant project management issue?
4. What are four costs that can result from a construction site accident that typically are not covered by insurance?
5. What is the purpose of a job hazard analysis? What three elements are involved in the analysis?
6. What are three ways to reduce the risk created by a hazard on a job site?
7. Why is substance abuse an important safety issue on a construction job site?
8. How are substance abuse programs in the construction industry typically administered?
9. What are four types of personal protective equipment that are commonly used on construction projects?
10. What is a hazardous materials communication program? Why does OSHA require its use?
11. What are material safety data sheets? Why are they used on construction sites?
12. What is a project-specific phased safety plan? Why is it prepared?
13. What are three objectives of a job site accident investigation?
14. What type information must be reported to OSHA regarding a construction injury in which a worker broke his leg?
15. What is EMR? How does it affect a contractor's labor rate?

18.12 EXERCISES

1. Prepare a job hazard analysis for the construction of the roofing on the Huna Office Building project.
2. Develop a substance abuse policy letter for the Huna Office Building project.
3. Develop the section of the phased safety plan for the Huna Office Building project that covers the early site-preparation phase of the project.
4. What can you tell about a general contractor who has an EMR of 1.8? 0.4?
5. Which construction trade is likely to have a higher worker's compensation base rate:
   a. steel erector or landscaper?
   b. drywall installer or painter?
   c. carpet installer or high voltage electrician?

18.13 SOURCES OF ADDITIONAL INFORMATION

Civitello, Andrew M., Jr. *Construction Operations Manual of Policies and Procedures*. 3d ed. New York: McGraw-Hill, Inc., 2000.

Heberle, Dave. *Construction Safety Manual*. New York: McGraw-Hill, Inc., 1998.

Hinze, Jimmie W. *Construction Safety*. Upper Saddle River, N.J.: Prentice-Hall, Inc., 1997.

Levitt, Raymond E., and Nancy M. Samuelson. *Construction Safety Management*. 2d ed. New York: John Wiley and Sons, Inc., 1993.

MacCollum, David V. *Construction Safety Planning*. New York: Van Nostrand Reinhold, 1995.

Mincks, William R., and Hal Johnston. *Construction Jobsite Management*. Albany, N.Y.: Delmar Publishers, 1998.

U.S. Department of Labor, Occupational Safety and Health Administration. *Construction Industry Digest*. OSHA Publication 2202, Washington, D.C.: U.S. Government Printing Office, 1998.

U.S. Department of Labor, Occupational Safety and Health Administration. *Construction Industry—OSHA Safety and Health Standards*. OSHA Publication 2207, Washington, D.C.: U.S. Government Printing Office, 1996.

U.S. Department of Labor, Occupational Safety and Health Administration. *Job Hazard Analysis*. OSHA Publication 3071, Washington, D.C.: U.S. Government Printing Office, 1992.

19

Contract Change Orders

19.1 INTRODUCTION

A change order is an agreement signed by the general contractor, the architect, and the owner after the contract has been awarded that modifies some aspect of the scope of work and/or adjusting the contract sum or contract time, or both. Change orders also are known as contract modifications. They may be additive, if they add scope of work, or deductive, if they delete work items. Since they occur on most construction contracts, managing change orders is an important project management function. In this chapter, we will discuss the major issues involved in managing contract change orders.

Change orders originate from a variety of sources and for a variety of reasons. Figure 19–1 lists some of the more common sources of change orders. Most change orders come from design errors and owner-directed scope changes; they are not necessarily due to poor design. Sometimes designers do not have sufficient funds, resources, or time to do a complete design. Sometimes owners contract with the subconsultants (such as mechanical or electrical engineers) directly and not through the architect. This may result in multidiscipline documents that are not fully coordinated. Design errors can occur due to the complexity of the project or innocent human error or oversight. Uncovering unknown site conditions can be the most difficult type of change order for an owner to accept. These generally result from inadequate site exploration prior to starting design. Hidden or latent conflicts or conditions are common in site work (for example, unknown buried debris) or remodeling (for example, rotten wood structure). When the contractor encounters hidden site conditions that adversely impact construction, he or she must notify the architect and owner to provide the architect an opportunity to make an inspection. Article 4.3.4 of the AIA General Conditions in Appendix E contains this requirement.

The lack of coordination of not-in-contract (NIC), or owner-furnished, equipment and materials is one type of change order that is avoidable. Owners sometimes believe that they can contract directly with subcontractors and suppliers and save the general

- Architect generated scope changes, change in material specifications
- Contractor generated material or detail change or value engineering proposal
- Design errors, discrepancies, or lack of coordinated multi-discipline design
- Discovery of unknown or hidden conditions
- Municipality generated changes, code interpretations or permit review changes
- Not-in-contract equipment discrepancies, utility connections, size variations
- Owner scope changes, additions, or changes to the program
- Specified product is unavailable or no longer manufactured
- Interference from third party or another contractor not under the control of the general contractor
- Unusually adverse weather

FIGURE 19–1 Common Sources of Change Orders

contractor's fee. This is common with items such as kitchen equipment, auditorium equipment, furnishings, custom casework, and landscaping. Problems arise and the project is disrupted due to the lack of coordination of owner-furnished materials. Eventually owners often will pay much more to resolve these conflicts then they would have originally paid the general contractors in fees to manage this work.

19.2 CHANGE ORDER PROPOSALS

Change order proposals may be initiated either by the owner or by the general contractor. An owner-initiated change order proposal request provides a description of the proposed change in the scope of work and requests that the contractor provide an estimate of additional cost (if the proposal adds scope of work) or deductive cost (if the proposal deletes scope of work). If the proposed change extends the project duration, the contractor also requests additional time when responding to the owner's change order proposal request. A contractor-initiated change order proposal generally results either from a differing site condition or from a response to a field question. The contractor's proposal describes the proposed change to the scope of work and provides any requested adjustments to contract price and time. An example of a contractor's change order proposal is shown in Figure 19–2. The procedures used on the Huna Office Building project are shown in Section 01035 of the contract specifications in Appendix F. Change order proposals do not modify the construction contract. Only change orders and construction change directives, which are discussed in Section 19.6, modify the contract.

Many change order proposals are initiated by subcontractors. For example, the carpet subcontractor submits a field question to the project manager stating that carpet is not clearly identified for Room 210. The floor plan (drawing A202) indicates office space, and the specifications indicate that all office spaces receive loop carpet. But the finish schedule (drawing A200) shows the floor finish in Room 210 is to be unfinished concrete. The carpet subcontractor assumed that there was not any carpet in this room and has asked a field question for verification. Another way this could have surfaced would have been through a submittal drawing of planned floor covering materials. Remember that field questions and submittals are methods for voicing discrepancies and therefore are part of the active quality management process discussed in Chapter 17. The project manager should research the issue and forward the question or submittal to the architect. The architect responds to the field question and indicates that the subcontractor's interpretation is incorrect and that carpet is required in Room 210.

NORTHWEST CONSTRUCTION COMPANY
1242 First Avenue, Cascade, Washington 98202
(206) 239-1422
Huna Office Building

CHANGE ORDER PROPOSAL NUMBER: **3** Date: 10/27/00

Description of work: Enclose pipes and conduits in pipe chase in the first floor lobby

Referenced documents: Field Question #5, CCD #2, and Sketch #6

	ESTIMATE SUMMARY:		Subtotal	Total
1	Direct Labor		$750	
2	Supervision	15%	$113	
3	Labor Burden	46%	$397	
4	Safety	2%	$25	
5	Total Labor:			$1,285
6	Direct Materials and Equipment		$150	
7	Small Tools	3%	$39	
8	Consumables	3%	$39	
9	Total Materials and Equipment:			$227
10	Subtotal Direct Work (Items 1 through 9)			$1,512
11	Subcontractors (See attached subcontractor quotes)			$2,515
12	5% Overhead on Direct Work Items		$76	
13	5% Fee on Direct Work Items		$79	
14	5% Fee on Subcontractors		$126	
15	Subtotal Overhead and Fee:			$281
16	Subtotal all costs:			$4,308
17	Liability Insurance (1.0%)			$43
18	Total this COP #	**3**		**$4,351**

This added work has an impact on the overall project schedule, the extent of which cannot be thoroughly analyzed until after the change is incorporated into the contract and the work has been completed.
Please indicate acceptance by signing and returning one copy to our office within five days of origination. This work is in process as directed by CCD #2.

Approved by:

Huna Totem Corporation Date

cc: JYL Architects, NWCC Superintendent
Job No. 9821/File Code: COP #03

FIGURE 19–2 Contractor's Change Order Proposal

The architect's response to the field question may contain a request for a change order proposal. If not, the subcontractor will notify the project manager regarding any cost and time impacts of the architect's response. If the project manager believes a change order is warranted, he or she will send a change order request to the subcontractor using a form similar to the one shown in Chapter 8 (Figure 8–8). The project manager uses the subcontractor's response to the change order request to prepare a change order proposal similar to the one illustrated in Figure 19–2. The following guidelines should be used when preparing a change order proposal:

- Each proposal should be numbered sequentially.
- The description of the proposed changes should be clear.
- Direct labor, hours, labor burden, supervision costs are separated, itemized, and indicated.
- Direct material and equipment costs should be summarized.
- Subcontract costs are listed separate from direct costs.
- Mark-ups should include overhead (home office vs. field), fees, taxes, insurance, and bonds.
- A line should be provided for the owner to sign approval.

The project manager should do everything possible to sell the change order proposal to the architect and owner. All relevant supporting documents should be attached. Some examples of attached documents include:

- The originating field question or submittal
- Copies of areas of all relevant drawings and specification sections
- Subcontractor and supplier quotations
- All detailed quantity take-off and pricing recap sheets
- Any letters, memos, meeting notes, daily diaries, or phone records

The project manager should require similar documentation from the subcontractors.

All change order proposals should be tracked with a log. As soon as a potential changed condition arises, it should be assigned a number and entered in the log. An example change order proposal log is shown in Figure 19–3.

The owner may accept and sign the proposal, which makes the rest of the process straightforward. Often, however, there will be questions related to the request and subsequent negotiations. This is to be expected and is part of working as a team. Remember that the proposal is usually negotiable. The project manger is not taking a hard line approach at this time. A weekly change order proposal meeting outside of the regular construction coordination meeting is a good way to discuss and resolve change issues. It is beneficial to keep change order discussions out of the coordination meeting as the discussion of extra costs has a way of undermining the communication process.

19.3 IMPACT ANALYSIS

When analyzing the impact of a proposed change order, the project manager determines the direct cost of additional materials, labor, equipment, and subcontractors and the impact of the change on the scheduled completion of the project. If the change delays critical activities, additional contract time generally is justified. To determine time impacts, the construction schedule is updated by adding the additional scope of work contained in the proposed change order and evaluating its impact on the scheduled completion date for the project. If additional contract time is not granted, the

NORTHWEST CONSTRUCTION COMPANY
1242 First Avenue, Cascade, Washington 98202
(206) 239-1422

CHANGE ORDER PROPOSAL LOG

Project No.: *9821* Project Name: *Huna Office Building* Project Manager: *Ted Jones*

COP No.	Originating Document	Description	Originating Date	COP Date	Amount Requested	Date Approved	Approved Amount	CO No.	Comments
1	*CCD #1*	*Permit documents*	*8/15/00*	*9/1/00*	*0*	*9/1/00*	*0*	*1*	*No impact*
2		*Over excavation for footings*	*9/15/00*	*10/1/00*	*1,500*	*10/10/00*	*1,250*	*1*	
3	*FQ #1/CCD #2*	*Pipe chase*	*10/12/00*	*10/27/00*	*4,351*	*11/1/00*	*4,351*	*1*	*in process*
4	*Submittal*	*Column rebar change*	*10/12/00*	*10/15/00*	*222*	*11/15/00*	*222*	*1*	
5	*Submittal*	*Carpet manufacture change*	*10/12/00*	*11/1/00*	*-1,200*	*11/1/00*	*-1,200*	*1*	
6		*Toilet accessory backing*	*11/1/00*	*11/15/00*	*475*	*NA*	*NA*	*NA*	*Rejected*
7	*FQ #3*	*Beam and duct conflict*	*11/1/00*						
8	*CCD #3*	*Low voltage light controls*	*11/15/00*	*12/1/00*	*3,500*	*12/1/00*	*3,600*	*2*	

FIGURE 19–3 Change Order Proposal Log

project manager may need to accelerate some activities to compensate for the additional work. The indirect, or overhead, costs associated with these impacts also need to be estimated and included in the change order price.

The timing and volume of change orders may disrupt the planned flow of work among project team members. This impact is difficult to quantify and may be equally difficult to negotiate with the owner. The best approach is to compare the as-built schedule with the as-planned schedule at the end of the project to determine what inefficiencies were created by the timing and volume of change orders. If adverse impacts occurred due to the timing and volume of change orders, the project manager should submit a claim for compensation using the procedures described in the contract general conditions.

19.4 PRICING CHANGE ORDERS

The ultimate goal for the project manager with respect to change orders is to have them approved so that he or she can get paid. The easiest way to achieve this goal is be realistic with respect to pricing on direct and subcontract cost estimates. Overly inflated prices will only delay the process. Quantity measurements generally are verifiable and should not be inflated. Wage rates paid to craft employees are verifiable and should not be inflated. Subcontractor quotes should be passed through as-is without adjustment (unless incomplete) from the project manager to the owner. The subcontractors and suppliers should practice the same procedures with their second- and third-tier firms. Labor productivity rates should be derived from preapproved resources. Material prices should be actual and verified with invoices or quotations.

Mark-ups or percentage add-ons are used to recover indirect costs such as:

- Bonds
- Cleanup
- Consumables
- Detailing
- Dumpsters or rubbish removal
- Fee on direct work
- Fee on subcontracted work
- Field overhead
- Foremen costs
- Hoisting
- Home office overhead
- Insurance
- Labor burden
- Material transportation and handling
- Safety equipment
- Small tools
- Supervision costs
- Taxes

It is possible to see a series of mark-ups which could double the cost of the direct work. Owners often get frustrated with these add-ons. They do not understand why they have to pay more for the change than simply the direct costs. Many of these items are required, and sometimes it is just the presentation that makes them difficult to sell. There are several ways to smooth the process and reinforce fairness for all parties.

Sometimes, general contractors (and subcontractors) are asked to propose mark-up rates with their bid proposals. This eliminates the need to negotiate a mark-up rate for change orders. Some mark-ups are stated in the contract documents. This is another reason to carefully read the contract prior to preparing the estimate. Some designers will try to lump the subcontractor and general contractor mark-ups together to prevent compounded mark-ups.

Another system is for the project manager to negotiate mark-up rates with each subcontractor and the owner soon after receiving the notice to proceed before many changes have occurred. This will avoid negotiating mark-up rates for each change order separately.

Installing Exterior Waterproofing on Third Floor Mechanical Room on Huna Office Building

Mark-up rates for general contractors typically range from 5 to 10%. This rate is usually the same percentage fee that was used on the original estimate and is stated in the negotiated contract. Home office overhead costs are assumed to be included in this fee. Job site general conditions are not allowed unless they can be substantiated on individual change issues or it can be proven that the scope of the change will extend the project schedule.

Subcontractors tend to receive higher fees because their volumes of work generally are less than those of general contractors and their labor risk, which is determined by the ratio of direct labor to subcontract value, is higher. Subcontractors may receive a 10% fee and an additional 10% overhead. Both of these rates will depend on how many of the items listed earlier in this section are anticipated to be included in the base estimate, are in the fee or overhead, or are allowed in addition to the fee.

19.5 CHANGE ORDER PROCESS

If the architect or owner and the project manager have negotiated a mutually acceptable adjustment in the contract price, time, or both, a change order is executed modifying both the scope of work and the terms of the contract. If a mutually acceptable adjustment has not been negotiated for an owner-initiated change, the owner may choose to withdraw the change order proposal request. If the owner does not agree to a change order proposal submitted by the project manager, the project manager may withdraw the proposal or submit a claim using procedures that will be discussed in Chapter 20. If the owner and the project manager have not negotiated a mutually agreeable contract adjustment, but the owner wants to proceed with the change, a construction change directive is issued. Both the contract change order and the construction change directive are discussed in more detail in the next section of this chapter.

Erecting Prefabricated Lobby Framing on Huna Office Building

Section 01035 of the specifications in Appendix F contains the change order procedures for the Huna Office Building project. Article 7 of the AIA General Conditions in Appendix E contain additional instructions regarding making changes to the contract.

19.6 DOCUMENTATION

The two documents used to modify construction contracts are the change order and the construction change directive. Both documents generally are prepared by the architect. The change order, which is illustrated in Figure 19–4, is used when the owner and the project manager have agreed to an appropriate adjustment to the contract price and time. The construction change directive, which is illustrated in Figure 19–5 on page 246, is used when the owner and the project manager have not agreed on an appropriate adjustment to the contract price and time. The construction change directive also is used when the change must be implemented before the project manager has had time to evaluate its cost and time impacts.

A change order may be used to incorporate several approved change order proposals into the construction contract. Some owners choose to issue monthly change orders incorporating all change order proposals approved during the month. Change order proposals do not modify the terms of the contract and are not added to the schedule of values for pay purposes until incorporated into the contract by change order. The contract documents should be annotated with all scope changes contained in each change order. Once the change order has been signed by the architect, owner, and contractor, the contract scope, price, and time have been modified. The contractor's signature indicates that he or she agrees that the adjustment in price and time adequately compensate for the added scope of work. After the general contractor's contract has been modified, the project manager should modify appropriate subcontracts using the procedures discussed in Chapter 8.

2000 EDITION

AIA DOCUMENT G701-2000

Change Order

(Instructions on reverse side)

PROJECT:
(Name and address)
Huna Office Building
9301 Glacier Highway
Juneau, Alaska 99801

CHANGE ORDER NUMBER: 1
DATE: November 15, 2000
ARCHITECT'S PROJECT NUMBER: 937
CONTRACT DATE: August 15, 2000
CONTRACT FOR: Construction of office building

OWNER ☒
ARCHITECT ☒
CONTRACTOR ☒
FIELD ☐
OTHER ☐

TO CONTRACTOR:
(Name and address)
Northwest Construction Co.
1242 First Avenue
Cascade, Washington 98202

THE CONTRACT IS CHANGED AS FOLLOWS:
(Include, where applicable, any undisputed amount attributable to previously executed Construction Change Directives.)

Incorporate Change Order Proposals 1, 2, 3, 4, and 5 per attached Change Order Proposal Log

The original (~~Contract Sum~~) (Guaranteed Maximum Price) was $ 1,760,000.00

The net change by previously authorized Change Orders $ NA

The (~~Contract Sum~~) (Guaranteed Maximum Price) prior to this Change Order was $ 1,760,000.00

The (~~Contract Sum~~) (Guaranteed Maximum Price) will be (increased) (~~decreased~~)

(~~unchanged~~) by this Change Order in the amount of $ 4,623.00

The new (~~Contract Sum~~) (Guaranteed Maximum Price) including this Change Order will be $ 1,764,623.00

The Contract Time will be (~~increased~~) (~~decreased~~) (unchanged) by Zero (0) days.

The date of Substantial Completion as of the date of this Change Order therefore is June 3, 2001

NOTE: This Change Order does not include changes in the Contract Sum, Contract Time or Guaranteed Maximum Price which have been authorized by Construction Change Directive for which the cost or time are in dispute as described in Subparagraph 7.3.8 of AIA Document A201.

Not valid until signed by the Architect, Contractor and Owner.

ARCHITECT	CONTRACTOR	OWNER
Jensen Yorba Lott	Northwest Const.	Huna Totem
ARCHITECT *(Typed name)*	**CONTRACTOR** *(Typed name)*	**OWNER** *(Typed name)*
Norm Riley	Sam Peters	Robert Smith
(Signature)	*(Signature)*	*(Signature)*
Norm Riley	Sam Peters	Robert Smith
BY	**BY**	**BY**
Nov. 15, 2000	Nov. 15, 2000	Nov. 15, 2000
DATE	**DATE**	**DATE**

1

The American Institute of Architects
1735 New York Avenue, N.W.
Washington, D.C. 20006-5292

FIGURE 19–4 Change Order

CONSTRUCTION CHANGE DIRECTIVE

AIA DOCUMENT G714

OWNER	☒
ARCHITECT	☒
CONTRACTOR	☒
FIELD	☐
OTHER	☐

(Instructions on reverse side. This document replaces AIA Document G713, Construction Change Authorization.)

PROJECT: (name, address) Huna Office Building, 9301 Glacier Highway, Juneau, Alaska 99801

TO CONTRACTOR: (name, address) Northwest Construction Co., 1242 First Avenue, Cascade, Washington 98202

DIRECTIVE NO: 2

DATE: Oct. 12, 2000

ARCHITECT'S PROJECT NO: 937

CONTRACT DATE: Aug. 15, 2000

CONTRACT FOR: Construction of office building

You are hereby directed to make the following change(s) in this Contract:

Construct first floor lobby pipe chase per Field Question 5 and Sketch 6

PROPOSED ADJUSTMENTS

1. The proposed basis of adjustment to the Contract Sum or Guaranteed Maximum Price is:

   ☐ Lump Sum (increase) (decrease) of $__________.

   ☐ Unit Price of $__________ per __________.

   ☐ as provided in Subparagraph 7.3.6 of AIA Document A201, 1987 edition.

   ☒ as follows: Proceed with Work and provide detailed Change Order Proposal

2. The Contract Time is proposed to ~~(be adjusted)~~ (remain unchanged). ~~The proposed adjustment, if any, is (an increase of~~ __________ ~~days) (a decrease of~~ __________ ~~days)~~.

When signed by the Owner and Architect and received by the Contractor, this document becomes effective IMMEDIATELY as a Construction Change Directive (CCD), and the Contractor shall proceed with the change(s) described above.

Signature by the Contractor indicates the Contractor's agreement with the proposed adjustments in Contract Sum and Contract Time set forth in this Construction Change Directive.

ARCHITECT	OWNER	CONTRACTOR
Jensen Yorba Lott	Huna Totem	Northwest Construction
Address: 522 W. 10th Street, Juneau, Alaska 99801	Address: 9309 Glacier Highway, Juneau, Alaska 99801	Address:
BY Norm Riley	BY Robert Smith	BY
DATE Oct. 12, 2000	DATE Oct. 12, 2000	DATE

AIA **CAUTION: You should sign an original AIA document which has this caution printed in red. An original assures that changes will not be obscured as may occur when documents are reproduced.**

FIGURE 19–5 Construction Change Directive

The construction change directive modifies the scope of the construction contract and may adjust the contract price. Often construction change directives indicate that the general contractor is to proceed with the changes and that an appropriate adjustment to contract price and time will be negotiated later. These are sometimes referred to as unpriced change orders. Upon receipt of a construction change directive, the project manager determines the impact of the change on the project and submits a change order proposal requesting an appropriate adjustment of contract price and time. He or she also must issue appropriate direction to affected subcontractors and suppliers. While the construction change directive does change the contract scope when signed by the architect and owner, it does not change the contract price or time unless signed by the contractor. If the contractor refuses to sign the construction change directive, any change in contract price and time will occur only after the architect, owner, and contractor have negotiated a separate change order.

19.7 SUMMARY

Change orders occur on most construction projects. The most common causes are design errors, owner-directed scope changes, and differing site conditions. Change order proposals may be initiated either by the owner or by the project manager. An owner-initiated proposal request contains a description of the proposed change in the scope of work and requests that the project manager provide an estimate of the cost and time impact on the project. A project manager-initiated proposal describes the proposed change in the scope of work and requests an appropriate adjustment to the contract price and time. The project manager maintains a change order proposal log to track all change order proposals whether generated by the owner or the project manager. Once the project manager and the owner have negotiated a mutually agreeable adjustment in contract price and time, a change order is executed modifying the contract. If the owner wants to proceed with a change but has not negotiated an appropriate adjustment to the contract price and time, a construction change directive is issued directing the work to be accomplished. The project manager later submits a change order proposal responding to the construction change directive with a proposed adjustment to the contract price and time.

19.8 REVIEW QUESTIONS

1. What is a change order to a construction contract?
2. What are five causes of change orders on a typical construction project?
3. Why does using owner-furnished equipment on a project sometimes result in change orders?
4. What is the difference between an owner-initiated change order proposal and a contractor-initiated change order proposal?
5. How do designer responses to field questions sometimes result in change orders?
6. What factors should a project manager consider when analyzing the impact of a proposed change order on a construction project?
7. What recourse does a project manager have if the owner denies a change order proposal?
8. How does a change order proposal become a change order?
9. What is the difference between a change order and a construction change directive?

10. What action does a project manager take upon receipt of a construction change directive?
11. Why might an owner decide to issue a construction change directive?

19.9 EXERCISES

1. Prepare a change order proposal with a value greater than $1,000. Include a cover letter that allows the owner to sign and approve. Include all relevant supporting documents such as quantity sheets, recap sheets, subcontractor quotes, sketches, field questions, submittals, and memorandums.
2. Prepare a change order incorporating the change order proposal prepared in Exercise 1. Note the schedule impact, if any.

19.10 SOURCES OF ADDITIONAL INFORMATION

Bartholomew, Stuart H. *Construction Contracting: Business and Legal Principles.* Upper Saddle River, N.J.: Prentice-Hall, Inc., 1998.

Fisk, Edward R. *Construction Project Administration.* 6th ed. Upper Saddle River, N.J.: Prentice-Hall, Inc., 2000.

Grimes, J. Edward. *Construction Paperwork: An Efficient Management System.* Kingston, Mass.: R. S. Means Company, Inc., 1989.

Hinze, Jimmie. *Construction Contracts.* New York: McGraw-Hill, Inc., 1993.

Mincks, William R., and Hal Johnston. *Construction Jobsite Management.* Albany, N.Y.: Delmar Publishers, 1998.

20

Claims and Disputes

20.1 INTRODUCTION

Sometimes issues occur on construction projects that cannot be resolved among project participants. Such issues from a contractor's perspective typically involve requests for additional money or time for work performed beyond that required by the construction contract. The project manager submits a change order proposal for the contract adjustment using the procedures discussed in Chapter 19. If the owner agrees with the project manager, a change order is negotiated and executed adjusting the contract duration and/or price using the procedures discussed in Chapter 19. If the owner does not agree with the project manager's request, the result may be a contract ***claim***. Procedures for processing claims typically are prescribed in the general conditions of the contract. Sections 4.3 through 4.6 of the AIA General Conditions in Appendix E outline the procedures used on the Huna Office Building project. The normal procedure is for the project manager to formally submit the request for additional compensation and/or time to the owner or the architect along with documentation supporting the project manager's position. The owner or the architect formally responds to the contractor's request either agreeing completely, agreeing in part, or rejecting the contractor's claim. If the project manager does not agree with the response, the claim becomes a contract ***dispute***, and one of the dispute resolution techniques discussed in Section 20.3 is used to settle it. It is to the advantage of both the contractor and the owner to resolve the dispute quickly. The farther from the project level the dispute reaches, the more likely it is to become adversarial, time consuming, and expensive. The partnering and team-building techniques discussed in Chapter 7 have been adopted by many in the construction industry in an attempt to reduce the number of claims and disputes. The frequent meetings and the issue escalation system are used to resolve issues at the project level in a timely manner.

20.2 SOURCES OF CLAIMS

Construction claims typically result from one of the following causes:

- Constructive acceleration where the contractor is required to perform a task or tasks at a faster rate than planned
- Constructive changes where the scope of work was modified by the owner
- Cumulative impact of numerous change orders
- Defective or deficient contract documents
- Delay caused by the owner or the owner's agents
- Site conditions that differ from those described in the contract documents
- Unresponsive contract administration
- Weather

Any of these issues will affect the project manager's ability to complete the project within budget and the prescribed duration. The major issues in claims and disputes are:

- What are the issues?
- Who is responsible?
- What are the cost and time impacts?

Time impacts are determined by assessing the impact of the disputed work on the construction schedule. Cost impacts are determined by evaluating the actual costs for any additional work and the overhead costs incurred by the contractor for being on the project any extra time.

20.3 DISPUTE RESOLUTION TECHNIQUES

There are several methods used by the construction industry to resolve disputes. Negotiation typically is the first technique attempted because it is relatively cheap and not time consuming. If negotiation does not result in resolution, other techniques may be selected in an attempt to find resolution. Litigation or going to court usually is the last resort, as it is the most expensive and time consuming. ***Mediation***, ***arbitration***, ***minitrials***, and ***dispute review boards*** are alternative techniques for dispute resolution that have been adopted in lieu of litigation. Figure 20–1 ranks the various resolution techniques in terms of cost and time, with negotiation being the least costly and litigation the most costly.

Negotiation

Negotiation involves both parties to the dispute sitting down, discussing both sides of the issue, and reaching agreement on an appropriate resolution. This is the most efficient and least expensive method of resolution and does not rely on any outside support. Negotiation should be attempted as soon as the dispute surfaces to avoid creating an adversarial relationship between the contractor's field personnel and those of the owner. Early negotiation may prove successful if attempted before the parties have had a chance to formulate strong positions regarding the dispute.

FIGURE 20–1
Relative Cost of Different Dispute Resolution Techniques

Dispute Resolution Techniques Ranked in Order of Increasing Cost and Time to Resolution
1. Negotiation
2. Mediation
3. Dispute Review Board
4. Minitrial
5. Arbitration
6. Litigation

Mediation

Mediation is an assisted negotiation process in which settlement discussions are facilitated by a neutral third party. Both the contractor and the owner may agree to bring in an outside mediator, or it may be required by the construction contract. Section 4.5 of the AIA General Conditions (Appendix E) requires mediation prior to taking a dispute to arbitration. The individual selected as mediator must be acceptable to both parties. As a consequence, this person must be credible and knowledgeable of the issues in question. The mediator listens to both parties' positions and attempts to help them reach a consensus. The mediator does not render any decision on the issues, but serves as an intermediary between the parties to the dispute. Most mediation sessions last only one day, but occasionally they may extend into a second day.

Prior to the mediation session, both parties submit brief memorandums to the mediator, setting forth their positions with regard to the issues that need to be resolved. Mediation starts with an initial joint session during which each side presents its position. After the opening statements are completed, the representatives of the contractor and those of the owner are assigned to separate rooms. Once assigned to different rooms, the parties are not assembled together again until a resolution has been reached. The mediator meets separately with each party and discusses the strengths and weaknesses of each position in an attempt to craft an agreement. Once both parties to the dispute reach a consensus, the mediator prepares a formal agreement document and the parties sign.

For mediation to be successful, both parties must have a desire to reach a settlement, the representatives participating must have authority to settle, and the mediator must have the trust of both parties. Not all mediations are successful; sometimes the mediator is unable to identify an acceptable solution. The sessions are kept confidential, and there is no written record kept of the process.

Arbitration

Arbitration is a formalized alternative to litigation in which the disputing parties present their case to a neutral third party, called the arbitrator, who is empowered to make a decision. Arbitration can be binding or nonbinding. Binding arbitration means that the arbitrator's decision is final, and nonbinding arbitration means that either party

Installing Siding on Huna Office Building

may pursue litigation after arbitration. If the losing party in nonbinding arbitration decides to litigate, the arbitration award may be entered as evidence in court. Both the contractor and the owner may agree to take their dispute to arbitration, or it may be required by the construction contract. Article 4.6 of the AIA General Conditions (Appendix E) requires the use of binding arbitration to resolve disputes. Arbitration generally is a more efficient process than litigation because it is quicker and less expensive. Even so, arbitration of large, complicated cases can still be time consuming and expensive. In addition, arbitrators typically have more expertise in the technical subject matter under dispute than do judges.

Most arbitration of construction disputes is conducted in accordance with the Construction Industry Arbitration Rules of the American Arbitration Association (AAA). Arbitration is initiated by the claimant (for example, the contractor) giving written notice to the respondent (for example, the owner) and the AAA regional office of its intent to demand arbitration of a dispute. The notice contains a description of the nature of the dispute and the remedy requested. Upon receipt of the written notice, the AAA regional office furnishes both parties a list of qualified, potential arbitrators with biographical information regarding each candidate. If both the claimant and the respondent agree to an arbitrator, the AAA will appoint the selected individual. Often, one party selects three candidates from the list, and the other party selects one from the list of three. If the parties cannot agree on an arbitrator, the AAA will designate one. A single arbitrator is used in most instances, but a panel of three arbitrators may be used on large, complex disputes. When the panel is used, one member is selected by the contractor, and a second is selected by the owner. The third member is selected by the other two members.

Arbitration hearings are similar in many respects to a trial. Both parties make opening statements and present their cases to the arbitrator or arbitrators. Case presentations may include witnesses and documentation. Rules of evidence and procedure are less formal in arbitration than they are in litigation. The arbitrator is the judge of the relevance and admissibility of the evidence offered. Written transcripts of the proceedings generally are not required.

Minitrial

A minitrial is a private, nonbinding structured settlement process that can blend together some components of negotiation, mediation, and litigation (adversarial case presentation). It is conducted only when both parties to a dispute agree to the procedure. Minitrials are used to resolve disputes quickly and avoid the cost of arbitration or litigation. Both parties select a neutral advisor who presides over the proceeding. The minitrial consists of two phases: first, attorneys for each side make abbreviated presentations before senior executives of the companies involved, then the executives discuss settlement following the hearing. If the executives are unable to settle the dispute, the neutral advisor may be empowered to provide a nonbinding advisory opinion.

The minitrial is a flexible procedure that may be tailored as desired by the parties to the dispute. The specific procedures to be followed are selected by the participating parties before initiating the process. A typical procedure would include provisions for exchanging key exhibits and evidence, selecting the neutral advisor, and choosing executives from each organization who will serve on the minitrial panel. The actual hearing is intended to be informal and rules of evidence and legal procedures typically are waived. While the hearing generally is limited to one day, the settlement discussions may take several.

Dispute Review Board

A dispute review board is quite different from the other techniques used for dispute resolution in that the board is organized before construction starts and any disputes arise. This proactive approach provides a panel of experienced construction professionals who are knowledgeable of the specific project. The board consists of three industry experts selected for their knowledge of the type of construction being accomplished. One member is nominated by the project owner, a second by the contractor, and the third by the other two members. All board members must be acceptable to both the owner and the contractor. The decision to use a dispute review board generally is made by the owner. If one is to be used, the construction contract will include a specification similar to the one illustrated in Figure 20–2. Once the board members are selected, they sign a three-party agreement obligating them to serve both parties fairly and equally. The agreement is signed by each board member, the contractor, and the owner.

The board members are provided copies of the contract plans and specifications to become familiar with the project and make periodic site visits to keep abreast of construction progress. Typically board members meet on the project site monthly or quarterly to review construction progress and hear any issues in dispute. Either the contractor or the owner may refer an issue to the dispute review board for a recommendation. The board review consists of an informal hearing at which each party explains its position and an examination of all appropriate documentation and evidence. After deliberation, the board renders a written, nonbinding recommendation for resolving the dispute together with an explanation of how the board arrived at its conclusions. It is up to the owner and the contractor to accept or reject the board's recommendation. If the recommendation is not accepted, the dispute would be resolved either by arbitration or litigation.

Litigation

Litigation means referring the disputed issue to a court for resolution. This involves hiring legal counsel, preparing necessary documentation, and scheduling an appearance before a judge. This typically is the most time consuming and expensive, as shown in Figure 20–1. Most contractors and owners attempt to resolve their disputes

DISPUTE REVIEW BOARD

1. A dispute review board will be established to assist in the resolution of disputes in connection with, or arising out of, performance of the work of this contract.
2. Either the owner or the contractor may refer a dispute to the board. Such referral shall be initiated as soon as it appears that the normal dispute resolution procedure is not working and prior to initiating other dispute resolution techniques.
3. The board shall consist of one member selected by the owner and one member selected by the contractor, with these two members to select the third member, who will serve as the board chair. The members shall be mutually acceptable to both the owner and the contractor. No member shall have a financial interest in the work, except for payment for services as a member of the board. The board will be considered established once a Three-Party Agreement among the owner, the contractor, and the board members has been signed. The agreement establishes the scope of board services and the rights and responsibilities of the parties.
4. The board will formulate it own rules of operation, except to the extent any such rules are provided for herein. To keep abreast of the work, the members shall regularly visit the project, keep a current file, and regularly meet with the other members of the board and representatives of the owner and contractor. The frequency of these visits shall be as agreed among the owner, the contractor, and the board.
5. Compensation for board members and board operating expenses shall be shared by the owner and the contractor in accordance with the following:
   a. Owner will pay the fee and travel expense for its selected member.
   b. Contractor shall pay the fee and travel expense for its selected member.
   c. Owner and contractor shall share equally in the third member's fee and travel expense and all board operating expenses. These shared expenses will be paid by the owner, and the contractor's share will be deducted from monies due the contractor.
   d. Owner will, at its cost, provide administrative services, such as meeting room and secretarial services, to the board.
6. Requests for board review of a dispute shall be submitted in writing to the board chair and the other party. The request for review shall state in full detail the specific issues of the dispute and provide full documentation. The board chair will establish a hearing schedule that provides adequate time for the other party to provide a written response to the requesting party's statement and for the board members to review the request, the response, and the supporting documentation prior to the hearing. Both the owner and the contractor will present their positions at a board hearing. Following the hearing, the board shall meet in private and reach a conclusion supported by at least 2 or more members. A written report of its findings and recommendations, together with its reasons, shall be submitted to both parties.
7. Board recommendations are not binding on either the contractor or the owner. Within 2 weeks of receipt of the board's recommendation, the owner and contractor shall provide written notice to the other of their acceptance or rejection of the board's recommendation.

FIGURE 20–2 Dispute Review Board Contract Provision

without resorting to litigation, but it might be used as a last resort. Litigation is not an expedient means of dispute resolution. It can take years before the matter proceeds to trial, and if appeals are made, the final result will be delayed further.

Litigation starts when the plaintiff (for example, the contractor) submits a formal complaint to the appropriate court. The complaint contains the names and addresses of the parties, the allegations that form the basis of the complaint, and the nature of the relief sought. The defendant (for example, the project owner) then submits a formal denial of the allegations contained in the plaintiff's complaint.

Before the case goes to trial, both parties go through a discovery process. Discovery refers to a number of procedures available to both parties prior to trial, the purpose of which is to learn as much as possible about the case. Procedures available include interrogatories, discovery of documents, deposition of witnesses, and inspection of the project site. Interrogatories are a series of written questions sent by one party to the other. Written responses must be provided within a specified time. Discovery of documents means that each party has a right to request copies of all pertinent files and documents of the other side. A deposition is a cross-examination of a witness taken under oath prior to trial. A verbatim record of the questions and answers is made by a court reporter.

Once discovery is completed, the complaint is scheduled for trial. A construction lawsuit is a civil proceeding rather than a criminal proceeding. The trial may be conducted by a judge without a jury or on demand of either party, the trial may be held before a jury. The purpose of the trial is first to determine the facts in the case and then to apply the law to render a decision. Court trials are formal proceedings, and every word spoken is recorded verbatim by a court reporter. The judge controls the type of exhibits and testimony that go into the trial record as evidence. There are strict rules regarding what is admissible and what is not. Each side is allowed to present its case starting with the plaintiff, followed by the defendant who presents a rebuttal. Once all the evidence has been presented, either the jury deliberates and renders a decision, or the proceedings are closed and the judge prepares a written decision. The judge's decision may not be issued until months after the trial. Either party has a right to appeal the trial court's decision to an appellate court that will delay final resolution.

20.4 SUMMARY

Sometimes issues occur on construction projects that cannot be resolved between the contractor and the owner. Such issues result in claims that are formally submitted by the contractor using the procedures specified in the construction contract. Unresolved claims which become disputes should be resolved in the most efficient, least costly manner. Several techniques for dispute resolution have been adopted by the construction industry.

Negotiation involves both parties sitting down, discussing the issue, and reaching an appropriate resolution. Mediation is an assisted negotiation process in which both parties agree to use a neutral facilitator, or mediator. The mediator listens to both parties' positions and attempts to help them reach a consensus regarding resolution.

Arbitration involves two parties presenting their case to a neutral third party for a decision. The arbitrator requests written position papers and supporting documentation from both sides. Once the documentation has been reviewed, the arbitrator conducts a hearing allowing both sides to present their positions and renders a written decision.

A minitrial is a private, nonbinding settlement procedure in which both sides make summary presentations to senior executives from the contractor's and the owner's organizations. A neutral advisor presides and may make recommendations regarding settlement if the executives are unable to reach agreement.

A dispute review board is a panel of three industry experts convened prior to the start of construction. The board periodically meets at the project site to review progress on the project and hear any issues in dispute. Either the contractor or the owner can refer an issue to the dispute review board for a recommendation. Informal but comprehensive hearings are held and the board makes a recommendation. Board recommendations are not binding on the contractor or owner.

Litigation means referring the dispute to a court for resolution. This involves hiring legal counsel, preparing necessary documentation, and scheduling an appearance in court. This typically is very time consuming and expensive. Most contractors and owners attempt to resolve their disputes without litigation, but it might be used as a last resort.

20.5 REVIEW QUESTIONS

1. What are three potential causes of claims on a construction project?
2. What is mediation and how is it conducted?
3. What are the differences between mediation and litigation? What are the similarities?
4. What are the differences between mediation and a minitrial?
5. What is arbitration and how is it conducted?
6. How are minitrials conducted?
7. What is a dispute review board? When are its members selected?
8. Why do dispute review board members make periodic visits to the construction project site?
9. What is the discovery process that is used in litigation?
10. Why is litigation generally the most expensive of the methods of dispute resolution discussed in this chapter?

20.6 EXERCISES

1. A contractor has been selected to construct an elementary school. The AIA General Conditions (Appendix E) were included in his contract. The project manager believes the contractor is owed additional time and money because of an owner-caused delay. What procedure should the project manager use in submitting the claim?
2. How can the partnering techniques discussed in Chapter 7 be used to resolve issues between the contractor and the owner?
3. You are the project manager for Northwest Construction Company on the Huna Office Building project and have a dispute with the owner. You and the owner have decided to use mediation to attempt to resolve the dispute. What experience and abilities are you looking for when you select the mediator?
4. As project manager for Northwest Construction Company for the Huna Office Building project, you are required to nominate a member for the dispute review board. What criteria would you use to select a nominee?
5. As project manager for Northwest Construction Company for the Huna Office Building project, you have been asked to prepare an agenda for the quarterly site meeting of the dispute review board. What agenda would you propose?

20.7 SOURCES OF ADDITIONAL INFORMATION

American Arbitration Association. *Construction Industry Arbitration Rules*. New York: 1996.

American Arbitration Association. *Construction Industry Dispute Review Board Procedures*. New York: 1993.

American Arbitration Association. *Construction Industry Mediation Rules*. New York: 1992.

Ashley Phillips, Barbara. *Finding Common Ground: A Field Guide to Mediation*. Austin: Hells Canyon Publishing, 1994.

Carbonneau, Thomas E. *Alternate Dispute Resolution: Melting the Lances and Dismounting the Steeds*. Urbana, Ill.: University of Illinois Press, 1989.

Matyas, Robert M., Al A. Mathews, Robert J. Smith, and P. E. (Joe) Sperry. *Construction Dispute Review Board Manual*. New York: McGraw-Hill Companies, Inc., 1996.

Samuels, Brian M. *Construction Law*. Englewood Cliffs, N.J.: Prentice-Hall, Inc., 1996.

Technical Committee on Contracting Practices of the Underground Technology Research Council. *Avoiding Disputes During Construction: Successful Practices and Guidelines*. New York: ASCE, 1991.

Vorster, Michael C. *Dispute Prevention and Resolution*. Source Document 95, Construction Industry Institute. Austin: 1993.

21

Project Close-Out

21.1 INTRODUCTION

When physical construction on a project nears completion, the project manager develops a plan for project ***close-out*** to manage the numerous activities involved in finishing the project. Just as the project start-up activities described in Chapter 10 are essential when initiating work on a project, good project close-out procedures are essential to timely completion of all contractual requirements and receipt of final payment. Not only is efficient project close-out good for the general contractor, but it is also good for the owner. The project manager wants to close out a project quickly and move on to another. Minimizing the duration of close-out activities generally maximizes the profit on a project, since it limits project overhead costs and facilitates early receipt of final payment and any retention. Efficient close-out and turnover procedures also minimize the contractor's interference with the owner's move-in and start-up activities. Project managers sometimes lose credibility with owners because of inefficient close-out procedures. Dissatisfied owners rarely give contractors a second chance; instead, they award future projects to other contractors.

21.2 CLOSE-OUT PROCESS

Project close-out is the process of completing all of the construction tasks and all documentation required to close out the contract and consider the job complete. Article 9.10 of the AIA General Conditions in Appendix E addresses requirements for final completion and final payment. Close-out unfortunately can take up to a year after the receipt of a ***certificate of occupancy***. For purposes of discussion, we have divided the close-out process into the following four categories:

- Construction close-out
- Financial close-out
- Contract close-out
- Project Manager's close-out

21.3 CONSTRUCTION CLOSE-OUT

Many of the items related to completing the construction on a project and closing out the physical aspects are the responsibility of the project superintendent, similar to the physical mobilization of the project discussed in Chapter 10. Major construction activities associated with close-out are:

- Ensuring that all construction tasks have been completed in accordance with contract requirements.
- Obtaining certificates of substantial completion and occupancy.
- Demobilizing.

Punch List

Throughout the construction of the project, the superintendent and quality control staff should be inspecting completed work and identifying any deficiencies as part of the active quality management program discussed in Chapter 17. When the project is nearing completion, the project manager requests a pre-final inspection from the owner and architect. The list of deficiencies identified during this inspection is known as the punch list. An example punch list is shown in Figure 21–1. All items on the punch list must be corrected before the project can be considered complete. The punch list usually is developed by the architect, but some owners prepare their own. Some consultant design team members, such as the mechanical or electrical engineers, may also develop punch lists. Many groups within an owner's organization may develop separate punch lists depending upon their specialization. How many punch lists should a project manager receive? He or she should try to receive just one. If numerous lists are received, items may be overlooked, duplicated, lost, or even contradictory to one another. The best method is for all parties who are interested in inspecting the project to walk the job site together. One punch list form should be used. The architect can collect all of the input and issue the list to the project manager.

The inspection should occur early enough to allow the superintendent and the subcontractors sufficient time to complete the corrections prior to the owner taking occupancy. If the team is still developing the punch list after the owner has moved in, it is difficult to determine who did what damage. It also is a mistake to start the process too early. If there still are basic construction activities to complete, there may be additional damage that was not listed on the original punch list. The punch list should be prepared as soon as all major construction activities are completed.

The general contractor and subcontractors should take no more than two weeks to complete all of the work on the punch list. If the process takes too long, the responsible parties may have demobilized, and it may be difficult to get them back to the job site. The punch list should be signed off by the responsible parties as deficiencies are corrected. A copy of the annotated punch list should be sent to the architect. The architect may then wish to revisit each punch list item and verify its completion or may perform spot checks on items or rooms. The architect will then notify the owner that all deficiencies on the punch list have been corrected.

NORTHWEST CONSTRUCTION COMPANY
1242 First Ave, Cascade, Washington 98202
(206) 239-1422

PUNCH LIST

Project: *Huna Totem Office Building* Inspection Date: *4/5/01*
Area/System: *Exterior/shell/site* Status Date: *4/10/01*

Inspection Participants: *Norm Riley, Jim Bates, Robert Smith, Mary Peterson*

Item	Description	Complete?	Verified?
1	*Downspout splash blocks not installed*	*NIC*	*OK*
2	*Front door hardware requires adjustment*	*Yes*	*OK*
3	*Phase II sitework pending spring weather*		
4	*Parking lot requires sweeping*	*Yes*	*OK*
5	*Two handicap signs to be squared and straightened*	*Yes*	
6	*Re-paint entrance arrows, too light*	*Yes*	*OK*
7	*Fuel oil tank certificate requires exterior display*	*Yes*	*OK*
8	*Remove temp silt fence along stream (next spring)*		
9	*Remove GC's project sign*	*Yes*	*OK*
10	*Add building address for fire marshal*	*Yes*	
11	*Remove dumpster*		
12	*Clean exterior of windows*	*Yes*	*OK*
13	*Incorrect door mat installed: check specifications*		
14	*General site clean-up*	*Ongoing*	*Partial*

FIGURE 21–1 Punch List for Huna Office Building

Sometimes items will appear on the punch list that are outside the scope of the contract, or at least the project manager may believe so. The superintendent should not perform punch list work that is not required by the contract and then request a change order to pay for it. The project manager should respond to the architect and owner as soon as possible so that they can decide if they want to pay to have the extra work performed. There ultimately may be disagreements regarding some of these items. The project manager will need to meet with the owner and work out any differences prior to the project being completely closed out.

Certificates of Completion

There are two basic certificates of completion. The ***certificate of substantial completion*** is issued by the architect. It indicates that the project is sufficiently completed such that it can be used for its intended purpose but that there may be some minor deficiencies that need correction. ***Substantial completion*** is addressed in Article 9.8 of the AIA General Conditions in Appendix E. All items on the punch list may not have been corrected, but the architect agrees that the facility can be used. A copy of the corrected punch list should be attached to the certificate. An example certificate of substantial completion is shown in Figure 21–2. Substantial completion is a significant contractual event. It ends the general contractor's liability for liquidated damages. The contractual completion date stated in the contract agreement is the date by which substantial completion is to be achieved. Article 4.3 of the contract agreement in Appendix D states this requirement for the Huna Office Building project.

The certificate of occupancy is issued by the city, county, or municipality having jurisdiction over the project site, which is usually the same agency that issued the original building permit. The certificate of occupancy signifies that all code-related issues have been accounted for and that the building is approved and safe to use. It is often a formality which follows completion of all of the various inspections and subsequent approval of all other construction permits. The most important aspect of the certificate of occupancy is inspection by the fire marshal for life safety issues. The project may have minor deficiencies that are not related to life safety and still be approved for occupancy. For example, the landscaping may not yet be installed because there is three feet of snow on the ground. In this case, the project manager may have to post a bond with the city which guarantees completion of this portion of the project even though the certificate of occupancy was approved. An example certificate of occupancy for the Huna Office Building is shown in Figure 21–3 on page 264.

Occupancy

When will the owner occupy the completed project? Usually as soon as the city permits occupation, whether it is totally finished or not. Joint occupancy occurs when the owner accepts and occupies a portion of the building while the contractor is still working in another portion. This may be dictated by the owner's need to begin business in the new facility by a certain date or by the owner's desire to begin moving equipment into the new facility. Joint, dual, or conditional occupancies often are unavoidable and can be problematic if not managed properly. The project manager and superintendent may have problems differentiating the owner's cleanup and maintenance from punch list and warranty work. Payment of permanent utility bills also may be an issue. Labor problems may occur when construction and operations personnel begin to work together in a building. It is better for all parties if occupancy is delayed until the certificates of completion have been obtained and all items on the punch list corrected. If the contractor and the owner cannot avoid joint occupancy, the project manager should work with the owner to establish good procedures early and to communicate clearly about each other's expectations. The owner's right to take partial occupancy of an uncompleted project is described in Article 9.9 of the AIA General Conditions in Appendix E.

Demobilization

Although demobilizing, or physically moving off the site, sounds easy, it can involve considerable work and be expensive, especially to the general contractor. At that time, there may not be funds that can be dedicated to a foreman and a small crew to clean up the site. Similar to mobilization, most estimators do not put a line item in their original estimate for demobilization. The question always arises as to whose garbage is piled up; seldom do subcontractors claim the surplus cardboard or pallets. Similar to the discussion regarding joint occupancy, garbage accumulation can become mixed between the construction crews and the owner, as the owner is busy moving in.

Demobilization involves closing the project office and removing all contractor-owned materials and equipment from the project site. Utility companies are notified to disconnect temporary utilities, and vendors are informed that project accounts should be closed. The project staff is phased out and reassigned to other projects. The project files are collected and taken to the construction firm's records holding area.

2000 EDITION

AIA DOCUMENT G704-2000

Certificate of Substantial Completion

(Instructions on reverse side)

PROJECT: Huna Office Bldg
(Name and address) 9301 Glacier Hwy
Juneau, AK 99801

PROJECT NUMBER: 937
CONTRACT FOR: Office building
CONTRACT DATE: Aug. 15, 2000

TO OWNER: Huna Totem Corp.
(Name and address) 9309 Glacier Hwy
Juneau, AK 99801

TO CONTRACTOR: Northwest Construction
(Name and address) 1242 First Avenue
Cascade, WA 98202

OWNER ☒
ARCHITECT ☒
CONTRACTOR ☒
FIELD ☐
OTHER ☐

PROJECT OR PORTION OF THE PROJECT DESIGNATED FOR PARTIAL OCCUPANCY OR USE SHALL INCLUDE:

Sitework, shell, and tenant improvement work per contract documents

The Work performed under this Contract has been reviewed and found, to the Architect's best knowledge, information and belief, to be substantially complete. Substantial Completion is the stage in the progress of the Work when the Work or designated portion is sufficiently complete in accordance with the Contract Documents so that the Owner can occupy or utilize the Work for its intended use. The date of Substantial Completion of the Project or portion designated above is the date of issuance established by this Certificate, which is also the date of commencement of applicable warranties required by the Contract Documents, except as stated below:

Jensen Yorba Lott	Norm Riley	April 9, 2001
ARCHITECT	**BY**	**DATE OF ISSUANCE**

A list of items to be completed or corrected is attached hereto. The failure to include any items on such list does not alter the responsibility of the Contractor to complete all Work in accordance with the Contract Documents. Unless otherwise agreed to in writing, the date of commencement of warranties for items on the attached list will be the date of issuance of the final Certificate of Payment or the date of final payment. List shown below*

Cost estimate of Work that is incomplete or defective: $12,750.00

The Contractor will complete or correct the Work on the list of items attached hereto within Sixty (60) days from the above date of Substantial Completion.

Northwest Construction	Ted Jones	April 9, 2001
CONTRACTOR	**BY**	**DATE**

The Owner accepts the Work or designated portion as substantially complete and will assume full possession at 8:00 a.m. *(time)* on April 9, 2001 *(date)*.

Huna Totem Corp.	Robert Smith	April 9, 2001
OWNER	**BY**	**DATE**

The responsibilities of the Owner and Contractor for security, maintenance, heat, utilities, damage to the Work and insurance shall be as follows:

(Note: Owner's and Contractor's legal and insurance counsel should determine and review insurance requirements and coverage.)

*Includes Phase II Sitework pending spring weather.

1

The American Institute of Architects
1735 New York Avenue, N.W.
Washington, D.C. 20006-5292

FIGURE 21–2 Certificate of Substantial Completion

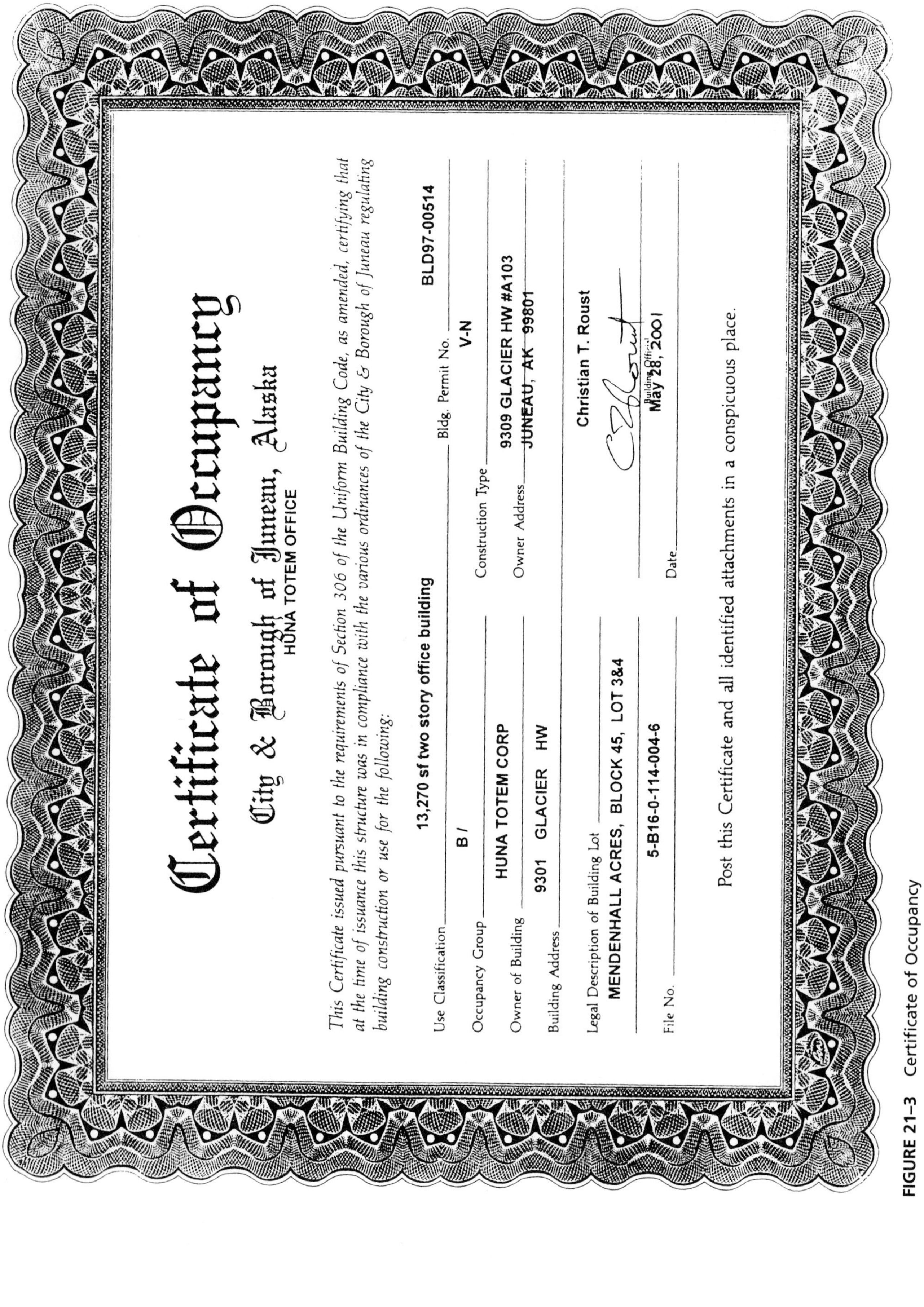

Certificate of Occupancy

City & Borough of Juneau, Alaska

HUNA TOTEM OFFICE

This Certificate issued pursuant to the requirements of Section 306 of the Uniform Building Code, as amended, certifying that at the time of issuance this structure was in compliance with the various ordinances of the City & Borough of Juneau regulating building construction or use for the following:

Use Classification: 13,270 sf two story office building — Bldg. Permit No.: BLD97-00514

Occupancy Group: B / — Construction Type: V-N

Owner of Building: HUNA TOTEM CORP — Owner Address: 9309 GLACIER HW #A103, JUNEAU, AK 99801

Building Address: 9301 GLACIER HW

Legal Description of Building Lot: MENDENHALL ACRES, BLOCK 45, LOT 3&4

Christian T. Roust

Building Official

File No.: 5-B16-0-114-004-6 — Date: May 28, 2001

Post this Certificate and all identified attachments in a conspicuous place.

FIGURE 21–3 Certificate of Occupancy

21.4 FINANCIAL CLOSE-OUT

The financial close-out of a project is not the accountant's or the officer-in-charge's responsibility, although they often become involved, nor is it the project engineer's duty. The project manager is responsible to financially close out the project with both the owner and the subcontractors. The items involved in financial termination of a project are discussed in this section.

Application for Final Payment

The request for final payment is submitted at ***final completion*** once all items on the punch list have been completed and all required documentation has been handed in. It asks for the release of all retention as well as any work completed since the preceding payment request was submitted. A final lien release and a waiver of claims generally are required to accompany the application for final payment.

Lien Releases

The general contractor will be required to provide a final and unconditional lien release to the owner, and most likely the owner will require similar releases from all subcontractors. Whether or not the owner requires them, the project manager should obtain final and unconditional lien releases from all subcontractors and suppliers before submitting the final lien release to the owner. Unconditional lien releases were discussed in Chapter 15 as a part of the request for payment process. The final lien release ends the contractor's right to place a lien on the project. It indicates that all financial accounts with the owner have been settled. All materialman's notices should be reviewed and each subcontractor and supplier required to obtain final and unconditional lien releases from all of their second- and third-tier subcontractors and suppliers, regardless of their contract values. If a company was concerned enough to reserve its lien rights, then it needs to release those rights in order to receive its retention. The contractor's release, without final releases from the subcontractors and suppliers, has little value. Even though the contractor has released its rights, the subcontractors can still place a lien on the job for alleged lack of payment. It is because of this that most experienced owners also will require the project manager to collect as many final releases from subcontractors and suppliers as possible and forward them to the owner.

Change Orders

All change order proposals and construction change directives must be negotiated and settled prior to closing out the contract. After the project manager receives the final change order from the owner, he or she should issue a final modification to each subcontractor and supplier. The word *final* is important. Even though a subcontractor may not have any cost issues in the last change order with the owner, the project manager should still issue a final modification to each subcontract and major purchase order for $0.00. This way they are officially notified that there will not be any other opportunities to collect on change orders. The final subcontract change order should be issued on a form similar to the one shown in Chapter 8 (Figure 8–9).

21.5 CONTRACT CLOSE-OUT

One of the first steps in contract close-out is to check the specifications for close-out requirements. Section 01700 of the specifications in Appendix F contain the close-out requirements for the Huna Office Building project. The project manager should

Completed Huna Office Building

make a list of what he or she thinks needs to be done and then ask the designer for verification, similar to an early submittal log. The major items the project manger will be required to prepare and submit as part of the contract close-out process are discussed in this section.

As-Built Drawings

As-built drawings are one of the most significant close-out deliverables. They were introduced in Chapter 11. Actual dimensions and conditions of the installed work are noted on the contract drawings. Field questions and sketches attached to the back of the preceding drawing, as discussed in Chapter 13, can be a big help. The project manager should collect all of the as-built drawings from the subcontractors. Mechanical, electrical, and civil disciplines are of the utmost importance because they include hidden systems that would cause severe damage if cut or may need to be accessed during a future remodel. Usually the general contractor will develop as-built drawings for the architectural, structural, and sometimes civil portions of the work. The as-built drawings should be submitted to the owner using the same procedures as were discussed in Chapter 14 for shop drawings. The best person to mark up the as-built drawings is the foreman or assistant superintendent who oversaw the work.

Operation and Maintenance Manuals

Operation and maintenance (O & M) manuals are the collection and organization of manufacturers' data regarding operating procedures and preventive maintenance and repair procedures for all of the operational equipment, as well as many of the finish items. This information should be collected from all the subcontractors and suppliers and organized in binders to be presented to the owner. Sometimes the contract specifications dictate the organization of these documents. Section 01700 of the specifications in Appendix F describes the required organization of the O & M manuals for the Huna Office Building project. The O & M manuals should be processed as a submittal using the procedures discussed in Chapter 14 to request designer approval. This is sometimes required and always a good idea. Some designers will request that draft copies be submitted for comment prior to submission of the final copy. This also should be well received by the construction team. The project manager cannot allow the project team simply to collect previous submittal data and place it into a three-ring binder. The information needed by the owner is not sales information, but operation and maintenance information.

Warranties

The project manager collects written, original, and signed warranties and guarantees from all of the subcontractors and suppliers, which can be inserted as a section in the O & M manuals. An example subcontractor warranty is shown in Chapter 22. The owner may also request an overall warranty document from the general contractor.

Test Reports

Throughout the course of the job, various materials, installations, and systems were tested. This includes balancing reports for the mechanical systems. All of these test reports also may be bound in the O & M manuals. Accurate record keeping and diligent filing throughout the course of the project will help with this.

Extra Materials

The specifications may require that extra quantities, say one to three percent, of some finish materials be supplied to the owner upon completion. This would include materials such as paint (amount of each color used), ceramic tile, carpet, and ceiling tile. This assists the owner with future repairs and remodels.

Permits

The project manager should require each subcontractor to provide an approved, signed permit from the authority having jurisdiction over the trade. This indicates that the subcontractor's work was performed in conformance with code requirements. The project manager also may be required by contract to submit to the designer all interim inspection reports or signature cards received from the city or county throughout the course of the job.

Close-Out Log

How does the project manager track completion of the O & M manual from the plumbing subcontractor, the warranty from the electrical subcontractor, the surplus rubber base material, the touch-up paint included on the painting subcontractor's punch list, and the lien release from the drywall subcontractor? It is done by use of a ***close-out log*** similar to the one shown in Figure 21–4. This log should be developed early in the project. The project manager should review the specification sections for each of the subcontractors and list all close-out items required. The log should be issued to the subcontractors and suppliers early and often to remind them of their

NORTHWEST CONSTRUCTION COMPANY

1242 First Avenue, Cascade, Washington 98202
(206) 239-1422

SUBCONTRACTOR AND SUPPLIER CLOSE-OUT LOG

Project No.: *9821* Project Name: *Huna Office Building* Project Manager: *Ted Jones*

Description	Site Work	Supply Doors	Utilities	Plumbing	HVAC	Electrical	Drywall	Tile	Flooring	Paint	Insulation	Supply Rebar
Complete punchlist	*10/1/00*	*NA*	*10/5/00*									*NA*
Sign final change order	*10/1/00*	*11/13/00*	*10/10/00*									*12/1/00*
Turn in permits	*NA*	*NA*					*NA*	*NA*	*NA*	*NA*	*NA*	*NA*
Extra materials	*NA*	*NA*	*NA*	*NA*	*NA*		*NA*				*NA*	*NA*
O&M manuals	*NA*						*NA*			*NA*	*NA*	*NA*
As-built drawings	*NA*											
Final lien release	*10/15/00*											
Second tier lien releases	*10/15/00*											
Test certificates	*NA*											
Union affidavits	*10/15/00*											
Back charges clear	*Yes*											
Demobilized	*Yes*											
Warranties	*NA*											
Retention released	*11/1/00*											

FIGURE 21–4 Close-Out Log

contractual responsibilities. A general letter can be sent out, repeatedly if necessary, listing all open issues. Many subcontractors are slow at closing out their portions of the project. The project manager must work closely with the subcontractors and suppliers to get the project closed out, as discussed in Chapter 15.

Some of the reasons the project manager should pursue a timely close-out include:

- To receive the final progress payment, which is different than retention. Although the last progress payment should not be tied to close-out, some owners may hold it as an incentive for timely close-out. Remember that cash is a useful tool. The project manager should help the owner by being proactive in the close-out process.
- To receive release of retention. The retention held may be approximately equal to the fee on the project. Therefore, the project manager cannot realize a profit on the project until retention has been collected. The request for release of retention is prepared and submitted using the same procedures as those discussed in Chapter 15 for monthly payment requests. Sometimes this is best resolved by keeping the final pay request, which bills up to 100% complete, separate from the release of retention request.
- To begin the clock on the warranty and guarantee.
- To close out the subcontracts and purchase orders as soon as possible. It is not recommended that the project manager hold their retention any longer than the owner holds the general contractor's retention. This is to ensure fair treatment of these key members of the construction team.
- To maintain good relations with the owner, designer, and subcontractors. The project manager will work with all of these people again on another project. It is important that everyone leave the project with a sense of teamwork and accomplishment.
- To minimize project overhead costs. Using the project manager and superintendent to oversee project close-out can be expensive, and some contractors rely on project engineers and foremen to manage close-out. This is not a good practice and may alienate owners.

21.6 PROJECT MANAGER'S CLOSE-OUT

There are a few additional close-out activities that are the responsibility of the project manager. These include:

- Preparation of an as-built estimate. If it is not maintained throughout construction or prepared near completion of the project, it never will be developed. Considerable work went into tracking actual costs. This is valuable input to the firm's ongoing ability to improve its estimating accuracy. Input of the as-built estimate into the firm's estimating database is necessary if the database is to be kept current.
- Analysis of the final forecast of project costs versus contract amount and the resultant fee. A narrative should be developed with a chart tracking the fee forecast throughout the project. This lessons-learned paper will help the project manager on subsequent similar projects, perhaps with the same owner or designer.
- Conducting a postproject meeting with the owner and designers. They should be asked to fill out a report card that serves as an evaluation of the construction firm's performance.

- Conducting a postproject meeting with all the field and office project personnel and the officer-in-charge. The meeting should include any staff personnel who may have some input, for example safety, accounting, estimating, and scheduling. Lessons learned should be applied on future projects.

21.7 SUMMARY

Project close-out is the process of completing all of the construction tasks and documentation required to close out the contract and consider the project complete. The project manager and the superintendent work closely together to ensure close-out procedures are comprehensive and efficient. Good close-out procedures typically result in higher contractor profits and satisfied owners. Issues relating to physical completion of the construction are the responsibility of the superintendent, while management of close-out documentation is the responsibility of the project manager.

When the project is nearing completion, the project manager asks the owner and architect to conduct a pre-final inspection. Any deficiencies noted during this inspection are placed on the punch list for future re-inspection, which must be corrected before the contract can be closed out. A significant project milestone is achieving substantial completion, which indicates that the project can be used for its intended purpose. The architect decides when the project is substantially complete and issues a certificate of substantial completion. Even though the project is substantially complete, the owner cannot move in until a certificate of occupancy is issued by the local permitting authority.

The project manager is responsible for the financial and contractual close-out of the project. This involves issuing final change orders to subcontractors and major suppliers and securing final and unconditional lien releases from them. As-built drawings, O & M manuals, warranties, and test reports must be submitted. The project manager should develop a close-out log early in the project to manage the timely submission of all close-out documents. The objective is to close out all project activities expeditiously so the contractor can receive the final payment and release of any retention. As a part of close-out activities, the project manager should conduct a postproject analysis to determine owner satisfaction and any lessons learned that can be applied on future projects.

21.8 REVIEW QUESTIONS

1. What is a punch list? When is it developed?
2. What action should the project manager take if he or she believes that some of the punch list items are outside the scope of the contract?
3. What does substantial completion mean in the context of a construction contract?
4. Why is substantial completion a significant contractual milestone?
5. Who issues the certificate of substantial completion?
6. What is a certificate of occupancy?
7. Who issues a certificate of occupancy?
8. What are final and unconditional lien releases?
9. Why do some owners require that project managers submit final and unconditional lien releases from subcontractors?

10. Where does the project manager obtain the information for the O & M manuals that are submitted to the designer for approval?
11. What items are tracked by the project manager on a close-out log?
12. What type of postproject analyses are performed as part of the project manager's close-out activities on a project?

21.9 EXERCISES

1. Prepare a close-out log for a project. Include at least ten subcontract and supplier categories.
2. Prepare a final and unconditional lien release for Richardson Electrical for the Huna Office Building project.
3. Prepare a request for release of retention on the Huna Office Building project.

21.10 SOURCES OF ADDITIONAL INFORMATION

Civitello, Andrew M., Jr. *Construction Operations Manual of Policies and Procedures.* 3d ed. New York: McGraw-Hill, Inc., 2000.

Fisk, Edward R. *Construction Project Administration.* 6th ed. Upper Saddle River, N.J.: Prentice-Hall, Inc., 2000.

Mincks, William R., and Hal Johnston. *Construction Jobsite Management.* Albany, N.Y.: Delmar Publishers, 1998.

22

Warranty Management

22.1 INTRODUCTION

Once the owner has accepted the completed project, he or she wants assurance that the project was completed in accordance with contract requirements. This assurance generally is provided in the form of a warranty. Article 3.5 of the AIA General Conditions in Appendix E discusses warranty. It states that the contractor warrants or guarantees that:

- All materials and equipment used on the project were new and met contract requirements, and
- All work is free from defects and meets contract requirements.

The warranty period required by most construction contracts is one year from substantial completion. Warranty would start earlier on any portions of the project occupied by the owner prior to substantial completion. Article 12.2.2 of the AIA General Conditions in Appendix E contains the one-year requirement. Longer warranties may be required in the technical specifications for selected components, such as the roof or electric motors. General contractors typically impose the same warranty requirements on their subcontractors and suppliers as are contained in the general contract with the owner.

As discussed in Chapter 21, the collection of subcontractor and supplier warranties is a part of project close-out activities. All warranties should be submitted by subcontractors and suppliers on their own letterhead, using text similar to the example shown in Figure 22–1. Warranty submission should be monitored and tracked in the close-out log as illustrated in Figure 21–4 in Chapter 21. Final payments to subcontractors and suppliers should not be made until warranty documents have been received. Supplier warranties may be inserted in the operation and maintenance materials provided to the owner. Subcontractor performance bonds should not be cancelled until the end of the warranty period to protect against subcontractor failure to respond to warranty claims.

Richardson Electric, Inc.
800 Pacific Highway
Juneau, Alaska 99802

WARRANTY FOR: Electrical Work

We hereby warrant and guarantee all electrical work which we have installed and/or furnished in the Huna Office Building project at Juneau, Alaska in compliance with the contract documents for one year from the date of substantial completion.

We agree to repair or replace to the satisfaction of the Architect all work that may prove defective in workmanship or materials within that period, ordinary wear and tear and unusual abuse or neglect excepted, together with all other work which may have been damaged or displaced in so doing.

All repairs or replacements shall have a warranty period equal to the original warranty period as herein stated, dated from the final acceptance or repairs or replacement.

In the event of our failure to comply with the above-mentioned conditions within a reasonable time after being notified in writing, we collectively and separately do hereby authorize the Owner to proceed to have defects repaired and made good at our expense, and will pay the costs and charges therefore immediately upon demand.

Date: April 11, 2001

Rick Richardson
Richardson Electric, Inc.

Ted Jones
Northwest Construction Company

FIGURE 22–1 Subcontractor Warranty

22.2 WARRANTY SERVICE REQUESTS

The project manager needs to organize a responsive warranty service that

- Satisfies the customer
- Ensures warranty costs are reasonable
- Minimizes conflicts
- Maximizes the potential for repeat business.

When a warranty claim is made, the project manager should review the project records and determine which subcontractors need to be notified. Appropriate subcontractors should immediately be notified orally and in writing that the owner has made a warranty claim. If the claim involves contractor-performed work, appropriate craftspeople should be sent to the site to inspect and make appropriate repairs. In emergency situations, the project manager may tell the owner to notify the appropriate subcontractor directly and then inform the project manager. The project manager needs to be aware of all warranty claims so he or she can ensure they have been resolved. Warranty procedures need to be explained by the project manager to both the owner and the subcontractors during the contract close-out so all parties understand the procedures to be used.

The project manager needs a system for tracking all warranty claims. A ***warranty service log*** similar to the one illustrated in Figure 22–2 can be used. Once the work on a warranty claim has been completed, the owner should be asked to sign a release indicating a satisfactory remedy. This tells the project manager that the warranty claim has been resolved.

22.3 WARRANTY RESPONSE AS CUSTOMER SERVICE

Warranty response is an important aspect of customer service. Just as customers expect quality work on their projects, they also expect timely response to warranty calls. Contractors who are poor at responding to warranty calls may not be invited to submit proposals on future projects. Subcontractors who are not responsive to warranty calls should not be used on future projects because their poor performance may affect the customer's opinion of the general contractor's warranty support. A reputation for good warranty support can be an important tool when marketing the construction firm's services. The best way to minimize warranty claims and associated costs is an active quality management program as discussed in Chapter 17. Using quality materials and skilled craftspeople who produce quality work should result in fewer warranty claims.

Project managers should contact owners just before the expiration of the warranty period and arrange for a joint inspection (owner and project manager) of the completed project. The purpose of the inspection is to identify any items that should be corrected under warranty. Owners tend to be impressed by the project manager's initiative and may be influenced to use the same construction firm on future projects.

22.4 SUMMARY

Most construction contracts contain a warranty provision that requires the contractor to repair any defective work or replace any defective equipment identified by the owner within one year after substantial completion. Similar provisions should be included in all subcontracts to cover work performed by subcontractors. Subcontractor warranty documentation is collected during project close-out. Warranty claims need to be investigated and resolved. Generally the owner submits any claims to the general contractor, who either notifies the appropriate subcontractors or sends an appropriate craftsperson to investigate. The contractor would send a craftsperson only when the claim involves work that was performed by the contractor's own workforce. The project manager should maintain a log to track all warranty claims and ensure their timely resolution. Warranty response is an important aspect of customer service. Poor support may jeopardize the contractor's ability to obtain future projects from the owner.

22.5 REVIEW QUESTIONS

1. What does the warranty provision in a construction contract cover?
2. When does the warranty period begin?
3. From whom should the project manager obtain written warranties?

NORTHWEST CONSTRUCTION COMPANY
1242 First Avenue, Cascade, Washington 98202
(206) 239-1422

WARRANTY SERVICE LOG

Project No.: *9821*   Project Name: *Huna Office Building*   Project Manager: *Ted Jones*

Item	Date Claim Received	Date Subcontractor Notified	Date Claim Resolved	Remarks
Fan in Room 205 inoperable	*July 10, 2001*	*July 19, 2001*	*July 22, 2001*	*Fan replaced*

FIGURE 22–2 Warranty Service Log

Completed Mechanical Room in Huna Office Building

4. Where in the contract would you find which components require warranties that are longer than the one year required in the general conditions?
5. What is a warranty claim?
6. Why is warranty response an important customer service?

22.6 EXERCISES

1. You were the project manager for the construction of a new high school. The school principal has made a warranty claim regarding the failure of a ventilating unit. You have notified the mechanical subcontractor, but the subcontractor has failed to take any action. What action should you take?
2. Draw a flow chart of the material procurement process starting at the selection of the supplier and ending with receipt of the product warranty.

22.7 SOURCES OF ADDITIONAL INFORMATION

Civitello, Andrew M., Jr. *Construction Operations Manual of Policies and Procedures*. 3d ed. New York: McGraw-Hill, Inc., 2000.

Hinze, Jimmie. *Construction Contracts*. New York: McGraw-Hill, Inc., 1993.

23

Advanced Topics in Project Management

23.1 INTRODUCTION

This chapter addresses several advanced project management topics. The first section describes human resource management responsibilities of the project manager. The design of the project management organization was discussed in Chapter 1, and here we will discuss staffing, performance measurement, and employee development. Preconstruction services are discussed in the second section of the chapter. These are services that the project manager may perform for the owner prior to the completion of the design and the start of construction. The third section discusses value engineering, which may be performed as a preconstruction service or during the construction of the project. The last section introduces some of the automated tools that may be used for project management. The use of automated project management tools will increase as additional capabilities are developed and fielded by software manufacturers.

23.2 HUMAN RESOURCE MANAGEMENT

Human resource management involves the design of the project management organization, recruitment and selection of new employees, management of subordinates' work performance, and professional development of subordinates. Organizational design involves identification of the basic project management organizational structure and determination of the specific responsibilities of each position. The result is an organization chart (see Chapter 1) and a ***job description*** and set of ***job specifications*** for each position. The job description defines the major tasks and duties to be performed by the person selected for the position. The job specifications identify the knowledge, abilities, and skills needed to be able to perform the tasks and duties contained in the job description. An example job description and set of job specifications for an administrative assistant are shown in Figure 23–1.

Both the job description and the job specifications are used when advertising for new applicants. The job description also is used by the project manager to establish an appropriate compensation rate for the position. Some construction firms have standard

Job Title: Administrative Assistant

Reports to: Project Manager

General Responsibilities: Provides clerical and reception services for project field office. Assists project personnel in the preparation and processing of written, verbal, and electronic communications. Responsible for the operation and maintenance of project office equipment.

Specific Responsibilities:

1. Provides reception services for the project office. Receives, records, and directs site visitors, telephone communications, electronic mail, internal distribution, parcel deliveries, and postal mail.
2. Assists the project manager in maintaining project files. Copies project documents as required by the project manager and company operating procedures.
3. Provides data processing support to the project office. Inputs data as required into computer database management, spreadsheet, and other applications programs.
4. Prepares final copies of letters, memorandums, typed standard forms, and other written communications using conventional typewriters and word processing programs.
5. Prepares timesheets for hourly employees.
6. Coordinates maintenance of field office and office equipment to maintain a presentable, efficient, and functional environment. Ensures that all critical office equipment are operational at all times. Responsible for maintaining an operational stock of consumable office supplies.

Required Knowledge, Skills, and Abilities:

1. Knowledge of construction terms and construction documents.
2. Knowledge of the operation and user-level maintenance of standard office equipment.
3. Knowledge of computer database management, word processing, and spreadsheet software applications.
4. Skilled in keyboard operations for fast and accurate typing and data input.
5. Able to communicate effectively in person and over the telephone. Able to maintain a focus on customer service and to represent the company at the project in a professional, courteous manner.
6. Able to organize, plan, and prioritize work efficiently. Must be able to work independently and productively with limited resources.

Experience Requirements: This position requires a minimum of 5 years experience in office administrative support functions, with a minimum of 2 years experience in construction field offices.

FIGURE 23–1 Job Description and Job Specifications for an Administrative Assistant

compensation schedules that list all types of positions, while others allow more flexibility to the project manager. Compensation decisions generally are based on the relative worth of the work to be performed and compensation levels for comparable positions in other construction firms. The objective is to make the position attractive to qualified individuals.

Once the job descriptions and job specifications have been developed, the project manager determines which positions are to be filled with current employees of the construction firm and which are to be filled with outside applicants. Recruiting applicants for positions to be externally filled may be through an employment agency, newspaper advertising, Internet advertising, or university or technical school recruiting. Most construction firms require each applicant to submit a standard application form, such as the example shown in Figure 23–2. In addition, resumes also may be required.

Once the applications have been received, the project manager must decide to whom to offer each position. Information used in making the decision generally is the information contained on the application form, any letters of recommendation provided, applicant's resume, contacts with listed references, and applicant interviews. Most project managers want to select qualified individuals who are self-motivated and will relate well with other team members. The written documentation typically is used to screen the candidates and select the most qualified individuals. The top-ranked candidates should be interviewed to assess their qualities and qualifications for the position and to provide them information regarding the position. Interviews must be planned carefully to ensure each candidate is evaluated using the same criteria. Once new employees are selected, they must be oriented regarding company policies and the specific jobs that they are to perform as members of the project management organization.

Performance management involves establishment of ***performance standards*** for each position and creation of a ***performance appraisal*** system. Performance standards typically are developed jointly by the employee and his or her supervisor. An example set of performance standards for an administrative assistant is shown in Figure 23–3 on page 284. A performance appraisal is a written evaluation of an employee's performance during a specific review period, typically one year. Forms similar to the one shown in Figure 23–4 on page 285 are used to document the evaluation. The appraisal is prepared by the employee's supervisor and describes how well the employee has performed during the review period. The appraisal should focus only on performance attributes that relate to organizational success. Appraisals often are used to determine compensation increases, annual bonuses, and employee training needs. The appraisal system works best when there is frequent feedback and mentoring provided by the supervisor to the employee throughout the review period, not just when the appraisal form is completed.

The last human resource management topic that we will discuss is employee development. There are two important aspects to employee development. The first is skill-enhancement training designed to improve employee performance in his or her current position. The second aspect is development training to provide the employee with the necessary skills to allow him or her to compete for higher level positions within the company. Both aspects are important. The first step in developing an employee development program is to assess the needs of each employee for skill-enhancement training and for professional development. Next specific training programs are either developed or identified. Employees are sent to specific training programs, and their performance is monitored to ascertain the effectiveness of the individual training programs. An individual development plan should be developed for each employee as a part of the appraisal process. This plan should be developed jointly by the employee and his or her supervisor. Training needs should be prioritized because most construction firms have limited training budgets.

Northwest Construction Company
Employment Application Form

ALL INFORMATION FURNISHED IN THIS APPLICATION MUST BE ACCURATE AND COMPLETE (IN INK). ANY FALSE STATEMENTS OR OMISSIONS OF ANY KIND ARE GROUNDS FOR DENYING EMPLOYMENT.

IDENTIFICATION

Name: Last ______________________ First ______________________ Middle __________

Social Security Number: ______________________

Date of Birth: Month __________ Day __________ Year __________

Home Address: ____

Street City State Zip

Home Telephone (Area Code and Number): ______________________

Work Telephone (Area Code and Number): ______________________

U.S. Citizen: Yes ______ No ______

If No, Type of Visa and Expiration Date: ______________________

Alien Registration Number: ______________________

EMPLOYMENT INFORMATION

Are you a former employee of Northwest Construction Company? Yes ______ No ______

Former Northwest Construction Company Employment: From __________ to __________

Month/Year Month/Year

Employment Desired: Full Time ______ Temporary ______ Summer ______

Date Available: ______________

Month/Year

Expected Salary/Wage: ______________

Will You Accept Overtime Work, if Offered? Yes ______ No ______

EDUCATION

Circle Highest Grade Completed: Elementary 1 2 3 4 5 6 Secondary 7 8 9 10 11 12 Advanced 13 14 15 16 17 18

Vocational Training/Special Courses of Study: ______________________

____

List Any Professional Certificates or Licenses You Have Obtained: ______________________

____

List All Post High School Education Below. Show Degrees Received or Expected and Date.

School Name City and State	Dates Attended Month/Year	Major Minor	Degree Date (Month/Year)
	From		
	To		
	From		
	To		
	From		
	To		

FIGURE 23–2 Employment Application Form

EMPLOYMENT HISTORY

BEGINNING NOW, ACCOUNT FOR EVERY MONTH OF EMPLOYMENT OR UNEMPLOYMENT WITHIN THE LAST 48 MONTHS (4 YEARS). A RESUME MAY BE ATTACHED, BUT THIS SECTION MUST BE COMPLETED.

Firm Name: ______
Address: ______ City: ______ State: ______
Position Title/Duties: ______

Date Employed: From ______ (Month/Year) to ______ (Month/Year)
Reason for Leaving: ______

Firm Name: ______
Address: ______ City: ______ State: ______
Position Title/Duties: ______

Date Employed: From ______ (Month/Year) to ______ (Month/Year)
Reason for Leaving: ______

Firm Name: ______
Address: ______ City: ______ State: ______
Position Title/Duties: ______

Date Employed: From ______ (Month/Year) to ______ (Month/Year)
Reason for Leaving: ______

REFERENCES

PLEASE PROVIDE 3 REFERENCES WHO ARE KNOWLEDGEABLE OF YOUR QUALIFICATIONS.

Name: ______ Years Known: ______
Occupation: ______ Employed By: ______
Address: ______ City: ______ State: ______
Telephone Number (Area Code and Number): ______

Name: ______ Years Known: ______
Occupation: ______ Employed By: ______
Address: ______ City: ______ State: ______
Telephone Number (Area Code and Number): ______

Name: ______ Years Known: ______
Occupation: ______ Employed By: ______
Address: ______ City: ______ State: ______
Telephone Number (Area Code and Number): ______

SIGNATURE

THIS APPLICATION IS COMPLETE AND ACCURATE TO THE BEST OF MY KNOWLEDGE.

Signature: ______ Date: ______

FIGURE 23–2 Employment Application Form *(Continued)*

Performance Standards for Administrative Assistant
Huna Office Building Project Office

Name of Employee: Janet Smith

Supervisor: Ted Jones

Performance Standards:

1. Receive visitors, record their presence, and direct to appropriate office with no more than one error per month.
2. Receive telephone communications, electronic mail, and written documents and direct to appropriate individual with no more than 2 errors per month.
3. Maintain project files and misfile no more than 2 documents per month.
4. Prepare final copies of written communication with no more than one error per week.
5. Maintain time sheets for hourly employees without error and submit on time to payroll office.
6. Ensure reception area in project office is well organized and presents a professional image to visitors.
7. Keep office reproduction and facsimile machines operational by contacting appropriate vendor to perform any needed repairs.
8. Maintain a 30-day supply of consumable office supplies.

Employee Signature: Janet Smith Date: Aug. 23, 2000

Supervisor Signature: Ted Jones Date: Aug. 23, 2000

FIGURE 23–3 Performance Standards for Administrative Assistant

23.3 PRECONSTRUCTION SERVICES

The project owner may choose to select the construction contractor during the development of the project design and ask the contractor to perform preconstruction services. Such services may include:

- Consultation
- Preliminary cost estimating
- Preliminary project scheduling
- Constructability analysis
- Value engineering
- Site logistics planning

Northwest Construction Company
Annual Performance Appraisal

Name of Employee: ______________________

Name of Supervisor: ______________________

Evaluation Period: From ____________ to ____________

For each applicable performance area, mark the box that most closely reflects the employee's performance using the following scale: 1 = unacceptable; 2 = needs improvement; 3 = satisfactory; 4 = above average; and 5 = outstanding

Performance Area	1	2	3	4	5
Ability to make job-related decisions					
Accepts responsibility					
Attendance					
Attitude					
Cooperation					
Dependability					
Effective under stress					
Initiative					
Leadership					
Operation and care of equipment					
Quality of work					
Safety practices					
Technical abilities					

Job Strengths: ______________________

Areas for Improvement: ______________________

Training Needed: ______________________

Supervisor Comments: ______________________

Employee Comments: ______________________

Employee Signature: ______________________ Date: ____________

Supervisor Signature: ______________________ Date: ____________

FIGURE 23–4 Performance Appraisal Form

Consultation involves attending design coordination and review meetings and providing advice regarding the use of materials, systems, and equipment, as well as cost and schedule implications of design proposals. Preliminary cost estimates are developed using conceptual cost estimating techniques and refined as the design is completed to ensure that the estimated cost of the project is within the owner's budget. A preliminary schedule may be developed to assess the time impacts of design alternatives. Constructability analysis is reviewing the proposed design for its impact on the cost and ease of construction. Value engineering, which is described in more detail in the next section of this chapter, seeks to find the most economical building components from a ***life-cycle cost*** perspective. Site logistics planning involves analysis of construction site access and staging sequences.

Preconstruction services are more prevalent on privately-funded projects than they are on public projects. This is because private owners are not restricted to the public bidding procedures that many public owners are. Contractors may negotiate a lump-sum contract with an owner for preconstruction services or a time and materials contract, as illustrated in Figure 23–5. The owner must first define the set of preconstruction services desired and then negotiate a service contract with the construction contractor. Some owners use construction management firms to perform preconstruction services if the owners are not able to select construction contractors before the designs are completed. Some public agencies use this approach. Owners hire contractors or construction managers to minimize cost, schedule, and constructability issues during construction by performing preconstruction services and providing construction expertise during design development.

23.4 VALUE ENGINEERING

Value engineering is a systematic evaluation of a project design to obtain the most value for the cost of construction. It includes analyzing selected building components to find creative ways of performing the same function as the original components at a lower life-cycle cost without sacrificing reliability, performance, or maintainability. Value engineering studies may be performed by consultants during design development as a contractor-performed preconstruction service, or by the contractor during construction. The most effective time to conduct such studies is during design development. Some construction contracts contain a value-engineering incentive provision that allows the contractor to share in the savings that results from approved value engineering change proposals. Value-engineering change proposals submitted by the contractor are reviewed by the architect and owner for acceptability. If approved, up to 50% of the savings in construction cost may go to the contractor. The percentage split between the owner and the contractor will be stated in the value-engineering provision of the contract.

The value of a component or system can be defined as its function plus quality divided by its life-cycle cost. The formula to compute life-cycle cost is:

$$\text{initial or construction cost} + \text{operating cost} + \text{maintenance cost} \\ + \text{replacement cost} - \text{any salvage value}$$

Value-engineering studies are conducted to select the highest-value design components or systems. These studies generally are conducted using the following five-step process:

1. Information gathering
2. Speculation through creative thinking
3. Evaluation through preliminary life-cycle costing

4. Development of technical solutions
5. Presentation of alternative options

The information-gathering phase involves studying the design to identify potential components or systems for detailed study. The essential functions of each component or system are studied to estimate the potential for value improvement. The study team needs to understand the rationale used by the designer in developing the plan and the assumptions made in establishing design criteria and selecting materials and equipment.

PRECONSTRUCTION SERVICES AGREEMENT

This agreement made this 27th day of September, 2000 between

the **Owner**:	Horizon Hotel Company 215 Fourth Avenue Seattle, Washington 98104
and the **Contractor**:	Northwest Construction Company 1242 First Avenue Cascade, Washington 98202

for the following project: Horizon Pacific Hotel

The **Owner** and the **Contractor** agree as follows:

1. That during the development of the design and prior to the start of construction, the **Contractor** will provide preconstruction services as follows:

- Attend weekly coordination meetings.
- Prepare budget estimates at the completion of conceptual documents, design development documents, during construction document development, and as otherwise required.
- Develop cost analyses of design options.
- Conduct value engineering studies as necessary to achieve budget goals.
- Develop and maintain preconstruction/construction schedule.
- Develop site logistics plan.
- Meet with consultants and/or subcontractors and suppliers, as necessary, to assist in the development of the design.
- Conduct constructability review at completion of design development documents, 90% construction documents, and as otherwise required.

2. That preconstruction services will be billed at the following rates:

Project manager	$75 per hour
Project superintendent	$80 per hour
Estimator	$65 per hour
Project engineer	$50 per hour
Administrative/clerical	$35 per hour

3. That all cost of materials and equipment associated with providing preconstruction services shall be reimbursed at actual cost to the **Contractor**.

FIGURE 23–5 Preconstruction Services Agreement

4. That all costs incurred by the **Contractor** prior to construction will be billed on a monthly basis for payment, by the **Owner**, by the 10th of the following month.

5. That it is the **Owner's** intent to enter into an agreement with the **Contractor** for the construction of the project assuming that:

- The negotiated guaranteed maximum price meets the **Owner's** budget.
- The final construction schedule meets the **Owner's** occupancy requirements.
- Contractual terms and conditions can be negotiated to mutual agreement.

6. That the **Owner** has the right to terminate this agreement at any time prior to start of construction. In the event of termination, all charges incurred or committed to date of termination will be reimbursed.

7. That the above agreement is hereby acknowledged and shall serve as the preconstruction services agreement between the **Owner** and the **Contractor**.

Northwest Construction Company	**Horizon Hotel Company**
Sam Peters	Jeffrey Jackson
Sam Peters, Vice President	Jeffrey Jackson, Vice President

FIGURE 23–5 Preconstruction Services Agreement *(Continued)*

The purpose of the speculation or creative phase is to identify alternative ways to accomplish the essential functions of the items selected for study. The intent is to develop a list of alternative materials or components that might be used. No intent is made to evaluate the identified alternatives, but rather to generate ideas that will be evaluated in the next step of the study process.

The evaluation phase involves determining the most promising alternatives from the set identified in the speculation phase. Preliminary cost data is generated and functional comparisons are made between the potential design components being studied. The intent is to determine which alternatives will meet the owner's functional requirements and provide more value to the completed project.

The development phase involves creating design concepts for the alternatives identified during the evaluation phase. This involves developing detailed functional and economic data for each alternative. Estimated life-cycle cost data is developed for each alternative and compared with the estimated life-cycle cost of the components under study. The advantages and disadvantages of each alternative are identified. Alternatives are compared, and the ones representing the best value are selected for presentation to the designer and the owner.

The final step is the preparation of the value engineering proposals, in which detailed technical and cost data are developed to support the recommendations. The advantages and disadvantages of each recommendation are described. The proposals are submitted to the designer and the owner for approval. If approved, the proposals are incorporated into the design. If not approved, the design is not changed.

Construction project managers involved in value engineering studies, whether as a preconstruction service or during construction, typically use a log similar to the one shown in Figure 23–6 to keep track of their proposals. Value-engineering proposals approved during construction must be incorporated into the contract by change orders. A simple approval does not provide the project manager the authority to deviate from the requirements of the contract plans and specifications.

NORTHWEST CONSTRUCTION COMPANY
1242 First Avenue, Cascade, Washington 98202
(206) 239-1422

VALUE ENGINEERING PROPOSAL LOG

Project No.: *9821* Project Name: *Huna Office Building* Project Manager: *Ted Jones*

Item	Description	Location	Sheet/ Spec No.	Redesign Impact	Schedule Impact	Confirmed Cost	Proposed Budget Revision	Owner Action		Remarks
				Y/N?	Y/N?	Y/N?		Accept	Reject	
1	*Substitute vinyl tile for carpet*	*Room 204, 2nd Floor*	*A200*	*N*	*N*	*Y*	*($5,000)*	*X*		
2	*Eliminate sliding doors in casework*	*Room 234, 2nd Floor*	*A501*	*N*	*N*	*Y*	*($6,400)*		*X*	

FIGURE 23–6 Value Engineering Proposal Log

23.5 AUTOMATED PROJECT MANAGEMENT

Many of the project management documents discussed in this text can be generated using word-processing or spreadsheet software. Standardized templates can be created that can be used on all projects managed by the construction firm. Some contractors have developed database systems to track submittals, field questions, drawings, and purchase orders. Many construction firms are using electronic mail for coordination with subcontractors, suppliers, architects, and owners.

Several manufacturers have developed computer-based project management software to automate many of the project management functions. Two commonly used software programs are Primavera's Expedition and Meridian's Prolog Manager. These programs generally have the following capabilities:

- Contract management
  - Track change order proposals, construction change directives, and change orders
  - Create bid packages for subcontractors
  - Prepare subcontracts
  - Analyze subcontractor bids
  - Generate subcontractor change orders
  - Track subcontractor insurance certificates
- Material management
  - Generate and track purchase orders
  - Track scheduled and actual deliveries
- Cost control
  - Track buyout
  - Track costs and compare with budgeted values
  - Manage material invoices
  - Prepare monthly payment requests
- Communication management
  - Generate transmittals and transmit copies to appropriate team members
  - Produce and distribute meeting notices and meeting minutes
  - Track open issues
  - Post reports on Internet for access by authorized individuals
- Project engineering
  - Generate submittal coversheets and track submittals
  - Submission of field questions and track them
  - Maintain drawing log
  - Generate punch lists and track deficiency correction
  - Track close-out activities
- Superintendent issues
  - Distribute daily report
  - Track labor and equipment usage
  - Track safety notices
  - Track quality control notices
  - Track quality control testing

When establishing a project in either of these programs, the project manager determines who should have access to the input screens and reports and the type of access. Users may be granted read only access or read-and-write access. Only those with write access can enter or change data. Documents can be transmitted to other people either by electronic mail or by facsimile. These project management programs can be linked to scheduling software, such as Primavera Project Planner or SureTrak, to share common data.

The newest trend is to develop project web sites for managing construction projects. Some of the web-based project management software systems available include Buzzsaw, Hard Dollar, Vista 2000, Constructware, and e-Builder. The project web site becomes the portal to all project information, both document based (such as spreadsheets, drawings, and photographs) and system based (such as software applications and propriety databases). Information is stored in project-specific databases on the web instead of on a computer or a network server. Stored information may include contract drawings, specifications, progress photographs, and project management documentation. Security systems can be used to limit access to project participants.

Correspondence can be generated and sent to its recipient with a copy left on the web site for review by others. Field questions can be posted to the web with attached drawings, and an email is automatically sent to the reviewer indicating the new posting. Management logs can be maintained on the web to indicate the status of field questions, submittals, drawings, purchase orders, material deliveries, change order proposals, change orders, and close-out activities. Meetings can be announced, conducted, and minutes posted on the web. Punch lists can be developed on the web and updated as deficiencies are corrected. These may be individual subcontractor punch lists or overall project punch lists. Each document placed on the web may be assigned an owner, permitting only the owner to make changes to the document.

Project web sites enable owners, architects, design consultants, general contractors, and subcontractors to communicate, interact, and share information in real time. Use of these web sites requires trust among project participants because all project-related information is available to all team members. The result of using project web sites is enhanced communication and collaboration among all members of the project delivery team.

23.6 SUMMARY

Human resources management involves the design of the project management organization, recruitment and selection of new employees, management of subordinates' work performance, and professional development of subordinates. Once the organizational structure has been developed for the project office, a job description and job specifications are prepared for each position. These are used in recruiting new employees and developing performance standards. Performance appraisals are used to evaluate and document subordinate performance and identify any training needed.

Preconstruction services are services the project manager may perform for the owner before the start of construction. These may include consultation, preliminary cost estimating, preliminary project scheduling, constructability analysis, value engineering, and site logistics planning. Preconstruction services are more commonly performed on privately-funded projects than they are on publicly-funded projects. Owners hire contractors to perform preconstruction services to minimize cost, schedule, and constructability issues during construction.

Value engineering is a systematic evaluation of a project design to obtain the most value for the cost of construction. It may be performed by the contractor as a preconstruction service or during construction. Value-engineering studies generally are conducted using a five-step process. The first step is to identify design components or systems for study. Next, potential alternative components or systems are identified. The alternatives are then evaluated to determine whether or not they represent greater value than the components or systems selected by the designer. The next step is to develop design concepts for those alternative components or systems that represent the best value to the owner. The final step is to prepare the value engineering proposals and supporting documentation.

Many of the project management documents described in this text can be generated using word-processing or spreadsheet software. Some contractors use computer- or web-based software systems to manage their projects. These systems enhance collaboration among project participants and reduce the time required to manage project documentation.

23.7 REVIEW QUESTIONS

1. What is a job description, and what is it used for?
2. What are job specifications, and what are they used for?
3. What type of written documentation would you use when selecting applicants for interviews?
4. What are performance standards, and what are they used for?
5. Who prepares the performance appraisal, and what is it used for?
6. How would you prepare an individual development plan for a subordinate employee?
7. What are preconstruction services, and why might an owner decide to pay a contractor to perform them?
8. What are four types of preconstruction services?
9. What is the difference between constructability analysis and value engineering?
10. What is meant by the term life-cycle cost when conducting value engineering studies?
11. How are value engineering proposals that are submitted by a contractor during construction and approved by the owner and architect incorporated into the contract?
12. What advantages do web-based project management systems offer over computer-based project management systems?

23.8 EXERCISES

1. Prepare a job description for a field engineer.
2. Prepare a performance standard for a field engineer.

23.9 SOURCES OF ADDITIONAL INFORMATION

Bernardin, H. John, and Joyce E. A. Russell. *Human Resource Management: An Experiential Approach*. New York: McGraw-Hill, Inc., 1993.

Dell'Isola, Alphonse. *Value Engineering: Practical Applications*. Kingston, Mass.: R. S. Means Company, Inc., 1997.

Gomez-Mejia, Luis R., David B. Balkin, and Robert L. Cardy. *Managing Human Resources*. Englewood Cliffs, N.J.: Prentice-Hall, Inc., 1995.

APPENDIX A

List of Abbreviations

AAA	American Arbitration Association
AGC	Associated General Contractors of America
AIA	American Institute of Architects
ASTM	American Society for Testing and Materials
ATB	asphalt tile base
CAD	computer-aided design
BF	backfill
CCD	construction change directive
CEO	chief executive officer
CO	change order
COP	change order proposal
CSF	100 square feet
CSI	Construction Specifications Institute
CY	cubic yard
DBIA	Design Build Institute of America
EA	each
EJCDC	Engineers Joint Council Document Committee
EMR	experience-modification rating
EMT	electrical metallic conduit, thin wall
FICA	Federal Insurance Contributors Act (Social Security)
FOB	free on board
FQ	field question
GC	general conditions
GMP	guaranteed maximum price
HVAC	heating, ventilating, and air conditioning
ISO	International Organization for Standardization
JYL	Jensen Yorba Lott, Incorporated
LF	linear feet

LS	lump sum
MSDS	material safety data sheets
NA	not applicable
NAHB	National Association of Home Builders
NIC	not-in-contract
NWCC	Northwest Construction Company
O & M	operation and maintenance
OSHA	Occupational Safety and Health Administration
PVC	polyvinyl chloride
PSI	pounds per square inch
QTO	quantity take-off
QTY	quantity
RFI	request for information
RFP	request for proposal
ROM	rough order-of-magnitude
SF	square feet
SFCA	square feet of contact area
SK	sketch
SOG	slab on grade
TCY	truck or loose cubic yards
TQM	total quality management
UMH	unit man-hours
UP	unit price
WBS	work breakdown structure

APPENDIX B

Glossary

Active quality management program – process that anticipates and prevents quality control problems rather than just responding to and correcting deficiencies.

Activity duration – the estimated length of time required to complete an activity.

Addenda – additions to or changes in bid documents issued prior to bid and contract award.

Additive alternates – alternates which add to the base bid if selected by the owner.

Agency construction management delivery method – a delivery method in which the owner has three contracts: one with the architect, one with the general contractor, and one with the construction manager. The construction manager acts as the owner's agent but has no contractual authority over the architect or the general contractor.

Agreement – a document that sets forth the provisions, responsibilities, and obligations of parties to a contract. Standard forms of agreement are available from professional organizations.

Allowance – an amount stated in the contract for inclusion in the contract sum to cover the cost of prescribed items, the full description of which is not known at the time of bidding. The actual cost of such items is determined by the contractor at the time of selection by the architect or owner, and the total contract amount is adjusted accordingly.

Alternates – selected items of work for which bidders are required to provide prices.

Alternative dispute resolution – a method of resolving disagreements other than by litigation.

Amendments – see *addenda*.

American Institute of Architects (AIA) – a national association that promotes the practice of architecture and publishes many standard contract forms used in the construction industry.

Application for payment – see *payment request.*

Arbitration – method of dispute resolution in which an arbitrator or a panel of arbitrators evaluates the arguments of the respective parties and renders a decision.

Arrow-diagramming method – scheduling technique that uses arrows to depict activities and nodes to depict events or dates.

As-built drawings – contractor-corrected construction drawings depicting actual dimensions, elevations, and conditions of in-place constructed work.

As-built estimate – assessment in which actual costs incurred are applied to the quantities installed to develop unit prices and productivity rates.

As-built schedule – marked-up, detailed schedule depicting actual start and completion dates, durations, deliveries, and restraint activities.

Associated General Contractors of America (AGC) – a national trade association primarily made up of construction firms and construction industry professionals. It publishes many standard contract forms used in the construction industry.

Automobile insurance – protects the contractor against claims from another party for bodily injury or property damage caused by contractor-owned, -leased, or -rented automobiles and equipment operated over the highway.

Back charge – general contractor charge against a subcontractor for work the general contractor performed on behalf of the subcontractor.

Bar chart schedule – time-dependent schedule system without nodes that may or may not include restraint lines.

Bid bond – a surety instrument that guarantees that the contractor, if awarded the contract, will enter into a binding contract for the price bid and provide all required bonds. A commonly used form is AIA document A310.

Bid security – money placed in escrow, a cashier's check, or bid bond offered as assurance to an owner that the bid is valid and that the bidder will enter into a contract for that price.

Bid shopping – unethical general contractor activity of sharing subcontractor bid values with the subcontractor's competitors in order to drive down prices.

Blanket purchase order – see *open purchase order.*

Bridging delivery method – a hybrid of the traditional and the design-build delivery methods. The owner contracts with a design firm for the preparation of partial design documents, then selects a design-build firm to complete the design and construct the project.

Builder's risk insurance – protects the contractor in the event that the project is damaged or destroyed while under construction.

Build-operate-transfer delivery method – a delivery method in which a single contractor is responsible for financing the design and construction of a project and is paid an annual fee to operate the completed project for a period of time, such as thirty years.

Buyout – the process of awarding subcontracts and issuing purchase orders for materials and equipment.

Buyout log – a project management document that is used for planning and tracking the buyout process.

Cash flow curve – a plot of the estimated value of work to be completed each month during the construction of a project.

Cash-loaded schedule – a schedule in which the value of each activity is distributed across the activity, and monthly costs are summed to produce a cash flow curve.

Certificate of insurance – a document issued by an authorized representative of an insurance company stating the types, amounts, and effective dates of insurance for a designated insured.

Certificate of occupancy – a certificate issued by the city or municipality indicating that the completed project has been inspected and meets all code requirements.

Certificate of substantial completion – a certificate signed by the owner, architect, and contractor indicating the date that substantial completion was achieved.

Change order (CO) – modification to contract documents made after contract award that incorporate changes in scope and adjustments in contract price and time. A commonly used form is AIA document G701.

Change order proposal (COP) – a request for a change order submitted to the owner by the contractor, or a proposed change sent to the contractor by the owner requesting pricing data.

Change order proposal log – a log listing all change order proposals indicating dates of initiation, approval, and incorporation as final change orders.

Claim – an unresolved request for a change order.

Close-out – the process of completing all construction and paperwork required to finish the project and complete the contract.

Close-out log – a list of all close-out tasks that is used to manage project completion.

Commissioning – a process of assuring that all equipment is working properly and that operators are trained in equipment use.

Conceptual cost estimate – cost estimates developed using incomplete project documentation.

Conditional lien release – a lien release that indicates that the issuer gives up his or her lien rights on the condition that the money requested is paid.

Constructability analysis – an evaluation of preferred and alternative materials and construction methods.

Construction change directive (CCD) – a directive issued by the owner to the contractor to proceed with the described change.

Construction-manager-at-risk delivery method – a delivery method in which the owner has two contracts: one with the architect and one with the construction manager/general contractor. The general contractor usually is hired early in the design process to perform preconstruction services. Once the design is completed, the construction manager/general contractor constructs the project.

Construction manager/general contractor delivery method – see *construction-manager-at-risk delivery method.*

Construction Specifications Institute (CSI) – the professional organization that developed the sixteen-division MasterFormat that is used to organize the technical specifications.

Contract – a legally enforceable agreement between two parties.

Contract time – the period of time allotted in the contract documents for the contractor to achieve substantial completion.

Corrected estimate – estimate that is adjusted based on buyout costs.

Cost codes – codes established in the firm's accounting system that are used for recording specific types of costs.

Cost estimating – process of preparing the best educated anticipated cost of a project given the parameters available.

Cost-plus-award-fee contract – a kind of cost-plus contract in which the contractor's fee has two components; a fixed component and an award component based on the contractor's performance. The award component is decided at periodic intervals, for example quarterly, based on an owner-established set of criteria. Criteria might include cost control, quality of construction, safety performance, and meeting an agreed schedule.

Cost-plus contract – a contract in which the contractor is reimbursed for stipulated direct and indirect costs associated with the construction of a project and is paid a fee to cover profit and company overhead.

Cost-plus contract with guaranteed maximum price – also known as a *guaranteed maximum price contract.* A cost-plus contract in which the contractor agrees to bear any construction costs that exceed the guaranteed maximum price unless the project scope of work is increased.

Cost-plus-fixed-fee contract – a cost-plus contract in which the contractor is guaranteed a fixed fee irrespective of the actual construction costs.

Cost-plus-incentive-fee contract – a cost-plus contract in which the contractor's fee is based on measurable incentives, such as actual construction cost or construction time. Higher fees are paid for lower construction costs and shorter project durations.

Cost-plus-percentage-fee contract – a cost-plus contract in which the contractor's fee is a percentage of the actual construction costs.

Cost-reimbursable contract – a contract in which the contractor is reimbursed stipulated direct and indirect costs associated with the construction of a project. The contractor may or may not receive an additional fee to cover profit and company overhead.

Craftspeople – non-managerial field labor force who construct the work, such as carpenters and electricians.

Critical path – the sequence of activities on a network schedule that determine the overall project duration.

Daily job diary – also know as *daily journal* or *daily report.* A daily report prepared by the superintendent that documents important daily events including weather, visitors, work activities, deliveries, and any problems.

Davis-Bacon wage rates – prevailing wage rates determined by the U.S. Department of Labor that must be met or exceeded by contractors and subcontractors on federally-funded construction projects.

Deductive alternates – alternates which subtract from the base bid if selected by the owner.

Design-build delivery method – a delivery method in which the owner hires a single contractor who designs and constructs the project.

Design-build-operate delivery method – a delivery method in which the contractor designs the project, constructs it, and operates it for a period of time, for example twenty years.

Detailed cost estimate – extensive estimate based on definitive design documents. Includes separate labor, material, equipment, and subcontractor quantities. Unit prices are applied to material quantity take-offs for every item of work.

Direct construction costs – labor, material, equipment, and subcontractor costs for the contractor, exclusive of any mark-ups.

Dispute – a contract claim between the owner and the general contractor that has not been resolved.

Dispute review board – a panel of experts selected for a project to make recommendations regarding resolution of disputes.

Earned value – a technique for determining the estimated or budgeted value of the work completed to date and comparing it with the actual cost of the work completed. Used to determine the cost and schedule status of an activity or the entire project.

Eighty–twenty rule – on most projects, about 80% of the costs are included in 20% of the work items.

Electronic mail – Internet tool for sending communications and attached documents.

Equipment floater insurance – protects the contractor against financial loss due to physical damage to equipment from named perils or all risks and theft.

Errors and omissions insurance – also known as *professional liability insurance*. Protects design professionals from financial loss resulting from claims for damages sustained by others as a result of negligence, errors, or omissions in the performance of professional services.

Estimate schedule – management document used to plan and forecast the activities and durations associated with preparing the cost estimate. Not a construction schedule.

Exhibits – important documents that are attached to a contract, such as a summary cost estimate, schedule, and document list.

Expediting – process of monitoring and actively ensuring vendor's compliance with the purchase order requirements.

Expediting log – a spreadsheet used to track material delivery requirements and commitments.

Experience-modification rating (EMR) – a factor, unique to a construction firm, that reflects a company's past claims history. This factor is used to increase or decrease the company's workers' compensation insurance premium rates.

Fast-track construction – also known as *phased construction*. Overlapping design and construction activities so that some are performed in parallel rather than in series. Allows construction to begin while the design is being completed.

Fee – contractor's income after direct project and job site general conditions are subtracted. Generally includes home office overhead costs and profit.

Field question (FQ) – document used to clarify discrepancies between differing contract documents and between assumed and actual field conditions.

Field question log – spreadsheet for tracking field questions from initiation through designer response.

Filing system – organized system for storage and retrieval of project documents.

Final completion – the stage of construction when all work required by the contract has been completed.

Final inspection – final review of project by owner and architect to determine whether final completion has been achieved.

Final lien release – a lien release issued by the contractor to the owner or by a subcontractor to the general contractor at the completion of a project indicating that all payments have been made and that no liens will be placed on the completed project.

Float – the flexibility available to schedule activities not on the critical path without delaying the overall completion of the project.

Foreman – direct supervisor of craft labor on a project.

Free on board (FOB) – an item whose quoted price includes delivery at the point specified. Any additional shipping costs are to be paid by the purchaser of the item.

Front loading – a tactic used by a contractor to place an artificially high value on early activities in the schedule of values to improve cash flows.

General conditions (GC) – a part of the construction contract that contains a set of operating procedures that the owner typically uses on all projects. They describe the relationship between the owner and the contractor, the authority of the owner's representatives or agents, and the terms of the contract. The general conditions contained in AIA document A201 is used by many owners.

General contractor – the party to a construction contract who agrees to construct the project in accordance with the contract documents.

General liability insurance – protects the contractor against claims from a third party for bodily injury or property damage.

Geotechnical report – also known as a *soils report.* A report prepared by a geotechnical engineering firm that includes the results of soil borings or test pits and recommends systems and procedures for foundations, roads, and excavation work.

Guaranteed maximum price (GMP) contract – a type of cost–plus contract in which the contractor agrees to construct the project at or below a specified cost.

Indirect construction costs – expenses indirectly incurred and not directly related to a specific project or construction activity, such as home office overhead.

Initial inspection – a quality-control inspection to ensure that workmanship and dimensional requirements are satisfactory.

Invitation to bid – a portion of the bidding documents soliciting bids for a project.

ISO 9000 international standards – quality management and quality assurance standards published by the International Organization for Standardization (ISO).

Job description – a description of the major tasks and duties to be performed by the person occupying a certain position.

Job hazard analysis – the process of identifying all hazards associated with a construction operation and selecting measures for eliminating, reducing, or responding to the hazards.

Job site general conditions costs – field indirect costs which cannot be tied to an item of work, but which are project specific, and in the case of cost reimbursable contracts are considered part of the cost of the work.

Job specifications – the knowledge, abilities, and skills a person must possess to be able to perform the tasks and duties required.

Joint check agreement – a check issued jointly to a subcontractor and its supplier or third-tier subcontractor paying for materials provided by the supplier or work performed by the third-tier subcontractor.

Joint venture – a contractual collaboration of two or more parties to undertake a project.

Just-in-time delivery of materials – a material management philosophy in which supplies are delivered to the job site just in time to support construction activities. This minimizes the amount of space needed for on-site storage of materials.

Labor and material payment bond – a surety instrument that guarantees that the contractor (or subcontractor) will make payments to his or her craftspeople, subcontractors, and suppliers. A commonly used form is AIA document A312.

Letter of intent – a letter, in lieu of a contract, notifying the contractor that the owner intends to enter into a contract pending resolution of some restraining factors, such as permits or financing.

Lien – a legal encumbrance against real or financial property for work, material, or services rendered to add value to that property.

Lien release – a document signed by a subcontractor or the general contractor releasing its rights to place a lien on the project.

Life-cycle cost – the sum of all acquisition, operation, maintenance, use, and disposal costs for a product over its useful life.

Liquidated damages – an amount specified in the contract that is owed by the contractor to the owner as compensation for damaged incurred as a result of the contractor's failure to complete the project by the date specified in the contract.

Litigation – a court process for resolving disputes.

Long-form purchase order – a contract for the acquisition of materials that is used by the project manager or the construction firm's purchasing department to procure major materials for a project.

Lump-sum contract – also known as *fixed-price contract* or *stipulated-sum contract.* A contract that provides a specific price for a defined scope of work.

Mark-up – percentage added to the direct cost of the work to cover such items as overhead, fee, taxes, and insurance.

MasterFormat – a sixteen-division numerical system of organization developed by the Construction Specifications Institute that is used to organize contract specifications and cost estimates.

Materialman's notice – a notice sent to the owner as notice that the supplier will be delivering materials to the project.

Material safety data sheets (MSDS) – short technical reports that identify all known hazards associated with particular materials and provide procedures for using, handling, and storing the materials safely.

Material supplier – vendor who provides materials but no on-site craft labor.

Mediation – a method of resolving disputes in which a neutral mediator is used to facilitate negotiations between the parties to the dispute.

Meeting agenda – a sequential listing of topics to be addressed in a meeting.

Meeting notes – a written record of meeting attendees, topics addressed, decisions made, open issues, and responsibilities for open issues.

Meeting notice – a written announcement of a meeting. It generally contains the date, time, and location of the meeting, as well as the topics to be addressed.

Minitrial – a method of resolving disputes that blends together some components of mediation, negotiation, and adversarial case presentation.

Mock-ups – stand-alone samples of completed work, such as a 6-foot-by-6-foot sample of a brick wall.

Network diagrams – schedule that shows the relationships among the project activities with a series of nodes and connecting lines.

Notice to proceed – written communication issued by the owner to the contractor, authorizing the contractor to proceed with the project and establishing the date for project commencement.

Occupational Safety and Health Administration (OSHA) – federal agency responsible for establishing job site safety standards and enforcing them through inspection of construction work sites.

Officer-in-charge – general contractor's principal individual who supervises the project manager and is responsible for overall contract compliance.

Open purchase order – a purchase order that specifies unit prices for specific materials, but does not specify an exact quantity for each material. It may cover a specific period of time and contain a maximum total price. Delivery orders are made when the materials are needed, and invoices are provided with each delivery at the unit prices contained in the open purchase order.

Operation and maintenance (O & M) manuals – a collection of descriptive data needed by the owner to operate and maintain equipment installed on a project.

Overbilling – requesting payment for work that has not been completed.

Overhead – expenses incurred that do not directly relate to a specific project, for example, rent on the contractor's home office.

Overhead burden – a percentage mark-up that is applied to the total estimated direct cost of a project to cover overhead or indirect costs.

Partnering – a cooperative approach to project management that recognizes the importance of all members of the project team, establishes harmonious working relationships among team members, and resolves issues in a timely manner.

Partnering charter – documents the results of the partnering workshop. It contains the project team's mission, identifies their collective goals, and is signed by workshop participants.

Performance appraisal – a written evaluation of an individual's work performance during a specific review period.

Performance bond – a surety instrument that guarantees that the contractor will complete the project in accordance with the contract. It protects the owner from the general contractor's default and the general contractor from the subcontractor's default. A commonly used form is AIA document A312.

Performance standards – standards a person is expected to achieve in the performance of his or her job.

Plugs – general contractor's cost estimates for subcontracted scopes of work.

Postproject analysis – reviewing all aspects of the completed project to determine lessons that can be applied to future projects.

Pre-bid conference – meeting of bidding contractors with the project owner and architect. The purpose of the meeting is to explain the project and bid process and solicit questions regarding the design or contract requirements.

Precedence-diagramming method – scheduling technique that uses nodes to depict activities and arrows to depict relationships among the activities. Used by most scheduling software.

Preconstruction agreement – a short contract that describes the contractor's responsibilities and compensation for preconstruction services.

Preconstruction conference – meeting conducted by owner or designer to introduce project participants and to discuss project issues and management procedures.

Preconstruction services – services that a construction contractor performs for a project owner during design development and before construction starts.

Pre-final inspection – an inspection conducted when the project is near completion to identify all work that needs to be completed or corrected before the project can be considered completed.

Preparatory inspection – a quality-control inspection to ensure that all preliminary work has been completed on a project site before starting the next phase of work.

Pre-proposal conference – meeting of potential contractors with the project owner and architect. The purpose of the meeting is to explain the project, the negotiating process and selection criteria, and solicit questions regarding the design or contract requirements.

Prequalification of contractors – investigating and evaluating prospective contractors based on selected criteria prior to inviting them to submit bids or proposals.

Process action team – also known as *quality improvement team.* A small team organized to study a specific process and identify means for improving it.

Product data sheet – also known as *material data* or *cut sheets.* Information furnished by a manufacturer to illustrate a material, product, or system for some portion of the project which includes illustrations, standard schedules, performance data, instructions, and warranty.

Profit – the contractor's net income after all expenses have been subtracted.

Progress payment request – document or package of documents requesting progress payments for work performed during the period covered by the request, usually monthly.

Progress payments – periodic (usually monthly) payments made during the course of a construction project to cover the value of work satisfactorily completed during the previous period.

Project close-out – completing the physical construction of the project, submitting all required documentation to the owner, and financially closing out the project.

Project control – the methods a project manager uses to anticipate, monitor, and adjust to risks and trends in controlling costs and schedules.

Project engineer – project management team member who assists the project manager on larger projects. Responsible for management of technical issues on the job site.

Project labor curve – a plot of estimated labor hours required per month for the duration of the project.

Project management – application of knowledge, skills, tools, and techniques to the many activities necessary to complete a project successfully.

Project management organization – the contractor's project management group headed by the officer-in-charge, including field supervision and staff.

Project manager – the leader of the contractor's project team who is responsible for ensuring that all contract requirements are achieved safely and within the desired budget and time frame.

Project manual – a volume usually containing the instructions to bidders, the bid form, general conditions, and special conditions. It also may include a geotechnical report.

Project planning – the process of selecting the construction methods and the sequence of work to be used on a project.

Project-specific phased safety plan – a detailed accident prevention plan that is focused directly on the hazards that will exist on a specific project and measures that can be taken to reduce the likelihood of accidents.

Project start-up – mobilizing the project management team, establishing the project management office, and creating project document management systems.

Project team – individuals from one or several organizations who work together as a cohesive team to construct a project.

Project team list – list of all team members with their addresses and telephone contact information.

Property damage insurance – protects the contractor against financial loss due to damage to the contractor's property.

Punch list – a list of items that need to be corrected or completed before the project can be considered completed.

Purchase orders – written contracts for the purchase of materials and equipment from suppliers.

Quality control – process to assure materials and installation meet or exceed the requirements of the contract documents.

Quantity take-off (QTO) – one of the first steps in the estimating process to measure and count items of work to which unit prices will later be applied to determine a project cost estimate.

Reading file – correspondence gathered in increments, for example daily or weekly, routed among project staff, and then filed.

Reimbursable costs – costs incurred on a project that are reimbursed by the owner. The categories of costs that are reimbursable are specifically stated in the contract agreement.

Request for information – see *field question.*

Request for proposals (RFP) – document containing instructions to prospective contractors regarding documentation required and the process to be used in selecting the contractor for a project.

Request for qualifications – a request for prospective contractors or subcontractors to submit a specific set of documents to demonstrate the firm's qualifications for a specific project.

Request for quotation – a request for a prospective subcontractor to submit a quotation for a defined scope of work.

Retention – also known as *retainage*. A portion of money withheld from progress payments to contractors and subcontractors to create an account for finishing the work of any parties not able to or unwilling to do so.

Rough order-of-magnitude (ROM) estimate – a conceptual cost estimate usually based on the size of the project. It is prepared early in the estimating process to establish a preliminary budget and to decide whether or not to pursue the project.

Routing stamp – a stamp placed on documents that are routed among the project staff. Each staff member initials on the stamp, indicating that he or she has read the document.

Schedule of submittals – a listing of all submittals required by the contract specifications.

Schedule of values – an allocation of the entire project cost to each of the various work packages required to complete a project. Used to develop a cash flow curve for an owner and to support requests for progress payments. Serves as the basis for AIA document G703, which is used to justify pay requests.

Schedule update – schedule revision to reflect the actual time spent on each activity to date.

Self-performed work – project work performed by the general contractor's work force rather than by a subcontractor.

Shop drawing – drawing prepared by a contractor, subcontractor, vendor, or manufacturer to illustrate construction materials, dimensions, installation, or other information relating to the incorporation of the items into a construction project.

Short-form purchase order – purchase orders used on project sites by superintendents to order materials from local suppliers.

Short-interval schedule – schedule that lists the activities to be completed during a short interval (two to four weeks). Also known as *look-ahead schedule*. Used by the superintendent and foremen to manage the work.

Soils report – see *geotechnical report.*

Special conditions – also known as *supplementary conditions.* A part of the construction contract that supplements and may also modify, add to, or delete portions of the general conditions.

Specialty contractors – construction firms that specialize in specific areas of construction work, such as painting, roofing, or mechanical. Such firms typically are involved in construction projects as subcontractors.

Start-up checklist – a listing of items that should be completed during project start-up, together with the date of completion for each item.

Start-up log – a spreadsheet used to manage start-up activities relating to suppliers and subcontractors.

Subcontractors – specialty contractors who contract with and are under the supervision of the general contractor.

Subcontractor call sheet – a form used to list all of the bidding firms from which the general contractor is soliciting subcontractor and vendor quotations.

Subcontractor preconstruction meeting – a meeting the project manager and/or superintendent conduct with each subcontractor before allowing him or her to start work on a project.

Subcontracts – written contracts between the general contractor and specialty contractors who provide craft labor and usually material for specialized areas of work.

Submittal register – see *schedule of submittals.*

Submittals – shop drawings, product data sheets, and samples submitted by contractors and subcontractors for verification by the design team that the materials purchased for installation comply with the design intent.

Substantial completion – state of a project when it is sufficiently completed, that the owner can use it for its intended purpose.

Summary schedule – abbreviated version of a detailed construction schedule that may include ten to twenty major activities.

Superintendent – individual from the contractor's project team who is the leader on the job site and who is responsible for supervision of daily field operations on the project.

Surety – a company that provides a bond guaranteeing that another company will perform in accordance with the terms of a contract.

Technical specifications – a part of the construction contract that provides the qualitative requirements for a project in terms of materials, equipment, and workmanship.

Telephone memorandum – a written summary of a telephone conversation.

Third-tier subcontractor – a subcontractor who is hired by a firm that has a subcontract with the general contractor.

Time-and-materials contract – a cost-plus contract in which the owner and the contractor agree to a labor rate that includes the contractor's profit and overhead. Reimbursement to the contractor is made based on the actual costs for materials and the agreed labor rate times the number of hours worked.

Total quality management (TQM) – a management philosophy that focuses on continuous process improvement and customer satisfaction.

Traditional project delivery method – a delivery method in which the owner has a contract with an architect to prepare a design for a project. When the design is completed, the owner hires a contractor to construct the project.

Transmittal – a form used as a cover sheet for formally transmitting documents between parties.

Umbrella liability insurance – provides coverage against liability claims exceeding that covered by standard general liability or automobile insurance.

Unconditional lien release – a lien release indicating that the issuer has received a certain amount of payment and releases all lien rights associated with that amount.

Unit-price contract – a contract that contains an estimated quantity for each element of work and a unit price. The actual cost is determined once the work is completed and the total quantity of work measured.

Value engineering – a study of the relative value of various materials and construction techniques to identify the least costly alternative without sacrificing quality or performance.

Warranty – a guarantee that all materials furnished are new and able to perform as specified and that all work is free from defects in material or workmanship.

Warranty service log – a spread sheet used to track all warranty claims from receipt to resolution.

Work breakdown structure (WBS) – a list of significant work items that will have associated cost or schedule implications.

Workers' compensation insurance – protects the contractor from a claim due to injury or death of an employee on the project site.

Work package – a defined segment of the work required to complete a project.

APPENDIX C

Selected Project Plans for Huna Office Building

All documents in Appendix C are used courtesy of Jensen Yorba Lott, Inc.

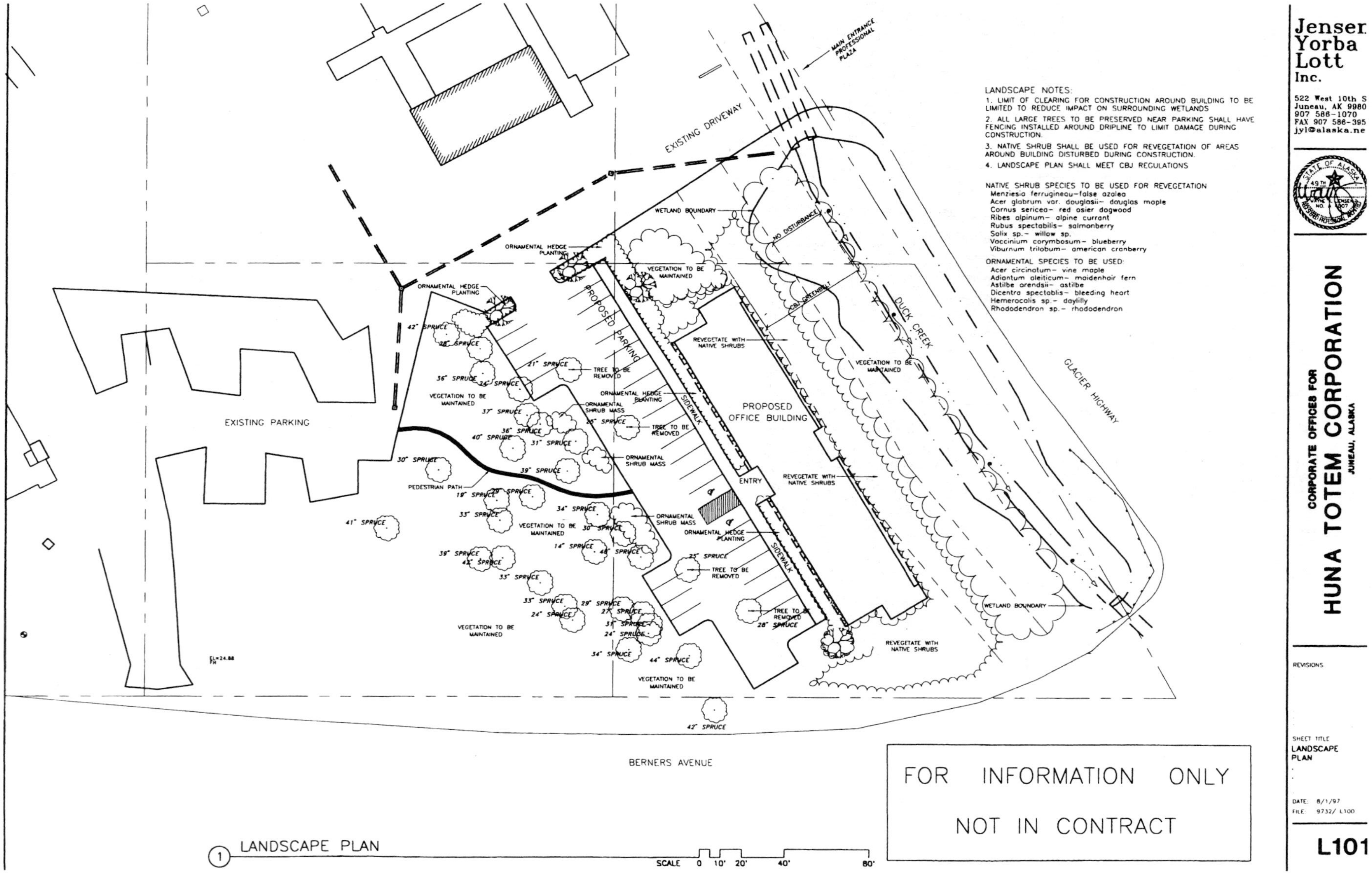
LANDSCAPE NOTES:
1. LIMIT OF CLEARING FOR CONSTRUCTION AROUND BUILDING TO BE LIMITED TO REDUCE IMPACT ON SURROUNDING WETLANDS
2. ALL LARGE TREES TO BE PRESERVED NEAR PARKING SHALL HAVE FENCING INSTALLED AROUND DRIPLINE TO LIMIT DAMAGE DURING CONSTRUCTION.
3. NATIVE SHRUB SHALL BE USED FOR REVEGETATION OF AREAS AROUND BUILDING DISTURBED DURING CONSTRUCTION.
4. LANDSCAPE PLAN SHALL MEET CBJ REGULATIONS
NATIVE SHRUB SPECIES TO BE USED FOR REVEGETATION
Menziesia ferrugineau– false azalea
Acer glabrum var. douglasii– douglas maple
Cornus sericea– red osier dogwood
Ribes alpinum– alpine currant
Rubus spectabilis– salmonberry
Salix sp.– willow sp.
Vaccinium corymbosum– blueberry
Viburnum trilobum– american cranberry
ORNAMENTAL SPECIES TO BE USED:
Acer circinatum– vine maple
Adiantum aleiticum– maidenhair fern
Astilbe arendsii– astilbe
Dicentra spectablis– bleeding heart
Hemerocalis sp.– daylilly
Rhododendron sp.– rhododendron
Jenser Yorba Lott Inc.
522 West 10th S
Juneau, AK 9980
907 586-1070
FAX 907 586-395
jyl@alaska.ne
CORPORATE OFFICES FOR
HUNA TOTEM CORPORATION
JUNEAU, ALASKA
REVISIONS
SHEET TITLE
LANDSCAPE PLAN
DATE: 8/1/97
FILE: 9732/ L100
L101
FOR INFORMATION ONLY
NOT IN CONTRACT
MAIN ENTRANCE PROFESSIONAL PLAZA
EXISTING DRIVEWAY
EXISTING PARKING
WETLAND BOUNDARY
NO DISTURBANCE
CBJ GREENBELT
DUCK CREEK
GLACIER HIGHWAY
VEGETATION TO BE MAINTAINED
REVEGETATE WITH NATIVE SHRUBS
PROPOSED OFFICE BUILDING
PROPOSED PARKING
SIDEWALK
ENTRY
ORNAMENTAL HEDGE PLANTING
ORNAMENTAL SHRUB MASS
TREE TO BE REMOVED
PEDESTRIAN PATH
BERNERS AVENUE
1 LANDSCAPE PLAN
SCALE 0 10' 20' 40' 80'

Figure C–1

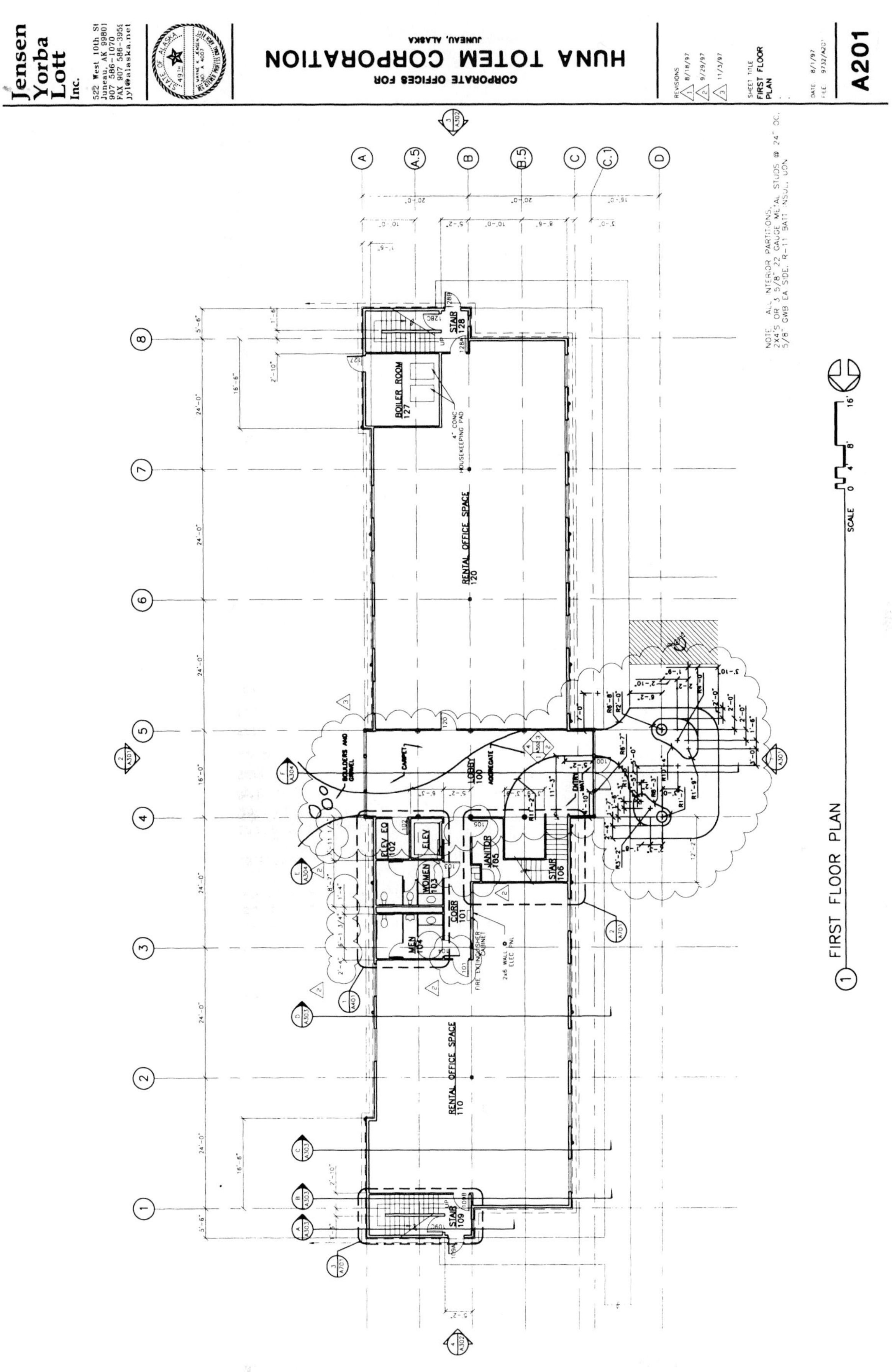
Jensen Yorba Lott Inc.
522 West 10th St
Juneau, AK 99801
907 586-1070
FAX 907 586-3959
jyl@alaska.net
CORPORATE OFFICES FOR
HUNA TOTEM CORPORATION
JUNEAU, ALASKA
REVISIONS
8/18/97
9/29/97
11/3/97
SHEET TITLE
FIRST FLOOR PLAN
DATE 8/1/97
A201
NOTE: ALL INTERIOR PARTITIONS, 2X4'S OR 3 5/8" 22 GAUGE METAL STUDS @ 24" OC, 5/8" GWB EA SIDE, R-11 BATT INSUL. UON
BOILER ROOM 127
STAIR 128
4" CONC HOUSEKEEPING PAD
RENTAL OFFICE SPACE 120
LOBBY 100
BOULDERS AND GRAVEL
CARPET
AGGREGATE
ELEV EQ 102
ELEV
WOMEN 103
MEN 104
CORR 101
JANITOR 105
STAIR 106
FIRE EXTINGUISHER CABINET
RENTAL OFFICE SPACE 110
STAIR 109
FIRST FLOOR PLAN
SCALE 0 4' 8' 16'

Figure C-2

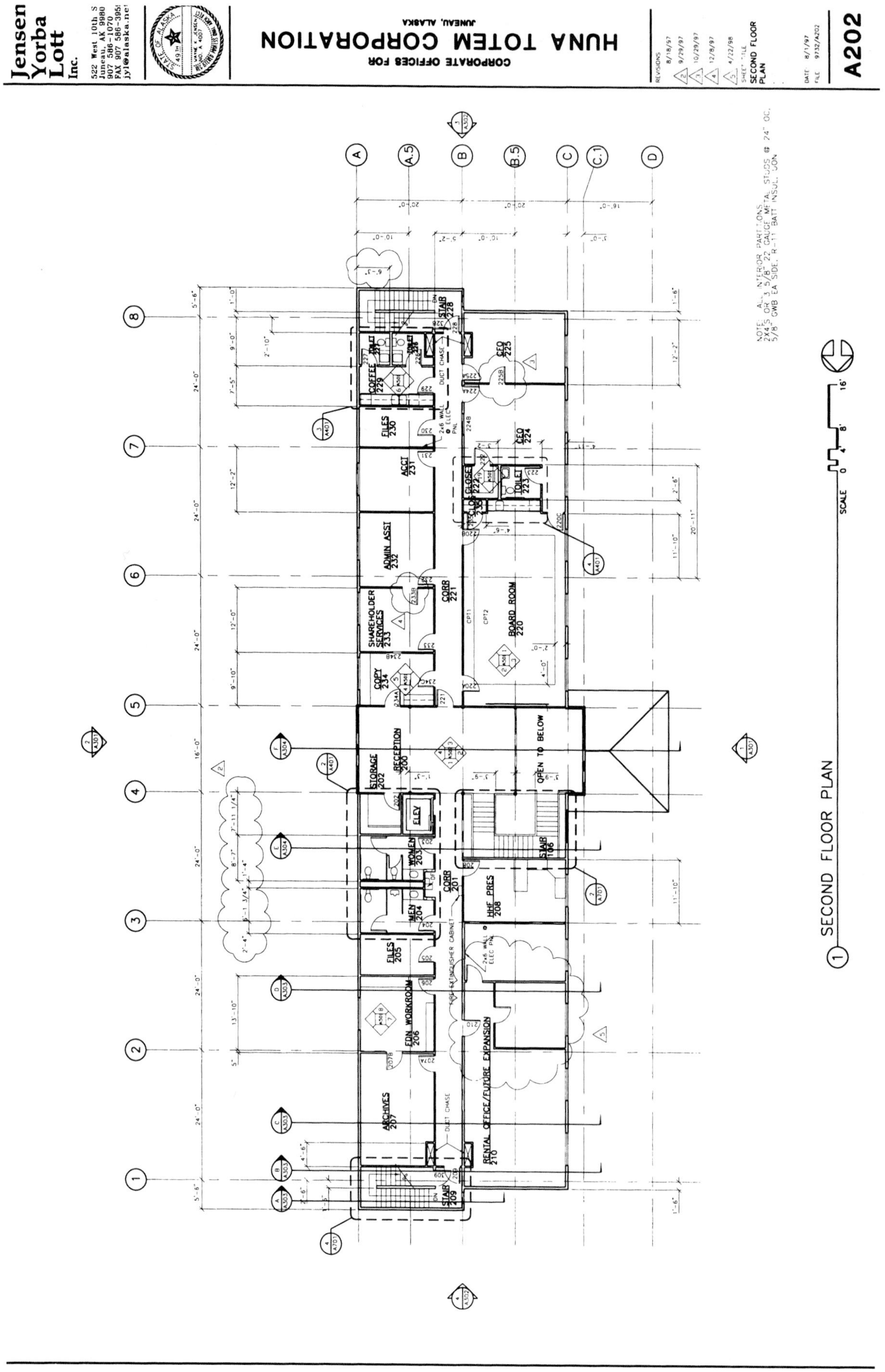
Jensen
Yorba
Lott
Inc.
CORPORATE OFFICES FOR
HUNA TOTEM CORPORATION
JUNEAU, ALASKA
SECOND FLOOR PLAN
A202

Figure C–3

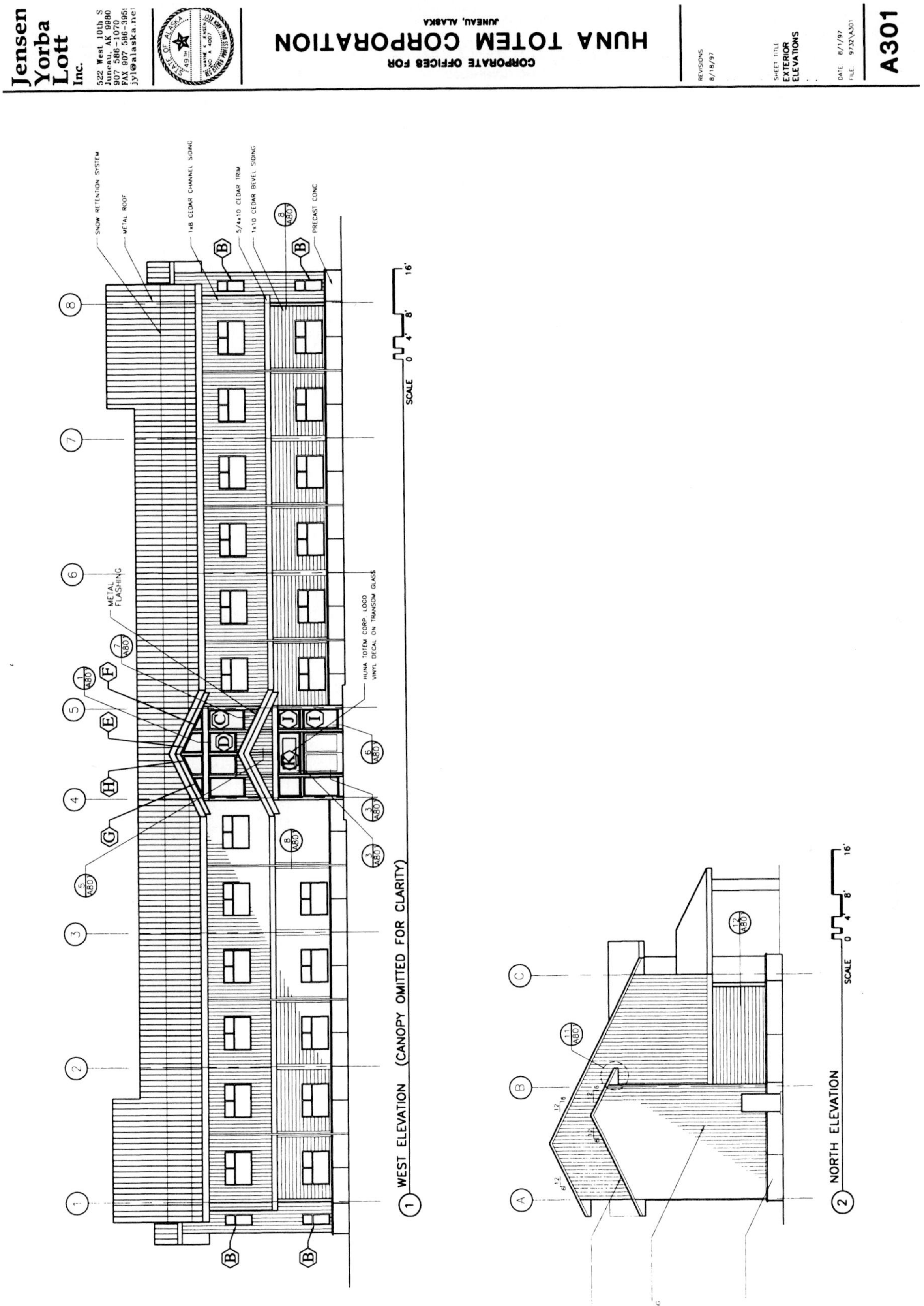
Jensen
Yorba
Lott
Inc.
HUNA TOTEM CORPORATION
CORPORATE OFFICES FOR
JUNEAU, ALASKA
SHEET TITLE
EXTERIOR
ELEVATIONS
A301
WEST ELEVATION (CANOPY OMITTED FOR CLARITY)
NORTH ELEVATION
SNOW RETENTION SYSTEM
METAL ROOF
1x8 CEDAR CHANNEL SIDING
5/4x10 CEDAR TRIM
1x10 CEDAR BEVEL SIDING
PRECAST CONC
METAL FLASHING
HUNA TOTEM CORP. LOGO
VINYL DECAL ON TRANSOM GLASS
SCALE

Figure C–4

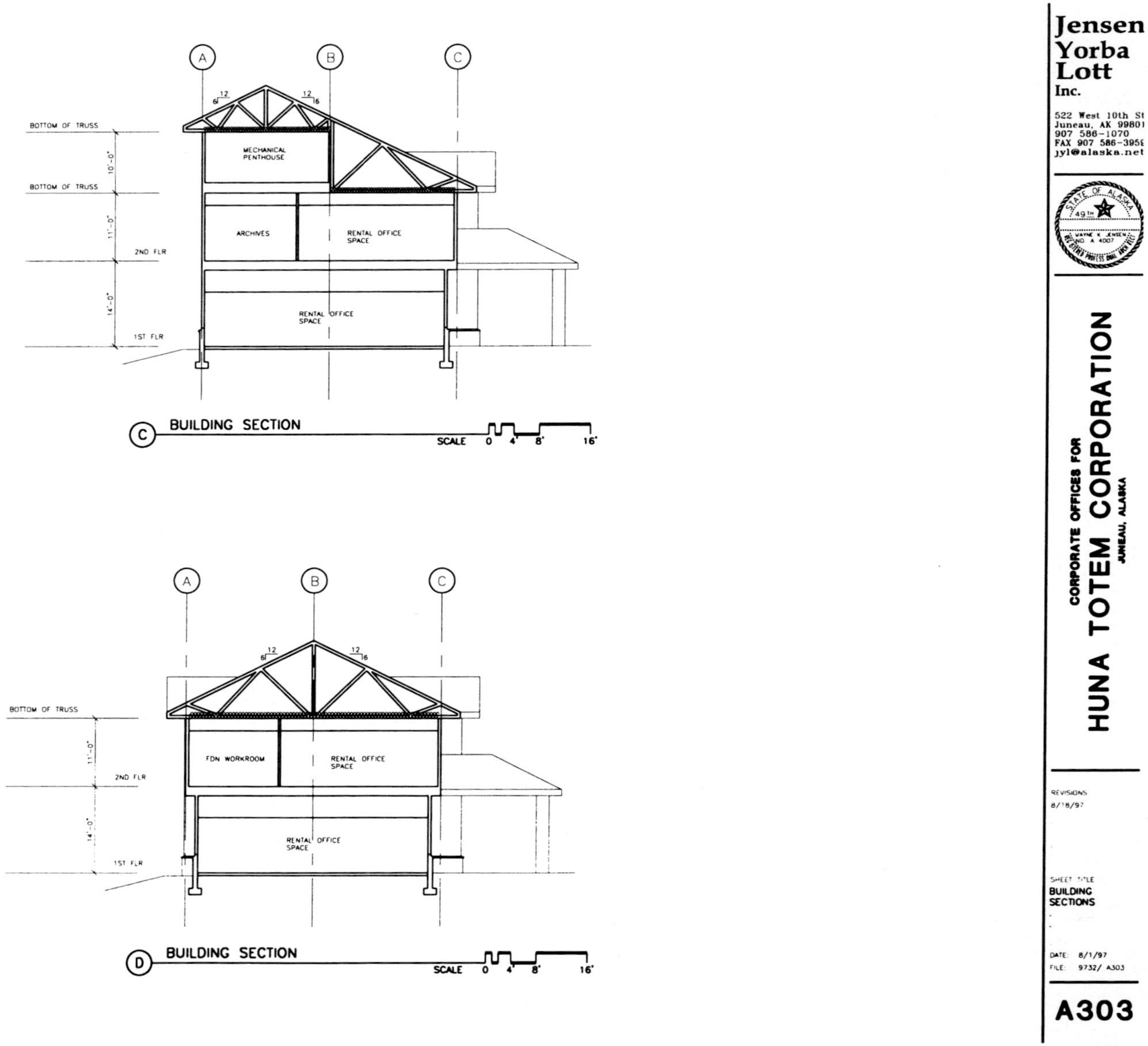

BOTTOM OF TRUSS
10'-0"
BOTTOM OF TRUSS
11'-0"
2ND FLR
14'-0"
1ST FLR
MECHANICAL PENTHOUSE
ARCHIVES
RENTAL OFFICE SPACE
RENTAL OFFICE SPACE
C BUILDING SECTION
SCALE 0 4' 8' 16'
BOTTOM OF TRUSS
11'-0"
2ND FLR
14'-0"
1ST FLR
FDN WORKROOM
RENTAL OFFICE SPACE
RENTAL OFFICE SPACE
D BUILDING SECTION
SCALE 0 4' 8' 16'
Jensen
Yorba
Lott
Inc.
522 West 10th St
Juneau, AK 99801
907 586-1070
FAX 907 586-3959
jyl@alaska.net
CORPORATE OFFICES FOR
HUNA TOTEM CORPORATION
JUNEAU, ALASKA
REVISIONS
8/18/97
SHEET TITLE
BUILDING SECTIONS
DATE: 8/1/97
FILE: 9732/ A303
A303

Figure C–5

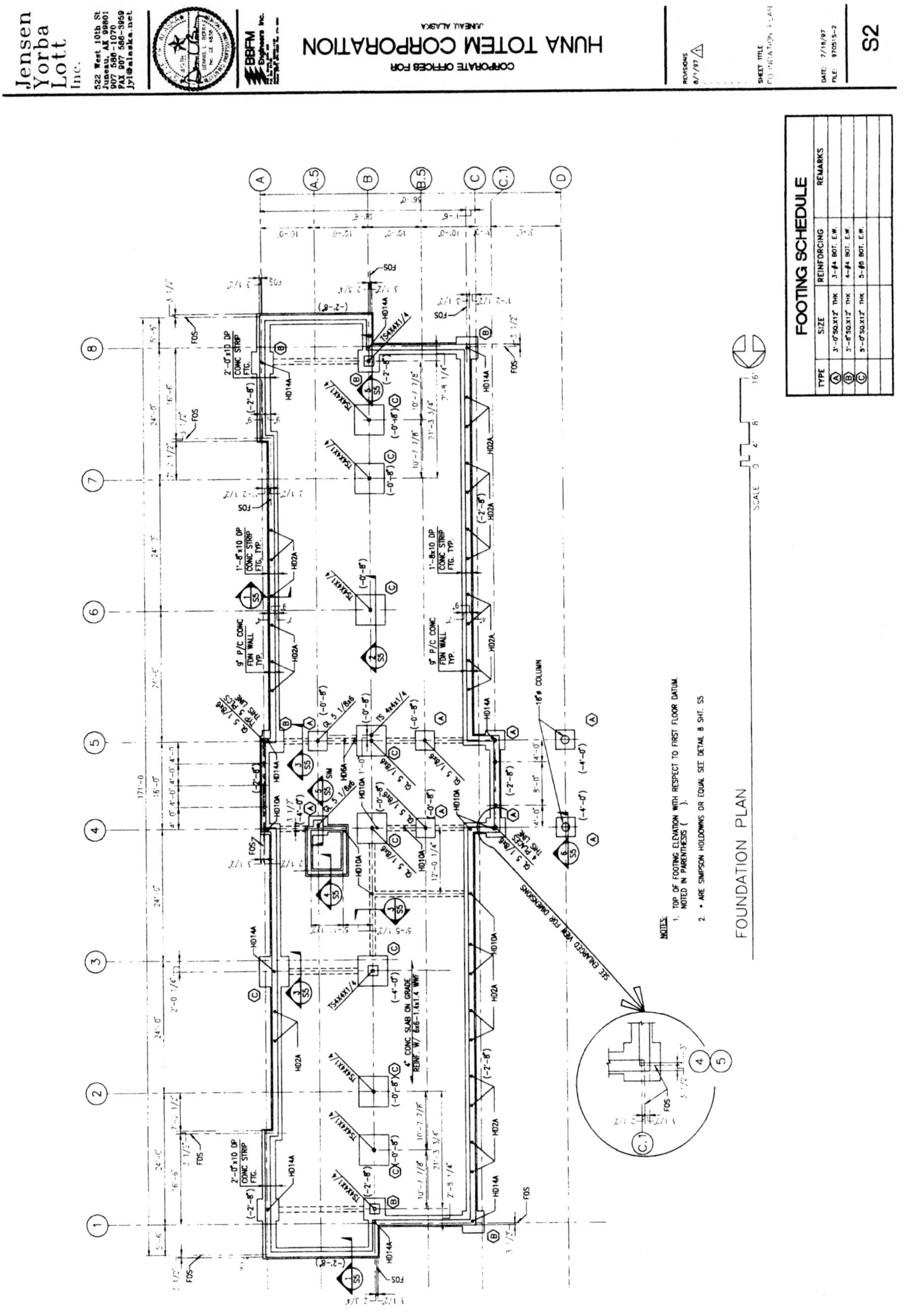
Jensen Yorba Lott Inc.
522 West 10th St
Juneau, AK 99801
HUNA TOTEM CORPORATION
CORPORATE OFFICES FOR
JUNEAU, ALASKA
S2
FOUNDATION PLAN
FOOTING SCHEDULE
TYPE SIZE REINFORCING REMARKS
A 3'-0"SQ.X12" THK 3-#4 BOT. E.W.
B 3'-6"SQ.X12" THK 4-#4 BOT. E.W.
C 5'-0"SQ.X12" THK 5-#5 BOT. E.W.
NOTES:
1. TOP OF FOOTING ELEVATION WITH RESPECT TO FIRST FLOOR DATUM. NOTED IN PARENTHESIS ( ).
2. • ARE SIMPSON HOLDOWNS OR EQUAL SEE DETAIL 8 SHT. S5
SEE ENLARGED VIEW FOR DIMENSIONS
16"ø COLUMN
4" CONC. SLAB ON GRADE REINF. W/ 6x6-1.4x1.4 WWF

Figure C–6

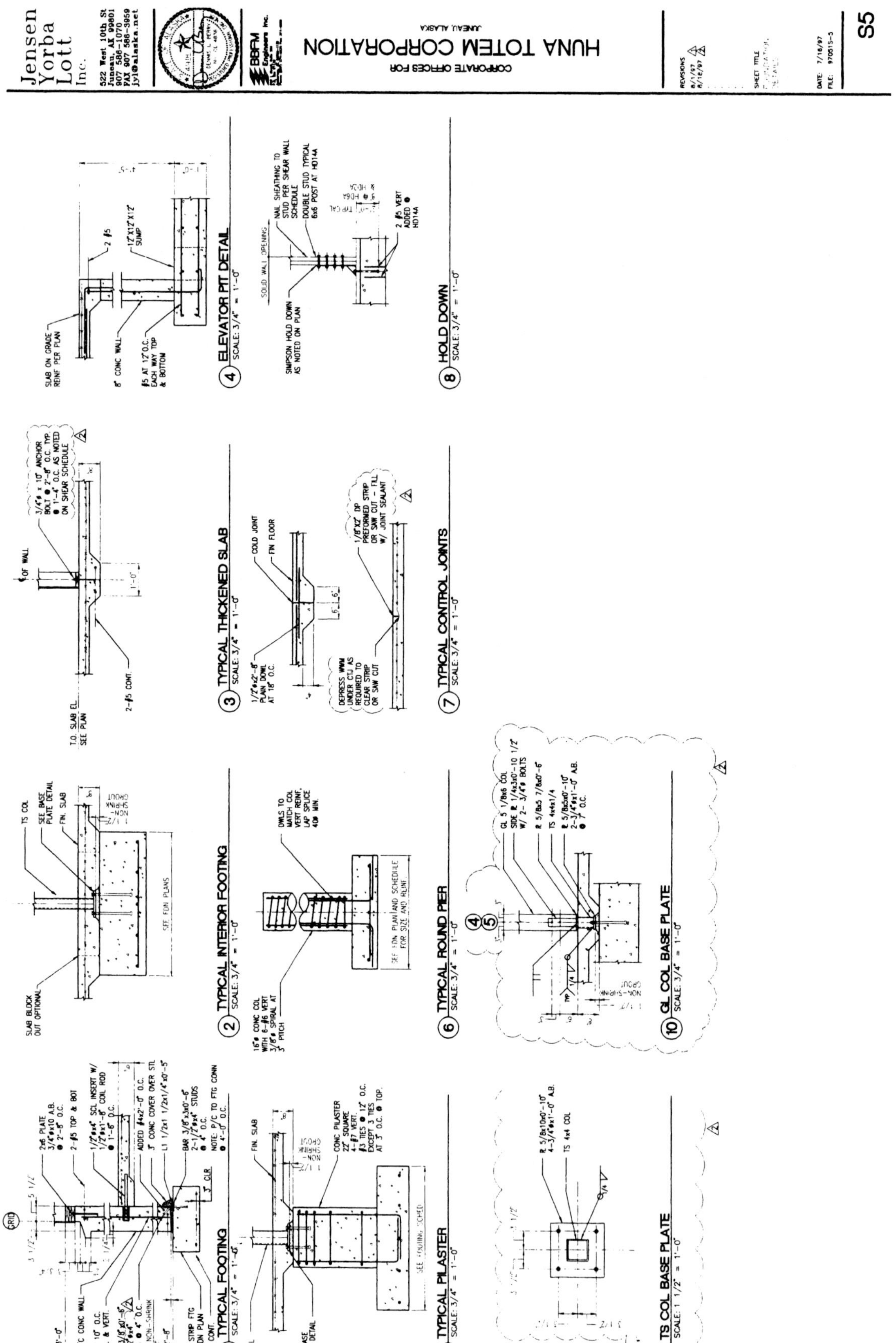
Jensen Yorba Lott Inc.
522 West 10th St. Juneau, AK 99801
HUNA TOTEM CORPORATION
CORPORATE OFFICES FOR
JUNEAU, ALASKA
S5
1 TYPICAL FOOTING SCALE: 3/4" = 1'-0"
2 TYPICAL INTERIOR FOOTING SCALE: 3/4" = 1'-0"
3 TYPICAL THICKENED SLAB SCALE: 3/4" = 1'-0"
4 ELEVATOR PIT DETAIL SCALE: 3/4" = 1'-0"
5 TYPICAL PILASTER SCALE: 3/4" = 1'-0"
6 TYPICAL ROUND PIER SCALE: 3/4" = 1'-0"
7 TYPICAL CONTROL JOINTS SCALE: 3/4" = 1'-0"
8 HOLD DOWN SCALE: 3/4" = 1'-0"
9 TS COL BASE PLATE SCALE: 1 1/2" = 1'-0"
10 GL COL BASE PLATE SCALE: 3/4" = 1'-0"

Figure C-7

APPENDIX D

Contract Agreement for Huna Office Building (AIA A111–1997)

AIA DOCUMENT A111-1997

Standard Form of Agreement Between Owner and Contractor

where the basis for payment is the COST OF THE WORK PLUS A FEE with a negotiated Guaranteed Maximum Price

AGREEMENT made as of the Fifteenth day of August in the year Two Thousand
(In words, indicate day, month and year)

BETWEEN the Owner:
(Name, address and other information)

Huna Totem Corporation
9309 Glacier Highway
Juneau, Alaska 99801

and the Contractor:
(Name, address and other information)

Northwest Construction Company
1242 First Avenue
Cascade, Washington 98202

The Project is:
(Name and address)

Huna Office Building
9301 Glacier Highway
Juneau, Alaska 99801

The Architect is:
(Name, address and other information)

Jensen Yorba Lott, Inc.
522 West 10th Street
Juneau, Alaska 99801

The Owner and Contractor agree as follows.

This document has important legal consequences. Consultation with an attorney is encouraged with respect to its completion or modification.

This document is not intended for use in competitive bidding.

AIA Document A201-1997, General Conditions of the Contract for Construction, is adopted in this document by reference.

This document has been approved and endorsed by The Associated General Contractors of America.

The American Institute of Architects
1735 New York Avenue, N.W.
Washington, D.C. 20006-5292

ARTICLE 1 THE CONTRACT DOCUMENTS

The Contract Documents consist of this Agreement, Conditions of the Contract (General, Supplementary and other Conditions), Drawings, Specifications, Addenda issued prior to execution of this Agreement, other documents listed in this Agreement and Modifications issued after execution of this Agreement; these form the Contract, and are as fully a part of the Contract as if attached to this Agreement or repeated herein. The Contract represents the entire and integrated agreement between the parties hereto and supersedes prior negotiations, representations or agreements, either written or oral. An enumeration of the Contract Documents, other than Modifications, appears in Article 15. If anything in the other Contract Documents is inconsistent with this Agreement, this Agreement shall govern.

ARTICLE 2 THE WORK OF THIS CONTRACT

The Contractor shall fully execute the Work described in the Contract Documents, except to the extent specifically indicated in the Contract Documents to be the responsibility of others.

ARTICLE 3 RELATIONSHIP OF THE PARTIES

The Contractor accepts the relationship of trust and confidence established by this Agreement and covenants with the Owner to cooperate with the Architect and exercise the Contractor's skill and judgment in furthering the interests of the Owner; to furnish efficient business administration and supervision; to furnish at all times an adequate supply of workers and materials; and to perform the Work in an expeditious and economical manner consistent with the Owner's interests. The Owner agrees to furnish and approve, in a timely manner, information required by the Contractor and to make payments to the Contractor in accordance with the requirements of the Contract Documents.

ARTICLE 4 DATE OF COMMENCEMENT AND SUBSTANTIAL COMPLETION

4.1 The date of commencement of the Work shall be the date of this Agreement unless a different date is stated below or provision is made for the date to be fixed in a notice to proceed issued by the Owner.

(Insert the date of commencement, if it differs from the date of this Agreement or, if applicable, state that the date will be fixed in a notice to proceed.) *Date of commencement will be approximately August 15, 2000 pending receipt of: (a) verification of financing, (b) building permit, (c) signed contract, and (d) notice to proceed.*

If, prior to commencement of the Work, the Owner requires time to file mortgages, mechanic's liens and other security interests, the Owner's time requirement shall be as follows:

4.2 The Contract Time shall be measured from the date of commencement.

4.3 The Contractor shall achieve Substantial Completion of the entire Work not later than 165 work days from the date of commencement, or as follows:
(Insert number of calendar days. Alternatively, a calendar date may be used when coordinated with the date of commencement. Unless stated elsewhere in the Contract Documents, insert any requirements for earlier Substantial Completion of certain portions of the Work.) Refer to attached project schedule, Exhibit A, dated August 15, 2000, which by this reference is made a part hereof.

, subject to adjustments of this Contract Time as provided in the Contract Documents.
(Insert provisions, if any, for liquidated damages relating to failure to complete on time, or for bonus payments for early completion of the Work.)

Not applicable

ARTICLE 5 BASIS FOR PAYMENT

5.1 CONTRACT SUM

5.1.1 The Owner shall pay the Contractor the Contract Sum in current funds for the Contractor's performance of the Contract. The Contract Sum is the Cost of the Work as defined in Article 7 plus the Contractor's Fee.

5.1.2 The Contractor's Fee is: 5% of the estimated cost of the Work
(State a lump sum, percentage of Cost of the Work or other provision for determining the Contractor's Fee, and describe the method of adjustment of the Contractor's Fee for changes in the Work.) Which is a lump sum of $85,000.00. In the case of approved changes in the Work, the contractor's fee will be adjusted as follows: 5% for increases in scope and 0% for decreases in scope.

5.2 GUARANTEED MAXIMUM PRICE

5.2.1 The sum of the Cost of the Work and the Contractor's Fee is guaranteed by the Contractor not to exceed One million seven hundred sixty thousand Dollars ($1,760,000), subject to additions and deductions by Change Order as provided in the Contract Documents. Such maximum sum is referred to in the Contract Documents as the Guaranteed Maximum Price. Costs which would cause the Guaranteed Maximum Price to be exceeded shall be paid by the Contractor without reimbursement by the Owner.
(Insert specific provisions if the Contractor is to participate in any savings.) Refer to attached Exhibit B, dated August 15, 2000, which by this reference is made a part hereof. If the actual cost of the Work plus the contractor's fee is less than the estimated cost of the Work as adjusted by approved change orders, the resultant savings will be distributed as follows: 70% to the owner and 30% to the contractor.

5.2.2 The Guaranteed Maximum Price is based on the following alternates, if any, which are described in the Contract Documents and are hereby accepted by the Owner:
(State the numbers or other identification of accepted alternates. If decisions on other alternates are to be made by the Owner subsequent to the execution of this Agreement, attach a schedule of such other alternates showing the amount for each and the date when the amount expires.)

Not applicable

The American Institute of Architects
1735 New York Avenue, N.W.
Washington, D.C. 20006-5292

5.2.3 Unit prices, if any, are as follows:

Not applicable

5.2.4 Allowances, if any, are as follows:
(Identify and state the amounts of any allowances, and state whether they include labor, materials, or both.)

Not applicable

5.2.5 Assumptions, if any, on which the Guaranteed Maximum Price is based are as follows:

Not applicable

5.2.6 To the extent that the Drawings and Specifications are anticipated to require further development by the Architect, the Contractor has provided in the Guaranteed Maximum Price for such further development consistent with the Contract Documents and reasonably inferable therefrom. Such further development does not include such things as changes in scope, systems, kinds and quality of materials, finishes or equipment, all of which, if required, shall be incorporated by Change Order.

ARTICLE 6 CHANGES IN THE WORK

6.1 Adjustments to the Guaranteed Maximum Price on account of changes in the Work may be determined by any of the methods listed in Subparagraph 7.3.3 of AIA Document A201-1997.

6.2 In calculating adjustments to subcontracts (except those awarded with the Owner's prior consent on the basis of cost plus a fee), the terms "cost" and "fee" as used in Clause 7.3.3.3 of AIA Document A201-1997 and the terms "costs" and "a reasonable allowance for overhead and profit" as used in Subparagraph 7.3.6 of AIA Document A201-1997 shall have the meanings assigned to them in AIA Document A201-1997 and shall not be modified by Articles 5, 7 and 8 of this Agreement. Adjustments to subcontracts awarded with the Owner's prior consent on the basis of cost plus a fee shall be calculated in accordance with the terms of those subcontracts.

6.3 In calculating adjustments to the Guaranteed Maximum Price, the terms "cost" and "costs" as used in the above-referenced provisions of AIA Document A201-1997 shall mean the Cost of the Work as defined in Article 7 of this Agreement and the terms "fee" and "a reasonable allowance for overhead and profit" shall mean the Contractor's Fee as defined in Subparagraph 5.1.2 of this Agreement.

The American Institute of Architects
1735 New York Avenue, N.W.
Washington, D.C. 20006-5292

6.4 If no specific provision is made in Paragraph 5.1 for adjustment of the Contractor's Fee in the case of changes in the Work, or if the extent of such changes is such, in the aggregate, that application of the adjustment provisions of Paragraph 5.1 will cause substantial inequity to the Owner or Contractor, the Contractor's Fee shall be equitably adjusted on the basis of the Fee established for the original Work, and the Guaranteed Maximum Price shall be adjusted accordingly.

ARTICLE 7 COSTS TO BE REIMBURSED

7.1 COST OF THE WORK

The term Cost of the Work shall mean costs necessarily incurred by the Contractor in the proper performance of the Work. Such costs shall be at rates not higher than the standard paid at the place of the Project except with prior consent of the Owner. The Cost of the Work shall include only the items set forth in this Article 7.

7.2 LABOR COSTS

7.2.1 Wages of construction workers directly employed by the Contractor to perform the construction of the Work at the site or, with the Owner's approval, at off-site workshops.

7.2.2 Wages or salaries of the Contractor's supervisory and administrative personnel when stationed at the site with the Owner's approval. Including contractor's project manager.
(If it is intended that the wages or salaries of certain personnel stationed at the Contractor's principal or other offices shall be included in the Cost of the Work, identify in Article 14 the personnel to be included and whether for all or only part of their time, and the rates at which their time will be charged to the Work.)

7.2.3 Wages and salaries of the Contractor's supervisory or administrative personnel engaged, at factories, workshops or on the road, in expediting the production or transportation of materials or equipment required for the Work, but only for that portion of their time required for the Work.

7.2.4 Costs paid or incurred by the Contractor for taxes, insurance, contributions, assessments and benefits required by law or collective bargaining agreements and, for personnel not covered by such agreements, customary benefits such as sick leave, medical and health benefits, holidays, vacations and pensions, provided such costs are based on wages and salaries included in the Cost of the Work under Subparagraphs 7.2.1 through 7.2.3.

7.3 SUBCONTRACT COSTS

7.3.1 Payments made by the Contractor to Subcontractors in accordance with the requirements of the subcontracts.

7.4 COSTS OF MATERIALS AND EQUIPMENT INCORPORATED IN THE COMPLETED CONSTRUCTION

7.4.1 Costs, including transportation and storage, of materials and equipment incorporated or to be incorporated in the completed construction.

7.4.2 Costs of materials described in the preceding Subparagraph 7.4.1 in excess of those actually installed to allow for reasonable waste and spoilage. Unused excess materials, if any, shall become the Owner's property at the completion of the Work or, at the Owner's option, shall be sold by the Contractor. Any amounts realized from such sales shall be credited to the Owner as a deduction from the Cost of the Work.

7.5 COSTS OF OTHER MATERIALS AND EQUIPMENT, TEMPORARY FACILITIES AND RELATED ITEMS

7.5.1 Costs, including transportation and storage, installation, maintenance, dismantling and removal of materials, supplies, temporary facilities, machinery, equipment, and hand tools not customarily owned by construction workers, that are provided by the Contractor at the site and

The American Institute
of Architects
1735 New York Avenue, N.W.
Washington, D.C. 20006-5292

fully consumed in the performance of the Work; and cost (less salvage value) of such items if not fully consumed, whether sold to others or retained by the Contractor. Cost for items previously used by the Contractor shall mean fair market value.

7.5.2 Rental charges for temporary facilities, machinery, equipment, and hand tools not customarily owned by construction workers that are provided by the Contractor at the site, whether rented from the Contractor or others, and costs of transportation, installation, minor repairs and replacements, dismantling and removal thereof. Rates and quantities of equipment rented shall be subject to the Owner's prior approval.

7.5.3 Costs of removal of debris from the site.

7.5.4 Costs of document reproductions, facsimile transmissions and long-distance telephone calls, postage and parcel delivery charges, telephone service at the site and reasonable petty cash expenses of the site office.

7.5.5 That portion of the reasonable expenses of the Contractor's personnel incurred while traveling in discharge of duties connected with the Work.

7.5.6 Costs of materials and equipment suitably stored off the site at a mutually acceptable location, if approved in advance by the Owner.

7.6 MISCELLANEOUS COSTS

7.6.1 That portion of insurance and bond premiums that can be directly attributed to this Contract

7.6.2 Sales, use or similar taxes imposed by a governmental authority that are related to the Work.

7.6.3 Fees and assessments for the building permit and for other permits, licenses and inspections for which the Contractor is required by the Contract Documents to pay.

7.6.4 Fees of laboratories for tests required by the Contract Documents, except those related to defective or nonconforming Work for which reimbursement is excluded by Subparagraph 13.5.3 of AIA Document A201-1997 or other provisions of the Contract Documents, and which do not fall within the scope of Subparagraph 7.7.3.

7.6.5 Royalties and license fees paid for the use of a particular design, process or product required by the Contract Documents; the cost of defending suits or claims for infringement of patent rights arising from such requirement of the Contract Documents; and payments made in accordance with legal judgments against the Contractor resulting from such suits or claims and payments of settlements made with the Owner's consent. However, such costs of legal defenses, judgments and settlements shall not be included in the calculation of the Contractor's Fee or subject to the Guaranteed Maximum Price. If such royalties, fees and costs are excluded by the last sentence of Subparagraph 3.17.1 of AIA Document A201-1997 or other provisions of the Contract Documents, then they shall not be included in the Cost of the Work.

7.6.6 Data processing costs related to the Work.

7.6.7 Deposits lost for causes other than the Contractor's negligence or failure to fulfill a specific responsibility to the Owner as set forth in the Contract Documents.

The American Institute of Architects
1735 New York Avenue, N.W.
Washington, D.C. 20006-5292

7.6.8 Legal, mediation and arbitration costs, including attorneys' fees, other than those arising from disputes between the Owner and Contractor, reasonably incurred by the Contractor in the performance of the Work and with the Owner's prior written approval; which approval shall not be unreasonably withheld.

7.6.9 Expenses incurred in accordance with the Contractor's standard personnel policy for relocation and temporary living allowances of personnel required for the Work, if approved by the Owner.

7.7 OTHER COSTS AND EMERGENCIES

7.7.1 Other costs incurred in the performance of the Work if and to the extent approved in advance in writing by the Owner.

7.7.2 Costs due to emergencies incurred in taking action to prevent threatened damage, injury or loss in case of an emergency affecting the safety of persons and property, as provided in Paragraph 10.6 of AIA Document A201-1997.

7.7.3 Costs of repairing or correcting damaged or nonconforming Work executed by the Contractor, Subcontractors or suppliers, provided that such damaged or nonconforming Work was not caused by negligence or failure to fulfill a specific responsibility of the Contractor and only to the extent that the cost of repair or correction is not recoverable by the Contractor from insurance, sureties, Subcontractors or suppliers.

ARTICLE 8 COSTS NOT TO BE REIMBURSED

8.1 The Cost of the Work shall not include:

8.1.1 Salaries and other compensation of the Contractor's personnel stationed at the Contractor's principal office or offices other than the site office, except as specifically provided in Subparagraphs 7.2.2 and 7.2.3 or as may be provided in Article 14.

8.1.2 Expenses of the Contractor's principal office and offices other than the site office.

8.1.3 Overhead and general expenses, except as may be expressly included in Article 7.

8.1.4 The Contractor's capital expenses, including interest on the Contractor's capital employed for the Work.

8.1.5 Rental costs of machinery and equipment, except as specifically provided in Subparagraph 7.5.2.

8.1.6 Except as provided in Subparagraph 7.7.3 of this Agreement, costs due to the negligence or failure to fulfill a specific responsibility of the Contractor, Subcontractors and suppliers or anyone directly or indirectly employed by any of them or for whose acts any of them may be liable.

8.1.7 Any cost not specifically and expressly described in Article 7.

8.1.8 Costs, other than costs included in Change Orders approved by the Owner, that would cause the Guaranteed Maximum Price to be exceeded.

ARTICLE 9 DISCOUNTS, REBATES AND REFUNDS

9.1 Cash discounts obtained on payments made by the Contractor shall accrue to the Owner if (1) before making the payment, the Contractor included them in an Application for Payment

The American Institute of Architects
1735 New York Avenue, N.W.
Washington, D.C. 20006-5292

and received payment therefor from the Owner, or (2) the Owner has deposited funds with the Contractor with which to make payments; otherwise, cash discounts shall accrue to the Contractor. Trade discounts, rebates, refunds and amounts received from sales of surplus materials and equipment shall accrue to the Owner, and the Contractor shall make provisions so that they can be secured.

9.2 Amounts that accrue to the Owner in accordance with the provisions of Paragraph 9.1 shall be credited to the Owner as a deduction from the Cost of the Work.

ARTICLE 10 SUBCONTRACTS AND OTHER AGREEMENTS

10.1 Those portions of the Work that the Contractor does not customarily perform with the Contractor's own personnel shall be performed under subcontracts or by other appropriate agreements with the Contractor. The Owner may designate specific persons or entities from whom the Contractor shall obtain bids. The Contractor shall obtain bids from Subcontractors and from suppliers of materials or equipment fabricated especially for the Work and shall deliver such bids to the Architect. The Owner shall then determine, with the advice of the Contractor and the Architect, which bids will be accepted. The Contractor shall not be required to contract with anyone to whom the Contractor has reasonable objection.

10.2 If a specific bidder among those whose bids are delivered by the Contractor to the Architect (1) is recommended to the Owner by the Contractor; (2) is qualified to perform that portion of the Work; and (3) has submitted a bid that conforms to the requirements of the Contract Documents without reservations or exceptions, but the Owner requires that another bid be accepted, then the Contractor may require that a Change Order be issued to adjust the Guaranteed Maximum Price by the difference between the bid of the person or entity recommended to the Owner by the Contractor and the amount of the subcontract or other agreement actually signed with the person or entity designated by the Owner.

10.3 Subcontracts or other agreements shall conform to the applicable payment provisions of this Agreement, and shall not be awarded on the basis of cost plus a fee without the prior consent of the Owner.

ARTICLE 11 ACCOUNTING RECORDS

The Contractor shall keep full and detailed accounts and exercise such controls as may be necessary for proper financial management under this Contract, and the accounting and control systems shall be satisfactory to the Owner. The Owner and the Owner's accountants shall be afforded access to, and shall be permitted to audit and copy, the Contractor's records, books, correspondence, instructions, drawings, receipts, subcontracts, purchase orders, vouchers, memoranda and other data relating to this Contract, and the Contractor shall preserve these for a period of three years after final payment, or for such longer period as may be required by law.

ARTICLE 12 PAYMENTS

12.1 PROGRESS PAYMENTS

12.1.1 Based upon Applications for Payment submitted to the Architect by the Contractor and Certificates for Payment issued by the Architect, the Owner shall make progress payments on account of the Contract Sum to the Contractor as provided below and elsewhere in the Contract Documents.

12.1.2 The period covered by each Application for Payment shall be one calendar month ending on the last day of the month, or as follows:

AIA DOCUMENT A111-1997
OWNER-CONTRACTOR AGREEMENT

The American Institute of Architects
1735 New York Avenue, N.W.
Washington, D.C. 20006-5292

12.1.3 Provided that an Application for Payment is received by the Architect not later than the 30th day of a month, the Owner shall make payment to the Contractor not later than the 10th day of the following month. If an Application for Payment is received by the Architect after the application date fixed above, payment shall be made by the Owner not later than 30 days after the Architect receives the Application for Payment.

12.1.4 With each Application for Payment, the Contractor shall submit payrolls, petty cash accounts, receipted invoices or invoices with check vouchers attached, and any other evidence required by the Owner or Architect to demonstrate that cash disbursements already made by the Contractor on account of the Cost of the Work equal or exceed (1) progress payments already received by the Contractor; less (2) that portion of those payments attributable to the Contractor's Fee; plus (3) payrolls for the period covered by the present Application for Payment.

12.1.5 Each Application for Payment shall be based on the most recent schedule of values submitted by the Contractor in accordance with the Contract Documents. The schedule of values shall allocate the entire Guaranteed Maximum Price among the various portions of the Work, except that the Contractor's Fee shall be shown as a single separate item. The schedule of values shall be prepared in such form and supported by such data to substantiate its accuracy as the Architect may require. This schedule, unless objected to by the Architect, shall be used as a basis for reviewing the Contractor's Applications for Payment.

12.1.6 Applications for Payment shall show the percentage of completion of each portion of the Work as of the end of the period covered by the Application for Payment. The percentage of completion shall be the lesser of (1) the percentage of that portion of the Work which has actually been completed; or (2) the percentage obtained by dividing (a) the expense that has actually been incurred by the Contractor on account of that portion of the Work for which the Contractor has made or intends to make actual payment prior to the next Application for Payment by (b) the share of the Guaranteed Maximum Price allocated to that portion of the Work in the schedule of values.

12.1.7 Subject to other provisions of the Contract Documents, the amount of each progress payment shall be computed as follows:

- **.1** take that portion of the Guaranteed Maximum Price properly allocable to completed Work as determined by multiplying the percentage of completion of each portion of the Work by the share of the Guaranteed Maximum Price allocated to that portion of the Work in the schedule of values. Pending final determination of cost to the Owner of changes in the Work, amounts not in dispute shall be included as provided in Subparagraph 7.3.8 of AIA Document A201-1997;
- **.2** add that portion of the Guaranteed Maximum Price properly allocable to materials and equipment delivered and suitably stored at the site for subsequent incorporation in the Work, or if approved in advance by the Owner, suitably stored off the site at a location agreed upon in writing;
- **.3** add the Contractor's Fee, less retainage of five percent (5.0%). The Contractor's Fee shall be computed upon the Cost of the Work described in the two preceding Clauses at the rate stated in Subparagraph 5.1.2 or, if the Contractor's Fee is stated as a fixed sum in that Subparagraph, shall be an amount that bears the same ratio to that fixed-sum fee as the Cost of the Work in the two preceding Clauses bears to a reasonable estimate of the probable Cost of the Work upon its completion;
- **.4** subtract the aggregate of previous payments made by the Owner;
- **.5** subtract the shortfall, if any, indicated by the Contractor in the documentation required by Paragraph 12.1.4 to substantiate prior Applications for Payment, or resulting from errors subsequently discovered by the Owner's accountants in such documentation; and
- **.6** subtract amounts, if any, for which the Architect has withheld or nullified a Certificate for Payment as provided in Paragraph 9.5 of AIA Document A201-1997.

The American Institute of Architects
1735 New York Avenue, N.W.
Washington, D.C. 20006-5292

12.1.8 Except with the Owner's prior approval, payments to Subcontractors shall be subject to retainage of not less than *five* percent (*5.0* %). The Owner and the Contractor shall agree upon a mutually acceptable procedure for review and approval of payments and retention for Subcontractors.

12.1.9 In taking action on the Contractor's Applications for Payment, the Architect shall be entitled to rely on the accuracy and completeness of the information furnished by the Contractor and shall not be deemed to represent that the Architect has made a detailed examination, audit or arithmetic verification of the documentation submitted in accordance with Subparagraph 12.1.4 or other supporting data; that the Architect has made exhaustive or continuous on-site inspections or that the Architect has made examinations to ascertain how or for what purposes the Contractor has used amounts previously paid on account of the Contract. Such examinations, audits and verifications, if required by the Owner, will be performed by the Owner's accountants acting in the sole interest of the Owner.

12.2 FINAL PAYMENT

12.2.1 Final payment, constituting the entire unpaid balance of the Contract Sum, shall be made by the Owner to the Contractor when:

.1 the Contractor has fully performed the Contract except for the Contractor's responsibility to correct Work as provided in Subparagraph 12.2.2 of AIA Document A201-1997, and to satisfy other requirements, if any, which extend beyond final payment; and

.2 a final Certificate for Payment has been issued by the Architect.

12.2.2 The Owner's final payment to the Contractor shall be made no later than 30 days after the issuance of the Architect's final Certificate for Payment, or as follows: *Final release of retention is predicated upon completion of all close-out activities including submission of full and unconditional lien releases from the general contractor and all second tier subcontractors and suppliers.*

12.2.3 The Owner's accountants will review and report in writing on the Contractor's final accounting within 30 days after delivery of the final accounting to the Architect by the Contractor. Based upon such Cost of the Work as the Owner's accountants report to be substantiated by the Contractor's final accounting, and provided the other conditions of Subparagraph 12.2.1 have been met, the Architect will, within seven days after receipt of the written report of the Owner's accountants, either issue to the Owner a final Certificate for Payment with a copy to the Contractor, or notify the Contractor and Owner in writing of the Architect's reasons for withholding a certificate as provided in Subparagraph 9.5.1 of the AIA Document A201-1997. The time periods stated in this Subparagraph 12.2.3 supersede those stated in Subparagraph 9.4.1 of the AIA Document A201-1997.

12.2.4 If the Owner's accountants report the Cost of the Work as substantiated by the Contractor's final accounting to be less than claimed by the Contractor, the Contractor shall be entitled to demand arbitration of the disputed amount without a further decision of the Architect. Such demand for arbitration shall be made by the Contractor within 30 days after the Contractor's receipt of a copy of the Architect's final Certificate for Payment; failure to demand arbitration within this 30-day period shall result in the substantiated amount reported by the Owner's accountants becoming binding on the Contractor. Pending a final resolution by arbitration, the Owner shall pay the Contractor the amount certified in the Architect's final Certificate for Payment.

12.2.5 If, subsequent to final payment and at the Owner's request, the Contractor incurs costs described in Article 7 and not excluded by Article 8 to correct defective or nonconforming Work, the Owner shall reimburse the Contractor such costs and the Contractor's Fee applicable thereto on the same basis as if such costs had been incurred prior to final payment, but not in excess of the Guaranteed Maximum Price. If the Contractor has participated in savings as provided in Paragraph 5.2, the amount of such savings shall be recalculated and appropriate credit given to the Owner in determining the net amount to be paid by the Owner to the Contractor.

ARTICLE 13 TERMINATION OR SUSPENSION

13.1 The Contract may be terminated by the Contractor, or by the Owner for convenience, as provided in Article 14 of AIA Document A201-1997. However, the amount to be paid to the Contractor under Subparagraph 14.1.3 of AIA Document A201-1997 shall not exceed the amount the Contractor would be entitled to receive under Paragraph 13.2 below, except that the Contractor's Fee shall be calculated as if the Work had been fully completed by the Contractor, including a reasonable estimate of the Cost of the Work for Work not actually completed.

13.2 The Contract may be terminated by the Owner for cause as provided in Article 14 of AIA Document A201-1997. The amount, if any, to be paid to the Contractor under Subparagraph 14.2.4 of AIA Document A201-1997 shall not cause the Guaranteed Maximum Price to be exceeded, nor shall it exceed an amount calculated as follows:

13.2.1 Take the Cost of the Work incurred by the Contractor to the date of termination;

13.2.2 Add the Contractor's Fee computed upon the Cost of the Work to the date of termination at the rate stated in Subparagraph 5.1.2 or, if the Contractor's Fee is stated as a fixed sum in that Subparagraph, an amount that bears the same ratio to that fixed-sum Fee as the Cost of the Work at the time of termination bears to a reasonable estimate of the probable Cost of the Work upon its completion; and

13.2.3 Subtract the aggregate of previous payments made by the Owner.

13.3 The Owner shall also pay the Contractor fair compensation, either by purchase or rental at the election of the Owner, for any equipment owned by the Contractor that the Owner elects to retain and that is not otherwise included in the Cost of the Work under Subparagraph 13.2.1. To the extent that the Owner elects to take legal assignment of subcontracts and purchase orders (including rental agreements), the Contractor shall, as a condition of receiving the payments referred to in this Article 13, execute and deliver all such papers and take all such steps, including the legal assignment of such subcontracts and other contractual rights of the Contractor, as the Owner may require for the purpose of fully vesting in the Owner the rights and benefits of the Contractor under such subcontracts or purchase orders.

13.4 The Work may be suspended by the Owner as provided in Article 14 of AIA Document A201-1997; in such case, the Guaranteed Maximum Price and Contract Time shall be increased as provided in Subparagraph 14.3.2 of AIA Document A201-1997 except that the term "profit" shall be understood to mean the Contractor's Fee as described in Subparagraphs 5.1.2 and Paragraph 6.4 of this Agreement.

ARTICLE 14 MISCELLANEOUS PROVISIONS

14.1 Where reference is made in this Agreement to a provision AIA Document A201-1997 or another Contract Document, the reference refers to that provision as amended or supplemented by other provisions of the Contract Documents.

The American Institute of Architects
1735 New York Avenue, N.W.
Washington, D.C. 20006-5292

14.2 Payments due and unpaid under the Contract shall bear interest from the date payment is due at the rate stated below, or in the absence thereof, at the legal rate prevailing from time to time at the place where the Project is located.
(Insert rate of interest agreed upon, if any.) Two percent above the prime rate as established by the Juneau Metropolitan Bank.

(Usury laws and requirements under the Federal Truth in Lending Act, similar state and local consumer credit laws and other regulations at the Owner's and Contractor's principal places of business, the location of the Project and elsewhere may affect the validity of this provision. Legal advice should be obtained with respect to deletions or modifications, and also regarding requirements such as written disclosures or waivers.)

14.3 The Owner's representative is:
(Name, address and other information.)

Robert Smith
Huna Totem Corporation
9309 Glacier Highway
Juneau, Alaska 99801

14.4 The Contractor's representative is:
(Name, address and other information.)

Sam Peters
Northwestern Construction Company
1242 First Avenue
Cascade, Washington 98202

14.5 Neither the Owner's nor the Contractor's representative shall be changed without ten days' written notice to the other party.

14.6 Other provisions:

Not applicable

ARTICLE 15 ENUMERATION OF CONTRACT DOCUMENTS

15.1 The Contract Documents, except for Modifications issued after execution of this Agreement, are enumerated as follows:

15.1.1 The Agreement is this executed 1997 edition of the Standard Form of Agreement Between Owner and Contractor, AIA Document A111-1997.

15.1.2 The General Conditions are the 1997 edition of the General Conditions of the Contract for Construction, AIA Document A201-1997.

AIA DOCUMENT A111-1997
OWNER-CONTRACTOR AGREEMENT

The American Institute of Architects
1735 New York Avenue, N.W.
Washington, D.C. 20006-5292

15.1.3 The Supplementary and other Conditions of the Contract are those contained in the Project Manual dated *August 18, 1997* , and are as follows:

Document	Title	Pages
See attached document, Exhibit C, dated August 15, 2000		

15.1.4 The Specifications are those contained in the Project Manual dated as in Subparagraph 15.1.3, and are as follows:
(Either list the Specifications here or refer to an exhibit attached to this Agreement.)

Section	Title	Pages
See attached document, Exhibit C, dated August 15, 2000		

15.1.5 The Drawings are as follows, and are dated unless a different date is shown below:
(Either list the Drawings here or refer to an exhibit attached to this Agreement.)

Number	Title	Date
See attached document, Exhibit C, dated August 15, 2000		

The American Institute of Architects
1735 New York Avenue, N.W.
Washington, D.C. 20006-5292

15.1.6 The Addenda, if any, are as follows:

Number	Date	Pages
Not applicable		

Portions of Addenda relating to bidding requirements are not part of the Contract Documents unless the bidding requirements are also enumerated in this Article 15.

15.1.7 Other Documents, if any, forming part of the Contract Documents are as follows:
(List here any additional documents, such as a list of alternates that are intended to form part of the Contract Documents. AIA Document A201-1997 provides that bidding requirements such as advertisement or invitation to bid, Instructions to Bidders, sample forms and the Contractor's bid are not part of the Contract Documents unless enumerated in this Agreement. They should be listed here only if intended to be part of the Contract Documents.)

The following Exhibits are attached to this agreement and by this reference are made a part hereof:

Exhibit A, Project Schedule, dated August 15, 2000
Exhibit B, Summary Estimate, dated August 15, 2000
Exhibit C, Document List, dated August 15, 2000

ARTICLE 16 INSURANCE AND BONDS

(List required limits of liability for insurance and bonds. AIA Document A201-1997 gives other specific requirements for insurance and bonds.)

This Agreement is entered into as of the day and year first written above and is executed in at least three original copies, of which one is to be delivered to the Contractor, one to the Architect for use in the administration of the Contract, and the remainder to the Owner.

Robert Smith

OWNER *(Signature)*

Robert Smith
Chief Executive Officer

(Printed name and title)

Sam Peters

CONTRACTOR *(Signature)*

Sam Peters
Vice President

(Printed name and title)

CAUTION: *You should sign an original AIA document or a licensed reproduction. Originals contain the AIA logo printed in red; licensed reproductions are those produced in accordance with the Instructions to this document.*

The American Institute of Architects
1735 New York Avenue, N.W.
Washington, D.C. 20006-5292

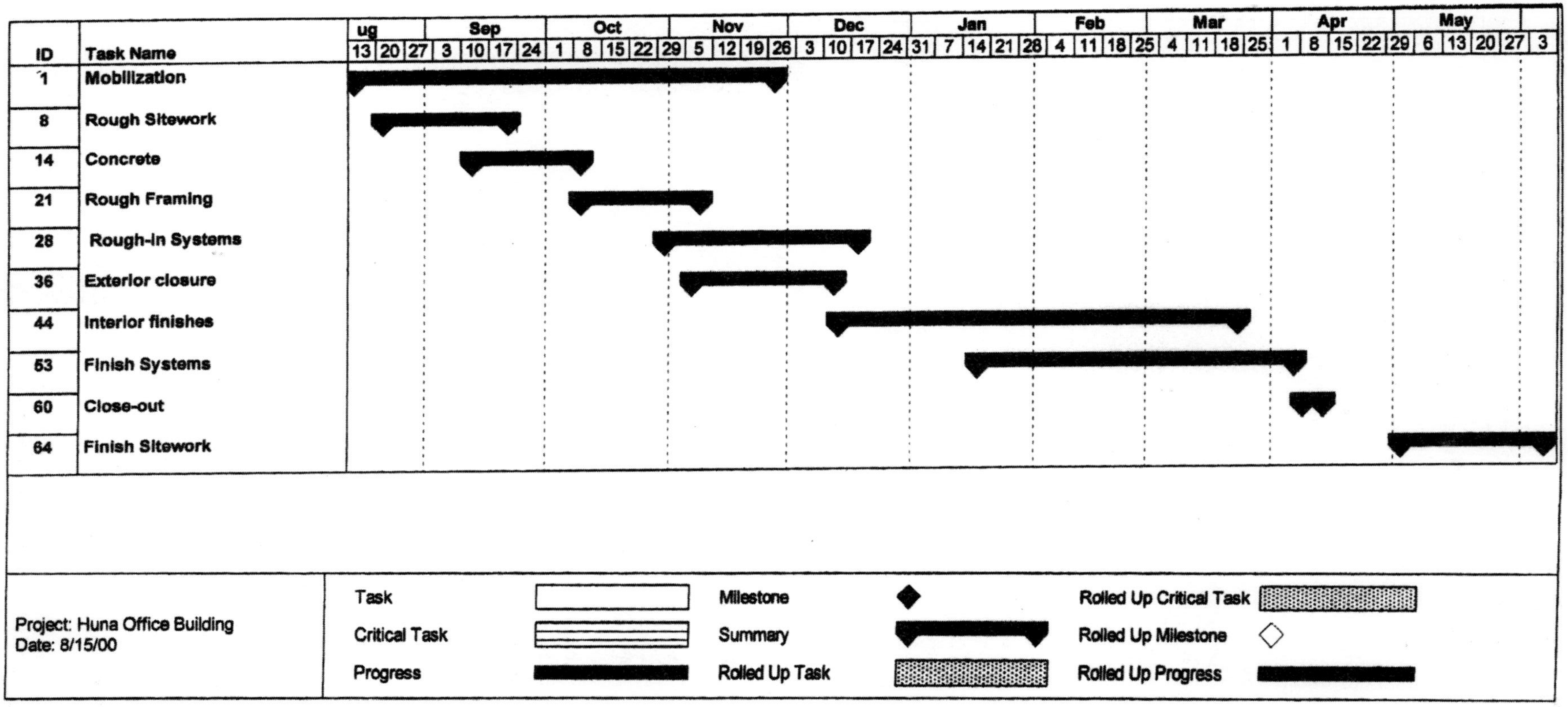

Project Schedule, Exhibit A

NORTHWEST CONSTRUCTION COMPANY
1242 First Avenue, Cascade, Washington 98202
1242 First Avenue, Cascade, Washington 98202

Huna Office Building
Summary Estimate, Exhibit B
8/15/00

Line Item	Description	Value
1	General Conditions	$205,000
2.1	Earthwork and Utilities	$124,000
2.2	Paving	$24,000
2.3	Miscellaneous Site	$48,000
	Subtotal Site:	$196,000
3.1	Reinforcement	$13,000
3.2	Foundations	$42,000
3.3	Walls and Slabs	$82,000
	Subtotal Concrete:	$137,000
4	Masonry	$0
5	Steel	$6,000
6.1	Rough Carpentry and Siding	$384,000
6.2	Finish Carpentry	$85,000
	Subtotal Carpentry:	$469,000
7.1	Insulation	$19,000
7.2	Roofing	$59,000
7.3	Gutters	$3,000
	Subtotal Div. 7:	$81,000
8.1	Doors & Frames	$29,000
8.2	Glazing	$19,000
8.3	Door Hardware	$15,000
	Subtotal Div. 8:	$63,000
9.1	Drywall	$25,000
9.2	Painting	$28,000
9.3	Acoustical Ceilings	$8,000
9.4	Carpet	$23,000
9.5	Balance of Floorcovering	$17,000
	Subtotal Finishes:	$101,000
10	Specialties	$11,000
11, 12, 13	Equipment	$0
14	Elevator	$30,000
15.1	Plumbing	$49,000
15.2	Fire Protection	$29,000
15.3	HVAC	$145,000
15.4	Controls	$35,000
	Subtotal Mechanical	$258,000
16	Electrical	$120,000
	Subtotal Job Costs:	$1,677,000
	Fee	$83,000
	Total	$1,760,000

NORTHWEST CONSTRUCTION COMPANY
1242 First Avenue, Cascade, Washington 98202
(206) 239-1422

Huna Office Building
Document List, Exhibit C
8/15/00
Page 1 of 2

Document Number	Description	Revision Number	Date
	ARCHITECTURAL DRAWINGS:		
A001	Cover and Administrative Information	1	8/18/97
A102	Site Section	1	8/18/97
A200	Door and Finish Schedules	1	8/18/97
A201	First Floor Plan	1	8/18/97
A202	Second Floor Plan	1	8/18/97
A203	Mechanical Penthouse Plan	1	8/18/97
A204	Roof Plan	1	8/18/97
A301	Exterior Elevations	1	8/18/97
A302	Exterior Elevations	1	8/18/97
A303	Building Sections	1	8/18/97
A304	Building Sections	1	8/18/97
A305	Building Sections	1	8/18/97
A306	Wall Sections	1	8/18/97
A307	Wall Sections	1	8/18/97
A401	Toilet Rooms	1	8/18/97
A501	Interior Elevations	1	8/18/97
A502	Interior Elevations	1	8/18/97
A601	First Floor Reflected Ceiling Plan	1	8/18/97
A602	Second Floor Reflected Ceiling Plan	1	8/18/97
A701	Elevator Section	1	8/18/97
A801	Exterior Details	1	8/18/97
A901	Interior Details	1	8/18/97
	CIVIL DRAWINGS:		
C1	Existing Site Conditions	1	7/23/97
C2	Soil Test Logs	1	7/23/97
C3	Site Grading Plan	2	7/29/97
C4	Construction Details	2	7/29/97
C5	Construction Details	2	7/29/97
C6	Site Cross Sections	2	7/30/98
C7	Striping and Signing Plan	2	7/29/97
C8	Erosion Control Plan	2	7/29/97
	LANDSCAPE DRAWINGS:		
L101	Landscape Plan	3	2/12/98
L102	Planting Plan	3	2/12/98
L103	Planting Schedule	3	2/12/98

NORTHWEST CONSTRUCTION COMPANY
1242 First Avenue, Cascade, Washington 98202
(206) 239-1422

Huna Office Building
Document List, Exhibit C
8/15/00
Page 2 of 2

Document Number	Description	Revision Number	Date
	STRUCTURAL DRAWINGS:		
S1	General Notes	2	8/18/97
S2	Foundation Plan	1	8/1/97
S3	First Floor Framing Plan	1	8/18/97
S4	Roof Framing Plan	1	8/18/97
S5	Foundation Details	2	8/18/97
S6	Structural Framing Details	1	8/18/97
S7	Structural Framing Details	2	8/18/97
	MECHANICAL DRAWINGS:		
M0.1	Schedules and Legend	NA	8/18/97
M1.1	Plumbing Plans	NA	8/18/97
M2.1	Heating and Ventilation Plans	NA	8/18/97
M3.1	Enlarged Plans	NA	8/18/97
M3.2	Enlarged Plans	NA	8/18/97
M4.1	Details	NA	8/18/97
	ELECTRICAL DRAWINGS:		
E0.1	Legend and Calculations	0	8/18/97
E0.2	Electrical Site Plan	0	8/18/97
E1.1	Electrical Lighting Plans	0	8/18/97
E2.1	Electrical Power Plans	0	8/18/97
E3.1	Electrical Signal Plans	0	8/18/97
E4.1	Panel Schedules	0	8/18/97
	MISCELLANEOUS DOCUMENTS:		
	Technical Specifications Book	1	8/18/97
	Soils Report	NA	5/15/97

APPENDIX E

Contract General Conditions for Huna Office Building (AIA A201–1997)

1997 EDITION

AIA DOCUMENT A201-1997

General Conditions of the Contract for Construction

This document has important legal consequences. Consultation with an attorney is encouraged with respect to its completion or modification

This document has been approved and endorsed by The Associated General Contractors of America.

TABLE OF ARTICLES

©1997 AIA®
AIA DOCUMENT A201-1997
GENERAL CONDITIONS OF THE CONTRACT FOR CONSTRUCTION

The American Institute of Architects
1735 New York Avenue, N.W.
Washington, D.C. 20006-5292

INDEX

AIA DOCUMENT A201-1997
GENERAL CONDITIONS OF THE CONTRACT FOR CONSTRUCTION

The American Institute of Architects
1735 New York Avenue, N.W.
Washington, D.C. 20006-5292

AIA DOCUMENT A201-1997
GENERAL CONDITIONS OF THE CONTRACT FOR CONSTRUCTION

The American Institute of Architects
1735 New York Avenue, N.W.
Washington, D.C. 20006-5292

©1997 AIA®
AIA DOCUMENT A201-1997
GENERAL CONDITIONS OF THE CONTRACT FOR CONSTRUCTION

The American Institute of Architects
1735 New York Avenue, N.W.
Washington, D.C. 20006-5292

AIA DOCUMENT A201-1997
GENERAL CONDITIONS OF THE CONTRACT FOR CONSTRUCTION

The American Institute of Architects
1735 New York Avenue, N.W.
Washington, D.C. 20006-5292

The American Institute of Architects
1735 New York Avenue, N.W.
Washington, D.C. 20006-5292

ARTICLE 1 GENERAL PROVISIONS

1.1 BASIC DEFINITIONS

1.1.1 THE CONTRACT DOCUMENTS

The Contract Documents consist of the Agreement between Owner and Contractor (hereinafter the Agreement), Conditions of the Contract (General, Supplementary and other Conditions), Drawings, Specifications, Addenda issued prior to execution of the Contract, other documents listed in the Agreement and Modifications issued after execution of the Contract. A Modification is (1) a written amendment to the Contract signed by both parties, (2) a Change Order, (3) a Construction Change Directive or (4) a written order for a minor change in the Work issued by the Architect. Unless specifically enumerated in the Agreement, the Contract Documents do not include other documents such as bidding requirements (advertisement or invitation to bid, Instructions to Bidders, sample forms, the Contractor's bid or portions of Addenda relating to bidding requirements).

1.1.2 THE CONTRACT

The Contract Documents form the Contract for Construction. The Contract represents the entire and integrated agreement between the parties hereto and supersedes prior negotiations, representations or agreements, either written or oral. The Contract may be amended or modified only by a Modification. The Contract Documents shall not be construed to create a contractual relationship of any kind (1) between the Architect and Contractor, (2) between the Owner and a Subcontractor or Sub-subcontractor, (3) between the Owner and Architect or (4) between any persons or entities other than the Owner and Contractor. The Architect shall, however, be entitled to performance and enforcement of obligations under the Contract intended to facilitate performance of the Architect's duties.

1.1.3 THE WORK

The term "Work" means the construction and services required by the Contract Documents, whether completed or partially completed, and includes all other labor, materials, equipment and services provided or to be provided by the Contractor to fulfill the Contractor's obligations. The Work may constitute the whole or a part of the Project.

1.1.4 THE PROJECT

The Project is the total construction of which the Work performed under the Contract Documents may be the whole or a part and which may include construction by the Owner or by separate contractors.

1.1.5 THE DRAWINGS

The Drawings are the graphic and pictorial portions of the Contract Documents showing the design, location and dimensions of the Work, generally including plans, elevations, sections, details, schedules and diagrams.

1.1.6 THE SPECIFICATIONS

The Specifications are that portion of the Contract Documents consisting of the written requirements for materials, equipment, systems, standards and workmanship for the Work, and performance of related services.

1.1.7 THE PROJECT MANUAL

The Project Manual is a volume assembled for the Work which may include the bidding requirements, sample forms, Conditions of the Contract and Specifications.

1.2 CORRELATION AND INTENT OF THE CONTRACT DOCUMENTS

1.2.1 The intent of the Contract Documents is to include all items necessary for the proper execution and completion of the Work by the Contractor. The Contract Documents are

The American Institute of Architects
1735 New York Avenue, N.W.
Washington, D.C. 20006-5292

complementary, and what is required by one shall be as binding as if required by all; performance by the Contractor shall be required only to the extent consistent with the Contract Documents and reasonably inferable from them as being necessary to produce the indicated results.

1.2.2 Organization of the Specifications into divisions, sections and articles, and arrangement of Drawings shall not control the Contractor in dividing the Work among Subcontractors or in establishing the extent of Work to be performed by any trade.

1.2.3 Unless otherwise stated in the Contract Documents, words which have well-known technical or construction industry meanings are used in the Contract Documents in accordance with such recognized meanings.

1.3 CAPITALIZATION

1.3.1 Terms capitalized in these General Conditions include those which are (1) specifically defined, (2) the titles of numbered articles and identified references to Paragraphs, Subparagraphs and Clauses in the document or (3) the titles of other documents published by the American Institute of Architects.

1.4 INTERPRETATION

1.4.1 In the interest of brevity the Contract Documents frequently omit modifying words such as "all" and "any" and articles such as "the" and "an," but the fact that a modifier or an article is absent from one statement and appears in another is not intended to affect the interpretation of either statement.

1.5 EXECUTION OF CONTRACT DOCUMENTS

1.5.1 The Contract Documents shall be signed by the Owner and Contractor. If either the Owner or Contractor or both do not sign all the Contract Documents, the Architect shall identify such unsigned Documents upon request.

1.5.2 Execution of the Contract by the Contractor is a representation that the Contractor has visited the site, become generally familiar with local conditions under which the Work is to be performed and correlated personal observations with requirements of the Contract Documents.

1.6 OWNERSHIP AND USE OF DRAWINGS, SPECIFICATIONS AND OTHER INSTRUMENTS OF SERVICE

1.6.1 The Drawings, Specifications and other documents, including those in electronic form, prepared by the Architect and the Architect's consultants are Instruments of Service through which the Work to be executed by the Contractor is described. The Contractor may retain one record set. Neither the Contractor nor any Subcontractor, Sub-subcontractor or material or equipment supplier shall own or claim a copyright in the Drawings, Specifications and other documents prepared by the Architect or the Architect's consultants, and unless otherwise indicated the Architect and the Architect's consultants shall be deemed the authors of them and will retain all common law, statutory and other reserved rights, in addition to the copyrights. All copies of Instruments of Service, except the Contractor's record set, shall be returned or suitably accounted for to the Architect, on request, upon completion of the Work. The Drawings, Specifications and other documents prepared by the Architect and the Architect's consultants, and copies thereof furnished to the Contractor, are for use solely with respect to this Project. They are not to be used by the Contractor or any Subcontractor, Sub-subcontractor or material or equipment supplier on other projects or for additions to this Project outside the scope of the Work without the specific written consent of the Owner, Architect and the Architect's consultants. The Contractor, Subcontractors, Sub-subcontractors and material or equipment suppliers are authorized to use and reproduce applicable portions of the Drawings, Specifications and other documents prepared by the Architect and the Architect's consultants appropriate to and for use in the execution of their Work under the Contract Documents. All copies made under this authorization shall bear the statutory copyright notice, if any, shown on the Drawings, Specifications and other documents prepared by the Architect and the Architect's consultants. Submittal or distribution to meet official regulatory requirements or for other purposes in connection with this Project is not to be construed as publication in derogation of the Architect's or Architect's consultants' copyrights or other reserved rights.

ARTICLE 2 OWNER

2.1 GENERAL

2.1.1 The Owner is the person or entity identified as such in the Agreement and is referred to throughout the Contract Documents as if singular in number. The Owner shall designate in writing a representative who shall have express authority to bind the Owner with respect to all matters requiring the Owner's approval or authorization. Except as otherwise provided in Subparagraph 4.2.1, the Architect does not have such authority. The term "Owner" means the Owner or the Owner's authorized representative.

2.1.2 The Owner shall furnish to the Contractor within fifteen days after receipt of a written request, information necessary and relevant for the Contractor to evaluate, give notice of or enforce mechanic's lien rights. Such information shall include a correct statement of the record legal title to the property on which the Project is located, usually referred to as the site, and the Owner's interest therein.

2.2 INFORMATION AND SERVICES REQUIRED OF THE OWNER

2.2.1 The Owner shall, at the written request of the Contractor, prior to commencement of the Work and thereafter, furnish to the Contractor reasonable evidence that financial arrangements have been made to fulfill the Owner's obligations under the Contract. Furnishing of such evidence shall be a condition precedent to commencement or continuation of the Work. After such evidence has been furnished, the Owner shall not materially vary such financial arrangements without prior notice to the Contractor.

2.2.2 Except for permits and fees, including those required under Subparagraph 3.7.1, which are the responsibility of the Contractor under the Contract Documents, the Owner shall secure and pay for necessary approvals, easements, assessments and charges required for construction, use or occupancy of permanent structures or for permanent changes in existing facilities.

2.2.3 The Owner shall furnish surveys describing physical characteristics, legal limitations and utility locations for the site of the Project, and a legal description of the site. The Contractor shall be entitled to rely on the accuracy of information furnished by the Owner but shall exercise proper precautions relating to the safe performance of the Work.

2.2.4 Information or services required of the Owner by the Contract Documents shall be furnished by the Owner with reasonable promptness. Any other information or services relevant to the Contractor's performance of the Work under the Owner's control shall be furnished by the Owner after receipt from the Contractor of a written request for such information or services.

2.2.5 Unless otherwise provided in the Contract Documents, the Contractor will be furnished, free of charge, such copies of Drawings and Project Manuals as are reasonably necessary for execution of the Work.

2.3 OWNER'S RIGHT TO STOP THE WORK

2.3.1 If the Contractor fails to correct Work which is not in accordance with the requirements of the Contract Documents as required by Paragraph 12.2 or persistently fails to carry out Work in

The American Institute of Architects
1735 New York Avenue, N.W.
Washington, D.C. 20006-5292

accordance with the Contract Documents, the Owner may issue a written order to the Contractor to stop the Work, or any portion thereof, until the cause for such order has been eliminated; however, the right of the Owner to stop the Work shall not give rise to a duty on the part of the Owner to exercise this right for the benefit of the Contractor or any other person or entity, except to the extent required by Subparagraph 6.1.3.

2.4 OWNER'S RIGHT TO CARRY OUT THE WORK

2.4.1 If the Contractor defaults or neglects to carry out the Work in accordance with the Contract Documents and fails within a seven-day period after receipt of written notice from the Owner to commence and continue correction of such default or neglect with diligence and promptness, the Owner may after such seven-day period give the Contractor a second written notice to correct such deficiencies within a three-day period. If the Contractor within such three-day period after receipt of such second notice fails to commence and continue to correct any deficiencies, the Owner may, without prejudice to other remedies the Owner may have, correct such deficiencies. In such case an appropriate Change Order shall be issued deducting from payments then or thereafter due the Contractor the reasonable cost of correcting such deficiencies, including Owner's expenses and compensation for the Architect's additional services made necessary by such default, neglect or failure. Such action by the Owner and amounts charged to the Contractor are both subject to prior approval of the Architect. If payments then or thereafter due the Contractor are not sufficient to cover such amounts, the Contractor shall pay the difference to the Owner.

ARTICLE 3 CONTRACTOR

3.1 GENERAL

3.1.1 The Contractor is the person or entity identified as such in the Agreement and is referred to throughout the Contract Documents as if singular in number. The term "Contractor" means the Contractor or the Contractor's authorized representative.

3.1.2 The Contractor shall perform the Work in accordance with the Contract Documents.

3.1.3 The Contractor shall not be relieved of obligations to perform the Work in accordance with the Contract Documents either by activities or duties of the Architect in the Architect's administration of the Contract, or by tests, inspections or approvals required or performed by persons other than the Contractor.

3.2 REVIEW OF CONTRACT DOCUMENTS AND FIELD CONDITIONS BY CONTRACTOR

3.2.1 Since the Contract Documents are complementary, before starting each portion of the Work, the Contractor shall carefully study and compare the various Drawings and other Contract Documents relative to that portion of the Work, as well as the information furnished by the Owner pursuant to Subparagraph 2.2.3, shall take field measurements of any existing conditions related to that portion of the Work and shall observe any conditions at the site affecting it. These obligations are for the purpose of facilitating construction by the Contractor and are not for the purpose of discovering errors, omissions, or inconsistencies in the Contract Documents; however, any errors, inconsistencies or omissions discovered by the Contractor shall be reported promptly to the Architect as a request for information in such form as the Architect may require.

3.2.2 Any design errors or omissions noted by the Contractor during this review shall be reported promptly to the Architect, but it is recognized that the Contractor's review is made in the Contractor's capacity as a contractor and not as a licensed design professional unless otherwise specifically provided in the Contract Documents. The Contractor is not required to ascertain that the Contract Documents are in accordance with applicable laws, statutes, ordinances, building codes, and rules and regulations, but any nonconformity discovered by or made known to the Contractor shall be reported promptly to the Architect.

The American Institute
of Architects
1735 New York Avenue, N.W.
Washington, D.C. 20006-5292

3.2.3 If the Contractor believes that additional cost or time is involved because of clarifications or instructions issued by the Architect in response to the Contractor's notices or requests for information pursuant to Subparagraphs 3.2.1 and 3.2.2, the Contractor shall make Claims as provided in Subparagraphs 4.3.6 and 4.3.7. If the Contractor fails to perform the obligations of Subparagraphs 3.2.1 and 3.2.2, the Contractor shall pay such costs and damages to the Owner as would have been avoided if the Contractor had performed such obligations. The Contractor shall not be liable to the Owner or Architect for damages resulting from errors, inconsistencies or omissions in the Contract Documents or for differences between field measurements or conditions and the Contract Documents unless the Contractor recognized such error, inconsistency, omission or difference and knowingly failed to report it to the Architect.

3.3 SUPERVISION AND CONSTRUCTION PROCEDURES

3.3.1 The Contractor shall supervise and direct the Work, using the Contractor's best skill and attention. The Contractor shall be solely responsible for and have control over construction means, methods, techniques, sequences and procedures and for coordinating all portions of the Work under the Contract, unless the Contract Documents give other specific instructions concerning these matters. If the Contract Documents give specific instructions concerning construction means, methods, techniques, sequences or procedures, the Contractor shall evaluate the jobsite safety thereof and, except as stated below, shall be fully and solely responsible for the jobsite safety of such means, methods, techniques, sequences or procedures. If the Contractor determines that such means, methods, techniques, sequences or procedures may not be safe, the Contractor shall give timely written notice to the Owner and Architect and shall not proceed with that portion of the Work without further written instructions from the Architect. If the Contractor is then instructed to proceed with the required means, methods, techniques, sequences or procedures without acceptance of changes proposed by the Contractor, the Owner shall be solely responsible for any resulting loss or damage.

3.3.2 The Contractor shall be responsible to the Owner for acts and omissions of the Contractor's employees, Subcontractors and their agents and employees, and other persons or entities performing portions of the Work for or on behalf of the Contractor or any of its Subcontractors.

3.3.3 The Contractor shall be responsible for inspection of portions of Work already performed to determine that such portions are in proper condition to receive subsequent Work.

3.4 LABOR AND MATERIALS

3.4.1 Unless otherwise provided in the Contract Documents, the Contractor shall provide and pay for labor, materials, equipment, tools, construction equipment and machinery, water, heat, utilities, transportation, and other facilities and services necessary for proper execution and completion of the Work, whether temporary or permanent and whether or not incorporated or to be incorporated in the Work.

3.4.2 The Contractor may make substitutions only with the consent of the Owner, after evaluation by the Architect and in accordance with a Change Order.

3.4.3 The Contractor shall enforce strict discipline and good order among the Contractor's employees and other persons carrying out the Contract. The Contractor shall not permit employment of unfit persons or persons not skilled in tasks assigned to them.

3.5 WARRANTY

3.5.1 The Contractor warrants to the Owner and Architect that materials and equipment furnished under the Contract will be of good quality and new unless otherwise required or permitted by the Contract Documents, that the Work will be free from defects not inherent in the quality required or permitted, and that the Work will conform to the requirements of the Contract

Documents. Work not conforming to these requirements, including substitutions not properly approved and authorized, may be considered defective. The Contractor's warranty excludes remedy for damage or defect caused by abuse, modifications not executed by the Contractor, improper or insufficient maintenance, improper operation, or normal wear and tear and normal usage. If required by the Architect, the Contractor shall furnish satisfactory evidence as to the kind and quality of materials and equipment.

3.6 TAXES

3.6.1 The Contractor shall pay sales, consumer, use and similar taxes for the Work provided by the Contractor which are legally enacted when bids are received or negotiations concluded, whether or not yet effective or merely scheduled to go into effect.

3.7 PERMITS, FEES AND NOTICES

3.7.1 Unless otherwise provided in the Contract Documents, the Contractor shall secure and pay for the building permit and other permits and governmental fees, licenses and inspections necessary for proper execution and completion of the Work which are customarily secured after execution of the Contract and which are legally required when bids are received or negotiations concluded.

3.7.2 The Contractor shall comply with and give notices required by laws, ordinances, rules, regulations and lawful orders of public authorities applicable to performance of the Work.

3.7.3 It is not the Contractor's responsibility to ascertain that the Contract Documents are in accordance with applicable laws, statutes, ordinances, building codes, and rules and regulations. However, if the Contractor observes that portions of the Contract Documents are at variance therewith, the Contractor shall promptly notify the Architect and Owner in writing, and necessary changes shall be accomplished by appropriate Modification.

3.7.4 If the Contractor performs Work knowing it to be contrary to laws, statutes, ordinances, building codes, and rules and regulations without such notice to the Architect and Owner, the Contractor shall assume appropriate responsibility for such Work and shall bear the costs attributable to correction.

3.8 ALLOWANCES

3.8.1 The Contractor shall include in the Contract Sum all allowances stated in the Contract Documents. Items covered by allowances shall be supplied for such amounts and by such persons or entities as the Owner may direct, but the Contractor shall not be required to employ persons or entities to whom the Contractor has reasonable objection.

3.8.2 Unless otherwise provided in the Contract Documents:

.1 allowances shall cover the cost to the Contractor of materials and equipment delivered at the site and all required taxes, less applicable trade discounts;

.2 Contractor's costs for unloading and handling at the site, labor, installation costs, overhead, profit and other expenses contemplated for stated allowance amounts shall be included in the Contract Sum but not in the allowances;

.3 whenever costs are more than or less than allowances, the Contract Sum shall be adjusted accordingly by Change Order. The amount of the Change Order shall reflect (1) the difference between actual costs and the allowances under Clause 3.8.2.1 and (2) changes in Contractor's costs under Clause 3.8.2.2.

3.8.3 Materials and equipment under an allowance shall be selected by the Owner in sufficient time to avoid delay in the Work.

The American Institute of Architects
1735 New York Avenue, N.W.
Washington, D.C. 20006-5292

3.9 SUPERINTENDENT

3.9.1 The Contractor shall employ a competent superintendent and necessary assistants who shall be in attendance at the Project site during performance of the Work. The superintendent shall represent the Contractor, and communications given to the superintendent shall be as binding as if given to the Contractor. Important communications shall be confirmed in writing. Other communications shall be similarly confirmed on written request in each case.

3.10 CONTRACTOR'S CONSTRUCTION SCHEDULES

3.10.1 The Contractor, promptly after being awarded the Contract, shall prepare and submit for the Owner's and Architect's information a Contractor's construction schedule for the Work. The schedule shall not exceed time limits current under the Contract Documents, shall be revised at appropriate intervals as required by the conditions of the Work and Project, shall be related to the entire Project to the extent required by the Contract Documents, and shall provide for expeditious and practicable execution of the Work.

3.10.2 The Contractor shall prepare and keep current, for the Architect's approval, a schedule of submittals which is coordinated with the Contractor's construction schedule and allows the Architect reasonable time to review submittals.

3.10.3 The Contractor shall perform the Work in general accordance with the most recent schedules submitted to the Owner and Architect.

3.11 DOCUMENTS AND SAMPLES AT THE SITE

3.11.1 The Contractor shall maintain at the site for the Owner one record copy of the Drawings, Specifications, Addenda, Change Orders and other Modifications, in good order and marked currently to record field changes and selections made during construction, and one record copy of approved Shop Drawings, Product Data, Samples and similar required submittals. These shall be available to the Architect and shall be delivered to the Architect for submittal to the Owner upon completion of the Work.

3.12 SHOP DRAWINGS, PRODUCT DATA AND SAMPLES

3.12.1 Shop Drawings are drawings, diagrams, schedules and other data specially prepared for the Work by the Contractor or a Subcontractor, Sub-subcontractor, manufacturer, supplier or distributor to illustrate some portion of the Work.

3.12.2 Product Data are illustrations, standard schedules, performance charts, instructions, brochures, diagrams and other information furnished by the Contractor to illustrate materials or equipment for some portion of the Work.

3.12.3 Samples are physical examples which illustrate materials, equipment or workmanship and establish standards by which the Work will be judged.

3.12.4 Shop Drawings, Product Data, Samples and similar submittals are not Contract Documents. The purpose of their submittal is to demonstrate for those portions of the Work for which submittals are required by the Contract Documents the way by which the Contractor proposes to conform to the information given and the design concept expressed in the Contract Documents. Review by the Architect is subject to the limitations of Subparagraph 4.2.7. Informational submittals upon which the Architect is not expected to take responsive action may be so identified in the Contract Documents. Submittals which are not required by the Contract Documents may be returned by the Architect without action.

3.12.5 The Contractor shall review for compliance with the Contract Documents, approve and submit to the Architect Shop Drawings, Product Data, Samples and similar submittals required by

The American Institute of Architects
1735 New York Avenue, N.W.
Washington, D.C. 20006-5292

the Contract Documents with reasonable promptness and in such sequence as to cause no delay in the Work or in the activities of the Owner or of separate contractors. Submittals which are not marked as reviewed for compliance with the Contract Documents and approved by the Contractor may be returned by the Architect without action.

3.12.6 By approving and submitting Shop Drawings, Product Data, Samples and similar submittals, the Contractor represents that the Contractor has determined and verified materials, field measurements and field construction criteria related thereto, or will do so, and has checked and coordinated the information contained within such submittals with the requirements of the Work and of the Contract Documents.

3.12.7 The Contractor shall perform no portion of the Work for which the Contract Documents require submittal and review of Shop Drawings, Product Data, Samples or similar submittals until the respective submittal has been approved by the Architect.

3.12.8 The Work shall be in accordance with approved submittals except that the Contractor shall not be relieved of responsibility for deviations from requirements of the Contract Documents by the Architect's approval of Shop Drawings, Product Data, Samples or similar submittals unless the Contractor has specifically informed the Architect in writing of such deviation at the time of submittal and (1) the Architect has given written approval to the specific deviation as a minor change in the Work, or (2) a Change Order or Construction Change Directive has been issued authorizing the deviation. The Contractor shall not be relieved of responsibility for errors or omissions in Shop Drawings, Product Data, Samples or similar submittals by the Architect's approval thereof.

3.12.9 The Contractor shall direct specific attention, in writing or on resubmitted Shop Drawings, Product Data, Samples or similar submittals, to revisions other than those requested by the Architect on previous submittals. In the absence of such written notice the Architect's approval of a resubmission shall not apply to such revisions.

3.12.10 The Contractor shall not be required to provide professional services which constitute the practice of architecture or engineering unless such services are specifically required by the Contract Documents for a portion of the Work or unless the Contractor needs to provide such services in order to carry out the Contractor's responsibilities for construction means, methods, techniques, sequences and procedures. The Contractor shall not be required to provide professional services in violation of applicable law. If professional design services or certifications by a design professional related to systems, materials or equipment are specifically required of the Contractor by the Contract Documents, the Owner and the Architect will specify all performance and design criteria that such services must satisfy. The Contractor shall cause such services or certifications to be provided by a properly licensed design professional, whose signature and seal shall appear on all drawings, calculations, specifications, certifications, Shop Drawings and other submittals prepared by such professional. Shop Drawings and other submittals related to the Work designed or certified by such professional, if prepared by others, shall bear such professional's written approval when submitted to the Architect. The Owner and the Architect shall be entitled to rely upon the adequacy, accuracy and completeness of the services, certifications or approvals performed by such design professionals, provided the Owner and Architect have specified to the Contractor all performance and design criteria that such services must satisfy. Pursuant to this Subparagraph 3.12.10, the Architect will review, approve or take other appropriate action on submittals only for the limited purpose of checking for conformance with information given and the design concept expressed in the Contract Documents. The Contractor shall not be responsible for the adequacy of the performance or design criteria required by the Contract Documents.

3.13 USE OF SITE

3.13.1 The Contractor shall confine operations at the site to areas permitted by law, ordinances, permits and the Contract Documents and shall not unreasonably encumber the site with materials or equipment.

3.14 CUTTING AND PATCHING

3.14.1 The Contractor shall be responsible for cutting, fitting or patching required to complete the Work or to make its parts fit together properly.

3.14.2 The Contractor shall not damage or endanger a portion of the Work or fully or partially completed construction of the Owner or separate contractors by cutting, patching or otherwise altering such construction, or by excavation. The Contractor shall not cut or otherwise alter such construction by the Owner or a separate contractor except with written consent of the Owner and of such separate contractor; such consent shall not be unreasonably withheld. The Contractor shall not unreasonably withhold from the Owner or a separate contractor the Contractor's consent to cutting or otherwise altering the Work.

3.15 CLEANING UP

3.15.1 The Contractor shall keep the premises and surrounding area free from accumulation of waste materials or rubbish caused by operations under the Contract. At completion of the Work, the Contractor shall remove from and about the Project waste materials, rubbish, the Contractor's tools, construction equipment, machinery and surplus materials.

3.15.2 If the Contractor fails to clean up as provided in the Contract Documents, the Owner may do so and the cost thereof shall be charged to the Contractor.

3.16 ACCESS TO WORK

3.16.1 The Contractor shall provide the Owner and Architect access to the Work in preparation and progress wherever located.

3.17 ROYALTIES, PATENTS AND COPYRIGHTS

3.17.1 The Contractor shall pay all royalties and license fees. The Contractor shall defend suits or claims for infringement of copyrights and patent rights and shall hold the Owner and Architect harmless from loss on account thereof, but shall not be responsible for such defense or loss when a particular design, process or product of a particular manufacturer or manufacturers is required by the Contract Documents or where the copyright violations are contained in Drawings, Specifications or other documents prepared by the Owner or Architect. However, if the Contractor has reason to believe that the required design, process or product is an infringement of a copyright or a patent, the Contractor shall be responsible for such loss unless such information is promptly furnished to the Architect.

3.18 INDEMNIFICATION

3.18.1 To the fullest extent permitted by law and to the extent claims, damages, losses or expenses are not covered by Project Management Protective Liability insurance purchased by the Contractor in accordance with Paragraph 11.3, the Contractor shall indemnify and hold harmless the Owner, Architect, Architect's consultants, and agents and employees of any of them from and against claims, damages, losses and expenses, including but not limited to attorneys' fees, arising out of or resulting from performance of the Work, provided that such claim, damage, loss or expense is attributable to bodily injury, sickness, disease or death, or to injury to or destruction of tangible property (other than the Work itself), but only to the extent caused by the negligent acts or omissions of the Contractor, a Subcontractor, anyone directly or indirectly employed by them or anyone for whose acts they may be liable, regardless of whether or not such claim, damage, loss or expense is caused in part by a party indemnified hereunder. Such obligation shall not be construed to negate, abridge, or reduce other rights or obligations of indemnity which would otherwise exist as to a party or person described in this Paragraph 3.18.

3.18.2 In claims against any person or entity indemnified under this Paragraph 3.18 by an employee of the Contractor, a Subcontractor, anyone directly or indirectly employed by them or anyone for whose acts they may be liable, the indemnification obligation under Subparagraph 3.18.1 shall not be limited by a limitation on amount or type of damages, compensation or benefits payable by or for the Contractor or a Subcontractor under workers' compensation acts, disability benefit acts or other employee benefit acts.

ARTICLE 4 ADMINISTRATION OF THE CONTRACT

4.1 ARCHITECT

4.1.1 The Architect is the person lawfully licensed to practice architecture or an entity lawfully practicing architecture identified as such in the Agreement and is referred to throughout the Contract Documents as if singular in number. The term "Architect" means the Architect or the Architect's authorized representative.

4.1.2 Duties, responsibilities and limitations of authority of the Architect as set forth in the Contract Documents shall not be restricted, modified or extended without written consent of the Owner, Contractor and Architect. Consent shall not be unreasonably withheld.

4.1.3 If the employment of the Architect is terminated, the Owner shall employ a new Architect against whom the Contractor has no reasonable objection and whose status under the Contract Documents shall be that of the former Architect.

4.2 ARCHITECT'S ADMINISTRATION OF THE CONTRACT

4.2.1 The Architect will provide administration of the Contract as described in the Contract Documents, and will be an Owner's representative (1) during construction, (2) until final payment is due and (3) with the Owner's concurrence, from time to time during the one-year period for correction of Work described in Paragraph 12.2. The Architect will have authority to act on behalf of the Owner only to the extent provided in the Contract Documents, unless otherwise modified in writing in accordance with other provisions of the Contract.

4.2.2 The Architect, as a representative of the Owner, will visit the site at intervals appropriate to the stage of the Contractor's operations (1) to become generally familiar with and to keep the Owner informed about the progress and quality of the portion of the Work completed, (2) to endeavor to guard the Owner against defects and deficiencies in the Work, and (3) to determine in general if the Work is being performed in a manner indicating that the Work, when fully completed, will be in accordance with the Contract Documents. However, the Architect will not be required to make exhaustive or continuous on-site inspections to check the quality or quantity of the Work. The Architect will neither have control over or charge of, nor be responsible for, the construction means, methods, techniques, sequences or procedures, or for the safety precautions and programs in connection with the Work, since these are solely the Contractor's rights and responsibilities under the Contract Documents, except as provided in Subparagraph 3.3.1.

4.2.3 The Architect will not be responsible for the Contractor's failure to perform the Work in accordance with the requirements of the Contract Documents. The Architect will not have control over or charge of and will not be responsible for acts or omissions of the Contractor, Subcontractors, or their agents or employees, or any other persons or entities performing portions of the Work.

4.2.4 Communications Facilitating Contract Administration. Except as otherwise provided in the Contract Documents or when direct communications have been specially authorized, the Owner and Contractor shall endeavor to communicate with each other through the Architect about matters arising out of or relating to the Contract. Communications by and with the Architect's consultants shall be through the Architect. Communications by and with Subcontractors and material suppliers shall be through the Contractor. Communications by and with separate contractors shall be through the Owner.

4.2.5 Based on the Architect's evaluations of the Contractor's Applications for Payment, the Architect will review and certify the amounts due the Contractor and will issue Certificates for Payment in such amounts.

4.2.6 The Architect will have authority to reject Work that does not conform to the Contract Documents. Whenever the Architect considers it necessary or advisable, the Architect will have authority to require inspection or testing of the Work in accordance with Subparagraphs 13.5.2 and 13.5.3, whether or not such Work is fabricated, installed or completed. However, neither this authority of the Architect nor a decision made in good faith either to exercise or not to exercise such authority shall give rise to a duty or responsibility of the Architect to the Contractor, Subcontractors, material and equipment suppliers, their agents or employees, or other persons or entities performing portions of the Work.

4.2.7 The Architect will review and approve or take other appropriate action upon the Contractor's submittals such as Shop Drawings, Product Data and Samples, but only for the limited purpose of checking for conformance with information given and the design concept expressed in the Contract Documents. The Architect's action will be taken with such reasonable promptness as to cause no delay in the Work or in the activities of the Owner, Contractor or separate contractors, while allowing sufficient time in the Architect's professional judgment to permit adequate review. Review of such submittals is not conducted for the purpose of determining the accuracy and completeness of other details such as dimensions and quantities, or for substantiating instructions for installation or performance of equipment or systems, all of which remain the responsibility of the Contractor as required by the Contract Documents. The Architect's review of the Contractor's submittals shall not relieve the Contractor of the obligations under Paragraphs 3.3, 3.5 and 3.12. The Architect's review shall not constitute approval of safety precautions or, unless otherwise specifically stated by the Architect, of any construction means, methods, techniques, sequences or procedures. The Architect's approval of a specific item shall not indicate approval of an assembly of which the item is a component.

4.2.8 The Architect will prepare Change Orders and Construction Change Directives, and may authorize minor changes in the Work as provided in Paragraph 7.4.

4.2.9 The Architect will conduct inspections to determine the date or dates of Substantial Completion and the date of final completion, will receive and forward to the Owner, for the Owner's review and records, written warranties and related documents required by the Contract and assembled by the Contractor, and will issue a final Certificate for Payment upon compliance with the requirements of the Contract Documents.

4.2.10 If the Owner and Architect agree, the Architect will provide one or more project representatives to assist in carrying out the Architect's responsibilities at the site. The duties, responsibilities and limitations of authority of such project representatives shall be as set forth in an exhibit to be incorporated in the Contract Documents.

4.2.11 The Architect will interpret and decide matters concerning performance under, and requirements of, the Contract Documents on written request of either the Owner or Contractor.

The American Institute
of Architects
1735 New York Avenue, N.W.
Washington, D.C. 20006-5292

The Architect's response to such requests will be made in writing within any time limits agreed upon or otherwise with reasonable promptness. If no agreement is made concerning the time within which interpretations required of the Architect shall be furnished in compliance with this Paragraph 4.2, then delay shall not be recognized on account of failure by the Architect to furnish such interpretations until 15 days after written request is made for them.

4.2.12 Interpretations and decisions of the Architect will be consistent with the intent of and reasonably inferable from the Contract Documents and will be in writing or in the form of drawings. When making such interpretations and initial decisions, the Architect will endeavor to secure faithful performance by both Owner and Contractor, will not show partiality to either and will not be liable for results of interpretations or decisions so rendered in good faith.

4.2.13 The Architect's decisions on matters relating to aesthetic effect will be final if consistent with the intent expressed in the Contract Documents.

4.3 CLAIMS AND DISPUTES

4.3.1 Definition. A Claim is a demand or assertion by one of the parties seeking, as a matter of right, adjustment or interpretation of Contract terms, payment of money, extension of time or other relief with respect to the terms of the Contract. The term "Claim" also includes other disputes and matters in question between the Owner and Contractor arising out of or relating to the Contract. Claims must be initiated by written notice. The responsibility to substantiate Claims shall rest with the party making the Claim.

4.3.2 Time Limits on Claims. Claims by either party must be initiated within 21 days after occurrence of the event giving rise to such Claim or within 21 days after the claimant first recognizes the condition giving rise to the Claim, whichever is later. Claims must be initiated by written notice to the Architect and the other party.

4.3.3 Continuing Contract Performance. Pending final resolution of a Claim except as otherwise agreed in writing or as provided in Subparagraph 9.7.1 and Article 14, the Contractor shall proceed diligently with performance of the Contract and the Owner shall continue to make payments in accordance with the Contract Documents.

4.3.4 Claims for Concealed or Unknown Conditions. If conditions are encountered at the site which are (1) subsurface or otherwise concealed physical conditions which differ materially from those indicated in the Contract Documents or (2) unknown physical conditions of an unusual nature, which differ materially from those ordinarily found to exist and generally recognized as inherent in construction activities of the character provided for in the Contract Documents, then notice by the observing party shall be given to the other party promptly before conditions are disturbed and in no event later than 21 days after first observance of the conditions. The Architect will promptly investigate such conditions and, if they differ materially and cause an increase or decrease in the Contractor's cost of, or time required for, performance of any part of the Work, will recommend an equitable adjustment in the Contract Sum or Contract Time, or both. If the Architect determines that the conditions at the site are not materially different from those indicated in the Contract Documents and that no change in the terms of the Contract is justified, the Architect shall so notify the Owner and Contractor in writing, stating the reasons. Claims by either party in opposition to such determination must be made within 21 days after the Architect has given notice of the decision. If the conditions encountered are materially different, the Contract Sum and Contract Time shall be equitably adjusted, but if the Owner and Contractor cannot agree on an adjustment in the Contract Sum or Contract Time, the adjustment shall be referred to the Architect for initial determination, subject to further proceedings pursuant to Paragraph 4.4.

The American Institute
of Architects
1735 New York Avenue, N.W.
Washington, D.C. 20006-5292

4.3.5 **Claims for Additional Cost.** If the Contractor wishes to make Claim for an increase in the Contract Sum, written notice as provided herein shall be given before proceeding to execute the Work. Prior notice is not required for Claims relating to an emergency endangering life or property arising under Paragraph 10.6.

4.3.6 If the Contractor believes additional cost is involved for reasons including but not limited to (1) a written interpretation from the Architect, (2) an order by the Owner to stop the Work where the Contractor was not at fault, (3) a written order for a minor change in the Work issued by the Architect, (4) failure of payment by the Owner, (5) termination of the Contract by the Owner, (6) Owner's suspension or (7) other reasonable grounds, Claim shall be filed in accordance with this Paragraph 4.3.

4.3.7 CLAIMS FOR ADDITIONAL TIME

4.3.7.1 If the Contractor wishes to make Claim for an increase in the Contract Time, written notice as provided herein shall be given. The Contractor's Claim shall include an estimate of cost and of probable effect of delay on progress of the Work. In the case of a continuing delay only one Claim is necessary.

4.3.7.2 If adverse weather conditions are the basis for a Claim for additional time, such Claim shall be documented by data substantiating that weather conditions were abnormal for the period of time, could not have been reasonably anticipated and had an adverse effect on the scheduled construction.

4.3.8 **Injury or Damage to Person or Property.** If either party to the Contract suffers injury or damage to person or property because of an act or omission of the other party, or of others for whose acts such party is legally responsible, written notice of such injury or damage, whether or not insured, shall be given to the other party within a reasonable time not exceeding 21 days after discovery. The notice shall provide sufficient detail to enable the other party to investigate the matter.

4.3.9 If unit prices are stated in the Contract Documents or subsequently agreed upon, and if quantities originally contemplated are materially changed in a proposed Change Order or Construction Change Directive so that application of such unit prices to quantities of Work proposed will cause substantial inequity to the Owner or Contractor, the applicable unit prices shall be equitably adjusted.

4.3.10 **Claims for Consequential Damages.** The Contractor and Owner waive Claims against each other for consequential damages arising out of or relating to this Contract. This mutual waiver includes:

.1 damages incurred by the Owner for rental expenses, for losses of use, income, profit, financing, business and reputation, and for loss of management or employee productivity or of the services of such persons; and

.2 damages incurred by the Contractor for principal office expenses including the compensation of personnel stationed there, for losses of financing, business and reputation, and for loss of profit except anticipated profit arising directly from the Work.

This mutual waiver is applicable, without limitation, to all consequential damages due to either party's termination in accordance with Article 14. Nothing contained in this Subparagraph 4.3.10 shall be deemed to preclude an award of liquidated direct damages, when applicable, in accordance with the requirements of the Contract Documents.

4.4 RESOLUTION OF CLAIMS AND DISPUTES

4.4.1 Decision of Architect. Claims, including those alleging an error or omission by the Architect but excluding those arising under Paragraphs 10.3 through 10.5, shall be referred initially to the Architect for decision. An initial decision by the Architect shall be required as a

The American Institute of Architects
1735 New York Avenue, N.W.
Washington, D.C. 20006-5292

condition precedent to mediation, arbitration or litigation of all Claims between the Contractor and Owner arising prior to the date final payment is due, unless 30 days have passed after the Claim has been referred to the Architect with no decision having been rendered by the Architect. The Architect will not decide disputes between the Contractor and persons or entities other than the Owner.

4.4.2 The Architect will review Claims and within ten days of the receipt of the Claim take one or more of the following actions: (1) request additional supporting data from the claimant or a response with supporting data from the other party, (2) reject the Claim in whole or in part, (3) approve the Claim, (4) suggest a compromise, or (5) advise the parties that the Architect is unable to resolve the Claim if the Architect lacks sufficient information to evaluate the merits of the Claim or if the Architect concludes that, in the Architect's sole discretion, it would be inappropriate for the Architect to resolve the Claim.

4.4.3 In evaluating Claims, the Architect may, but shall not be obligated to, consult with or seek information from either party or from persons with special knowledge or expertise who may assist the Architect in rendering a decision. The Architect may request the Owner to authorize retention of such persons at the Owner's expense.

4.4.4 If the Architect requests a party to provide a response to a Claim or to furnish additional supporting data, such party shall respond, within ten days after receipt of such request, and shall either provide a response on the requested supporting data, advise the Architect when the response or supporting data will be furnished or advise the Architect that no supporting data will be furnished. Upon receipt of the response or supporting data, if any, the Architect will either reject or approve the Claim in whole or in part.

4.4.5 The Architect will approve or reject Claims by written decision, which shall state the reasons therefor and which shall notify the parties of any change in the Contract Sum or Contract Time or both. The approval or rejection of a Claim by the Architect shall be final and binding on the parties but subject to mediation and arbitration.

4.4.6 When a written decision of the Architect states that (1) the decision is final but subject to mediation and arbitration and (2) a demand for arbitration of a Claim covered by such decision must be made within 30 days after the date on which the party making the demand receives the final written decision, then failure to demand arbitration within said 30 days' period shall result in the Architect's decision becoming final and binding upon the Owner and Contractor. If the Architect renders a decision after arbitration proceedings have been initiated, such decision may be entered as evidence, but shall not supersede arbitration proceedings unless the decision is acceptable to all parties concerned.

4.4.7 Upon receipt of a Claim against the Contractor or at any time thereafter, the Architect or the Owner may, but is not obligated to, notify the surety, if any, of the nature and amount of the Claim. If the Claim relates to a possibility of a Contractor's default, the Architect or the Owner may, but is not obligated to, notify the surety and request the surety's assistance in resolving the controversy.

4.4.8 If a Claim relates to or is the subject of a mechanic's lien, the party asserting such Claim may proceed in accordance with applicable law to comply with the lien notice or filing deadlines prior to resolution of the Claim by the Architect, by mediation or by arbitration.

4.5 MEDIATION

4.5.1 Any Claim arising out of or related to the Contract, except Claims relating to aesthetic effect and except those waived as provided for in Subparagraphs 4.3.10, 9.10.4 and 9.10.5 shall, after initial decision by the Architect or 30 days after submission of the Claim to the Architect, be subject to mediation as a condition precedent to arbitration or the institution of legal or equitable proceedings by either party.

4.5.2 The parties shall endeavor to resolve their Claims by mediation which, unless the parties mutually agree otherwise, shall be in accordance with the Construction Industry Mediation Rules of the American Arbitration Association currently in effect. Request for mediation shall be filed in writing with the other party to the Contract and with the American Arbitration Association. The request may be made concurrently with the filing of a demand for arbitration but, in such event, mediation shall proceed in advance of arbitration or legal or equitable proceedings, which shall be stayed pending mediation for a period of 60 days from the date of filing, unless stayed for a longer period by agreement of the parties or court order.

4.5.3 The parties shall share the mediator's fee and any filing fees equally. The mediation shall be held in the place where the Project is located, unless another location is mutually agreed upon. Agreements reached in mediation shall be enforceable as settlement agreements in any court having jurisdiction thereof.

4.6 ARBITRATION

4.6.1 Any Claim arising out of or related to the Contract, except Claims relating to aesthetic effect and except those waived as provided for in Subparagraphs 4.3.10, 9.10.4 and 9.10.5, shall, after decision by the Architect or 30 days after submission of the Claim to the Architect, be subject to arbitration. Prior to arbitration, the parties shall endeavor to resolve disputes by mediation in accordance with the provisions of Paragraph 4.5.

4.6.2 Claims not resolved by mediation shall be decided by arbitration which, unless the parties mutually agree otherwise, shall be in accordance with the Construction Industry Arbitration Rules of the American Arbitration Association currently in effect. The demand for arbitration shall be filed in writing with the other party to the Contract and with the American Arbitration Association, and a copy shall be filed with the Architect.

4.6.3 A demand for arbitration shall be made within the time limits specified in Subparagraphs 4.4.6 and 4.6.1 as applicable, and in other cases within a reasonable time after the Claim has arisen, and in no event shall it be made after the date when institution of legal or equitable proceedings based on such Claim would be barred by the applicable statute of limitations as determined pursuant to Paragraph 13.7.

4.6.4 Limitation on Consolidation or Joinder. No arbitration arising out of or relating to the Contract shall include, by consolidation or joinder or in any other manner, the Architect, the Architect's employees or consultants, except by written consent containing specific reference to the Agreement and signed by the Architect, Owner, Contractor and any other person or entity sought to be joined. No arbitration shall include, by consolidation or joinder or in any other manner, parties other than the Owner, Contractor, a separate contractor as described in Article 6 and other persons substantially involved in a common question of fact or law whose presence is required if complete relief is to be accorded in arbitration. No person or entity other than the Owner, Contractor or a separate contractor as described in Article 6 shall be included as an original third party or additional third party to an arbitration whose interest or responsibility is insubstantial. Consent to arbitration involving an additional person or entity shall not constitute consent to arbitration of a Claim not described therein or with a person or entity not named or described therein. The foregoing agreement to arbitrate and other agreements to arbitrate with an additional person or entity duly consented to by parties to the Agreement shall be specifically enforceable under applicable law in any court having jurisdiction thereof.

The American Institute of Architects
1735 New York Avenue, N.W.
Washington, D.C. 20006-5292

4.6.5 Claims and Timely Assertion of Claims. The party filing a notice of demand for arbitration must assert in the demand all Claims then known to that party on which arbitration is permitted to be demanded.

4.6.6 Judgment on Final Award. The award rendered by the arbitrator or arbitrators shall be final, and judgment may be entered upon it in accordance with applicable law in any court having jurisdiction thereof.

ARTICLE 5 SUBCONTRACTORS

5.1 DEFINITIONS

5.1.1 A Subcontractor is a person or entity who has a direct contract with the Contractor to perform a portion of the Work at the site. The term "Subcontractor" is referred to throughout the Contract Documents as if singular in number and means a Subcontractor or an authorized representative of the Subcontractor. The term "Subcontractor" does not include a separate contractor or subcontractors of a separate contractor.

5.1.2 A Sub-subcontractor is a person or entity who has a direct or indirect contract with a Subcontractor to perform a portion of the Work at the site. The term "Sub-subcontractor" is referred to throughout the Contract Documents as if singular in number and means a Sub-subcontractor or an authorized representative of the Sub-subcontractor.

5.2 AWARD OF SUBCONTRACTS AND OTHER CONTRACTS FOR PORTIONS OF THE WORK

5.2.1 Unless otherwise stated in the Contract Documents or the bidding requirements, the Contractor, as soon as practicable after award of the Contract, shall furnish in writing to the Owner through the Architect the names of persons or entities (including those who are to furnish materials or equipment fabricated to a special design) proposed for each principal portion of the Work. The Architect will promptly reply to the Contractor in writing stating whether or not the Owner or the Architect, after due investigation, has reasonable objection to any such proposed person or entity. Failure of the Owner or Architect to reply promptly shall constitute notice of no reasonable objection.

5.2.2 The Contractor shall not contract with a proposed person or entity to whom the Owner or Architect has made reasonable and timely objection. The Contractor shall not be required to contract with anyone to whom the Contractor has made reasonable objection.

5.2.3 If the Owner or Architect has reasonable objection to a person or entity proposed by the Contractor, the Contractor shall propose another to whom the Owner or Architect has no reasonable objection. If the proposed but rejected Subcontractor was reasonably capable of performing the Work, the Contract Sum and Contract Time shall be increased or decreased by the difference, if any, occasioned by such change, and an appropriate Change Order shall be issued before commencement of the substitute Subcontractor's Work. However, no increase in the Contract Sum or Contract Time shall be allowed for such change unless the Contractor has acted promptly and responsively in submitting names as required.

5.2.4 The Contractor shall not change a Subcontractor, person or entity previously selected if the Owner or Architect makes reasonable objection to such substitute.

5.3 SUBCONTRACTUAL RELATIONS

5.3.1 By appropriate agreement, written where legally required for validity, the Contractor shall require each Subcontractor, to the extent of the Work to be performed by the Subcontractor, to be bound to the Contractor by terms of the Contract Documents, and to assume toward the Contractor all the obligations and responsibilities, including the responsibility for safety of the

The American Institute of Architects
1735 New York Avenue, N.W.
Washington, D.C. 20006-5292

Subcontractor's Work, which the Contractor, by these Documents, assumes toward the Owner and Architect. Each subcontract agreement shall preserve and protect the rights of the Owner and Architect under the Contract Documents with respect to the Work to be performed by the Subcontractor so that subcontracting thereof will not prejudice such rights, and shall allow to the Subcontractor, unless specifically provided otherwise in the subcontract agreement, the benefit of all rights, remedies and redress against the Contractor that the Contractor, by the Contract Documents, has against the Owner. Where appropriate, the Contractor shall require each Subcontractor to enter into similar agreements with Sub-subcontractors. The Contractor shall make available to each proposed Subcontractor, prior to the execution of the subcontract agreement, copies of the Contract Documents to which the Subcontractor will be bound, and, upon written request of the Subcontractor, identify to the Subcontractor terms and conditions of the proposed subcontract agreement which may be at variance with the Contract Documents. Subcontractors will similarly make copies of applicable portions of such documents available to their respective proposed Sub-subcontractors.

5.4 CONTINGENT ASSIGNMENT OF SUBCONTRACTS

5.4.1 Each subcontract agreement for a portion of the Work is assigned by the Contractor to the Owner provided that:

.1 assignment is effective only after termination of the Contract by the Owner for cause pursuant to Paragraph 14.2 and only for those subcontract agreements which the Owner accepts by notifying the Subcontractor and Contractor in writing; and

.2 assignment is subject to the prior rights of the surety, if any, obligated under bond relating to the Contract.

5.4.2 Upon such assignment, if the Work has been suspended for more than 30 days, the Subcontractor's compensation shall be equitably adjusted for increases in cost resulting from the suspension.

ARTICLE 6 CONSTRUCTION BY OWNER OR BY SEPARATE CONTRACTORS

6.1 OWNER'S RIGHT TO PERFORM CONSTRUCTION AND TO AWARD SEPARATE CONTRACTS

6.1.1 The Owner reserves the right to perform construction or operations related to the Project with the Owner's own forces, and to award separate contracts in connection with other portions of the Project or other construction or operations on the site under Conditions of the Contract identical or substantially similar to these including those portions related to insurance and waiver of subrogation. If the Contractor claims that delay or additional cost is involved because of such action by the Owner, the Contractor shall make such Claim as provided in Paragraph 4.3.

6.1.2 When separate contracts are awarded for different portions of the Project or other construction or operations on the site, the term "Contractor" in the Contract Documents in each case shall mean the Contractor who executes each separate Owner-Contractor Agreement.

6.1.3 The Owner shall provide for coordination of the activities of the Owner's own forces and of each separate contractor with the Work of the Contractor, who shall cooperate with them. The Contractor shall participate with other separate contractors and the Owner in reviewing their construction schedules when directed to do so. The Contractor shall make any revisions to the construction schedule deemed necessary after a joint review and mutual agreement. The construction schedules shall then constitute the schedules to be used by the Contractor, separate contractors and the Owner until subsequently revised.

6.1.4 Unless otherwise provided in the Contract Documents, when the Owner performs construction or operations related to the Project with the Owner's own forces, the Owner shall be deemed to be subject to the same obligations and to have the same rights which apply to the

The American Institute of Architects
1735 New York Avenue, N.W.
Washington, D.C. 20006-5292

Contractor under the Conditions of the Contract, including, without excluding others, those stated in Article 3, this Article 6 and Articles 10, 11 and 12.

6.2 MUTUAL RESPONSIBILITY

6.2.1 The Contractor shall afford the Owner and separate contractors reasonable opportunity for introduction and storage of their materials and equipment and performance of their activities, and shall connect and coordinate the Contractor's construction and operations with theirs as required by the Contract Documents.

6.2.2 If part of the Contractor's Work depends for proper execution or results upon construction or operations by the Owner or a separate contractor, the Contractor shall, prior to proceeding with that portion of the Work, promptly report to the Architect apparent discrepancies or defects in such other construction that would render it unsuitable for such proper execution and results. Failure of the Contractor so to report shall constitute an acknowledgment that the Owner's or separate contractor's completed or partially completed construction is fit and proper to receive the Contractor's Work, except as to defects not then reasonably discoverable.

6.2.3 The Owner shall be reimbursed by the Contractor for costs incurred by the Owner which are payable to a separate contractor because of delays, improperly timed activities or defective construction of the Contractor. The Owner shall be responsible to the Contractor for costs incurred by the Contractor because of delays, improperly timed activities, damage to the Work or defective construction of a separate contractor.

6.2.4 The Contractor shall promptly remedy damage wrongfully caused by the Contractor to completed or partially completed construction or to property of the Owner or separate contractors as provided in Subparagraph 10.2.5.

6.2.5 The Owner and each separate contractor shall have the same responsibilities for cutting and patching as are described for the Contractor in Subparagraph 3.14.

6.3 OWNER'S RIGHT TO CLEAN UP

6.3.1 If a dispute arises among the Contractor, separate contractors and the Owner as to the responsibility under their respective contracts for maintaining the premises and surrounding area free from waste materials and rubbish, the Owner may clean up and the Architect will allocate the cost among those responsible.

ARTICLE 7 CHANGES IN THE WORK

7.1 GENERAL

7.1.1 Changes in the Work may be accomplished after execution of the Contract, and without invalidating the Contract, by Change Order, Construction Change Directive or order for a minor change in the Work, subject to the limitations stated in this Article 7 and elsewhere in the Contract Documents.

7.1.2 A Change Order shall be based upon agreement among the Owner, Contractor and Architect; a Construction Change Directive requires agreement by the Owner and Architect and may or may not be agreed to by the Contractor; an order for a minor change in the Work may be issued by the Architect alone.

7.1.3 Changes in the Work shall be performed under applicable provisions of the Contract Documents, and the Contractor shall proceed promptly, unless otherwise provided in the Change Order, Construction Change Directive or order for a minor change in the Work.

The American Institute of Architects
1735 New York Avenue, N.W.
Washington, D.C. 20006-5292

7.2 CHANGE ORDERS

7.2.1 A Change Order is a written instrument prepared by the Architect and signed by the Owner, Contractor and Architect, stating their agreement upon all of the following:

.1 change in the Work;

.2 the amount of the adjustment, if any, in the Contract Sum; and

.3 the extent of the adjustment, if any, in the Contract Time.

7.2.2 Methods used in determining adjustments to the Contract Sum may include those listed in Subparagraph 7.3.3.

7.3 CONSTRUCTION CHANGE DIRECTIVES

7.3.1 A Construction Change Directive is a written order prepared by the Architect and signed by the Owner and Architect, directing a change in the Work prior to agreement on adjustment, if any, in the Contract Sum or Contract Time, or both. The Owner may by Construction Change Directive, without invalidating the Contract, order changes in the Work within the general scope of the Contract consisting of additions, deletions or other revisions, the Contract Sum and Contract Time being adjusted accordingly.

7.3.2 A Construction Change Directive shall be used in the absence of total agreement on the terms of a Change Order.

7.3.3 If the Construction Change Directive provides for an adjustment to the Contract Sum, the adjustment shall be based on one of the following methods:

.1 mutual acceptance of a lump sum properly itemized and supported by sufficient substantiating data to permit evaluation;

.2 unit prices stated in the Contract Documents or subsequently agreed upon;

.3 cost to be determined in a manner agreed upon by the parties and a mutually acceptable fixed or percentage fee; or

.4 as provided in Subparagraph 7.3.6.

7.3.4 Upon receipt of a Construction Change Directive, the Contractor shall promptly proceed with the change in the Work involved and advise the Architect of the Contractor's agreement or disagreement with the method, if any, provided in the Construction Change Directive for determining the proposed adjustment in the Contract Sum or Contract Time.

7.3.5 A Construction Change Directive signed by the Contractor indicates the agreement of the Contractor therewith, including adjustment in Contract Sum and Contract Time or the method for determining them. Such agreement shall be effective immediately and shall be recorded as a Change Order.

7.3.6 If the Contractor does not respond promptly or disagrees with the method for adjustment in the Contract Sum, the method and the adjustment shall be determined by the Architect on the basis of reasonable expenditures and savings of those performing the Work attributable to the change, including, in case of an increase in the Contract Sum, a reasonable allowance for overhead and profit. In such case, and also under Clause 7.3.3.3, the Contractor shall keep and present, in such form as the Architect may prescribe, an itemized accounting together with appropriate supporting data. Unless otherwise provided in the Contract Documents, costs for the purposes of this Subparagraph 7.3.6 shall be limited to the following:

.1 costs of labor, including social security, old age and unemployment insurance, fringe benefits required by agreement or custom, and workers' compensation insurance;

.2 costs of materials, supplies and equipment, including cost of transportation, whether incorporated or consumed;

.3 rental costs of machinery and equipment, exclusive of hand tools, whether rented from the Contractor or others;

The American Institute of Architects
1735 New York Avenue, N.W.
Washington, D.C. 20006-5292

.4 costs of premiums for all bonds and insurance, permit fees, and sales, use or similar taxes related to the Work; and

.5 additional costs of supervision and field office personnel directly attributable to the change.

7.3.7. The amount of credit to be allowed by the Contractor to the Owner for a deletion or change which results in a net decrease in the Contract Sum shall be actual net cost as confirmed by the Architect. When both additions and credits covering related Work or substitutions are involved in a change, the allowance for overhead and profit shall be figured on the basis of net increase, if any, with respect to that change.

7.3.8 Pending final determination of the total cost of a Construction Change Directive to the Owner, amounts not in dispute for such changes in the Work shall be included in Applications for Payment accompanied by a Change Order indicating the parties' agreement with part or all of such costs. For any portion of such cost that remains in dispute, the Architect will make an interim determination for purposes of monthly certification for payment for those costs. That determination of cost shall adjust the Contract Sum on the same basis as a Change Order, subject to the right of either party to disagree and assert a claim in accordance with Article 4.

7.3.9 When the Owner and Contractor agree with the determination made by the Architect concerning the adjustments in the Contract Sum and Contract Time, or otherwise reach agreement upon the adjustments, such agreement shall be effective immediately and shall be recorded by preparation and execution of an appropriate Change Order.

7.4 MINOR CHANGES IN THE WORK

7.4.1 The Architect will have authority to order minor changes in the Work not involving adjustment in the Contract Sum or extension of the Contract Time and not inconsistent with the intent of the Contract Documents. Such changes shall be effected by written order and shall be binding on the Owner and Contractor. The Contractor shall carry out such written orders promptly.

ARTICLE 8 TIME

8.1 DEFINITIONS

8.1.1 Unless otherwise provided, Contract Time is the period of time, including authorized adjustments, allotted in the Contract Documents for Substantial Completion of the Work.

8.1.2 The date of commencement of the Work is the date established in the Agreement.

8.1.3 The date of Substantial Completion is the date certified by the Architect in accordance with Paragraph 9.8.

8.1.4 The term "day" as used in the Contract Documents shall mean calendar day unless otherwise specifically defined.

8.2 PROGRESS AND COMPLETION

8.2.1 Time limits stated in the Contract Documents are of the essence of the Contract. By executing the Agreement the Contractor confirms that the Contract Time is a reasonable period for performing the Work.

8.2.2 The Contractor shall not knowingly, except by agreement or instruction of the Owner in writing, prematurely commence operations on the site or elsewhere prior to the effective date of insurance required by Article 11 to be furnished by the Contractor and Owner. The date of commencement of the Work shall not be changed by the effective date of such insurance. Unless the date of commencement is established by the Contract Documents or a notice to proceed given by the Owner, the Contractor shall notify the Owner in writing not less than five days or other agreed period before commencing the Work to permit the timely filing of morgages, mechanic's liens and other security interests.

8.2.3 The Contractor shall proceed expeditiously with adequate forces and shall achieve Substantial Completion within the Contract Time.

8.3 DELAYS AND EXTENSIONS OF TIME

8.3.1 If the Contractor is delayed at any time in the commencement or progress of the Work by an act or neglect of the Owner or Architect, or of an employee of either, or of a separate contractor employed by the Owner, or by changes ordered in the Work, or by labor disputes, fire, unusual delay in deliveries, unavoidable casualties or other causes beyond the Contractor's control, or by delay authorized by the Owner pending mediation and arbitration, or by other causes which the Architect determines may justify delay, then the Contract Time shall be extended by Change Order for such reasonable time as the Architect may determine.

8.3.2 Claims relating to time shall be made in accordance with applicable provisions of Paragraph 4.3.

8.3.3 This Paragraph 8.3 does not preclude recovery of damages for delay by either party under other provisions of the Contract Documents.

ARTICLE 9 PAYMENTS AND COMPLETION

9.1 CONTRACT SUM

9.1.1 The Contract Sum is stated in the Agreement and, including authorized adjustments, is the total amount payable by the Owner to the Contractor for performance of the Work under the Contract Documents.

9.2 SCHEDULE OF VALUES

9.2.1 Before the first Application for Payment, the Contractor shall submit to the Architect a schedule of values allocated to various portions of the Work, prepared in such form and supported by such data to substantiate its accuracy as the Architect may require. This schedule, unless objected to by the Architect, shall be used as a basis for reviewing the Contractor's Applications for Payment.

9.3 APPLICATIONS FOR PAYMENT

9.3.1 At least ten days before the date established for each progress payment, the Contractor shall submit to the Architect an itemized Application for Payment for operations completed in accordance with the schedule of values. Such application shall be notarized, if required, and supported by such data substantiating the Contractor's right to payment as the Owner or Architect may require, such as copies of requisitions from Subcontractors and material suppliers, and reflecting retainage if provided for in the Contract Documents.

9.3.1.1 As provided in Subparagraph 7.3.8, such applications may include requests for payment on account of changes in the Work which have been properly authorized by Construction Change Directives, or by interim determinations of the Architect, but not yet included in Change Orders.

9.3.1.2 Such applications may not include requests for payment for portions of the Work for which the Contractor does not intend to pay to a Subcontractor or material supplier, unless such Work has been performed by others whom the Contractor intends to pay.

9.3.2 Unless otherwise provided in the Contract Documents, payments shall be made on account of materials and equipment delivered and suitably stored at the site for subsequent incorporation in the Work. If approved in advance by the Owner, payment may similarly be made for materials and equipment suitably stored off the site at a location agreed upon in writing. Payment for materials and equipment stored on or off the site shall be conditioned upon compliance by the Contractor with procedures satisfactory to the Owner to establish the Owner's title to such materials and equipment or otherwise protect the Owner's interest, and shall include the costs of applicable insurance, storage and transportation to the site for such materials and equipment stored off the site.

9.3.3 The Contractor warrants that title to all Work covered by an Application for Payment will pass to the Owner no later than the time of payment. The Contractor further warrants that upon submittal of an Application for Payment all Work for which Certificates for Payment have been previously issued and payments received from the Owner shall, to the best of the Contractor's knowledge, information and belief, be free and clear of liens, claims, security interests or encumbrances in favor of the Contractor, Subcontractors, material suppliers, or other persons or entities making a claim by reason of having provided labor, materials and equipment relating to the Work.

9.4 CERTIFICATES FOR PAYMENT

9.4.1 The Architect will, within seven days after receipt of the Contractor's Application for Payment, either issue to the Owner a Certificate for Payment, with a copy to the Contractor, for such amount as the Architect determines is properly due, or notify the Contractor and Owner in writing of the Architect's reasons for withholding certification in whole or in part as provided in Subparagraph 9.5.1.

9.4.2 The issuance of a Certificate for Payment will constitute a representation by the Architect to the Owner, based on the Architect's evaluation of the Work and the data comprising the Application for Payment, that the Work has progressed to the point indicated and that, to the best of the Architect's knowledge, information and belief, the quality of the Work is in accordance with the Contract Documents. The foregoing representations are subject to an evaluation of the Work for conformance with the Contract Documents upon Substantial Completion, to results of subsequent tests and inspections, to correction of minor deviations from the Contract Documents prior to completion and to specific qualifications expressed by the Architect. The issuance of a Certificate for Payment will further constitute a representation that the Contractor is entitled to payment in the amount certified. However, the issuance of a Certificate for Payment will not be a representation that the Architect has (1) made exhaustive or continuous on-site inspections to check the quality or quantity of the Work, (2) reviewed construction means, methods, techniques, sequences or procedures, (3) reviewed copies of requisitions received from Subcontractors and material suppliers and other data requested by the Owner to substantiate the Contractor's right to payment, or (4) made examination to ascertain how or for what purpose the Contractor has used money previously paid on account of the Contract Sum.

9.5 DECISIONS TO WITHHOLD CERTIFICATION

9.5.1 The Architect may withhold a Certificate for Payment in whole or in part, to the extent reasonably necessary to protect the Owner, if in the Architect's opinion the representations to the Owner required by Subparagraph 9.4.2 cannot be made. If the Architect is unable to certify payment in the amount of the Application, the Architect will notify the Contractor and Owner as provided in Subparagraph 9.4.1. If the Contractor and Architect cannot agree on a revised amount, the Architect will promptly issue a Certificate for Payment for the amount for which the Architect is able to make such representations to the Owner. The Architect may also withhold a Certificate for Payment or, because of subsequently discovered evidence, may nullify the whole or a part of a Certificate for Payment previously issued, to such extent as may be necessary in the Architect's

The American Institute of Architects
1735 New York Avenue, N.W.
Washington, D.C. 20006-5292

opinion to protect the Owner from loss for which the Contractor is responsible, including loss resulting from acts and omissions described in Subparagraph 3.3.2, because of:

.1 defective Work not remedied;

.2 third party claims filed or reasonable evidence indicating probable filing of such claims unless security acceptable to the Owner is provided by the Contractor;

.3 failure of the Contractor to make payments properly to Subcontractors or for labor, materials or equipment;

.4 reasonable evidence that the Work cannot be completed for the unpaid balance of the Contract Sum;

.5 damage to the Owner or another contractor;

.6 reasonable evidence that the Work will not be completed within the Contract Time, and that the unpaid balance would not be adequate to cover actual or liquidated damages for the anticipated delay; or

.7 persistent failure to carry out the Work in accordance with the Contract Documents.

9.5.2 When the above reasons for withholding certification are removed, certification will be made for amounts previously withheld.

9.6 PROGRESS PAYMENTS

9.6.1 After the Architect has issued a Certificate for Payment, the Owner shall make payment in the manner and within the time provided in the Contract Documents, and shall so notify the Architect.

9.6.2 The Contractor shall promptly pay each Subcontractor, upon receipt of payment from the Owner, out of the amount paid to the Contractor on account of such Subcontractor's portion of the Work, the amount to which said Subcontractor is entitled, reflecting percentages actually retained from payments to the Contractor on account of such Subcontractor's portion of the Work. The Contractor shall, by appropriate agreement with each Subcontractor, require each Subcontractor to make payments to Sub-subcontractors in a similar manner.

9.6.3 The Architect will, on request, furnish to a Subcontractor, if practicable, information regarding percentages of completion or amounts applied for by the Contractor and action taken thereon by the Architect and Owner on account of portions of the Work done by such Subcontractor.

9.6.4 Neither the Owner nor Architect shall have an obligation to pay or to see to the payment of money to a Subcontractor except as may otherwise be required by law.

9.6.5 Payment to material suppliers shall be treated in a manner similar to that provided in Subparagraphs 9.6.2, 9.6.3 and 9.6.4.

9.6.6 A Certificate for Payment, a progress payment, or partial or entire use or occupancy of the Project by the Owner shall not constitute acceptance of Work not in accordance with the Contract Documents.

9.6.7 Unless the Contractor provides the Owner with a payment bond in the full penal sum of the Contract Sum, payments received by the Contractor for Work properly performed by Subcontractors and suppliers shall be held by the Contractor for those Subcontractors or suppliers who performed Work or furnished materials, or both, under contract with the Contractor for which payment was made by the Owner. Nothing contained herein shall require money to be placed in a separate account and not commingled with money of the Contractor, shall create any fiduciary liability or tort liability on the part of the Contractor for breach of trust or shall entitle any person or entity to an award of punitive damages against the Contractor for breach of the requirements of this provision.

9.7 FAILURE OF PAYMENT

9.7.1 If the Architect does not issue a Certificate for Payment, through no fault of the Contractor, within seven days after receipt of the Contractor's Application for Payment, or if the Owner does not pay the Contractor within seven days after the date established in the Contract Documents the amount certified by the Architect or awarded by arbitration, then the Contractor may, upon seven additional days' written notice to the Owner and Architect, stop the Work until payment of the amount owing has been received. The Contract Time shall be extended appropriately and the Contract Sum shall be increased by the amount of the Contractor's reasonable costs of shut-down, delay and start-up, plus interest as provided for in the Contract Documents.

9.8 SUBSTANTIAL COMPLETION

9.8.1 Substantial Completion is the stage in the progress of the Work when the Work or designated portion thereof is sufficiently complete in accordance with the Contract Documents so that the Owner can occupy or utilize the Work for its intended use.

9.8.2 When the Contractor considers that the Work, or a portion thereof which the Owner agrees to accept separately, is substantially complete, the Contractor shall prepare and submit to the Architect a comprehensive list of items to be completed or corrected prior to final payment. Failure to include an item on such list does not alter the responsibility of the Contractor to complete all Work in accordance with the Contract Documents.

9.8.3 Upon receipt of the Contractor's list, the Architect will make an inspection to determine whether the Work or designated portion thereof is substantially complete. If the Architect's inspection discloses any item, whether or not included on the Contractor's list, which is not sufficiently complete in accordance with the Contract Documents so that the Owner can occupy or utilize the Work or designated portion thereof for its intended use, the Contractor shall, before issuance of the Certificate of Substantial Completion, complete or correct such item upon notification by the Architect. In such case, the Contractor shall then submit a request for another inspection by the Architect to determine Substantial Completion.

9.8.4 When the Work or designated portion thereof is substantially complete, the Architect will prepare a Certificate of Substantial Completion which shall establish the date of Substantial Completion, shall establish responsibilities of the Owner and Contractor for security, maintenance, heat, utilities, damage to the Work and insurance, and shall fix the time within which the Contractor shall finish all items on the list accompanying the Certificate. Warranties required by the Contract Documents shall commence on the date of Substantial Completion of the Work or designated portion thereof unless otherwise provided in the Certificate of Substantial Completion.

9.8.5 The Certificate of Substantial Completion shall be submitted to the Owner and Contractor for their written acceptance of responsibilities assigned to them in such Certificate. Upon such acceptance and consent of surety, if any, the Owner shall make payment of retainage applying to such Work or designated portion thereof. Such payment shall be adjusted for Work that is incomplete or not in accordance with the requirements of the Contract Documents.

9.9 PARTIAL OCCUPANCY OR USE

9.9.1 The Owner may occupy or use any completed or partially completed portion of the Work at any stage when such portion is designated by separate agreement with the Contractor, provided such occupancy or use is consented to by the insurer as required under Clause 11.4.1.5 and authorized by public authorities having jurisdiction over the Work. Such partial occupancy or use may commence whether or not the portion is substantially complete, provided the Owner and Contractor have accepted in writing the responsibilities assigned to each of them for payments, retainage, if any, security, maintenance, heat, utilities, damage to the Work and insurance, and

AIA DOCUMENT A201-1997
GENERAL CONDITIONS OF THE CONTRACT FOR CONSTRUCTION

The American Institute of Architects
1735 New York Avenue, N.W.
Washington, D.C. 20006-5292

have agreed in writing concerning the period for correction of the Work and commencement of warranties required by the Contract Documents. When the Contractor considers a portion substantially complete, the Contractor shall prepare and submit a list to the Architect as provided under Subparagraph 9.8.2. Consent of the Contractor to partial occupancy or use shall not be unreasonably withheld. The stage of the progress of the Work shall be determined by written agreement between the Owner and Contractor or, if no agreement is reached, by decision of the Architect.

9.9.2 Immediately prior to such partial occupancy or use, the Owner, Contractor and Architect shall jointly inspect the area to be occupied or portion of the Work to be used in order to determine and record the condition of the Work.

9.9.3 Unless otherwise agreed upon, partial occupancy or use of a portion or portions of the Work shall not constitute acceptance of Work not complying with the requirements of the Contract Documents.

9.10 FINAL COMPLETION AND FINAL PAYMENT

9.10.1 Upon receipt of written notice that the Work is ready for final inspection and acceptance and upon receipt of a final Application for Payment, the Architect will promptly make such inspection and, when the Architect finds the Work acceptable under the Contract Documents and the Contract fully performed, the Architect will promptly issue a final Certificate for Payment stating that to the best of the Architect's knowledge, information and belief, and on the basis of the Architect's on-site visits and inspections, the Work has been completed in accordance with terms and conditions of the Contract Documents and that the entire balance found to be due the Contractor and noted in the final Certificate is due and payable. The Architect's final Certificate for Payment will constitute a further representation that conditions listed in Subparagraph 9.10.2 as precedent to the Contractor's being entitled to final payment have been fulfilled.

9.10.2 Neither final payment nor any remaining retained percentage shall become due until the Contractor submits to the Architect (1) an affidavit that payrolls, bills for materials and equipment, and other indebtedness connected with the Work for which the Owner or the Owner's property might be responsible or encumbered (less amounts withheld by Owner) have been paid or otherwise satisfied, (2) a certificate evidencing that insurance required by the Contract Documents to remain in force after final payment is currently in effect and will not be canceled or allowed to expire until at least 30 days' prior written notice has been given to the Owner, (3) a written statement that the Contractor knows of no substantial reason that the insurance will not be renewable to cover the period required by the Contract Documents, (4) consent of surety, if any, to final payment and (5), if required by the Owner, other data establishing payment or satisfaction of obligations, such as receipts, releases and waivers of liens, claims, security interests or encumbrances arising out of the Contract, to the extent and in such form as may be designated by the Owner. If a Subcontractor refuses to furnish a release or waiver required by the Owner, the Contractor may furnish a bond satisfactory to the Owner to indemnify the Owner against such lien. If such lien remains unsatisfied after payments are made, the Contractor shall refund to the Owner all money that the Owner may be compelled to pay in discharging such lien, including all costs and reasonable attorneys' fees.

9.10.3 If, after Substantial Completion of the Work, final completion thereof is materially delayed through no fault of the Contractor or by issuance of Change Orders affecting final completion, and the Architect so confirms, the Owner shall, upon application by the Contractor and certification by the Architect, and without terminating the Contract, make payment of the balance due for that portion of the Work fully completed and accepted. If the remaining balance for Work not fully completed or corrected is less than retainage stipulated in the Contract Documents, and if bonds have been furnished, the written consent of surety to payment of the balance due for that

The American Institute of Architects
1735 New York Avenue, N.W.
Washington, D.C. 20006-5292

portion of the Work fully completed and accepted shall be submitted by the Contractor to the Architect prior to certification of such payment. Such payment shall be made under terms and conditions governing final payment, except that it shall not constitute a waiver of claims.

9.10.4 The making of final payment shall constitute a waiver of Claims by the Owner except those arising from:

.1 liens, Claims, security interests or encumbrances arising out of the Contract and unsettled;
.2 failure of the Work to comply with the requirements of the Contract Documents; or
.3 terms of special warranties required by the Contract Documents.

9.10.5 Acceptance of final payment by the Contractor, a Subcontractor or material supplier shall constitute a waiver of claims by that payee except those previously made in writing and identified by that payee as unsettled at the time of final Application for Payment.

ARTICLE 10 PROTECTION OF PERSONS AND PROPERTY

10.1 SAFETY PRECAUTIONS AND PROGRAMS

10.1.1 The Contractor shall be responsible for initiating, maintaining and supervising all safety precautions and programs in connection with the performance of the Contract.

10.2 SAFETY OF PERSONS AND PROPERTY

10.2.1 The Contractor shall take reasonable precautions for safety of, and shall provide reasonable protection to prevent damage, injury or loss to:

.1 employees on the Work and other persons who may be affected thereby;
.2 the Work and materials and equipment to be incorporated therein, whether in storage on or off the site, under care, custody or control of the Contractor or the Contractor's Subcontractors or Sub-subcontractors; and
.3 other property at the site or adjacent thereto, such as trees, shrubs, lawns, walks, pavements, roadways, structures and utilities not designated for removal, relocation or replacement in the course of construction.

10.2.2 The Contractor shall give notices and comply with applicable laws, ordinances, rules, regulations and lawful orders of public authorities bearing on safety of persons or property or their protection from damage, injury or loss.

10.2.3 The Contractor shall erect and maintain, as required by existing conditions and performance of the Contract, reasonable safeguards for safety and protection, including posting danger signs and other warnings against hazards, promulgating safety regulations and notifying owners and users of adjacent sites and utilities.

10.2.4 When use or storage of explosives or other hazardous materials or equipment or unusual methods are necessary for execution of the Work, the Contractor shall exercise utmost care and carry on such activities under supervision of properly qualified personnel.

10.2.5 The Contractor shall promptly remedy damage and loss (other than damage or loss insured under property insurance required by the Contract Documents) to property referred to in Clauses 10.2.1.2 and 10.2.1.3 caused in whole or in part by the Contractor, a Subcontractor, a Sub-subcontractor, or anyone directly or indirectly employed by any of them, or by anyone for whose acts they may be liable and for which the Contractor is responsible under Clauses 10.2.1.2 and 10.2.1.3, except damage or loss attributable to acts or omissions of the Owner or Architect or anyone directly or indirectly employed by either of them, or by anyone for whose acts either of them may be liable, and not attributable to the fault or negligence of the Contractor. The foregoing obligations of the Contractor are in addition to the Contractor's obligations under Paragraph 3.18.

The American Institute
of Architects
1735 New York Avenue, N.W.
Washington, D.C. 20006-5292

10.2.6 The Contractor shall designate a responsible member of the Contractor's organization at the site whose duty shall be the prevention of accidents. This person shall be the Contractor's superintendent unless otherwise designated by the Contractor in writing to the Owner and Architect.

10.2.7 The Contractor shall not load or permit any part of the construction or site to be loaded so as to endanger its safety.

10.3 HAZARDOUS MATERIALS

10.3.1 If reasonable precautions will be inadequate to prevent foreseeable bodily injury or death to persons resulting from a material or substance, including but not limited to asbestos or polychlorinated biphenyl (PCB), encountered on the site by the Contractor, the Contractor shall, upon recognizing the condition, immediately stop Work in the affected area and report the condition to the Owner and Architect in writing.

10.3.2 The Owner shall obtain the services of a licensed laboratory to verify the presence or absence of the material or substance reported by the Contractor and, in the event such material or substance is found to be present, to verify that it has been rendered harmless. Unless otherwise required by the Contract Documents, the Owner shall furnish in writing to the Contractor and Architect the names and qualifications of persons or entities who are to perform tests verifying the presence or absence of such material or substance or who are to perform the task of removal or safe containment of such material or substance. The Contractor and the Architect will promptly reply to the Owner in writing stating whether or not either has reasonable objection to the persons or entities proposed by the Owner. If either the Contractor or Architect has an objection to a person or entity proposed by the Owner, the Owner shall propose another to whom the Contractor and the Architect have no reasonable objection. When the material or substance has been rendered harmless, Work in the affected area shall resume upon written agreement of the Owner and Contractor. The Contract Time shall be extended appropriately and the Contract Sum shall be increased in the amount of the Contractor's reasonable additional costs of shut-down, delay and start-up, which adjustments shall be accomplished as provided in Article 7.

10.3.3 To the fullest extent permitted by law, the Owner shall indemnify and hold harmless the Contractor, Subcontractors, Architect, Architect's consultants and agents and employees of any of them from and against claims, damages, losses and expenses, including but not limited to attorneys' fees, arising out of or resulting from performance of the Work in the affected area if in fact the material or substance presents the risk of bodily injury or death as described in Subparagraph 10.3.1 and has not been rendered harmless, provided that such claim, damage, loss or expense is attributable to bodily injury, sickness, disease or death, or to injury to or destruction of tangible property (other than the Work itself) and provided that such damage, loss or expense is not due to the sole negligence of a party seeking indemnity.

10.4 The Owner shall not be responsible under Paragraph 10.3 for materials and substances brought to the site by the Contractor unless such materials or substances were required by the Contract Documents.

10.5 If, without negligence on the part of the Contractor, the Contractor is held liable for the cost of remediation of a hazardous material or substance solely by reason of performing Work as required by the Contract Documents, the Owner shall indemnify the Contractor for all cost and expense thereby incurred.

10.6 EMERGENCIES

10.6.1 In an emergency affecting safety of persons or property, the Contractor shall act, at the Contractor's discretion, to prevent threatened damage, injury or loss. Additional compensation or

The American Institute
of Architects
1735 New York Avenue, N.W.
Washington, D.C. 20006-5292

extension of time claimed by the Contractor on account of an emergency shall be determined as provided in Paragraph 4.3 and Article 7.

ARTICLE 11 INSURANCE AND BONDS

11.1 CONTRACTOR'S LIABILITY INSURANCE

11.1.1 The Contractor shall purchase from and maintain in a company or companies lawfully authorized to do business in the jurisdiction in which the Project is located such insurance as will protect the Contractor from claims set forth below which may arise out of or result from the Contractor's operations under the Contract and for which the Contractor may be legally liable, whether such operations be by the Contractor or by a Subcontractor or by anyone directly or indirectly employed by any of them, or by anyone for whose acts any of them may be liable:

- .1 claims under workers' compensation, disability benefit and other similar employee benefit acts which are applicable to the Work to be performed;
- .2 claims for damages because of bodily injury, occupational sickness or disease, or death of the Contractor's employees;
- .3 claims for damages because of bodily injury, sickness or disease, or death of any person other than the Contractor's employees;
- .4 claims for damages insured by usual personal injury liability coverage;
- .5 claims for damages, other than to the Work itself, because of injury to or destruction of tangible property, including loss of use resulting therefrom;
- .6 claims for damages because of bodily injury, death of a person or property damage arising out of ownership, maintenance or use of a motor vehicle;
- .7 claims for bodily injury or property damage arising out of completed operations; and
- .8 claims involving contractual liability insurance applicable to the Contractor's obligations under Paragraph 3.18.

11.1.2 The insurance required by Subparagraph 11.1.1 shall be written for not less than limits of liability specified in the Contract Documents or required by law, whichever coverage is greater. Coverages, whether written on an occurrence or claims-made basis, shall be maintained without interruption from date of commencement of the Work until date of final payment and termination of any coverage required to be maintained after final payment.

11.1.3 Certificates of insurance acceptable to the Owner shall be filed with the Owner prior to commencement of the Work. These certificates and the insurance policies required by this Paragraph 11.1 shall contain a provision that coverages afforded under the policies will not be canceled or allowed to expire until at least 30 days' prior written notice has been given to the Owner. If any of the foregoing insurance coverages are required to remain in force after final payment and are reasonably available, an additional certificate evidencing continuation of such coverage shall be submitted with the final Application for Payment as required by Subparagraph 9.10.2. Information concerning reduction of coverage on account of revised limits or claims paid under the General Aggregate, or both, shall be furnished by the Contractor with reasonable promptness in accordance with the Contractor's information and belief.

11.2 OWNER'S LIABILITY INSURANCE

11.2.1 The Owner shall be responsible for purchasing and maintaining the Owner's usual liability insurance.

11.3 PROJECT MANAGEMENT PROTECTIVE LIABILITY INSURANCE

11.3.1 Optionally, the Owner may require the Contractor to purchase and maintain Project Management Protective Liability insurance from the Contractor's usual sources as primary coverage for the Owner's, Contractor's and Architect's vicarious liability for construction operations under the Contract. Unless otherwise required by the Contract Documents, the Owner shall reimburse the Contractor by increasing the Contract Sum to pay the cost of purchasing and maintaining such optional insurance coverage, and the Contractor shall not be responsible for purchasing any other liability insurance on behalf of the Owner. The minimum limits of liability purchased with such coverage shall be equal to the aggregate of the limits required for Contractor's Liability Insurance under Clauses 11.1.1.2 through 11.1.1.5.

11.3.2 To the extent damages are covered by Project Management Protective Liability insurance, the Owner, Contractor and Architect waive all rights against each other for damages, except such rights as they may have to the proceeds of such insurance. The policy shall provide for such waivers of subrogation by endorsement or otherwise.

11.3.3 The Owner shall not require the Contractor to include the Owner, Architect or other persons or entities as additional insureds on the Contractor's Liability Insurance coverage under Paragraph 11.1.

11.4 PROPERTY INSURANCE

11.4.1 Unless otherwise provided, the Owner shall purchase and maintain, in a company or companies lawfully authorized to do business in the jurisdiction in which the Project is located, property insurance written on a builder's risk "all-risk" or equivalent policy form in the amount of the initial Contract Sum, plus value of subsequent Contract modifications and cost of materials supplied or installed by others, comprising total value for the entire Project at the site on a replacement cost basis without optional deductibles. Such property insurance shall be maintained, unless otherwise provided in the Contract Documents or otherwise agreed in writing by all persons and entities who are beneficiaries of such insurance, until final payment has been made as provided in Paragraph 9.10 or until no person or entity other than the Owner has an insurable interest in the property required by this Paragraph 11.4 to be covered, whichever is later. This insurance shall include interests of the Owner, the Contractor, Subcontractors and Sub-subcontractors in the Project.

11.4.1.1 Property insurance shall be on an "all-risk" or equivalent policy form and shall include, without limitation, insurance against the perils of fire (with extended coverage) and physical loss or damage including, without duplication of coverage, theft, vandalism, malicious mischief, collapse, earthquake, flood, windstorm, falsework, testing and startup, temporary buildings and debris removal including demolition occasioned by enforcement of any applicable legal requirements, and shall cover reasonable compensation for Architect's and Contractor's services and expenses required as a result of such insured loss.

11.4.1.2 If the Owner does not intend to purchase such property insurance required by the Contract and with all of the coverages in the amount described above, the Owner shall so inform the Contractor in writing prior to commencement of the Work. The Contractor may then effect insurance which will protect the interests of the Contractor, Subcontractors and Sub-subcontractors in the Work, and by appropriate Change Order the cost thereof shall be charged to the Owner. If the Contractor is damaged by the failure or neglect of the Owner to purchase or maintain insurance as described above, without so notifying the Contractor in writing, then the Owner shall bear all reasonable costs properly attributable thereto.

11.4.1.3 If the property insurance requires deductibles, the Owner shall pay costs not covered because of such deductibles.

11.4.1.4 This property insurance shall cover portions of the Work stored off the site, and also portions of the Work in transit.

11.4.1.5 Partial occupancy or use in accordance with Paragraph 9.9 shall not commence until the insurance company or companies providing property insurance have consented to such partial

The American Institute
of Architects
1735 New York Avenue, N.W.
Washington, D.C. 20006-5292

occupancy or use by endorsement or otherwise. The Owner and the Contractor shall take reasonable steps to obtain consent of the insurance company or companies and shall, without mutual written consent, take no action with respect to partial occupancy or use that would cause cancellation, lapse or reduction of insurance.

11.4.2 Boiler and Machinery Insurance. The Owner shall purchase and maintain boiler and machinery insurance required by the Contract Documents or by law, which shall specifically cover such insured objects during installation and until final acceptance by the Owner; this insurance shall include interests of the Owner, Contractor, Subcontractors and Sub-subcontractors in the Work, and the Owner and Contractor shall be named insureds.

11.4.3 Loss of Use Insurance. The Owner, at the Owner's option, may purchase and maintain such insurance as will insure the Owner against loss of use of the Owner's property due to fire or other hazards, however caused. The Owner waives all rights of action against the Contractor for loss of use of the Owner's property, including consequential losses due to fire or other hazards however caused.

11.4.4 If the Contractor requests in writing that insurance for risks other than those described herein or other special causes of loss be included in the property insurance policy, the Owner shall, if possible, include such insurance, and the cost thereof shall be charged to the Contractor by appropriate Change Order.

11.4.5 If during the Project construction period the Owner insures properties, real or personal or both, at or adjacent to the site by property insurance under policies separate from those insuring the Project, or if after final payment property insurance is to be provided on the completed Project through a policy or policies other than those insuring the Project during the construction period, the Owner shall waive all rights in accordance with the terms of Subparagraph 11.4.7 for damages caused by fire or other causes of loss covered by this separate property insurance. All separate policies shall provide this waiver of subrogation by endorsement or otherwise.

11.4.6 Before an exposure to loss may occur, the Owner shall file with the Contractor a copy of each policy that includes insurance coverages required by this Paragraph 11.4. Each policy shall contain all generally applicable conditions, definitions, exclusions and endorsements related to this Project. Each policy shall contain a provision that the policy will not be canceled or allowed to expire, and that its limits will not be reduced, until at least 30 days' prior written notice has been given to the Contractor.

11.4.7 Waivers of Subrogation. The Owner and Contractor waive all rights against (1) each other and any of their subcontractors, sub-subcontractors, agents and employees, each of the other, and (2) the Architect, Architect's consultants, separate contractors described in Article 6, if any, and any of their subcontractors, sub-subcontractors, agents and employees, for damages caused by fire or other causes of loss to the extent covered by property insurance obtained pursuant to this Paragraph 11.4 or other property insurance applicable to the Work, except such rights as they have to proceeds of such insurance held by the Owner as fiduciary. The Owner or Contractor, as appropriate, shall require of the Architect, Architect's consultants, separate contractors described in Article 6, if any, and the subcontractors, sub-subcontractors, agents and employees of any of them, by appropriate agreements, written where legally required for validity, similar waivers each in favor of other parties enumerated herein. The policies shall provide such waivers of subrogation by endorsement or otherwise. A waiver of subrogation shall be effective as to a person or entity even though that person or entity would otherwise have a duty of indemnification, contractual or otherwise, did not pay the insurance premium directly or indirectly, and whether or not the person or entity had an insurable interest in the property damaged.

The American Institute
of Architects
1735 New York Avenue, N.W.
Washington, D.C. 20006-5292

11.4.8 A loss insured under Owner's property insurance shall be adjusted by the Owner as fiduciary and made payable to the Owner as fiduciary for the insureds, as their interests may appear, subject to requirements of any applicable mortgagee clause and of Subparagraph 11.4.10. The Contractor shall pay Subcontractors their just shares of insurance proceeds received by the Contractor, and by appropriate agreements, written where legally required for validity, shall require Subcontractors to make payments to their Sub-subcontractors in similar manner.

11.4.9 If required in writing by a party in interest, the Owner as fiduciary shall, upon occurrence of an insured loss, give bond for proper performance of the Owner's duties. The cost of required bonds shall be charged against proceeds received as fiduciary. The Owner shall deposit in a separate account proceeds so received, which the Owner shall distribute in accordance with such agreement as the parties in interest may reach, or in accordance with an arbitration award in which case the procedure shall be as provided in Paragraph 4.6. If after such loss no other special agreement is made and unless the Owner terminates the Contract for convenience, replacement of damaged property shall be performed by the Contractor after notification of a Change in the Work in accordance with Article 7.

11.4.10 The Owner as fiduciary shall have power to adjust and settle a loss with insurers unless one of the parties in interest shall object in writing within five days after occurrence of loss to the Owner's exercise of this power; if such objection is made, the dispute shall be resolved as provided in Paragraphs 4.5 and 4.6. The Owner as fiduciary shall, in the case of arbitration, make settlement with insurers in accordance with directions of the arbitrators. If distribution of insurance proceeds by arbitration is required, the arbitrators will direct such distribution.

11.5 PERFORMANCE BOND AND PAYMENT BOND

11.5.1 The Owner shall have the right to require the Contractor to furnish bonds covering faithful performance of the Contract and payment of obligations arising thereunder as stipulated in bidding requirements or specifically required in the Contract Documents on the date of execution of the Contract.

11.5.2 Upon the request of any person or entity appearing to be a potential beneficiary of bonds covering payment of obligations arising under the Contract, the Contractor shall promptly furnish a copy of the bonds or shall permit a copy to be made.

ARTICLE 12 UNCOVERING AND CORRECTION OF WORK

12.1 UNCOVERING OF WORK

12.1.1 If a portion of the Work is covered contrary to the Architect's request or to requirements specifically expressed in the Contract Documents, it must, if required in writing by the Architect, be uncovered for the Architect's examination and be replaced at the Contractor's expense without change in the Contract Time.

12.1.2 If a portion of the Work has been covered which the Architect has not specifically requested to examine prior to its being covered, the Architect may request to see such Work and it shall be uncovered by the Contractor. If such Work is in accordance with the Contract Documents, costs of uncovering and replacement shall, by appropriate Change Order, be at the Owner's expense. If such Work is not in accordance with the Contract Documents, correction shall be at the Contractor's expense unless the condition was caused by the Owner or a separate contractor in which event the Owner shall be responsible for payment of such costs.

12.2 CORRECTION OF WORK

12.2.1 BEFORE OR AFTER SUBSTANTIAL COMPLETION

12.2.1.1 The Contractor shall promptly correct Work rejected by the Architect or failing to conform to the requirements of the Contract Documents, whether discovered before or after Substantial Completion and whether or not fabricated, installed or completed. Costs of correcting such rejected Work, including additional testing and inspections and compensation for the Architect's services and expenses made necessary thereby, shall be at the Contractor's expense.

12.2.2 AFTER SUBSTANTIAL COMPLETION

12.2.2.1 In addition to the Contractor's obligations under Paragraph 3.5, if, within one year after the date of Substantial Completion of the Work or designated portion thereof or after the date for commencement of warranties established under Subparagraph 9.9.1, or by terms of an applicable special warranty required by the Contract Documents, any of the Work is found to be not in accordance with the requirements of the Contract Documents, the Contractor shall correct it promptly after receipt of written notice from the Owner to do so unless the Owner has previously given the Contractor a written acceptance of such condition. The Owner shall give such notice promptly after discovery of the condition. During the one-year period for correction of Work, if the Owner fails to notify the Contractor and give the Contractor an opportunity to make the correction, the Owner waives the rights to require correction by the Contractor and to make a claim for breach of warranty. If the Contractor fails to correct nonconforming Work within a reasonable time during that period after receipt of notice from the Owner or Architect, the Owner may correct it in accordance with Paragraph 2.4.

12.2.2.2 The one-year period for correction of Work shall be extended with respect to portions of Work first performed after Substantial Completion by the period of time between Substantial Completion and the actual performance of the Work.

12.2.2.3 The one-year period for correction of Work shall not be extended by corrective Work performed by the Contractor pursuant to this Paragraph 12.2.

12.2.3 The Contractor shall remove from the site portions of the Work which are not in accordance with the requirements of the Contract Documents and are neither corrected by the Contractor nor accepted by the Owner.

12.2.4 The Contractor shall bear the cost of correcting destroyed or damaged construction, whether completed or partially completed, of the Owner or separate contractors caused by the Contractor's correction or removal of Work which is not in accordance with the requirements of the Contract Documents.

12.2.5 Nothing contained in this Paragraph 12.2 shall be construed to establish a period of limitation with respect to other obligations which the Contractor might have under the Contract Documents. Establishment of the one-year period for correction of Work as described in Subparagraph 12.2.2 relates only to the specific obligation of the Contractor to correct the Work, and has no relationship to the time within which the obligation to comply with the Contract Documents may be sought to be enforced, nor to the time within which proceedings may be commenced to establish the Contractor's liability with respect to the Contractor's obligations other than specifically to correct the Work.

12.3 ACCEPTANCE OF NONCONFORMING WORK

12.3.1 If the Owner prefers to accept Work which is not in accordance with the requirements of the Contract Documents, the Owner may do so instead of requiring its removal and correction, in which case the Contract Sum will be reduced as appropriate and equitable. Such adjustment shall be effected whether or not final payment has been made.

The American Institute
of Architects
1735 New York Avenue, N.W.
Washington, D.C. 20006-5292

ARTICLE 13 MISCELLANEOUS PROVISIONS

13.1 GOVERNING LAW

13.1.1 The Contract shall be governed by the law of the place where the Project is located.

13.2 SUCCESSORS AND ASSIGNS

13.2.1 The Owner and Contractor respectively bind themselves, their partners, successors, assigns and legal representatives to the other party hereto and to partners, successors, assigns and legal representatives of such other party in respect to covenants, agreements and obligations contained in the Contract Documents. Except as provided in Subparagraph 13.2.2, neither party to the Contract shall assign the Contract as a whole without written consent of the other. If either party attempts to make such an assignment without such consent, that party shall nevertheless remain legally responsible for all obligations under the Contract.

13.2.2 The Owner may, without consent of the Contractor, assign the Contract to an institutional lender providing construction financing for the Project. In such event, the lender shall assume the Owner's rights and obligations under the Contract Documents. The Contractor shall execute all consents reasonably required to facilitate such assignment.

13.3 WRITTEN NOTICE

13.3.1 Written notice shall be deemed to have been duly served if delivered in person to the individual or a member of the firm or entity or to an officer of the corporation for which it was intended, or if delivered at or sent by registered or certified mail to the last business address known to the party giving notice.

13.4 RIGHTS AND REMEDIES

13.4.1 Duties and obligations imposed by the Contract Documents and rights and remedies available thereunder shall be in addition to and not a limitation of duties, obligations, rights and remedies otherwise imposed or available by law.

13.4.2 No action or failure to act by the Owner, Architect or Contractor shall constitute a waiver of a right or duty afforded them under the Contract, nor shall such action or failure to act constitute approval of or acquiescence in a breach thereunder, except as may be specifically agreed in writing.

13.5 TESTS AND INSPECTIONS

13.5.1 Tests, inspections and approvals of portions of the Work required by the Contract Documents or by laws, ordinances, rules, regulations or orders of public authorities having jurisdiction shall be made at an appropriate time. Unless otherwise provided, the Contractor shall make arrangements for such tests, inspections and approvals with an independent testing laboratory or entity acceptable to the Owner, or with the appropriate public authority, and shall bear all related costs of tests, inspections and approvals. The Contractor shall give the Architect timely notice of when and where tests and inspections are to be made so that the Architect may be present for such procedures. The Owner shall bear costs of tests, inspections or approvals which do not become requirements until after bids are received or negotiations concluded.

13.5.2 If the Architect, Owner or public authorities having jurisdiction determine that portions of the Work require additional testing, inspection or approval not included under Subparagraph 13.5.1, the Architect will, upon written authorization from the Owner, instruct the Contractor to make arrangements for such additional testing, inspection or approval by an entity acceptable to the Owner, and the Contractor shall give timely notice to the Architect of when and where tests and inspections are to be made so that the Architect may be present for such procedures. Such costs, except as provided in Subparagraph 13.5.3, shall be at the Owner's expense.

The American Institute of Architects
1735 New York Avenue, N.W.
Washington, D.C. 20006-5292

13.5.3 If such procedures for testing, inspection or approval under Subparagraphs 13.5.1 and 13.5.2 reveal failure of the portions of the Work to comply with requirements established by the Contract Documents, all costs made necessary by such failure including those of repeated procedures and compensation for the Architect's services and expenses shall be at the Contractor's expense.

13.5.4 Required certificates of testing, inspection or approval shall, unless otherwise required by the Contract Documents, be secured by the Contractor and promptly delivered to the Architect.

13.5.5 If the Architect is to observe tests, inspections or approvals required by the Contract Documents, the Architect will do so promptly and, where practicable, at the normal place of testing.

13.5.6 Tests or inspections conducted pursuant to the Contract Documents shall be made promptly to avoid unreasonable delay in the Work.

13.6 INTEREST

13.6.1 Payments due and unpaid under the Contract Documents shall bear interest from the date payment is due at such rate as the parties may agree upon in writing or, in the absence thereof, at the legal rate prevailing from time to time at the place where the Project is located.

13.7 COMMENCEMENT OF STATUTORY LIMITATION PERIOD

13.7.1 As between the Owner and Contractor:

.1 **Before Substantial Completion.** As to acts or failures to act occurring prior to the relevant date of Substantial Completion, any applicable statute of limitations shall commence to run and any alleged cause of action shall be deemed to have accrued in any and all events not later than such date of Substantial Completion;

.2 **Between Substantial Completion and Final Certificate for Payment.** As to acts or failures to act occurring subsequent to the relevant date of Substantial Completion and prior to issuance of the final Certificate for Payment, any applicable statute of limitations shall commence to run and any alleged cause of action shall be deemed to have accrued in any and all events not later than the date of issuance of the final Certificate for Payment; and

.3 **After Final Certificate for Payment.** As to acts or failures to act occurring after the relevant date of issuance of the final Certificate for Payment, any applicable statute of limitations shall commence to run and any alleged cause of action shall be deemed to have accrued in any and all events not later than the date of any act or failure to act by the Contractor pursuant to any Warranty provided under Paragraph 3.5, the date of any correction of the Work or failure to correct the Work by the Contractor under Paragraph 12.2, or the date of actual commission of any other act or failure to perform any duty or obligation by the Contractor or Owner, whichever occurs last.

ARTICLE 14 TERMINATION OR SUSPENSION OF THE CONTRACT

14.1 TERMINATION BY THE CONTRACTOR

14.1.1 The Contractor may terminate the Contract if the Work is stopped for a period of 30 consecutive days through no act or fault of the Contractor or a Subcontractor, Sub-subcontractor or their agents or employees or any other persons or entities performing portions of the Work under direct or indirect contract with the Contractor, for any of the following reasons:

.1 issuance of an order of a court or other public authority having jurisdiction which requires all Work to be stopped;

.2 an act of government, such as a declaration of national emergency which requires all Work to be stopped;

The American Institute of Architects
1735 New York Avenue, N.W.
Washington, D.C. 20006-5292

.3 because the Architect has not issued a Certificate for Payment and has not notified the Contractor of the reason for withholding certification as provided in Subparagraph 9.4.1, or because the Owner has not made payment on a Certificate for Payment within the time stated in the Contract Documents; or

.4 the Owner has failed to furnish to the Contractor promptly, upon the Contractor's request, reasonable evidence as required by Subparagraph 2.2.1.

14.1.2 The Contractor may terminate the Contract if, through no act or fault of the Contractor or a Subcontractor, Sub-subcontractor or their agents or employees or any other persons or entities performing portions of the Work under direct or indirect contract with the Contractor, repeated suspensions, delays or interruptions of the entire Work by the Owner as described in Paragraph 14.3 constitute in the aggregate more than 100 percent of the total number of days scheduled for completion, or 120 days in any 365-day period, whichever is less.

14.1.3 If one of the reasons described in Subparagraph 14.1.1 or 14.1.2 exists, the Contractor may, upon seven days' written notice to the Owner and Architect, terminate the Contract and recover from the Owner payment for Work executed and for proven loss with respect to materials, equipment, tools, and construction equipment and machinery, including reasonable overhead, profit and damages.

14.1.4 If the Work is stopped for a period of 60 consecutive days through no act or fault of the Contractor or a Subcontractor or their agents or employees or any other persons performing portions of the Work under contract with the Contractor because the Owner has persistently failed to fulfill the Owner's obligations under the Contract Documents with respect to matters important to the progress of the Work, the Contractor may, upon seven additional days' written notice to the Owner and the Architect, terminate the Contract and recover from the Owner as provided in Subparagraph 14.1.3.

14.2 TERMINATION BY THE OWNER FOR CAUSE

14.2.1 The Owner may terminate the Contract if the Contractor:

.1 persistently or repeatedly refuses or fails to supply enough properly skilled workers or proper materials;

.2 fails to make payment to Subcontractors for materials or labor in accordance with the respective agreements between the Contractor and the Subcontractors;

.3 persistently disregards laws, ordinances, or rules, regulations or orders of a public authority having jurisdiction; or

.4 otherwise is guilty of substantial breach of a provision of the Contract Documents.

14.2.2 When any of the above reasons exist, the Owner, upon certification by the Architect that sufficient cause exists to justify such action, may without prejudice to any other rights or remedies of the Owner and after giving the Contractor and the Contractor's surety, if any, seven days' written notice, terminate employment of the Contractor and may, subject to any prior rights of the surety:

.1 take possession of the site and of all materials, equipment, tools, and construction equipment and machinery thereon owned by the Contractor;

.2 accept assignment of subcontracts pursuant to Paragraph 5.4; and

.3 finish the Work by whatever reasonable method the Owner may deem expedient. Upon request of the Contractor, the Owner shall furnish to the Contractor a detailed accounting of the costs incurred by the Owner in finishing the Work.

14.2.3 When the Owner terminates the Contract for one of the reasons stated in Subparagraph 14.2.1, the Contractor shall not be entitled to receive further payment until the Work is finished.

The American Institute of Architects
1735 New York Avenue, N.W.
Washington, D.C. 20006-5292

14.2.4 If the unpaid balance of the Contract Sum exceeds costs of finishing the Work, including compensation for the Architect's services and expenses made necessary thereby, and other damages incurred by the Owner and not expressly waived, such excess shall be paid to the Contractor. If such costs and damages exceed the unpaid balance, the Contractor shall pay the difference to the Owner. The amount to be paid to the Contractor or Owner, as the case may be, shall be certified by the Architect, upon application, and this obligation for payment shall survive termination of the Contract.

14.3 SUSPENSION BY THE OWNER FOR CONVENIENCE

14.3.1 The Owner may, without cause, order the Contractor in writing to suspend, delay or interrupt the Work in whole or in part for such period of time as the Owner may determine.

14.3.2 The Contract Sum and Contract Time shall be adjusted for increases in the cost and time caused by suspension, delay or interruption as described in Subparagraph 14.3.1. Adjustment of the Contract Sum shall include profit. No adjustment shall be made to the extent:

.1 that performance is, was or would have been so suspended, delayed or interrupted by another cause for which the Contractor is responsible; or

.2 that an equitable adjustment is made or denied under another provision of the Contract.

14.4 TERMINATION BY THE OWNER FOR CONVENIENCE

14.4.1 The Owner may, at any time, terminate the Contract for the Owner's convenience and without cause.

14.4.2 Upon receipt of written notice from the Owner of such termination for the Owner's convenience, the Contractor shall:

.1 cease operations as directed by the Owner in the notice;

.2 take actions necessary, or that the Owner may direct, for the protection and preservation of the Work; and

.3 except for Work directed to be performed prior to the effective date of termination stated in the notice, terminate all existing subcontracts and purchase orders and enter into no further subcontracts and purchase orders.

14.4.3 In case of such termination for the Owner's convenience, the Contractor shall be entitled to receive payment for Work executed, and costs incurred by reason of such termination, along with reasonable overhead and profit on the Work not executed.

APPENDIX F

Selected Contract Specifications for Huna Office Building

SECTION 01035 - MODIFICATION PROCEDURES

1.1 GENERAL

A. Minor Changes in the Work: The Architect will issue instructions authorizing minor changes in the Work on AIA Form G710.

B. Owner-Initiated Change Order Proposal Requests: The Architect will issue a description of proposed changes in the Work that require adjustment to the Contract Sum or Time. The description may include supplemental or revised Drawings and Specifications.

1. Proposal requests are for information only. Do not consider them an instruction to stop work or to execute the proposed change.
2. Within 20 days of receipt, submit an estimate of cost necessary to execute the change for the Owner's review.

    a. Include an itemized list of products required and unit costs, with the total amount of purchases.
    b. Indicate taxes, delivery charges, equipment rental, and amounts of trade discounts.
    c. Indicate the effect the change will have on the Contract Time.

C. Contractor-Initiated Proposals: When unforeseen conditions require modifications, the Contractor may submit a request for a change to the Architect.

1. Describe the proposed change. Indicate reasons for the change and the effect of the change on the Contract Sum and Time.
2. Include an itemized list of products required and unit costs, with the total amount of purchases.
3. Indicate taxes, delivery charges, equipment rental, and amounts of trade discounts.

D. Proposal Request Form: Use AIA Document G709.

E. Allowance Adjustment: Base Change Order Proposals on the difference between the purchase amount and the allowance, multiplied by the measurement of work-in-place. Allow for cutting losses, tolerances, mixing wastes, normal product imperfections, and similar margins.

1. Include installation costs only where indicated as part of the allowance.
2. Prepare explanations and documentation to substantiate margins claimed.

F. Submit claims for increased costs because of a change in the allowance, whether for purchase order amount or handling, labor, installation, overhead, and profit. Submit claims within 21 days of receipt of authorization to proceed. The Owner will reject claims submitted later than 21 days.

1. Do not include indirect expense in cost amount unless the Work has changed from that described in Contract Documents.
2. No change to indirect expense is permitted for selection of higher- or lower-priced materials or systems of the same scope and nature as originally indicated.

G. Construction Change Directive: When Owner and Contractor disagree on the terms of a Proposal Request, the Architect may issue a Construction Change Directive on AIA Form G714 instructing the Contractor to proceed with a change.

1. The Construction Change Directive contains a description of the change and designates the method to be followed to determine change in the Contract Sum or Time.

H. Documentation: Maintain detailed records on a time and material basis of work required by the Construction Change Directive.

1. After completing the change, submit an itemized account and supporting data to substantiate Contract adjustments.

I. Change Order Procedures: Upon the Owner's approval of a Proposal Request, the Architect will issue a Change Order on AIA Form G701.

1.2 PRODUCTS (Not Applicable)

1.3 EXECUTION (Not Applicable)

END OF SECTION 01035

SECTION 01200 - PROJECT MEETINGS

1.1 GENERAL

A. This Section specifies administrative and procedural requirements for project meetings, including, but not limited to, the following:

1. Preconstruction conferences.
2. Preinstallation conferences.
3. Progress meetings.

B. Preconstruction Conference: Schedule a preconstruction conference before starting construction. Review responsibilities and personnel assignments.

C. Attendees: Authorized representatives of the Owner, Architect, and their consultants; the Contractor and its superintendent; major subcontractors; and other concerned parties shall attend.

1. Participants shall be familiar with the Project and authorized to conclude matters relating to the Work.

D. Agenda: Discuss items that could affect progress, including the following:

1. Tentative construction schedule.
2. Critical work sequencing.
3. Submittal of Shop Drawings, Product Data, and Samples.
4. Use of the premises.

E. Preinstallation Conferences: Conduct a conference before each activity that requires coordination with other operations.

F. Attendees: The Installer and representatives of manufacturers and fabricators involved in or affected by the installation shall attend. Advise the Architect of scheduled meeting dates.

1. Review the progress of other operations and preparations for the activity under consideration at each preinstallation conference, including requirements for the following:

   a. Compatibility problems and acceptability of substrates.
   b. Time schedules and deliveries.
   c. Manufacturer's recommendations.
   d. Warranty requirements.
   e. Inspecting and testing requirements.

2. Record significant discussions and agreements and disagreements, and the approved schedule. Promptly distribute the record of the meeting to everyone concerned, including the Owner and the Architect.
3. Do not proceed with the installation if the conference cannot be successfully concluded. Initiate actions necessary to resolve problems and reconvene the conference.

G. Progress Meetings: Conduct progress meetings at the Project Site at regular intervals. Notify the Owner and the Architect of scheduled dates. Coordinate meeting dates with preparation of the payment request.

H. Attendees: The Owner, Architect, and other entities concerned with current progress or involved in planning, coordination, or future activities shall be represented. Participants shall be authorized to conclude matters relating to the Work.

I. Agenda: Review and correct or approve minutes of the previous meeting. Review items of significance that could affect progress. Include topics for discussion appropriate to Project status.

1. Contractor's Construction Schedule: Review progress since the last meeting. Determine where each activity is in relation to the Contractor's Construction Schedule. Determine how to expedite construction behind schedule; secure commitments from parties involved to do so. Discuss revisions required to insure subsequent activities will be completed within the Contract Time.
2. Review the present and future needs of each entity present, including the following:

    a. Time.
    b. Sequences.
    c. Status of submittals.
    d. Deliveries and off-site fabrication problems.
    e. Temporary facilities and services.
    f. Quality and work standards.
    g. Change Orders.

3. Reporting: Distribute meeting minutes to each party present and to parties who should have been present. Include a summary of progress since the previous meeting and report.
4. Schedule Updating: Revise the Contractor's Construction Schedule after each meeting where revisions have been made. Issue the revised schedule concurrently with the report of each meeting.

1.2 PRODUCTS (Not Applicable)

1.3 EXECUTION (Not Applicable)

END OF SECTION 01200

SECTION 01300 - SUBMITTALS

1.1 GENERAL

A. Submittal Procedures: Coordinate submittal preparation with construction, fabrication, other submittals, and activities that require sequential operations. Transmit in advance of construction operations to avoid delay.

1. Coordinate submittals for related operations to avoid delay because of the need to review submittals concurrently for coordination. The Architect reserves the right to withhold action on a submittal requiring coordination until related submittals are received.
2. Processing: Allow 2 weeks for initial review. Allow more time if the Architect must delay processing to permit coordination. Allow 2 weeks for reprocessing.

   a. No extension of Contract Time will be authorized because of failure to transmit submittals sufficiently in advance of the Work to permit processing.

3. Submittal Preparation: Place a permanent label on each submittal for identification. Provide a 4- by 5-inch space on the label or beside title block to record review and approval markings and action taken. Include the following information on the label for processing and recording action taken.

   a. Project name.
   b. Date.
   c. Name and address of the Architect.
   d. Name and address of the Contractor.
   e. Name and address of the subcontractor.
   f. Name and address of the supplier.
   g. Name of the manufacturer.
   h. Number and title of appropriate Specification Section.
   i. Drawing number and detail references, as appropriate.

4. Submittal Transmittal: Package each submittal appropriately. Transmit with a transmittal form. The Architect will not accept submittals from sources other than the Contractor.

B. Contractor's Construction Schedule: Prepare a horizontal bar-chart-type, contractor's construction schedule. Provide a separate time bar for each activity and a vertical line to identify the first working day of each week. Use the same breakdown of Work indicated in the "Schedule of Values." Indicate estimated completion in 10 percent increments. As Work progresses, mark each bar to indicate actual completion.

1. Prepare the schedule on stable transparency, or other reproducible media, of width to show data for the entire construction period.
2. Secure performance commitments from parties involved. Coordinate each element with other activities; include minor elements involved in the Work. Show each activity in proper sequence. Indicate sequences necessary for completion of related Work.
3. Coordinate with the Schedule of Values, list of subcontracts, Submittal Schedule, payment requests, and other schedules.
4. Indicate completion in advance of Substantial Completion. Indicate Substantial Completion to allow time for the Architect's procedures necessary for certification of Substantial Completion.

5. Schedule Distribution: Distribute copies of the Contractor's Construction Schedule to the Architect, Owner, subcontractors, and parties required to comply with submittal dates. Post copies in the field office.

   a. When revisions are made, distribute to the same parties and post in the same locations. Delete parties from distribution when they have completed their Work and are no longer involved in construction activities.
   b. Updating: Revise the schedule after each meeting or activity where revisions have been made. Issue the updated schedule concurrently with the report of each meeting.

C. Shop Drawings: Submit newly prepared information drawn to scale. Indicate deviations from the Contract Documents. Do not reproduce Contract Documents or copy standard information. Include the following information:

1. Dimensions.
2. Identification of products and materials included by sheet and detail number.
3. Compliance with standards.
4. Notation of coordination requirements.
5. Notation of dimensions established by field measurement.
6. Sheet Size: Except for templates and full-size Drawings, submit one correctable, reproducible print and one blue- or black-line print on sheets at least 8-1/2 by 11 inches but no larger than 36 by 48 inches. The Architect will return the reproducible print.

   a. Do not use Shop Drawings without an appropriate final stamp indicating action taken.

D. Product Data: Collect Product Data into a single submittal for each element of construction. Mark each copy to show applicable choices and options. Where Product Data includes information on several products, mark copies to indicate applicable information.

1. Include the following information:

   a. Manufacturer's printed recommendations.
   b. Compliance with trade association standards.
   c. Compliance with recognized testing agency standards.
   d. Application of testing agency labels and seals.
   e. Notation of dimensions verified by field measurement.
   f. Notation of coordination requirements.

2. Submittals: Submit 5 copies; submit 6 copies where required for maintenance manuals. The Architect and Owner will retain three and return the others marked with action taken.

   a. Unless noncompliance with Contract Documents is observed, the submittal serves as the final submittal.

3. Distribution: Furnish copies to installers, subcontractors, suppliers, and others required for performance of construction activities. Show distribution on transmittal forms. Do not proceed with installation until a copy of Product Data is in the Installer's possession.

   a. Do not use unmarked Product Data for construction.

E. Samples: Submit full-size Samples cured and finished as specified and identical with the material proposed. Mount Samples to facilitate review of qualities.

1. Include the following:

   a. Specification Section number and reference.
   b. Generic description of the Sample.
   c. Sample source.
   d. Product name or name of the manufacturer.
   e. Compliance with recognized standards.
   f. Availability and delivery time.

2. Submit Samples for review of size, kind, color, pattern, and texture, for a check of these characteristics, and for a comparison of these characteristics between the final submittal and the actual component as delivered and installed. Where variations are inherent in the material, submit at least 3 units that show limits of the variations.

3. Preliminary Submittals: Submit a full set of choices where Samples are submitted for selection of color, pattern, texture, or similar characteristics from standard choices. The Architect will review and return submittals indicating selection and other action.

F. Architect's Action: Except for submittals for the record or information, where action and return are required, the Architect will review each submittal, mark to indicate action taken, and return. Compliance with specified characteristics is the Contractor's responsibility.

1. Action Stamp: The Architect will stamp each submittal with an action stamp. The Architect will mark the stamp appropriately to indicate the action taken.

1.2 PRODUCTS (Not Applicable)

1.3 EXECUTION (Not Applicable)

END OF SECTION 01300

SECTION 01700 - CONTRACT CLOSEOUT

1.1 GENERAL

A. Closeout requirements for specific construction activities are included in the appropriate Sections in Divisions 2 through 16.

B. Substantial Completion: Before requesting inspection for certification of Substantial Completion, complete the following:

1. In the Application for Payment that coincides with, or first follows, the date Substantial Completion is claimed, show 100 percent completion for the Work claimed as substantially complete.

   a. Include supporting documentation for completion and an accounting of changes to the Contract Sum.

2. Advise the Owner of pending insurance changeover requirements.
3. Submit specific warranties, workmanship bonds, maintenance agreements, final certifications, and similar documents.
4. Submit record drawings, maintenance manuals,.
5. Deliver tools, spare parts, extra stock, and similar items.
6. Changeover locks and transmit keys to the Owner.
7. Complete startup testing of systems and instruction of operation and maintenance personnel. Remove temporary facilities, mockups, construction tools, and similar elements.
8. Complete final cleanup requirements, including touchup painting.
9. Touch up and repair and restore marred, exposed finishes.

C. Inspection Procedures: On receipt of a request for inspection, the Architect will proceed or advise the Contractor of unfilled requirements. The Architect will prepare the Certificate of Substantial Completion following inspection or advise the Contractor of construction that must be completed or corrected before the certificate will be issued.

1. The Architect will repeat inspection when requested and assured that the Work is substantially complete.
2. Results of the completed inspection will form the basis of requirements for final acceptance.

D. Final Acceptance: Before requesting inspection for certification of final acceptance and final payment, complete the following:

1. Final payment request with releases and supporting documentation. Include insurance certificates where required.
2. Submit a statement, accounting for changes to the Contract Sum.
3. Submit a copy of the final inspection list stating that each item has been completed or otherwise resolved for acceptance.
4. Submit final meter readings for utilities, a record of stored fuel, and similar data as of the date of Substantial Completion.
5. Submit consent of surety to final payment.
6. Submit a final settlement statement.

7. Submit evidence of continuing insurance coverage complying with insurance requirements.

E. Reinspection Procedure: The Architect will reinspect the Work upon receipt of notice that the Work has been completed, except for items whose completion is delayed under circumstances acceptable to the Architect.

1. Upon completion of reinspection, the Architect will prepare a certificate of final acceptance. If the Work is incomplete, the Architect will advise the Contractor of Work that is incomplete or obligations that have not been fulfilled but are required.
2. If necessary, reinspection will be repeated.

F. Record Document Submittals: Do not use record documents for construction. Protect from loss in a secure location. Provide access to record documents for the Architect's reference.

G. Record Drawings: Maintain a set of prints of Contract Drawings and Shop Drawings. Mark the set to show the actual installation where the installation varies substantially from the Work as originally shown. Mark the drawing most capable of showing conditions fully and accurately. Give attention to concealed elements.

1. Mark sets with red pencil. Use other colors to distinguish between variations in separate categories of the Work.
2. Organize record drawing sheets into manageable sets. Bind with durable-paper cover sheets; print titles, dates, and other identification on the cover of each set.

H. Record Specifications: Maintain one copy of the Project Manual, including addenda. Mark to show variations in Work performed in comparison with the text of the Specifications and modifications. Give attention to substitutions and selection of options and information on concealed construction. Note related record drawing information and Product Data.

1. Upon completion of the Work, submit record Specifications to the Architect for the Owner's records.

I. Maintenance Manuals: Organize operation and maintenance data into sets of manageable size. Bind in individual, heavy-duty, 2-inch, 3-ring, binders, with pocket folders for folded sheet information. Mark identification on front and spine of each binder. Include the following information:

1. Emergency instructions.
2. Spare parts list.
3. Copies of warranties.
4. Wiring diagrams.
5. Shop Drawings and Product Data.

1.2 PRODUCTS (Not Applicable)

1.3 EXECUTION

A. Operation and Maintenance Instructions: Arrange for each Installer of equipment that requires maintenance to provide instruction in proper operation and maintenance. Include a detailed review of the following items:

1. Maintenance manuals.
2. Spare parts, tools, and materials.
3. Lubricants and fuels.
4. Identification systems.
5. Control sequences.
6. Hazards.
7. Warranties and bonds.
8. Maintenance agreements and similar continuing commitments.

B. As part of instruction for operating equipment, demonstrate the following:

1. Startup and shutdown.
2. Emergency operations and safety procedures.
3. Noise and vibration adjustments.

C. Final Cleaning: Employ experienced cleaners for final cleaning. Clean each surface or unit to the condition expected in a normal, commercial building cleaning and maintenance program. Complete the following operations before requesting inspection for certification of Substantial Completion.

1. Remove labels that are not permanent labels.
2. Clean transparent materials, including mirrors and glass. Remove glazing compounds. Replace chipped or broken glass.
3. Clean exposed finishes to a dust-free condition, free of stains, films, and foreign substances. Leave concrete floors broom clean. Vacuum carpeted surfaces.
4. Wipe surfaces of mechanical and electrical equipment. Remove excess lubrication. Clean plumbing fixtures. Clean light fixtures and lamps.
5. Clean the site of rubbish, litter, and foreign substances. Sweep paved areas; remove stains, spills, and foreign deposits. Rake grounds to a smooth, even-textured surface.

D. Removal of Protection: Remove temporary protection and facilities.

E. Compliance: Comply with regulations of authorities having jurisdiction and safety standards for cleaning. Remove waste materials and dispose of lawfully.

END OF SECTION 01700

SECTION 06100 - ROUGH CARPENTRY

1.1 GENERAL

A. Submittals: Submit the following:

1. Product Data for engineered wood products and underlayment,.

1.2 PRODUCTS

A. Lumber, General: Comply with DOC PS 20 and with applicable grading rules of inspection agencies certified by the American Lumber Standards Committee's (ALSC) Board of Review. Provide dressed lumber, S4S, with each piece factory marked with grade stamp of inspection agency.

1. Provide lumber with 15 percent maximum moisture content at time of dressing for 2-inch nominal thickness or less, unless otherwise indicated.

B. Wood-Preservative-Treated Materials: Comply with applicable requirements of AWPA C2 (lumber) and AWPA C9 (plywood). Mark each treated item with the Quality Mark Requirements of an inspection agency approved by ALSC's Board of Review.

1. Pressure treat aboveground items with waterborne preservatives to a minimum retention of 0.25 lb/cu. ft. After treatment, kiln-dry lumber and plywood to a maximum moisture content of 19 and 15 percent, respectively. Treat indicated items and the following:

a. Wood sills and similar concealed members in contact with concrete.
b. Wood floor plates installed over concrete slabs directly in contact with earth.

C. Dimension Lumber: Provide dimension lumber of grades indicated according to the ALSC National Grading Rule (NGR) provisions of the inspection agency indicated.

1. Non-Load-Bearing Interior Partitions: Provide Douglas Fir, No. 2 grade.
2. Framing Other than Non-Load-Bearing Partitions: As indicated on drawings.
3. Exposed Framing: Provide material hand-selected from lumber of species and grade indicated below for uniformity of appearance and freedom from characteristics that would impair finish appearance.

a. Species and Grade: As indicated on drawings.

D. Engineered Wood Products: Acceptable to authorities having jurisdiction and for which current model code research or evaluation reports exist that evidence compliance with building code in effect for Project. Provide engineered wood products with allowable design stresses, as published by manufacturer, that meet or exceed those indicated. Manufacturer's published values shall be determined from empirical data or by rational engineering analysis, and demonstrated by comprehensive testing performed by a qualified independent testing agency.

1. Prefabricated Wood I-Joists: Units manufactured by bonding stress-graded lumber flanges to wood-based structural-use panel webs with exterior-type adhesives complying with ASTM D 2559, to produce I-shaped joists complying with the following requirements:

a. Structural Capacities: Establish and monitor structural capacities according to ASTM D 5055.

E. Wood-Based Structural-Use Panels: Provide either all-veneer, mat-formed, or composite panels complying with DOC PS 2, "Performance Standard for Wood-Based Structural-Use Panels," unless otherwise indicated. Provide plywood panels complying with DOC PS 1, "U.S. Product Standard for Construction and Industrial Plywood," where plywood is indicated.

1. Trademark: Factory mark structural-use panels with APA trademark evidencing compliance with grade requirements.
2. Span Ratings: Provide panels with span ratings required to suit support spacing indicated.
3. Subflooring: APA-rated sheathing, Exposure 1.
4. Wall Sheathing: APA-rated sheathing, Exposure 1.
5. Roof Sheathing: APA-rated sheathing, Exterior.

F. Fiberboard Underlayment: Sound deadening carpet underlayment, complying with the following requiremtents:

Size: 5/8 inch thick, 4 feet by 8 feet panels.
Density: 1.5 pounds per square foot.
Available Product: "440 Carpet Board," Homasote Company.

G. Air-Infiltration Barrier: Air retarder complying with ASTM E 1677; made from polyolefins; either cross-laminated films, woven strands, or spunbonded fibers; coated or uncoated; with or without perforations to transmit water vapor but not liquid water; and with minimum water-vapor transmission of 10 perms when tested according to ASTM E 96, Procedure A.

H. Fasteners: Size and type indicated. Where rough carpentry is exposed to weather, in ground contact, or in area of high relative humidity, provide fasteners with a hot-dip zinc coating per ASTM A 153 or of Type 304 stainless steel.

I. Metal Framing Anchors: Provide galvanized steel framing anchors of structural capacity, type, and size indicated and as follows:

1. Research or Evaluation Reports: Provide products for which model code research or evaluation reports exist that are acceptable to authorities having jurisdiction and that evidence compliance of metal framing anchors for application indicated with building code in effect for Project.
2. Allowable Design Loads: Provide products with allowable design loads, as published by manufacturer, that meet or exceed those indicated. Manufacturer's published values shall be determined from empirical data or by rational engineering analysis, and demonstrated by comprehensive testing performed by a qualified independent testing agency.
3. Galvanized Steel Sheet: Hot-dip, zinc-coated steel sheet complying with ASTM A 653, G60 coating designation; structural, commercial, or lock-forming quality, as standard with manufacturer for type of anchor indicated.

J. Sill-Sealer Gaskets: Glass-fiber-resilient insulation, fabricated in strip form, for use as a sill sealer; 1-inch nominal thickness, compressible to 1/32 inch; selected from manufacturer's standard widths to suit width of sill members indicated.

K. Adhesives for Field Gluing Panels to Framing: Formulation complying with APA AFG-01 that is approved for use with type of construction panel indicated by both adhesive and panel manufacturers.

1.3 EXECUTION

A. Set rough carpentry to required levels and lines, with members plumb, true to line, cut, and fitted.

B. Fit rough carpentry to other construction; scribe and cope as required for accurate fit. Correlate location of furring, nailers, blocking, grounds, and similar supports to allow attachment of other construction.

C. Securely attach rough carpentry work to substrate by anchoring and fastening as indicated, complying with the following:

1. Published requirements of metal framing anchor manufacturer.
2. "Table 23-I-Q--Nailing Schedule" of the Uniform Building Code.

D. Use hot-dip galvanized or stainless-steel nails.

E. Framing Standard: Comply with AFPA's "Manual for Wood Frame Construction," unless otherwise indicated.

F. Installation of Structural-Use Panels: Comply with applicable recommendations contained in APA Form No. E30, "APA Design/Construction Guide: Residential & Commercial," for types of structural-use panels and applications indicated.

1. Fastening Methods: Fasten panels as indicated below:

a. Subflooring: Glue and nail to framing throughout.
b. Sheathing: Nail to framing.
c. Underlayment: Nail to subflooring.

G. Air-Infiltration Barrier: Cover sheathing with air-infiltration barrier to comply with manufacturer's written instructions.

1. Apply air-infiltration barrier to cover upstanding flashing with 4-inch overlap.

END OF SECTION 06100

SECTION 09255 - GYPSUM BOARD ASSEMBLIES

1.1 GENERAL

1.2 PRODUCTS

A. Manufacturers: Subject to compliance with requirements, provide products by one of the following:

1. Steel Framing and Furring:

   a. Dale Industries, Inc.
   b. Marino/Ware (formerly Marino Industries Corp.).
   c. National Gypsum Co.; Gold Bond Building Products Division.
   d. Unimast, Inc.

2. Gypsum Board and Related Products:

   a. Domtar Gypsum.
   b. Georgia-Pacific Corp.
   c. National Gypsum Co.; Gold Bond Building Products Division.
   d. United States Gypsum Co.

B. Steel Framing for Walls and Partitions: Provide steel framing members complying with the following requirements:

1. Steel Studs and Runners: ASTM C 645, in depth indicated and with 0.0179-inch minimum base metal thickness, unless otherwise indicated.

   a. Provide 0.0329-inch minimum base metal thickness for head runner, sill runner, jamb, and cripple studs at door and other openings.
   b. Provide 0.0329-inch minimum base metal thickness in locations to receive cementitious backer units.

2. Z-Furring Members: Manufacturer's standard Z-shaped furring members with slotted or nonslotted web, fabricated from steel sheet complying with ASTM A 653 or ASTM A 568; with a minimum base metal (uncoated) thickness of 0.0179 inch, face flange of 1-1/4 inch, wall-attachment flange of 7/8 inch, and of depth required to fit insulation thickness indicated.

C. Fasteners for Metal Framing: Type, material, size, corrosion resistance, holding power, and other properties required to fasten steel framing and furring members securely to substrates involved; complying with the recommendations of gypsum board manufacturers for applications indicated.

D. Gypsum Board Products: Types indicated in maximum lengths available that will minimize end-to-end butt joints in each area indicated to receive gypsum board application.

1. Gypsum Wallboard: ASTM C 36, in thickness indicated.

   a. Type: Regular for vertical surfaces, unless otherwise indicated.

b. Edges: Tapered and featured (rounded or beveled) for prefilling.

2. Water-Resistant Gypsum Backing Board: ASTM C 630, in thickness indicated.

a. Type: Regular, unless otherwise indicated.

E. Accessories for Interior Installation: Cornerbead, edge trim, and control joints complying with ASTM C 1047, formed metal or plastic, with metal complying with the following requirement:

1. Steel sheet zinc coated by hot-dip process or rolled zinc.

F. Joint Treatment Materials: Provide joint treatment materials complying with ASTM C 475 and the recommendations of both the manufacturers of sheet products and of joint treatment materials for each application indicated.

1. Joint Tape for Gypsum Board: Paper reinforcing tape, unless otherwise indicated.

2. Setting-Type Joint Compounds for Gypsum Board: Factory-packaged, job-mixed, chemical-hardening powder products formulated for uses indicated.

a. For prefilling gypsum board joints, use formulation recommended by gypsum board manufacturer.
b. For filling joints and treating fasteners of water-resistant gypsum backing board behind base for ceramic tile, use formulation recommended by gypsum board manufacturer.
c. For topping compound, use sandable formulation.

3. Drying-Type Joint Compounds for Gypsum Board: Factory-packaged vinyl-based products complying with the following requirements for formulation and intended use.

a. Ready-Mixed Formulation: Factory-mixed product.
b. Job-Mixed Formulation: Powder product for mixing with water at Project site.

1) Taping compound formulated for embedding tape and for first coat over fasteners and face flanges of trim accessories.
2) Topping compound formulated for fill (second) and finish (third) coats.
3) All-purpose compound formulated for both taping and topping compounds.

G. Miscellaneous Materials: Provide auxiliary materials for gypsum board construction that comply with referenced standards and recommendations of gypsum board manufacturer.

1. Steel drill screws complying with ASTM C 1002 for the following applications:

a. Fastening gypsum board to steel members less than 0.033 inch thick.
b. Fastening gypsum board to wood members.

2. Gypsum Board Nails: ASTM C 514.

H. Texture Finish: As follows:

1. Primer: Of type recommended by texture finish manufacturer.
2. Aggregate Finish: Factory-packaged proprietary drying-type powder product formulated with aggregate for mixing with water at Project site for spray application to produce texture selected by Architect from manufacturer's full range of textures.

1.3 EXECUTION

A. Install steel framing to comply with ASTM C 754 and with ASTM C 840 requirements that apply to framing installation.

1. Install supplementary framing, blocking, and bracing at terminations in gypsum board assemblies to support fixtures, equipment services, heavy trim, grab bars, toilet accessories, furnishings, or similar construction.

B. Installing Steel Framing for Walls and Partitions: Install steel studs and furring at spacings indicated.

1. Extend partition framing full height to structural supports or substrates above suspended ceilings. Continue framing over frames for doors and openings and frame around ducts penetrating partitions above ceiling to provide support for gypsum board.
2. Cut studs 1/2 inch short of full height to provide perimeter relief.
3. Frame door openings to comply with GA-219, and with applicable published recommendations of gypsum board manufacturer, unless otherwise indicated.
4. Install Z-furring members and thermal insulation as indicated and to comply with requirements of manufacturer's directions.
installation of gypsum board or other construction.

C. Gypsum Board Application and Finishing Standards: Install and finish gypsum panels to comply with ASTM C 840 and GA-216.

1. Install sound-attenuation blankets, where indicated, prior to installing gypsum panels unless blankets are readily installed after panels have been installed on one side.
2. Install ceiling board panels across framing to minimize the number of abutting end joints and to avoid abutting end joints in the central area of each ceiling. Stagger abutting end joints of adjacent panels not less than one framing member.
3. Space fasteners in gypsum panels according to referenced gypsum board application and finishing standard and manufacturer's recommendations.
4. Space fasteners in panels that are tile substrates a maximum of 8 inches o.c.
5. Install water-resistant gypsum backing board panels as substrate for ceramic tile.
6. Single-Layer Fastening Methods: Apply gypsum panels to supports as follows:

   a. Fasten with screws.

D. Installing Trim Accessories: For trim accessories with back flanges, fasten to framing with the same fasteners used to fasten gypsum board. Otherwise, fasten trim accessories according to accessory manufacturer's directions for type, length, and spacing of fasteners.

1. Install cornerbead at external corners.
2. Install edge trim where edge of gypsum panels would otherwise be exposed. Provide edge trim type with face flange formed to receive joint compound, except where other types are indicated.

E. Finishing Gypsum Board Assemblies: Treat gypsum board joints, interior angles, flanges of cornerbead, edge trim, control joints, penetrations, fastener heads, surface defects, and elsewhere as required to prepare gypsum board surfaces for decoration.

1. Prefill open joints, rounded or beveled edges, and damaged areas using setting-type joint compound.

2. Apply joint tape over gypsum board joints and to flanges of trim accessories as recommended by trim accessory manufacturer.
3. Levels of Gypsum Board Finish: Provide the following levels of gypsum board finish per GA-214.

    a. Level 1 for ceiling plenum areas.
    b. Level 2 where panels form substrates for tile or wainscot and where indicated.
    c. Level 4 for gypsum board surfaces, unless otherwise indicated.

4. For Level 4 gypsum board finish, embed tape in joint compound and apply first, fill (second), and finish (third) coats of joint compound over joints, angles, fastener heads, and accessories. Touch up and sand between coats and after last coat as needed to produce a surface free of visual defects and ready for decoration.
5. Where Level 2 gypsum board finish is indicated, embed tape in joint compound and apply first coat of joint compound.
6. Where Level 1 gypsum board finish is indicated, embed tape in joint compound.

F. Applying Texture Finishes: As follows:

1. Surface Preparation and Primer: Prepare and apply primer to gypsum panels and other surfaces receiving texture finishes according to texture finish manufacturer's instructions. Apply primer only to surfaces that are clean, dry, and smooth.
2. Texture Finish Application: Mix and apply finish to gypsum panels and other surfaces indicated to receive texture finish according to texture finish manufacturer's directions. Using powered spray equipment, produce a uniform texture free of starved spots or other evidence of thin application or of application patterns.
3. Prevent texture finishes from coming into contact with surfaces not indicated to receive texture finish by covering them with masking agents, polyethylene film, or other means. If, despite these precautions, texture finishes contact these surfaces, immediately remove droppings and overspray as recommended by texture finish manufacturer to prevent damage.

END OF SECTION 09255

APPENDIX G

Standard Form Subcontract (AGC 655–1998)

THE ASSOCIATED GENERAL CONTRACTORS OF AMERICA

AGC DOCUMENT NO. 655
STANDARD FORM OF AGREEMENT BETWEEN CONTRACTOR AND SUBCONTRACTOR
(Where the Contractor and Subcontractor Share the Risk of Owner Payment)

TABLE OF ARTICLES

This Agreement has important legal and insurance consequences. Consultation with an attorney and an insurance consultant is encouraged with respect to its completion or modification.

AGC DOCUMENT NO.655
STANDARD FORM OF AGREEMENT
BETWEEN CONTRACTOR AND SUBCONTRACTOR
(Where the Contractor and Subcontractor Share the Risk of Owner Payment)

ARTICLE 1

AGREEMENT

This Agreement is made this ____________________ day of ____________________

in the year ______________., by and between the

CONTRACTOR
(Name and Address)

and the
SUBCONTRACTOR
(Name and Address)

for services in connection with the
SUBCONTRACT WORK

for the following
PROJECT

whose
OWNER is
(Name and Address)

The **ARCHITECT/ENGINEER** for the Project is
(Name and Address)

Notice to the parties shall be given at the above addresses.

ARTICLE 2

SCOPE OF WORK

2.1 **SUBCONTRACT WORK** The Contractor contracts with the Subcontractor as an independent contractor to provide all labor, materials, equipment and services necessary or incidental to complete the work described in Article 1 for the Project in accordance with, and reasonably inferable from, that which is indicated in the Subcontract Documents, and consistent with the Progress Schedule, as may change from time to time. The Subcontractor shall perform the Subcontract Work under the general direction of the Contractor and in accordance with the Subcontract Documents.

2.2 **CONTRACTOR'S WORK** The Contractor's work is the construction and services required of the Contractor to fulfill its obligations pursuant to its agreement with the Owner (the Work). The Subcontract Work is a portion of the Work.

2.3 **SUBCONTRACT DOCUMENTS** The Subcontract Documents include this Agreement, the Owner-Contractor agreement, special conditions, general conditions, specifications, drawings, addenda, Subcontract Change Orders, amendments and any pending and exercised alternates. The Contractor shall make available to the Subcontractor, prior to the execution of the Subcontract Agreement, copies of the Subcontract Documents to which the Subcontractor will be bound. The Subcontractor similarly shall make copies of applicable portions of the Subcontract Documents available to its proposed subcontractors and suppliers. Nothing shall prohibit the Subcontractor from obtaining copies of the Subcontract Documents from the Contractor at any time after the Subcontract Agreement is executed. The Subcontract Documents existing at the time of the execution of this Agreement are set forth in Article 13.

2.4 **CONFLICTS** In the event of a conflict between this Agreement and the other Subcontract Documents, this Agreement shall govern.

2.5 **EXTENT OF AGREEMENT** Nothing in this Agreement shall be construed to create a contractual relationship between persons or entities other than the Contractor and Subcontractor. This Agreement is solely for the benefit of the parties, represents the entire and integrated agreement between the parties, and supersedes all prior negotiations, representations, or agreements, either written or oral.

2.6 **DEFINITIONS**

.1 Wherever the term Progress Schedule is used in this Agreement, it shall be read as Project Schedule when that term is used in the Subcontract Documents.

.2 Whenever the term Change Order is used in this Agreement, it shall be read as Change Document when that term is used in the Subcontract Documents.

.3 Unless otherwise indicated, the term Day shall mean calendar day.

ARTICLE 3

SUBCONTRACTOR'S RESPONSIBILITIES

3.1 **OBLIGATIONS** The Contractor and Subcontractor are hereby mutually bound by the terms of this Subcontract. To the extent the terms of the prime contract between the Owner and Contractor apply to the work of the Subcontractor, then the Contractor hereby assumes toward the Subcontractor all the obligations, rights, duties, and redress that the Owner under the prime contract assumes toward the Contractor. In an identical way, the Subcontractor hereby assumes toward the Contractor all the same obligations, rights, duties, and redress that the Contractor assumes toward the Owner and Architect under the prime contract. In the event of an inconsistency among the documents, the specific terms of this Subcontract shall govern.

3.2 **RESPONSIBILITIES** The Subcontractor agrees to furnish its best skill and judgment in the performance of the Subcontract Work and to cooperate with the Contractor so that the Contractor may fulfill its obligations to the Owner. The Subcontractor shall furnish all of the labor, materials, equipment, and services, including but not limited to, competent supervision, shop drawings, samples, tools, and scaffolding as are necessary for the proper performance of the Subcontract Work. The Subcontractor shall provide the Contractor a list of its proposed subcontractors and suppliers, and be responsible for taking field dimensions, providing tests, obtaining required permits related to the Subcontract Work and affidavits, ordering of materials and all other actions as required to meet the Progress Schedule.

3.3 **INCONSISTENCIES AND OMISSIONS** The Subcontractor shall make a careful analysis and comparison of the drawings, specifications, other Subcontract Documents and information furnished by the Owner relative to the Subcontract Work. Such analysis and comparison shall be solely for the purpose of facilitating the Subcontract Work and not for the discovery of errors, inconsistencies or omissions in the Subcontract Documents nor for ascertaining if the Subcontract Documents are in accordance with applicable laws, statutes, ordinances, building codes, rules or regulations. Should the Subcontractor discover any errors, inconsistencies or omissions in the Subcontract Documents, the Subcontractor shall report such discoveries to the Contractor in writing within three (3) days. Upon receipt of notice, the Contractor shall instruct the Subcontractor as to the measures to be taken and the Subcontractor shall comply with the Contractor's instructions. If the Subcontractor performs work knowing it to be contrary to any applicable laws, statutes, ordinances, building codes, rules or regulations without notice to the Contractor and advance approval by appropriate authorities, including the Contractor, the Subcontractor shall assume appropriate responsibility for such work and shall bear all associated costs, charges, fees and expenses necessarily incurred to remedy the violation. Nothing in this Paragraph 3.3 shall relieve the Subcontractor of responsibility for its own errors, inconsistencies and omissions.

3.4 **SITE VISITATION** Prior to performing any portion of the Subcontract Work, the Subcontractor shall conduct a visual inspection of the Project site to become generally familiar with local conditions and to correlate site observations with the Subcontract Documents. If the Subcontractor discovers any discrepancies between its site observations and the Subcontract Documents, such discrepancies shall be promptly reported to the Contractor.

3.5 **INCREASED COSTS AND/OR TIME** The Subcontractor may assert a Claim as provided in Article 7 if Contractor's clarifications or instructions in responses to requests for information are believed to require additional time or cost. If the Subcontractor fails to perform the reviews and comparisons required in Paragraphs 3.3 and 3.4, above, to the extent the Contractor is held liable to the Owner because of the Subcontractor's failure, the Subcontractor shall pay the costs and damages to the Contractor that would have been avoided if the Subcontractor had performed those obligations.

3.6 COMMUNICATIONS Unless otherwise provided in the Subcontract Documents and except for emergencies, Subcontractor shall direct all communications related to the Project to the Contractor.

3.7 SUBMITTALS

3.7.1 The Subcontractor promptly shall submit for approval to the Contractor all shop drawings, samples, product data, manufacturers' literature and similar submittals required by the Subcontract Documents. The Subcontractor shall be responsible to the Contractor for the accuracy and conformity of its submittals to the Subcontract Documents. The Subcontractor shall prepare and deliver its submittals to the Contractor in a manner consistent with the Progress Schedule and in such time and sequence so as not to delay the Contractor or others in the performance of the Work. The approval of any Subcontractor submittal shall not be deemed to authorize deviations, substitutions or changes in the requirements of the Subcontract Documents unless express written approval is obtained from the Contractor and Owner authorizing such deviation, substitution or change. In the event that the Subcontract Documents do not contain submittal requirements pertaining to the Subcontract Work, the Subcontractor agrees upon request to submit in a timely fashion to the Contractor for approval any shop drawings, samples, product data, manufacturers' literature or similar submittals as may reasonably be required by the Contractor, Owner or Architect.

3.7.2 The Contractor, Owner, and Architect are entitled to rely on the adequacy, accuracy and completeness of any professional certifications required by the Subcontract Documents concerning the performance criteria of systems, equipment or materials, including all relevant calculations and any governing performance requirements.

3.8 DESIGN DELEGATION

3.8.1 If the Subcontract Documents (1) specifically require the Subcontractor to provide design services and (2) specify all design and performance criteria, the Subcontractor shall provide those design services necessary to satisfactorily complete the Subcontract Work. Design services provided by the Subcontractor shall be procured from licensed design professionals retained by the Subcontractor as permitted by the law of the place where the Project is located (the Designer).The Designer's signature and seal shall appear on all drawings, calculations, specifications, certifications, Shop Drawings and other submittals prepared by the Designer. Shop Drawings and other submittals related to the Subcontract Work designed or certified by the Designer, if prepared by others, shall bear the Subcontractor's and the Designer's written approvals when submitted to the Contractor. The Contractor shall be entitled to rely upon the adequacy, accuracy and completeness of the services, certifications or approvals performed by the Designer.

3.8.2 If the Designer is an independent professional, the design services shall be procured pursuant to a separate agreement between the Subcontractor and the Designer. The Subcontractor-Designer agreement shall not provide for any limitation of liability, except to the extent that consequential damages are waived pursuant to Paragraph 5.4, or exclusion from participation in the multiparty proceedings requirement of Paragraph 11.4. The Designer(s) is (are) ______________________________.◆ The Subcontractor shall notify the Contractor in writing if it intends to change the Designer. The Subcontractor shall be responsible for conformance of its design with the information given and the design concept expressed in the Subcontract Documents. The Subcontractor shall not be responsible for the adequacy of the performance or design criteria required by the Subcontract Documents.

3.8.3 The Subcontractor shall not be required to provide design services in violation of any applicable law.

3.9 TEMPORARY SERVICES Subcontractor's responsibilities for temporary services are set forth in Exhibit _____. ◆

3.10 COORDINATION The Subcontractor shall:

.1 cooperate with the Contractor and all others whose work may interface with the Subcontract Work;

.2 specifically note and immediately advise the Contractor of any such interface with the Subcontract Work; and

.3 participate in the preparation of coordination drawings and work schedules in areas of congestion.

3.11 SUBCONTRACTOR'S REPRESENTATIVE The Subcontractor shall designate a person, subject to Contractor's approval, who shall be the Subcontractor's authorized representative. This representative shall be the only person to whom the Contractor shall issue instructions, orders or directions, except in an emergency. The Subcontractor's representative is ______________________________,◆ who is agreed to by the Contractor.

3.12 TESTS AND INSPECTIONS The Subcontractor shall schedule all required tests, approvals and inspections of the Subcontract Work at appropriate times so as not to delay the progress of the work. The Subcontractor shall give proper written notice to all required parties of such tests, approvals and inspections. The Subcontractor shall bear all expenses associated with tests, inspections and approvals required of the Subcontractor by the Subcontract Documents which, unless otherwise agreed to, shall be conducted by an independent testing laboratory or entity approved by the Contractor and Owner. Required certificates of testing, approval or inspection shall, unless otherwise required by the Subcontract Documents, be secured by the Subcontractor and promptly delivered to the Contractor.

3.13 CLEANUP

3.13.1 The Subcontractor shall at all times during its performance of the Subcontract Work keep the work site clean and free from debris resulting from the Subcontract Work. Prior to discontinuing the Subcontract Work in an area, the Subcontractor shall clean the area and remove all its rubbish and its construction equipment, tools, machinery, waste and surplus materials. Subcontractor shall make provisions to minimize and confine dust and debris resulting from its construction activities. The Subcontractor shall not be held responsible for unclean conditions caused by others.

3.13.2 If the Subcontractor fails to commence compliance with cleanup duties within forty-eight (48) hours after written notification from the Contractor of non-compliance, the Contractor may implement appropriate cleanup measures without further notice and the cost thereof shall be deducted from any amounts due or to become due the Subcontractor.

3.14 SAFETY

3.14.1 The Subcontractor is required to perform the Subcontract Work in a safe and reasonable manner. The Subcontractor shall seek to avoid injury, loss or damage to persons or property by taking reasonable steps to protect:

.1 employees and other persons at the site;

.2 materials and equipment stored at the site or at off-site locations for use in performance of the Work; and

.3 all property and structures located at the site and adjacent to work areas, whether or not said property or structures are part of the Project or involved in the Work.

3.14.2 The Subcontractor shall give all required notices and comply with all applicable rules, regulations, orders and other lawful requirements established to prevent injury, loss or damage to persons or property.

3.14.3 The Subcontractor shall implement appropriate safety measures pertaining to the Subcontract Work and the Project, including establishing safety rules, posting appropriate warnings and notices, erecting safety barriers, and establishing proper notice procedures to protect persons and property at the site and adjacent to the site from injury, loss or damage.

3.14.4 The Subcontractor shall exercise extreme care in carrying out any of the Subcontract Work which involves explosive or other dangerous methods of construction or hazardous procedures, materials or equipment. The Subcontractor shall use properly qualified individuals or entities to carry out the Subcontract Work in a safe and reasonable manner so as to reduce the risk of bodily injury or property damage.

3.14.5 Damage or loss not insured under property insurance which may arise from the performance of the Subcontract Work, to the extent of the negligence attributed to such acts or omissions of the Subcontractor, or anyone for whose acts the Subcontractor may be liable, shall be promptly remedied by the Subcontractor. Damage or loss attributable to the acts or omissions of the Contractor and not to the Subcontractor shall be promptly remedied by the Contractor.

3.14.6 The Subcontractor is required to designate an individual at the site in the employ of the Subcontractor who shall act as the Subcontractor's designated safety representative with a duty to prevent accidents. Unless otherwise identified by the Subcontractor in writing to the Contractor, the designated safety representative shall be the Subcontractor's project superintendent.

3.14.7 The Subcontractor has an affirmative duty not to overload the structures or conditions at the site and shall take reasonable steps not to load any part of the structures or site so as to give rise to an unsafe condition or create an unreasonable risk of bodily injury or property damage. The Subcontractor shall have the right to request, in writing, from the Contractor loading information concerning the structures at the site.

3.14.8 The Subcontractor shall give prompt written notice to the Contractor of any accident involving bodily injury requiring a physician's care, any property damage exceeding Five Hundred Dollars ($500.00) in value, or any failure that could have resulted in serious bodily injury, whether or not such an injury was sustained.

3.14.9 Prevention of accidents at the site is the responsibility of the Contractor, Subcontractor, and all other subcontractors, persons and entities at the site. Establishment of a safety program by the Contractor shall not relieve the Subcontractor or other parties of their safety responsibilities. The Subcontractor shall establish its own safety program implementing safety measures, policies and standards conforming to those required or recommended by governmental and quasi-governmental authorities having jurisdiction and by the Contractor and Owner, including, but not limited to, requirements imposed by the Subcontract Documents. The Subcontractor shall comply with the reasonable recommendations of insurance companies having an interest in the Project, and shall stop any part of the Subcontract Work which the Contractor deems unsafe until corrective measures satisfactory to the Contractor shall have been taken. The Contractor's failure to stop the Subcontractor's unsafe practices shall not relieve the Subcontractor of the responsibility therefor. The Subcontractor shall notify the Contractor immediately following an accident and promptly confirm the notice in writing. A detailed written report shall be furnished if requested by the Contractor. Each party to this Agreement shall indemnify the other party from and against fines or penalties imposed as a result of safety violations, but only to the extent that such fines or penalties are caused by its failure to comply with applicable safety requirements.

3.15 PROTECTION OF THE WORK The Subcontractor shall take necessary precautions to properly protect the Subcontract Work and the work of others from damage caused by the Subcontractor's operations. Should the Subcontractor cause damage to the Work or property of the Owner, the Contractor or others, the Subcontractor shall promptly remedy such damage to the satisfaction of the Contractor, or the Contractor may remedy the damage and deduct its cost from any amounts due or to become due the Subcontractor, unless such costs are recovered under applicable property insurance.

3.16 PERMITS, FEES, LICENSES AND TAXES The Subcontractor shall give timely notices to authorities pertaining to the Subcontract Work, and shall be responsible for all permits, fees, licenses, assessments, inspections, testing and taxes necessary to complete the Subcontract Work in accordance with the Subcontract Documents. To the extent reimbursement is obtained by the Contractor from the Owner under the Owner-Contractor agreement, the Subcontractor shall be compensated for additional costs resulting from taxes enacted after the date of this Agreement.

3.17 ASSIGNMENT OF SUBCONTRACT WORK The Subcontractor shall not assign the whole nor any part of the Subcontract Work without prior written approval of the Contractor.

3.18 HAZARDOUS MATERIALS To the extent that the Contractor has rights or obligations under the Owner-Contractor agreement or by law regarding hazardous materials as defined by the Subcontract Document within the scope of the Subcontract Work, the Subcontractor shall have the same rights or obligations.

3.19 MATERIAL SAFETY DATA (MSD) SHEETS The Subcontractor shall submit to the Contractor all Material Safety Data Sheets required by law for materials or substances necessary for the performance of the Subcontract Work. MSD sheets obtained by the Contractor from other subcontractors or sources shall be made available to the Subcontractor by the Contractor.

3.20 LAYOUT RESPONSIBILITY AND LEVELS The Contractor shall establish principal axis lines of the building and site, and benchmarks. The Subcontractor shall lay out and be strictly responsible for the accuracy of the Subcontract Work and for any loss or damage to the Contractor or others by reason of the Subcontractor's failure to lay out or perform Subcontract Work correctly. The Subcontractor shall exercise prudence so that the actual final conditions and details shall result in alignment of finish surfaces.

3.21 WARRANTIES The Subcontractor warrants that all materials and equipment furnished under this Agreement shall be new, unless otherwise specified, of good quality, in conformance with the Subcontract Documents, and free from defective workmanship and materials. Warranties shall commence on the date of Substantial Completion of the Work or a designated portion.

3.22 UNCOVERING/CORRECTION OF SUBCONTRACT WORK

3.22.1 UNCOVERING OF SUBCONTRACT WORK

3.22.1.1 If required in writing by the Contractor, the Subcontractor must uncover any portion of the Subcontract Work which has been covered by the Subcontractor in violation of the Subcontract Documents or contrary to a directive issued to the Subcontractor by the Contractor. Upon receipt of a written directive from the Contractor, the Subcontractor shall uncover such work for the Contractor's or Owner's inspection and restore the uncovered Subcontract Work to its original condition at the Subcontractor's time and expense.

3.22.1.2 The Contractor may direct the Subcontractor to uncover portions of the Subcontract Work for inspection by the Owner or Contractor at any time. The Subcontractor is required to uncover such work whether or not the Contractor or Owner had requested to inspect the Subcontract Work prior to it being covered. Except as provided in Clause 3.22.1.1, this Agreement shall be adjusted by change order for the cost and time of uncovering and restoring any work which is uncovered for inspection and proves to be installed in accordance with the Subcontract Documents, provided the Contractor had not previously instructed the Subcontractor to leave the work uncovered. If the Subcontractor uncovers work pursuant to a directive issued by the Contractor, and such work upon inspection does not comply with the Subcontract Documents, the Subcontractor shall be responsible for all costs and time of uncovering, correcting and restoring the work so as to make it conform to the Subcontract Documents. If the Contractor or some other entity for which the Subcontractor is not responsible caused the nonconforming condition, the Contractor shall be required to adjust this Agreement by change order for all such costs and time.

3.22.2 CORRECTION OF WORK

3.22.2.1 If the Architect or Contractor rejects the Subcontract Work or the Subcontract Work is not in conformance with the Subcontract Documents, the Subcontractor shall promptly correct the Subcontract Work whether it had been fabricated, installed or completed. The Subcontractor shall be responsible for the costs of correcting such Subcontract Work, any additional testing, inspections, and compensation for services and expenses of the Architect and Contractor made necessary by the defective Subcontract Work.

3.22.2.2 In addition to the Subcontractor's obligations under Paragraph 3.21, the Subcontractor agrees to promptly correct, after receipt of a written notice from the Contractor, all Subcontract Work performed under this Agreement which proves to be defective in workmanship or materials within a period of one year from the date of Substantial Completion of the Subcontract Work or for a longer period of time as may be required by specific warranties in the Subcontract Documents. Substantial Completion of the Subcontract Work, or of a designated portion, occurs on the date when construction is sufficiently complete in accordance with the Subcontract Documents so that the Owner can occupy or utilize the Project, or a designated portion, for the use for which it is intended. If, during the one-year period, the Contractor fails to provide the Subcontractor with prompt written notice of the discovery of defective or nonconforming Subcontract Work, the Contractor shall neither have the right to require the Subcontractor to correct such Subcontract Work nor the right to make claim for breach of warranty. If the Subcontractor fails to correct defective or nonconforming Subcontract Work within a reasonable time after receipt of notice from the Contractor, the Contractor may correct such Subcontract Work pursuant to Subparagraph 10.1.1.

3.22.3 The Subcontractor's correction of Subcontract Work pursuant to this Paragraph 3.22 shall not extend the one-year period for the correction of Subcontract Work, but if Subcontract Work is first performed after Substantial Completion, the one-year period for corrections shall be extended by the time period after Substantial Completion and the performance of that portion of Subcontract Work. The Subcontractor's obligation to correct Subcontract Work within one year as described in this Paragraph 3.22 does not limit the enforcement of Subcontractor's other obligations with regard to the Agreement and the Subcontract Documents.

3.22.4 If the Subcontractor's correction or removal of Subcontract Work destroys or damages completed or partially completed work of the Owner, the Contractor or any separate contractors, the Subcontractor shall be responsible for the cost of correcting such destroyed or damaged construction.

3.22.5 If portions of Subcontract Work which do not conform with the requirements of the Subcontract Documents are neither corrected by the Subcontractor nor accepted by the Contractor, the Subcontractor shall remove such Subcontract Work from the Project site if so directed by the Contractor.

3.23 MATERIALS OR EQUIPMENT FURNISHED BY OTHERS In the event the scope of the Subcontract Work includes installation of materials or equipment furnished by others, it shall be the responsibility of the Subcontractor to exercise proper care in receiving, handling, storing and installing such items, unless otherwise provided in the Subcontract Documents. The Subcontractor shall examine the items provided and report to the Contractor in writing any items it may discover that do not conform to requirements of the Subcontract Documents. The Subcontractor shall not proceed to install nonconforming items without further instructions from the Contractor. Loss or damage due to acts or omissions of the Subcontractor shall be deducted from any amounts due or to become due the Subcontractor.

3.24 SUBSTITUTIONS No substitutions shall be made in the Subcontract Work unless permitted in the Subcontract Documents, and only upon the Subcontractor first receiving all approvals required under the Subcontract Documents for substitutions.

3.25 USE OF CONTRACTOR'S EQUIPMENT The Subcontractor, its agents, employees, subcontractors or suppliers shall use the Contractor's equipment only with the express written permission of the Contractor's designated representative and in accordance with the Contractor's terms and conditions for such use. If the Subcontractor or any of its agents, employees, subcontractors or suppliers utilize any of the Contractor's equipment, including machinery, tools, scaffolding, hoists, lifts or similar items owned, leased or under the control of the Contractor, the Subcontractor shall defend, indemnify and be liable to the Contractor as provided in Article 9 for any loss or damage (including bodily injury or death) which may arise from such use, except to the extent that such loss or damage is caused by the negligence of the Contractor's employees operating the Contractor's equipment.

3.26 WORK FOR OTHERS Until final completion of the Subcontract Work, the Subcontractor agrees not to perform any work directly for the Owner or any tenants, or deal directly with the Owner's representatives in connection with the Subcontract Work, unless otherwise approved in writing by the Contractor.

3.27 SUBCONTRACT BONDS

3.27.1 The Subcontractor ☐ shall ☐ shall not furnish to ◆ the Contractor, as the named Obligee, appropriate surety bonds to secure the faithful performance of the Subcontract Work and to satisfy all Subcontractor payment obligations related to Subcontract Work.

3.27.2 If a performance or payment bond, or both, are required of the Subcontractor under this Agreement, the bonds shall be in a form and by a surety mutually agreeable to the Contractor and Subcontractor, and in the full amount of the Subcontract Amount, unless otherwise specified.

3.27.3 The Subcontractor shall be reimbursed, without retainage, for the cost of any required performance or payment bonds simultaneously with the first progress payment. The reimbursement amount for the subcontractor bonds shall not exceed __________ percent (__________%) of the Subcontract ◆ Amount, which sum is included in the Subcontract Amount.

3.27.4 In the event the Subcontractor shall fail to promptly provide any required bonds, the Contractor may terminate this Agreement and enter into a subcontract for the balance of the Subcontract Work with another subcontractor. All Contractor costs and expenses incurred by the Contractor as a result of said termination shall be paid by the Subcontractor.

3.28 SYSTEMS AND EQUIPMENT STARTUP With the assistance of the Owner's maintenance personnel and the Contractor, the Subcontractor shall direct the check-out and operation of systems and equipment for readiness, and assist in their initial startup and the testing of the Subcontract Work.

3.29 COMPLIANCE WITH LAWS The Subcontractor agrees to be bound by, and at its own costs comply with, all federal, state and local laws, ordinances and regulations (the Laws) applicable to the Subcontract Work, including but not limited to, equal employment opportunity, minority business enterprise, women's business enterprise, disadvantaged business enterprise, safety and all other Laws with which the Contractor must comply. The Subcontractor shall be liable to the Contractor and the Owner for all loss, cost and expense attributable to any acts of commission or omission by the Subcontractor, its employees and agents resulting from the failure to comply with Laws, including, but not limited to, any fines, penalties or corrective measures, except as provided in Subparagraph 3.14.9.

3.30 CONFIDENTIALITY To the extent the Owner-Contractor agreement provides for the confidentiality of any of the Owner's proprietary or otherwise confidential information disclosed in connection with the performance of this Agreement, the Subcontractor is equally bound by the Owner's confidentiality requirements.

3.31 ROYALTIES, PATENTS AND COPYRIGHTS The Subcontractor shall pay all royalties and license fees which may be due on the inclusion of any patented or copyrighted materials, methods or systems selected by the Subcontractor and incorporated in the Subcontract Work. The Subcontractor shall defend, indemnify and hold the Contractor and Owner harmless from all suits or claims for infringement of any patent rights or copyrights arising out of such selection. The Subcontractor shall be liable for all loss, including all costs, expenses, and attorneys' fees, but shall not be responsible for such defense or loss when a particular design, process or product of a particular manufacturer or manufacturers is required by the Subcontract Documents. However, if the Subcontractor has reason to believe that a particular design, process or product required by the Subcontract Documents is an infringement of a patent, the Subcontractor shall promptly furnish such information to the Contractor or be responsible to the Contractor and Owner for any loss sustained as a result.

3.32 LABOR RELATIONS (Insert here any conditions, obligations or requirements relative to labor relations and their effect on the project. Legal counsel is recommended.) ◆

ARTICLE 4

CONTRACTOR'S RESPONSIBILITIES

4.1 CONTRACTOR'S REPRESENTATIVE The Contractor shall designate a person who shall be the Contractor's authorized representative. The Contractor's representative shall be the only person the Subcontractor shall look to for instructions, orders and/or directions, except in an emergency. The Contractor's representative is______________________

____.◆

4.2 PAYMENT BOND REVIEW The Contractor ☐ has ☐ has not provided the Owner a payment bond. The ◆ Contractor's payment bond for the Project, if any, shall be made available by the Contractor for review and copying by the Subcontractor.

4.3 OWNER'S ABILITY TO PAY

4.3.1 The Subcontractor shall have the right upon request to receive from the Contractor such information as the Contractor has obtained relative to the Owner's financial ability to pay for the Work, including any subsequent material variation in such information. The Contractor, however, does not warrant the accuracy or completeness of the information provided by the Owner.

4.3.2 If the Subcontractor does not receive the information referenced in Subparagraph 4.3.1 with regard to the Owner's ability to pay for the Work as required by the Contract Documents, the Subcontractor may request the information from the Owner and/or the Owner's lender.

4.4 CONTRACTOR APPLICATION FOR PAYMENT Upon request, the Contractor shall give the Subcontractor a copy of the most current Contractor application for payment reflecting the amounts approved and/or paid by the Owner for the Subcontract Work performed to date.

4.5 INFORMATION OR SERVICES The Subcontractor is entitled to request through the Contractor any information or services relevant to the performance of the Subcontract Work which is under the Owner's control. To the extent the Contractor receives such information and services, the Contractor shall provide them to the Subcontractor. The Contractor, however, does not warrant the accuracy or completeness of the information provided by the Owner.

4.6 STORAGE AREAS The Contractor shall allocate adequate storage areas, if available, for the Subcontractor's materials and equipment during the course of the Subcontract Work. Unless otherwise agreed upon, the Contractor shall reimburse the Subcontractor for the additional costs of having to relocate such storage areas at the direction of the Contractor.

4.7 TIMELY COMMUNICATIONS The Contractor shall transmit to the Subcontractor, with reasonable promptness, all submittals, transmittals, and written approvals relative to the Subcontract Work. Unless otherwise specified in the Subcontract Documents, communications by and with the Subcontractor's subcontractors, materialmen and suppliers shall be through the Subcontractor.

4.8 USE OF SUBCONTRACTOR'S EQUIPMENT The Contractor, its agents, employees or suppliers shall use the Subcontractor's equipment only with the express written permission of the Subcontractor's designated representative and in accordance with the Subcontractor's terms and conditions for such use. If the Contractor or any of its agents, employees or suppliers utilize any of the Subcontractor's equipment, including machinery, tools, scaffolding, hoists, lifts or similar items owned, leased or under the control of the Subcontractor, the Contractor shall defend, indemnify and be liable to the Subcontractor as provided in Article 9 for any loss or damage (including bodily injury or death) which may arise from such use, except to the extent that such loss or damage is caused by the negligence of the Subcontractor's employees operating the Subcontractor's equipment.

ARTICLE 5

PROGRESS SCHEDULE

5.1 TIME IS OF THE ESSENCE Time is of the essence for both parties. They mutually agree to see to the performance of their respective obligations so that the entire Project may be completed in accordance with the Subcontract Documents and particularly the Progress Schedule as set forth in Exhibit _____.◆

5.2 SCHEDULE OBLIGATIONS The Subcontractor shall provide the Contractor with any scheduling information proposed by the Subcontractor for the Subcontract Work. In consultation with the Subcontractor, the Contractor shall prepare the schedule for performance of the Work (the Progress Schedule) and shall revise and update such schedule, as necessary, as the Work progresses. Both the Contractor and the Subcontractor shall be bound by the Progress Schedule. The Progress Schedule and all subsequent changes and additional details shall be submitted to the Subcontractor promptly and reasonably in advance of the required performance. The Contractor shall have the right to determine and, if necessary, change the time, order and priority in which the various portions of the Work shall be performed and all other matters relative to the Subcontract Work.

5.3 DELAYS AND EXTENSIONS OF TIME

5.3.1 OWNER CAUSED DELAY Subject to Subparagraph 5.3.2, if the commencement and/or progress of the Subcontract Work is delayed without the fault or responsibility of the Subcontractor, the time for the Subcontract Work shall be extended by Subcontract Change Order to the extent obtained by the Contractor under the Subcontract Documents, and the Progress Schedule shall be revised accordingly.

5.3.2 CLAIMS RELATING TO OWNER The Subcontractor agrees to initiate all claims for which the Owner is or may be liable in the manner and within the time limits provided in the Subcontract Documents for like claims by the Contractor upon the Owner and in sufficient time for the Contractor to initiate such claims against the Owner in accordance with the Subcontract Documents. At the Subcontractor's request and expense to the extent agreed upon in writing, the Contractor agrees to permit the Subcontractor to prosecute a claim in the name of the Contractor for the use and benefit of the Subcontractor in the manner provided in the Subcontract Documents for like claims by the Contractor upon the Owner.

5.3.3 CONTRACTOR CAUSED DELAY Nothing in this Article shall preclude the Subcontractor's recovery of delay damages caused by the Contractor.

5.3.4 CLAIMS RELATING TO CONTRACTOR The Subcontractor shall give the Contractor written notice of all claims not included in Subparagraph 5.3.2 within seven (7) days of the Subcontractor's knowledge of the facts giving rise to the event for which claim is made; otherwise, such claims shall be deemed waived. All unresolved claims, disputes and other matters in question between the Contractor and the Subcontractor not relating to claims included in Subparagraph 5.3.2 shall be resolved in the manner provided in Article 11.

5.3.5 DAMAGES If the Subcontract Documents provide for liquidated or other damages for delay beyond the completion date set forth in the Subcontract Documents, and such damages are assessed, the Contractor may assess a share of the damages against the Subcontractor in proportion to the Subcontractor's share of the responsibility for the delay. However, the amount of such assessment shall not exceed the amount assessed against the Contractor. This Paragraph 5.3 shall not limit the Subcontractor's liability to the Contractor for the Contractor's actual delay damages caused by the Subcontractor's delay.

5.4 MUTUAL WAIVER OF CONSEQUENTIAL DAMAGES

5.4.1 To the extent the Owner-Contractor agreement provides for a mutual waiver of consequential damages by the Owner and the Contractor, the Contractor and Subcontractor waive claims against each other for consequential damages arising out of or relating to this Agreement, including to the extent provided in the Owner-Contractor agreement, damages for principal office expenses and the compensation of personnel stationed there; loss of financing, business and reputation; and for loss of profit. Similarly, the Subcontractor shall obtain from its sub-subcontractors mutual waivers of consequential damages that correspond to the Subcontractor's waiver of consequential damages herein. To the extent applicable, this mutual waiver applies to consequential damages due to termination by the Contractor or the Owner in accordance with this Agreement or the Owner-Contractor agreement. To the extent the Owner-Contractor agreement does not preclude the award of liquidated damages, nothing contained in this Paragraph 5.4 shall preclude the imposition of such damages, if applicable in accordance with the requirements of the Subcontract Documents.

5.4.2 To the extent the Owner-Contractor agreement provides for a mutual waiver of consequential damages by the Owner and the Contractor, damages for which the Contractor is liable to the Owner including those related to Subparagraph 9.1.1 are not consequential damages for the purpose of this waiver. Similarly, to the extent the Subcontractor-sub-subcontractor agreement provides for a mutual waiver of consequential damages by the Owner and the Contractor, damages for which the Subcontractor is liable to lower-tiered parties due to the fault of the Owner or Contractor are not consequential damages for the purpose of this waiver.

ARTICLE 6

SUBCONTRACT AMOUNT

As full compensation for performance of this Agreement, Contractor agrees to pay Subcontractor in current funds for the satisfactory performance of the Subcontract Work subject to all applicable provisions of the Subcontract:

(a) the fixed-price of______________________________
____
Dollars ($_____________________________________)◆
subject to additions and deductions as provided for in the Subcontract Documents; and/or

(b) unit prices in accordance with the attached schedule of Unit Prices and estimated quantities, which is incorporated by reference and identified as Exhibit__________;◆ and/or

(c) time and material rates and prices in accordance with the attached Schedule of Labor and Material Costs which is incorporated by reference and identified as Exhibit____.◆

The fixed price, unit prices and/or time and material rates and prices are referred to as the Subcontract Amount.

ARTICLE 7

CHANGES IN THE SUBCONTRACT WORK

7.1 **SUBCONTRACT CHANGE ORDERS** When the Contractor orders in writing, the Subcontractor, without nullifying this Agreement, shall make any and all changes in the Subcontract Work which are within the general scope of this Agreement. Any adjustment in the Subcontract Amount or Subcontract Time shall be authorized by a Subcontract Change Order. No adjustments shall be made for any changes performed by the Subcontractor that have not been ordered by the Contractor. A Subcontract Change Order is a written instrument prepared by the Contractor and signed by the Subcontractor stating their agreement upon the change in the Subcontract Work.

7.2 **CONSTRUCTION CHANGE DIRECTIVES** To the extent that the Subcontract Documents provide for Construction Change Directives in the absence of agreement on the terms of a Subcontract Change Order, the Subcontractor shall promptly comply with the Construction Change Directive and be entitled to apply for interim payment if the Subcontract Documents so provide.

7.3 **UNKNOWN CONDITIONS** If in the performance of the Subcontract Work the Subcontractor finds latent, concealed or subsurface physical conditions which differ materially from those indicated in the Subcontract Documents or unknown physical conditions of an unusual nature, which differ materially from those ordinarily found to exist and not generally recognized as inherent in the kind of work provided for in this Agreement, the Subcontract Amount and/or the Progress Schedule shall be equitably adjusted by a Subcontract Change Order within a reasonable time after the conditions are first observed. The adjustment which the Subcontractor may receive shall be limited to the adjustment the Contractor receives from the Owner on behalf of the Subcontractor, or as otherwise provided under Subparagraph 5.3.2.

7.4 **ADJUSTMENTS IN SUBCONTRACT AMOUNT** If a Subcontract Change Order requires an adjustment in the Subcontract Amount, the adjustment shall be established by one of the following methods:

.1 mutual acceptance of an itemized lump sum;

.2 unit prices as indicated in the Subcontract Documents or as subsequently agreed to by the parties; or

.3 costs determined in a manner acceptable to the parties and a mutually acceptable fixed or percentage fee; or

.4 another method provided in the Subcontract Documents.

7.5 **SUBSTANTIATION OF ADJUSTMENT** If the Subcontractor does not respond promptly or disputes the method of adjustment, the method and the adjustment shall be determined by the Contractor on the basis of reasonable expenditures and savings of those performing the Work attributable to the change, including, in the case of an increase in the Subcontract Amount , an allowance for overhead and profit of the percentage provided in Paragraph 7.6. The Subcontractor may contest the reasonableness of any adjustment determined by the Contractor. The Subcontractor shall maintain for the Contractor's review and approval an appropriately itemized and substantiated accounting of the following items attributable to the Subcontract Change Order:

.1 labor costs, including Social Security, health, welfare, retirement and other fringe benefits as normally required, and state workers' compensation insurance;

.2 costs of materials, supplies and equipment, whether incorporated in the Subcontract Work or consumed, including transportation costs;

.3 costs of renting machinery and equipment other than hand tools;

.4 costs of bond and insurance premiums, permit fees and taxes attributable to the change; and

.5 costs of additional supervision and field office personnel services necessitated by the change.

7.6 Adjustments shall be based on net change in Subcontractor's reasonable cost of performing the changed Subcontract Work plus, in case of a net increase in cost, an agreed upon sum for overhead and profit not to exceed ________percent (____________%). ◆

7.7 NO OBLIGATION TO PERFORM The Subcontractor shall not perform changes in the Subcontract Work until a Subcontract Change Order has been executed or written instructions have been issued in accordance with Paragraphs 7.2 and 7.9.

7.8 EMERGENCIES In an emergency affecting the safety of persons and/or property, the Subcontractor shall act, at its discretion, to prevent threatened damage, injury or loss. Any change in the Subcontract Amount and/or the Progress Schedule on account of emergency work shall be determined as provided in this Article.

7.9 INCIDENTAL CHANGES The Contractor may direct the Subcontractor to perform incidental changes in the Subcontract Work which do not involve adjustments in the Subcontract Amount or Subcontract Time. Incidental changes shall be consistent with the scope and intent of the Subcontract Documents. The Contractor shall initiate an incidental change in the Subcontract Work by issuing a written order to the Subcontractor. Such written notice shall be carried out promptly and are binding on the parties.

ARTICLE 8

PAYMENT

8.1 SCHEDULE OF VALUES As a condition to payment, the Subcontractor shall provide a schedule of values satisfactory to the Contractor not more than fifteen (15) days from the date of execution of this Agreement.

8.2 PROGRESS PAYMENTS

8.2.1 APPLICATIONS The Subcontractor's applications for payment shall be itemized and supported by substantiating data as required by the Subcontract Documents. If the Subcontractor is obligated to provide design services pursuant to Paragraph 3.8, Subcontractor's applications for payment shall show the Designer's fee and expenses as a separate cost item. The Subcontractor's application shall be notarized if required and if allowed under the Subcontract Documents may include properly authorized Subcontract Construction Change Directives. The Subcontractor's progress payment application for the Subcontract Work performed in the preceding payment period shall be submitted for approval of the Contractor in accordance with the schedule of values if required and Subparagraphs 8.2.2, 8.2.3, and 8.2.4. The Contractor shall incorporate the approved amount of the Subcontractor's progress payment application into the Contractor's payment application to the Owner for the same period and submit it to the Owner in a timely fashion. The Contractor shall immediately notify the Subcontractor of any changes in the amount requested on behalf on the Subcontractor.

8.2.2 RETAINAGE The rate of retainage shall be______________percent (_____________________%)◆ which is equal to the percentage retained from the Contractor's payment by the Owner for the Subcontract Work. If the Subcontract Work is satisfactory and the Subcontract Documents provide for reduction of retainage at a specified percentage of completion, the Subcontractor's retainage shall also be reduced when the Subcontract Work has attained the same percentage of completion and the Contractor's retainage for the Subcontract Work has been so reduced by the Owner.

8.2.3 TIME OF APPLICATION The Subcontractor shall submit progress payment applications to the Contractor no later than the_____________________________________◆ day of each payment period for the Subcontract Work performed up to and including the_______________________◆ day of the payment period indicating work completed and, to the extent allowed under Subparagraph 8.2.4, materials suitably stored during the preceding payment period.

8.2.4 STORED MATERIALS Unless otherwise provided in the Subcontract Documents, and if approved in advance by the Owner, applications for payment may include materials and equipment not incorporated in the Subcontract Work but delivered to and suitably stored at the site or at some other location agreed upon in writing. Approval of payment applications for such stored items on or off the site shall be conditioned upon submission by the Subcontractor of bills of sale and applicable insurance or such other procedures satisfactory to the Owner and Contractor to establish the Owner's title to such materials and equipment, or otherwise to protect the Owner's and Contractor's interest including transportation to the site.

8.2.5 TIME OF PAYMENT Receipt of payment by the Contractor from the Owner for the Subcontract Work is a condition precedent to payment by the Contractor to the Subcontractor. The Subcontractor hereby acknowledges that it relies on the credit of the Owner, not the Contractor for payment of Subcontract Work. Progress payments received from the Owner for the Subcontractor for satisfactory performance of the Subcontract Work shall be made no later than seven (7) days after receipt by the Contractor of payment from the Owner for the Subcontract Work.

8.2.6 PAYMENT DELAY If the Contractor has received payment from the Owner and if for any reason not the fault of the Subcontractor, the Subcontractor does not receive a progress payment from the Contractor within seven (7) days after the date such payment is due, as defined in Subparagraph 8.2.5, the Subcontractor, upon giving seven (7) days' written notice to the Contractor, and without prejudice to and in addition to any other legal remedies, may stop work until payment of the full amount owing to the Subcontractor has been received. The Subcontract Amount and Time shall be adjusted by the amount of the Subcontractor's reasonable and verified cost of shutdown, delay, and startup, which shall be effected by an appropriate Subcontractor Change Order.

8.2.7 PAYMENTS WITHHELD The Contractor may reject a Subcontractor payment application or nullify a previously approved Subcontractor payment application, in whole or in part, as may reasonably be necessary to protect the Contractor from loss or damage based upon:

.1 the Subcontractor's repeated failure to perform the Subcontract Work as required by this Agreement;

.2 loss or damage arising out of or relating to this Agreement and caused by the Subcontractor to the Owner, Contractor or others to whom the Contractor may be liable;

.3 the Subcontractor's failure to properly pay for labor, materials, equipment or supplies furnished in connection with the Subcontract Work;

.4 rejected, nonconforming or defective Subcontract Work which has not been corrected in a timely fashion;

.5 reasonable evidence of delay in performance of the Subcontract Work such that the Work will not be completed within the Subcontract Time, and that the unpaid balance of the Subcontract Amount is not sufficient to offset the liquidated damages or actual damages that may be sustain by the Contractor as a result of the anticipated delay caused by the Subcontractor;

.6 reasonable evidence demonstrating that the unpaid balance of the Subcontract Amount is insufficient to cover the cost to complete the Subcontract Work;

.7 third party claims involving the Subcontractor or reasonable evidence demonstrating that third party claims are likely to be filed unless and until the Subcontractor furnishes the Contractor with adequate security in the form of a surety bond, letter of credit or other collateral or commitment which are sufficient to discharge such claims if established.

The Contractor shall give written notice to the Subcontractor, at the time of disapproving or nullifying an application for payment stating its specific reasons for such disapproval or nullification. When the above reasons for disapproving or nullifying an application for payment are removed, payment will be made for amounts previously withheld.

8.3 FINAL PAYMENT

8.3.1 **APPLICATION** Upon acceptance of the Subcontract Work by the Owner and the Contractor and receipt from the Subcontractor of evidence of fulfillment of the Subcontractor's obligations in accordance with the Subcontract Documents and Subparagraph 8.3.2, the Contractor shall incorporate the Subcontractor's application for final payment into the Contractor's next application for payment to the Owner without delay, or notify the Subcontractor if there is a delay and the reasons therefor.

8.3.2 **REQUIREMENTS** Before the Contractor shall be required to incorporate the Subcontractor's application for final payment into the Contractor's next application for payment, the Subcontractor shall submit to the Contractor:

.1 an affidavit that all payrolls, bills for materials and equipment, and other indebtedness connected with the Subcontract Work for which the Owner or its property or the Contractor or the Contractor's surety might in any way be liable, have been paid or otherwise satisfied;

.2 consent of surety to final payment, if required;

.3 satisfaction of required closeout procedures;

.4 certification that insurance required by the Subcontract Documents to remain in effect beyond final payment pursuant to Clauses 9.2.3.1 and 9.2.6 is in effect and will not be cancelled or allowed to expire without at least thirty (30) days' written notice to the Contractor unless a longer period is stipulated in this Agreement;

.5 other data, if required by the Contractor or Owner, such as receipts, releases, and waivers of liens to the extent and in such form as may be designated by the Contractor or Owner;

.6 written warranties, equipment manuals, startup and testing required in Paragraph 3.28; and

.7 as-built drawings if required by the Subcontract Documents.

8.3.3 **TIME OF PAYMENT** Receipt of final payment by the Contractor from the Owner for the Subcontract Work is a condition precedent to payment by the Contractor to the Subcontractor. The Subcontractor hereby acknowledges that it relies on the credit of the Owner, not the Contractor for payment of Subcontract Work. Final payment of the balance due of the Contract Price shall be made to the Subcontractor:

.1 upon receipt of the Owner's waiver of all claims related to the Subcontract Work except for unsettled liens, unknown defective work, and non-compliance with the Subcontract Documents or warranties; and

.2 within seven (7) days after receipt by the Contractor of final payment from the Owner for such Subcontract Work.

8.3.4 **FINAL PAYMENT DELAY** If the Owner or its designated agent does not issue a certificate for final payment or the Contractor does not receive such payment for any cause which is not the fault of the Subcontractor, the Contractor shall promptly inform the Subcontractor in writing. The Contractor shall also diligently pursue, with the assistance of the Subcontractor, the prompt release by the Owner of the final payment due for the Subcontract Work. At the Subcontractor's request and expense, to the extent agreed upon in writing, the Contractor shall institute reasonable legal remedies to mitigate the damages and pursue payment of the Subcontractor's final payment including interest.

8.3.5 **WAIVER OF CLAIMS** Final payment shall constitute a waiver of all claims by the Subcontractor relating to the Subcontract Work, but shall in no way relieve the Subcontractor of liability for the obligations assumed under Paragraphs 3.21 and 3.22, or for faulty or defective work or services discovered after final payment.

8.4 **LATE PAYMENT INTEREST** To the extent obtained by the Contractor under the Subcontract Documents, progress payments or final payment due and unpaid under this Agreement shall bear interest from the date payment is due at the rate provided in the Subcontract Documents.

8.5 **CONTINUING OBLIGATIONS** Provided the Contractor is making payments on or has made payments to the Subcontractor in accordance with the terms of this Agreement, the Subcontractor shall reimburse the Contractor for any costs and expenses for any claim, obligation or lien asserted before or after final payment is made that arises from the performance of the Subcontract Work. The Subcontractor shall reimburse the Contractor for costs and expenses including attorneys' fees and costs and expenses incurred by the Contractor in satisfying, discharging or defending against any such claims, obligation or lien including any action brought or judgment recovered. In the event that any applicable law, statute, regulation or bond requires the Subcontractor to take any action prior to the expiration of the reasonable time for payment referenced in Subparagraph 8.2.5 in order to preserve or protect the Subcontractor's rights, if any, with respect to mechanic's lien or bond claims, then the Subcontractor may take that action prior to the expiration of the reasonable time for payment and such action will not create the reimbursement obligation recited above nor be in violation of this Agreement or considered premature for purposes of preserving and protecting the Subcontractor's rights.

8.6 PAYMENT USE RESTRICTION Payments received by the Subcontractor shall be used to satisfy the indebtednessowed by the Subcontractor to any person furnishing labor or materials, or both, for use in performing the Subcontract Work through the most current period applicable to progress payments received from the Contractor before it is used for any other purpose. In the same manner, payments received by the Contractor from the Owner for the Subcontract Work shall be dedicated to payment to the Subcontractor. This provision shall bear on this Agreement only, and is not for the benefit of third parties. Moreover, it shall not be construed by the parties to this Agreement or third parties to require that dedicated sums of money or payments be deposited in separate accounts, or that there be other restrictions on commingling of funds. Neither shall these mutual covenants be construed to create any fiduciary duty on the Subcontractor or Contractor, nor create any tort cause of action or liability for breach of trust, punitive damages, or other equitable remedy or liability for alleged breach.

8.7 PAYMENT USE VERIFICATION If the Contractor has reason to believe that the Subcontractor is not complying with the payment terms of this Agreement, the Contractor shall have the right to contact the Subcontractor's subcontractors and suppliers to ascertain whether they are being paid by the Subcontractor in accordance with this Agreement.

8.8 PARTIAL LIEN WAIVERS AND AFFIDAVITS As a prerequisite for payments, the Subcontractor shall provide, in a form satisfactory to the Owner and Contractor, partial lien or claim waivers in the amount of the application for payment and affidavits covering its subcontractors and suppliers for completed Subcontract Work. Such waivers may be conditional upon payment. In no event shall Contractor require the Subcontractor to provide an unconditional waiver of lien or claim, either partial or final, prior to receiving payment or in an amount in excess of what it has been paid.

8.9 SUBCONTRACTOR PAYMENT FAILURE Upon payment by the Contractor, the Subcontractor shall promptly pay its subcontractors and suppliers the amounts to which they are entitled. In the event the Contractor has reason to believe that labor, material or other obligations incurred in the performance of the Subcontract Work are not being paid, the Contractor may give written notice of a potential claim or lien to the Subcontractor and may take any steps deemed necessary to assure that progress payments are utilized to pay such obligations, including but not limited to the issuance of joint checks. If upon receipt of notice, the Subcontractor does not (a) supply evidence to the satisfaction of the Contractor that the moneys owing have been paid; or (b) post a bond indemnifying the Owner, the Contractor, the Contractor's surety, if any, and the premises from a claim or lien, the Contractor shall have the right to withhold from any payments due or to become due to the Subcontractor a reasonable amount to protect the Contractor from any and all loss, damage or expense including attorneys' fees that may arise out of or relate to any such claim or lien.

8.10 SUBCONTRACTOR ASSIGNMENT OF PAYMENTS The Subcontractor shall not assign any moneys due or to become due under this Agreement without the written consent of the Contractor, unless the assignment is intended to create a new security interest within the scope of Article 9 of the Uniform Commercial Code. Should the Subcontractor assign all or any part of any moneys due or to become due under this Agreement to create a new security interest or for any other purpose, the instrument of assignment shall contain a clause to the effect that the assignee's right in and to any money due or to become due to the Subcontractor shall be subject to the claims of all persons, firms and corporations for services rendered or materials supplied for the performance of the Subcontract Work.

8.11 PAYMENT NOT ACCEPTANCE Payment to the Subcontractor does not constitute or imply acceptance of any portion of the Subcontract Work.

ARTICLE 9

INDEMNITY, INSURANCE AND WAIVER OF SUBROGATION

9.1 INDEMNITY

9.1.1 INDEMNITY To the fullest extent permitted by law, the Subcontractor shall defend, indemnify and hold harmless the Contractor, the Contractor's other subcontractors, the Architect/Engineer, the Owner and their agents, consultants and employees (the Indemnitees) from all claims for bodily injury and property damage that may arise from the performance of the Subcontract Work to the extent of the negligence attributed to such acts or omissions by the Subcontractor, the Subcontractor's subcontractors or anyone employed directly or indirectly by any of them or by anyone for whose acts any of them may be liable.

9.1.2 NO LIMITATION ON LIABILITY In any and all claims against the Indemnitees by any employee of the Subcontractor, anyone directly or indirectly employed by the Subcontractor or anyone for whose acts the Subcontractor may be liable, the indemnification obligation shall not be limited in any way by any limitation on the amount or type of damages, compensation or benefits payable by or for the Subcontractor under workers' compensation acts, disability benefit acts or other employee benefit acts.

9.2 INSURANCE

9.2.1 SUBCONTRACTOR'S INSURANCE Before commencing the Subcontract Work, and as a condition of payment, the Subcontractor shall purchase and maintain insurance that will protect it from the claims arising out of its operations under this Agreement, whether the operations are by the Subcontractor, or any of its consultants or subcontractors or anyone directly or indirectly employed by any of them, or by anyone for whose acts any of them may be liable.

9.2.2 MINIMUM LIMITS OF LIABILITY The Subcontractor shall maintain at least the limits of liability in a company satisfactory to the Contractor as set forth in Exhibit ___________.◆

9.2.3 PROFESSIONAL LIABILITY INSURANCE

9.2.3.1 PROFESSIONAL LIABILITY INSURANCE The Subcontractor shall require the Designer(s) to maintain Project Specific Professional Liability Insurance with a company satisfactory to the Contractor, including contractual liability insurance against the liability assumed in Paragraph 3.8, and including coverage for any professional liability caused by any of the Designer's(s') consultants. Said insurance shall have specific minimum limits as set forth below:

Limit of $___________per claim. ◆

General Aggregate of $___________ for the subcontract services rendered. ◆

The Professional Liability Insurance shall contain prior acts coverage sufficient to cover all subcontract services rendered by the Designer. Said insurance shall be continued in effect with an extended period of __________ years following final◆ paymentto the Designer.

Such insurance shall have a maximum deductible amount of $______________________________________◆ per occurrence. The deductible shall be paid by the Subcontractor or Designer.

9.2.3.2 The Subcontractor shall require the Designer to furnish to the Subcontractor and Contractor, before the Designer commences its services, a copy of its professional liability policy evidencing the coverages required in this Paragraph. No policy shall be cancelled or modified without thirty (30) days' prior written notice to the Subcontractor and Contractor.

9.2.4 NUMBER OF POLICIES Commercial General Liability Insurance and other liability insurance may be arranged under a single policy for the full limits required or by a combination of underlying policies with the balance provided by an Excess or Umbrella Liability Policy.

9.2.5 CANCELLATION, RENEWAL AND MODIFICATION The Subcontractor shall maintain in effect all insurance coverages required under this Agreement at the Subcontractor's sole expense and with insurance companies acceptable to the Contractor. The policies shall contain a provision that coverage will not be cancelled or not renewed until at least thirty (30) days' prior written notice has been given to the Contractor. Certificates of insurance showing required coverage to be in force pursuant to Subparagraph 9.2.2 shall be filed with the Contractor prior to commencement of the Subcontract Work. In the event the Subcontractor fails to obtain or maintain any insurance coverage required under this Agreement, the Contractor may purchase such coverage as desired for the Contractor's benefit and charge the expense to the Subcontractor, or terminate this Agreement.

9.2.6 CONTINUATION OF COVERAGE The Subcontractor shall continue to carry Completed Operations Liability Insurance for at least ______________________ years after either ninety (90) days following Substantial Completion of the Work or final payment to the Contractor, whichever is earlier. The Subcontractor shall furnish the Contractor evidence of such insurance at final payment and one year from final payment.

9.2.7 BUILDER'S RISK INSURANCE

9.2.7.1 Upon written request of the Subcontractor, the Contractor shall provide the Subcontractor with a copy of the Builder's Risk policy of insurance or any other property or equipment insurance in force for the Project and procured by the Owner or Contractor. The Contractor will advise the Subcontractor if a Builder's Risk policy of insurance is not in force.

9.2.7.2 If the Owner or Contractor has not purchased Builder's Risk insurance satisfactory to the Subcontractor, the Subcontractor may procure such insurance as will protect the interests of the Subcontractor, its subcontractors and their subcontractors in the Subcontract Work.

9.2.7.3 If not covered under the Builder's Risk policy of insurance or any other property or equipment insurance required by the Subcontract Documents, the Subcontractor shall procure and maintain at the Subcontractor's own expense property and equipment insurance for the Subcontract Work including portions of the Subcontract Work stored off the site or in transit, when such portions of the Subcontract Work are to be included in an application for payment under Article 8.

9.2.8 WAIVER OF SUBROGATION

9.2.8.1 The Contractor and Subcontractor waive all rights against each other, the Owner and the Architect/Engineer, and any of their respective consultants, subcontractors, and sub-subcontractors, agents and employees, for damages caused by perils to the extent covered by the proceeds of the insurance provided in Clause 9.2.7.1, except such rights as they may have to the insurance proceeds. The Subcontractor shall require similar waivers from its subcontractors.

9.2.9 ENDORSEMENT If the policies of insurance referred to in this Article require an endorsement to provide for continued coverage where there is a waiver of subrogation, the owners of such policies will cause them to be so endorsed.

ARTICLE 10

CONTRACTOR'S RIGHT TO PERFORM SUBCONTRACTOR'S RESPONSIBILITIES AND TERMINATION OF AGREEMENT

10.1 FAILURE OF PERFORMANCE

10.1.1 NOTICE TO CURE If the Subcontractor refuses or fails to supply enough properly skilled workers, proper materials, or maintain the Progress Schedule, or fails to make prompt payment to its workers, subcontractors or suppliers, or disregards laws, ordinances, rules, regulations or orders of any public authority having jurisdiction, or otherwise is guilty of a material breach of a provision of this Agreement, the Subcontractor shall be deemed in default of this Agreement. If the Subcontractor fails within three (3) days after written notification to commence and continue satisfactory correction of the default with diligence and promptness, then the Contractor without prejudice to any other rights or remedies, shall have the right to any or all of the following remedies:

.1 supply workers, materials, equipment and facilities as the Contractor deems necessary for the completion of the Subcontract Work or any part which the Subcontractor has failed to complete or perform after written notification, and charge the cost, including reasonable overhead, profit, attorneys' fees, costs and expenses to the Subcontractor;

.2 contract with one or more additional contractors to perform such part of the Subcontract Work as the Contractor determines will provide the most expeditious completion of the Work, and charge the cost to the Subcontractor as provided under Clause 10.1.1.1; and/or

.3 withhold any payments due or to become due the Subcontractor pending corrective action in amounts sufficient to cover losses and compel performance to the extent required by and to the satisfaction of the Contractor.

In the event of an emergency affecting the safety of persons or property, the Contractor may proceed as above without notice, but the Contractor shall give the Subcontractor notice promptly after the fact as a precondition of cost recovery.

10.1.2 TERMINATION BY CONTRACTOR If the Subcontractor fails to commence and satisfactorily continue correction of a default within three (3) days after written notification issued under Subparagraph 10.1.1, then the Contractor may, in lieu of or in addition to Subparagraph 10.1.1, issue a second written notification, to the Subcontractor and its surety, if any. Such notice shall state that if the Subcontractor fails to commence and continue correction of a default within seven (7) days of the written notification, the Agreement will be deemed terminated. A written notice of termination shall be issued by the Contractor to the Subcontractor at the time the Subcontractor is terminated. The Contractor may furnish those materials, equipment and/or employ such workers or subcontractors as the Contractor deems necessary to maintain the orderly progress of the Work. All costs incurred by the Contractor in performing the Subcontract Work, including reasonable overhead, profit and attorneys' fees, costs and expenses, shall be deducted from any moneys due or to become due the Subcontractor. The Subcontractor shall be liable for the payment of any amount by which such expense may exceed the unpaid balance of the Subcontract Amount. At the Subcontractor's request, the Contractor shall provide a detailed accounting of the costs to finish the Subcontract Work.

10.1.3 USE OF SUBCONTRACTOR'S EQUIPMENT If the Contractor performs work under this Article, either directly or through other subcontractors, the Contractor or other subcontractors shall have the right to take and use any materials, implements, equipment, appliances or tools furnished by, or belonging to the Subcontractor and located at the Project site for the purpose of completing any remaining Subcontract Work. Immediately upon completion of the Subcontract Work, any remaining materials, implements, equipment, appliances or tools not consumed or incorporated in performance of the Subcontract Work, and furnished by, belonging to, or delivered to the Project by or on behalf of the Subcontractor, shall be returned to the Subcontractor in substantially the same condition as when they were taken, normal wear and tear excepted.

10.2 BANKRUPTCY

10.2.1 TERMINATION ABSENT CURE If the Subcontractor files a petition under the Bankruptcy Code, this Agreement shall terminate if the Subcontractor or the Subcontractor's trustee rejects the Agreement or, if there has been a default, the Subcontractor is unable to give adequate assurance that the Subcontractor will perform as required by this Agreement or otherwise is unable to comply with the requirements for assuming this Agreement under the applicable provisions of the Bankruptcy Code.

10.2.2 INTERIM REMEDIES If the Subcontractor is not performing in accordance with the Progress Schedule at the time a petition in bankruptcy is filed, or at any subsequent time, the Contractor, while awaiting the decision of the Subcontractor or its trustee to reject or to assume this Agreement and provide adequate assurance of its ability to perform, may avail itself of such remedies under this Article as are reasonably necessary to maintain the Progress Schedule. The Contractor may offset against any sums due or to become due the Subcontractor all costs incurred in pursuing any of the remedies provided including, but not limited to, reasonable overhead, profit and attorneys' fees. The Subcontractor shall be liable for the payment of any amount by which costs incurred may exceed the unpaid balance of the Subcontract Price.

10.3 SUSPENSION BY OWNER Should the Owner suspend the Work or any part which includes the Subcontract Work and such suspension is not due to any act or omission of the Contractor, or any other person or entity for whose acts or omissions the Contractor may be liable, the Contractor shall notify the Subcontractor in writing and upon receiving notification the Subcontractor shall immediately suspend the Subcontract Work. In the event of Owner suspension, the Contractor's liability to the Subcontractor shall be limited to the extent of the Contractor's recovery on the Subcontractor's behalf under the Subcontract Documents. The Contractor agrees to cooperate with the Subcontractor, at the Subcontractor's expense, in the prosecution of any Subcontractor claim arising out of an Owner suspension and to permit the Subcontractor to prosecute the claim, in the name of the Contractor, for the use and benefit of the Subcontractor.

10.4 TERMINATION BY OWNER Should the Owner terminate its contract with the Contractor or any part which includes the Subcontract Work, the Contractor shall notify the Subcontractor in writing within three (3) days of the termination and upon written notification, this Agreement shall be terminated and the Subcontractor shall immediately stop the Subcontract Work, follow all of Contractor's instructions, and mitigate all costs. In the event of Owner termination, the Contractor's liability to the Subcontractor shall be limited to the extent of the Contractor's recovery on the Subcontractor's behalf under the Subcontract Documents. The Contractor agrees to cooperate with the Subcontractor, at the Subcontractor's expense, in the prosecution of any Subcontractor claim arising out of the Owner termination and to permit the Subcontractor to prosecute the claim, in the name of the Contractor, for the use and benefit of the Subcontractor, or assign the claim to the Subcontractor.

10.5 CONTINGENT ASSIGNMENT OF THIS AGREEMENT The Contractor's contingent assignment of this Agreement to the Owner, as provided in the Owner-Contractor agreement , is effective when the Owner has terminated the Owner-Contractor agreement for cause and has accepted the assignment by notifying the Subcontractor in writing. This contingent assignment is subject to the prior rights of a surety that may be obligated under the Contractor's bond, if any. Subcontractor consents to such assignment and agrees to be bound to the assignee by the terms of this Agreement, provided that the assignee fulfills the obligations of the Contractor.

10.6 SUSPENSION BY CONTRACTOR The Contractor may order the Subcontractor in writing to suspend all or any part of the Subcontract Work for such period of time as may be determined to be appropriate for the convenience of the Contractor. Phased Work or interruptions of the Subcontract Work for short periods of time shall not be considered a suspension. The Subcontractor, after receipt of the Contractor's order, shall notify the Contractor in writing in sufficient time to permit the Contractor to provide timely notice to the Owner in accordance with the Owner-Contractor agreement of the effect of such order upon the Subcontract Work. The Subcontract Amount or Progress Schedule shall be adjusted by Subcontract Change Order for any increase in the time or cost of performance of this Agreement caused by such suspension. No claim under this Paragraph shall be allowed for any costs incurred more than fourteen (14) days prior to the Subcontractor's notice to the Contractor. Neither the Subcontract Amount nor the Progress Schedule shall be adjusted for any suspension, to the extent that performance would have been suspended, due in whole or in part to the fault or negligence of the Subcontractor or by a cause for which Subcontractor would have been responsible. The Subcontract Amount shall not be adjusted for any suspension to the extent that performance would have been suspended by a cause for which the Subcontractor would have been entitled only to a time extension under this Agreement.

10.7 WRONGFUL EXERCISE If the Contractor wrongfully exercises any option under this Article, the Contractor shall be liable to the Subcontractor solely for the reasonable value of Subcontract Work performed by the Subcontractor prior to the Contractor's wrongful action, including reasonable overhead and profit on the Subcontract Work performed, less prior payments made, together with reasonable overhead and profit on the Subcontract Work not executed, and other costs incurred by reason of such action.

10.8 TERMINATION BY SUBCONTRACTOR If the Subcontract Work has been stopped for thirty (30) days because the Subcontractor has not received progress payments or has been abandoned or suspended for an unreasonable period of time not due to the fault or neglect of the Subcontractor, then the Subcontractor may terminate this Agreement upon giving the Contractor seven (7) days' written notice. Upon such termination, Subcontractor shall be entitled to recover from the Contractor payment for all Subcontract Work satisfactorily performed but not yet paid for, including reasonable overhead, profit and attorneys' fees, costs and expenses, subject to the terms of Paragraphs 8.2 and 8.3. The Contractor's liability for any other damages claimed bythe Subcontractor under such circumstances shall be extinguished by the Contractor pursuing said damages and claims against the Owner, on the Subcontractor's behalf, in the manner provided for in Subparagraphs 10.3 and 10.4 of this Agreement.

ARTICLE 11

DISPUTE RESOLUTION

11.1 INITIAL DISPUTE RESOLUTION If a dispute arises out of or relates to this Agreement or its breach, the parties shall endeavor to settle the dispute first through direct discussions. If the dispute cannot be resolved through direct discussions, the parties shall participate in mediation under the Construction Industry Mediation Rules of the American Arbitration Association before recourse to any other form of binding dispute resolution. The location of the mediation shall be the location of the Project. Once a party files a request for mediation with the other party and with the American Arbitration Association, the parties agree to commence such mediation within thirty (30) days of filing of the request. Either party may terminate the mediation at any time after the first session, but the decision to terminate must be delivered in person to the other party and the mediator. Engaging in mediation is a condition precedent to any other form of binding dispute resolution.

11.2 WORK CONTINUATION AND PAYMENT Unless otherwise agreed in writing, the Subcontractor shall continue the Subcontract Work and maintain the Progress Schedule during any dispute resolution proceedings. If the Subcontractor continues to perform, the Contractor shall continue to make payments in accordance with this Agreement.

11.3 NO LIMITATION OF RIGHTS OR REMEDIES Nothing in this Article shall limit any rights or remedies not expressly waived by the Subcontractor which the Subcontractor may have under lien laws or payment bonds.

11.4 MULTIPARTY PROCEEDING The parties agree that to the extent permitted by Subcontract Document all parties necessary to resolve a claim shall be parties to the same dispute resolution proceeding. To the extent disputes between the Contractor and Subcontractor involve in whole or in part disputes between the Contractor and the Owner, disputes between the Subcontractor and the Contractor shall be decided by the same tribunal and in the same forum as disputes between the Contractor and the Owner.

11.5 DISPUTES BETWEEN CONTRACTOR AND SUBCONTRACTOR In the event that the provisions for resolution of disputes between the Contractor and the Owner contained in the Subcontract Documents do not permit consolidation or joinder with disputes of third parties, such as the Subcontractor, resolution of disputes between the Subcontractor and the Contractor involving in whole or in part disputes between the Contractor and the Owner shall be stayed pending conclusion of any dispute resolution proceeding between the Contractor and the Owner. At the conclusion of those proceedings, disputes between the Subcontractor and the Contractor shall be submitted again to mediation pursuant to Paragraph 11.1. Any disputes not resolved by mediation shall be decided in the manner selected in the agreement between the Owner and the Contractor.

11.6 COST OF DISPUTE RESOLUTION The cost of any mediation proceeding shall be shared equally by the parties participating. The prevailing party in any dispute arising out of or relating to this Agreement or its breach that is resolved by a dispute resolution procedure designated in the Subcontract Documents shall be entitled to recover from the other party reasonable attorneys' fees, costs and expenses incurred by the prevailing party in connection with such dispute resolution process.

ARTICLE 12

MISCELLANEOUS PROVISIONS

12.1 GOVERNING LAW This Agreement shall be governed by the law in effect at the location of the Project.

12.2 SEVERABILITY The partial or complete invalidity of any one or more provisions of this Agreement shall not affect the validity or continuing force and effect of any other provision.

12.3 NO WAIVER OF PERFORMANCE The failure of either party to insist, in any one or more instances, upon the performance of any of the terms, covenants or conditions of this Agreement, or to exercise any of its rights, shall not be construed as a waiver or relinquishment of term, covenant, condition or right with respect to further performance.

12.4 TITLES The titles given to the Articles of this Agreement are for ease of reference only and shall not be relied upon or cited for any other purpose.

12.5 OTHER PROVISIONS AND DOCUMENTS Other provisions and documents applicable to the Subcontract Work are set forth in Exhibit ________. ◆

12.6 JOINT DRAFTING The parties expressly agree that this Agreement was jointly drafted, and that they both had opportunity to negotiate its terms and to obtain the assistance of counsel in reviewing its terms prior to execution. Therefore, this Agreement shall be construed neither against nor in favor of either party, but shall be construed in a neutral manner.

ARTICLE 13

EXISTING SUBCONTRACT DOCUMENT

As defined in Paragraph 2.3, the following Exhibits are a part of this Agreement.

EXHIBIT_____◆ The Subcontract Work, ______________________________ pages.◆

EXHIBIT_____◆ The Drawings, Specifications, General and other conditions, addenda and other information. (Attach a complete listing by title, date and number of pages.)

EXHIBIT_____◆ Progress Schedule, ______________________________ pages.◆

EXHIBIT_____◆ Alternates and Unit Prices, include dates when alternates and unit prices no longer apply, ______________________________ pages.◆

EXHIBIT_____◆ Temporary Services, stating specific responsibilities of the Subcontractor, ______________________________ pages.◆

EXHIBIT_____◆ Insurance Provisions, ______________________________ pages.◆

EXHIBIT_____◆ Other Provisions and Documents, ______________________________ pages.◆

This Agreement is entered into as of the date entered in Article 1.

CONTRACTOR______________________________◆

ATTEST: ______________________________◆ BY: ______________________________◆

PRINT NAME: ______________________________◆

PRINT TITLE: ______________________________◆

SUBCONTRACTOR: ______________________________◆

ATTEST: ______________________________◆ BY: ______________________________◆

PRINT NAME: ______________________________◆

PRINT TITLE: ______________________________◆

APPENDIX H

Standard Construction Bond Forms

THE AMERICAN INSTITUTE OF ARCHITECTS

AIA Document A310

Bid Bond

KNOW ALL MEN BY THESE PRESENTS, that we Northwest Construction
(Here insert full name and address or legal title of Contractor)
Company, 1242 First Avenue, Cascade, Washington 98202
as Principal, hereinafter called the Principal, and Reliance Surety, 700 Fifth Avenue,
(Here insert full name and address or legal title of Surety)
Seattle, Washington 98104

a corporation duly organized under the laws of the State of Washington
as Surety, hereinafter called the Surety, are held and firmly bound unto Western Financial
(Here insert full name and address or legal title of Owner)
Group, 5000 Fourth Avenue, Seattle, Washington 98104

as Obligee, hereinafter called the Obligee, in the sum of Six Hundred Thousand******
***Dollars ($ 600,000.00),
for the payment of which sum well and truly to be made, the said Principal and the said Surety, bind ourselves, our heirs, executors, administrators, successors and assigns, jointly and severally, firmly by these presents.

WHEREAS, the Principal has submitted a bid for
(Here insert full name, address and description of project)

Pacific Towers
2805 Western Avenue
Seattle, Washington 98121

NOW, THEREFORE, if the Obligee shall accept the bid of the Principal and the Principal shall enter into a Contract with the Obligee in accordance with the terms of such bid, and give such bond or bonds as may be specified in the bidding or Contract Documents with good and sufficient surety for the faithful performance of such Contract and for the prompt payment of labor and material furnished in the prosecution thereof, or in the event of the failure of the Principal to enter such Contract and give such bond or bonds, if the Principal shall pay to the Obligee the difference not to exceed the penalty hereof between the amount specified in said bid and such larger amount for which the Obligee may in good faith contract with another party to perform the Work covered by said bid, then this obligation shall be null and void, otherwise to remain in full force and effect.

Signed and sealed this 17th day of April 2001

Jim Jones
(Witness)

Sam Peters
(Principal) (Seal)
Vice President
Northwest Construction Company
(Title)

Mary Smith
(Witness)

William Brown
(Surety) (Seal)
Principal, Reliance Surety
(Title)

THE AMERICAN INSTITUTE OF ARCHITECTS

AIA Document A312

Performance Bond

Any singular reference to Contractor, Surety, Owner or other party shall be considered plural where applicable.

CONTRACTOR (Name and Address):
Northwest Construction Company
1242 First Avenue
Cascade, Washington 98202

SURETY (Name and Principal Place of Business):
Reliance Surety
700 Fifth Avenue
Seattle, Washington 98104

OWNER (Name and Address):
Western Financial Group
5000 Fourth Avenue
Seattle, Washington 98104

CONSTRUCTION CONTRACT
Date: May 10, 2001
Amount: $12,000,000.00
Description (Name and Location): Pacific Towers, 2805 Western Avenue
Seattle, Washington 98121

BOND
Date (Not earlier than Construction Contract Date): May 10, 2001
Amount: $12,000,000.00
Modifications to this Bond: ☒ None ☐ See Page 3

CONTRACTOR AS PRINCIPAL
Company: Northwest Construction Company (Corporate Seal)
Signature: Sam Peters
Name and Title: Sam Peters, Vice Pres.

SURETY
Company: Reliance Surety (Corporate Seal)
Signature: William Brown
Name and Title: William Brown, Principa

(Any additional signatures appear on page 3)

(FOR INFORMATION ONLY—Name, Address and Telephone)
AGENT or BROKER:
Smith, Jones and Blair
400 Pine Street, Suite 500
Seattle, Washington 98104
Tel: 206-718-5361

OWNER'S REPRESENTATIVE (Architect, Engineer or other party):

1 The Contractor and the Surety, jointly and severally, bind themselves, their heirs, executors, administrators, successors and assigns to the Owner for the performance of the Construction Contract, which is incorporated herein by reference.

2 If the Contractor performs the Construction Contract, the Surety and the Contractor shall have no obligation under this Bond, except to participate in conferences as provided in Subparagraph 3.1.

3 If there is no Owner Default, the Surety's obligation under this Bond shall arise after:

3.1 The Owner has notified the Contractor and the Surety at its address described in Paragraph 10 below that the Owner is considering declaring a Contractor Default and has requested and attempted to arrange a conference with the Contractor and the Surety to be held not later than fifteen days after receipt of such notice to discuss methods of performing the Construction Contract. If the Owner, the Contractor and the Surety agree, the Contractor shall be allowed a reasonable time to perform the Construction Contract, but such an agreement shall not waive the Owner's right, if any, subsequently to declare a Contractor Default; and

3.2 The Owner has declared a Contractor Default and formally terminated the Contractor's right to complete the contract. Such Contractor Default shall not be declared earlier than twenty days after the Contractor and the Surety have received notice as provided in Subparagraph 3.1; and

3.3 The Owner has agreed to pay the Balance of the Contract Price to the Surety in accordance with the terms of the Construction Contract or to a contractor selected to perform the Construction Contract in accordance with the terms of the contract with the Owner.

4 When the Owner has satisfied the conditions of Paragraph 3, the Surety shall promptly and at the Surety's expense take one of the following actions:

4.1 Arrange for the Contractor, with consent of the Owner, to perform and complete the Construction Contract; or

4.2 Undertake to perform and complete the Construction Contract itself, through its agents or through independent contractors; or

4.3 Obtain bids or negotiated proposals from qualified contractors acceptable to the Owner for a contract for performance and completion of the Construction Contract, arrange for a contract to be prepared for execution by the Owner and the contractor selected with the Owner's concurrence, to be secured with performance and payment bonds executed by a qualified surety equivalent to the bonds issued on the Construction Contract, and pay to the Owner the amount of damages as described in Paragraph 6 in excess of the Balance of the Contract Price incurred by the Owner resulting from the Contractor's default; or

4.4 Waive its right to perform and complete, arrange for completion, or obtain a new contractor and with reasonable promptness under the circumstances:

.1 After investigation, determine the amount for which it may be liable to the Owner and, as soon as practicable after the amount is determined, tender payment therefor to the Owner; or

.2 Deny liability in whole or in part and notify the Owner citing reasons therefor.

5 If the Surety does not proceed as provided in Paragraph 4 with reasonable promptness, the Surety shall be deemed to be in default on this Bond fifteen days after receipt of an additional written notice from the Owner to the Surety demanding that the Surety perform its obligations under this Bond, and the Owner shall be entitled to enforce any remedy available to the Owner. If the Surety proceeds as provided in Subparagraph 4.4, and the Owner refuses the payment tendered or the Surety has denied liability, in whole or in part, without further notice the Owner shall be entitled to enforce any remedy available to the Owner.

6 After the Owner has terminated the Contractor's right to complete the Construction Contract, and if the Surety elects to act under Subparagraph 4.1, 4.2, or 4.3 above, then the responsibilities of the Surety to the Owner shall not be greater than those of the Contractor under the Construction Contract, and the responsibilities of the Owner to the Surety shall not be greater than those of the Owner under the Construction Contract. To the limit of the amount of this Bond, but subject to commitment by the Owner of the Balance of the Contract Price to mitigation of costs and damages on the Construction Contract, the Surety is obligated without duplication for:

6.1 The responsibilities of the Contractor for correction of defective work and completion of the Construction Contract;

6.2 Additional legal, design professional and delay costs resulting from the Contractor's Default, and resulting from the actions or failure to act of the Surety under Paragraph 4; and

6.3 Liquidated damages, or if no liquidated damages are specified in the Construction Contract, actual damages caused by delayed performance or non-performance of the Contractor.

7 The Surety shall not be liable to the Owner or others for obligations of the Contractor that are unrelated to the Construction Contract, and the Balance of the Contract Price shall not be reduced or set off on account of any such unrelated obligations. No right of action shall accrue on this Bond to any person or entity other than the Owner or its heirs, executors, administrators or successors.

8 The Surety hereby waives notice of any change, including changes of time, to the Construction Contract or to related subcontracts, purchase orders and other obligations.

9 Any proceeding, legal or equitable, under this Bond may be instituted in any court of competent jurisdiction in the location in which the work or part of the work is located and shall be instituted within two years after Contractor Default or within two years after the Contractor ceased working or within two years after the Surety refuses or fails to perform its obligations under this Bond, whichever occurs first. If the provisions of this Paragraph are void or prohibited by law, the minimum period of limitation available to sureties as a defense in the jurisdiction of the suit shall be applicable.

10 Notice to the Surety, the Owner or the Contractor shall be mailed or delivered to the address shown on the signature page.

11 When this Bond has been furnished to comply with a statutory or other legal requirement in the location where the construction was to be performed, any provision in this Bond conflicting with said statutory or legal requirement shall be deemed deleted herefrom and provisions conforming to such statutory or other legal requirement shall be deemed incorporated herein. The intent is that this Bond shall be construed as a statutory bond and not as a common law bond.

12 DEFINITIONS

12.1 Balance of the Contract Price: The total amount payable by the Owner to the Contractor under the Construction Contract after all proper adjustments have been made, including allowance to the Contractor of any amounts received or to be received by the Owner in settlement of insurance or other claims for damages to which the Contractor is entitled, reduced by all valid and proper payments made to or on behalf of the Contractor under the Construction Contract.

12.2 Construction Contract: The agreement between the Owner and the Contractor identified on the signature page, including all Contract Documents and changes thereto.

12.3 Contractor Default: Failure of the Contractor, which has neither been remedied nor waived, to perform or otherwise to comply with the terms of the Construction Contract.

12.4 Owner Default: Failure of the Owner, which has neither been remedied nor waived, to pay the Contractor as required by the Construction Contract or to perform and complete or comply with the other terms thereof.

MODIFICATIONS TO THIS BOND ARE AS FOLLOWS:

(Space is provided below for additional signatures of added parties, other than those appearing on the cover page.)

CONTRACTOR AS PRINCIPAL		SURETY	
Company:	(Corporate Seal)	Company:	(Corporate Seal)
Signature: ______________________		Signature: ______________________	
Name and Title:		Name and Title:	
Address:		Address:	

AIA Document A312

Payment Bond

Any singular reference to Contractor, Surety, Owner or other party shall be considered plural where applicable.

CONTRACTOR (Name and Address):
Northwest Construction Company
1242 First Avenue
Cascade, Washington 98202

SURETY (Name and Principal Place of Business):
Reliance Surety
700 Fifth Avenue
Seattle, Washington 98104

OWNER (Name and Address):
Western Financial Group
5000 Fourth Avenue
Seattle, Washington 98104

CONSTRUCTION CONTRACT
Date: May 10, 2001
Amount: $12,000,000.00
Description (Name and Location): Pacific Towers, 2805 Western Avenue, Seattle, Washington 98121

BOND
Date (Not earlier than Construction Contract Date): May 10, 2001
Amount: $12,000,000.00
Modifications to this Bond: ☒ None ☐ See Page 6

CONTRACTOR AS PRINCIPAL
Company: Northwest Construction Company (Corporate Seal)

Signature: Sam Peters
Name and Title: Sam Peters, Vice Pres.

SURETY
Company: Reliance Surety (Corporate Seal)

Signature: William Brown
Name and Title: William Brown, Principal

(Any additional signatures appear on page 6)

(FOR INFORMATION ONLY—Name, Address and Telephone)
AGENT or BROKER:
Smith, Jones and Blair
400 Pine Street, Suite 500
Seattle, Washington 98104
Tel: 206-718-5361

OWNER'S REPRESENTATIVE (Architect, Engineer or other party):

1 The Contractor and the Surety, jointly and severally, bind themselves, their heirs, executors, administrators, successors and assigns to the Owner to pay for labor, materials and equipment furnished for use in the performance of the Construction Contract, which is incorporated herein by reference.

2 With respect to the Owner, this obligation shall be null and void if the Contractor:

2.1 Promptly makes payment, directly or indirectly, for all sums due Claimants, and

2.2 Defends, indemnifies and holds harmless the Owner from claims, demands, liens or suits by any person or entity whose claim, demand, lien or suit is for the payment for labor, materials or equipment furnished for use in the performance of the Construction Contract, provided the Owner has promptly notified the Contractor and the Surety (at the address described in Paragraph 12) of any claims, demands, liens or suits and tendered defense of such claims, demands, liens or suits to the Contractor and the Surety, and provided there is no Owner Default.

3 With respect to Claimants, this obligation shall be null and void if the Contractor promptly makes payment, directly or indirectly, for all sums due.

4 The Surety shall have no obligation to Claimants under this Bond until:

4.1 Claimants who are employed by or have a direct contract with the Contractor have given notice to the Surety (at the address described in Paragraph 12) and sent a copy, or notice thereof, to the Owner, stating that a claim is being made under this Bond and, with substantial accuracy, the amount of the claim.

4.2 Claimants who do not have a direct contract with the Contractor:

.1 Have furnished written notice to the Contractor and sent a copy, or notice thereof, to the Owner, within 90 days after having last performed labor or last furnished materials or equipment included in the claim stating, with substantial accuracy, the amount of the claim and the name of the party to whom the materials were furnished or supplied or for whom the labor was done or performed; and

.2 Have either received a rejection in whole or in part from the Contractor, or not received within 30 days of furnishing the above notice any communication from the Contractor by which the Contractor has indicated the claim will be paid directly or indirectly; and

.3 Not having been paid within the above 30 days, have sent a written notice to the Surety (at the address described in Paragraph 12) and sent a copy, or notice thereof, to the Owner, stating that a claim is being made under this Bond and enclosing a copy of the previous written notice furnished to the Contractor.

5 If a notice required by Paragraph 4 is given by the Owner to the Contractor or to the Surety, that is sufficient compliance.

6 When the Claimant has satisfied the conditions of Paragraph 4, the Surety shall promptly and at the Surety's expense take the following actions:

6.1 Send an answer to the Claimant, with a copy to the Owner, within 45 days after receipt of the claim, stating the amounts that are undisputed and the basis for challenging any amounts that are disputed.

6.2 Pay or arrange for payment of any undisputed amounts.

7 The Surety's total obligation shall not exceed the amount of this Bond, and the amount of this Bond shall be credited for any payments made in good faith by the Surety.

8 Amounts owed by the Owner to the Contractor under the Construction Contract shall be used for the performance of the Construction Contract and to satisfy claims, if any, under any Construction Performance Bond. By the Contractor furnishing and the Owner accepting this Bond, they agree that all funds earned by the Contractor in the performance of the Construction Contract are dedicated to satisfy obligations of the Contractor and the Surety under this Bond, subject to the Owner's priority to use the funds for the completion of the work.

9 The Surety shall not be liable to the Owner, Claimants or others for obligations of the Contractor that are unrelated to the Construction Contract. The Owner shall not be liable for payment of any costs or expenses of any Claimant under this Bond, and shall have under this Bond no obligations to make payments to, give notices on behalf of, or otherwise have obligations to Claimants under this Bond.

10 The Surety hereby waives notice of any change, including changes of time, to the Construction Contract or to related subcontracts, purchase orders and other obligations.

11 No suit or action shall be commenced by a Claimant under this Bond other than in a court of competent jurisdiction in the location in which the work or part of the work is located or after the expiration of one year from the date (1) on which the Claimant gave the notice required by Subparagraph 4.1 or Clause 4.2.3, or (2) on which the last labor or service was performed by anyone or the last materials or equipment were furnished by anyone under the Construction Contract, whichever of (1) or (2) first occurs. If the provisions of this Paragraph are void or prohibited by law, the minimum period of limitation available to sureties as a defense in the jurisdiction of the suit shall be applicable.

12 Notice to the Surety, the Owner or the Contractor shall be mailed or delivered to the address shown on the signature page. Actual receipt of notice by Surety, the Owner or the Contractor, however accomplished, shall be sufficient compliance as of the date received at the address shown on the signature page.

13 When this Bond has been furnished to comply with a statutory or other legal requirement in the location where the construction was to be performed, any provision in this Bond conflicting with said statutory or legal requirement shall be deemed deleted herefrom and provisions conforming to such statutory or other legal requirement shall be deemed incorporated herein. The intent is that this

Bond shall be construed as a statutory bond and not as a common law bond.

14 Upon request by any person or entity appearing to be a potential beneficiary of this Bond, the Contractor shall promptly furnish a copy of this Bond or shall permit a copy to be made.

15 DEFINITIONS

15.1 Claimant: An individual or entity having a direct contract with the Contractor or with a subcontractor of the Contractor to furnish labor, materials or equipment for use in the performance of the Contract. The intent of this Bond shall be to include without limitation in the terms "labor, materials or equipment" that part of water, gas, power, light, heat, oil, gasoline, telephone service or rental equipment used in the Construction Contract, architectural and engineering services required for performance of the work of the Contractor and the Contractor's subcontractors, and all other items for which a mechanic's lien may be asserted in the jurisdiction where the labor, materials or equipment were furnished.

15.2 Construction Contract: The agreement between the Owner and the Contractor identified on the signature page, including all Contract Documents and changes thereto.

15.3 Owner Default: Failure of the Owner, which has neither been remedied nor waived, to pay the Contractor as required by the Construction Contract or to perform and complete or comply with the other terms thereof.

MODIFICATIONS TO THIS BOND ARE AS FOLLOWS:

(Space is provided below for additional signatures of added parties, other than those appearing on the cover page.)

CONTRACTOR AS PRINCIPAL
Company: (Corporate Seal)

Signature: ______________________
Name and Title:
Address:

SURETY
Company: (Corporate Seal)

Signature: ______________________
Name and Title:
Address:

INDEX OF FORMS

INDEX